The Rise of Political Action Committees

The Rise of Political Action Committees

Interest Group Electioneering and the Transformation of American Politics

EMILY J. CHARNOCK

OXFORD
UNIVERSITY PRESS

OXFORD
UNIVERSITY PRESS

Oxford University Press is a department of the University of Oxford. It furthers
the University's objective of excellence in research, scholarship, and education
by publishing worldwide. Oxford is a registered trade mark of Oxford University
Press in the UK and certain other countries.

Published in the United States of America by Oxford University Press
198 Madison Avenue, New York, NY 10016, United States of America.

© Oxford University Press 2020

Library of Congress Cataloging-in-Publication Data
Names: Charnock, Emily J., author.
Title: The rise of political action committees : interest group
electioneering and the transformation of American politics / Emily J. Charnock.
Description: New York, NY : Oxford University Press, 2020. |
Series: Studies in postwar American political development |
Includes bibliographical references and index.
Identifiers: LCCN 2020006628 (print) | LCCN 2020006629 (ebook) |
ISBN 9780190075514 (hardback) | ISBN 9780190075538 (epub)
Subjects: LCSH: Political action committees—United States—History. |
Campaign funds—United States—History. | Lobbying—United
States—History | Pressure groups—United States—History.
Classification: LCC JK1991 .C45 2020 (print) | LCC JK1991 (ebook) |
DDC 324/.40973—dc23
LC record available at https://lccn.loc.gov/2020006628
LC ebook record available at https://lccn.loc.gov/2020006629

1 3 5 7 9 8 6 4 2

Printed by Integrated Books International, United States of America

CONTENTS

Introduction

"Going into Politics"

The charges laid before Congress were dire indeed. The United States Brewers' Association, a Senate resolution thundered, had been making "contributions to political campaigns on a great scale without precedent in the political history of the country and in violation of the laws of the land." And the outrages did not stop there. The Brewers had "exacted pledges from candidates to office . . . before election" so as "to control legislation in State and Nation." They had compiled "political surveys of States, counties, and districts tabulating the men and forces for and against them." They had "paid large sums of money to citizens of the United States to advocate their cause and interests," and "for the furthering of their political enterprises" had even "erected a political organization." The Brewers were attempting, in sum, "to build up in the country . . . a political influence which can be turned to one or the other party, thus controlling electoral results."[1]

What constituted allegations worthy of congressional investigation in 1918, when the Senate passed this resolution, are largely considered normal interest group activities today. That the Brewers might employ individuals "to advocate their cause and interests"—to hire a *lobbyist,* that is—would raise few eyebrows in contemporary Washington, DC. But even back then, senators were less concerned with lobbying than with the far more pernicious type of activity, as they saw it, of *electioneering* by "special interests." Such interests were controversial to begin with, of course—easily denounced as selfish cliques, only concerned with their own financial gain—but few were more so than the Brewers' Association in 1918. With the United States embroiled overseas in a war against Germany, the brewing industry's Teutonic ties raised questions of patriotism. And as temperance fervor gripped the nation at home, the Brewers' moral fiber was in doubt too.[2] Yet concern about electioneering was by no means limited to such questionable trade associations.

That same year, the National Security League—an avowedly patriotic organization that had urged "preparedness" ahead of America's entry into the First

The Rise of Political Action Committees. Emily J. Charnock, Oxford University Press (2020). © Oxford University Press.
DOI: 10.1093/oso/9780190075514.001.0001

World War—also faced investigation for trying to sway the electoral fortunes of congressmen.[3] And while the Anti-Saloon League of America fanned the flames of temperance sentiment all the way to a constitutional amendment in 1919, it would find its own electoral practices under scrutiny soon enough.[4] Even a veritable arbiter of Americanism like the National Association of the Motion Picture Industry could find itself under the watchful eye of lawmakers. As calls for "morality" in the movies threatened to translate into federal censorship, its leadership threatened to "get into politics"—that is, to mobilize in elections.[5] The US Senate, at least, responded with its own threat: to investigate the entire industry and its political practices.[6] "Going into politics," it seemed, would not be taken lying down.

And yet from these hesitant, controversial beginnings, interest group electioneering would expand dramatically over the next several decades, even as new laws repeatedly sought to constrain and regulate it. Partly in response to such measures, in fact, interest group electioneering would become more formalized and specialized, as reflected in the creation of political action committees or PACs from the 1940s onward. As the years wore on, moreover, electioneering would become, for many interest groups, ever more important to the pursuit of their goals. Indeed, interest groups today are considered crucial electoral players, with an extensive body of scholarship examining their spending in campaigns— via PACs or similar entities—and their wider political influence.[7] We know very little, however, about their rise to electoral prominence, the contours of this development, and its wider implications in the political world.

Historically, interest group lobbying has been a more dominant focus for scholars—a reflection of its prominence in the early twentieth century, when interest groups first emerged in a recognizably "modern" organized form. As Elisabeth S. Clemens has shown, these new entities were bureaucratic in operation and technocratic in orientation, and they embraced a wider range of concerns beyond the commercial aims traditionally identified with special interests, such as promoting ideas and policies or advocating for those less economically advantaged in society.[8] To do so, they developed new modes of engagement in the political sphere that primarily revolved around lobbying. Interest groups tried to persuade lawmakers to support their favored policies, whether directly through personal entreaties or indirectly by appealing to the public, hoping thereby to build a groundswell of popular support for their aims and influence how lawmakers voted. Electioneering was not entirely absent from this model of "pressure politics," as it came to be known, but it was originally a limited and secondary activity, engaged in by only a handful of interest groups and carefully presented so as to limit potential criticism.

In the political culture of the United States in the early twentieth century, electioneering was widely considered the appropriate pursuit of party organizations alone. Even candidates campaigning too openly for office were viewed askance for violating a sacred tenet of republican virtue, in which prospective politicians should be drafted into public service on the basis of their reputation and credentials and thus need merely *stand* for office rather than *run* for it.[9] Similarly, despite the Madisonian model of pluralist harmony in America, traditional special interests were controversial exactly because they appeared to promote their selfish aims at the expense of the public interest, going against another republican ideal.[10] Even newer groups pushing agendas with substantial popular support could be accused of promoting "class legislation" that would set different elements of American society against each other. For critics of either type of group, their turn to lobbying was bad enough. But to promote such aims in *elections* raised more basic fears for American democracy, whether the "corruption" of voters or lawmakers by wealthy interests using their money in campaigns, or the undue influence that popular groups might have over the votes of their members or supporters, thus debasing the electoral process. Accordingly, interest groups ventured only warily into electoral territory and undertook their efforts with persuasion in mind.

For those that dared, the approach was simple: they threatened wavering lawmakers with punishment at the polls, hoping thereby to bolster their legislative influence and carry the day for their preferred policies. As such, they pursued what Mark J. Rozell, Clyde Wilcox, and Michael M. Franz have labeled an "access, or legislative strategy," in which electioneering serves "as an adjunct to lobbying efforts," and a distinctly junior one.[11] This kind of threat, in fact, was the ultimate backstop to the pressure politics of the 1910s and 1920s, premised on the idea, as the Senate's resolution implied, of turning votes to one side or the other to swing an election. But it was a threat that was rarely acted upon. To the extent a group could credibly claim influence over a large bloc of voters, it might have some effect on a lawmaker's decision calculus. Yet this effectiveness was best demonstrated less by *actual* electioneering than by the *absence* thereof; the threat itself keeping a lawmaker in line.[12] In those rare cases in which groups had to make good on their warnings, their actions were typically limited in scope both geographically and substantively—to circulating literature or staging rallies in a handful of constituencies, for example—and they often generated a significant backlash. Their activities were also temporary in nature, being undertaken for only a short time in the run-up to an election, and they were largely punitive in orientation. Such interest groups typically sought to defeat their "enemies" in the legislature or other offices and only occasionally to help their "friends."

This picture of limited electoral engagement, forged in the political conflicts and context of the early twentieth century, contrasts starkly with subsequent developments, as more groups appeared willing to weather the criticism and embrace electioneering far more actively. In the 1930s electioneering would thus become much more prominent, as new campaign groups associated with labor unions and business interests undertook overt and coordinated nationwide activity in presidential and congressional contests. In the 1940s the Congress of Industrial Organizations (CIO)—the major industrial union federation in the United States—institutionalized this more assertive form of electioneering with the creation of its "Political Action Committee." This original "P.A.C." and its many subsequent imitators were permanent, dedicated campaign organizations that would keep electoral objectives in sight even in the lengthy interludes between elections. Formally, PACs were vehicles designed to circumvent campaign finance laws, which had recently banned labor unions from contributing money in federal election campaigns, a ban previously applied to corporations. As a legal device for channeling money into politics, PACs became an important source of funding *for* friendly candidates, providing resources on a regularized and reliable basis. But there was far more to PACs than money alone. They did not simply contribute directly to candidates but often campaigned on their behalf, making "independent expenditures," as such practices came to be known. Meanwhile, adopting the mantra that "elections are won between campaigns," they launched ongoing publicity campaigns designed to make the wider political environment more receptive to their aims.[13] In so doing, they moved beyond the sporadic, threat-based, and largely punitive electoral activity with which "pressure groups" had been identified to a more permanent and positive form of "political action," as it came to be known.

For those interest groups that created PACs or adopted some of their political practices, the embrace of electioneering represented an important strategic shift, moving away from attempts to persuade incumbent lawmakers to see their point of view toward the election of candidates who already embraced that viewpoint. The new approach lessened the strategic emphasis on lobbying since, in theory at least, such reliable friends would need no further persuasion when in office. With this shift, interest group leaders came closer to embracing what Rozell, Wilcox, and Franz have called an "electoral strategy": looking to elections themselves as a means of altering the composition of government and achieving legislative aims.[14] Yet this shift in interest group orientation did not simply affect the composition of government. It had important implications for party politics, too. For as interest group electoral involvement became increasingly positive, it also became increasingly *partisan*, even as those involved pretended otherwise.

For both cultural and strategic reasons, pressure politics in the early twentieth century had been conducted and justified along nonpartisan lines. On the rhetorical front, "nonpartisanship" had been an important device through which interest groups defined themselves and tried to justify their activity in the face of criticism. This language was intended to distance them from the seedy world of party politics, which had come under attack at the dawn of the Progressive

Era, while elevating their own reputation along the way. If parties were a species of "faction" that might go against the public interest—as many Americans increasingly believed—then claiming to be "nonpartisan" was meant to clothe interest groups in a more benign façade and downplay their own divisiveness.[15] Nonpartisanship was important in strategic terms, too, as the threat of electoral punishment only worked if groups were willing to swing their support either way. Since opinion on few, if any, political issues divided cohesively along party lines at this time, there was little reason for an interest group to hew only to one side.

In the mid-twentieth century, prominent political scientists would develop this strategic insight into a fully fledged theory of party–interest group relations that placed nonpartisanship at its core. E. E. Schattschneider, for example, himself no fan of "pressure groups," concluded in 1942 that they had "sound strategical reasons for avoiding affiliation with either of the major parties" in elections.[16] This was not simply a matter of credibility in making their electoral threats but of avoiding possible fallout from partisan behavior. Pressure groups feared *isolation,* he said, and could not afford to be too closely identified with one party side, lest the opposing side won office and left them out in the political wilderness. It was often "unwise to back either party," Schattschneider's contemporary V. O. Key similarly observed, and far better "to have friends in both camps, for the group must promote its objectives whatever party is in power."[17] To the extent electioneering risked appearing partisan, such considerations would counsel against it. The presidential contest was especially dangerous territory, since backing a party's nominee was widely viewed as tantamount to endorsing that party. Pressure groups might occasionally wade into congressional waters with a "threat of retaliation at the polls," Key acknowledged, where apparent partisan preferences might be balanced out or diluted across multiple candidates.[18] But they would otherwise confine themselves to lobbying, Schattschneider and Key believed, exerting a substantial and, in their view, pernicious influence over lawmakers.

By 1948 Schattschneider had channeled these ideas into a broader generalization, succinctly expressed in the title of a short but influential article, "Pressure Groups versus Political Parties,"[19] in which he described these important political actors as oppositional forces, noting that "pressure groups thrive on the weaknesses of the parties."[20] This was a more subtle statement than it at first appeared, grounded in Schattschneider's long-held belief that pressure groups were only influential because American parties were so ideologically diffuse—a characteristic he linked, in turn, to the latter's decentralized organization and the weakness of their national institutions. Dominated by local politicians more concerned with patronage than policy, the parties had few cohesive and consistent positions on the issues. This gave pressure groups an opening in Congress,

Schattschneider argued, as lawmakers looked elsewhere for guidance on legislation and proved receptive to their pleas. Were parties to develop stronger national institutions capable of imposing greater discipline on policy, he believed, they could "shut out" pressure group influence.[21] Schattschneider was himself a passionate advocate of such national party institutions and of the more programmatic, ideologically cohesive parties they could bring about, promoting this position as chair of the American Political Science Association's (APSA) Committee on Political Parties, as reflected in its famous 1950 report, "Toward a More Responsible Two-Party System."[22]

Nonetheless, in much ensuing scholarship on parties and pressure groups it was the stark opposition of Schattschneider's 1948 publication that stuck. Stripped of its context and caveats, this formulation became entrenched in the lore of political science for decades thereafter as a statement of "rivalry," even a claim of inverse relative strength with distinctly causal overtones.[23] And yet this characterization of rivalry between party and pressure group—whether in its weak or strong variety—and the analysis of pressure group strategy to which it was linked, increasingly stood at odds with the facts on the ground. For not only did group electoral involvement increase in volume and visibility in the very period that Schattschneider and Key were articulating these ideas, it also became increasingly partisan in form.

Not every interest group created a PAC at mid-century or engaged in some form of electioneering. Not all who did came to rely on it heavily or, indeed, exclusively. But those that embraced electioneering most fully tended to embrace partisanship, too. In general, early interest group PACs and related organizations would come to be viewed as reliable allies for one major party or the other, though they provided resources "independently" of them. The CIO P.A.C., for example, and labor unions more broadly, were considered by the 1950s to be close allies of the Democratic Party. PACs linked to business interests, which first became prominent in the 1960s, came to be associated with the Republican Party. These identifications might appear "natural" to us now, but given the controversies over interest group partisanship, intertwined as it was with electioneering, and the very lack of consistent policy or ideological divisions between the parties for much of the early to mid-twentieth century, they are less obvious in hindsight.

The parties are, of course, far more divided in the twenty-first century. Programmatic concerns have come to predominate over those of patronage, and ideological discipline now reigns supreme—much as Schattschneider had hoped. If anything, the concern today is that the division has gone too far—that party "responsibility" has been replaced with a toxic "polarization" that threatens to bring American governance to a standstill.[24] Certainly Schattschneider did not anticipate such an outcome, nor did he live to see it realized—though he did begin to discern some movement in his preferred direction by the late 1950s. Indeed, it appears that by that point some of Schattschneider's views had shifted. He no longer felt that interest groups would be entirely "shut out" by more responsible parties, but rather that they would be *subordinated*. Where parties took distinct and opposing views on significant policy questions, groups would be forced to pick a side, becoming harnessed thereby to a party's larger aims and agenda. This helped him to account for, though not entirely reconcile with his earlier expectations, the evidence already emerging of enduring alliances between parties and certain interest groups.[25]

By the early 1960s both Schattschneider and Key noted significant relationships between labor unions and the Democratic Party, for example, and between business interests and the Republicans, among others.[26] And to the extent that they explained these relationships, they did so in terms of partisan change. A strengthening of the party system—that is, a clearer division between the two major parties—would exert a "centripetal" effect on interest groups, Schattschneider argued in 1960, drawing pressure groups "into the vortex of party conflict."[27] This would in turn affect their tactical calculations. As Key noted in a 1964 update of his earlier book, "the interests of some groups are so completely identified with those of a party that *they might as well* join the fray and risk the consequences."[28] The "fray" he had in mind was the electoral arena, since Key meant that groups now had far less to fear from campaigning. In fact, they had much more to gain. For if one party was already opposed to their legislative aims, then political "isolation" would be all but guaranteed if that party won control of the government; lobbying would simply have no effect on lawmakers predisposed against them. A group "might as well" back the friendlier side in that case, because it would be, in truth, their only hope.

Neither Schattschneider nor Key fully developed these later insights or linked them back to their previous claims. But in essence, they portray interest groups as purely *reactive* actors, allying with parties in response to partisan change and embracing elections once the fear of appearing partisan no longer mattered. Such an explanation is appealing but not necessarily convincing. If the parties were already changing in the 1950s and early 1960s, they were certainly not perfectly divided by this point, raising questions about the point at which an interest group would be "forced" to pick a side. Democratic presidents such as Franklin Roosevelt and Harry Truman may have offered a "liberal" political vision in the 1930s and 1940s, for example, but their Republican successor in the 1950s, Dwight D. Eisenhower, adopted many of their social policies, offering a moderate consensus alternative rather than a clearly conservative one. And in Congress, an influential "conservative coalition" of (mostly) Southern Democrats and midwestern Republicans confused any simple correlation of party and ideology.

How or why the parties might be changing, moreover, was never fully addressed. American parties had "no system of quality control so as to be able to deliver a standard product under their trade-mark," Key had explained in a 1957 lecture, noting their decentralized structure and the widespread use of primary elections. "The customer has to beware," he warned.[29] Indeed, the 1950 APSA committee had bemoaned the lack of national party institutions that might impose such "quality control," in Key's phrase. Yet no such institutions had emerged by 1964 to explain why parties might appear more distinctive or divided. In his account, Schattschneider pointed toward a decline in sectional voting patterns, evident since the "critical election" of 1932, which had made both parties more competitive nationally and thereby strengthened the party system.[30] Yet exactly how this might translate into more ideologically cohesive parties was not made clear.

At the same time, those interest groups that came to ally with parties in the mid-twentieth century were neither "shut out" nor subordinated, as Schattschneider had predicted they would be. Today, many interest groups, PACs, and other related organizations have become influential inside players, long-term allies who form part of a party's broader "network," as contemporary political scientists now conceive their relations—working alongside the formal party committees to promote legislative goals and get candidates elected.[31] Indeed, the relationship now appears so close that some contemporary scholars such as Bawn and colleagues have effectively reversed the "rivalry" thesis, presenting a theoretical framework in which parties and interest groups enjoy a cooperative relationship, even a *constitutive* one: "[P]arties in the United States are best understood as coalitions of interest groups and activists seeking to capture and use government for their particular goals," they argue, and partisan electioneering (with a focus on securing sympathetic candidates) plays an important role in their theory.[32] But this approach ignores important changes in interest group organization and tactics over time, not least the strategic and cultural prohibitions that once constrained partisan electioneering.[33] Bawn and colleagues therefore neglect what is an important and consequential historical development. Nonetheless, they effectively describe and explain a very different political environment today, in which *both* parties and interest groups appear powerful. Importantly, they also depict interest groups as potential catalysts for partisan change.[34]

Bridging these two waves of scholarship, this book argues that interest groups were far from merely reactive players responding to clear-cut changes in party politics. Rather, they were proactive, adopting new electoral strategies prior to significant party shifts. Indeed, interest group leaders are *agents* in the story told here, who came to reject the strategic calculus that had counseled nonpartisanship and an emphasis on lobbying—a calculus articulated by mid-century political scientists and enshrined in subsequent scholarship as a kind of political gospel—instead seeing greater potential in electioneering and, ultimately, in partisanship. This relationship between electioneering and partisanship was neither automatic nor logically necessary, however, as Bawn and colleagues intimate.[35] Rather, it was a product of contingency, an evolving presidential context, organizational learning and experience, and competitive pressures from within the interest group world. It was facilitated, moreover, by institutional developments, particularly the rise of primaries, which created opportunities for outside actors to influence parties from within.

Crucially, interest group partisanship was never *static*; interest groups did not simply pick a side and blindly promote its fortunes. Rather, they began to see new opportunities to promote their own causes by advancing them first within a major party, thus exhibiting a dynamic type of partisanship. By promoting candidates with sympathetic views in primaries and general elections, these nonparty actors sought to gradually but steadily alter a party's positions on a range of policy issues, devising new electoral tactics to help them achieve their aims. Those issues were increasingly woven into broader ideological worldviews. Following the political convulsions of the 1930s, the opposing economic goals desired by key interest groups, particularly labor and business, and their attendant vision of the federal government's role, provided the foundations for modern liberalism and conservatism. Beginning in the 1940s, then, from the very birth of PACs, interest groups sought not merely to advance their policy goals through electioneering but to make the parties more cohesively *liberal* or *conservative* in general—to make them more "responsible," as scholars had once hoped, by offering the "quality control" that major parties could not.

Their efforts would help to remake the patronage-based Democratic and Republican Parties of old as programmatic and ideological parties of the Left and Right and to transform the decentralized and diffuse American party system into the nationalized and polarized system of today.[36] Far from being "shut out" or subordinated by polarized parties, therefore, interest groups were among the instruments of their creation. But "polarization" was not the language they themselves used or conceptualized; it is a contemporary term for what is now seen as a modern malaise. Rather, interest group leaders believed they were promoting a *realignment* of the party system around a new dimension of conflict—primarily the role and reach of the federal government—which had been a long-cherished aim especially of progressive activists. They proffered a new understanding of how that realignment could be achieved. As traditionally understood, realignment required a third party to channel popular discontent into the electoral sphere and break apart the existing configuration and commitments of the party system, a purely progressive or conservative vehicle that would displace a major party and force the other to take a clear opposing stance. The creation of PACs committed to partisan political action reflected a new belief in the possibility of transformation without such an external shock, through gradual internal change of the existing parties, and offered a new organizational model for achieving it. The rise of PACs has accordingly lessened recourse to third parties in American politics, while refashioning the major parties to more closely resemble them.

This book seeks to explain why some interest groups adopted this new partisan electoral strategy and explores the broader implications of that choice. It does so, in the first instance, by sketching out the contours of electoral action in the early twentieth century. Drawing on a series of congressional investigations conducted between 1912 and 1957, as well as related data on the early 1960s, the first chapter offers a novel overview of the electoral environment, identifying those interest groups and related entities, including early PACs, that participated in elections during this period. The major groups so identified—primarily business organizations, labor unions, and related ideological groups—form the spine of the narrative told in later chapters. The second chapter examines the relatively limited involvement of business and labor groups in early twentieth-century congressional elections, their nonpartisan claims and emphasis on lobbying, and the techniques of pressure politics perfected by temperance groups like the Anti-Saloon League (ASL). It looks also at the hesitant involvement of the ASL in the 1928 presidential election, amid the rise of a powerful new opponent with ties to business leaders— the Association Against the Prohibition Amendment—and considers how backing one party's nominee challenged nonpartisan pretensions and played out differently for each side.

If the battle over Prohibition provided a preview, the 1930s saw a more significant shift, as the presidency of Franklin Roosevelt and his New Deal policies sparked intense political conflict over the power and reach of the federal government. Ideological terms like "liberal" and "conservative," in fact, were reconfigured in this period, taking on their modern meanings on each side of that conflict. Labor and business groups took opposing sides too, with support of or opposition to the New Deal mobilizing them politically in new ways. The third chapter thus looks to the 1936 election, when campaign groups associated with the labor and business communities—Labor's Non-Partisan League (LNPL) and the Liberty League—squared off in the presidential election. These groups resembled proto-PACs, pumping large amounts of money into the election in support of opposing party nominees, but still tried to justify their support in nonpartisan terms by emphasizing individual candidates rather than parties.

Founded largely with CIO support, the LNPL remained active after the 1936 campaign, when it shifted its sights from electing the president to electing his supporters, as discussed in chapter 4. In so doing, its actions began to take on a more partisan hue, for LNPL support went predominantly to Democrats and few, if any, Republicans. But it opposed some Democrats too, mostly conservative southerners, suggesting a nascent interest in partisan change. Roosevelt himself had pointed in this direction with his 1938 "Purge" campaign, in which he sought to unseat his most bitter Democratic critics by urging their defeat in primary elections. While his interventions proved largely unsuccessful, Roosevelt's attempt to make his party more liberal proved instructive for some CIO leaders. They began to look beyond a strategy of "rewarding and punishing" to envisaging a cohesive, disciplined, and supportive Democratic Party as a vehicle through which labor's aims could be better achieved over the long term.

The CIO set about making its new vision a reality, with the creation of its P.A.C. in 1943 proving a critical point in this strategic transformation, as discussed in chapter 5. Through interventions in primary elections and the targeted provision of support for sympathetic Democratic candidates in general elections, the CIO P.A.C. sought to reshape the Democratic Party along more uniformly pro-labor and more broadly liberal lines. The PAC wanted to install supportive "friends" from the outset—seeking out candidates who were precommitted to labor's goals. But in line with a strategy of dynamic partisanship, they chose not to look for allies on both sides of the aisle, instead favoring liberal Democrats over liberal Republicans—seeking to impress Franklin Roosevelt's New Deal vision onto the Democratic Party as a whole.

This new organizational form and strategy soon attracted imitators in the interest group world—among other labor groups and sympathetic liberal interests but also among conservative opponents too, who would ultimately, though not immediately, turn to the Republican Party as a counterweight. Chapter 6 traces the diffusion of the PAC model from labor unions through ideological groups of the Left, together forging an extensive labor-liberal electoral constellation by the 1950s. Chapter 7 shows the same process occurring on the Right, as conservative electoral groups were formed to counter liberal ones, with the business community following suit by the early 1960s. Business groups had not entirely ignored elections to this point, but as the chapter explores, they had concentrated their energies on lobbying and publicity campaigns and resisted forming a PAC. They had also placed greater faith in the "conservative coalition" and thus only reluctantly adopted a partisan counterstrategy centered on the Republican Party, reacting to what they saw as labor "infiltration" on the Democratic side.

This reactive process culminated in the presidential election of 1964, the first in which labor and business PACs were arrayed against each other, and a contest to which the roots of modern partisan "polarization" are often traced, as discussed in chapter 8. Indeed, as explored in the conclusion, the emergence of partisan interest group PACs played an important and neglected role in fostering the polarization of American politics, a development that has raised concern in recent decades. Seeking to reconfigure party politics around specific policy issues—more broadly, to *realign* the party system along an ideological dimension of conflict—these PACs helped make the parties more distinct and more deeply divided over time. They did so via electoral tools and tactics that are now ubiquitous in political life but rarely probed in scholarship. Exploring the role of PACs, therefore, can illuminate the very mechanisms through which party change was brought about, as much as its wider meaning.

What this book offers, then, is a developmental narrative that highlights the complex process leading interest groups into the electoral sphere, and into the arms of the parties. It suggests a process of competitive emulation whereby the PAC organizational form and the strategy of dynamic partisanship diffused across the interest group environment, as labor groups mobilized for partisan political action, as liberal and conservative groups joined the fray on different sides, and as business groups moved to counteract in like form. This was the first major wave of reactive partisan mobilization, but a similar pattern has appeared since—on social issues such as abortion from the 1970s onward, for example, or constitutional controversies over the Second Amendment right to bear arms. As more groups with opposing aims gravitate to different parties, they exacerbate partisan divisions and escalate electoral activity. Indeed, the competitive dynamics of electioneering, rooted in underlying antagonisms within the interest group realm, have seen interest groups caught in an arms race that once begun elicits ever greater commitment of resources to the electoral sphere. At the same time, it brings diminishing returns to that commitment, since organized opposition reduces the chances of fully achieving electoral and therefore policy aims. Even in the face of disappointment, however, interest groups can no longer walk away; the polarized, hypercompetitive party system they have helped to create has closed off any return to nonpartisan lobbying. Allied interest groups are thus effectively stuck with "their" sides and can only cling harder to their electoral advancement.

Reckoning with the current dysfunction in American politics requires understanding interest group electioneering. The shift away from nonpartisan lobbying toward partisan campaigning is a major organizational, cultural, and strategic change in the mode of modern interest group activity—one that has gained a level of cultural acceptability, even respectability, that was unimaginable a century ago. Urging Congress to investigate the movie industry in 1920, the Reverend William Chase declared that he "recognize[d] the right of every man to enter politics, and the right to advocate his own measures . . . but there is an excess to which no interests ought to go."[37] For Chase, "going into politics" at all was a step too far for interest groups. Yet today it is a fundamental fact of political life. While controversy might still swirl around the *scale* of their financial involvement, the electoral participation of interest groups is taken as a given.

This book seeks to understand that transformation and its effects. It suggests that the rise of interest group electioneering, especially as embodied in PACs and associated with a partisan form of "political action," is a crucial and consequential twentieth-century political development. Interest group electioneering, in sum, has helped remake the political world.

1

"Interests" and Elections

If an era can be embodied in a type of person, a particular kind of character, then for the Gilded Age, the lobbyist was the man of his time. From statehouses to the US Senate, the lobbyist strode the halls of power in pursuit of his clients' objectives. In Texas he served up "beefsteak, bourbon, and blondes" for the state's part-time legislators.[1] In Washington, DC, he installed himself at a hotel near the Capitol and proceeded to seek out lawmakers for a quiet word or a friendly drink, all in pursuit of a friendly vote. A liberal supply of money and favors were the key to his influence, drawn from the deep pockets of the industrialists, railroad magnates, and financiers who employed his services. And his masters, along with his methods, made him the object of popular scorn. For these corporate behemoths looked to their own "special interests" rather than the public interest, critics railed, and their actions corrupted democracy.

Where their lobbyists' persuasive charm might falter, corporate interests were accused of purchasing lawmakers' support for their favored bills and projects, whether through outright bribes, kickbacks, or more veiled financial assistance. Entire state legislatures were said to be "bought" in such fashion, and even the august members of the US Congress were not immune, as a series of scandals attested.[2] But the clandestine activities of "special interests," were never entirely confined to the legislative sphere. They were accused of purchasing support *for* lawmakers, too, by paying citizens directly for their votes—and to the extent such charges were corroborated, their "corruptions" reached outward, into the world of elections. And there was growing concern in the late nineteenth century with a more subtle way that business might corrupt the electoral process, as corporate money became the dominant source of national party campaign funds on both the Republican and Democratic sides.[3]

The Gilded Age, of course, was as famed for its exuberant elections as for its underwhelming candidates. From the local wards all the way to Washington, DC, party organizations sought to elect their men to office and then distribute the spoils: the federal and state patronage jobs that fueled the era's

The Rise of Political Action Committees. Emily J. Charnock, Oxford University Press (2020). © Oxford University Press.
DOI: 10.1093/oso/9780190075514.001.0001

"machine" politics, especially at the local level, where powerful party "bosses" held sway. For presidential campaigns they offered political theater on a grand scale: forming military-style marching bands and drilling in the streets, illuminating neighborhoods with dramatic torchlight parades, and staging mass rallies to energize and express popular passions—all in pursuit of votes.[4] The expense of such entertainments had initially been borne by the postmasters, customs inspectors, and clerks who owed their federal jobs to the party's favor and in return paid part of their salaries back to its coffers. But patronage politics attracted powerful critics in the late nineteenth century: urban reformers who objected to the poor administration of government and the graft that so often came with it. They pushed for new merit requirements for US civil service appointments, first applied in the 1880s, which eventually put an end to this internal source of party funding.[5] Corporations soon stepped in to fill the void, but in doing so they raised a new concern among the very critics who had helped bring about this development. Business interests, they realized, would likely *want* something in return for their donations—a quid pro quo—and that something, they surmised, was favorable policies. The 1896 election helped to crystallize this concern, when Marc Hanna—chairman of the Republican National Committee (RNC)—solicited huge corporate contributions to aid the GOP's presidential candidate William McKinley, portraying him as the defender of business interests against the unabashed populism of Democratic contender William Jennings Bryan. Hanna proceeded to raise at least $3 million, and by some estimates as much as $10 million, for McKinley's campaign, exacerbating concerns over the role of money in elections.[6]

As the century drew to a close, therefore, both special interests *and* political parties found themselves subject to intense and intertwined criticism. Reformist zeal for "clean government" was morphing into broader national demands for a "purer" democracy—less susceptible to corporate influence, boss rule, and machine politics, and much more responsive to the people. The early twentieth century saw a wave of legislation embodying this reformist spirit—the Progressive spirit—including primary elections in many states, designed to enhance popular control over party nomination contests, and new laws intended to stop the influx of corporate money into politics. In New York, for example, a 1905 investigation into financial malpractice among life insurance companies revealed extensive corporate campaign contributions to state lawmakers, and the ensuing public outcry prompted the legislature to ban the practice altogether.[7] This scandal had national ramifications, too, for the investigation also uncovered massive donations to the RNC in 1904, embarrassing McKinley's successor as president—Theodore Roosevelt—who had styled himself as a champion of business regulation. Roosevelt responded late in 1905 by calling for an outright ban on corporate contributions in federal elections, along with requirements to publicize other campaign donations and spending.[8] A new advocacy group was even formed to promote these measures, the "National Publicity Bill Organization," which lobbied Congress to act.[9]

What eventually emerged was the Tillman Act of 1907. Named for its Senate sponsor, South Carolina Democrat "Pitchfork" Ben Tillman, it was the first federal law to regulate campaign finance and banned corporate contributions "in connection with" congressional or presidential elections altogether.[10] It did not eliminate corporate influence entirely, since the law applied only to federal contests, the enforcement regime was weak, and it did nothing to prevent an *individual* businessman making donations. But the attempt suggested something important about the electoral scene and the way "special interests" participated in it: that the dominant mode of corporate involvement in elections was understood to be *financial*, and that corporations or their representatives did not so much *electioneer* as help to finance the campaigns of those who did.

Indeed, at the time of the law's passage those major electoral combatants were still party organizations, whether Democratic, Republican, or sometimes third parties. Numerous third or "independent" parties, as they were then known, had reared their heads since the end of the Civil War, expressing societal discontent or advocating new causes: whether the pursuit of greater legal rights for women and African Americans as embodied in the Equal Rights Party of 1872, the drive for "temperance" by restraining alcohol consumption, as promoted by the Prohibition Party from the 1870s, or the protests of farmers and industrial workers that culminated in the People's Party of the 1890s. But in the early twentieth century, other electoral actors were coming into view.

The growth of primary elections during the Progressive Era meant that candidates for office, for example, increasingly had to wage their own campaigns before receiving the party's label and assistance—encouraging a range of new personalized campaign organizations, especially at the presidential level. But new campaign finance laws hinted at other developments. In 1910 Congress enacted further reforms requiring the disclosure of congressional campaign contributions and expenditures, just as Roosevelt had urged five years before.[11] The Publicity Act of 1910 applied to all "political committees," instructing them to file financial reports with the Clerk of the House of Representatives and, after amendments to the Publicity Act were passed in 1911, with the Secretary of the Senate too.[12] (The amendments further extended such disclosure requirements to candidates and placed limitations on their spending, while also bringing Senate and primary elections under the auspices of the law, alongside the House contests it had originally applied to.)[13] The term "political committee," while mainly intended to embrace the national and congressional party committees, was defined broadly so as to embrace *any* group that sought to influence federal elections and was active in more than one state.[14] The legislation did not elaborate further, but a new type of political organization emerging at the turn of the century would increasingly fit the bill: the modern "interest group."

Embracing a wider range of economic, societal, and ideational concerns than traditional special interests and organized along more bureaucratic lines, this period saw the emergence of new or reformulated labor unions, farmers' associations, and issue-oriented groups, alongside a growing number of trade associations, which pursued specific policy goals at the national level. These early interest groups developed novel modes of lobbying that drew on public opinion as a source of influence and generally focused their attention on legislative and administrative affairs, as scholars such as Clemens have explored.[15] But some did venture into electoral territory, as subsequent campaign finance laws make clear. By 1943, for example, labor unions were sufficiently engaged in elections to prompt a federal ban on their campaign contributions altogether, just as corporations had been restricted more than three decades before. That ban, written into the War Labor Disputes Act of 1943—popularly known as the Smith-Connally Act—would prompt the formation of the first "political action committee" (PAC) that same year, as well as further waves of legislation to regulate this new mode of electoral engagement.

This sketch, drawing on campaign finance law itself, suggests a changing electoral environment in the twentieth century in which at least some interest groups came to participate. But we know very little about the specific contours of that environment prior to the 1970s, when major campaign finance reforms required systematic monitoring of parties and nonparty electoral actors. This chapter seeks to address that deficiency and offer a framework for understanding the rise of interest group electioneering by reconstructing the universe of organized electoral participants in this earlier period, examining *who* was active and *when* they were active and considering their organizational characteristics. It does so by drawing on a neglected legacy of the Publicity Act and its amendments, a series of congressional investigations into campaign expenditures and wider electoral activity conducted in the first half of the twentieth century, supplemented by other relevant congressional data. In this same time frame, Congress also conducted several investigations into lobbying and erected a separate legislative framework to regulate this aspect of interest group activity. These lobbying investigations provide further detail on the interest group environment and offer a comparative perspective, indicating to what extent groups were active across both realms.

Though electioneering was predominantly a party activity at the beginning of the century, these investigations reveal an expanding electoral field, as organized interest groups and other nonparty entities increasingly entered the fray. The focus in this chapter is on identifying relevant groups, while subsequent chapters examine the nature of their activities more closely and their orientation toward political parties. Indeed, the analysis offered here highlights the key actors on which the rest of the book focuses and provides the spine for the larger story it tells: showing the rise of new types of campaign organization and suggesting waves of interest group electoral mobilization, often reactive in character, that would have important implications for party politics in the United States.

Identifying Electoral Actors

Organizations participating actively in elections are relatively easy to identify today. Major campaign finance reforms in the 1970s clarified and codified a wide range of economic activities in elections—whether direct contributions to candidates and parties or forms of indirect spending with electoral implications—and required much more rigorous financial reporting from groups that engaged in them. These reforms also created a new federal institution to monitor compliance and oversee implementation of the laws, the Federal Election Commission (FEC). Since 1974 FEC information has offered a detailed picture of the electoral environment, documenting a dramatic increase in the number of PACs, in particular.

Originally, PACs were vehicles designed to circumvent outright bans on financial participation by labor unions and corporations in elections. By drawing on separate "voluntary" funds solicited from union members or corporate officers rather than resources from the central treasury, they offered an alternative avenue for financial participation, whether it was making direct contributions to candidates or party organizations, should the PAC's directors so choose, or spending money separately in support of particular candidates or causes. This latter possibility became more significant after 1947, when restrictions on labor unions were tightened to include any *expenditures* in elections, not simply their contributions.[16] The legality of the PAC form, however, was never directly tested in the mid-twentieth century. Only in 1971, with passage of the Federal Election Campaign Act (FECA), was the concept legally codified, described in the statute itself and subjected to fundraising and spending limitations. So began a sharp rise in the number of PACs. The newly created FEC (established by amendments to the FECA passed that year) identified 608 PACs active on the national scene in 1974. By the end of the 1970s there would be over 2,000 in existence, and there were over 8,000 in the most recent count.[17]

Some of these contemporary PACs are freestanding or "unconnected" to any other organization, though they may themselves be dedicated to promoting particular economic interests, issues, or ideological goals. In this sense, they can be embraced within the larger category of "interest group" as proposed by Truman, since they are forged on the basis of "shared attitudes," which they hope to advance in the political sphere.[18] Others are "connected PACs," often linked to prominent interest groups as traditionally understood, in line with the original PAC concept. Such groups have created affiliated PACs to legally participate in elections but may also undertake other politically relevant activities themselves, such as lobbying, or may engage in entirely nonpolitical activities for the benefit of their members or adherents, such as offering insurance schemes or discount programs.[19]

The dramatic growth in the number of PACs since the 1970s has led most scholars of interest group electioneering to focus their attention on the late twentieth century and to place particular emphasis on the growth of PACs associated with corporations or business groups.[20] But the 1971 law did not create the concept of a PAC; it merely integrated it formally into the body of campaign finance law and in some sense legitimized what had been a legally ambiguous and somewhat controversial mode of organization. PACs did exist prior to the campaign finance reforms of the 1970s, at least thirty by 1964 and more than a hundred by 1970, according to contemporary sources.[21] Other groups, moreover, though not formally classified as PACs, were already operating in elections in significant ways well before the 1970s. And yet there is a dearth of systematic information on interest groups that became actively involved in earlier federal elections. Though scholars usually offer a brief list of highlights, including Labor's Non-Partisan League (LNPL) in 1936, the original P.A.C. created by the Congress of Industrial Organizations (CIO) in 1943, or the American Medical Association's Political Action Committee (AMPAC), created in 1961, none have delved deeply into the origins of modern interest group electioneering.[22]

Some sources do help to identify interest groups more broadly in the earlier twentieth century. The US Commerce Department began tracking the number of trade associations in the late 1910s, for example, and added other "national associations," including professional and civic groups, in the 1940s.[23] From 1956 onward, moreover, the *Encyclopedia of Associations* offered a comprehensive guide to national interest groups, as do a range of more recent sources.[24] Scholars such as Walker have used these sources to try to reconstruct a historical directory, based on the formation dates of interest groups that appear there.[25] Tichenor and Harris, however, have criticized this approach because it necessarily omits shorter-lived organizations. Instead, they look to Congress and its wide range of oversight and legislative hearings as a contemporary source of information, identifying representatives of organized interests that appeared before its committees to track new groups in real time.[26]

To an extent, then, what Tichenor and Harris identify are *lobbies*, interest groups that sought to influence proposed legislation by offering their views before Congress. Since the 1920s, in fact, earlier generations of political scientists had sought to do just that, using Washington, DC, phone directories or office tenant lists, for example.[27] After 1946, moreover, individuals and organizations that undertook lobbying activities were required to register with congressional officials under the terms of the Federal Regulation of Lobbying Act of that year, passed amid an upswing in lobbying as Congress debated major legislation following World War II.[28] Government publications thus provide comprehensive lists of registered lobbies from that point.[29] But interest group representatives appearing before Congress were not always there to lobby. They might not even have appeared voluntarily, if compelled by committee chairmen using their subpoena power, or they might have testified at oversight or investigative hearings rather than those concerned with prospective legislation. To the extent it is possible to determine the nature of their activity, therefore, we might be better served by looking at the nature of the hearings themselves.

In the early to mid-twentieth century, Congress held a series of investigative hearings examining lobbying specifically, considering its practitioners, their methods, and the scope of their influence, which can shed light on those interest groups whose activities were considered worthy of attention. In this same period, moreover, Congress held oversight hearings to assess compliance with existing campaign finance laws, which by 1925 had been revised to take account of the US Supreme Court's 1921 decision in *Newberry v. United States,* which rejected congressional authority to regulate campaign spending in primaries or other prenomination contests and thus struck down those aspects of the Publicity Act amendments (this judicial prohibition would eventually be reversed in 1941).[30] Congress had responded with the Federal Corrupt Practices Act of 1925, which increased the spending limits for congressional candidates in general election contests and extended disclosure requirements to all "political committees" active in presidential campaigns as well as congressional races.[31] Although some additional restrictions would be introduced thereafter, including overall caps on spending by political committees and bans on labor union activity, the revised Federal Corrupt Practices Act would serve as the main regulatory framework for campaign finance until the 1970s.[32]

The oversight hearings thus shed light on the electoral environment these laws governed, providing one of the few sources of information on the disclosure reports filed by political committees, for example, since the Publicity Laws neither placed requirements on the House Clerk or Senate Secretary to keep or publish them nor provided effective mechanisms forcing anyone to file them in the first place.[33] More generally, considering the organizational affiliations of the witnesses appearing before these committees offers insight into who was active in campaigns—whether they self-identified as political committees or not. By adapting Tichenor and Harris's methodology, therefore, but looking only to these subsets of hearings, we can both identify interest groups and associate them with a particular type of activity. Using the campaign expenditure subset in particular, we can build a picture of the early electoral environment and the role of interest groups therein.

Between 1912—the first election year in which the amended publicity laws would operate—and 1974—when Congress established the Federal Election Commission as an independent agency charged with monitoring campaign finance activities—Congress formed thirty-six committees to assess different aspects of campaign activity. At first these were ad hoc affairs, formed at varying intervals when controversies over campaign finance bubbled to the surface in the national discourse. Over time they became more regularized, with one or both chambers typically creating a campaign investigation committee each election cycle, though these were sometimes inactive, being held in reserve to examine any potential violations of the law that might emerge in the campaign. Of those that were active, some looked only at congressional elections in specific states, in response to local scandals or specific charges of impropriety. But others took on a more general or national aspect, whether by virtue of examining the presidential race or by looking to congressional elections at large. Fourteen such investigations took place in this period, as detailed in table 1.1.

Congress also undertook a number of investigations into lobbying activities in this same period, usually in response to notable scandals. Again, some of these committees investigated specific charges of impropriety or particular organizations, and some examined lobbying practices at large. At least twenty separate committees examined lobbying with a narrower focus, while four took a more general view, as shown in tables 1.2 and 1.3. These general investigations into lobbying and electioneering were conducted separately in all but one case, the 1956–1957 Special Committee to Investigate Political Activities, Lobbying, and Campaign Contributions, chaired by Senator John L. McClellan. And yet testimony before both types of lobbying committee often touched on concerns about *electoral* practices. (The apparently pernicious electioneering of the United States Brewers' Association, for example, was examined under the guise of a *lobbying* investigation.)[34]

The tendency to separate these investigations points to an initial belief that lobbying and electioneering were theoretically distinct types of activity undertaken in different realms—despite testimony that often revealed their interaction—which helps explain why Congress established different legal regimes to regulate them. Yet the McClellan committee suggests a growing awareness of connections between them over time.[35] This investigation had been prompted, after all, by charges that an oil company had promised a large campaign contribution to a senator in return for a favorable vote on a natural gas bill, exactly the kind of quid pro quo that linked lobbying and campaigning in the most corrupting light.[36] Drawing on the lobbying investigations, therefore, can shed light on when and how these two spheres intersected.

Table 1.1 **National-Level/General Campaign Contribution and Expenditure Investigations, 1912–1974**

Committee	Chairman	Chamber	Year/ Congress
Committee on Privileges and Elections, Subcommittee	Moses E. Clapp (R-MN)	Senate	1912–1913 (62nd)
Committee on Privileges and Elections, Subcommittee on S. Res. 357	William S. Kenyon (R-IA)	Senate	1920 (66th)
Special Committee on Campaign Expenditures	William E. Borah (R-ID)	Senate	1924 (68th)
Special Committee Investigating Presidential Campaign Expenditures	Frederick Steiwer (R-OR)	Senate	1928 (70th)
Select Committee on Senatorial Campaign Expenditures	Gerald P. Nye (R-ND)	Senate	1930–31 (71st–72nd)
Special Committee on Investigation of Campaign Expenditures	Robert B. Howell (R-NE) / Tom Connally (D-TX)	Senate	1932–33 (72nd-73rd)
Special Committee to Investigate Campaign Expenditures of Presidential, Vice Presidential, and Senatorial Candidates in 1936	Augustine Lonergan (D-CT)	Senate	1936–1937 (74th–75th)
Special Committee Investigating Campaign Expenditures	Guy M. Gillette (D-IA)	Senate	1940–1941 (76th–77th)
Committee to Investigate Campaign Expenditures	Clinton P. Anderson (D-NM)	House	1944 (78th)
Special Committee to Investigate Campaign Expenditures of Presidential, Vice Presidential, and Senatorial Candidates	Theodore F. Green (D-RI)	Senate	1944 (78th)
Committee to Investigate Campaign Expenditures	J. Percy Priest (D-TN)	House	1946 (79th)
Special Committee to Investigate Campaign Expenditures	Hale Boggs (D-LA)	House	1952 (82nd)

Table 1.1 **Continued**

Committee	Chairman	Chamber	Year/ Congress
Committee on Rules and Administration, Subcommittee on Privileges and Elections	Albert Gore (D-TN)	Senate	1956 (84th)
Special Committee to Investigate Political Activities, Lobbying, and Campaign Contributions	John L. McClellan (D-AR)	Senate	1956–1957 (84th)

The McClellan committee would prove to be the last major investigation into either lobbying or campaign expenditures prior to the electoral reforms of the 1970s. Though the House would set up pro forma electoral committees beyond this point, they only examined a handful of subnational controversies.[37] Congress instead shifted its attention to legislative reform, holding a number of hearings on proposed campaign finance legislation in the 1960s that culminated in passage of the FECA in 1971.[38] The hearings identified in these tables offer information on lobbying and electoral practices through the late 1950s.

The electoral hearings, moreover, offer insight into the specific organizations involved in campaigns during this period. Despite occasional chronological gaps—such as 1916, when no committee was formed in either chamber, or 1936, when a Senate committee issued a report but held no hearings—these hearings offer a systematic source of information on electoral participants, utilizing the Tichenor and Harris methodology.[39] Though necessarily an imperfect measure, identifying the organizational affiliations of witnesses who appeared can indicate which groups were active on the electoral scene.[40] Comparison to the lobbying hearings can suggest to what extent groups were active in both realms or if they tended to focus their attentions on one, providing a more nuanced picture of interest group political activity in general.

Tables 1.4 and 1.5 show those national organizations whose representatives appeared at congressional hearings for major electoral and lobbying investigations from 1912 through 1957.[41] Table 1.4 displays this information prior to 1940, arrayed by committee, while Table 1.5 shows the same information post-1940. These hearings cover eight of the twelve presidential elections held between 1912 and 1957—with the exceptions of 1916, 1932, 1936, and 1948—and include one congressional midterm election in 1946 (most midterm investigations focused on particular contests in which problems had emerged rather than nationwide or general patterns, with this exception). The organizations are categorized based on their relationships with or commitment to political

Table 1.2 **Investigations of Lobbying by Specific Groups/in Particular Sectors, 1900–1974**

Committee	Chairman	Chamber	Year /Congress	Groups/ Corporations Investigated
Select Committee Under House Resolution 288	Henry S. Boutell (R-IL)	House	1908 (60th)	Investigation of Corrupt Practices in Lobbying Congress, Charges Against Electric Boat Co. and Lake Torpedo Boat Co.
Subcommittee of the House Judiciary Committee in relation to H. Res. 482	John A. Sterling (R-IL)	House	1910 (61st)	Investigation of Charges Relative to Ship Subsidy Legislation
Committee on Investigation of United States Steel Corporation	Augustus O. Stanley (D-KY)	House	1911–1912 (62nd)	United States Steel Corporation
Select Committee to Investigate Lobby Charges	Finis J. Garrett (D-TN)	House	1913–1914 (63rd)	Charges Against Members of the House and Lobby Activities of the National Association of Manufacturers of the US and Others
Special Committee on Lobbying	Thomas J. Walsh (D-MT)	Senate	1914–1916 (63rd–64th)	Maintenance of a Lobby to Influence Legislation on the Ship Purchase Bill
Special Committee to Investigate National Security League	Ben Johnson (D-KY)	House	1918–1919 (65th)	National Security League
Committee on Judiciary	Lee S. Overman (D-NC)	Senate	1918–1919 (65th)	Brewing and Liquor Interests and German and Bolshevik Propaganda (United States Brewers' Association)

Table 1.2 **Continued**

Committee	Chairman	Chamber	Year /Congress	Groups/ Corporations Investigated
Committee on Banking and Currency	Louis T. McFadden (R-PA)	House	1921 (66th)	Farm Organizations
Subcommittee on S. Res. 110, of the Committee on Agriculture and Forestry	Henry W. Keyes (R-NH)	Senate	1922 (67th)	Investigation of Organizations Engaged in Combating Legislation for the Relief of Agriculture
Subcommittee on S. Res. 142, Committee on Judiciary	Samuel M. Shortridge (R-CA)	Senate	1922 (67th)	Proposed Investigation of the Motion-Picture Industry
Subcommittee on S. Res. 77, Committee on Judiciary	Samuel M. Shortridge (R-CA)	Senate	1922 (67th)	Alleged Dye Monopoly (and maintenance of lobbies)
Special Committee to Investigate Air Mail and Ocean Mail Contracts	Hugo L. Black (D-AL)	Senate	1934 (72nd)	Investigation of Air Mail and Ocean Mail Contracts
Special Committee Investigating Munitions Industry	Gerald P. Nye (R-ND)	Senate	1934–1936 (73rd–74th)	Munitions Industry
Special Committee to Investigate American Retail Federation	Wright Patman (D-TX)	House	1935–1936 (74th)	Investigation of the Lobbying Activities of the American Retail Federation/ Investigation of the Trade Practices of Big Scale Retail and Wholesale Buying and Selling Organizations
Select Committee Investigating Old-Age Pension Organizations	C. Jasper Bell (D-MO)	House	1936 (74th)	Old-Age Pension Plans and Organizations

(continued)

Table 1.2 **Continued**

Committee	Chairman	Chamber	Year /Congress	Groups/ Corporations Investigated
Special Committee to Investigate Contracts under National Defense Program	Harry S. Truman (D-MO)	Senate	1941 (77th)	Investigation of the National Defense Program
Subcommittee on Publicity and Propaganda of the Committee on Expenditures in Executive Departments	Forest A. Harness (R-IN)	House	1947 (80th)	Investigation of Agricultural Adjustment Agency and Production and Marketing Administration Publicity and Propaganda in Nebraska
Subcommittee on Investigations of the Committee on Expenditures in Executive Departments	Clyde R. Hoey (D-NC)	House	1951 (82nd)	Influence in Government Procurement
Subcommittee on Public Works and Resources, of the Committee on Government Operations	Earl Chudoff (D-PA)	House	1955–1956 (84th)	Private Electric Utilities' Organized Efforts to Influence the Secretary of the Interior (Ebasco Services, Inc., and Rocky Mountain Group)
Special Committee to Investigate Political Activities, Lobbying, and Campaign Contributions	John L. McClellan (D-AR)	Senate	1956 (84th)	Oil and Gas Lobby Investigation
Senate Committee on Foreign Relations	J. William Fulbright (D-AR)	Senate	1963 (88th)	Activities of Nondiplomatic Representatives of Foreign Principals in the US

Table 1.3 **General Lobbying Investigations, 1900–1974**

Committee/Investigation	Chairman	Chamber	Year /Congress
Subcommittee on S. Res. 92, Committee on Judiciary ("Maintenance of a Lobby to Influence Legislation")	Lee S. Overman (D-NC)	Senate	1913–1914 (63rd)
Subcommittee on S. Res. 20, Committee on Judiciary ("Lobby Investigation")	Thaddeus H. Caraway (D-AR)	Senate	1929–1931 (71st–72nd)
Special Committee to Investigate Lobbying Activities ("Investigation of Lobbying Activities")	Hugo L. Black (D-AL)/Sherman Minton (D-IN)	Senate	1935–1938 (74th–75th)
Select Committee on Lobbying Activities ("Role of Lobbying In Representative Self-Government")	Frank Buchanan (D-PA)	House	1950 (81st)

parties, presidential candidates, economic and professional communities, or specific causes. This categorization looks beyond organizational names, however, for in many cases these are uninformative or misleading—particularly where parties or economic interests formed "front groups" designed to appeal to specific communities while obscuring their true provenance, as discussed in more detail later in this chapter.[42]

Although these hearings can tell us much about the electoral environment in the early to mid-twentieth century in themselves, supplementary information can help to round out the picture, compensating for the missing years previously noted (which includes significant contests such as 1936 and 1948) and bringing us further forward in time toward the end of the old campaign finance regime, before the major reforms of the 1970s. As noted, some committees that did not hold hearings still issued significant reports.[43] Moreover, various studies that analyzed these reports, or drew directly from financial disclosures made by political committees themselves, touch on these missing or later years.[44] In this respect, the work of early campaign finance scholars such as James Pollock, Louise Overacker, Alexander Heard, and Herbert Alexander is particularly valuable.

Overacker, for example, published a series of important *American Political Science Review* articles detailing spending in each presidential election cycle from 1932 to 1944.[45] Although she focused more heavily on individual contributions than organizational ones, she increasingly identified important "nonparty" or "independent" groups, as she labeled them, that had been active in each campaign.

Table 1.4 **National Organizations Represented at Campaign/Lobbying Hearings, before 1940**

	Campaign Expenditure Hearings				Lobbying Hearings		
	CLAPP (1912)	KENYON (1920)	BORAH (1924)	STEIWER (1928)	OVERMAN (1913)	CARAWAY (1929)	BLACK (1935)
Political Parties							
Democratic	Democratic Congressional Campaign Committee Democratic Executive Committee Democratic National Committee (DNC)	Democratic Congressional Campaign Committee DNC					
Republican		Republican Congressional Campaign Committee		RNC			

Republican National Committee (RNC)	RNC		
Republican Senatorial Campaign Committee			
National Young Men's Republican League			
Third Party	Progressive Party	Farmer-Labor Party	LaFollette-Wheeler National Progressive Committee
	Socialist Labor Party		Progressive Party

Candidate Centered Groups

Hoover National Republican Club	Engineers National Committee

(*continued*)

Table 1.4 Continued

	Campaign Expenditure Hearings				Lobbying Hearings		
	CLAPP (1912)	KENYON (1920)	BORAH (1924)	STEIWER (1928)	OVERMAN (1913)	CARAWAY (1929)	BLACK (1935)
		Leonard Wood League		Hoover for President Association			
Economic Interests							
Farm						American Farm Bureau Federation	
Labor		Plumb Plan League	Order of Railway Conductors		American Federation of Labor (AFL)		
Professional						National Council of State Legislatures	
Business	American Association of Foreign Language Newspapers	National Retail Liquor Dealers Association			American Cane Growers Association	American Bottlers of Carbonated Beverages	American Federation of Utility Investors

National Association of Manufacturers (NAM)	American Press Association	American Fruit Growers, Inc.	American Gas Association
	Diamond Trade Tariff League	American Tariff League	Committee of Public Utility Executives
	Home Market Club	Chamber of Commerce of the United States	Edison Electric Institute
	NAM	Independent Petroleum Association	National Conference of Investors
	National Association of Hosiery Manufacturers	National Association of Wool Manufacturers	
	National Association of Wool Manufacturers	National Council of American Importers and Traders	
	National Council for Industrial Defense	National Dry Goods Association	

(*continued*)

Table 1.4 Continued

	Campaign Expenditure Hearings				Lobbying Hearings		
	CLAPP (1912)	KENYON (1920)	BORAH (1924)	STEIWER (1928)	OVERMAN (1913)	CARAWAY (1929)	BLACK (1935)
					National Wool Growers Association	Southern Tariff Association	
					US Beet Sugar Association	Tennessee River Improvement Association	
						US Beet Sugar Association	
						US Sugar Association	
Issues/Ideological Interests							
		League to Enforce Peace		Anti-Saloon League of America	American Antitrust League	Anti-Saloon League of America	American Taxpayers League
				Association Against the Prohibition Amendment	Carnegie Endowment for International Peace	Association Against the Prohibition Amendment	Crusaders
Veterans							

Ku Klux Klan	National Committee on Prison Labor	Board of Temperance, Prohibition, and Public Morals—Methodist Episcopal Church	Farmers Independence Council of America
	National Civic League	National Tariff Commission Association	National Committee to Uphold Constitutional Government
			Sentinels of the Republic

Sources: "Campaign Contributions," Vols. I-II of *Hearings before a Subcommittee of the Committee on Privileges and Elections*, US Senate, 62nd Cong., 2nd–3rd sess. (Washington, DC: Government Printing Office, 1912–1913) [**Clapp Committee**]; "Presidential Campaign Expenses," Vols. I-II of *Hearings before a Subcommittee of the Committee on Privileges and Elections*, US Senate, 66th Cong., 2nd sess. (Washington, DC: Government Printing Office, 1921) [**Kenyon Committee**]; "Campaign Expenditures," Vols. I-III of *Hearings before the Special Committee on Campaign Expenditures*, US Senate, 68th Cong., 2nd sess. (Washington, DC: Government Printing Office, 1925) [**Borah Committee**]; "Presidential Campaign Expenditures," Parts 1–4 of *Hearings before the Special Committee Investigating Presidential Campaign Expenditures*, US Senate, 70th Cong., 1st-2nd sess. (Washington, DC: Government Printing Office, 1928) [**Steiwer Committee**]; "Maintenance of a Lobby to Influence Legislation," Vols I-IV and Parts 49–65 of *Hearings before the Subcommittee on S. Res. 92, Committee on the Judiciary*, US Senate, 63rd Cong., 1st-2nd sess. (Washington, DC: Government Printing Office, 1913–1914) [**Overman Committee**]; "Lobby Investigation," Vols I-IV of *Hearings before the Subcommittee on S. Res. 20, Committee on the Judiciary*, US Senate, 71st–72nd Cong. (Washington, DC: Government Printing Office, 1931–32) [**Caraway Committee**]; "Investigation of Lobbying Activities," Parts 1–8 of *Hearings before the Special Committee to Investigate Lobbying Activities*, 74th–75th Cong. (Washington, DC: Government Printing Office, 1936–1938) [**Black/Minton Committee**]. (Note: Senator Sherman Minton of Indiana took over the chairmanship of this committee following Senator Hugo Black's appointment to the Supreme Court in August 1937).

Table 1.5 **National Organizations Represented at Campaign/Lobbying Hearings, after 1940**

	Campaign Expenditure Hearings						Lobbying Hearings	Lobbying/ Campaign Hearings
	GILLETTE (1940)	ANDERSON (1944)	GREEN (1944)	PRIEST (1946)	BOGGS (1952)	GORE (1956)	BUCHANAN (1950)	McCLELLAN (1956/57)
Political Parties								
Democratic	DNC					DNC		DNC
						Young Democratic Club of America		
Republican	RNC					National Federation of Republican Women		RNC
	United Republican Finance Committee of New York					RNC		
						United Republican Finance Committee		

Third	Communist Party of USA	American Democratic National Committee	American Democratic National Committee	Young Republican National Campaign Committee	Socialist Labor Party of America
		America First Party		Young Republican National Federation	

Candidate Centered Groups

	Associated Willkie Clubs of America		Citizens for Eisenhower-Nixon	Citizens for Eisenhower-Nixon	Citizens for Eisenhower-Nixon
	Democrats for Willkie		Volunteers for Stevenson	Volunteers for Stevenson	Volunteers for Stevenson-Kefauver

(continued)

Table 1.5 Continued

	Campaign Expenditure Hearings						Lobbying Hearings	Lobbying/ Campaign Hearings
	GILLETTE (1940)	ANDERSON (1944)	GREEN (1944)	PRIEST (1946)	BOGGS (1952)	GORE (1956)	BUCHANAN (1950)	McCLELLAN (1956/57)
First Voters League								
Independent Business Men's Committee								
National Committee for Agriculture								
National Committee of Independent Voters								
Economic Interests								
Farm								American Farm Bureau Federation

Labor	CIO-PAC	AFL	CIO-PAC	AFL-CIO	CIO	AFL-CIO
Labor	Congress of Industrial Organizations Political Action Committee (CIO-PAC)			AFL-CIO Committee on Political Education (COPE)		COPE
	National Citizens Political Action Committee (NCPAC)	American Federation of Musicians	(AFL) Labor's League for Political Education	International Brotherhood of Teamsters	Public Affairs Institute	United Steelworkers of America
		Brotherhood of Railroad Trainmen		United Automobile Workers		International Association of Machinists
		CIO-PAC				
		International Brotherhood of Teamsters				
		NCPAC				
		United Garment Workers				

(continued)

Table 1.5 **Continued**

	Campaign Expenditure Hearings						Lobbying Hearings	Lobbying/ Campaign Hearings
	GILLETTE (1940)	ANDERSON (1944)	GREEN (1944)	PRIEST (1946)	BOGGS (1952)	GORE (1956)	BUCHANAN (1950)	McCLELLAN (1956/57)
Professional								American Medical Association
Business	People's Committee to Defend Life Insurance and Savings	NAM		NAM	National Drainage, Levee, and Irrigation Association	American Publishers Association	National Association of Home Builders	American Automobile Association
					National Association of Radio and TV Broadcasters	Chamber of Commerce of US	National Association of Real Estate Boards	American Sugar Beet Industry Policy Committee

	National Association of Real Estate Brokers—Realtors Washington Committee	American Sugar Cane League
National Association of Radio and Television Broadcasters		
	National Retail Lumber Dealers Association	American Trucking Association
	Twenty Percent Cabaret Tax Committee	Association of American Railroads
		Association of Sugar Producers of Puerto Rico
		Chamber of Commerce of US
		National Milk Producers Federation
		National Rural Electric Cooperative Association

(continued)

Table 1.5 **Continued**

	Campaign Expenditure Hearings						Lobbying Hearings	Lobbying/Campaign Hearings
	GILLETTE (1940)	ANDERSON (1944)	GREEN (1944)	PRIEST (1946)	BOGGS (1952)	GORE (1956)	BUCHANAN (1950)	McCLELLAN (1956/57)
								US Cuban Sugar Council
Veterans								American Legion
Issues/Ideological Interests								
	Anti-Third Term Association	Committee for Constitutional Government		American Action, Inc.		Americans for Democratic Action	Americans for Democratic Action	National Committee for an Effective Congress
	National Committee to Uphold Constitutional Government					For America	Civil Rights Congress	
	Communist Political Association						Committee for Constitutional Government	
	Constitutional Educational League						Constitutional Educational League	
	Friends of Democracy							

Union for Democratic Action
Federation for Economic Education
National Economic Council
National Housing Conference

Sources: Vols 1–9 of *Hearings before the Special Committee Investigating Campaign Expenditures, 1940,* US Senate, 76th-77th Cong. (Washington, DC: Ward & Paul, 1940–1941) [**Gillette Committee**]; "Campaign Expenditures," Parts 1–12 of *Hearings before the Committee to Investigate Campaign Expenditures,* US House of Representatives, 78th Cong, 2nd sess. (Washington, DC: Government Printing Office, 1944) [**Anderson Committee**]; "Presidential, Vice Presidential, and Senatorial Campaign Expenditures, 1944," Part 1 of *Hearings before the Special Committee to Investigate Presidential, Vice Presidential, and Senatorial Campaign Expenditures, 1944,* US Senate, 78th Cong, 2nd sess. (Washington, DC: Government Printing Office, 1944) [**Green Committee**]; "Investigation of Presidential, Vice Presidential, and Senatorial Campaign Expenditures, 1944," Report of the Special Committee to Investigate Presidential, Vice Presidential, and Senatorial Campaign Expenditures, 1944, US Senate, 79th Cong, 1st sess, March 15, 1945, S. Rep. No. 101 [**Green Committee Report**] (This report mentions testimony not published separately); "Campaign Expenditures," Parts 1–7 of *Hearings before the Committee to Investigate Campaign Expenditures,* US House of Representatives, 79th Cong, 2nd sess. (Washington DC: Government Printing Office, 1946) [**Priest Committee**]; "Campaign Expenditures," *Hearings before the Special Committee to Investigate Campaign Expenditures,* 82nd Cong, 2nd sess. (Washington, DC: Government Printing Office, 1952) [**Boggs Committee**]; "1956 Presidential and Senatorial Campaign Contributions and Practices," Parts 1–2 of *Hearings before the Subcommittee on Privileges and Elections of the Committee on Rules and Administration,* US Senate, 84th Cong, 2nd sess. (Washington, DC: Government Printing Office, 1956) [**Gore Committee**]; Parts 1–10 of *Hearings before the Select Committee on Lobbying Activities,* US House of Representatives, 81st Cong, 2nd sess. (Washington, DC: Government Printing Office, 1950) [**Buchanan Committee**]; "Campaign Contributions, Political Activities, and Lobbying," Hearings before the Special Committee to Investigate Political Activities, Lobbying, and Campaign Contributions, US Senate, 84th Cong, 2nd sess. (Washington, DC: Government Printing Office, 1957) [**McClellan Committee**].

From 1936 onward, in fact, she provided extensive tables listing the most important examples, measured in terms of financial impact.[46] She also clarified her terminology over time, reserving the label "independent" for groups that raised money *independently* of the party organizations, even if they contributed some *to* the parties or spent money promoting their candidates. (In today's parlance we might call them "outside" groups, since they existed beyond the party's formal apparatus or the candidate's official reach but nonetheless participated in campaigns.)[47] Furthermore, Overacker indicated which presidential candidate a group was aiding—whether implicitly or explicitly—which raises questions about the partisan orientation of such groups, particularly those associated with organized interest groups, which typically proclaimed their "nonpartisanship" in this period. Her 1936 data, therefore, can supplement information drawn from the hearings, while her 1940 and 1944 lists provide a partial comparability check, as shown in table 1.6.[48]

Similar information is available for the early 1960s, courtesy of the Citizens Research Foundation (CRF). The CRF was an early campaign finance watchdog organization headed by Alexander Heard, a noted scholar of campaign finance who had served as an expert adviser for the Senate's 1956 campaign expenditure investigation, chaired by Senator Albert Gore (D-TN).[49] V. O. Key was a member of the advisory board, and Herbert Alexander became the executive director, eventually taking over and continuing Heard's work. (In this respect, he continued Overacker's work too, since the CRF had adopted her methods and acquired her research files.)[50]

In regular surveys of campaign financing, the CRF began to identify national organizations that were active in federal elections, including some that could be classified as PACs (that is, groups formed for the purposes of making campaign contributions to candidates, especially from parent organizations otherwise restricted by the law). In 1960, for example, a CRF study authored by Herbert Alexander identified at least thirty-nine national nonparty organizations that were financially active in elections. By 1964 the number had risen to fifty-six. The majority of these organizations were associated with labor unions, but others were "miscellaneous" groups identified with a range of business interests, professional associations, or particular policies and social issues.[51] The most financially notable of each type are shown in table 1.7 (all spent more than $100,000 on their political activities during the campaign, a benchmark Overacker first employed to distinguish the most important groups in her 1944 list).[52] Indeed, 1964 is chosen as the last election year for consideration here because the range of "miscellaneous" groups active in that election suggests an important culminating point, as discussed more in the following sections.

So what can these various sources tell us about the electoral and legislative worlds in the early to mid-twentieth century? Who were the main actors in each

Table 1.6 **Important Nonparty or Independent Organizations, 1936–1944 (National Only)**

	1936	1940	1944
Political Parties			
Democratic	Young Democratic Club of America	Young Democratic Clubs of America	
Republican	Women's National Republican Club	Women's National Republican Club	
Third Party			American Democratic National Committee*
Candidate Centered Groups			
	Committee of One	Associated Willkie Clubs of America*	Business Men for Roosevelt
	Good Neighbor League	Business Men's League for Roosevelt	Democrats for Dewey
	Independent Coalition of American Women	Citizens Information Committee	National Independent Committee for Roosevelt and Truman
	Progressive National Committee	Democrats for Willkie*	One Thousand Club
	Progressive Republican Committee for Franklin D. Roosevelt	Hollywood for Roosevelt Committee	Roosevelt Campaign Committee
	Roosevelt Agricultural Committee	Independent Willkie Advertising Campaign	
		National Committee for Agriculture*	
		National Committee of Independent Voters [for Roosevelt and Wallace]*	
		Willkie War Veterans	

(continued)

Table 1.6 **Continued**

	1936	*1940*	*1944*
		Economic Interests	
Farm			
Labor	Labor's Non-Partisan League		CIO-PAC*
			International Ladies' Garment Workers Union Campaign Committee for Roosevelt-Truman
			NCPAC*
Professional		*National Committee of Physicians for Willkie*	
Business	*Liberty League*	*People's Committee to Defend Life Insurance and Savings**	
Veterans			
		Issues/Ideological Interests	
		*National Committee to Uphold Constitutional Government**	Hollywood Democratic Committee
		[National Association of] Pro-America	

Note: Groups listed in Roman font supported the Democratic presidential candidate; groups listed in italics supported the Republican candidate.

* Groups marked with an asterisk in 1940 and 1944 also appear in congressional hearings/witness data for those years.

Sources: Adapted from "Table II—Expenditures of Important Non-Party Organizations in 1936," in Louise Overacker, "Campaign Funds in the Presidential Election of 1936," *American Political Science Review* 31, no. 3 (1937): 478; "Table IV—Expenditures of Important Non-Party Organizations in 1940," in Louise Overacker, "Campaign Finance in the Presidential Election of 1940," *American Political Science Review* 35, no. 4 (1941): 709; and "Table III—Receipts and Expenditures of Finance Committees and Important Independent Organizations in 1944," in Louise Overacker, "Presidential Campaign Funds, 1944," *American Political Science Review* 39, no. 5 (1945), 902. Subnational organizations and party-linked finance committees specified in the 1944 list have been excluded.

Table 1.7 **Labor and "Miscellaneous" National Committees, 1960–1964**

1960	1964
Political Parties	
–	–
Candidate-Centered Groups	
–	–
Economic Interests	
Farm	
Labor AFL-CIO Committee on Political Education (COPE)	Apparel Industry for Johnson-Humphrey
International Ladies Garment Workers Union	AFL-CIO COPE
Machinists' Non-Partisan Political League General and Educational Fund	[United Autoworkers] Committee for Good Government
United Steelworkers of America	Communications Workers of America
	[Teamsters] Democratic, Republican, Independent Voter Education (DRIVE)
	International Ladies Garment Workers Union
	Machinists' Non-Partisan League, General and Educational Fund
	Seafarers International Union
	United Autoworkers (UAW)
	United Steel Workers of America
Professional	American Medical Association Political Action Committee (AMPAC)
Business	Business-Industry Political Action Committee (BIPAC)
Veterans	

(*continued*)

Table 1.7 **Continued**

1960	1964
Issues/Ideological Interests	
Americans for Constitutional Action	Americans for Constitutional Action
Americans for Democratic Action	Americans for Democratic Action
Christian Nationalist Crusade	Christian Nationalist Crusade
National Committee for an Effective Congress	Council for a Livable World
	National Committee for an Effective Congress (Campaign Fund)

Note: In 1960 two other funds associated with the NCEC were also listed but are here subsumed within it: "A Clean Politics Appeal" and "Fund for Case, Cooper & Boggs." There were a further four unidentified "miscellaneous" committees. In 1964 five minor miscellaneous committees were listed, identified as the Conservative Action Committee, the Committee for a Conservative Congress, the Committee of the Hundred, the National Good Government Committee, and the Shoe Manufacturers Good Government Committee.

Sources: Adapted from Table 6 in Herbert E. Alexander, *Financing the 1960 Election* (Princeton, NJ: Citizens' Research Foundation, 1962), 42–43; and Table 13 in Herbert E. Alexander, *Financing the 1964 Election* (Princeton, NJ: Citizens' Research Foundation, 1966), 64–65.

setting? And in particular, what do they suggest about the contours of interest group involvement in elections?

Exploring Congressional Investigations

The major hearings themselves—both campaign expenditure and lobbying—heard over one thousand different witnesses representing more than one hundred different organizations.[53] Some of these organizations appeared across both types of hearings, others in only one type. Some appeared on only a single occasion, while others kept appearing before different committees over time. (Indeed, some individual witnesses themselves appeared multiple times.) Many organizations defied easy categorization, blending aspects of the four major types identified in the tables: formal party committees or party-affiliated groups, those promoting individual candidates, those advocating particular issues or causes, and those associated with a particular economic sector or professional community. Nonetheless, organizations that can be closely identified with each type did appear across the hearings. And the range appearing in the campaign expenditure investigations, in particular, suggests at least some nonparty involvement in elections from the outset.

Formal party organizations such as the RNC and Democratic National Committee (DNC) appeared regularly in the hearings, but only in those considering campaign expenditures rather than lobbying, which points to the dominant association of parties with the electoral field. Various party "auxiliaries" also appeared in the electoral hearings—affiliated groups usually founded and funded by the parties, such as the Young Men's Republican League in 1920 or the Young Democrats in 1956. These kinds of organizations primarily emerged in the 1920s and 1930s in an effort to broaden a party's appeal with particular demographic groups. Whereas the Young Men's Republican League was a temporary campaign group, the Young Democrats, founded in 1932, was a permanent auxiliary, reflecting the newfound permanence of the national party committees themselves (prior to the late 1920s, they had largely closed their doors between elections, operating with only a skeleton staff).[54]

A variety of third-party organizations also appear in the electoral hearings, such as the Progressive Party of 1912, although this category itself embraces some variations. The Progressive Party of 1924, for example, only fielded a candidate at the presidential level, making Senator Robert La Follette's campaign more of an independent presidential bid than a true third-party effort. (The La Follette-Wheeler National Progressive Committee, which appeared in 1924, supports that characterization.) Others were closer to intraparty factions (and proved to be far less electorally significant), such as the America First Party and American Democratic National Committee of 1944, which opposed Franklin Roosevelt as the Democratic nominee.[55] In contrast, the Communist Party of the United States (CPUSA), which had appeared as a third party in 1940, was dissolved and reformulated in 1944 as the Communist Political Association, which *supported* Roosevelt at the top of the ticket rather than field a presidential candidate of its own. It is therefore classified as an ideologically based interest group in 1944.[56]

The CPUSA's brief transformation (it was reconstituted as a party in 1945), in fact, suggests the growing importance of presidential candidates as a focus for organization. Indeed, an array of purely candidate-centered groups appear across the electoral hearings (and again, only in this arena). They were originally formed to contest primary elections and thereby aid an individual's campaign for a major party nomination. Though primaries were not determinative in presidential nominations until the later twentieth century, a strong showing could demonstrate a candidate's popular appeal and help create a "bandwagon" among regular convention delegates. Thus groups like the Hoover National Republican Club and the Leonard Wood League of 1920 sought to promote their respective candidates for the Republican nomination (though unsuccessfully in both cases that year).[57] But if their candidates were successfully nominated, such groups might continue to operate during the general election campaign too. Thus the Hoover for President Association of 1928 remained active after the GOP convention, securing a better outcome for its favored candidate that time around.[58]

Since they typically emerged during primary contests from which the parties themselves were barred, such groups were organizationally and financially independent.[59] They usually denied any official connections to their favored candidates, moreover, for a blend of cultural and legal reasons. For one, this stance allowed candidates to appear disinterested in their own election, as traditional conceptions of republican virtue required, and distanced them from the unseemly business of campaigning. It had certain legal benefits, too, since both the Publicity Act Amendments of 1911 and the Federal Corrupt Practices Act of 1925 imposed spending restrictions on federal candidates but did not restrict what others might do to aid their campaigns, ostensibly without the candidate's knowledge. As Overacker noted, "the astute candidate" must simply be "discreetly ignorant of what his friends are doing" in order to circumvent the law.[60]

From the 1930s, however, the Democratic Party itself began to embrace the candidate-centered mode of organizing in the general election context. The Committee of One for the Re-Election of Franklin D. Roosevelt, for example, received significant funding from the DNC itself in 1936, as did the Good Neighbor League, another group formed to promote Roosevelt's reelection, also discussed by Overacker. Like permanent auxiliaries, they were designed to expand the party's support, but in this case by downplaying the party connection and focusing instead on a candidate's personal appeal. Through such means the Democrats sought to attract voters in specific demographic, professional, and economic communities. The Roosevelt Agricultural Committee of 1936, for example, reached out to farmers and was almost entirely party funded, while the National Committee for Agriculture of 1940 was partially financed by the DNC.[61] They even sought to appeal to voters on ideological rather than partisan grounds. The National Progressive League in 1932, for example, mentioned by Overacker, was a Democratic-funded attempt to attract progressive Republican votes for Roosevelt. A similar group formed in 1936, the Progressive National Committee, however, was financed independently of the party.[62]

This portended an important shift toward independent financing more generally. The various groups supporting Republican presidential candidates in 1936 and 1940 were already independently financed, and all of the candidate groups appearing from 1944 onward had separate financing. Changes to the campaign finance laws in 1940 actually encouraged the formation of such groups, since amendments to the recently passed Hatch Act imposed an overall cap on spending by any one political committee, including the national party committees and their congressional counterparts. In 1940, therefore, there was a proliferation of alternative vehicles through which to raise and spend campaign cash on both sides, some of which appear in the hearings, like the National Committee of Independent Voters for Roosevelt and Wallace or the Associated Willkie Clubs of America (though the latter's formation actually predated the change in the law).[63] A subtle shift is also apparent in the form of some of these groups. Whereas a 1936 congressional report described "emergency committees" appearing for the duration of the campaign, some became more enduring organizations, even continuing their activities beyond Election Day.[64] The Willkie Clubs, for example, rebranded as the "Independent Clubs" after Willkie's defeat and remained in existence until December 1941.[65] More prominently, the Citizens for Eisenhower group, formed to advance the presidential candidacy of Dwight D. Eisenhower in 1952, was placed on a long-term footing thereafter, aiding his Republican congressional allies in 1954 and planning for his reelection in 1956, when it again appeared before a campaign expenditure committee.[66]

The electoral hearings and supplementary information thus suggest that a range of nonparty organizations were active in campaigns throughout the time frame under consideration, with their main unifying feature being the promotion of a particular presidential candidate. Some of these groups, as noted, reached out to or identified with specific economic or professional communities, temporarily at least. But those communities often formed their own groups to represent them politically on a permanent basis: interest groups as traditionally understood. This typically involved the promotion of beneficial legislation (or opposing laws that might hurt members' interests); accordingly, interest groups appear regularly in the lobbying hearings while parties and candidate-centered organizations do not. Yet interest groups also appear in some of the campaign expenditure hearings too, suggesting at least some electoral involvement on their part.

In terms of traditional economic interests, groups representing all three major sectors—business, labor, and agriculture—are evident across the hearings overall, but there are significant differences in where and how extensively they appear. First, across both sets of hearings, fewer farm groups appeared than those representing labor or business. The American Farm Bureau Federation, for example, the most prominent national farm group, only appeared twice—once before a lobbying committee in 1929 and again before the dual investigation into lobbying and campaigning in 1957, where its representatives were primarily questioned on legislative affairs.[67] While some apparently farm-related groups did appear in the dedicated electoral hearings and supplementary information, they did not necessarily have relationships with its major representative *interest* groups. The Roosevelt Agricultural League of 1936, as noted, was a party-funded campaign group whose efforts were directed by the DNC, while the National Committee for Agriculture of 1940 was a semi-independent version.[68] A similar entity mentioned in the 1928 campaign expenditure committee's report, the Independent Agricultural League, may have had informal links to the Farm Bureau, but this was a regional rather than a national effort, and Farm Bureau representatives were not questioned about it.[69] Similarly, the Farmer-Labor Party of 1920 drew some support from the Farmers' Union—an organization formed to protect small landowners and tenant farmers—yet the Farmers' Union itself does not appear elsewhere in the hearings.[70]

In contrast, business organizations were much more evident across both sets of hearings and the supplementary information.[71] Dedicated trade associations were especially numerous in the lobbying hearings, reinforcing the long-standing association of business and industrial interests with that realm. But they were not entirely absent from the electoral arena. In 1920, for example, the National Retail Liquor Dealers Association appeared in a campaign expenditure investigation, apparently fighting a rearguard electoral action to protect its industry following the enactment of nationwide Prohibition. More generally, however, the business organizations appearing in the electoral hearings tended to be umbrella groups rather than sector-specific trade associations. In 1912, for example, in the very first electoral investigation, the National Association of Manufacturers (NAM) appeared.[72] The following year its representatives appeared before a lobbying committee alongside an affiliated legislative group, the National Council for Industrial Defense. But the NAM came back into the campaign spotlight in 1944 and 1946. The Chamber of Commerce of the United States also made several appearances, once before the 1929 lobbying investigation, again before the campaign investigation of 1956, and finally before the combined investigation of 1956/1957. The two most prominent national business groups, therefore, were examined in both the lobbying and campaign contexts over time. Officers of both groups, moreover, were linked to an important business-backed effort in the 1936 election—the American Liberty League—that opposed the New Deal policies of President Franklin Roosevelt and campaigned against his re-election. The Liberty League, in fact, might be classified as a business-oriented interest group in itself, since it was not a formal affiliate of these major business organizations and conducted its own policy advocacy and fundraising prior to entering the 1936 campaign.

Most prominent in the electoral hearings, however, are labor organizations, particularly from the 1940s onward, though they are notable even before that point.[73] In 1920, for example, the Plumb Plan League made an appearance, a group formed by the Railroad Brotherhoods that sought to make reprivatization of railroads after World War I an issue in the campaign.[74] In 1924 the Brotherhoods leant their support to Robert La Follette's independent presidential bid, and in this connection the head of the Order of Railroad Conductors testified before the Senate's Special Committee on Campaign Expenditures that year.[75] Just over two decades later, in 1946, the Brotherhood of Railroad Trainmen also appeared, alongside representatives of a range of craft and industrial union organizations, including the American Federation of Labor (AFL) and the CIO, the two national labor union federations.[76] Both federations would appear multiple times in the electoral hearings, either directly or via affiliated groups, and also in the lobbying hearings.

The AFL, the older of the two organizations, had first appeared in 1913 before a lobbying investigation. The CIO emerged in the mid-1930s as a breakaway group from the AFL, dedicating itself to industrial rather than craft unionism. Already in 1936, Overacker points to a new campaign organization established by the CIO, the LNPL, which supported Roosevelt in the 1936 election.[77] Like some of the candidate committees, the LNPL was financially independent of the Democratic Party, but it was longer lasting, continuing to operate until 1940. Rozell, Wilcox, and Franz have identified the LNPL as an important predecessor to the CIO's P.A.C., which itself appeared before Congress in 1944, just a year after its founding, with its representatives testifying before both the House and Senate campaign investigations.[78] P.A.C. representatives would appear before four congressional electoral investigations overall, while another CIO-fostered group designed to appeal to a liberal audience beyond union members, the National Citizens Political Action Committee (NCPAC), appeared twice.

By 1948, in fact, a congressional report on campaign expenditures observed that "[t]he period following the summer of 1943 is noteworthy for the appearance on the political scene of so-called political action committees and educational leagues." Describing these groups as "instrumentalities for the application of political pressure or for participation in political activities sponsored indirectly by labor unions," the report listed several others.[79] These included Labor's League for Political Education (LLPE), a PAC created by the AFL in 1947, which would subsequently appear in the 1952 electoral hearings, and various PACs associated with the Railroad Brotherhoods or particular international unions.[80] The LLPE would ultimately merge with the CIO P.A.C. in 1955, when the two labor federations reunited as the AFL-CIO. Their combined political action committee, the Committee on Political Education (COPE), would appear before the Senate's campaign expenditure investigation in 1956 and was the most financially important labor PAC identified by Alexander in 1960 and 1964.[81]

Compared to labor and business organizations, or indeed to farm interests more broadly, professional groups and veterans' organizations were far less prevalent in both types of hearing. The most prominent veterans' group, the American Legion, appeared only once before the combined investigation of

1956/1957. Its legislative director was primarily asked about his lobbying activities, but he also denied that the group made any campaign contributions,
endorsed candidates, or formed political committees to aid in elections—
reflecting the American Legion's unease with these more public and overtly
"political" activities, lest they be criticized for seeking to subvert the electoral process.[82] One of its former national commanders did head up a campaign group in the 1940 election—the Willkie War Veterans mentioned
by Overacker. This group appealed to former servicemen and women,
emphasizing Willkie's own status as a World War I veteran. But it does not appear to have been fostered by the American Legion itself, hence its classification as a candidate-centered group.[83] In contrast, Overacker mentions another
1940 campaign organization, this one for medical doctors, that does appear to
have been linked to a preexisting professional group. The National Committee
of Physicians for Willkie was organized, in part, by the National Physicians'
Committee (NPC), a pressure group formed in 1939 to oppose federal health
insurance. The NPC, in turn, had an informal but apparently substantial relationship with the American Medical Association (AMA), the most prominent national organization for medical professionals.[84] In 1940, however, the
Physicians for Willkie group was a relatively minor player in the campaign,
spending less than $12,000 (compared to the Willkie War Veterans' $78,000,
and the Associated Willkie Clubs' nearly $1.4 million).[85]

The AMA itself would be more renowned for its lobbying efforts in the 1940s
and 1950s—both directly in Congress and indirectly through publicity—most
notably in its campaign against President Truman's proposal for national health
insurance in 1949.[86] Yet somewhat surprisingly, AMA representatives did not
appear before the 1950 lobbying investigation (though their efforts against the
healthcare bill were noted and discussed in one of that committee's reports).[87]
Several AMA officials did, however, appear before the 1956/1957 combined
investigation's hearings, primarily to discuss their lobbying activities.[88] At that
time, they denied any involvement in electoral politics, whether through campaign contributions, endorsements, or "healing arts" groups which sometimes
sprang up during campaigns—which they described as local volunteer efforts
without formal links to any medical societies.[89] But the AMA would soon become much more electorally active. Amid renewed talk of federal healthcare
legislation at the start of President John F. Kennedy's administration in 1961,
it became the first professional association to form a PAC, offering financial
support to lawmakers who opposed such a measure.[90] AMPAC thus appears
in Alexander's 1964 list of "miscellaneous" political committees and is widely
noted in overviews of PAC development.[91] Nonetheless, for all AMPAC's
prominence, professional interests are largely overshadowed in the hearings

and supplementary information by other types of interests, whether economic or ideational.

Indeed, far more prevalent are issue-oriented or ideological groups, often labeled "advocacy" organizations today. Several appeared in the early lobbying hearings, where their varying policy concerns included prison labor, the tariff, and foreign affairs.[92] Foreign policy concerns were evident in the electoral hearings too, with the League to Enforce Peace, which promoted international cooperation in the wake of World War I, appearing in 1920 for example.[93] But the dominant issue across both sets of hearings prior to 1940 was Prohibition. The two main groups on either side of that question, the Anti-Saloon League and the Association Against the Prohibition Amendment (AAPA), both appeared before electoral hearings in 1928 and lobbying hearings in 1929. Both were prominently involved in the 1928 presidential election, with the Anti-Saloon League offering indirect support to Republican nominee Herbert Hoover and the AAPA effectively backing Democratic nominee Al Smith. (The appearance of the Ku Klux Klan and National Civic League in 1928, moreover, was also tied to their support for Prohibition.)[94]

The Prohibition question, however, confuses the normal identification of advocacy groups with *purposive* rather than *material* incentives; typically, members or adherents do not benefit economically from the policies they promote.[95] At least some opposition to Prohibition was informed by economic considerations, since brewers and liquor interests stood to gain financially from its repeal. It was also intertwined with a larger ideological concern about the power of the federal government, which itself could have material implications for individual citizens and specific communities in terms of taxes or regulation. The AAPA, for example, was closely tied to leading industrialists who opposed federal encroachment into the economy. Some groups that began as anti-Prohibition vehicles, therefore, actually appear later in the hearings advocating a more general antistatist message, such as the Crusaders discussed in the 1935 lobbying hearings. In fact, the Crusaders had close ties to the Liberty League, which itself was linked to the earlier AAPA, so the league's categorization as a "business" group should not obscure the ideological nature of its anti–New Deal message.[96]

Indeed, a number of broadly ideological groups appear in the hearings beyond this point, in both contexts, which are difficult to entirely separate from economic interests given their ideas about governance and the state. The National Committee to Uphold Constitutional Government (NCUCG), for example (later the Committee for Constitutional Government), which appeared before the 1935 and 1950 lobbying committees along with 1940 and 1944 electoral committees, made philosophical arguments for constitutional limitations on the federal government (including opposition to Roosevelt's third and fourth terms) that also had practical economic implications. For those chafing under federal regulation, including some businesses, they promised financial gains. For those who benefited from regulation, including many workers by that point, they threatened significant losses. What came to be labeled "conservative" or "liberal" positions in the wake of the New Deal would be closely identified with the economic communities who stood to gain from them, primarily business and labor. The Union for Democratic Action (UDA), for example, which appeared before the 1944 House electoral investigation, and its successor Americans for Democratic Action (ADA), which appeared in 1956, were liberal groups with close connections to the labor movement.

The ADA appears in Alexander's list of "miscellaneous" political committees in both 1960 and 1964, suggesting it was an active financial participant in election campaigns (spending nearly $150,000 on election-related activities in 1960 and almost $180,000 in 1964, he calculated).[97] Alexander also lists Americans for Constitutional Action in both years, a conservative organization explicitly designed to emulate and counter the liberal ADA (it spent nearly $190,000 in 1960 and over $200,000 in 1964).[98] Drawing on Alexander's figures, the ACA was one of the highest spending nonlabor organizations in 1960, with the ADA not too far behind (COPE topped the list at nearly $800,000), though both were outspent in 1964 by other non-labor groups, including the National Committee for an Effective Congress, a liberal group, and the AMA's AMPAC, whose opposition to federal intervention in healthcare located it on the conservative side of the spectrum. (COPE kept the top spot by spending almost $1 million that year.)[99] Indeed, that ideological-interest group connection on the right would be further enhanced in 1964 by the appearance of one other notable group, just behind the ACA in its 1964 spending: the Business-Industry Political Action Committee (BIPAC).[100]

While AMPAC appears in most brief histories of PACS, far less attention has been paid to BIPAC.[101] But it is particularly significant, since it was a formal PAC created by the National Association of Manufacturers and, as such, a "business PAC" born well before the campaign finance reforms of the 1970s. Its appearance, moreover, suggests the importance of competitive emulation in the realm of interest group electioneering. Much like the ACA, which was formed as a conservative counterpart to the ADA, BIPAC was intended to be a rival to COPE and other labor PACs. Where the NAM may have flirted with electoral politics in the past alongside its lobbying work, and drawn some congressional scrutiny of its activities along the way, BIPAC formalized its commitment to campaigns and placed its electoral work on a permanent footing. By 1964, therefore, PACs associated with both major labor and business organizations were doing battle in the electoral arena, anchoring a growing set of ideological groups with complementary views.

The Contours of Electoral Participation

This overview of organizations appearing before campaign expenditure committees or mentioned in supplemental information speaks to the changing contours of electoral participation in the first half of the twentieth century. It suggests an expanding universe of nonparty electoral actors in national campaigns, though quantitative assessments should be made with caution because the available sources cannot produce a definitive count of *all* participants, only those national organizations that came to congressional notice or whose financial activities were extensive and documented. Nonetheless, a qualitative assessment highlights emerging organizational features and developmental themes, particularly in terms of the "interests" with which electoral participants were associated and the nature of the organizations through which they pursued their political aims.

At the outset, nonparty electoral actors were typically temporary entities, sometimes fostered by the parties themselves. Over time, however, they exhibited increasing organizational and financial independence from parties, as well as greater organizational endurance, with semipermanent and even permanent campaign groups emerging by the 1930s and 1940s. Some were forged by individual citizens aiming to promote a particular candidate, others to promote an issue or a larger ideology, and where they persisted beyond Election Day they came to constitute a kind of interest group in themselves.[102] Others were created by preexisting economic interest groups to channel their electoral activity, including experiments in the 1930s that appear much like proto-PACs, along with the first true PACs of the 1940s and beyond. In these cases there appears to have been a specialization of activity, too, with direct lobbying and nonpolitical tasks left to the parent group, allowing for some detachment from the controversies surrounding interest group electioneering and a dash of deniability. As discussed in later chapters, PACs were not only active close to election contests but waged an early form of permanent campaigning through ongoing research, candidate cultivation, voter-registration drives, and what was termed "political education"—publicity campaigns designed to promote a positive electoral environment for the group's broader aims. Indeed, although campaign finance data are useful in identifying electoral actors, the wide range of election-oriented activities in which PACs engaged beyond donating to candidates or spending on their behalf—all embraced under the general heading of "political action"—suggests that we need to examine them in far more than financial, numerical terms.

The hearings point toward other developments too, though more impressionistically. Third parties, for example, appear somewhat less prominent over time, raising questions about the strategic dynamics of protest and whether the availability of new organizational forms lessened recourse to third parties among discontented elements in American society. The PAC form provided a means of electoral engagement without the attendant challenges of creating a full-blown political party, particularly one that would compete nationwide, and thus presented an attractive alternative.[103] Even existing third parties were influenced by the expanded organizational portfolio, the Communist Party's short-lived transformation into the Communist Political Association supporting Franklin Roosevelt for president in 1944 being a case in point. More generally, how non-party groups related to the major parties is an important question to consider because, as Overacker indicates, most promoted a Democratic or Republican presidential nominee. How such support squared with the "nonpartisan" claims of interest groups, moreover, is especially important, since this orientation was supposedly key to their cultural acceptability and strategic success, as noted in the introduction. Indeed, since the hearings suggest many interest groups did "go into politics" despite the apparent dangers of doing so, we must consider *why* they took this course of action, and how they sought to justify it.

To help answer such questions and explore these developments more fully, the rest of this book focuses in depth on a handful of organizations discussed here. Primarily, it looks to those interest groups that appeared most extensively in the hearings, either as parent organizations or via affiliated entities. These are groups that feature in both the lobbying and electoral subsets and across the entire time frame of the hearings and beyond, thus illuminating the contours of electoral action over time, its relationship to lobbying, and group relations with political parties more generally. And they are groups that represent the two core and oppositional economic interests in twentieth-century American life: business and labor. As indicated earlier, the American Federation of Labor, the Congress of Industrial Organizations, the US Chamber of Commerce, and the National Association of Manufacturers appear most often in the hearings and supplementary information reviewed here.

It was the CIO, of course, that created the first PAC, in 1943, following its LNPL experiment in 1936. The AFL followed suit in 1947, creating the LLPE to channel money and manpower into elections. Following the AFL-CIO merger in 1955, their joint PAC, COPE, appeared soon after, while the NAM created its own PAC, BIPAC, in 1963. Though the Chamber of Commerce did not create a PAC in this period, it did come under scrutiny in the 1950s for "political ed-ucation" activities that encouraged business executives to get more involved in election campaigns. Officials of both groups, moreover, had loose ties to another important proto-PAC active in the 1936 election, one directly opposed to the LNPL: the Liberty League.[104]

These groups form the spine of the story told in this book, though others from the hearings or supplementary sources also appear to the extent they illuminate the contours of electoral action across this period and offer comparative and developmental insight into the activities of these core economic groups. Issue-oriented groups—primarily those for and against Prohibition—were particularly important in the 1910s and 1920s because they refined electoral techniques with which both the NAM and the AFL had experimented and began to test the bounds and benefits of "nonpartisanship." Likewise, ideological groups became especially relevant in the 1940s and 1950s because they were connected to these economic communities in important ways. As subsequent chapters show, liberal groups worked in interlinked fashion with labor PACs, while conservative groups spurred business groups toward more overt and formalized electoral action.

The 1936 election is thus a critical moment in this story, when proto-electoral groups associated with the labor and business communities—the LNPL and the Liberty League—squared off in a presidential election. By extension, 1964 offers a culminating moment, when fully formed PACs associated with both business and labor contested a presidential election for the first time. It suggests the completion of an initial wave of PAC development, as interest group opponents mobilized to fight each other on the electoral field. In doing so, they placed electioneering at the forefront of their political strategies. But along with this came an increasing embrace of partisanship, as subsequent chapters show—with labor unions gravitating to the Democratic Party and business organizations to the GOP. To understand how electioneering and partisanship became intertwined, then, we must first consider why interest groups once feared them both. The next chapter thus explores the background to interest groups' involvement in the political world, exploring their once fraught relationship with political parties and their hesitant, early experimentation in the electoral arena.

"Pressure" as Prologue

Waves of popular discontent had washed over Gilded Age America. From the South and West had come the protests of farmers, raging against the discriminatory rates set by railroads and a perceived conspiracy of eastern bankers to deprive them of credit. From the industrial North and Midwest came the cries of laborers, striving for higher wages and safer working conditions. Both movements sought ways to counter the power of corporations and financial interests—those intent, as they saw it, on keeping them down. They found their strength not in money but in manpower, forming the great fraternal associations of the nineteenth century—the Grange and the Knights of Labor—initially to help themselves, then increasingly to recruit the government to aid them.[1] And when they first looked to the political sphere to achieve their aims, they turned to elections as the most obvious arena in which "the people" might have their say. Rebuffed by the major parties, they created new independent parties to contest those elections, hoping to send their own people—committed to their favored policies—straight into government.

But these third-party efforts—the Greenback Party, the Socialist Labor Party, and the People's Party, among others—repeatedly failed to gain electoral traction. Even after "fusion" with the Democrats in 1896, in which they set their hopes on the presidential candidacy of William Jennings Bryan, the Populists lost in a landslide. Agrarian and labor parties were never quite able to forge the alliances across regions and economic sectors—uniting South and West, farm and labor—that would be necessary for national success.[2] And their electoral failures would do much to undermine the fraternal organizations themselves, which rapidly lost members and influence.[3] A better method had to be found. And to find it, as Clemens explains, a new wave of popular associations looked to the despised corporate interests for guidance, developing a populist answer to the corporate "lobby."[4]

Big business had found success by pursuing a narrow legislative agenda aimed squarely at its own self-interest, promoting such aims through its lobbyists and financial largesse and working with both of the major parties.[5] Indeed, business

The Rise of Political Action Committees. Emily J. Charnock, Oxford University Press (2020). © Oxford University Press.
DOI: 10.1093/oso/9780190075514.001.0001

interests had a distinctly pragmatic approach to partisanship, putting their interests above party loyalty. As Jay Gould, president of the Erie Railroad and a robber baron par excellence, once explained: "In a Democratic state, I am a Democrat; in a Republican state, I am a Republican; in a doubtful state, I am doubtful, but I am always for Erie."[6] Though businessmen might lean Republican at the national level, especially after the 1896 election, they were content to work with Democrats whenever doing so would be productive, particularly on the state and local stages.[7] Thus corporate America was often bipartisan in its approach to politics, lobbying both sides of the aisle and, as noted in the previous chapter, giving generously to the campaign treasuries of both major parties until 1907, when the Tillman Act was passed.[8]

Popular associations, Clemens argues—including new farm organizations and labor unions, and especially groups seeking women's suffrage—would adapt this approach, developing an alternative that drew on their mass membership and popular appeal as a currency of power, seeking to harness the emerging concept of "public opinion" to their cause. (Women's suffrage groups, in fact, were central to this development, since their outright exclusion from the electoral system forced them to seek influence via a more limited set of tools.)[9] Where third parties had to take positions on a wide range of national issues, these associations emphasized the key issues they truly cared about. And they set out to "educate" their members, the wider public, and lawmakers to prioritize them, supplying "expert witnesses" to testify before legislative committees, holding public conferences to draw media attention, and waging large-scale publicity campaigns to promote specific legislative goals.[10] In doing so, they invented a new form of indirect lobbying, bringing it outside the halls of Congress and into the heartland, appealing to the public as constituents, imploring them to communicate with their representatives about specific policy matters, and invoking that sentiment in their own appeals to lawmakers.[11]

Like business interests, popular associations now directed those appeals to lawmakers affiliated with both major parties, but their experiences left them wary of being closely identified with either.[12] Rather than a bipartisan approach, they proclaimed their "nonpartisanship"—a term that conveyed both the rejection of third parties and of unquestioning loyalty to a major party. Distancing themselves from traditional party politics, in fact, helped popular associations to cast their new approach in a more positive light, tapping into a burgeoning Progressive critique of parties as a corrupt world of machines and bosses, propped up by unthinking popular support for a favored team. Similarly, by portraying their policy aims as technical solutions to social problems and framing their persuasive efforts as "educational," popular associations elevated their efforts above those of sordid and selfish "special interests." Through such rhetorical means, popular associations sought to justify their activities and gain broader cultural acceptance, in an era increasingly hostile to other modes of political activity.[13]

What they created, in sum, was the "modern" interest group: more bureaucratic in organization than its nineteenth-century predecessors, avowedly "nonpartisan" in orientation, and set on achieving specific policy goals, primarily through new techniques of indirect lobbying.[14] So appealing was this model, Clemens observes, that more traditional special interests soon adopted it. Smaller businesses and specific industries had already begun to create trade associations and representative groups in the late nineteenth century.[15] And these new membership associations (along with those corporations large enough to fund their own lobbying operations) increasingly emulated the educational publicity methods of their "popular" rivals. Indeed, as Sheingate observes, an entire *business* of political consulting began to emerge at this time, as interests and individuals sought out self-professed experts in the new arts of propaganda, public relations, and marketing to aid their appeals.[16]

"Many years ago the lobbying that was carried on here in Washington was of a very much coarser kind," Senator Robert La Follette of Wisconsin observed in a 1913 congressional hearing, but it had been "changing in form" before their very eyes.[17] "[T]hat old, raw, bargain-and-sale system of lobbying is out of fashion," he reflected, "the interests, I think, found a better way."[18] That "better way" involved *publicity*—reaching out beyond the proverbial smoke-filled room to attract popular support for their preferred policies, even to create the artificial appearance of it where genuine sentiment might be lacking.[19] As the *Washington Post* explained in 1912, commenting on this "New Lobby," "[t]he new method is not to bribe statesmen, but to create a public sentiment in their districts which will impel or compel them to vote this way or that."[20]

But elections were not entirely absent from modern interest group politics, or "pressure politics" as it was known by the 1920s.[21] For as lawmakers recognized, those constituents who expressed their opinion might also vote in line with it. And thus underlying a group's ability to "impel or compel" a congressman— to apply *pressure*—was the prospect that its members or supporters might do just that.[22] The question, however, was how explicitly, and how actively, interest groups might encourage them to do so. The practice of lobbying in itself remained somewhat controversial, even as it had been harnessed to more popular ends and justified in more palatable terms. To wade into electoral territory, therefore, was to invite further criticism for seeking to influence, even to subvert, the basic democratic process. It raised practical questions, too, of what electoral participation would look like short of forming a third party. Moreover, it posed challenges to the "nonpartisan" image that interest groups had carefully cultivated, since involvement risked visible identification with one side, particularly at the presidential level. Such identification raised strategic concerns as well as normative ones, as Schattschneider and Key would warn in their early scholarship, since a close association with the losing side would leave a group politically isolated, thus endangering its legislative goals.[23]

Indeed, in the strategic logic these early political scientists outlined, such partisan considerations would tend to discourage electoral forays altogether, unless "pressure groups" could find ways to participate without acquiring a partisan taint. The most prominent solution to that quandary was the "friends and enemies" strategy, in which interest groups placed their emphasis on individual candidates rather than parties and expressed their support or opposition on the basis of candidates' stances on the issues they cared about, irrespective of their party label. Its effectiveness was premised on the formation of a swing vote; if groups had properly educated their members or supporters to prioritize particular issues rather than blindly following party loyalty, they could control a bloc of voters who would move in either direction as the group desired. This also presumed a particular configuration of party competition, since the strategy only made sense in an environment where patronage still trumped policy and few issues, if any, split the parties neatly in two. If each party's candidates were already lined up on opposing sides of a question, there would be little reason to cultivate a swing vote rather than urge voters to switch parties. Opposing issue positions were distributed unevenly across the parties in the early twentieth century, meaning that the outcome of this nonpartisan strategy could reasonably be expected to appear "bipartisan," as groups would support or oppose *both* Democrats and Republicans in accordance with their policy stances.

Such patterns might never come to light, however, for—as understood theoretically—the effectiveness of the "friends and enemies" strategy was premised more on the *threat* of electoral intervention than any actual activity.[24] And formulated in that guise, it was the prospect of a group *opposing* its enemies that was most important; threatening punishment at the polls was a way of applying additional pressure on wavering lawmakers to vote a certain way on legislative proposals. The extent to which groups acted upon such threats, however, is unclear. Both Schattschneider and Key questioned whether any group could actually deliver a bloc vote, even if lawmakers often believed their claims to be credible.[25] And these scholars had little to say about the methods groups might employ to mobilize such a vote, should they ever try.

This chapter examines interest group strategy and tactics in the first three decades of the twentieth century. It looks primarily to major groups associated with business and labor, identified in the previous chapter as critical to this developmental study, such as the National Association of Manufacturers and the American Federation of Labor. But it also places a special emphasis on organizations promoting or opposing temperance—the Anti-Saloon League (ASL) and the Association Against the Prohibition Amendment (AAPA)—which were the signature pressure groups of the time. Drawing on the congressional hearings alongside other contemporary evidence, the chapter explores the nature and scope of any electioneering they contemplated, both as threatened and as acted upon. While all adopted a "friends and enemies" strategy, their actions show important variations within this broader type. There were also several alternative modes of both electoral and legislative influence apparent at this time, associated primarily with farm groups, which are explored here for comparative insight.

The resulting portrait of the early twentieth-century electoral scene is one of both controversy and complexity. At the beginning of this period, interest group electioneering was indeed limited, temporary, decentralized, and largely intended to enhance lobbying efforts—thus reflecting an "access, or legislative strategy" as Rozell, Wilcox, and Franz have labeled it, and in line with the theoretical vision sketched out by Key and Schattschneider.[26] But interest groups faced heavy criticism for their incursions "into politics"—a phrase then predominantly associated with the electoral arena. Much as they had defended their lobbying techniques, groups deployed claims of nonpartisanship to try to blunt the attack. Being "in politics" had an intertwined electoral and partisan meaning at that time; in common usage, it meant involvement in "party politics," aiding one side or the other in elections. Some groups therefore used their proclaimed nonpartisanship to downplay or even deny their involvement "in politics" at all. They also sought to reduce criticism by stressing their organizational detachment from parties or candidates—waging publicity campaigns "independently" rather than making direct financial contributions to their cause.

Yet as this chapter shows, such electioneering did not always live up to its nonpartisan reputation, particularly by the late 1920s. In the 1928 presidential election, especially, the activities of pro- and anti-temperance groups appeared distinctly partisan, assertive, and national in scope. Indeed, this very example helped to foster Key and Schattschneider's theory that partisanship was strategically *damaging* to pressure groups. But as we shall see, this theory was built atop a selective interpretation of the results. A closer examination of that election reveals contradictory lessons that shaped future interest group behavior in more complex ways, in both nonpartisan and partisan directions.

Business and Labor: Friends or Enemies?

The year 1912 would prove to be a dramatic election year, as former president Theodore Roosevelt challenged incumbent president William Howard Taft for the Republican nomination, bolted the party when he failed, and launched the new Progressive Party for the general election.[27] The rift between Taft

and Roosevelt also served to bring about the first congressional investigatic
into campaign expenditures, since Taft's allies in the Senate banded together
with Democrats who had long sought to expose Republican misdeeds in the
1904 elections (partially uncovered by the 1905 life insurance investigation in
New York that had been so damaging to then-president Roosevelt) to establish
an investigating committee. Chaired by Republican senator Moses E. Clapp
of Minnesota under the auspices of the Senate's Committee on Privileges and
Elections, it was initially charged with examining expenditures and "influence"
in the 1904 and 1908 congressional campaigns, and eventually the 1912 presidential nomination contests, too.[28] And its wide-ranging enquiries came to embrace one particularly prominent interest group: the National Association of
Manufacturers (NAM).

Formed in 1895, the NAM was the nation's premier business lobby. Originally
concerned with tariff policy, it had found a more rousing battle cry in the early
years of the new century calling for the "open shop" in the face of a burgeoning
labor movement. Its membership—composed of both trade associations and
individual corporations—had since grown dramatically, and it retained representatives in Washington, DC, to monitor legislation and express its views on
bills affecting business.[29] The NAM was well-financed and connected, and the
senators wanted to understand its methods and whether it had ever contributed
to federal election campaigns in pursuit of its business-friendly aims. To do so,
they called to testify Ferdinand C. Schwedtman, once personal secretary to the
NAM's late president, James Van Cleave.[30]

Schwedtman's testimony carefully downplayed any electoral dimension to
the NAM's activities, drawing a strong distinction between personal and organizational actions and distancing it from both "politics" and the parties.
He acknowledged that the NAM's officers had made campaign contributions
over the years, for example, especially to presidential contenders. But money
had never been donated from its organizational accounts, he said, even prior
to the Tillman Act (when, as an incorporated association, its making such
contributions became illegal).[31] Moreover, although Schwedtman acknowledged that these personal donations had largely favored Republican candidates
(since concern for the tariff and the "silver question" in 1896 had shaken many
of their former Democratic allegiance), he claimed that the NAM as an organization bore no partisan allegiance.[32] Indeed, he said that the NAM's charter
precluded any contributions, endorsements, or electioneering of any kind—
an intriguing admission that perhaps conveyed some awareness among the
NAM's founders of the controversy these activities might engender.[33] The
NAM was simply "not a political association" and "not interested in politics,"
Schwedtman affirmed, deploying the term with its intertwined partisan and
electoral glaze.[34] Instead, the NAM advocated for its principles, he declared.[35] It

-business policies, in essence, and left politicking to the discre-
lals.

ng investigation the following year cast the NAM's electoral in-
more substantial and nefarious light. This particular investigation came about at the behest of newly elected president Woodrow Wilson,
following a frenzy of lobbying on his proposed tariff reform bill in 1913. The
NAM had been a prominent opponent of the bill, seeking to preserve high tariff
protections for American manufacturers, while other interests had sprung into
action to seek favorable rates for their own industries or products. Wilson had
ultimately denounced this wider "tariff lobby" and called on Congress to investigate lobbying practices more generally.[36] Shortly thereafter, the *Chicago Tribune*
and *New York World* ran a series of sensational stories exposing the seedier side
of the NAM's lobbying methods. They revealed the role of one Martin Mulhall, a
sometime NAM employee, in strong-arming legislators to toe its line.[37] Mulhall
alleged that the NAM had tried to shape the composition of key congressional
committees like Judiciary and Labor and had paid pages and elevator operators
to keep tabs on activities behind the scenes.[38] But as the *Tribune* made clear,
Mulhall's activities had gone beyond direct *lobbying* to "political"—that is,
electoral—work, too.[39]

Mulhall claimed the NAM had a "system of campaigning" in which it helped
to finance the election campaigns of its "friends" in Congress while rallying
members against "enemies" who were hostile to its policy goals.[40] This might involve direct appeals from NAM officials to local manufacturers, he said, seeking
funds for particular candidates, or simply spreading the word about the NAM's
preference. He even claimed that some of the money he handled had been used
for "corrupting voters" by purchasing their votes, a throwback to Gilded Age
methods.[41] Through such activities in selected districts, the NAM sought to defeat unfriendly candidates. But its "system of campaigning" had a bigger picture
in view. "When the N.A.M. defeated a candidate, it spread the knowledge in
every direction," Mulhall explained—pursuing its legislative aims by the deploy-
ment of electoral threat. "By using these tactics and intimidating weak-kneed
members of congress that are elected by small majorities in other districts, the
N.A.M. compelled them to vote the ways its lobby wished them to."[42]

Mulhall was hardly an unimpeachable source, having been dismissed from
NAM employ in somewhat strained circumstances.[43] But his allegations gained
traction in a society still wrestling with the growth of corporate power. In response
to the scandal and Wilson's earlier entreaty, both chambers of Congress established special committees to investigate lobbying, and Ferdinand Schwedtman
would thus find himself called to testify before the Senate again. To this "Lobby
Investigation" committee, chaired by Democratic senator Lee Overman of
North Carolina, Schwedtman admitted that while its charter prohibited political

activities, the NAM's attorneys had advised that "the activities of a field man who might go into the district to call the attention of the manufacturers to the qualifications of a man, and who might raise among those manufacturers local funds, *would not come under the description of political activities.*"[44]

Indeed, the NAM had done just that in 1906, it emerged, seeking to aid Republican congressman Charles Littlefield in a difficult re-election contest in Maine. As Littlefield later told a companion investigating committee in the House, chaired by Representative Finis J. Garrett of Tennessee, the NAM had not directly contributed to his campaign fund.[45] Nonetheless, he conceded that "a substantial part of it came from men who were probably members of the National Association of Manufacturers" but "came from them individually, not as members."[46] What individuals chose to do with their own money—even with the NAM's encouragement—was their own affair, this legal interpretation seemed to imply.[47] Ultimately, the NAM itself was not sending checks or publicly associating itself with a candidate or his party. It was "interested in promoting certain economic and political principles," Schwedtman acknowledged, "but not partisan politics, and that is the difference."[48]

The NAM's efforts to support friends and defeat enemies, therefore, had a distinctly *monetary* flavor. It spearheaded at least some efforts to raise funds for a candidate's use, though it maintained organizational distance by emphasizing the *individual* nature of these donations. Though the local manufacturers it contacted might also urge their workers to vote a particular way—a form of employer coercion widely criticized at the time—the NAM's main electoral threat was not punishment at the polls through a swing vote it controlled but the large war chest it might help furnish an opponent with, which could be used against a lawmaker in the campaign. Its methods were also discreet and largely private; it did not seek to publicize its efforts to the wider constituency, but rather worked behind the scenes. In contrast, publicity was central to the techniques of the NAM's main interest group rival—the American Federation of Labor (AFL)— which would forge a more visible and assertive version of this tactic, premised on open appeals to its membership and the masses.

Although the AFL had not been called before the Clapp electoral investigation in 1912, its representatives did appear before both lobbying committees in 1913, where their electoral activities became a point of discussion. As AFL president Samuel Gompers acknowledged before the House's committee (a somewhat narrower investigation than its Senate counterpart), the AFL had been active in the 1906 Maine contest, too. Littlefield's "continued opposition to all legislation sought by the American Federation of Labor in the interests of the working people" had prompted its intervention, but only on the invitation of local members, Gompers insisted.[49] The AFL had spent about $1,500 there, he testified, but it did not donate this sum to Littlefield's opponent so much as mount its own campaign against the incumbent, paying for organizers, speakers, and the costs of circulating literature.[50]

Indeed, from 1906 onward the AFL had raised a "political fund" through the voluntary donations of its individual members and affiliated unions—about $8,000 in 1906, $8,500 in 1908, and $3,500 in 1910—and used those funds to support and oppose lawmakers in a variety of districts.[51] (General funds had occasionally been utilized, Gompers admitted, but the AFL was a voluntary association rather than a corporation, and thus not subject to the Tillman Act ban.)[52] The AFL had been especially active in 1908 and 1910, Gompers noted, seeking the election of lawmakers "nearer to our view of what was right politically."[53] And all of this was "entirely in the open," Gompers said. "As a matter of fact, the only degree of success we could attain was by publicity; so that as a matter of policy as well as of purpose publicity was our weapon."[54]

This active electoral stance was at odds, however, with the AFL's founding mantra. It had been formed in 1886 as the power of the Knights of Labor waned. And it was formed with the lessons of the Knights' third-party dalliance firmly in view. Under Gompers's leadership, the AFL initially stressed its determination to "keep out of politics," viewed in distinctly electoral and partisan terms, and emphasized private over political solutions to the problems of workers: "business unionism," as this philosophy became known.[55] This "nonpolitical" position did permit occasional lobbying of the government—promoting a limited legislative agenda designed to secure collective bargaining rights—but such objectives were to be pursued on a firmly nonpartisan basis.[56] In the late nineteenth century, Gompers associated the major parties with the corruptions of machine politics and saw both as equally bad when it came to aiding the workingman.[57] But he reserved his strongest vitriol for "independent" or third-party politics, seeing trade unions, not a labor party, as the key to achieving real progress.[58]

In 1906, however, this strongly "nonpolitical" stance gave way to a more assertive phase of political activity, as Greene has detailed, with the AFL launching a "systematic effort" in the electoral sphere.[59] "The reasons for that are plain," Gompers explained, citing the application of antitrust laws to unions, the growing use of injunctions in labor disputes, and "[t]he war that had been declared upon us by the officers of the National Association of Manufacturers"—a reference to the open shop campaign and its negative effects.[60] Rather than form a third party, however, the AFL determined to work within the existing party system, supporting friends of labor and opposing its foes, whatever their party label may be.[61] Most prominent in the AFL's sights was Littlefield, who drew its most "conspicuous" effort, Gompers recalled, along with another key opponent, House Speaker Joe Cannon of Illinois, among several others. The AFL appealed to workers to vote against these incumbents, both to punish Littlefield and Cannon and to demonstrate labor's electoral weight at large, thus sending a powerful warning to labor's enemies to change their ways or face defeat.

But if publicity had been a weapon in this effort, the AFL's very openness proved to be a double-edged sword. Cannon, for example, attacked Gompers for presuming to direct the choices of AFL members and "deliver" the vote en bloc. "Samuel Gompers, by the grace of God, these very laborers next Monday will put their foot on your proposition," he rallied a crowd just before the 1906 election, "because it is *undemocratic* and it is not according to the principles of your labor organization."[62] Critics cast doubt, too, on the AFL's purported nonpartisanship, thus limiting its effectiveness as a rhetorical defense. Cannon and Littlefield were both Republicans and, prior to the election, AFL leaders had publicized a "bill of grievances" against the GOP at large, promising punishment at the polls if labor's aims were neglected.[63] Though ostensibly targeting the Republicans as the "party in power," this was widely viewed as a partisan attack and elicited an "unprecedented" response from President Theodore Roosevelt, who rallied support for his fellow Republicans in public letters.[64] And when Election Day rolled around, both Littlefield and Cannon won handily, returning to Congress even more avowed "enemies" of labor than they had been before.

Nonetheless, the AFL persisted in this approach in 1908, veering even closer to outright partisanship through engagement in a presidential contest. That year, the AFL's Executive Council took the unprecedented step of endorsing the Democratic nominee, William Jennings Bryan, in his third bid for the presidency. In his testimony five years later, however, Gompers tried to cast even this decision in a nonpartisan light.[65] The AFL had evaluated both candidates and party platforms in terms of *issues*, Gompers explained, particularly their stances on antitrust and injunctions, and deemed the Democrat more favorable.[66] Its support for Bryan was principled, therefore, not partisan.[67] Yet as Greene reveals, the AFL went so far as to make a formal agreement with the Democratic National Committee in 1908 to work on its behalf. In a deal reached with Gompers, DNC chairman Norman Mack agreed to pay the salaries of union organizers assigned to campaign work, to underwrite the costs of AFL literature, and to assign more resources to districts in which the AFL was particularly interested, such as Cannon's.[68] Gompers made no mention of this arrangement in his testimony, asserting instead that the AFL was "not a partisan political organization," much as the NAM had claimed.[69]

Still, the 1908 elections went badly for the AFL, with Cannon being reelected and Bryan going down to another massive defeat.[70] The AFL's involvement had generated intense criticism, moreover, despite efforts to defend and justify it. The apparent promise to "deliver the labor vote" for Bryan was again attacked as undemocratic and even coercive by President Roosevelt, among others—though Gompers later framed it in terms of education and citizenship, claiming the AFL had simply encouraged individuals to exercise their vote in an informed manner.[71] Republican campaign managers also denounced unions as "special interests" working against the public interest, which suggests that the efforts of "modern" interest groups to distinguish themselves from traditional counterparts were not always successful.[72] And there were claims that labor was dominating a political party, with Gompers pulling strings behind the scenes.[73] Gompers himself saw the NAM's shadowy presence behind the attacks. "The men of labor were never so active in any political campaign as they were in the campaign of 1908," he noted, "but our very publicity, our very activity, was turned by the representatives of the National Association of Manufacturers and by the men of vested interests to their own account."[74] Nonetheless, these charges had resonated among AFL members themselves, as well as the broader public.[75]

Despite this hostility, 1910 proved a more auspicious year for the AFL. Amid Republican party infighting, the Democrats won a majority in the House of Representatives that year. To what extent the AFL's efforts contributed to this turn of events is unclear, but Gompers told the House lobbying committee that it had sought to "dislodge those who had been in power so long" and bring about a change in the political parties and "had made up our mind that if we accomplished nothing further than that, it would clear the atmosphere and make things brighter and better."[76] That change having been effected in the House, the AFL swiftly retired from the field—testament, perhaps, to the heavy reputational toll its electoral involvement had taken.[77] The AFL did not raise a political fund in 1912 or undertake on-the-ground activities in any districts, believing that its "campaign could be conducted much better without the publicity in 1912 than in 1908."[78] The organization might discuss the campaign to some extent in its newsletters or distribute "a circular here and there," but any systematic political efforts were essentially over.[79]

Diminishing resources may have played a role in the AFL's reduced political activities, too. The 1910 political fund, after all, had been less than half that raised in 1906 and 1908, for all Gompers claimed the AFL had been substantially active.[80] And in 1908, as Greene reports, the AFL had received money from the DNC to aid in its work. As AFL secretary Frank Morrison explained before the House lobbying committee in 1913, the federation had "very little funds" with which to do anything.[81] At the presidential level, the AFL retreated to the kind of distinction between individual and official activities that Schwedtman had claimed for the NAM. Gompers personally endorsed Democrat Woodrow Wilson in 1912, but the AFL otherwise stayed out of the presidential fray.[82] Moving forward, the national AFL renewed its emphasis on legislative lobbying, supplemented on occasion by "nonpartisan political action," as Morrison described it, by which he meant "friends and enemies" congressional campaigns conducted at the discretion of state and local federations, with limited research support provided by the national office.[83] Emphasizing the initiative and autonomy of its affiliates, in fact, became another way for the national AFL to distance itself from actual electioneering.[84] It distanced itself from the mere threat of it, too. Testifying in 1914 before the Senate's lobbying committee, the AFL's legislative agent, Arthur Holder, denied that the AFL ever made explicit "threats against men" or offered "promises of support" in future campaigns in its efforts to persuade lawmakers.[85]

If the NAM and the AFL were involved "in politics" in the early twentieth century, therefore, they were so on a limited basis. In the NAM's case, its leaders sought to downplay any organizational connection and understate their activity—most likely for legal reasons, but in part to avoid the kinds of negative publicity they had fanned against the AFL. The AFL's leaders, in contrast, acknowledged some organizational involvement for a handful of election cycles, before ostensibly withdrawing amid a backlash against their methods and a diminution of funds. Money, of course, was the NAM's main asset—urging its officers and sympathetic company executives to spread their largesse to sympathetic candidates—while the AFL's main asset was manpower—urging its members in a particular district to vote as it advised. Both sought to "reward or punish" lawmakers through different means, but to the same end: promoting support for legislative aims by convincing lawmakers that their electoral survival depended on it. This approach was initially formulated as a means of persuasion, designed to support and promote a much larger lobbying effort. And it was clothed in the language of nonpartisanship for both normative and strategic reasons. Strategically, nonpartisanship lessened the risk of political isolation, the main danger of being linked to a losing party. Normatively, it offered distance from the sordid world of political bosses and party combat, a way for "special interests" to seem *disinterested*, in line with the Progressive temper of the times. Such rhetorical claims were not always substantiated or successful in reducing criticism, but both groups advanced them consistently.

After 1912 the NAM's "system of campaigning" appears to have retreated from view, or at least did not attract any further congressional notice (representatives of the NAM did not appear before a major congressional electoral investigation again until 1944). Contemporary sources suggest that it poured its energies into shaping public opinion, without necessarily extending those efforts to the electoral arena. By the mid-1920s, Publicity was the "most important" of the NAM's four departments, a 1928 study suggested, more important than its Law Department, which handled traditional lobbying, and much more so than its Trade and Industrial Relations divisions.[86] The indirect lobbying engineered by the Publicity Department, through its "constant contact with the daily newspapers, with press associations, and with special correspondents," helped the NAM sustain its reputation as "one of the most powerful lobbies in Washington, D.C."[87]

Yet even this aspect of the NAM's activity did not generate further congressional inquiry. Somewhat surprisingly, its officials were not called to testify before the next major lobbying investigation in 1929, chaired by Democratic senator Thaddeus H. Caraway of Arkansas, a longtime advocate of tighter lobbying regulation.[88] Lawmakers' attention might have been diverted, however, by the rise of another prominent business organization: the United States Chamber of Commerce. The Chamber had been founded in 1912, just prior to the first lobbying investigations, at the instigation of President Taft and his commerce secretary and with the blessing of the NAM. It was designed to articulate a unified expression of "business" opinion across all commercial sectors, not just manufacturing, and quickly became a force to be reckoned with, taking advantage of its access to the executive branch and drawing strength from its local affiliates in dealing with Congress (unlike the NAM, the Chamber also allowed individual memberships).[89] The Caraway Committee took notice, questioning its chairman, Julius H. Barnes, as well as representatives from several smaller trade associations.[90] Yet the Chamber's activities, like the NAM's by this point, appeared primarily geared to direct and indirect lobbying, with few hints of an electoral backdrop.

Indeed, such methods appeared to be getting business groups what they wanted. Though their fortunes would soon tumble (the Caraway Committee opened its hearings in October 1929, just prior to the Wall Street crash), business had been riding high throughout the 1920s, politically, economically, and culturally. Successive Republican administrations had maintained high tariffs and minimal business regulation, Congress had held the line against labor legislation, and judicial decisions overwhelmingly favored management in its dealings with unions. Amid unprecedented economic growth, moreover, popular culture in the 1920s came to celebrate businessmen and corporate achievements as much as earlier generations of Americans had demonized their "corruptions." With their insider connections and newfound cultural cachet, business organizations had little need to venture into elections to get their legislative way.

In contrast, the AFL found itself drawn back into the electoral world in the 1920s—at least briefly—and in a manner quite different from its earlier experiments. For all its hostility to third parties, particularly under Gompers's leadership, their appeal had never entirely disappeared, especially among more radical labor activists.[91] The 1912 presidential election had helped to reignite such hopes, with Theodore Roosevelt delivering the best-ever showing by a third-party presidential candidate, gaining 27.4 percent of the popular vote, while Eugene Debs simultaneously delivered the Socialist Party's best-ever result with 6 percent.[92] These results offered succor to those who still saw an independent labor party as the only way to achieve progress for workers and considered both major parties to be fatally tarnished. The existing party system, they believed, must be "realigned" along a new dimension of political conflict, and this required transformation from *without* rather than working from *within*, breaking apart the existing system by breaking in with a new party. Party "realignment," in fact, would long be understood in terms of this third-party role, though it would come to be viewed differently over time.

Developments after 1912, however, were less promising for third parties. In 1916 Theodore Roosevelt returned to the Republican fold, leaving down-ballot Progressive candidates to wither along with his Bull Moose Party. Meanwhile, the ideological Left was riven with severe internal conflicts, and neither Debs nor any of his rivals were able to rally the various Communist, Socialist, and labor forces under a single banner.[93] In 1916, Debs was even forced off the Socialist presidential ticket for the first time since the party's founding fifteen years earlier, and support dropped to just over 3 percent of the popular vote.[94] Though the Socialists returned to Debs in 1920, when he famously campaigned from a prison cell (having been jailed for "seditious" speech during World War I), the results barely improved, though other third-party candidates performed even worse; Parley Christensen of the Farmer-Labor Party, for example, polled less than 1 percent of the vote.[95]

Christensen, in fact, was asked to testify before the Senate's campaign expenditure committee that year, chaired by Republican William Kenyon of Iowa, where he charged that both major parties were "financed by Wall Street" and controlled by a "capitalist combination" and requested some form of public financing to aid "minority" parties.[96] Despite his poor showing in November, the Farmer-Labor Party did have significant support in rural areas, especially in the Midwest, and marked another effort to bring industrial workers and farmers together under the same umbrella.[97] On the labor side of that equation, the party's support came mostly from the Railroad Brotherhoods, a group of independent unions representing brakemen, engineers, and other railroad employees. Their electoral foray, in fact, came on the heels of a failed lobbying campaign in which they unsuccessfully sought to defeat the Transportation Act of 1920, which would return the railroads from wartime federal control to private ownership. They had formed a grassroots pressure group to fight it in Congress—the Plumb Plan League, whose representatives also appeared before the Kenyon Committee—and poured energy into the Farmer-Labor Party as the general election came into view.[98]

The Brotherhoods continued to promote third-party politics even after 1920. They transformed the nearly six hundred branches of the Plumb Plan League into the Conference for Progressive Political Action and urged formation of a new third party in 1924. What they helped bring about was the presidential candidacy of progressive Republican senator Robert La Follette of Wisconsin, ostensibly as the nominee of a revamped Progressive Party, though it did not contest any other offices.[99] (Representatives of both the Progressive Party and the Order of Railway Conductors—one of the Railroad Brotherhoods—were called before the Senate's 1924 campaign expenditure investigation to discuss these efforts.)[100] The Socialist Party backed La Follette too, and other radicals, progressives, and sympathetic organizations rallied to his cause, including the AFL. With Gompers in declining health and perhaps unable to stem the momentum, the AFL's executive council officially endorsed La Follette. Significantly, though, it did *not* endorse the idea of a new party, suggesting another effort to downplay partisanship by emphasizing individual candidates, and the AFL appears to have played only a limited role in the campaign.[101] (Indeed, it did not attract the notice of the Senate investigators that year.)

Once again, however, the experience was a cautionary one. Though he polled nearly five million votes, amounting to almost 17 percent of the popular vote—then the second strongest performance by a third-party candidate since the Civil War—La Follette's success did little to erode support for Republican incumbent Calvin Coolidge, who won a substantial majority.[102] Thus the AFL retired from the field once more. Lacking the advantages of business organizations, it had oscillated between legislative and electoral approaches in the early twentieth century, placing a greater emphasis on one when frustrated with the other. But after 1924 a more enduring balance was struck, with the AFL placing its predominant emphasis on lobbying and reaffirming its commitment to nonpartisanship.[103] The AFL tried to accept the existing two-party system without becoming *part* of that system, neither challenging it from without through an independent party nor embracing it from within by allying with a major party. State and local affiliates might still launch "friends and enemies" campaigns in House and Senate races, but the national organization had only limited official involvement and steered clear of presidential campaigns. Indeed, Congress paid little attention to the AFL's subsequent activity, in either the legislative or electoral realms, for the next two decades at least. Not until 1946 would an AFL representative appear again before one of its major investigative committees. (The Railroad Brotherhoods, meanwhile, did not reappear.) Though never dead, the idea of "realignment" through a third party—"independent political action," as it was then known—seemed to have lost some of its luster, even among radicals.[104]

A similar disillusionment played out on the other side of the Farmer-Labor coalition, though the solution devised differed from that of the AFL. Farm groups, in fact, showed greater experimentation in terms of both electoral and legislative strategies in this period, but for their most prominent representative group, at least, these experiences would eventually lead out of the electoral realm altogether.

The Split Personality of Agricultural Politics

Though the Railroad Brotherhoods had backed the Farmer-Labor Party in 1920, the dominant impetus behind it was on the agricultural side. It drew support from the Farmers' Union, for example, a national organization representing tenant farmers and agricultural workers, which Clemens identifies as one of the first recognizably "modern" interest groups.[105] It also attracted a regional group called the Non-Partisan League (NPL), whose strength lay in the upper Midwest.[106] Neither of these organizations drew congressional scrutiny, yet the role of the NPL is important to consider, for its vision of nonpartisanship was quite different from that espoused by either the AFL or the NAM, and it looked to elections in a distinctive way.[107] Indeed, it might seem ironic that an avowedly "nonpartisan" organization would throw its support behind a third-party initiative. But the NPL had pioneered a range of electoral tactics that had brought it into close contact with various state parties, while maintaining distance from the idea of partisanship itself.

The NPL built a new strategy of political influence upon the edifice of Progressive Era electoral reforms, as antiparty sentiment translated into mechanisms of direct democracy like the initiative, the recall, and the direct primary election.[108] The primary concept swept across the country after 1901, when Minnesota introduced it for selecting candidates for the state legislature and the US House of Representatives.[109] A wave of other states followed suit, mainly in the Midwest and West, extending primary laws to cover US senators (after ratification of the Seventeenth Amendment in 1913) and even the presidency, with Oregon being the first state to pass a "presidential preference" primary law in 1910.[110] Elite reformers had advocated primaries as a means of loosening the grip of party leaders on candidate selection—a defining act of parties—so as to diminish the power of corrupt party machines.[111] But the NPL saw in primaries a way to *use* existing parties and achieve legislative aims directly, without the need to create a new "independent" party. It would not threaten incumbent lawmakers with defeat if they did not support a group's preferred policy. Rather, it would try to elect loyal allies who would need no further persuasion, looking to primaries as an arena in which farm voters could be mobilized and a small number could make a difference.[112]

Emerging first in North Dakota in 1915 and soon spreading elsewhere in the upper Midwest, the NPL tried to take over one party in the state and, in essence, make it look more like a third party. It usually set its sights on whichever party was dominant in a particular district or state, whether Republican or Democrat, so that the election of its slate of candidates would be all but guaranteed, providing they won the primaries.[113] Through these tactics the NPL was able to take over the Republican Party in North Dakota and infiltrate other parties in nearby midwestern and western states.[114] Yet as Huntington noted, the NPL employed a hierarchy of tactics, depending on context. Sometimes it entered NPL candidates in *both* major parties' primaries; sometimes it entered neither, waiting to see who would emerge and throwing its support to the most sympathetic candidate. If their favored candidates lost in the primaries, NPL leaders were not above running them as independents in the general election or, as a last resort, putting them on a farmer-labor party ticket, even as they distanced themselves from third-party aspirations more generally.[115]

And thus when the NPL turned its attention to national politics in 1920, its least favored method—farmer-labor party politics—won out. In part, this reflected the lesser significance of primaries in presidential contests, where party bosses still controlled the majority of convention delegates and thus determined the final outcome.[116] The national party apparatus, therefore, could not be commandeered in one go. But this also reflected the declining strength of the NPL's organization. It had burst into prominence in 1915 on a renewed wave of agrarian discontent, but record commodity and land prices during World War I had sapped the populist sentiment on which it fed.[117] By the time farm conditions plummeted to unprecedented lows in the postwar period, the NPL was already fatally weakened, its membership diminished, its leaders battling among themselves, and its methods the subject of widespread scorn.[118] (Despite the Progressive critique of partisanship, many recoiled from its opportunistic approach of picking different sides in different circumstances.) Accordingly, the NPL threw what weight it had left behind the Farmer-Labor Party of 1920 and sank further into ignominy as a result.

At that very moment, however, a new national farmers' organization was coming to prominence that would take agricultural politics in a new direction by focusing its attentions on lobbying and forging an explicitly *bipartisan* path. The American Farm Bureau Federation was founded in 1919, and its membership had grown to about 1.5 million by 1921.[119] Like the US Chamber of Commerce, its formation was linked to the federal government, in this case to the Department of Agriculture (USDA) and its "extension" programs, which were designed to promote new agricultural techniques in rural communities.[120] Beginning in 1914, the USDA encouraged the creation of local Farm Bureaus to support the work of the Extension Service, and they soon federated as a national organization.[121] The American Farm Bureau Federation quickly established a powerful presence in Washington, DC, headed up by the improbably named Gray Silver, who would become a prominent figure on Capitol Hill. By the early 1920s, in fact, Silver had managed to cultivate a core group of supportive lawmakers in both parties, dubbed the "Farm Bloc," to advance agricultural interests. And indeed this innovation, and the Farm Bureau's apparent power, has led generations of political scientists to view it as the quintessential modern "lobby."

The Farm Bureau's rapid rise to prominence drew notice from lawmakers at the time, and Silver was called to explain its activities before the House Banking Committee in 1921, which was holding a series of hearings on farm organizations. He proceeded to describe the Farm Bureau as an entirely "nonpolitical organization."[122] Like Ferdinand Schwedtman of the NAM, Silver appeared to view being "political" in both partisan and electoral terms, explaining that the Farm Bureau avoided anything to do with "party politics" and forbade its officers from seeking election themselves.[123] Throughout the 1920s, it was never called before a congressional electoral investigation, though Silver's successor, Chester Gray, did appear before the Senate's 1929 lobbying investigation. There, Gray reiterated Silver's earlier stance. "We are not in politics in the American Farm Bureau Federation," Gray said. "We are not playing the partisan wagon."[124]

Instead, the Farm Bureau would deploy nonpartisan legislative and administrative techniques and primarily pursue an inside track. Given its origins and connection to the USDA, the Farm Bureau had a natural affinity for bureaucratic lobbying and pursued part of its agenda in the executive branch.[125] But it also looked to the legislative realm. As Silver had explained in 1921, the Farm Bureau concentrated on gauging membership opinion on agricultural matters being considered by Congress and transmitting that information to receptive lawmakers, in essence a blend of direct and indirect lobbying.[126] The Farm Bloc was a novel formalization of that process, cultivating a reliable unit among lawmakers themselves rather than looking to a bloc of voters to support its lobbying efforts. This coalition of Republican and Democratic legislators who came together on agricultural issues was organized on an official basis from 1921 to 1923 and informally for several years thereafter.[127]

Yet despite some early legislative successes, the bipartisan Farm Bloc did not secure what would become the premier objective for all the major farm organizations in the 1920s: the McNary-Haugen bill.[128] With the postwar agricultural depression continuing to devastate their communities, farm leaders were convinced that some form of government aid was needed. Many considered it redress, in fact, for existing federal policy, since tariffs protected various American industries while hurting many farmers. Agriculture thus sought "parity" with industry through government intervention. The most popular plan was the brainchild of George Peek, a one-time farm equipment manufacturer turned agricultural economist, and the bill to enact it—sponsored by Republicans Charles McNary in the Senate and Gilbert Haugen in the House—would have established a federal agency to buy up agricultural surpluses, store, or sell them overseas, and thereby raise domestic prices.[129]

Congress passed two versions of the McNary-Haugen bill between 1924 and 1928 and debated several more. And President Coolidge vetoed it both times. Business interests voiced strong opposition to the bill, viewing it as a much greater federal intervention in the economy than tariff policy.[130] And while their entreaties may have failed with lawmakers, they had an ally in the White House, showing once more the advantaged position of business groups in promoting their aims, particularly when those aims were obstructive. (The American political system, after all, provides far more opportunities to hinder legislation than to help it.) Not only could Coolidge's actions be identified as pro-business, they also threatened to stamp opposition to McNary-Haugen with a partisan hue. Such a characterization was initially complicated, however, by the fact that Republican lawmakers had sponsored the bill in Congress, even as a Republican president had vetoed it. But by 1928 the Farm Bureau's leaders discerned a clearer party division emerging.

They had sought support for their pet measure at both party conventions but were rebuffed by the GOP's platform committee and further alienated by the nomination of commerce secretary Herbert Hoover, a known opponent of McNary-Haugen.[131] In contrast, they had received a warmer welcome at the Democratic convention and an encouraging if vague statement of support from its eventual nominee, Governor Al Smith of New York. The question arose, therefore, of whether the Farm Bureau should "go into politics" to support Smith's election, since its prized bill was otherwise all but lost.[132] This prospect, however, also raised the central strategic concern outlined by Schattschneider and Key: the fear of political isolation if Hoover won and his fellow Republicans kept control of Congress, ensuring a frosty reception for the Farm Bureau and imperiling its other legislative or bureaucratic aims. There were other concerns, too, about a possible public backlash against a "special interest" trying to "deliver the vote" in a presidential contest, as the AFL had experienced in 1908. And with many loyal Republicans among their own ranks, Farm Bureau leaders feared alienating their members.[133]

According to Orville Kile, a longtime Farm Bureau operative, it was George Peek himself who proposed a solution, through an organizational innovation. Rather than have the Farm Bureau endorse Smith or launch a publicity campaign on his behalf, Peek created a new entity, the Independent Agricultural League. This was a parallel campaign structure built around the county farm bureaus in key farm states but organized separately from them. It was supposedly separate from the Democratic Party machinery, too, encouraging voters in those areas to support Smith while touting its "independence," urging them to "Vote as Farmers, not Partisans."[134] Yet in reality, Peek's League was heavily dependent on the DNC for financing, much like the AFL in 1908, and much of the impetus for its formation had come from the party leadership.[135] Indeed, it is not clear how overt the connections to the Farm Bureau actually were or how significant this regional electoral effort ultimately was.[136] No representatives of either group were called before the Senate's 1928 campaign expenditures committee, chaired by Republican Frederick Steiwer of Oregon. Nonetheless, the League does briefly appear in the Steiwer Committee's report, where it is essentially portrayed as a Democratic entity, a temporary auxiliary as discussed in the last chapter, designed to expand the party's appeal within an economic community.[137]

Certainly the Independent Agricultural League failed to rally farm communities to vote en bloc for Smith, perhaps because of traditional Republican ties in much of the Midwest or because the party divisions were never as clear to the rank and file as they may have been to the Farm Bureau's leadership. Hoover was offering an extensive agricultural program built around a "federal farm board," after all, while Smith equivocated to some extent on his support for McNary-Haugen.[138] Perhaps most fundamentally, as Fite explains, the Farm Bureau failed to convince voters that McNary-Haugen was the critical issue in the campaign. Instead, the intertwined specters of Prohibition and religious identity predominated in 1928, cutting against economic interest for many farmers.[139] Still, although it did not achieve its ostensible aim, the Independent Agricultural League did succeed in protecting the Farm Bureau from both internal disarray and external rebuke.[140]

Farm organizations, then, had experimented with a range of electoral and legislative tactics in the 1910s and 1920s, finding some temporary successes but no enduring political solutions to the problems of farmers. The onset of the Great Depression would only exacerbate those economic woes, and it sent the membership of the Farm Bureau into freefall, down to under 200,000 by 1932.[141] In such straitened circumstances it took little active part in the presidential campaign that year, beyond a small-scale effort in the congressional arena mostly conducted through its member newsletter, urging support for the Farm Bureau's "friends" in Congress and the defeat of its opponents.[142] A preference for the Democratic presidential candidate, Franklin Roosevelt, was nevertheless palpable, even as the Farm Bureau declined to offer an official endorsement.[143] The DNC, for its part, launched a strong campaign in farm states, sensing in the economic devastation an opportunity to lure midwestern farmers away from their Republican moorings, and without the need for "front" groups or other disguise.[144]

The election of Roosevelt would usher in a dramatic shift in farm politics, through the fundamental achievement of the Farm Bureau's major legislative aim. Though the mechanism differed slightly from McNary-Haugen's, the Agricultural Adjustment Act (AAA) of 1933 and subsequent amendments solved the basic problem of overproduction that had long plagued farmers through production quotas and subsidies, and lodged care of their concerns in the administrative state.[145] The implications for interest group strategy were profound. After 1933, groups like the Farm Bureau increasingly concentrated their energies on the implementation of farm policies and minor changes in their funding and formulae, issues ripe for legislative and bureaucratic lobbying. As Hansen suggests, the Farm Bureau had "gained access"; that is, lawmakers came to rely on them for "advice and assistance" in agricultural matters, thus affording significant opportunities for insider influence.[146]

Though he emphasizes lobbying, elections do play a significant role in Hansen's theory of group access, in which influence partly depends on their having "competitive advantage over their rivals in meeting congressional reelection needs."[147] But he has little to say about *actual* electioneering, describing the Farm Bureau as largely "subtle" or "silent" in this regard, both before and after passage of the AAA.[148] Indeed, Hansen acknowledges that his study shows "influence" being achieved without outright "pressure" being applied.[149] Agricultural groups "did next to nothing in political campaigns," he concludes, finding "little evidence that they bought off political candidates . . . that they canvassed the countryside and knocked on all the doors," or "that whole legions of their loyalists marched off as directed to the polls," as a friends and enemies strategy might dictate.[150] In a sense, Hansen's theory formalizes a threat-based approach but presents it as "informational" rather than intimidating, in which a group's influence is premised on the intelligence it provides about constituency opinion rather than the votes it could potentially muster.[151] If a group reads voters' views correctly, and a lawmaker wins re-election after following its advice, then it gains "access." If it reads the constituency incorrectly, however, then both lose out.[152]

The Farm Bureau's intelligence was consistently accurate, Hansen suggests, throughout the 1930s and 1940s, when AAA programs proved immensely popular in farming communities. Despite originating with a Democratic administration, this widespread popularity ensured bipartisan consensus on the issue, Hansen explains.[153] Though a partisan split did briefly emerge in the 1950s and early 1960s over the specific nature of price supports, this division had subsided by the mid-1960s, rendering farm politics generally bipartisan thereafter.[154] During that brief partisan period, however, the Farm Bureau aligned itself with the Republican viewpoint, which Hansen links to a subsequent decline in its influence.[155] Drawing on Schattschneider's earlier work, in fact, Hansen theorizes that visible partisanship would hurt interest groups because the intelligence they offered lawmakers would now be identical to that the party provided, and thus their "comparative advantage" would be lost.[156] In this particular case, moreover, the Republican policy proved unpopular in congressional elections, meaning the Farm Bureau lost access to both sides. Neither the partisan orientation nor the loss of legislative influence, however, appears to have prompted experimentation with outright electioneering by the Farm Bureau. (It did not appear before any of the dedicated congressional campaign investigations in the 1940s and 1950s, and though it was called before the Senate's dual investigation into campaigning and lobbying in 1957, the discussion focused primarily on the latter.)[157]

The nature of agricultural politics may help to explain this. As an "interest," agriculture had no clear opponent, unlike business and labor.[158] Even within the agricultural sector, different representative groups often agreed on policy aims.[159] Furthermore, it enjoyed an elevated cultural status relative to other special interests, given the centrality of the "yeoman farmer" to the ideology of civic republicanism. These properties can themselves help to explain the bipartisan consensus on agricultural policy for most of the twentieth century, in addition to the popularity of the programs. The relative permanence and security of those programs, moreover, focused debate on incremental changes and administration rather than on existential questions that might mobilize farmers in elections.[160] Meanwhile, the relative efficacy of lobbying and the lack of organized opponents reduced competitive pressures to find new techniques.[161] For reasons both strategic and cultural, therefore, 1928 would prove to be the Farm Bureau's first and last presidential campaign.

Pressure Politics and Prohibition

The issue of Prohibition had loomed large over the 1928 presidential election. Ratified as a constitutional amendment in 1919 and implemented via the Volstead Act in 1920, the nationwide ban on alcohol had split public opinion from the outset into "dry" and "wet" camps, with both views cutting across the party divide. The dry forces had long been better organized and more visible, most prominently through the Anti-Saloon League, which had helped push the Eighteenth Amendment in the first place. To do so, the ASL had seemingly perfected the "nonpartisan" methods that utilized publicity to influence lawmakers and backed it up with electoral threats. In the 1920s, however, the "wet" forces began to regroup, and new organizations like the Association Against the Prohibition Amendment adopted similar methods for opposing ends. Their escalating competition led both into the presidential contest in 1928, though changing partisan dynamics also played an important role. Indeed, 1928 would prove to be a key inflection point in terms of pressure politics, electioneering, and partisanship, with important implications for subsequent interest group activity, the full contours of which were obscured in earlier scholarship by a lopsided focus on the ASL.

The Anti-Saloon League was a source of both fascination and fear in 1920s Washington, DC. It had, after all, ridden a seemingly far-fetched policy all the way to a constitutional amendment in 1919.[162] And this great victory appeared to vindicate its leaders' choice of tactics: using publicity to cultivate mass sentiment in favor of their aims. It was the exemplary pressure group of the age: bureaucratic, nonpartisan, and narrowly focused on a single issue.[163] The term "pressure politics," in fact, was coined with the ASL in mind, providing the title for Peter Odegard's 1928 account of its methods.[164] And its emergence mirrors the trajectory Clemens describes for business, labor, and women's groups. A federation of Protestant churches, state, and local leagues with a mass membership, the ASL was formed in 1893 as an explicit repudiation of third-party politics, following the repeated failures of the Prohibition Party in national elections.[165] Like labor unions, it had looked to business interests for a new model of activity, in this case the brewers and "liquor men" who supplied the American market with alcohol and bought the support of state lawmakers on both sides of the aisle. The ASL fashioned its own "nonpartisan" alternative and set out to spread its gospel of temperance.[166]

Starting small in Ohio with a drive for "local option" laws—permitting individual cities and counties to go "dry"—it soon took the idea elsewhere, gradually working upward to the national level.[167] Unlike the Prohibition Party, therefore, it sought alcohol restriction through incremental reform and kept its attention narrowly focused on this single issue.[168] Indeed, the ASL was insistently nonpartisan. It was explicitly "not a party," an official explained in 1908, "and, furthermore, refuses to become a part of any party."[169] Instead, it undertook massive "educational" publicity campaigns, as Odegard detailed, flooding the mails with leaflets and pamphlets warning of the dangers of alcohol and promoting specific legislative solutions.[170] But publicity alone did not make the ASL into the powerful entity it would become. Odegard acknowledged that its "influence in the lobby and committee room would have been negligible" had it not "demonstrated its ability to elect and defeat candidates for public office."[171] The ASL did not merely seek to sway public opinion or motivate constituents to express their views but to influence the way they would *vote*. Its propaganda "was not so much an educational as a political weapon," Odegard concluded. "Its purpose was to spur into action those voters who believed the liquor traffic to be an evil."[172]

Indeed, from the start, elections had been the backstop to the Anti-Saloon League's pressure. Much as drinkers must be convinced that temperance was best for their health and moral well-being, the ASL sought to convince lawmakers that supporting temperance legislation was best for their electoral welfare. Thus the ASL tracked how state and national lawmakers voted on such measures and sought pro-temperance pledges from new candidates for office. It made endorsements accordingly, clearly and openly, and when necessary, rallied supporters to the polls through its decentralized network of churches, exhorting them to reward "drys" and punish "wets" irrespective of party affiliation. By controlling a bloc of voters that could be mobilized for or against any candidate, the ASL sought to hold the balance of power in any given election.[173]

But it did not always want to deploy that bloc. Indeed, as with other groups using "friends and enemies" tactics, *threat* was the critical element—though in delivering such warnings, the ASL emphasized the candidate selection phase more than its counterparts. In its early years it hoped to induce both major parties to nominate dry candidates for office and only rewarded or punished in the general election if one did not.[174] As primary elections became more widespread in the early twentieth century, the ASL adapted its approach, encouraging its members to support dry candidates in primaries and make their general election choice accordingly. Again, in the ideal situation both parties would nominate a dry, in which case the ASL would have no further involvement in the campaign. Its preferred scenario, therefore, actually precluded the need for active electoral participation, in the general election at least.[175] Where it did participate, it would do so indirectly, promoting favored candidates through its member newsletters and wider publicity campaigns rather than donating money to a candidate or party. Through such veiled threats, and some indirect campaigning, the ASL claimed by 1908 to have influenced "thousands of victories at the polls" at the local, state, and federal levels.[176] By 1916 it had helped to ensure sufficient congressional support for a constitutional amendment.[177]

Attempts to mobilize a bloc vote had usually generated controversy and criticism. The AFL's 1908 efforts, after all, had been attacked as coercive, even subversive of democracy. But the ASL appeared relatively immune to such criticism, in the 1910s at least, perhaps because its aims could not be ascribed to economic self-interest. It claimed to be working for the public good, rooted its aims in moral and religious conviction, and had no financial stake in the laws it sought. In contrast, the United States Brewers' Association—which promoted the financial interests of beer producers and opposed restrictions on alcohol—found itself subject to a Senate investigation in 1918 for attempting to influence congressional elections.[178] While illegal campaign donations were a major concern here, along with the brewing industry's ties to Germany in a time of war, the Brewers were scrutinized for using methods similar to those of the ASL: "exacting pledges" from candidates, building "a political organization," and trying to create a swing vote, as noted in the Introduction.[179] The ASL's moral imperative, in contrast, helped it to rise above the fray of "special interests" and preempt criticism of its methods. It saw itself, as one ASL official put it in 1923, as a "political machine . . . built for good."[180]

Yet that exemption seemed to wane after Prohibition went into effect. Indeed, the ASL's standing and tactics shifted dramatically throughout the 1920s, as it adapted to a new position in defense of its policy gains, and as the enforcement of Prohibition began to alter the surrounding partisan dynamics. Prohibition had not been a clear "party" issue prior to ratification of the Eighteenth Amendment; indeed, party platforms had largely steered clear of the issue, while presidential candidates kept quiet.[181] The ASL's push for a constitutional amendment had instead centered on Congress, where support and opposition could be found on both sides. Enforcement, however, brought the presidency and the executive branch into the picture. And since throughout the 1920s it would be Republican presidents who bore that responsibility, Prohibition began to be imprinted with a Republican tint.[182] There were some who had long seen Prohibition as a more Republican project, of course—in line with the GOP's greater Protestant and nativist appeal, set against a Democratic Party more attuned to urban, immigrant, and Catholic voters. But the Southern Democrats had always complicated this picture; the Bible Belt was dry country, after all. As the 1920s progressed, however, and concerns about bootlegging, organized crime, and other negative effects of Prohibition grew, opposition began to cohere more clearly in Democratic circles.[183] And it was tied most visibly to the rising fortunes of New York governor Al Smith, who came close to winning his party's presidential nomination in 1924, and succeeded in 1928.

Smith was "the nation's best-known wet politician," whose Catholicism identified him with a constituency largely hostile to Prohibition and with a church viewed by many Protestants as deeply suspect, with adherents subject to the "foreign" influence of the pope.[184] The ASL had thus sprung into action in 1924, with its "legislative superintendent," Wayne Wheeler, working the Democratic convention to prevent Smith's nomination and promote adoption of a "dry" platform. (Wheeler also worked the Republican convention, for appearance's sake at least, since the threat of a "wet" candidate was never as strong there.) The ASL's leaders had breathed a sigh of relief with the eventual nomination of the "satisfactorily dry" John W. Davis and retreated from the presidential scene to focus on key congressional races.[185]

But in a changing popular and partisan context, the ASL's methods increasingly drew notice, even criticism, from Congress and the public at large. "[T]he politics of the Anti-Saloon league is being exposed in state after state as a thing without scruple," the *Chicago Tribune* declared in 1926, citing its unsavory partnership with the virulently racist and anti-Catholic Ku Klux Klan in Indiana as just one example.[186] Its singular focus on Prohibition, moreover, led the ASL to support candidates whose qualifications or stances might otherwise be wanting.[187] Such questionable means were sullying the ASL reputation, despite its elevated end. "[T]he Anti-Saloon league is showing no more regard for decent political action or for the consequences of its tactics than the booze barons," the *Tribune* railed, "and its pretense of moral motive does not cover the sordid truth."[188]

Congress, too, began to examine the ASL's "political action." There were campaign finance laws to consider, after all. Though the ASL was unincorporated and thus not subject to the Tillman Act's ban, the 1910 Publicity Act and its amendments required all "political committees" to disclose any electoral spending, something national ASL officials repeatedly declined to do.[189] The ASL claimed to be "educational" rather than "political" in purpose and thus exempt from the reach of the law. In 1920, however, after a specific request from the Clerk of the House of Representatives, the ASL did file a report, making sure to emphasize that it was done under protest.[190] In 1925, responding to a Supreme Court case, Congress passed the Federal Corrupt Practices Act, which reformulated the publicity laws and strengthened disclosure requirements.[191] But the ASL continued to file seemingly thin reports. And thus in 1926, when the Senate formed a committee to investigate midterm campaign expenditures, its Democratic chairman—Senator James Reed of Missouri—called Wheeler in to testify.[192]

The ASL "took an interest" in the election of dry candidates to office, Wheeler acknowledged, describing how it backed those who "stand right" on the Prohibition question, beginning in the primaries.[193] To Reed's chagrin, Wheeler even defended the ASL's practice of urging one party's primary voters to back the other's general election candidate, if only one "dry" emerged. Where Reed saw this as dishonorable, Wheeler claimed "it is far better citizenship to support a good man on an opposite ticket rather than a bad one on your own."[194] But his main objective was to downplay the ASL's electoral activities as a mere "incident of the work" compared to its ongoing "educational" publicity efforts promoting abstinence and law enforcement.[195] Since those efforts were not "political," Wheeler claimed, the ASL did not report the cost in its campaign disclosures, detailing only the specific funds raised for primary or general election use.[196] Reed strongly disputed the ASL's distinction between educational and political, and their disagreement would preview a more modern debate over "issue advertising" in campaigns, about whether advertising purportedly concerned with specific policies might aid the electoral fortunes of certain candidates (and thus be subject to regulation) without mentioning them by name.[197] Under Wheeler's rationale, the ASL would file just $2 of "political" expenditures in 1927, even as it sought to shape public opinion in ways that would benefit "dry" candidates in 1928.[198]

But the ASL was not the only organization with a deep interest in Prohibition to be called before Reed's committee. Representatives of the Association Against the Prohibition Amendment—a prominent anti-temperance group—also appeared. By the mid-1920s, anti-Prohibition sentiment outside of Congress had become increasingly organized, with critical voices channeled through an array of anti-temperance groups.[199] But loudest of all was the AAPA, a group with strong ties to the business community, and especially to the du Pont family, which put the ASL and its constitutional achievement directly in its sights.[200] The AAPA was explicitly modeled on the ASL, in fact, employing similar methods for opposing aims.[201] Founded late in 1918 by Baltimore lawyer William H. Stayton, it was originally intended to be a nonpartisan, mass membership organization, but it struggled early on to attract a level of support similar to that of the ASL or to replicate the latter's electoral successes.[202] In both 1922 and 1924, numerous congressional candidates actually disavowed the AAPA's endorsement, in part due to threats of punishment from the ASL.[203]

Despite massaging its membership figures, claiming to have in excess of 700,000 members by mid-1926, AAPA strategy shifted around that time, away from the masses and toward elite influence.[204] Stayton had already recruited a number of prominent Americans to its ranks, including Irénée and Pierre du Pont of the DuPont chemical company and their close associate John J. Raskob, vice president of General Motors. For the AAPA, the du Ponts' involvement offered a veneer of Protestant, philanthropic respectability, helping to counteract negative perceptions of the "wet" cause as morally suspect and predominantly associated with Catholics and immigrants.[205] For the du Ponts, the prospect of repealing Prohibition engaged both economic self-interest and political principle. On the one hand, the loss of liquor taxes had placed a greater burden on high-income individuals and corporations for federal revenue, a burden that repeal might shift elsewhere.[206] On the other, Prohibition represented a massive expansion of federal power, which the du Ponts opposed in itself, and they feared further encroachment into economic and civil life.[207] Thus at the end of 1927, the AAPA was effectively "refounded" by a group of eighteen prominent members, injecting new funds and renewed purpose into Stayton's organization.[208]

The new AAPA launched a massive publicity campaign to promote revision of the Volstead Act, state referenda on Prohibition, and ultimate repeal of the Eighteenth Amendment. And they continued working to defeat drys and install wets into state offices and the House of Representatives. "We are a comparatively young organization, and we have not gotten so ambitious as to take part in the election of Senators," Stayton told the Reed Committee in 1926.[209] But developments in 1928 would cause the AAPA to set its sights still higher. In that year the nation's most prominent "wet," Al Smith, would ultimately secure the Democratic nomination for president—in part through the efforts of prominent AAPA members, and despite the ASL's best efforts to stop him. Both organizations, in fact, would be called once more to explain their activities in Congress, this time before the Senate's 1928 campaign expenditure committee, chaired by Frederick Steiwer of Oregon.[210]

Even before the conventions the ASL was deeply opposed to the nomination of any "wet" candidate, Edward B. Dunford, the group's attorney, admitted.[211] Testifying in June, he noted that the ASL had raised $3,000 for a primary and preconvention fund, which it had used to circulate leaflets reviewing the records of prominent candidates on Prohibition—in effect, to denounce Smith's positions.[212] The ASL's national superintendent, Francis McBride, had then attended the conventions, pushing both parties to include a strong "law enforcement" plank in their platforms (that is, a promise to enforce Prohibition) and maneuvering against Smith at the Democratic conclave.[213] His efforts proved ineffectual, for as McBride later acknowledged, though both party planks were ultimately satisfactory, the Democratic candidate was not.[214] Smith installed the AAPA's John J. Raskob as his party chairman and proceeded to announce his support for some modification of the Eighteenth Amendment.[215] In contrast, though the Republican nominee floated an inquiry into the problems of Prohibition, he promised to faithfully enforce the law.[216] Given such divisions, the strategic calculus that had long counseled ASL restraint at the presidential level should have broken, as per Key's analysis.[217] The group might as well back Hoover because a Smith victory would be detrimental from its perspective. Likewise, the AAPA had little to lose by backing Smith.

Accordingly, both ventured into the presidential fray, though they did so cautiously, offering implicit support to their chosen candidates while seeking to carve out a nonpartisan model for their participation, challenging the presumption that backing a party's presidential nominee was a signature "partisan" act. Each emphasized that its preference was based on *issues*, thus extending the "friends and enemies" rationale in principle, even to a singular office where, in practice, neither could balance out its support by backing another candidate from the other side. Furthermore, both groups distanced themselves from the party organizations. Both raised significant amounts of money to spend on the campaign: almost half a million dollars for the AAPA, compared to under $200,000 for the ASL (though given the poor reporting system at the time, the actual amounts may well have been higher).[218] But neither contributed this money directly to candidates or party committees. Nor did either receive party funds. Rather, both spent "independently" of the official campaigns, through wider publicity efforts, organizing speakers and events, and communicating with their members.

They also looked for other ways to break the partisan connection. Neither made official endorsements of its favored candidate, and both placed a greater emphasis on attacking the opponent than on expressing their support.[219] The ASL circulated leaflets detailing Smith's "vile" record on the "liquor traffic," for example, while also fostering a whispering campaign centered on Smith's personal habits.[220] One of its leading officers, Methodist bishop James Cannon Jr., publicly denounced Smith as a "cocktail president," citing the Democratic nominee's reported penchant for "four to eight" alcoholic drinks a day.[221] Cannon also led a charge against Smith in the South, where his "wet" stance was straining traditional Democratic allegiances. Through a network of campaign committees dubbed the "Anti-Smith Democrats," Cannon sought to ease the psychic burden on southerners by urging them to vote *against* Smith rather than *for* Hoover, and to otherwise vote as "loyal" Democrats down-ballot.[222] This was a rhetorical mix of policy purity and party regularity, though officially distanced from both the regular party and the ASL (Cannon was acting purely as an individual, he declared).

The AAPA relied on similar distinctions between individual and organizational activity, much as Ferdinand Schwedtman had first claimed for the NAM in 1912. One of the AAPA's directors was serving as chairman of the DNC, after all, and practically bankrolling its campaign (Raskob personally contributed over $100,000 to the party's campaign coffers in 1928 and cleared its post-election debts).[223] Yet the separation was never as perfect as the rhetoric proclaimed. As Stayton wrote a California AAPA official in September, "We are keeping in touch with the Democratic National Committee so that we know what work they are doing, and we are merely trying to supplement it."[224] Though operating independently of the DNC in financial terms, the AAPA was complementing its activities, previewing another dimension of the modern campaign finance debate around the question of *coordination* between parties and nonparty groups, whether explicit or implicit, and how this might be regulated.

Nonetheless, even the AAPA's additional support could not prevent Smith's defeat. Hoover won almost 60 percent of the popular vote and forty states overall.[225] Smith's Catholicism, if not his views on Prohibition, was largely blamed for the result, with Protestants deserting the Democratic standard in droves. Even the "Solid South" was broken in 1928, as "Hoover Democrats" brought the Republican candidate victory in Virginia, North Carolina, Florida, Tennessee, and Texas, along with several border states, propelling him toward a landslide victory overall. Wets also appeared to lose ground elsewhere, with the largest ever dry contingent returned to Congress (eighty senators and more than three hundred representatives), and dry governors were installed in forty-three states.[226] On the surface, it appeared that partisanship had served the ASL well. Yet these results masked a deeper ambivalence about the Prohibition project nationally, and they obscured a growing discomfort in the aftermath of the campaign with the role temperance groups had played.

In 1929, when the Senate launched its second major inquiry into "the activities of . . . lobbying associations and lobbyists," Senator Caraway's committee called witnesses from both the ASL and the AAPA.[227] Though ostensibly concerned with legislative influence, the senators found themselves veering into electoral territory: campaign fundraising and reporting; the "publicity methods" these groups utilized to promote or oppose candidates; and even their authority to engage in electioneering at all.[228] Members of the committee began to press these witnesses on the ways election campaigns played into their overall efforts to shape legislation and expressed vocal disapproval of their techniques and lack of transparency.

Senator Caraway questioned the ASL's Francis McBride, for example, on a statement he made to supporters in 1930 that "more than 90% of Anti-Saloon League activities cluster about elections," which contradicted Wheeler's earlier claims that elections were just an "incident" of its larger work.[229] McBride tried to finesse the statement by claiming the outright "political phase" of its activities was very brief, and while its ongoing publicity work might "huddle up close" to elections, it still did not constitute political activity as defined by the law.[230] Yet he described its lobbying work in ways that directly implicated elections. "The drys' lobbying is done back home in the districts," he said, "and when well done there little more is needed in Washington."[231] While initially appearing to describe indirect lobbying through the cultivation of public opinion, McBride went on to frame this approach in distinctly *electoral* terms. "If the work is done right in the primary and election they work all right when they get here," he said.[232] In other words, grassroots pressure was best applied to influence the selection and election of dry candidates; if this was "done right," little else would be needed down the road. When Caraway probed, "If you elect your man, you don't have to keep the home fires burning under him?" McBride confirmed, "Not often, if it is done right."[233]

McBride's remark suggests that the ASL was drawing away from an "access, or legislative strategy," in which electoral activities are designed to enhance a group's legislative persuasiveness, and moving closer to an "electoral strategy," in which elections are themselves the vehicle for pursuing policy aims.[234] By emphasizing candidate *selection*, whether through primaries or party conclaves, the ASL approach changed the locus at which pressure was applied, making it more *active* than *reactive*. The emphasis on "standing right," moreover, hinted at the importance of what a candidate actually believed, not simply what he was prepared to say or do in office if his electoral fortunes were threatened. For its part, the AAPA denied that it "lobbied" at all, at least not directly. As AAPA president Henry Curran explained, the group sought repeal by "assembling and distributing to the American people information of the workings of this amendment," and "[b]y supporting the candidacies of those who agree with the object of our association," but did not approach lawmakers directly.[235] The implication, once more, was that electioneering "done right" could bring about legislative change without the need for direct entreaties or the persuasive arts of the traditional lobbyist.

But after 1928 electioneering "done right" increasingly had a partisan tinge, despite both organizations' continued "nonpartisan" protestations.[236] And partisan electoral successes could quickly turn into losses, as the ASL would soon discover. Its intervention in 1928 had already caused organizational damage. For all the South's discomfort with Al Smith, the ASL's implicit support for Herbert Hoover had been a step too far for many dry Southern Democrats, and the group saw its regional support erode.[237] Through its connections to Bishop Cannon, moreover, it was implicated in a serious scandal, since Cannon had improperly used large donations to his Anti-Smith Democrats for personal purposes.[238] In some ways, as Kerr suggests, the very shift from offense to defense had enervated the ASL at the grassroots throughout the 1920s, finding it harder to sustain enthusiasm for the cause once its main aim had been achieved. The Volstead Act, too, had been more restrictive than some drys had anticipated, setting the maximum alcohol content so low that it outlawed beer and wine as well as hard liquor. Accordingly, the ASL had already seen a sharp decline in financial contributions.[239] The stock market crash of October 1929 only worsened its financial straits. But the ensuing economic disaster also undermined its key practical argument for Prohibition. Drys had attributed the economic boom of the 1920s to Prohibition, claiming that money once spent on alcohol was now "the motive power of our prosperity."[240] The Great Depression would sweep away such claims, along with many other economic shibboleths.[241]

Sensing a shift in the public mood with the economic downturn, Prohibition's opponents in Congress stepped up their attacks. In early 1930, wets on the Judiciary Committee pushed for hearings on proposed changes to the Eighteenth Amendment, bringing the idea of outright repeal into the open.[242] At the same time, the independent inquiry Hoover had promised—the National Commission on Law Observance—concluded in its 1931 report that drinking was on the rise, along with a wider disrespect for the legal system.[243] The embattled president, however, chose to cling to Prohibition in some form, doing much to further the partisan divide first signaled in 1928 and to imbue the policy with his own unpopularity.[244] Hoover's stance carried the day at the 1932 Republican convention, though not without a serious struggle, with a platform plank proposing a modified constitutional amendment that would give states some say in whether they wanted to permit alcohol within their borders.[245]

Meanwhile, the Democrats increasingly saw a "damper" stance as playing to their advantage.[246] Far from retiring into the political wilderness, the AAPA was pushing the repeal message hard both publicly and privately, through its unofficial channels in the Democratic Party. And the Depression had provided a new and powerful argument: presenting legalized liquor as an economic recovery measure, offering the prospect of new jobs and a new source of revenue from excise taxes on alcoholic beverages. Democrats had already won back the House in 1930, and party leaders smelled victory on the horizon in 1932. If the AAPA-backed DNC chairman preferred outright repeal, however, the party's eventual presidential nominee—New York governor Franklin Roosevelt—maneuvered for a less definitive, pragmatic stance.[247] Nonetheless, with the prospect of federal patronage in sight, even Southern Democrats were willing to countenance some equivocation.[248] Ultimately, after a few convention skirmishes between the Raskob and Roosevelt forces, the Democratic platform came out for immediate modification of the Volstead Act "pending repeal" and took that plan to the country.[249]

In 1932, of course, it was the Democratic candidate who would win. And by extension, the AAPA would win. Though the AAPA had refrained from formally endorsing Roosevelt, its leaders had nonetheless worked to aid his victory.[250] The Volstead Act was modified to permit sale of some alcoholic beverages within Roosevelt's first hundred days, and the Twenty-First Amendment, repealing the Eighteenth, was ratified by the end of his first year in office. Its primary purpose thus achieved, the AAPA quietly dismantled much of its organizational machinery. The ASL, in contrast, suffered a more painful demise. Already a shadow of its former self, organizationally enfeebled by internal battles and financial losses, outspent and outmaneuvered by an opponent on the upswing, ASL leaders faced the fallout of having hitched their fortunes to the wrong horse after all.[251] They had scaled the heights of interest group influence, achieving a constitutional amendment, no less—a once inconceivable prospect. And little more than a decade later, they faced the once inconceivable reality of losing it.

Electioneering and Partisanship

For generations of political scientists, the ASL's rise and fall was told as a cautionary tale of the way partisanship would hurt an interest group that went "into politics." It shaped how Schattschneider and Key understood pressure politics and the dangers groups would face when they strayed into electoral territory and picked a party side: alienating potential allies across the aisle, facing "isolation" if the chosen party lost, and alienating their own membership or the public at large.[252] Nonpartisanship was a safer strategy, they argued, and to maintain it, avoiding presidential elections (at the very least) was a group's best bet. Only if parties diverged clearly on a policy issue might groups be induced to take a stand in national elections, and even then only reluctantly, as a last resort. The idea that groups might enter the electoral fray by *choice* never entered the equation for these scholars, nor did the possibility that pressure groups might *want* the parties to diverge on their issues of concern. Thus the ASL's Republican drift in the 1920s was seen as a matter of expedience rather than preference, a product of context, contingency, and particular presidential candidacies.[253] Groups simply responded to the structure of partisan conflict as they found it and chose their tactics accordingly.

But the AAPA's experience points to a different lesson, one these scholars ignored.[254] Its partisan electioneering eventually brought about success, despite initial failure in 1928. The configuration of interests and the nature of its aims help to explain why. On the one hand, the rise of the AAPA as a direct opponent to the ASL fostered an oppositional dynamic on the Prohibition question, framing it as a polar choice and encouraging lawmakers to pick a side. Meanwhile, the growing association of Prohibition with the GOP and the prominence of Al Smith in Democratic circles made the Democratic Party a more receptive vehicle for the AAPA's aims.[255] To that extent, then, the AAPA did respond to party changes, but its behind-the-scenes championing of Smith might also be construed as an attempt to *make* Prohibition into a partisan question. Though its leaders might try to maintain the appearance of nonpartisanship for cultural reasons—extending the rhetoric and self-presentation of "modern" interest groups forged in the early twentieth century—the AAPA had less to fear strategically from partisan alliance.

Unlike its rival's policy aim, the AAPA's objective was singular rather than serial; it only needed to win *once*. The ASL, as it had discovered to its displeasure in the 1920s, had to keep winning in order to enforce and maintain its prized policy. (As McBride told the Caraway Committee in 1930, "we thought we had won in the ninth inning and that the game was over," only to discover that, thanks to the wets, there was to be "a tenth inning on this game.")[256] With Prohibition so discredited, proponents of repeal had little reason to fear a new temperance movement resuscitating the cause and resurrecting the Eighteenth Amendment. If they could ride a partisan wave to success they were content to do so, since the issue would then be laid to rest. Following passage and ratification of the Twenty-First Amendment, in fact, the AAPA closed its doors, largely dismantling its organizational machinery and ceasing its main operations.

Such considerations are important to keep in mind when looking at future interest group activity. They caution us against the automatic assumption that interest group leaders would view partisanship as detrimental to their aims and that, accordingly, they would largely avoid elections. As the next chapter shows, the AAPA's partisan dalliance would actually come back to haunt its leaders, who soon perceived a new threat of federal aggrandizement from the same Democratic president they had helped to install. But their response once again embraced a form of partisan electioneering, in reality if not in rhetoric. Only this time, they switched sides.

A Tale of Two Leagues

As the 1936 presidential election approached, the journalist Max Lerner observed a "new phenomenon" in the world of campaign politics: the "fellow traveler." This label, he explained, applied to "someone who does not accept all your aims but has enough in common with you to accompany you in a comradely fashion part of the way."[1] Both major presidential candidates—incumbent Democratic president Franklin Roosevelt and his Republican challenger, Governor Alf Landon of Kansas—had acquired such comrades in the campaign, Lerner noted. "Coughlin, Townsend, Gerald Smith, Al Smith, the du Ponts," all were helping Landon "on his difficult trek to the White House," while "the forces of progressive labor, organized nationally as Labor's Non-Partisan League," hoped to keep Roosevelt there.[2] Lerner's list comprised a disparate set of personalized political movements, disaffected businessmen, newly prominent labor organizations, and third parties that would come up short. Differing in their structure, finances, motivations, and relations to major parties, they reflected a surge of organizational creativity in the electoral arena, born of the political and economic turmoil of the early New Deal.

Though Roosevelt had entered the White House on the back of a landslide victory, his resounding win in 1932 had failed to subdue all dissenting voices, and his administration would quickly create new enemies on both the left and right.[3] Some adopted the traditional posture of the third party as a means of channeling political opposition. Early in 1933, for example, the Socialists were already testing the waters for a potential run.[4] And by that fall, the League for Independent Political Action—a leftist group formed by the philosopher John Dewey—had called a convention to discuss a new third party. The result was the Farmer-Labor Political Federation, an interim body designed to bring about the longed-for union of agriculture and labor interests behind a new political agenda.[5] The Federation even toyed with the prospect of launching a national presidential campaign in 1936, looking to state-level third-party successes in Minnesota and Wisconsin for inspiration.[6] The urge to create a truly independent party at the

The Rise of Political Action Committees. Emily J. Charnock, Oxford University Press (2020). © Oxford University Press.
DOI: 10.1093/oso/9780190075514.001.0001

national level remained powerful for many radicals, even though prior efforts had repeatedly failed.

But other critics were adopting more novel forms of political organization. Across the country, charismatic political personalities were tapping into popular discontent, spurred by the Depression, and offering their own set of radical policy solutions. There was Father Charles Coughlin, the Catholic "radio priest" with a populist vision of social justice; Francis Townsend, a small-town doctor with a big idea—his revolving pensions for the elderly would solve the economic problems of the Depression *and* care for the aged, he claimed; and Gerald L. K. Smith, carrying the torch for the late Louisiana senator Huey Long, whose economic program had called for capping individual fortunes at $1 million and, unabashedly, spreading the rest around.[7] They had each created distinctive organizations to promote their legislative visions—personalized pressure groups, in effect—and then tried to parlay them into presidential politics. Ultimately they would merge to form the Union Party, a lackluster third-party committed less to its own victory than to drawing support away from Roosevelt, thus earning itself a place among Landon's fellow travelers.

The major parties were also experimenting with new kinds of personalized organization. As noted in chapter 1, a variety of party-funded campaign groups had begun to appear in 1932, primarily on the Democratic side, which sought to expand the appeal of the presidential candidate beyond loyal partisans by downplaying their partisan connections. Unlike the defined geographic communities around which the regular party machinery was structured, these groups appealed to broader constituencies united by "interests" in some sense: economics, occupation, demographics, even ideas. And they did so by stressing how the candidate's personal beliefs, principles, and policy positions might directly benefit such constituencies. They offered, in essence, a nonpartisan appeal to support their party's candidate, challenging the traditional idea that a presidential vote was an expression of partisanship—that to support a Democrat you had to *be* a Democrat. This perspective gained traction in the 1936 election, when voices within the world of "interests" reinforced the message that supporting a presidential candidate could be a limited commitment—that one could be more like a fellow traveler than a partisan.

The economic allegiances of one of these groups—Labor's Non-Partisan League (LNPL)—were obvious enough. But Lerner's reference to "Al Smith and the du Ponts" alluded to another group with less overt ties to an economic community: the business-backed American Liberty League. Combining elements of pressure group and party organization, these two leagues created a new hybrid in 1936 that crossed over from legislative lobbying—the traditional realm of special interests—into the world of presidential electioneering, long the exclusive domain of political parties. Their intrusion into that domain would exert a powerful influence on the election and beyond.

Both the LNPL and the Liberty League would build substantial organizations that participated in the election on their own terms, not as the creations or creatures of the parties. They oriented their campaigns toward or against particular presidential candidates on purportedly nonpartisan grounds and stressed their financial independence from the regular party organizations as a means of emphasizing a new kind of *political* independence, too. Indeed, that independent financial status, shared by a handful of similar organizations in 1936, would mark the start of an important new phase in which groups outside of the major parties, but operating within the existing party system, began contributing and controlling significant amounts of money in federal election campaigns, much more extensively and systematically than in 1928. At the same time, the LNPL and the Liberty League adopted different electoral strategies, modes of activity, and justifications for involvement in the electoral sphere that would shape future interest group electioneering along distinctive lines.

The 1936 election is often viewed through the lens of "critical" or "realigning" elections—those that transform voter preferences and shape party politics in enduring ways. Though scholars such as Mayhew have criticized the idea of a critical election and the body of "realignment theory" of which it forms part, it is clear that the policies of the Roosevelt administration became the object around which new ideological divisions in the American polity began to cohere, setting in motion a changing configuration of party policy priorities and voter preferences around support or opposition to the New Deal.[8] Whether the 1936 election was a "critical" one or not, developments in the 1936 campaign were certainly crucial to the long-term transformation of the Democratic and Republican Parties themselves, to their becoming more cohesively liberal and conservative entities. It was in this contest that the contours of modern electoral organization and politics first began to emerge, in large part through the innovations of prominent "fellow travelers" such as the LNPL and the Liberty League. And it was the new political forms and modes of action first realized in the 1936 election that would ultimately bring about that broader transformation of the party system.

The Idea of Political "Independence"

At the beginning of 1936, Franklin Roosevelt told Democratic National Committee (DNC) chairman James Farley that he was "very anxious that we start organizing different committees at once."[9] Roosevelt had in mind the handful of organizations that had aided his campaign in 1932, groups cultivated and funded by the DNC, designed to bolster its appeal to specific interest-based or ideological constituencies. A few days later the gears began turning, as aides reached out to potential allies like Senator George Norris, the progressive Republican from Nebraska who had supported Roosevelt's campaign four years earlier.[10]

In that contest, Norris had helped form the National Progressive League (NPL), a group composed of Republican and Democratic leaders who had urged all "progressives" to support Roosevelt's bid for the presidency. "What this country needs is another Roosevelt in the White House" the NPL proclaimed—a rallying cry coined by Norris, linking the Democratic candidate to his Republican kinsman, former president Theodore Roosevelt.[11] The slogan captured perfectly what the NPL itself sought to do: provide non-Democrats with a way to support the latest Roosevelt without identifying themselves with his party, challenging the traditional sense that voting for a presidential candidate was the defining act of partisanship.[12]

In this the NPL looked beyond progressive Republicans (whose defection at the top of the ticket they hoped to make more acceptable) and the relatively few political "independents" of the time, to radical leftists too—trying to make them feel less like "sellouts" if they chose to back Roosevelt. After all, powerful voices on the left had long denounced giving support to mainstream party candidates; Socialist and Communist leaders in the United States could barely tolerate each other, let alone condone cooperation with the major parties, and other left-leaning organizations, like the League for Independent Political Action (LIPA), still yearned for a truly independent, radical political party to contest American elections.[13]

The LIPA had been formed in 1929 by a group of intellectuals including John Dewey, W. E. B. Du Bois, the economist Paul Douglas, and Oswald Garrison Villard, editor of *The Nation*.[14] Though its popular appeal and profile remained limited (it makes no appearances in the congressional hearings or supplementary information reviewed in chapter 1, for example), the ideas it espoused are instructive. These intellectuals believed that changing social and economic realities in the United States, spurred by industrialization, were insufficiently reflected in the relatively static political environment. In essence, they sought a realignment of the party system around the key conflict in modern society, the struggle between capital and labor. Since they considered both the Democratic and Republican Parties to be capitalist in orientation, a realignment could only be brought about by adding a new, noncapitalist party into the mix.[15] Indeed, substantial change in the party system was generally understood at this time to be possible *only* through the disruptive force of a third party.

Yet the LIPA's leaders had also recognized that the electoral record of third parties on the national stage was far from encouraging, and that radical energies were ebbing (as one exhausted sympathizer wrote to Dewey in 1931, "WHAT'S THE USE?").[16] In light of such concerns, they had stopped short of forming a party outright and instead taken a leaf out of the pressure group playbook, adopting publicity techniques as part of a longer-term "campaign of political education" designed to build support for a new party in 1932 or at least to prepare the way for a viable independent presidential candidate.[17] LIPA's leaders had even quietly approached Norris in 1930, in the hopes that he might take up the mantle of independent candidate in the forthcoming presidential campaign.[18] But the Nebraska senator had refused—he had little faith in third-party politics or independent candidacies, preferring to maintain his personal political independence within the existing party system, as a nominal, but hardly regular, Republican.[19]

Amid continued economic hardship, moreover, Norris was increasingly concerned that the progressive vote might be diluted across several minor party presidential candidates in 1932, thereby permitting a conservative candidate to win. He had thus determined to support the most progressive major party candidate, whichever label he might bear.[20] Such a position was anathema to the LIPA, for whom a "good" candidate from one of the "old parties" was suspect no matter how much their professed political sympathies might align.[21] Thus where Dewey, the great exponent of philosophical pragmatism, would retain his third-party dreams in 1932, political pragmatism would be the order of the day for Norris. He helped forge the NPL and embarked upon a nationwide speaking tour, driving home the point that a vote for Roosevelt was a *personal* endorsement, based on an agreement of principles, to be sure, but not on partisanship.[22]

Yet even as Norris emphasized the separability of the candidate from his party, the NPL itself could not claim a perfect detachment. Despite Norris's leadership, the League's national committee was dominated by Democrats.[23] More important still, it was financially connected to the Democratic Party, receiving substantial support directly from the national committee's coffers.[24] Nonetheless, the results of the 1932 election suggested the nonpartisan message had resonated; Roosevelt swept into the White House and third-party candidates performed poorly.[25] Shortly thereafter, its purpose fulfilled, the NPL closed its doors. Like other campaign committees formed to that point, it was envisaged as a temporary effort, existing for the purposes of the immediate campaign. Though Norris and other NPL leaders had shown some initial interest in maintaining the League as an unofficial progressive Republican club of some form, the flicker soon went out. The NPL was put to rest, and the Democratic Party quietly acquired its membership list.[26]

Four years later Roosevelt's aides came knocking on Norris's door once more, hoping the senator would rally progressive forces again for Roosevelt's re-election. This time, Norris deferred to his younger colleagues, and other progressive leaders were prodded to organize a campaign committee.[27] Not until the summer of 1936 were things fully under way, coming to fruition in early September with a rousing conference held in Chicago, which officially voted to establish the Progressive National Committee (PNC). Senator Robert La Follette Jr., scion of Wisconsin's progressive Republican dynasty (and cofounder of the Wisconsin Progressive Party) was now primarily in charge, joined by a number of progressive luminaries from both sides of the aisle in Congress and the states, and by various labor leaders.[28] Floyd B. Olson, the Farmer-Labor governor of Minnesota, also came on board, abandoning his earlier calls for a national Farmer-Labor party to contest the 1936 election. Olson had simply become too afraid of splitting the progressive vote and allowing a "fascist Republican" to be elected.[29]

Like its predecessor, the PNC was explicitly framed as a nonpartisan organization, neither a third party in itself nor an open supporter of the Democratic Party as a whole.[30] The 1936 contest was "a conflict which is above party," a PNC speakers' manual explained.[31] Like the National Progressive League of 1932, it sought to translate support for progressive ideas, increasingly termed "liberal" ones, into support for an individual candidate.[32] Yet unlike that earlier effort, which had received significant funding from the party, the Progressive National Committee of 1936 was financially self-sufficient, raising and spending money as it saw fit.[33] This was an important distinction, relevant for considering other new organizations appearing in the 1936 election—for the PNC was far from alone in its quest to expand support for a presidential candidate beyond partisan appeals. A range of new groups emerged that year, appealing to intellectual circles, supporters of specific issues, economic communities, or demographic populations. While some remained tied to party funding, others were self-sufficient like the PNC. As such, they represented the first wave of fully fledged "outside groups" in federal elections: actors without formal or financial connections to parties or candidates.

As the Senate committee tasked with investigating campaign expenditures in 1936 observed, "*emergency* committees and organizations, varying in nature and purpose" were now created in every national campaign. "Ostensibly, they function independently of the regular national party organizations," its report continued, "but, in reality, they are closely affiliated with them in their political and financial endeavors."[34] Chaired by Senator Augustine Lonergan of Connecticut, the committee's investigations, however, had revealed that several groups were formally operating on a fully or partially independent financial basis in 1936. As Overacker concluded, drawing on the report, both major parties had "received important aid from auxiliary organizations *or from groups which functioned entirely independently*"—both of which she classified under the broader category of "non-party organizations."[35] But there were differences between the two sides. Where Overacker identified seven "important" nonparty organizations supporting the Democratic ticket in 1936, she noted just three on the Republican side. Yet all three of those Republican groups were financially independent, while five of the Democratic groups had received substantial funding from the DNC, making them "auxiliary organizations" in Overacker's classification, though all had undertaken some additional independent fundraising from other sources.[36]

On the Democratic side, the PNC was joined by auxiliary groups like the Committee of One, the Good Neighbor League, and the Roosevelt Agricultural Committee. Such vehicles were intended, as Spencer explains, "to attract voters who had a significant stake in the New Deal relief and recovery programs," along with progressives "who felt at ease supporting Roosevelt but not the Democratic party."[37] While the Roosevelt Agricultural Committee urged a specific occupational group—farmers—to support the president, the Good Neighbor League made a broader idealistic appeal, framing the New Deal as the realization of Roosevelt's "neighborly" Latin American policy at home, though it also targeted certain demographic groups judged "susceptible" to this message.[38] The Committee of One, meanwhile, made a purely personal appeal; its members simply "signed pledge cards to commit themselves to work as a Committee of One for the President."[39] In contrast to this Democratic variation, women were the only group overtly targeted on the Republican side, with the Independent Coalition of American Women and the Women's National Republican Club forming two of the three important nonparty groups backing the GOP ticket (the latter of which operated more like an official party auxiliary, even as it raised its money independently).[40]

The imbalance in the number and to some extent the *nature* of groups backing each side may reflect differing views of the electorate. As Weed describes, an increasingly nationalized electorate was emerging in the early 1930s, but Republican strategists continued to view voting patterns through a sectional lens.[41] Democratic strategists, in contrast, began to conceive of the electorate in terms of group identities or issue-based affiliations, a viewpoint informed by new social scientific research, especially ideas about marketing and nascent polling techniques, as Balogh and Sheingate have detailed.[42] The Democrats, in effect, were beginning to envisage a new kind of electoral coalition, one that could supplement geographically conditioned party loyalty with temporary supporters (who might eventually become converts) based on interests, identities, and issue positions.[43]

Yet there were two other organizations on each side that formed more comparable rivals. Both Labor's Non-Partisan League and the American Liberty League emerged out of particular economic communities—labor and business, respectively—and were entirely independent in their financing. Labor unions contributed almost $200,000 to the LNPL, plus more than $180,000 to the American Labor Party, a state-level third party that effectively operated as the LNPL branch in New York; a further $40,000 to the PNC; and over $250,000 directly to the DNC, thus injecting a significant amount of cash into the campaign.[44] Meanwhile, individual businessmen, industrialists, and other supporters contributed over $500,000 to the Liberty League and more to its state affiliates, far exceeding the amount raised by any single Democratic-leaning group. Nonetheless, each led the way in independent funding to aid its preferred presidential ticket—the LNPL for the Democrats, the Liberty League for the GOP—becoming the most prominent examples of a larger shift toward true outside groups in campaigns: groups that would be net contributors to a party's cause, rather than an expense.

Examining the contest between the LNPL and the Liberty League thus offers significant insight into this crucial wider development in the 1936 campaign. It can, moreover, illuminate what drove them "into politics" in the first place and how groups tied to special interests sought to navigate the complex set of norms and values surrounding their political activity. Financial independence, in fact, could be used to bolster claims of nonpartisanship that interest groups had used since the 1910s to try to defuse popular hostility and defend their tentative electoral involvement. Such claims could be difficult to sustain in the electoral context—particularly in presidential contests—as seen in the last chapter. But party-funded campaign auxiliaries were now making a similar attempt, trying to disconnect individual presidential candidates from a larger partisan identity. The LNPL and the Liberty League would go further, using their financial detachment from the party organizations to deny any partisan aim, subtly shifting the meaning of "independent" politics from a term associated with third parties *outside* of the existing two-party system to one associated with organized electoral activity *within* that system, if conducted independently of either side.

Business, the Depression, and Politics

"Ours is a business civilization," the journalist James Truslow Adams had pronounced in July 1929. "Our economic and social life has been dominated by the business man's point of view."[45] At the end of a decade of dramatic economic growth, the American businessman seemed to stand at unimpeachable heights: a pillar of his community, essential to its economic success, his voice without rival for political influence. But just a few months after Adams penned these lines, the Wall Street crash and ensuing Depression would serve to put that "business civilization" in jeopardy and bring the prestige of business to an unprecedented low.

"Business," of course, is a diffuse term that embraces multiple sectors, industries, and corporate interests that may not always be harmonious. Still, at the national level, the United States Chamber of Commerce and the National Association of Manufacturers (NAM) were seen as spokesmen for a broad swathe of business sentiment. Their ideas had "entered the stream of American political thought during the 1920's as *the* business viewpoint," Prothro noted.[46] And that viewpoint was far from universally hostile to government involvement in business affairs, as industries regularly seeking special tariff protections attested.[47] Linkages between government and business groups flowed in the opposite direction, too. The Department of Commerce played a crucial role in the formation of the US Chamber of Commerce in 1912, for example, while Herbert Hoover's vision of an "associative state" in the 1920s further encouraged the creation of trade associations as a means of self-regulation within industries.[48]

In the early stages of the Depression, these voices of business were supportive of federal government efforts to rationalize and restore the flailing economy. The Chamber had urged President Hoover to consider some form of cartelization of industry through suspension of the antitrust laws.[49] And after Roosevelt's election as president, they quickly leant their support to the National Industrial Recovery Act (NIRA) he proposed.[50] The NAM also recommended passage of the NIRA, if a little more reluctantly in its case.[51] And the NIRA itself, by requiring industry-wide representatives to help formulate the industrial codes it would enforce, would stimulate the creation of even more trade and business organizations.[52]

But this cooperative attitude would not last long. The NIRA may have offered trade associations a crucial role in shaping industrial regulations, but it had given other actors—most conspicuously labor—a seat at the table too, straining the enthusiasm of NAM and Chamber officials. Their support waned further as the National Recovery Administration (NRA) asserted its own regulatory authority more forcefully. And as the federal bureaucracy expanded dramatically alongside a ballooning federal deficit, a more strident opposition to the government's actions began to take hold within the NAM and the Chamber, as well as among other important business leaders.[53] By December 1934 both organizations were publicly criticizing the recovery program, and the administration more generally.[54] By the following year, "business leaders were calling directly for 'industrial mobilization' in order to end the New Deal," to overturn the "new economic order" the Roosevelt revolution was putting into place.[55]

Overturning an entire economic order was no easy task, however. The NAM responded in early 1934 much as a pressure group might be expected to do: it set up a public relations committee.[56] But dismantling the New Deal one press release at a time hardly seemed a sufficient response to the perceived crisis. The expression of political sentiment on a grander scale, however, was normally the preserve of political parties. Yet the Republican National Committee hardly appeared functional, let alone capable of channeling opposition. The national committees had only recently begun to do much more than maintain a skeleton staff between elections, but the Republican machinery was "practically dormant" between the 1932 and 1936 campaigns, Overacker observed.[57] Rudolph described the party as "moribund" in the wake of the 1932 election, spiritually defeated and organizationally defunct.[58] Business leaders thus looked for an alternative and ultimately channeled their hostility to the New Deal through an entirely new organization: the American Liberty League.

"At a time when the Republican party was bankrupt of leadership and purpose," Rudolph observed, "the American Liberty League became the spokesman for a business civilization," one seemingly besieged from all sides in the mid-1930s.[59] In a satirical sketch for the New Republic in July 1936, the journalist Hamilton Basso put it in blunter terms, envisaging a "Future Historian" recommending a book on the Liberty League's origins and presumed demise. The title said it all: "An Investigation into the Behavior of Millionaires When Affected by a Severe Case of the Jitters."[60]

Whether a case of the jitters or a deep-seated fear for a fundamental way of life, the Depression had certainly been a shock to the system for America's business elite. Accustomed to social and political dominance, the loss of prestige and power that paralleled the economic decline was proving difficult to accept or comprehend. Faced with new political realities from which prominent business leaders felt increasingly alienated, new questions arose among those for whom legislative lobbying had usually proved a successful tool of influence, and for whom the prospect of electoral action through a third party was almost anathema. The Liberty League was their solution, and its formation was announced to the world in August 1934.[61]

Among the founding members were prominent industrialists such as Pierre du Pont of the Du Pont chemical company and John J. Raskob, its vice president; Alfred Sloan of General Motors; and J. Howard Pew of Sun Oil, among other individuals linked to major corporations (and in some cases, to the major business organizations too).[62] All had become concerned that New Deal programs were fostering economic dependence and "communistic elements" in society. Letters circulated among them in early 1934 stressing a need "to definitively organize to protect society" from the dire consequences of believing "that all businessmen are crooks."[63] They needed "some plan for educating the people to the value of encouraging people to work; encouraging people to get rich," among other, loftier purposes.[64] As they publicly proclaimed, the overarching purpose of their new organization was "preserving the Constitution."

The Liberty League accordingly described itself as an "educational" organization dedicated to "teach[ing] the necessity of respect for the rights of person and property ... and the duty of government to encourage and protect individual and group initiative and enterprise, to foster the right to work, earn, save and acquire property and to preserve the ownership and lawful use of property when acquired."[65] Its vision of constitutional preservation was thus heavily infused with the protection of traditional property rights, as critics were quick to point out. Some questioned its methods too, seeing not an "educational" group so much as an electoral one. As Basso's "Future Historian" reflected: "It is fairly safe to say that the Liberty League was formed to defeat Roosevelt II."[66] Yet as tempting as this characterization may be, it is not so clear that the League intended to undertake electoral activity from the outset.

To be sure, the Liberty League's founders were by no means novices in traversing the line between "educational" and "electoral" activity. They had cut their political teeth in the temperance battles of the 1920s and early 1930s, backing the Association Against the Prohibition Amendment and, working closely with Democratic politicians, helping to bring about repeal of the Eighteenth Amendment in 1933.[67] Hostility to Prohibition had trumped other concerns among the AAPA's business leaders, unifying their support behind Franklin Roosevelt for the presidency in 1932. But as Roosevelt's policies began to cut more deeply against their generally conservative economic sensibilities, that union was increasingly strained. For the Democrats among them, the Liberty League offered a vehicle for opposition without severing their party ties altogether.[68] It would even attract the Democrats' own 1928 nominee, Al Smith, who was never particularly enamored of Roosevelt. Finding himself increasingly alienated from the president's style of progressivism, he would become one of the Liberty League's most prominent leaders.[69]

The AAPA even provided the skeleton organization upon which the Liberty League would be built. In its final act before disbanding after the repeal of Prohibition, the AAPA executive committee had authorized the "Repeal Associates," a small group whose members were instructed to "continue to meet from time to time" and be ready to form another major organization "in the event of danger to the Federal Constitution."[70] That danger would be quickly apparent in the scope of Roosevelt's New Deal policies, bringing the threat of federal intervention beyond alcohol sales and consumption into all aspects of the economy. With this foundation already laid, the Liberty League's machinery was quickly in place, and Jouett Shouse—Raskob's lieutenant at the DNC and former head of the AAPA—was installed as president.[71]

But that machinery was not clearly electoral in orientation, at least at first. Outright pronouncements of intent "to defeat Roosevelt II" were conspicuously absent from the League's initial rhetoric and activities.[72] As late as January 1936, at a gala dinner held in Washington's Mayflower Hotel, Al Smith in his keynote speech painted the New Deal as divisive, derided its complex web of agencies and acronyms, and denounced the circle of advisers Roosevelt had surrounded himself with—the Brains Trust—as an affront to traditional modes of governance. But Smith was more circumspect in his criticism of Roosevelt himself.[73]

To that point, the Liberty League had, in fact, acted much like an "educational" pressure group, engaging in publicity efforts aimed at particular pieces of legislation, if doing so on a massive scale. As Wolfskill observed, the League "launched an educational campaign that surpassed even that waged against the Eighteenth Amendment."[74] It offered a subscription news service for weekly newspapers and set up offices in the National Press Club, aiming—as a state leader told radio listeners in November 1934—to provide the citizenry with "the means for collective expression of public opinion" on the legislative measures being debated in Congress.[75] This claim to be channeling "public opinion" was a controversial one, of course, since the Liberty League's business ties raised the specter of professional lobbyists cultivating "artificial" opinion rather than genuine grassroots sentiment of the sort that the pioneering educational pressure groups—popular associations with mass memberships— might credibly marshal.[76]

But the Liberty League *did* seek to build a real mass membership, unlike business organizations like the NAM or the Chamber, whose "members" were primarily corporations or trade associations. By the beginning of January 1936 it had approximately 75,000 members, rising to about 150,000 at its high point.[77] This might be a somewhat lackluster figure when contrasted with the "Share Our Wealth" societies of Huey Long or the Townsend Clubs, but it still represents an unprecedented effort coming from this quarter.[78] Indeed, the Liberty League tried to distance itself from any identification with "business" at all. It organized state divisions, with active Liberty League headquarters in some twenty states by 1936.[79] And there were even plans for specialized divisions along economic lines, such as "homeowners, farmers, labor, savings depositors, life insurance policyholders, bondholders, and stockholders," though such plans never fully materialized.[80] (Only a student Liberty League and a special Lawyers' Committee emerged.)[81]

Far from pursuing the goals of a business elite, Liberty League leaders claimed that they stood against the pursuit of narrow interests. The League would give "the rank and file of the American people" a vehicle through which "to offset the influence of any and all groups working for selfish purposes," the platform declared.[82] Its leaders even attacked what they saw as a New Deal effort to *create* classes and conflict where none had existed before.[83] Yet it was hard to ignore the extent to which its leadership was *not* reflective of the "rank and file of the American people." Nonetheless, because it sought to "protect the Constitution"—a presumably universal and noble aim—the League's founders appear to have believed that the average man or woman would be eager to join, and that a mass membership would follow almost automatically (they were eventually persuaded to bring on a paid organizer).[84]

At the same time, despite its professed educational purpose and seemingly universalist aims, League spokesmen did acknowledge a political dimension to their activities prior to 1936, something earlier pressure groups had typically denied. *Educational* had long been a byword for *nonpolitical* among such groups, employed to elevate their activities above the sordid world of "politics." The League, however, filed a financial report with the House Clerk in January 1935 as a "political organization" was required to do, though Shouse blurred the issue by stating it was filing voluntarily rather than under any legal obligation. (The report showed close to $105,000 in receipts since its formation four months earlier, and expenditures of just over $95,000.)[85] Since "political organization" was a concept still largely conceived in terms of *party* committees, he also strongly denied that the Liberty League was either a party in itself or intent on becoming one.[86] "[W]hile the American Liberty League is in its very essence a political organization—because its objectives are political—it is in no sense a political party," he had told an audience at the Bond Club of New York in late 1934.[87] As Shouse clarified in a statement accompanying the January financial report, it was not a party because "it has no intention of placing its own candidates in the field for any public office."[88] Nor should it be considered an ally of one of the extant parties, either. "Its cooperation will not be partisan," Shouse had informed the Bond Club. "Its criticism will not be partisan."[89]

Thus where Shouse was prepared to admit that the League's legislative goals were political in some sense, he also sought to temper that admission by emphasizing nonpartisanship in pursuing them.[90] Shouse and other Liberty League leaders pointed to the mix of Democrats and Republicans among its founding members—he and Raskob, after all, were former DNC officials, while Smith was a former Democratic governor—and tried to downplay any partisan interpretation of their criticism of the administration.[91] "It is definitely not anti-Roosevelt," Shouse had told the press back in August 1934, when announcing plans for the League.[92] He had even met with the president prior to its launch, he said, gaining Roosevelt's seal of approval for its mission to "preserve" the Constitution.[93] Indeed, Shouse had claimed the League would "*appeal to both parties* to indorse its principles and . . . endeavor to persuade elected officers of Government to adhere to those principles," appearing to favor *lobbying* both sides of the aisle.[94]

The Liberty League was, in fact, largely categorized and understood as a "lobby" in its first year of activity. Democratic senator Pat Harrison of Mississippi derisively dubbed it the "American 'Lobby' League," and it was legislative rather than electoral activity that first drew the ire of the League's many critics, primarily its shadowy role as a unifying force behind a massive effort to defeat the

Public Utility Holding Company Act of 1935.[95] The bill targeted the holding company structures through which utility firms had consolidated massive monopolies. But the firms struck back with the methods of the "New Lobby," as journalist George Soule described in the *New Republic,* suggesting that artificial rather than real opinion was being deployed: "What the utility executives really tried to do was not so much to bring their own pressure directly to bear on Congress as representatives of their own interest, but to give Congress the impression that multitudes outside the inner group were opposed to the bill as a matter of public policy."[96]

They had plenty of help in the effort. Viewing the bill as an unconstitutional assault on property rights, a swathe of groups "formed to defend something that is variously called 'the American system,' 'the constitution,' or more simply, 'liberty'" set their sights on the holding company bill—groups with grandiloquent names like the Crusaders, the Sentinels of the Republic, and the National Committee to Uphold Constitutional Government.[97] Rudolph described them as part of a range of "all and sundry anti-New Deal groups," most of which were simply "masthead organizations," he said, lacking real memberships and "operated by professional publicists and lobbyists"—front groups, in effect.[98] So intensive was the lobbying that the Senate formed another investigating committee, this time chaired by Senator Hugo Black of Alabama, before which many of these groups would soon appear.

While Soule described the Liberty League as "the most impressive and the best financed" of these "liberty-saving" organizations, however, its representatives were not themselves called before Black's Committee.[99] Its influence was instead inferred from the interlinked patterns of leadership and financial backing among those groups that did appear.[100] Alfred Sloan, for example, was prominently associated with the Liberty League *and* the Crusaders (another group initially formed to oppose Prohibition).[101] Many of the publicists and lobbyists who populated these organizations were also "veterans of the prohibition repeal movement," Rudolph claimed.[102] Further, he added, they all "owed substantial financial backing to the same small group of industrialists who sponsored the Liberty League."[103] And while the groups themselves denied any formal connections or responsibilities, Soule discerned an interconnected set of "opinions and tactics" that could be classified "under the general head of Liberty League Liberty."[104]

Deriding the League's claims to popular appeal, Soule saw "Liberty League Liberty" as an elitist conception—a vision of the Constitution dedicated to property rights and little else, which presented the selfish claims of employers as arguments about the rights of workers themselves. Thus the "open shop" was pitched in terms of the worker's individual right to choose when and how he wished to work, though the only real right the worker enjoyed, Soule said, was "to work for what wages and hours the employer pleased, or not to work at all," since he had no power to negotiate.[105] Similarly, once collective bargaining rights were enshrined in Section 7(a) of the NIRA, business rhetoric had lambasted independent unions for interfering with the workers' right to bargain through a *company* union—those effectively controlled by employers themselves.[106] In essence, Soule summarized: "Liberty League liberty simply means fighting against government as a dangerous regulator or rival of private business enterprise."[107]

The "liberty-saving" organizations would lose out in the fight over the utility holding companies act, however. Despite expenditures in excess of $3.5 million on the effort (an amount Soule presciently noted was "more than an entire presidential campaign fund usually amounts to"), the Holding Company bill passed.[108] Legislative lobbying—the purported arena of business dominance— had thus failed spectacularly in this instance. Accordingly, the Liberty League looked for alternatives, though it did not immediately embrace an electoral approach. Well into 1935 it was still exploring another way to undo New Deal legislation, this time in the courts.

In May 1935 the Supreme Court had found Title I of the NIRA unconstitutional, offering a glimmer of hope to anti–New Deal forces.[109] Yet Congress had responded with the National Labor Relations Act (the "Wagner Act"), passed in July 1935, which guaranteed workers the right to join or organize a union and outlawed company unions, among other measures designed to strengthen labor protections. The League's National Lawyers' Committee soon declared that in its opinion the act was unconstitutional, and advised employer groups to ignore it. Moreover, the League offered free legal support to any employer caught up in litigation as a result.[110] In this regard, Vose drew analogies between the judicial tactics utilized so prominently in the 1950s by the National Association for the Advancement of Colored People (NAACP) and those adopted by the Liberty League for quite different purposes.[111] The idea of the businessman-as-protester is a jarring one—probably even for the individuals themselves. But the League helped assuage their concerns by denying any real disobedience. As Earl F. Reed from the Lawyers' Committee announced: "When a lawyer tells a client that a law is unconstitutional . . . it is then a nullity and he need no longer obey that law."[112] The result of this advice, however, was a new wave of intense labor-management strife, with increasing allegations of violence and intimidation on the part of employers, culminating in the sit-down strikes of 1936–1937.[113]

The NAM mounted a similar legal challenge to the Wagner Act, if a less aggressive version.[114] But as its general counsel James A. Emery remarked, such efforts were "not sufficient" since judicial rulings "afford no remedy against unsound policy."[115] The legal approach was thus proving inadequate, while traditional lobbying had failed so far; each technique was slow and specific, moving case by case or bill by bill. Meanwhile, the broader public education campaign designed to highlight the New Deal's constitutional dangers did not appear to have advanced much further. As Texas oilman and major Liberty League contributor J. S. Cullinan wrote to Shouse late in 1935, the League had "never quite fulfilled the aims and ends" that at least some of its founders had envisaged, to "reach all or practically all of our citizens regardless of party, and make them constitutionally conscious to the end that . . . all would be qualified to act or vote intelligently on all matters of public importance."[116]

Something more than constitutional "education" was needed; some greater "remedy against unsound policy" had to be found. And with that broader policy agenda now embodied in a single individual, an electoral possibility seemed to offer the Liberty League a last hope of reprieve: to restore the old constitutional order, it must defeat the architect of the new one.

Lobbying the Voters?

"[T]here was never any doubt," DNC chairman Jim Farley later remarked, "that the [Liberty] League would eventually support whatever Republican candidate was nominated."[117] Like Basso, he assumed that defeating Roosevelt had been its plan all along and depicted an unproblematic embrace of the Republican contender. But translating electoral aims into concrete activity posed normative and practical difficulties for the Liberty League. How could a pressure group become involved in a presidential election without becoming a third party or backing a major party candidate, either of which would violate the nonpartisan claim on which the authority of its opposition was presumed to rest? The League's answer would involve expanding the horizons of "publicity" activities and reshaping the meaning of *nonpartisanship* itself.

Indeed, the Liberty League's extensive publicity activities—attacking particular pieces of legislation or, increasingly, the New Deal in general—can be viewed within the context of a growing trend: employing the methods of grassroots lobbying in pursuit of a broader electoral goal. Issue-based educational efforts could still imply support or opposition to certain *candidates*, legislators were beginning to realize. Representative Howard W. Smith of Virginia, for example, was outraged after receiving a threat of electoral punishment from "The People's Lobby, Incorporated" (of which the now-defunct LIPA's John Dewey was honorary president) if he failed to oppose an upcoming agriculture bill.[118] Anticipating a campaign against him framed around that issue, Smith proposed extending the financial disclosure requirements of the Corrupt Practices Act to individuals or organizations trying to influence legislation, even if they denied any interest in federal elections.[119] "Suppose they don't in so many words *advocate*?" a House colleague asked Smith during a committee hearing on his bill in

February 1936. "For example, suppose that Father Coughlin did not advocate the defeat of my colleague from Pennsylvania . . . but did advocate the defeat of people who opposed his ideas with respect to the Frazier-Lemke bill. Would your bill meet that situation?"[120] Smith assured him that it would.[121]

In essence, Howard Smith was aiming to bring lobbying and electoral regulations under a single umbrella, in an effort to stifle an emerging system of "government by propaganda," as he called it.[122] Though his proposal ultimately went nowhere, it pointed to the ways in which mass publicity was becoming increasingly relevant in elections, where on-the-ground organizing had once held sway. As the Liberty League's publicity machine cranked into high gear in 1936, therefore, speculation mounted as to its electoral intentions, particularly as prominent members began to espouse more strident opposition to the president. In a lecture tour that summer Al Smith openly attacked Roosevelt, yet he tried to distinguish between his actions as an individual citizen and those of the League.[123] Wolfskill observes that the League's official position of neutrality "became untenable" at this point, though it continued to distance itself from any suggestion that it might lend support to the Republican cause.[124]

The Republican National Committee, moreover, appeared concerned to distance itself too. In February, after reports surfaced that the League would endorse the GOP candidate if the platform passed muster with its executive committee, RNC chairman Henry Fletcher publicly denied any prospect of coordination.[125] The extent of this dissociation is unclear; Shouse claimed that even as Fletcher was making such statements, strong pressure was emanating from his direction "to have the League endorse the Republican ticket."[126] But there was likely good reason for Fletcher's public hesitance; the Liberty League had already come under attack for its links to business and financial interests, despite its own claims to the contrary. Father Coughlin condemned it as "the mouthpiece" of the bankers, while Senator Pat Harrison savaged its organizers as "apostles of greed."[127] Such rhetoric supports a warning Schattschneider made, that much as partisanship could hurt interest groups, too close an association with an *unpopular* interest could be dangerous for a party, too.[128]

In April the League itself put out a statement reaffirming its status as a "nonpartisan organization founded to defend the Constitution."[129] Again it pointed to its bipartisan composition to bolster the claim, stressing that "that the League's membership is composed of thousands of Democrats and thousands of Republicans," and that it was not concerned with "promoting the special interests of any individual or group."[130] Yet by July, when both party conventions were over, the League appeared ready to take a more definitive position on its plans for the fall campaign and to finally, officially, embrace an electoral role. Since the GOP platform had fulfilled many of its hopes, it seemed clear which way policy and principle would lead.[131] But the League still avoided an outright endorsement of the person in whose candidacy its hopes would now rest: Republican nominee Alf Landon.[132] As a formal statement from the League's Executive Committee explained, the Liberty League would not embrace the Republican candidate so much as pursue "a *non-partisan opposition* to Franklin D. Roosevelt."[133]

Wolfskill derided this position as "a *non sequitur* peculiar to politics," and both liberal commentators at the time and historians since have largely mocked its pretentions of nonpartisanship.[134] Rudolph described it as an "obvious fiction" and an exercise in "gross hypocrisy," for example.[135] It was, moreover, a fiction that offered few benefits, Rudolph concluded, since it placed "two serious handicaps" on the Liberty League's campaign: "It fooled no one; and it amounted to a self-imposed limitation on the kind of attack which could be made upon the New Deal and Franklin Roosevelt."[136] A more open attack, Rudolph seemed to suggest, would have been less hypocritical and more effective. "[T]he New Dealers themselves had no qualms about their own partisanship," he observed.[137] And yet some of those very New Dealers did qualify their partisanship in similar, if not identical, terms. The Liberty League's main rival in the electoral realm, after all, had named itself "Labor's Non-Partisan League for the Re-Election of Franklin D. Roosevelt," to use its full title. *Both* the LNPL and the Liberty League sought to separate Roosevelt from his party. The LNPL simply came out *for* him rather than against. Indeed, observers noted how the president himself had become the dominant "issue" in the election, destabilizing traditional party alignments and creating something closer to a class divide.[138]

For both groups, moreover, the nonpartisan claim was proffered as a justification for entering the electoral arena. For the Liberty League, refusing to actively endorse Roosevelt's opponent was meant to enhance its posture of partisan detachment, reinforcing its emphasis on a bipartisan membership, denial of self-interested aims, vision of constitutional preservation as a universal goal, and financial separation from either party. The LNPL, however, would cast its claim to nonpartisanship in a somewhat different manner, offering a formulation that would prove more effective in the 1936 election and more influential over the longer term. Though it placed some emphasis on financial and organizational separation from the Democratic party, the LNPL offered an issue-based rationale for supporting Roosevelt that acknowledged its own economic interest while framing it in a more open, positive, and seemingly principled way.

Industrial Labor in Politics

"More significant than anything Mr. Landon may say in the coming campaign is the fact that he is being backed by the oil, steel and chemical industries," a *New Republic* editorial observed in September 1936, referencing the industries with which the Liberty League was most associated. "[M]ore significant than any-thing Mr. Roosevelt may say," it continued, "is the support he is receiving from Labor's Non-Partisan League."[139] In his discussion of fellow travelers Max Lerner had dismissed the Liberty League as a "desperate union of tories and fascists" that was "to be expected" in the circumstances. But "[t]he massing of labor al-most solidly behind a liberal Democrat deserves closer analysis," he urged. "The fate of workers and progressives in the fascist countries" had sufficiently "roused American workers from their traditional lethargy in politics," Lerner explained, and "led the more militant of them to abandon their former 'plague on both your houses' attitude and come out for Roosevelt."[140]

The vehicle through which such disaffected workers would channel that support—the LNPL—did not make its appearance on the political stage until early 1936. It was an outgrowth of the nascent Committee for Industrial Organization or CIO, a movement within the craft-based American Federation of Labor (AFL) pushing for industrial unionization.[141] The CIO had been formed in November 1935 by the presidents of eight international unions and quickly began organizing drives in the mass production industries, leading the AFL to sus-pend these unions in September 1936 (not until 1938 would the CIO reformu-late as a separate labor federation, the Congress of Industrial Organizations).[142] In April, though, the presidents of three of these CIO unions—John L. Lewis of the United Mine Workers, Sidney Hillman of the Amalgamated Clothing Workers of America, and George Berry of the Printing Pressmen's Union—had come together to form the LNPL, and it would gain most of its support, financial and otherwise, from unions aligned with the CIO.[143] Unlike the Liberty League, it declared its electoral intentions from the start and made no effort to lobby for legislation. At its inaugural convention in August, held in Washington, DC, an official resolution was adopted affirming the re-election of Roosevelt in 1936 as the League's "sole objective."[144] But this objective had not been chosen lightly; it was carefully crafted to maximize internal support from within the labor move-ment and to seek external legitimacy from the public at large.

As much as unions had made significant gains during Roosevelt's first term, some within the labor movement distrusted his long-term commitment to their aims. After all, there had been little indication in 1932 that his support would be forthcoming; the Democratic platform had not mentioned labor concerns, and the electoral strategy had been, as Brains Truster Raymond Moley described, "essentially agrarian" in its appeal.[145] John L. Lewis had himself backed Hoover that year, while the AFL had remained neutral.[146] Whether Roosevelt would be fully supportive beyond 1936 seemed equally unclear. For the most "militant" labor activists, then, an "independent" labor party had long been considered the only way to ensure fulfillment of labor's goals—even though such ideal-istic efforts had repeatedly failed in practice. Like the LIPA's supporters, these activists discerned little difference between the two major parties, seeing both as ultimately committed to capitalism and to elevating the desires of business over labor. To support the titular head of a major party was thus traditionally seen as a wholesale abandonment of their aim, since it was widely interpreted as an expression of wholesale partisan commitment, for all the parties might be decentralized, ill-disciplined entities at that time.

The now "traditional" political policy of the AFL also counseled against entanglements with either major party, even as it resolutely opposed the creation of an "independent" labor party too. As noted in the last chapter, after unsuccessful interventions in the presidential contests of 1908 and to a lesser extent in 1924, the AFL had stuck to a nonpartisan strategy in the electoral realm that involved limited campaigns to punish labor's congressional "enemies" and occasionally reward its "friends," irrespective of their party affiliation. This political stance was the counterpart to its "business unionism"—the idea that labor required only minimal state action to ensure fairness in its dealings with management, by limiting the use of injunctions, for example. In the traditional AFL view, labor would achieve its goals through *collective action* in the shop environment, not *political action* in the electoral realm.

CIO leaders saw things differently, however. As Taft observed, "The political methods of Gompers and his followers were based on assumptions derived in an environment unlike the present."[147] Taft pointed to new means of employer coercion, such as company unions and spies, and the threat of interregional economic competition from nonunionized areas as prompting a more favorable view of the state among leaders of industrial unions, along with a belief that far more than relief from injunctions was needed to redress the balance with management.[148] "Unlike the skilled workers in the early part of the century, they are unable to depend upon the special skills and a large treasury to bring the employer to terms," Taft explained. "Their experience as union men will therefore tend to direct their interest toward politics."[149] The political mindset of the CIO leaders, in particular, was much more attuned to "labor political action," he added—a fear of government was simply "alien to their mentality."[150] With the guarantees of the NIRA and Wagner Act largely responsible for the massive expansion of industrial unionism itself, their movement had effectively been born "in politics."[151]

But being "in politics" was still sufficiently controversial to require special precautions and special justifications. Recognizing that collective action was insufficient to the needs of industrial labor, that "friends and enemies" campaigns in congressional contests could not achieve their immediate aims, and that third parties were an impractical vehicle of political activism, the LNPL looked for a middle way. Taft would label its creation "a new departure in labor's political activity," one that might even augur "the long-looked-for political re-alignment."[152]

But it would neither be a party in itself nor formally attached to one. It would be organized separately from the regular Democratic machinery and separate from the CIO, too. Indeed, the choice to engage in political activity via a new entity, and to orient that entity toward the Democratic presidential candidate in the 1936 campaign, suggests organizational *learning* on the part of the unions— looking to auxiliary groups like the Independent Agricultural League of 1928 or the National Progressive League of 1932. Much as the Agricultural League had safeguarded the Farm Bureau's internal unity while lending regional support to Al Smith's 1928 campaign, the LNPL was meant to provide some distance for CIO unions from a potentially divisive presidential endorsement and also allow for participation by non-CIO union members.

Most important, the LNPL proclaimed nonpartisanship as a source of both cultural legitimacy and practical internal appeal. Labor's political orientation had long been conditioned by the AFL's hostility to partisanship, and even as the CIO embraced a more actively political stance, it sought to smooth over the transition with rhetorical continuity. It would do so by drawing on the "friends and enemies" philosophy as a justification for that nonpartisanship, while extending its application to the presidential contest. Connecting issue stances to the individual, the LNPL's leaders framed their support for Roosevelt in terms of his policy positions—his support for their basic economic interests—irrespective of the fact that he was a Democrat. This offered both a clearer principle of action and a more open acknowledgment of motivation than the Liberty League's questionable claims to a cross-class identity and universalist goal.

This rhetorical extension of "friends and enemies" to the presidential contest might appear to be an underwhelming step, but it was a critical one—it began a process by which nonpartisan claims might be detached from nonpartisan outcomes. That is, the AFL had generally avoided the presidential contest because, with only one office involved, there was no way in which to balance out the results by supporting or opposing at least some candidates from each side, a pattern that could be used to defend against accusations of favoritism. In translating a "friends and enemies" policy to the presidential context, the LNPL tried to make the nonpartisan case, knowing that the substantive outcome would ultimately be one-sided. Hence the importance of other claims that could bolster its assertion of party neutrality, such as a rhetorical separation of president and party or organizational separation from the party itself.

Nonetheless, the AFL did not seem to buy the distinction or its sustainability. Although the AFL might lean toward Roosevelt, it chose not to participate in the LNPL because it feared, as Hower explains, that it "would be used as a springboard for an independent labor party."[153] The AFL was not entirely wrong in this respect. The LNPL *was* heavily involved in creating a third party in 1936: the American Labor Party (ALP) in New York State, where "fusion" election laws permitted a third party to nominate a major party candidate for the presidential contest while putting forward its own candidates for other offices. The ALP could thereby fuse with the Socialists to offer a more traditional vision of "independent" labor politics, as long as one looked below the top of the ticket.[154] But in the national contest, the LNPL would embrace "independence" in the newer sense—undertaking electoral activity *within* the two-party system, in support of a major party presidential candidate.

A Contrast in Political Action

The LNPL threw itself actively into the fall campaign, as did labor unions more generally. Other than disclosure requirements, unions were relatively unencumbered by legal restrictions on their political spending at this point (their very existence had been precarious when the Corrupt Practices Act was revised in 1925, giving little indication of their future electoral potential).[155] Accordingly, as noted earlier, unions gave generously to the LNPL—nearly $230,000 to the national and state divisions combined—as well as large amounts to the ALP and the PNC.[156] Union funds also went to the Roosevelt Nominators Division, a party entity raising money for direct use by the DNC.[157] And some went straight to the DNC itself. The Lonergan Committee found nearly $130,000 in union contributions to the national party's coffers, of which $100,000 came from John L. Lewis's UMW (a further $50,000 was provided as a loan).[158] In total, the committee put the "combined financial assistance of all labor organizations to all political organizations" during the presidential campaign at just over $770,000, describing this as an "unprecedented" figure compared to any previous election.[159] (For comparison, the DNC spent just over $5.6 milllion.)[160]

These official figures might still underplay the actual amounts involved. Some estimates had the DNC receiving at least $500,000 from unions in 1936, much of which went unreported.[161] An internal CIO report later attributed such a sum to the UMW alone.[162] The LNPL amounts may have been higher too. Taft calculated that it "expended almost one million dollars" on behalf of the Democratic ticket in 1936, taking into account both its national and subnational affiliates.[163] And for all the LNPL's claims of organizational independence, the Lonergan Committee report shows at least one financial connection, a $1,000 contribution from the LNPL directly to the DNC.[164] Substantively, too, the LNPL worked closely with other Democratic-leaning independent and auxiliary committees, particularly the PNC, which its leaders had also helped to found and finance.[165] Lewis and Hillman both volunteered as spokesmen for the PNC's Speaker's Bureau, for example (something even AFL president William Green was prepared to do), which coordinated its activities carefully with the DNC.[166]

In late September, the LNPL even joined with the PNC and the Good Neighbor League for a series of radio programs highlighting Roosevelt's achievements and criticizing the Republican party, according to McCoy.[167] Yet much Democratic propaganda attacked the Liberty League and its links to nefarious business interests rather than the GOP itself, in line with a "battle order" issued by Jim Farley.[168]

For its part, the Liberty League struggled to convey a clear message to the electorate. In May, for example, the League's Executive Committee sent an open letter to the membership with plans for a major "get out the vote campaign."[169] Like the Committee of One, it urged members to sign a pledge to vote and ask ten nonmembers to do the same, returning their addresses to national headquarters so as to build the League's mailing list and expand the effort.[170] Unlike the Committee of One, however, the League did not ask its members to pledge their support to any one candidate or party, fearing that to do so would breach its neutrality—still its official position at that point.[171] Even Pierre du Pont tentatively questioned Shouse on the efficacy of this approach. "While I admire the frankness with which you state that you desire votes, but not votes for a particular party or purpose," du Pont wrote—a "sound doctrine," in his opinion—he wondered about enclosing an anti-administration leaflet with the letter, something that might have "popular appeal" du Pont said, perhaps recognizing that members might need a stronger hint.[172] Even once formally announced, the Liberty League's "nonpartisan opposition to Roosevelt" lacked the directive quality of the LNPL's affirmative campaign. Shouse had assured reporters that the League would not endorse *any* candidate or party in 1936, a position that informed its anti-Roosevelt formulation and, strictly interpreted, proscribed any overt expressions of support for Landon. Shouse danced around the subject in his speeches, offering little more than a mild recommendation that New Deal critics might vote Republican, if they so chose.[173]

The Liberty League also maintained more organizational distance from the party it aided. In addition to nonendorsement, Shouse told reporters in August that the League "has not contributed and will not contribute to any campaign fund."[174] The national League would end up spending more than $500,000 during the election year, but true to Shouse's declaration, none of that money went directly to the RNC.[175] In some ways, this was a matter of legal necessity. The Liberty League was incorporated and thus, on its face at least, forbidden by the Tillman Act of 1907 from "making money *contributions* in connection with political elections."[176] How it rationalized its financial involvement in the 1936 campaign is thus an open question. Perhaps it extended its "educational" claim into the campaign itself, mirroring those issue-based groups that Howard Smith had denounced, which sought to influence elections without admitting their involvement. Perhaps its lawyers had discerned a loophole permitting political *expenditures* if not contributions, made on behalf of a candidate or party, in effect, a position that would become far more important in the 1940s and beyond. (In either scenario, the Liberty League's refusal to actively endorse a candidate might bolster its legal case.) Or maybe its status as what we would now call a nonprofit corporation simply placed it in a gray area of the law.

Yet for Wolfskill, the League's purported financial distance was simply "part of the nonpartisan charade." As individuals, Liberty League members had contributed lavishly to the GOP and largely facilitated the Republican campaign, he noted. Members of the du Pont and Pew families alone provided $1 million to the RNC, which spent nearly $9 million overall.[177] "Without Liberty League money," incoming RNC chairman John Hamilton acknowledged after the election, "we couldn't have had a national headquarters."[178] Liberty League officials, however, might fall back on a distinction first offered by the NAM's Ferdinand Schwedtman more than two decades before: that there was a significant difference between the activities of individual members and the actions of the League itself. Irrespective of the larger financial picture, Shouse continued to claim that it was "neither an adjunct nor an ally of the Republican party."[179] Historians have perhaps underestimated the extent to which Shouse's organization saw itself as defending the Democratic Party against a liberal insurgency, rather than abandoning it for the GOP.

If the Liberty League differed from the LNPL in its financial and endorsement practices, its style of campaigning differed, too. Without a comparable membership to draw upon, the League lacked ground-level organizational manpower. This was a major deficiency in an era when, according to Wolfskill, elections were won on "a combination of many little things—ringing doorbells, stuffing envelopes, buttonholing voters, volunteering transportation—a thousand things that cannot be accomplished by network radio speeches or slick paper pamphlets."[180] In effect, the Liberty League campaigned to defeat Roosevelt on the basis of publicity alone.[181] Though the LNPL also launched publicity efforts, it could turn to local unions for organizational muscle on the ground. As Paul Ward observed in the *Nation* on the eve of the election, the LNPL was a "power in the campaign," its local machinery even "shouldering out the Democratic or Republican machines" in some areas.[182] In so doing, the LNPL had silenced the critics "who at the outset jeered at the league and its theory that labor's vote could be organized and delivered."[183] In the latter respect, Ward pointed to the underlying resource on which successful nonpartisan electioneering was presumed to rest: the mobilization of a bloc vote. But rather than merely *threaten* that prospect to punish a wavering lawmaker, the LNPL sought actively to *deliver* a large labor vote to reward an incumbent president. As Leuchtenburg concluded, "Never before had union leaders done so effective a job of mobilizing the labor vote in a national campaign."[184]

The Liberty League's pure publicity campaign, unaccompanied by ground-level organization or even clear guidance as to how Americans should vote, was far less effective. In September, when voters went to the polls in Maine, a local Republican leader did credit Landon's victory there to "the liberal supply of printing and the circulation and showing up of the present administration" that the Liberty League's publicity machine had provided.[185] But Maine was one of just two states to support Landon in the general election. As Maine went, only Vermont followed. The nation went for Roosevelt by a landslide.

The Lessons of Two Leagues

With Roosevelt swept back into office, the Liberty League was cast as a failure. In the post-election recriminations, significant weight was placed on Landon's inability to distance himself from the League's reactionary aura, despite his often pained efforts to do so.[186] The fault, moreover, was largely attributed to the League's big business image.[187] "[N]othing is more stupid," the RNC's chairman summarized, "than for an organization of big businessmen to get out and carry a flag in a political parade." As Wolfskill interprets this, "[w]hat he meant was that the Republican party wanted and needed help from these people, but as individuals, not as a flag-waving organization that the Democrats could readily discredit." For Jim Farley, the Liberty League spoke "as conclusively for the reactionaries and their party as does Mr. Hoover, the United States Chamber of Commerce and the National Manufacturers' Association."[188]

The denial of leading Liberty Leaguers that it was an organization of and for businessmen was given little credence by commentators at the time or since. Indeed, its classless posture, set against the class conflict it claimed the New Deal was fomenting, has usually evoked derision among historians.[189] For Rudolph, the League was simply "masquerading a defense of property and wealth as a popular movement."[190] This deception resulted in a discordant message that ultimately proved its downfall, appealing to the common man by defending "something which most Americans had very little of—property."[191] "[E]ven after its expiration," Rudolph adds, "the League was a symbol of selfish greed and special interests."[192]

But the *inaccuracy* of its claim to "classlessness" does not necessarily imply *insincerity*. Steeped in the "business civilization" of the 1920s, many business leaders associated with the Liberty League made no real distinction between their own economic interests and those of society as a whole. When insurance executive Fred G. Clark appeared before the Black Committee in his capacity as the Crusaders' "National Commander," for example, he vociferously denied the group was an "agent[] of big business," despite revelations he had failed to disclose large contributions from prominent businessmen.[193] As Soule described, "Mr. Clark protested, and *probably believed*, that the concealment was of no importance, because what is good for big business is good for everybody."[194] Among the wider public, any sense of mutual benefit between business and society was severely damaged by the Depression, and the League's emphasis on property rights accordingly missed the mark. But these universalist ideas would continue to shape the approach taken by business groups in the political realm, though individual economic rights would later be reframed in terms of wider freedoms.

Unlike typical campaign auxiliaries, the Liberty League itself intended to remain active, despite Roosevelt's decisive re-election. In mid-September, anticipating the result if perhaps not its scale, Pierre du Pont had already written Shouse to discuss post-election plans. "Should the electorate decide to continue Mr. Roosevelt as President for another term," du Pont wrote, "it would be a great misfortune and sign of admitted defeat if the League should disband." Citing a lack of financial backing as the only "possible cause" that could prevent its continued operations, he promised to maintain his support "and expect that others will do likewise."[195] Another member of the Liberty League's Executive Committee, George L. Buist, wrote too. "Let us admit that the Liberty League has been shot up a bit by the Michelson propaganda machine," Buist began, referring to the DNC's publicity director, Charley Michelson. "What of it?" The "struggle between diverse systems of government" would not be over in November, regardless of how the election turned out—thus the Liberty League must stay the course too.

The League must first work to repair its reputation, Buist urged, dedicating itself "to convincing the public that it is not a rich man's club, but is a large group of patriotic citizens who are seriously and sincerely concerned over the future welfare of our people, of all of our people in all walks of life." Then the League could turn to mobilizing Americans "who oppose the introduction into this country of experiments in government now so popular in Europe."[196] Looking beyond 1936, Buist's assessment brought a larger aim into view than just the defeat of Franklin Roosevelt. A party realignment was approaching, Buist said, in which the League had a role to play. The election showed that party divisions had "broken down" and "[t]he old names now serve only to confuse and mislead." He feared that, as in Europe, socialist and fascist parties would soon emerge, breaking apart the old party system. Against this threat there must be "an American party that believes that our system of government that has worked well for considerably over a century might serve us a trifle longer." *This* was where the League could make its mark, in "welding into a unit the American party." It would be "a work of education, a work of calling things by their right names, a work of organization."[197]

The LNPL would also continue its "work of organization." Flush with success, it showed no intention of closing its doors after November. It had, in fact, been formed with the long term in mind. At its inaugural convention in August 1936, alongside the resolution supporting Roosevelt, a measure was approved calling for the League to "be continued after the election as an instrumentality *for the furtherance of liberalism* in the United States."[198] LNPL leaders also foresaw a party realignment on the horizon, one that would array "liberal forces on one side opposed to the forces of reaction," as Sidney Hillman told the delegates. In that "great realignment . . . labor should take its place in an organized manner," Hillman said, by making the LNPL "a permanent, effective instrumentality for labor to fight for a constructive political program in the years to come.[199] As an LNPL brochure later described, "[s]peaker after speaker emphasized the imperative urgency of *independent political action* by labor" after 1936, through an organization that would be "maintained permanently." In so doing, labor would "be prepared for any future realignments in national politics."[200]

Where Buist feared the impending destruction of the traditional US party system, proposing an "American Party" as a last resort, Hillman appeared to welcome a realignment, though the role that the LNPL might play was less clear. Party realignment had been traditionally envisaged in terms of a third or "independent" party of the Left that would break apart the existing system and reframe its central conflict around attitudes to capitalism. Would the LNPL thus become, as the AFL had suspected, a springboard for a third party in 1940 after all? Or would it find other ways to "further liberalism" in the country, while continuing to work *within* the existing two-party system? As a campaign group created to contest a presidential election, moreover, how would it sustain itself while waiting for the next one? And what might "independent political action" come to involve? If the Liberty League was a pressure group that had ultimately turned to politics, the LNPL would forge a different path forward, offering a new vision of realignment along the way.

4

Electoral Afterlives

Labor's Non-Partisan League (LNPL) had emerged from the 1936 election as an apparent success story. Its favored candidate had won re-election in a resounding victory, signaling to all who cared to take notice that organized labor could be a significant actor in campaigns. But the LNPL had not pleased everyone, even those who ostensibly supported its aims. Writing in the *Nation*, Paul Ward expressed the residual disappointment of some on the left with its strategy, questioning whether the LNPL's apparently pragmatic support for the president had not evolved into something deeper.[1] It had started out "as the most promising step toward a farmer-labor party that this country has seen," Ward observed, but had failed to live up to expectations, ending the campaign "as a mere adjunct of the Democratic National Committee" (DNC) in his view. The Progressive National Committee (PNC), moreover, had been little more than a "lecture bureau" for the DNC, he charged, making it "just as much a false-front organization as the Liberty League."[2]

The LNPL was not supposed to end up as a Democratic adjunct. Its participation in Roosevelt's re-election campaign, as far as Ward discerned its founders' intent, was to be "a first strategic step toward the formation of a third party." [3] Instead the LNPL's leaders had "lost their heads and become hysterically orthodox supporters of the status quo," doing little more than aid a candidate who, Ward argued, "might have won without its help."[4] They had sought no commitments from the incumbent in return for their support, nor had they insisted he clarify any policy positions.[5] Thus for all Roosevelt's first administration had provided some aid to labor, there was no guarantee it would continue to do so.[6] "Risking all for Roosevelt," Ward warned, the LNPL had not even "had the courage to test its strength by entering the Congressional jousts in *truly nonpartisan support* of labor candidates," whatever party affiliation they might bear.[7]

For Ward, the LNPL needed to move beyond its temporary alliance with Roosevelt and toward a third party, since a president tied to a major party could never reliably promote labor's aims. As Max Lerner had written in the *Nation's* previous issue, the LNPL had been "working shoulder to shoulder

The Rise of Political Action Committees. Emily J. Charnock, Oxford University Press (2020). © Oxford University Press.
DOI: 10.1093/oso/9780190075514.001.0001

with Democratic politicians who represent the worst aspects of capitalism and of whom they will eventually have to sweep the polity clean."[8] And yet the prospects for an independent labor party, as such radical voices desired, seemed diminished in the aftermath of the 1936 election. The handful of minor parties that had participated fared poorly; the Union Party attracted under 2 percent of the popular vote, and others even less.[9] Public attitudes, moreover, seemed less than encouraging. When George Gallup's new American Institute of Public Opinion (AIPO) conducted a survey of the general public in December 1936, it found that 82 percent of respondents would *not* choose to "join a new farmer-labor party if one is organized."[10]

Yet just a few weeks later, when the United Auto Workers (UAW) organized the first of what became a wave of "sit-down strikes" in Flint, Michigan, Ward's concerns about Roosevelt appeared somewhat validated. During this fierce struggle between labor and management, which continued into 1937, the president studiously maintained a position of neutrality.[11] This did not stop his political opponents trying to make hay from the increasingly disruptive strikes, by linking the administration to the Committee for Industrial Organization (CIO) and its support for the strikers.[12] But relations between the CIO and the Roosevelt administration were becoming more strained. Speaking to a radio audience of more than twenty million on September 6, 1937—Labor Day— United Mine Workers (UMW) president John L. Lewis sounded the alarm. He who has "supped at labor's table" and "been sheltered in labor's house," Lewis warned, should not "curse with equal fervor and fine impartiality both labor and its adversaries when they become locked in deadly embrace."[13]

There was disillusionment, too, with congressional hostility toward further labor legislation, even from apparent New Dealers who proved less supportive once in office. The failure of legislation to regulate wages and hours in 1937, which the Rules Committee had first tried to bottle up in the House and was subsequently blocked by a recommittal motion, was particularly egregious to CIO leaders (in contrast, the American Federation of Labor's [AFL] leadership had thrown its weight behind recommittal, since it sought changes to the bill).[14] Indeed, the "conservative coalition" of Republicans and Southern Democrats that emerged on this vote, and on other New Deal measures in Roosevelt's second term, gave further credence to the leftist critique that both major parties were as bad as each other. With renewed economic problems at home, moreover—the "Roosevelt Recession" of 1937–1938—and rising tensions internationally, Lewis grew increasingly concerned about the administration and began to question the success of the LNPL's 1936 electoral strategy.[15] The only bright spot appeared to be the impact of hard times on CIO membership, which reached four million in 1937, exceeding the AFL's membership of around three million.[16] The following year, the CIO would finally reconstitute itself as a separate labor federation, moving from a "Committee" to a "Congress" of Industrial Organizations.[17]

Amid such developments, the American public seemed to grow more expectant of a new third-party movement, despite their reluctance to join it. In a nationwide poll conducted for *Fortune* magazine in May 1938, 38 percent of respondents believed that a "powerful new labor party" would emerge in the next decade, though only 22 percent *hoped* that would be the case.[18] The Gallup poll suggested similar levels of support for "a new farmer-labor party" if one was organized—ranging from 18 percent at the end of 1936, rising to 21 percent by the summer of 1937, and falling back to 15 percent by the start of 1938.[19] Such variable results might appear lukewarm at best, but they would nonetheless have registered in the upper echelons of third-party performance if translated into a proportion of the popular vote.

The LNPL was not to become the basis for that third party, as Ward had hoped, yet it did not disappear, either, as most groups organized for a presidential campaign had previously done. Rather, the LNPL would have an electoral "afterlife," forging a new model of ongoing political activity within the existing party system as an electorally oriented pressure group. For the time being, Lewis and other LNPL leaders chose not to abandon their electoral alliance with Franklin Roosevelt, despite their misgivings, but instead to augment and extend it in pursuit of New Deal policies. To ensure that "victories won at the ballot box were not to be lost in the halls of Congress," as an LNPL pamphlet later described, it turned its attention to the legislative sphere—using both direct and indirect lobbying methods, through grassroots publicity campaigns, to put "continuing pressure" on lawmakers and promote "the people's mandate for social legislation."[20]

Concurrently, the LNPL would seek out other elections in which to continue its campaign activities and promote its message, undertaking "independent political action" in state and local contests as well as congressional races—now an established reference to organizational and financial independence rather than a nod to third-party politics.[21] The LNPL would also continue to profess the "nonpartisanship" enshrined in its original name, yet its commitment to Roosevelt and his legislative aims would soon translate into lopsided electoral support for his Democratic allies in Congress, complicating its claims of neutrality. Indeed, the LNPL's involvement in the 1938 midterms partly complemented a nascent effort, launched by the president himself, to imprint the Democratic Party with New Deal liberalism by defeating the strongest critics on his own side. This electoral experiment would prove ineffective in the short term but influential in the longer term, by projecting a different vision of how party realignment might be brought about. And the LNPL's afterlife would have other enduring institutional effects.

Its ongoing electoral activities, alongside the growing financial involvement of unions in elections at all levels, would prompt a wave of new legislation intended to stymy labor's influence, backed by the conservative lawmakers that the LNPL so often opposed. Despite its sponsors' intentions, that legislation would channel labor political activity in different and ultimately more assertive directions, and would also have consequences for nonlabor groups, including the LNPL's erstwhile foe: the Liberty League. It too had hoped to carve out an electoral afterlife but had managed only a nominal existence before new financing rules introduced in 1940 forced it to finally close its doors. For very different reasons, the LNPL's afterlife would also be brought to an end in 1940, owing to internal disagreements rather than external constraints. The legacies of both groups would live on, however, in the political ideas they promoted and the new wave of organizations they inspired, including, soon enough, the first political action committee.

"Purging" the Party

The LNPL made its first post-1936 electoral outings in the municipal elections of 1937, a natural environment for the group since its affiliated union membership was concentrated in urban, industrial locations. In Pennsylvania, Connecticut, and New York, the League helped elect pro-labor candidates to office.[22] In this it extended its rationale for supporting Roosevelt, as a "friend" of labor, into a more traditional setting with multiple offices in play. The AFL had long pursued its "friends and enemies" approach in local, state, and congressional races, after all. But writing in 1937, labor economist Philip Taft described differences between the LNPL's tactics and the traditional AFL approach. "In contrast to the purely negative attitude of the American Federation of Labor, the League believes in conducting intensive campaigns *on behalf of* the candidates it supports for office," Taft noted, suggesting that LNPL actively supported its friends, while the AFL placed a greater emphasis on defeating enemies.[23] Where the AFL largely confined its efforts to general elections, moreover, the LNPL had also been active in some primaries for these municipal contests.

In so doing, the LNPL was moving beyond the AFL tradition of "rewarding or punishing" candidates in terms of their positions on labor issues, instead coming closer to the model pioneered by the old Non-Partisan League of the 1910s and early 1920s. "For the present the League is mainly interested in operating within one of the two major political parties," Taft explained. But its activity was "not limited to mere indorsement of candidates," he observed, with the LNPL going so far as to enter its own candidates in some primary contests, just as the Non-Partisan League had done.[24] In Taft's estimation, this made the

LNPL "an independent political party operating in the primaries instead of in the final election."[25] And it fueled speculation that the LNPL might ultimately pursue a third-party path. The League was "sufficiently flexible" to do so "whenever that becomes necessary," Taft noted, pointing to its existing involvement with the American Labor Party in New York.[26]

The LNPL's organizational flexibility could extend in other directions, however. Though elections might offer a regular if intermittent focus of activity, congressional opposition to legislation favored by the LNPL provided a more persistent target against which to rally. Accordingly, the LNPL would begin, as Key observed, "to lobby before Congress in support of New Deal measures," including prominent initiatives such as the Wages and Hours bill, to which it leant strong support.[27] On this issue, the LNPL would tie its legislative and electoral activities together in explicit ways. It pushed hard for the bill, which faced a significant hurdle when it was recommitted to the House Labor Committee in December 1937, normally a death-knell for legislation. In response, the LNPL identified lawmakers who had voted for recommittal and, adopting a punitive electoral stance, determined to defeat them in the 1938 midterms.[28] But it also intended to support incumbents who had backed New Deal policies more generally, using their stances as a principled and purportedly nonpartisan basis on which to justify electoral assistance.

LNPL staffers thus scrutinized the voting records of every lawmaker on a range of labor and social issues they cared about, while placing a special emphasis on the recommittal vote in the House, and produced a list of incumbents whom they urged sympathetic union members to support or oppose.[29] Beyond the circulation of this list to unions and, to some extent, the public at large, the LNPL's practical involvement was primarily directed to a handful of House rather than Senate contests, reflecting the importance of the recommittal vote and perhaps the smaller, more manageable size of House districts.[30] According to the LNPL's own assessment, it had accordingly been "[t]rue to its non-partisan policy," since it "threw its support to those candidates in either major party who stood for social progress."[31] In this respect, Key concluded that the League's activities had "not differed fundamentally from that of the A.F.L." Though it had "been much more vigorous in its political campaigning," it fundamentally sought "to exert electoral strength by swinging its support to that party and that candidate more favorable to labor rather than by forming a labor party," he observed.[32]

But Key's assessment, and the LNPL's own spin on its activities, were somewhat misleading. The LNPL's list had named both Democrats and Republicans it supported and opposed, yet the division was far from equal. In a novel exercise in political marketing, the LNPL had actually identified its friends and enemies by giving them letter grades—"A" for incumbents it supported and "D" for those it opposed—and then circulated in the press a selected list of about forty lawmakers in each category.[33] Almost all of the lawmakers graded "A" were Democrats, with just a smattering of Wisconsin Progressives, Minnesota Farmer-Laborites, and a single Republican earning that accolade, an imbalance that opened the LNPL to the charge of partisanship, even as it might claim that principle alone had guided its grading.[34] Most of the LNPL's "D"-listers, however, were Democrats too (though a good number of Republicans also found them-selves in that category).[35] Accordingly, this substantial *opposition* to Democrats might, at first glance, seem to offset its lopsided support for Democrats and bol-ster its nonpartisan claims. But closer examination points to a more subtle par-tisan bias at work.

The LNPL had claimed nonpartisanship in 1936 by focusing on Roosevelt alone and the policies he proposed, challenging the widespread belief that backing a presidential candidate was tantamount to endorsing his party. In 1938, moreover, it showed itself willing to oppose members of that party in support of those policies. But in promoting New Deal Democrats almost exclusively while seeking to defeat their conservative counterparts, the LNPL's efforts threatened to alter the composition of a *party* as much as the Congress, suggesting experi-mentation with a more dynamic form of partisanship rather than blind loyalty to one side. In so doing, they effectively endorsed Roosevelt's own vision for the Democratic party, which he hoped to see refashioned in a more liberal di-rection, more uniformly supportive of the New Deal. Indeed, Roosevelt himself would famously seek to realize this in the 1938 midterms, launching a personal campaign to "purge" the party of his most recalcitrant critics, primarily in its southern wing, by backing New Deal liberals against entrenched Southern Democrats in their primaries (since general elections were a forgone conclusion in the one-party South).[36]

The president's ire had been raised by southern opposition to two core initiatives of his second term: the executive reorganization plan, by which he sought to enhance presidential control over the expanded federal government, and the Judicial Procedures Reform Bill of 1937—the "court-packing" bill, through which he intended to appoint more liberal justices to the Supreme Court in the wake of its repeated rulings against New Deal legislation. Roosevelt's purge thus particularly targeted those Democrats who had voted against these measures, seeking to deploy his own popularity to punish internal enemies.[37] The effort proved controversial, however, both within and outside of the admin-istration. DNC chairman Jim Farley viewed it as an affront to the regular party organization and normal democratic procedures. As he would later write, the president had "violated a cardinal political creed which demanded that he keep out of local matters," since "voters naturally and rightfully resent the unwar-ranted invasion of outsiders."[38] Indeed, only the national party committees, and especially the "Hill Committees"—the senatorial and congressional campaign committees on each side—bore any wider responsibility for collective efforts to elect party members at this time. They did so, moreover, only in general election contests, in deference to local parties and the primary or caucus voters who would select party candidates in the first place.

But Roosevelt *was* trying to shape primary outcomes, and his example pointed to the possibility that other "outside" actors might do the same. The Non-Partisan League and the Anti-Saloon League had done so to some extent in the 1910s and 1920s, though they had worked within both parties. The LNPL was now trying something similar, but focusing more on the Democratic side. Still, its effort did not fully overlap with the president's purge. Where the administration emphasized Senate targets, most prominently in the South, and primarily based its opposition on the court-packing and executive reorganization votes, the LNPL stressed the wages and hours recommittal vote and looked more to House contests (the chamber in which the recommittal vote had taken place), including several outside of the South.[39] The LNPL did become embroiled in at least one Senate contest, in Pennsylvania, though this was largely due to the personal involvement of John L. Lewis. Against the preferences of the regular Democratic organization, Lewis backed a former miner and UMW official for the gubernatorial nomination, and the dispute soon spilled over into the Senate primaries.[40] Though it was not considered part of the wider "purge," conservative commentators charged the administration with lending some assistance behind the scenes—in gratitude for the large campaign contributions Lewis had engineered in 1936, as Frank Kent claimed in the *Los Angeles Times*.[41] Yet the Lewis-backed candidates ultimately failed to secure the nominations, casting doubt on the president's personal power and on the LNPL's influence, too.[42]

Elsewhere, Roosevelt's more overt personal interventions fared little better. His purge campaign was largely viewed as a disaster, with only one of the five Democratic lawmakers targeted by the administration going on to lose his primary: Congressman John O'Connor of New York, a non-southerner and the only non-senator. Meanwhile, the four senators who secured renomination despite his best efforts—Walter George of Georgia, "Cotton Ed" Smith of South Carolina, Millard Tydings of Maryland, and Guy Gillette of Iowa— all won re-election.[43] Despite its emphasis on House members, the LNPL had also given George and Tydings "D" grades, though it is unclear whether it provided any active campaign assistance in these contests.[44] In fact, in an organizational sense, it was Roosevelt's use of administrative resources in pursuit of his campaign aims that generated the most criticism, not the role of the LNPL. Accusations mounted that Roosevelt had widely turned to the Works Progress Administration (WPA)—the largest New Deal relief agency—to implement his political plans. The WPA was accused of distributing its funds to influence the primaries, encouraging partisan activity among its workers, and influencing the vote choice of those on its relief rolls.[45]

In contrast, the LNPL cast the primary results as a success story, with "[a]ll but one or two of the Congressional candidates" it supported winning their nominations, as the *CIO News* reported.[46] The LNPL had gained "new recognition on behalf of labor's political strength," with its endorsements "eagerly sought after," rendering the prospects "bright" for the general election.[47] But the November results would prove to be less positive. Amid growing public disapproval of disruptive strikes, an economic downturn, and a backlash against Roosevelt's campaign intervention, 1938 saw one of the largest swings away from the president's party in a midterm election, with Democrats losing seventy-one seats in the House and six in the Senate.[48] And it was the New Dealers who most often lost. With their constituencies generally safer to begin with, most of the conservative Democrats had retained their seats, and the results strengthened the incipient conservative coalition in Congress.[49] Key calculated that just three of the House incumbents the LNPL opposed were defeated in November, while the results for those candidates it supported broke somewhat evenly: ninety-eight winning and one hundred losing.[50] In an election postmortem, the LNPL highlighted a few victories in California and New York but admitted the need for more extensive organization, along with "intensive education" of "farmer and so-called middle class voters . . . in the identity of their interests with labor."[51]

From the president's perspective, the failure of the purge and the 1938 results did not so much discredit the end he had lurched toward as the means. According to Savage, Roosevelt had long hoped to transform the Democratic Party in a more liberal direction, but in the 1920s he had envisaged doing so through internal procedural reforms in the DNC.[52] With the purge campaign, Roosevelt had hoped his own activism could achieve something similar, but he had been swiftly disabused of the notion. As well as being practically unsuccessful, it had generated backlash from a public unaccustomed to the president playing such an overtly partisan role—or more accurately, a *factional* role. As a result, Milkis argues, Roosevelt determined to pursue his liberal objectives not via enduring party change so much as through the enlarged federal administrative apparatus his presidency was building.[53] Yet as both Milkis and Savage acknowledge, Roosevelt was not necessarily averse to letting others continue the struggle within the party. Both point to the DNC's special divisions and auxiliaries as important vehicles for these efforts, including the Good Neighbor League, for example, which had also been maintained after 1936 and would continue until 1939, when diminished party finances led to its demise.[54]

The LNPL's example shows another possibility, in which nonparty groups—those ostensibly "independent" of the party—might promote partisan change from the *outside* while remaining *inside* the two-party system.

If pursued consistently and systematically, its electoral approach might even bring about a full-scale realignment in the axis of party competition without the need for a disruptive third party; instead, an existing party might be gradually reshaped in a more ideologically cohesive direction. Such possibilities were not yet fully recognized or articulated in 1938, however. The LNPL's leaders were not entirely committed to a strategy of Democratic Party liberalization at this time, even as their patterns of support and opposition hinted toward it and partly overlapped with the president's "purge." These actions, however, would contribute to a legislative backlash by the newly empowered conservative coalition that would powerfully shape the future trajectory of nonparty electioneering and force labor leaders to reckon more fully with their partisan ties.

A New Assault on "Corruption"

MR. BIGGERS. I guess that corrupt practice law was a New Deal measure?

THE CHAIRMAN. No, sir; unfortunately it was put on the books during the earlier administration of Calvin Coolidge.

MR. BIGGERS. I thought it was a flaming New Dealer, a New Mexico man, responsible for it.

THE CHAIRMAN. Was that Senator Hatch? I would like to take the credit, but I have to be honest and tell you it was not a New Mexico person who sponsored the Corrupt Practices Act. It came in under Calvin Coolidge. He is not a New Dealer, is he?

MR. BIGGERS. No.

THE CHAIRMAN. To the best of your knowledge?

MR. BIGGERS. No.

THE CHAIRMAN. Therefore you don't like the corrupt practice law.

MR. BIGGERS. I thought it was a New Deal one.

— Congressman Clinton P. Anderson (D-NM) talks with E.M. Biggers
of the Biggers Printing Co., Houston, TX (1944)[55]

When members of the 76th Congress took their seats in 1939, hostility toward increasing labor union electioneering and indignation at Roosevelt's personal intervention would make reformers out of those more often labeled "reactionaries," at least when it came to corrupt practices legislation. With the 1940 presidential contest on the horizon, concern had arisen among Roosevelt's opponents that the growing federal workforce, which had expanded prodigiously with the New Deal state, might "become a permanent political force in the Democratic Party," as Corrado observes.[56] Or at least it might become a permanent force behind *Roosevelt's* vision of the party. The blurred lines between bureaucracy and politics reflected in the WPA's 1938 electoral activities had already elicited public disapproval, and they would now generate a legislative response.

Less a "flaming New Dealer" than a moderate Democrat, Senator Carl Hatch of New Mexico would lead the charge, moving to cut off this bureaucratic source of support for electoral candidates. The eponymous Hatch Act of 1939 (officially "An Act to Prevent Pernicious Political Activities") legally barred federal workers from engaging in partisan electoral activity.[57] Though Hatch was inspired primarily by a longtime progressive hostility to government corruption—from wherever it might emanate—he would gain substantial support for his measure from conservatives in both parties. The following year, concern with the growth of unions and their expanding financial role in campaigns would lead conservatives to support significant amendments to the Hatch Act too. In attempting to limit the flow of money into politics, these amendments would not target unions directly but impose constraints on those generally receiving their largesse—parties and candidates—as well as introducing other restrictions. In so doing, these legislative changes would have both profound and unintended consequences.

For a start, the 1940 amendments to the Hatch Act placed the first limitations on what individuals could contribute to federal campaigns, setting the limit at $5,000. They also capped the overall amount any political committee operating in two or more states could raise or spend in a given year at a maximum of $3 million.[58] The latter provision was aimed primarily at the national party committees—still the main multistate political committees at that time—though it appears to have been something of a legislative afterthought. Indeed, the initial impetus for amending the Hatch Act was simply to extend its original provisions to *state* government workers paid with federal funds. As Hayward points out, the caps on individual contributions and party spending were subsequently tacked on with little debate or discussion.[59] Hayward speculates that these measures may even have been "poison pills" intended to defeat the legislative package rather than reasoned commitments to a new vision of campaign finance reform.[60] If so, their unexpected survival would make the Hatch Act Amendments far more significant than originally intended. And far more disruptive.

The timing of the amendments' passage in 1940 meant the changes went into effect midway through a presidential election year. The national party committees unsurprisingly struggled to reorganize their affairs so as to comply with the new law immediately. And perhaps unsurprisingly, too, they soon looked for ways to get around it. Financially independent campaign groups offered a partial solution, as an outlet for contributions and spending in excess of the new limitations. So long as there were no official ties between them, the parties might tacitly encourage the creation of such groups and send donors in their direction, expecting those groups to return the favor with support. Or at least this was the position one could infer from the opinion of the RNC's legal counsel, Henry P. Fletcher.

Having consulted "with several prominent lawyers," Fletcher proffered his advice in August 1940. The $5,000 cap on individual contributions was not a fixed overarching limit, he explained, but a maximum amount an individual could contribute to any *one* federal candidate or political committee. The only catch was how the RNC itself would factor in. In Fletcher's view, since a contribution to the RNC could yield benefits to *all* Republican candidates, it might preclude an individual being able to give another $5,000 to a particular GOP candidate. The safest option, which he recommended, was thus to give the full amount to the RNC and direct any further contributions to the state or local party committees, which were beyond the law's reach.[61] Yet a more intuitive recommendation, and one that many contributors immediately grasped, was to avoid giving to the RNC altogether and instead distribute as many $5,000 contributions as they wished directly to candidates and to independent non-party committees.[62]

Of the $3 million limitation (which capped a committee's expenditures *and* the contributions it could receive), Fletcher noted an important loophole from the outset: it applied *only* to the calendar year. Most important, however, he interpreted the spending cap as applying separately to any distinct political committees, irrespective of whether they were working toward the same goals, such as promoting a specific presidential candidate. Thus the cap certainly applied to national committees like the RNC—as the lawmakers had intended— but the Republican congressional committees would have their own $3 million limits, too. As to whether an "independent Willkie-McNary committee" might be a possibility, referring to the Republican presidential and vice presidential nominees in 1940, Wendell Willkie and Charles McNary, Fletcher advised that so long as it was "unconnected with the Republican National Committee," it would also have a separate $3 million limit on what it could raise and spend. Such a group would be "unconnected," it seemed to Fletcher, as long as it was "independently organized and does not consist of members of the Republican National Committee," a relatively low bar that did not seem to preclude communication between the two entities and thus the possibility of outright coordination (still a thorny issue in regard to modern campaign finance regulation, since the possibility of coordination even *without* active communication, using only publicly available information, looms larger in the internet age).[63]

Many of those with Republican sensibilities apparently took this advice to heart. According to the Senate committee tasked with investigating campaign expenditures in the 1940 election (chaired by one of Roosevelt's intended "purge" victims, Senator Guy Gillette), there were eighty-nine "independent" groups operating in multiple states on behalf of the Republican presidential ticket in 1940, and forty-one such groups operating within a single state. The combined expenditures of these interstate committees came to just over $2.8 million, an amount somewhat higher than the $2.2 million spent by the RNC (though all came in under the $3 million mark).[64] The Democrats, in contrast, having earlier pioneered the formation of campaign auxiliaries, had only twenty interstate committees operating on a financially independent basis in 1940, and twenty-one more within particular states. The combined spending of their interstate committees came to approximately $550,000, about 20 percent of the amount spent by their Republican-leaning counterparts. The DNC, meanwhile, would spend more than the RNC this time around: over $2.4 million, likely reflecting its smaller network of independent committees.[65] But in total, the amounts deployed in support of the Republican ticket would dwarf the Democratic expenditure: $16.6 million compared to $6.1 million (with state party spending factored in), of which interstate independent committees provided approximately 17 percent and 9 percent, respectively.[66]

On the Republican side, almost half of the interstate independent spending came from a single organization: the Associated Willkie Clubs of America. It spent over $1.3 million in support of Wendell Willkie's bid for the presidency and was classified by Overacker as the most important nonparty organization supporting the Republican ticket.[67] Its spending far exceeded that of any other nonparty group active in 1940; its closest Republican-leaning rivals were the Democrats for Willkie, which spent more than $400,000, and the National Committee to Uphold Constitutional Government (NCUCG), which spent nearly $380,000. The Democratic-leaning groups were even further behind; the National Committee of Independent Voters for Roosevelt and Wallace spent the most, just over $250,000, some of which came from labor unions, followed by the National Committee for Agriculture, which spent approximately $130,000, though it received part of its funding from the DNC.[68]

The Associated Willkie Clubs was exactly the kind of "independent Willkie-McNary committee" Fletcher had alluded to in his opinion. And it was, in fact, already in existence prior to passage of the Hatch Act Amendments, having been formed to help secure the Republican nomination for Willkie in the first place—a dark horse candidate without prior political experience and, until recently, a registered Democrat. Ostensibly a popular movement springing from the localities, the clubs prompted Alice Roosevelt Longworth, daughter of former president Theodore Roosevelt and a cousin of the incumbent, to quip that Willkie's support came "from the grassroots of a thousand country clubs."[69] Willkie, after all, was a prominent business executive who had come to national attention as the crusading chairman of Commonwealth & Southern, a private utility company, challenging the Tennessee Valley Authority—a symbol of the New Deal state.[70] Whether or not it tapped into a genuine groundswell of opinion, the Willkie

Clubs had used the grassroots publicity techniques pioneered by lobbying groups to build apparent popular momentum for Willkie's candidacy, helping to convince the Republican convention to nominate him.[71]

In the case of the Willkie Clubs, a candidate-centered organization formed to promote a presidential nomination melded with newer ideas about "independent" campaign groups in general elections, which might, as auxiliary groups had done before, appeal to "independent" voters while contributing financially to the party's overall cause. As Evjen explains, Willkie had personally authorized the continuation of the clubs beyond the Republican convention, now organized under the national umbrella of the Associated Willkie Clubs, in order to promote his nonpartisan appeal.[72] Around four thousand local clubs affiliated with this national committee, directed by Oren Root Jr., translating into approximately 500,000 members.[73] But this large personal following also illustrated some of the problems that independent organizations might pose for the regular party apparatus. Where Franklin Roosevelt's campaigns had still been directed by the DNC, even as some independent groups emerged in 1936, Willkie lacked ties to the regular Republican Party, and it became clear that the Willkie Clubs would play a larger role. An understanding was reached with the RNC whereby the clubs would focus their efforts on independent voters but would retain significant autonomy in their operations.[74] Nevertheless, conflicts with the regular Republican organizations ensued, as the young political amateurs populating the clubs clashed with career politicians over strategy and authority, while Willkie himself frequently disagreed with his RNC advisors.[75] Such conflicts even threatened to continue beyond 1940, since the Willkie Clubs had a brief afterlife following Willkie's loss as the Independent Clubs, though it would permanently close in late 1941 with the outbreak of war.[76]

The prospect of competition, and the attendant loss of full party control over the presidential campaign, led a congressional committee to later conclude that parties had *discouraged* the creation of independent groups prior to the Hatch Act Amendments, since they were "not amenable to the discipline of an organized and responsible political party" and "tended to funnel away funds needed by the regular party organizations."[77] "With the passage of the Hatch Act," however, "the trend was reversed," it concluded. "Both national party organizations feverishly aided, openly or covertly, the establishment of numerous independent committees."[78] But the parties *had* encouraged some financially independent groups prior to the Hatch Act, alongside auxiliaries in the Democratic case, in part to strengthen their claim of partisan detachment in reaching out to independent voters. As noted in the previous chapter, significant impetus for the Democratic-leaning PNC of 1936 came from the White House, for example, while the GOP worked closely with the Women's National Republican Club (in this case effectively a party affiliate, though independently funded). Relations with the Liberty League had been less positive, however, perhaps informing the committee's view.

Nonetheless, whatever the risks from the party's perspective, the economic incentives now favored the formation of independent organizations rather than dependent party auxiliaries, so as to circumvent overall and individual spending caps. Of the ten most "important non-party organizations" favoring the Democratic ticket in 1940, as identified by Overacker, only the National Committee for Agriculture received funds from the DNC (constituting about 40 percent of its expenditures).[79] Yet previous incarnations of this agricultural outreach group, like the Roosevelt Agricultural Committee of 1936 or the Independent Agricultural League of 1928, had been almost entirely financed by the DNC, suggesting a transition from auxiliary to more independent forms of organization.[80] Accordingly, independent committees proliferated after passage of the Hatch Act Amendments in 1940, though their rapid growth may have owed something to preexisting familiarity with the model.[81] Lawmakers, for their part, had not anticipated this development and the way it would subvert their intent. As Senator Lister Hill (D-AL) observed during the Gillette Committee hearings in 1940, "If you have all these different organizations, each one setting its own budget limitations, each one spending what it sees fit . . . the law is not worth the paper it is written on."[82]

But there were other factors at work that would serve to undermine the value of the law. It was not simply *who* was spending what, but *what* they were saying. In the case of organizations classified as political committees, such as the RNC or the Willkie Clubs, their $3 million would be used for overt electoral activities: advocating for particular presidential candidates and encouraging voters to support them at the polls. Yet as Howard Smith had noted in 1936, there were other groups that seemed to orbit particular candidates while never explicitly advocating their cause. Such groups simply denied that they were political committees and thus considered themselves largely exempt from corrupt practices laws, including the new Hatch Act provisions. Thus a number of organizations opposed to Roosevelt's re-election in 1940 appeared before the Gillette Committee and claimed they had no real involvement in the campaign. These groups maintained that they opposed the president's policies and characterized their efforts to convey that disapproval to the wider public as merely "educational" rather than political, offering once again the questionable distinction that earlier pressure groups had invoked.

One such anti-Roosevelt group was the National Committee to Uphold Constitutional Government, which Overacker listed as an important nonparty group supporting the Republican ticket. But the NCUCG refused to admit to being "in politics" at all, least of all in support of Wendell Willkie. Closely associated with the political ambitions of newspaper publisher Frank E. Gannett, who had himself unsuccessfully sought the GOP nomination in 1940, the NCUCG had been formed as a "nonpartisan" pressure group in early 1937, mobilizing to fight Roosevelt's executive reorganization proposal and the court-packing bill, which it depicted as threats to the Constitution.[83] Gannett himself claimed that its membership was diverse in terms of party affiliation and ideological persuasion and noted that care had been taken "not to include anyone who had been prominent in party politics" among its leadership."[84] At the helm day to day was Edward A. Rumely, a master of the new forms of public persuasion, who knew how to target potential supporters and "develop sentiment" in the wider public using techniques the "new lobbies" of the 1920s had first developed.[85] Yet when called before the Senate's ongoing lobby investigation in 1938, Rumely would even deny that its activities constituted *lobbying* and refused to hand over financial documents on that basis.[86]

In any case, the NCUCG's sole concern with legislation did not last long. By late 1937 Gannett was growing disillusioned with both sides of the political aisle, as Polenberg explains. Though he and his followers disliked the New Deal Democrats, they also had little time for the monetary orthodoxy of the "Old Guard" Republicans. More generally, Gannett felt the Republican Party was "dying of dry rot."[87] Instead, they began to consider ways to mobilize a coalition of New Deal opponents, irrespective of their party affiliation, in the 1938 elections. This idea gained momentum when Roosevelt launched his purge campaign, which the NCUCG quickly branded a further affront to the Constitution that must be defended against.[88] An ambitious plan was sketched out in which the NCUCG would mobilize ten million voters—"Constitutional Freemen" as it labeled them—pledged to support congressional candidates "who are upholding our constitutional system" irrespective of their party affiliation.[89] And yet the NCUCG would not actively *endorse* such candidates.

Much like the Liberty League's position, Gannett and his close associates interpreted "nonpolitical" status as precluding open endorsements altogether. Yet they were comfortable with the notion of recruiting millions of "Constitutional Freemen" to vote. The idea seemed to be that as long as those individuals were not explicitly *instructed* how to vote through the mechanism of an endorsement, then their mobilization was educational and not political or partisan. Indeed, criticism of the AFL in the early twentieth century had revealed an underlying conservative discomfort with electoral instruction, framing it as a subversion of democracy. The Liberty League's reluctance to offer guidance to voters also reflected this sensibility. For his part, Gannett founded a new magazine, *America's Future*, to help "educate" voters in the right direction, though it was ostensibly "entirely separate" from the NCUCG.[90] Perhaps because of his restricted sense of what a "nonpolitical" group might do, Gannett ultimately hoped to institutionalize the anti–New Deal coalition as an independent party, one that could have "loftier ideals and finer objectives than either of the parties today."[91] Thus Gannett did not advocate refashioning an existing party from within at this point, expressing doubt, on a practical level, that Southern Democrats could ever be lured to the Republican side.[92]

Nonetheless, Gannett's personal ambitions led him to seek the Republican presidential nomination in 1940, and he turned over leadership of the NCUCG to Samuel B. Pettengill, a former Democratic congressman from Indiana.[93] It was Pettengill, then, who appeared before the Gillette Committee to explain the group's activities, which he claimed had been focused on "developing a strong Congress" by encouraging the best candidates to stand "wholly irrespective of party."[94] But the NCUCG was also interested in the presidential race, he acknowledged, even as Gannett's campaign had stalled. Thus the NCUCG set about "educating" voters on a new and dangerous threat to the Constitution: the third term. As Gannett himself later explained, when called before another campaign expenditure investigation in 1944, the NCUCG had viewed a third presidential term "as a violation of the *spirit* of the Constitution."[95] The group's activities had not been political, Gannett told the chairman of that committee, Representative Clinton Anderson (D-NM), since they had articulated a *principle*—opposition to a third term on constitutional grounds—rather than advocating for or against any particular candidate.[96] The transcript of the hearing reports laughter in response. As Anderson quizzed drily: "Well, there was only one third-term candidate, was there not?"[97]

That candidate, Franklin Roosevelt, successfully secured his third term in 1940, despite the NCUCG's best efforts. Shaken by bad publicity, internal splits over foreign policy, and the fallout from Gannett's own candidacy, it struggled with the result and ultimately ceased operations in April 1941, though a successor organization would later emerge.[98] In fact, the 1940 election would see a more general demise among the first wave of electoral groups forged in the mid-1930s, as their attempts to endure faced new challenges from within and without.

The Demise of Two Leagues

If the NCUCG had been notable among the conservative groups called before the Gillette Committee, the Liberty League had been notable for its absence. Despite encouragement from Pierre du Pont and George Buist late in 1936, urging its continuation—whether to channel opposition to Roosevelt or, as Buist had suggested, to foster a new "American party"—the League had quickly faltered.[99]

Initially, the third-party idea had gained some traction. The League's president, Jouett Shouse, circulated Buist's letter among other members of the executive committee, and according to Wolfskill, seriously contemplated ways to launch a new party. This marked something of a shift in the group's orientation, Wolfskill acknowledged, since the idea had "figured only remotely in Liberty League strategy for 1936," with its leaders well aware that the record of such parties was "not an impressive one."[100] He might have added that such parties had traditionally been associated with very different interests and actors: more "popular" interests or radical causes of the Left. Business leaders and wealthy individuals should have no need of such vehicles in leftist orthodoxy, since both major parties were meant to promote their political aims. The Liberty League's contemplation of this third-party alternative, then (and, indeed, the plans laid out by Gannett) suggest an intriguing transposition of strategies brought about by the New Deal, as labor organizations appeared to move in the opposite direction. Much as leftist radicals had looked to the disruptive power of a third party to break apart existing political conflicts, Shouse had long "visualized the League as the intellectual nucleus for a reorientation and realignment of parties," Wolfskill writes, "an idea that was often discussed in executive committee and one on which there was complete agreement."[101]

According to Wolfskill, Shouse commenced to shop around the third-party idea soon after the 1936 election, suggesting that the defeated Republican nominee Alf Landon and even the chairman of the RNC, John Hamilton, were receptive.[102] It was the president of General Motors, Alfred Sloan, who "carried the word" to Hamilton on behalf of the Liberty League's leading lights, "warning that if a new party were not undertaken before the next election they might withdraw their financial support from the Republicans."[103] How exactly such a wholesale reformulation was to occur is unclear, but Wolfskill goes on to suggest that Hamilton pursued it further, informally polling Republican leaders around the country and ultimately presenting "a lengthy report to the Republican National Committee" in which "he argued that the idea was neither desirable nor feasible."[104] As Wolfskill reports of the informal poll, "local Republican leaders laughed Hamilton out of town when he came to them with the third-party proposal," because they recognized—as perhaps few others did—that "[e]lections are won in the precincts, not in the dining room of the Metropolitan Club." The local level Republican organizations, moreover, were still "in surprisingly good shape."[105]

The Liberty League, however, was not. Its long list of wealthy backers had grown shorter in the wake of electoral defeat and the popular backlash against the League itself. With finances in limited supply, all but the League's Washington, DC, office were closed following the election and its state divisions dissolved.[106] "The Executive Committee, at the end of 1936, told us to stop all mail solicitation, and to keep as much out of the limelight as possible," noted the League's secretary, William Stanton.[107] The executive committee itself no longer met after that.[108] Throughout 1937, in fact, the League subsisted entirely on the contributions of two donors: Pierre du Pont, as he had promised, and his brother Irénée. Another du Pont brother, Lammot, was induced to contribute in early 1938, with a small additional sum from oil tycoon J. Howard Pew preventing the League from becoming an entirely du Pont project.[109] But it was merely limping along, a paper organization with little tangible existence beyond its letterhead.

What prompted its ultimate demise was, in fact, the Hatch Act Amendments— an irony because substantial support for those reforms had come from lawmakers sympathetic to the Liberty League's views, who had primarily intended to thwart groups aiding Roosevelt and his allies. Having subsisted for so long on the handouts of a few wealthy contributors, however, the effect of the $5,000 individual contribution limit was to cut off the Liberty League's life support.[110] Pierre du Pont could not carry its costs alone. As the *New York Times* stated simply in September 1940, after reporting that its Washington office had finally been closed and its skeleton staff dismissed, "the American Liberty League, organized in 1934 to oppose New Deal policies by an 'educational' campaign, has expired."[111]

The 1940 election would also spell the effective demise of the Liberty League's rival, the LNPL. But in this case, the Hatch Act would not be the cause. "Labor's Non-Partisan League was inactive in 1940," Overacker reported, adding that "it raised no funds and spent only $2,000."[112] Increasingly alienated from Roosevelt as the threat of international war loomed, John L. Lewis had clashed with fellow LNPL founder Sidney Hillman, who had forged stronger ties with Roosevelt and been appointed to the National Defense Advisory Board, readying the nation for conflict.[113] As Lewis remarked at the outset of 1940, "A political coalition . . . presupposes a post-election good faith," but "[t]he Democratic Party and its leadership have not preserved this faith." They had ignored the "views of labor," and Lewis now wished "to serve notice that labor is not to be *taken for granted*."[114] "Serving notice" would not involve creating a third party, however, though Lewis toyed with the idea once more.[115] He was, perhaps, dissuaded by the continued lack of public appetite for such a move. A Roper/*Fortune* survey in April 1940 found only 11 percent of respondents believing that unions "should form a national labor party" to compete with the existing major parties. A further 57 percent of respondents felt that labor unions should "keep out of politics altogether," though Lewis seemed less attuned to such signals of public discontent.[116]

Rather than building a new party or aiding an existing one, he would return to the idea of labor as a swing voting bloc, the basic strategy behind a "friends and enemies" policy: that the threat of *punishment*, more so than support, was the way to maintain a beneficial relationship with elected officials, and that the threat must be carried through if a warning did not suffice. Thus Lewis ultimately threw his support to Wendell Willkie in 1940, engineering the official support of the LNPL to go with him. In the ensuing fallout within the CIO, Lewis stepped down as president, and the UMW itself would eventually dissociate from it. The LNPL would be reconstituted as little more than a political fund of the UMW.[117] Though he had shown himself unable to command the vote of labor's rank and file in 1940, with union voters coming out strongly for Roosevelt, Lewis had been true to the nonpartisan justification the LNPL had offered back in 1936. He had supported Roosevelt when he considered him a friend and abandoned him when not.

But the fallout from Lewis's 1940 move would ultimately preclude any third-party possibilities he had once imagined. While the dream of a new party did not entirely disappear from within the industrial labor movement, "independent political action" within the extant two-party system would become the CIO's dominant strategy. And it would become a strategy of *dynamic partisanship,* as liberalizing the Democratic Party became the overarching goal. For the CIO had learned much from its experience with the LNPL. Though polls suggested a slight uptick in support for a third party early in 1941, the CIO soon rejected that approach outright.[118] As Key concluded, the LNPL had "perhaps pointed the way to a means for a more effective expression of labor's strength without the risks incident to operation through an independent labor party."[119] It had "provided a valuable lesson in political action," LaPalombara agreed, "a lesson which was not to be forgotten when labor supporters received a setback in the Congressional elections of 1942."[120] Nor was it forgotten the following year when a new law sought to constrain the political activities in which labor unions might engage. Drawing on the LNPL's example, the CIO moved to create a new and improved political committee. It was to be a truly permanent and proactive electoral organization; not merely a "fellow traveler" of President Roosevelt's, but a means of realizing his liberal vision of the Democratic Party.

Introducing P.A.C.

It was ostensibly a war measure. Passed in June 1943, the War Labor Disputes Act—more commonly known as the Smith-Connally Act after its legislative sponsors—was intended to stop labor disruptions from interfering with America's military mobilization. In the wake of the December 1941 attack on Pearl Harbor, which had prompted the United States to enter World War II, the leaders of both the American Federation of Labor (AFL) and the Congress of Industrial Organizations (CIO) had pledged that their member unions would not engage in strike action for the duration of the conflict. But a series of "wildcat" strikes had broken out anyway, including one led by erstwhile CIO president John L. Lewis earlier in 1943.[1] Amid popular frustration, Congress took action, approving a measure proposed by Representative Howard Smith of Virginia and Senator Tom Connally of Texas—both Southern Democrats— giving the president authority to seize and operate private production facilities threatened by strikes. Roosevelt himself had vetoed it, but with the conservative coalition strengthened in the 1942 midterms, Congress had overridden him the very same day.

Roosevelt had not objected to the main thrust of the Smith-Connally Act; indeed, he had claimed just such authority to seize private facilities eight weeks earlier, on the grounds that a strike might impede the war effort. Rather, as his veto message made clear, he opposed "certain extraneous matter" written into the bill, including a temporary prohibition on "political contributions by labor organizations" while the nation was at war.[2] This tacked-on provision would profoundly alter the political environment for all labor organizations, which now found themselves banned from making financial contributions "in connection with" federal election campaigns, much as corporations had been restricted since passage of the Tillman Act of 1907.[3]

Just two weeks after passage of the Smith-Connally Act, the CIO Executive Committee approved formation of a new "Political Action Committee," which came to be known by its acronym, "P.A.C."[4] This timing has led many scholars to characterize it as a straightforward response to the new legal framework. "The

The Rise of Political Action Committees. Emily J. Charnock, Oxford University Press (2020). © Oxford University Press.
DOI: 10.1093/oso/9780190075514.001.0001

CIO struck back at once," Mutch observes, by creating a new entity that "was not a 'labor organization' as defined in the National Labor Relations Act" and was thus outside the scope of the law.[5] Similarly, Urofsky describes how "[t]he unions circumvented" the new restrictions "with a device that would come to play a key role in the debate over campaign finance reform a half-century later, the political action committee, or PAC."[6] The CIO's P.A.C. would ultimately come to do so by collecting *voluntary* donations from union members to fund campaign contributions, rather than paying them out of union treasuries, forging the basic organizational model for future imitators.[7]

But P.A.C. was much more than a financial vehicle designed to get around new restrictions on union campaign contributions. It reflected and channeled earlier developments in industrial labor's orientation to the political realm, embodying a more active political stance that had been gathering steam for nearly a decade. A new CIO political organization, in fact, had been planned prior to the passage of Smith-Connally. The formation of P.A.C., moreover, placed that activity on a new trajectory, one that the law's requirements did not foreordain. Drawing on the CIO's experience over four previous election cycles via Labor's Non-Partisan League (LNPL) and the activism of individual member unions, P.A.C. forged an assertive model of "political action" that went beyond mere campaign contributions, bringing together targeted financial assistance with ground-level campaign work and wider publicity efforts, systematically coordinated on a national scale. It elaborated on the LNPL's experiment with dynamic partisanship, moreover, coming to view the liberalization of the Democratic Party as the key to labor's long-term success, grounding its pursuit of policy gains in partisan electoral activity. Indeed, many scholars point to the Democratic-labor alliance that solidified in the 1940s as something of a given, without considering the mechanics of its operation and the strategy behind it.[8] Understanding the emergence and activities of P.A.C. sheds light on both.

In sum, the CIO in the early 1940s, through its P.A.C., developed a characteristic form of electoral organization; a specific strategy of political action focused on a single party; and a set of legal and rhetorical arguments to justify both that would have profound effects on the nature of election campaigning, pressure group-party relations, and even the broader contours of the party system. The P.A.C. model would inspire liberal allies organizationally and strategically, but it would also energize opponents in Congress and beyond, prompting renewed efforts to constrain labor electioneering in the Taft-Hartley Act of 1947. Yet in spite of such legislative constraints, P.A.C. would endure. Indeed, Taft-Hartley would itself induce the American Federation of Labor—long hostile to the CIO's more assertive political posture and initially opposed to P.A.C.—to develop a similar organization. Through such emulation and combined electoral efforts, "political action" as P.A.C. came to define it would be the tool through which a new vision of party politics was forged.

"A More Perfect Organization"

In a basic respect, P.A.C. was simply one of several committees appointed by the CIO's executive board for various purposes, to consider issues such as war relief or racial discrimination, for example, or to coordinate its legislative affairs.[9] Where the CIO's Legislative Committee would be responsible for traditional direct lobbying, the new Political Action Committee would coordinate the CIO's electoral activity on a national scale, to be directed in 1944 toward the re-election of President Franklin Roosevelt and a Congress that would support him. To head up this effort, Amalgamated Clothing Workers president Sidney Hillman was appointed as chairman, with a vice chairman and secretary also named at the first meeting. With a national headquarters in New York, fourteen regional offices across the country, and a staff of 135 spread among them, P.A.C. set out to organize state and local subcommittees and mobilize members for the 1944 campaign.[10]

By this point, the CIO had been at the forefront of labor's political activity for almost a decade, and plans for a new national electoral organization—to replace the defunct LNPL—had already been set in motion prior to the passage of the Smith-Connally Act. While P.A.C. was launched in the summer of 1943, its second director, Jack Kroll, later told a congressional committee, "I do not think that the Labor Disputes Act, if you will as my opinion, had much to do with it."[11] Indeed, in a larger sense, P.A.C. was not a straightforward response to the law alone, created out of whole cloth in 1943, as some campaign finance scholars imply. Instead, it reflected a refinement and expansion of a more assertive strain of interest group electoral activity that had become particularly apparent over the previous decade, and in which labor organizations had played a major role.

With the growth of the industrial labor movement in the 1930s, embodied in the nascent CIO, a more overtly political face of labor had emerged. As the labor economist Philip Taft explained in 1937, the CIO had favored "political action" over "purely economic action" from the outset, rejecting the self-help philosophy of the AFL and its preference for workplace agreements and looking straight to government for assistance.[12] In Taft's view, this new orientation reflected a growing recognition of the larger forces impinging on unions' activity and outside of their control, such as capital flight to nonunionized states, and the need to protect labor's fundamental right to organize, first fully secured by federal government action with the Wagner Act of 1935.[13]

The need to engage politically seemed more pressing than ever in the early 1940s, even if the CIO's first political vehicle, the LNPL, had folded. For a start, labor's public image was suffering. The war effort had linked patriotism and industrial productivity in the public mind, and the business community enjoyed a post-Depression resurgence in prestige amid the "miracle" of wartime manufacturing.[14] This helped to erode any relative advantage in public opinion labor may have once enjoyed, and wildcat strikes contributed to a popular backlash. At the same time, for those unions that abided by it, the no-strike pledge took one of their most important tools of private influence off the table.[15] This made them more reliant on favorable government action, yet CIO leaders were becoming less sure of receiving it. With military considerations taking precedence, they viewed the various wartime government agencies dealing with labor issues warily, and they feared that presidential support for their aims was waning.[16] Roosevelt's decision to nationalize the mines in May 1943, for example, after John L. Lewis led his United Mine Workers out on an unauthorized strike (one of the major incidents prompting passage of the Smith-Connally Act), had shown where the president's priorities now lay. Congress also appeared an even less sympathetic environment since the 1942 midterms, with Republicans having secured their largest share of House seats since 1930, often at the expense of liberal Democrats, thereby enhancing the power of the conservative coalition. Hillman blamed "political apathy" for the results, placing both the cause and potential cure of labor's ills in the electoral realm.[17] Aware that legislative or bureaucratic decisions could quickly undo gains secured through collective bargaining, and fearing that lobbying alone could not prevent such outcomes, labor leaders now saw electoral action—for all the risks involved—as a necessity.

The CIO's leaders had already established a new Legislative Committee in early 1942 to improve communication with the administration and Congress, but they did not stop there, instructing it "to take steps toward the establishment of a political arm of the CIO."[18] In accordance with this goal, Nathan E. Cowan, John Brophy, and J. Raymond Walsh—the CIO's legislative representative, director of its industrial union councils, and director of education and research, respectively—produced a report for CIO president Phillip Murray assessing current political capabilities and providing a blueprint for a new organization. Thus by late 1942 plans were laid for a new CIO political vehicle of national scope, one that would pull together and build upon existing streams of activity and try to carve out a new path to influence.

"The general outlines of a national political organization . . . are already in existence," Cowan, Brophy, and Walsh observed, though they suggested this fact owed little to the prior operations of the LNPL.[19] For all the LNPL was an important development in terms of labor's financial role in election campaigns, they felt it had done little to build up grassroots organization across the country.

Those outlines had instead been established through more recent efforts. "[T]he neglect of detailed political work which characterized the administration of the first President of the CIO [John L. Lewis] made it necessary to begin building organizations and procedures anew from the ground up," Cowan and his colleagues explained.[20] Nonetheless, progress had been made, and there was now "considerable political machinery" at the subnational level and a skeleton national staff in place to coordinate it.[21]

Two national departments had shared primary responsibility for coordinating this activity: the Legislative Department, which liaised with the international unions and kept track of their "contacts with Congress and the administration," and the Council Department, which did the same with the industrial union councils (IUCs), the state-level coordinating bodies of the CIO.[22] The IUCs were the heart of extant political operations, the authors observed. "Even before the abandonment of Labor's Non-Partisan League, and very definitely since that time, the state industrial union councils have carried the primary responsibility for the political work of the CIO," they noted.[23] Indeed, Cowan and colleagues made a distinction between legislative lobbying activity and purely *electoral* activities—the sense in which "political" was usually meant—pointing out that the IUCs tended to separate lobbying and political tasks and locate the latter within specialized entities. They would emphasize this feature in their recommendations for a new national political action committee.[24]

The CIO's national office itself had already undertaken some electoral activity, they acknowledged. The 1942 midterm elections had provided opportunities to gain experience, and the Legislative and Council Departments had not simply gathered information about state political operations in those contests, but had also sought to stimulate activity and even, "[i]n one or two instances," had "participated directly in coordinating labor political campaigns."[25] One such instance involved the Eighth Congressional District of Virginia, chosen both for its proximity to Washington, DC, and the notoriety of its incumbent: none other than Howard W. Smith, a perennial labor foe.[26] Both here and in the sixth district of Virginia, where the CIO was also active, there were "unfortunate results," Cowan and colleagues admitted, "in which labor-endorsed candidates lost by wide margins," suggesting the need for better research and organization.[27] Perhaps most unfortunately for the CIO, Smith won re-election and proceeded to take his revenge, pushing the antistrike measure that soon bore his name—to which constraints on union political activity would be added—and proving a thorn in the side of labor for decades to come.

With few labor successes elsewhere in the 1942 elections, the report's authors concluded that "[t]he existing political structure . . . has many obvious faults and deficiencies." Nonetheless, it should serve as "the point of departure from which the development of a more perfect organization should be undertaken."[28]

Perfecting the CIO's political operations would involve several organizational innovations at the national level—innovations that served to advance longer-term trends in the interest group world. Most prominent would be the very *permanence* of P.A.C. itself. "We have not organized for 1944 alone," Sidney Hillman would inform the CIO's 1943 convention, and from the outset P.A.C. was designed as a permanent body.[29] In this respect, it would be more successful than earlier electoral groups that had tried to move in a more permanent direction, such as the Liberty League of 1936 or the Willkie Clubs of 1940, or even the LNPL (though P.A.C., unlike the LNPL, was never envisaged as a stepping stone to a third party, as discussed later in the chapter). In some ways, it even outdid the major parties, which still had a limited organizational footprint at the national level, even if they now had headquarters and a small permanent staff.[30] As E. E. Schattschneider observed in 1942, "only the transparent filaments of the ghost of a party" were visible at the national level.[31]

P.A.C. was also envisaged as a separate entity, distinct from the CIO itself, and a specialized one, dedicated to election-oriented activity. While predecessors like the LNPL or the Anti-Saloon League had combined *both* legislative and electoral activities within the same organization, P.A.C. would focus solely on the latter.[32] Murray had actually recommended that the existing Legislative Committee direct "at least the initial stages of political organization," but Cowan, Brophy, and Walsh pushed against this idea.[33] This drive for separation and specialization was not, however, purely a search for bureaucratic efficiency, as organizational historians might suggest.[34] Nor can it be explained in terms of legal necessity, as might be inferred from the later use of P.A.C. as a repository for voluntary campaign donations.[35]

To some extent, Cowan, Brophy, and Walsh recommended forming a separate organization so that it could focus exclusively on its specialized tasks.[36] They also felt that the CIO's existing structure was ill-suited to political activities, since it was built around industrial sectors rather than electoral geography.[37] But primarily, they wanted the new political arm to be distinct from the CIO, including its Legislative Committee and especially the state-level IUCs, in order to encourage participation by non-CIO labor groups and *nonlabor* groups. They recommended that membership be extended well beyond CIO unions, to AFL affiliates, Railroad Brotherhoods, farm organizations, and liberal groups in general, seeking to better realize the LNPL's professed goal of incorporating broader constituencies. It was this desire to foster "[a] much broader coalition of labor than has ever been achieved in the past" that made organizational separation from the CIO desirable, irrespective of any legal or financial considerations.[38]

In this respect, the Smith-Connally Act did have some eventual influence, even if it did not induce the initial separation of P.A.C. from the wider CIO structure. Rather, it served to undermine the original rationale for that separation, since the CIO leadership narrowed the scope of P.A.C.'s intended membership in response to the law. Instead, they sought to realize Cowan and colleagues' broader coalitional aims by creating another new organization in July 1944, the National Citizens' Political Action Committee (NCPAC), which was ostensibly a nonpartisan and nonlabor group but in reality was tightly linked to the CIO P.A.C. in both financial and organizational terms.[39] Sidney Hillman served as the director of both organizations, and they shared offices.[40] Testifying before the House committee investigating campaign expenditures in 1944, chaired by Representative Clinton Anderson, Hillman explained that it offered "progressives outside of the ranks of labor" who had been attracted by P.A.C.'s work "an opportunity for organized participation in political activity."[41] More cynically, it also expanded the pool of potential political donors, once contributions straight from union treasuries had been proscribed.[42]

It was on the financial front, of course, that the Smith-Connally law had its most important impact on the operations of both P.A.C. and the NCPAC. But it had different short and longer-term effects. The CIO's original intention was to finance the national organization through a combination of large donations from international unions and from a per capita tax levied on local unions—a tax presumably passed on to members via dues.[43] The law necessitated a different approach, since it banned the use of treasury funds—that is, funds derived from compulsory member dues—"in connection with" federal elections.[44] The CIO's initial response, however, looked for loopholes where treasury funds might still be used, rather than immediately adopting the model of individual voluntary contributions with which it would soon be associated.[45]

As Hillman explained to the Anderson Committee, all of P.A.C.'s original financing (approximately $700,000) came from CIO-affiliated union treasuries.[46] But it had only used that money in election contests it considered beyond the reach of the law: in state electoral contests, for example, and in primary contests for both state and federal positions.[47] According to Foster, P.A.C.'s legal counsel, John Abt, argued that "the Smith-Connally Act forbade union contributions to an election campaign," but "an election required a candidate, and any activity prior to the nomination of party candidates was not restricted."[48] At the presidential level, P.A.C. officials thus reasoned that the general election did not begin until the party conventions were concluded later that summer and thus continued to use treasury funds until July, even though they had publicly endorsed Roosevelt in May.[49] Only after that did P.A.C. turn to voluntary contributions from union members to fund its activities, which, P.A.C.'s legal team reasoned, could not be prohibited by law without infringing upon individual rights.

To drum up volunteers, in July the CIO launched an appeal to its members for one-dollar donations, half of which would go to the national P.A.C. fund and the other half of which would remain within the state.[50] This also served to encourage the formation of state- and local-level PACs, which offered a means of avoiding other legal restrictions, namely the disclosure requirements of the Federal Corrupt Practices Act, which only applied to electoral organizations active in more than one state. Testifying before the Senate's campaign expenditure committee in 1944, chaired by Theodore F. Green (D-RI), Hillman claimed that these subnational PACs were semiautonomous entities "not subordinate to the national organization" and "solely intrastate" in operation; thus they did not constitute "political committees" under the law.[51]

By August, P.A.C. had raised more than $17,000 in voluntary contributions, and it quickly set up internal machinery to deal with its different streams of income and their distinctive status, establishing an accounting system in which treasury funds and voluntary donations were kept separate (a system that modern "connected" PACs continue to use).[52] Exhibiting some legal caution, however, P.A.C. determined to freeze its treasury account following the conventions, relying on voluntary donations to fund its general overhead and maintenance costs during the general election period, in addition to its overtly political activities.[53] This stance overstretched P.A.C.'s nascent voluntary account, however, and it took a less cautious approach to dealing with the shortfall, soliciting about $40,000 in loans, which were to be paid back once sufficient voluntary donations had been collected.[54] Nonetheless, as Hillman clarified in his Anderson Committee testimony, P.A.C. officials believed that its activities could be separated into different categories as much as its funding could. "We would like to make it clear that it is our judgment that our operating expenses are purely educational," Hillman told lawmakers, and that "a number of the things we are doing are educational and no one would question that."[55] They had chosen to pay everything out of voluntary funds after the conventions simply to avoid controversy, he said, perhaps conscious of arousing public hostility.[56] "In other words, we believe we have a right to do a lot of things under the law, but we do not want to have any public debate as to whether we are or are not within our rights."[57]

Hillman's testimony points to an emerging set of legal and normative arguments put forth to justify the P.A.C. idea. Like earlier interest groups seeking to defend their electoral involvement, he sought to clothe some of its activity in an educational veneer—though unlike those earlier examples, P.A.C. would not consistently deny a "political" dimension to that activity, coming to embrace instead a blended concept of "political education" while still contrasting it to direct "political action." Hillman also tried to dispel any hint of compulsion or coercion of members in soliciting donations for P.A.C. (in this case for distinctly legal reasons, since a compulsory political donation might have the same status as required membership dues). And like previous group officials, he sought to wrap P.A.C. in the mantle of "nonpartisanship" as a means of justifying both its ends and its means. "Our committee is a nonpartisan organization," Hillman told the

Anderson Committee.[58] "We do not care what party a candidate belongs to," he said, but rather emphasized *issues* instead, supporting those candidates who shared the CIO's policy goals.[59] Yet as with each previous innovation in interest group electioneering, this new venture was met with criticism both within and beyond Congress, even before it had fully mobilized.

Among the most outraged was Congressman Howard Smith, coauthor of the very law that had set out to constrain labor's electoral involvement.[60] In early January 1944 he complained to Attorney General Francis Biddle that P.A.C. represented "a flagrant violation of the criminal provisions of the Federal Corrupt Practices Act, as amended by the War Labor Disputes Act."[61] But Biddle proceeded to pronounce P.A.C.'s basic financial structure and activities legally sound. An FBI investigation ordered in response to Smith's complaint had found no violations of the Corrupt Practices Act or the Hatch Act contribution limit, Biddle reported in his reply. Though P.A.C. had been established using union treasury funds, as Smith had drawn attention to in his initial complaint, it had not made any direct contributions to federal candidates for general election purposes using those funds and thus had not yet violated the law.[62] "If future action by the Committee of a nature prohibited by the Act should occur," Biddle assured the congressman, "appropriate action will be taken by this Department."[63]

But Smith was not alone in his disdain for P.A.C. Almost from the moment it was established, P.A.C. had generated scrutiny from the House Special Committee on Un-American Activities (HUAC), chaired by Martin Dies (D-TX).[64] Ever vigilant against Communist infiltration, Dies's committee launched an investigation into the CIO and P.A.C.'s purported links to Communists, fanning the flames of criticism even as its March 1944 report did little to substantiate its allegations of subversion.[65] Nonetheless, in August 1944 Dies took to writing Biddle too, this time questioning whether P.A.C. had violated Hatch Act restrictions on political activities by federal employees—perhaps referring to those members of the Roosevelt administration with whom P.A.C. appeared to have close ties.[66] But Biddle essentially dismissed this complaint, observing that the Hatch Act applied only to nonpolitical appointees anyway.[67] Still, Dies had already used the considerable power and resources of his committee to rail against P.A.C. and sow seeds of public suspicion.

Irrespective of a Communist threat, real or imagined, critics could tap into a deeper cultural discomfort with the idea of electoral activity by a "special interest." In terms of labor unions, public opinion polls in the early 1940s consistently showed majorities of Americans believing they should "keep out of politics altogether."[68] Polls also revealed recognition of, and some hostility toward, the specifically *financial* role unions were playing in campaigns. In a *Fortune* magazine poll conducted in April 1944, for example, 57 percent of respondents felt that labor unions "should *not* be allowed to contribute money to an election campaign" even if they wanted to.[69] Perhaps in recognition of this public concern, but also facing legal uncertainty surrounding its new organizational form, P.A.C. avoided making any direct campaign contributions from its voluntary funds in 1944, in either primary or general elections.

The question was whether P.A.C. and the NCPAC might count as "labor organizations" in themselves, under the meaning of the National Labor Relations Act, and would thereby be prohibited from making campaign contributions whatever the funding source, a point that Senator E. H. Moore (R-OK) raised with Biddle in September.[70] In fact, during the Anderson Committee hearings in August, Hillman and Abt had vehemently denied that the NCPAC was a "labor organization" in this technical sense.[71] As for P.A.C., Abt acknowledged that it was "a highly debatable question" but emphasized that P.A.C. did not "negotiate with employers, or have anything to do with the problem of wages, hours, or working conditions," which were defining features of labor organizations as he understood them.[72] Since the point was a debatable one, Abt explained that P.A.C. had proceeded along the most cautious route—as it had done with "every legal question which we have been confronted with"—assuming it *would* be classified as a labor organization and therefore determining that neither the CIO nor P.A.C. would make any "contributions whatever in connection with the elections."[73] Instead, P.A.C. would confine its activities to campaigning *on behalf of* federal candidates in 1944, rather than giving money to them directly or to their party committees.[74]

The NCPAC, in contrast, did offer financial support directly to candidates in the general election.[75] And it was here that Moore made his second objection, questioning the very distinction between treasury and voluntary contributions that would come to define the concept of a PAC. The NCPAC's funding structure, Moore argued, was "a mere technical effort expressly designed for the purpose of attempting to evade the provisions of the Federal Corrupt Practices Act, as amended by the Smith-Connally Act."[76] But Biddle did not agree. The law was designed "to restrict the use of union and corporate funds," he acknowledged, but Congress had not intended "to restrict the political activities of individuals."[77] *Even if* the NCPAC were a "labor organization," Biddle argued—a classification he himself strongly doubted—the law's prohibition could not extend to the actions it had funded through voluntary contributions.[78] "Any other construction of the statute would require me to assume that Congress intended to place the persons who belonged to labor organizations or who hold stock in national banks, or in corporations organized by authority of Federal law, under a special disability and to deny to them a privilege that belongs to all other citizens." The plan of the NCPAC, then, complied with "both the spirit and the letter of the law," in Biddle's view.[79] By implication, this statement authorized other PACs to make direct campaign contributions using voluntary funds in future years.

But Moore had one last trick up his sleeve: highlighting the ways that unions themselves might *aid* a candidate without directly contributing to his or her campaign, by distributing pamphlets or editorials, for example, or engaging in other promotional activities that appeared to advocate for their election, all of which cost money.[80] The concern Moore raised would later become a highly contentious area of legal debate, considering just what an organization could say or do in the electoral sphere without giving funds directly to a candidate or party. But in 1944, Biddle remained unmoved. Section 9 of the Smith-Connally Act only prohibited *contributions* from labor organizations to federal candidates or party committees, Biddle observed. It did not prohibit *expenditures*, he explained, including the costs incurred in producing such literature.[81] And prohibiting groups from spending money as they saw fit could be seen as an abridgment of fundamental freedoms, he warned, as much as prohibiting individuals from making contributions could be. While Biddle did not dismiss the possibility that some forms of expression might fall under the statutes, those that Moore had emphasized were "very similar to many of the editorials appearing in newspapers and other periodicals during this campaign, and I hardly conceive that Congress should have intended that expressions of opinion by labor unions or by newspapers should be covered by the statutes."[82]

Biddle's letter appeared to validate theoretical rights-based arguments that P.A.C. officials had made from the outset, even as they took a more cautious approach during the general election period by relying on voluntary funds after the conventions. The Corrupt Practices Act made a "very clear distinction between contributions and expenditures," P.A.C. counsel John Abt had explained to the Green Committee in June 1944, stressing that only the former were restricted.[83] Thus, as a letter to P.A.C.'s regional directors in December 1943 affirmed, P.A.C. believed in principle that its "expenditures" on publicity—whether "the distribution of leaflets, the holding of meetings of members of organized labor and the general public, the use of radio time, etc."—even where they involved explicit candidate advocacy, could not be limited.[84] "These activities on the part of the committee are merely the exercise of its constitutional right of free speech, press and assembly. They are not and cannot be prohibited by law."[85] On this interpretation, P.A.C.'s lawyers argued that union treasury money—that derived from required member dues—could, in fact, be used to aid or promote particular candidates, so long as it was not given directly to them and the activities it funded were not explicitly prearranged or coordinated with them.[86] (In taking this latter position, P.A.C. would tap into a longer stream of arguments about what a candidate's "friends" might do on his or her behalf, ostensibly without that person's knowledge.)[87] They argued, in essence, that an "independent" publicity campaign could still be waged on a candidate's behalf, Smith-Connally Act or not, and the attorney general had effectively upheld them.

Still somewhat uncertain in its first outing, P.A.C. did not push this theory to its logical conclusion—that treasury funds might be used throughout the general election period too, at least for "expenditures," choosing instead to switch to voluntary funds.[88] But it had already spent extensively prior to that point: more than $478,000 in trade union funds up to the conventions, and over $470,000 in voluntary funds afterward.[89] Nonetheless, P.A.C. officials were concerned to play down the financial dimensions of their work, stressing instead the popular support those voluntary contributions represented. As the headline of a September *CIO News* article pronounced, "People Not Money Power Behind PAC."[90] Since those voluntary contributions did not go directly to candidates, moreover, the substance of P.A.C.'s activities, beyond the financial, must be considered in more detail.

P.A.C. in Action

"For many years each of the affiliated unions of the CIO have conducted their own programs of political activity and political education," Sidney Hillman told the Anderson Committee in 1944, in explaining P.A.C.'s larger purpose. "It is the function of our committee to coordinate and make more effective the work which our constituent unions have heretofore carried on independently."[91] P.A.C. would pursue this purpose, Hillman explained, by working toward three related aims:[92] "to bring the issues at stake to the attention of the people," "to secure the widest possible participation in the determination of those issues through the use of the ballot," and "to assist [the American people] in using their ballot intelligently and effectively."[93] Roughly speaking, these aims would be fulfilled by three different streams of activity: political education, which involved the discussion or promotion of specific issues and policy positions without outright advocacy of candidates; voter mobilization, through registration drives and ground-level activity on Election Day; and direct political action, through the provision of financial support to candidates, endorsements, and publicity advocating their election.

Bringing key issues to public attention was a matter of political education, of building publicity campaigns around individual issues or broader themes.[94] For 1944, the CIO's national convention endorsed a strong commitment to the war effort with an eye on a "sound and progressive post-war program" at home, one that "could give full employment to our people, provide an adequate system of social security in times of unemployment, sickness, and old age, and lay the basis for a more secure and abundant life."[95] Although the resolution was drafted by the national P.A.C., Hillman emphasized the collaborative process by which it had been formulated.[96] The program "represents the collective thinking of the

CIO," Hillman claimed, "as well as of the *many other groups and organizations* which participated in the discussions which preceded its formulation."[97] Exactly *which* groups had given input was unclear, but the point was to portray both CIO and P.A.C. aims in less exclusively union terms.[98] Theirs was "not a narrow labor program," nor "framed in the interest of any special group" Hillman went on, seeking to defuse the continuing stigma associated with special interests. Indeed, he went so far as to suggest that P.A.C. offered "a basis for unity and common action by all Americans in every walk of life, regardless of formal party affiliation."[99] That is, the issue-based P.A.C. program was neither labor-dominated in focus nor partisan in form.

Beyond specific issues, Hillman linked P.A.C.'s program of political education to the basic duties of citizenship, encouraging "the full and enlightened exercise" of those responsibilities.[100] Concerned with the drop in voter turnout in 1942, P.A.C. undertook an extensive registration campaign in 1944, "working in close cooperation with other labor groups as well as with civic, businessmen's, and other organizations."[101] "[W]e are interested in assuring the largest possible ballot in 1944," he explained.[102] To be sure, there was an instrumental purpose as much as idealistic motivation behind this particular aim. Apathy among labor voters, particularly low turnout in northern industrial cities, was widely blamed for what the CIO saw as poor midterm results in 1942, contributing to a strengthened conservative coalition in Congress.[103] But as Foster explains, P.A.C. promoted a broader concept of the "union voter" that sought to tie together the civic, the instrumental, and the ideological, in essence.[104] Its rejection of a "narrow labor program" was not mere rhetoric designed to distance P.A.C. from self-interested concerns (though ironically, it would distance P.A.C. from the approach pioneered by the first "modern" interest groups, which had focused on a limited range of issues in order to distinguish themselves from parties and disrupt the party loyalties of voters). Rather, through educational publicity and local events, P.A.C. encouraged union members to embrace a wide array of "liberal" policy positions and to conceive of their political obligations in both civic and communal terms, as having a responsibility to vote, to encourage others to vote, and contribute to P.A.C.'s efforts. "All of us must register. All of us must vote. All of us must help get out the vote. All of us must contribute to campaign expenses," one of P.A.C.'s early pamphlets exhorted.[105]

Hillman professed to be unconcerned with *how* union members registered, whether as Democrats or Republicans.[106] But P.A.C. was concerned with how those members ultimately voted, encouraging support for the incumbents and challengers most sympathetic to the CIO's aims. Thus the final strand of P.A.C. activity, its program of direct political action, involved efforts to guide voters toward preferred candidates and to provide tangible assistance to those candidates in their campaigns—whether through outright endorsements, the production and distribution of publicity materials and advertisements, or the provision of field workers to guide and support local P.A.C. efforts. In terms of endorsements, however, Hillman was careful to clarify the decentralized nature of this process. As he told the Green Committee, the national P.A.C. made official recommendations only at the presidential level: backing President Roosevelt in 1944 for a fourth term in office, which the CIO Executive Committee soon affirmed. Revealing continued sensitivity to the controversies of 1938, he asserted that P.A.C. otherwise had "no purge list, either in public or secret." Rather, state and local PACs were responsible for giving their official backing to congressional candidates, though Hillman acknowledged that the national committee often gave advice in this regard.[107]

This advisory role, in fact, helped the national P.A.C. to frame some of its guidance to voters and affiliate PACs as educational rather than explicitly political. As Hillman explained: "We do not think it is sufficient merely to bring issues to the attention of the people. We also believe that it is one of our important functions to show people how they can participate in deciding those issues in their own best interest."[108] This would be done, in part, by bringing "to the American people the record of the candidates who solicit their support."[109] Those records—usually an analysis of roll-call votes for incumbent lawmakers or an overview of a challenger's issue positions—showed the extent to which an existing or prospective elective official was in agreement with P.A.C.'s desired policy aims. Justified as a means of aiding citizens "in using their ballot intelligently and effectively," P.A.C. developed such records, and its research activities more broadly, into powerful political weapons.[110]

Interest groups had experimented with roll-call analysis since the early twentieth century. The AFL, for example, was already publicizing roll calls on some individual measures by 1910 and tracking lawmaker's votes on "measures of vital importance" to labor, providing those voting records to members on request.[111] But as Clemens points out, such records, or "scorecards," as they came to be known, were often highly controversial. When unions in California and elsewhere began publicizing the records of state legislators on labor issues in the early 1910s, they faced significant criticism.[112] Californians "found the legitimacy of this technique *extremely* questionable," she says, while lawmakers themselves "looked upon it as black-listing."[113] Certainly, in accordance with electoral practices at the time, this was a way of identifying "friends" and "enemies" whom union members should support or oppose. But some rank-and-file workers were equally troubled by its apparently imperative quality. To offset these various criticisms, interest group leaders sought to justify the practice as "educational."[114] As AFL president Samuel Gompers told a congressional committee in 1913, such information was intended to help members "form their own conclusions," not instruct them how to vote.[115]

P.A.C.'s promotion of voting records owed much to its first congressional strategist, former Wisconsin congressman Thomas Amlie, and to his lengthy experience in radical and liberal politics. Amlie had briefly served in Congress as a Republican in 1931–1932, and again from 1935 as a Wisconsin Progressive, though he subsequently lost his bid for a Senate nomination in 1938 and retired from the House. He also had a background in Socialist politics and had been involved with the Non-Partisan League in the late 1910s and early '20s, before chairing the Farmer-Labor Political Federation in the early 1930s, which had hoped to launch a new nationwide third party.[116] During this time he toured the country as a spokesman for leftist causes and learned a powerful lesson about appearance and reality in politics. Even in crowds sympathetic to his most radical ideas, he would find enthusiasm for local congressmen whom he considered "reactionary."[117] Constituents simply lacked any real sense of their congressman's record, Amlie concluded. "As a result of these experiences I learned that in the Northern States, a congressman could vote liberal on from 10 to 20% of the recorded votes and maintain a reputation as a liberal with his constituents," he would later write.[118] Publicizing roll-call data might help to correct their false impressions, he believed, and thereby aid in the election or re-election of candidates more sympathetic to liberal goals.

In early 1942 Amlie had been hired by a newly formed liberal organization, the Union for Democratic Action (UDA), where he first put his insight about congressional records to work. The UDA itself reflected the expanding sphere of electorally oriented pressure groups in the early 1940s, formed to articulate a liberal viewpoint in international and domestic affairs and to promote that message assertively in elections.[119] With midterms coming up, the UDA hoped to defeat isolationist lawmakers who had opposed US entry into World War II and often showed hostility to New Deal programs at home—"obstructionists," as the UDA labeled them. To aid that effort, Amlie compiled an extensive legislative scorecard showing how lawmakers had voted on key foreign policy and domestic votes in recent years, which was published as a special supplement in the *New Republic*.[120] Though previous groups, including the LNPL, had experimented with roll-call analysis and scorecards of various types, they had typically confined their focus to single votes or a series of votes on single issues.[121] The UDA's effort compiled a multi-vote and multi-issue scorecard that approximated, as Amlie saw it, varying aspects of the liberal worldview, and the *New Republic* publicized it widely. Its prominence in the 1942 campaign thus brought roll-call analysis to wider notice, though it also generated extensive criticism.[122]

By 1944 Amlie had moved on from the UDA to P.A.C., helping to set up its research operations in time for the next campaign.[123] A congressional scorecard duly appeared, published as a special legislative supplement to the *CIO News* in June.[124] (An earlier scorecard attributed to P.A.C., "Keeping Score to

Win the War," was singled out by HUAC in its March 1944 report as being identical to one circulated by the Communist Party, though it appears to have been compiled originally by the United Auto Workers and was then distributed by the CIO.)[125] Amlie and his team were still careful how they framed and presented these records, providing extensive tables, with lawmakers' names listed in rows and their positions on various bills indicated across columns with a plus or minus sign. While these signs offered a sense of the CIO's viewpoint on their position, whether positive or negative, the interpretive key did not describe any vote as "right" or "wrong." The labels were hardly neutral, though, describing plus votes as being "for labor and the nation's win-the-war program," while minus votes went against it.[126] "Learn the record and apply it as the acid test for election support," the CIO News urged its readers in October.[127] But readers would have to wade through the entire list to find their representatives, look over their various votes, and compare them with the CIO's explanation—a time-consuming task.

The point of such a presentation was to appear informational rather than instructive, as Jack Kroll, P.A.C.'s second director, made plain in his testimony before a 1946 campaign expenditures committee. Asked by a congressman whether P.A.C. ever explicitly pointed out "the person that you consider has been a friend of yours, of your organization" in its various publications, Kroll explained that P.A.C. did not.[128] "We do make the issues known," he said, "and whether we think that particular thing is good or bad from our viewpoint. Then we make known the voting record on that particular act, see?" "We do not single out an individual and say, 'Here is Bill Smith; Bill Smith is altogether bad,'" he continued. "We say, 'We are for this issue. Here is how all the Congressmen voted on it.'"[129] If P.A.C. talked in general terms about legislators who had supported or opposed a bill it desired, "we do not mention any individual names," Kroll assured. "Now, that we are very careful not to do from the national organization," he emphasized.[130] While this format might help assuage the concerns of congressmen to a degree, it made early P.A.C. voting records less useful as a propaganda tool in and of themselves.

But those records did have other crucial uses. For a start, they provided the underlying research on which state and local PAC endorsement decisions were based and could be used for publicity materials praising or attacking the records of individual lawmakers.[131] More important, they offered a means by which the national P.A.C. could standardize and publicize its criteria for what made a "good" lawmaker: a pro-labor, liberal one. And in that sense, they offer insight into the political strategy of the CIO and P.A.C. These records might appear, and indeed were defended as, scientific or "objective" analysis, technical and apparently nonpartisan in form. But the votes upon which they were based were carefully selected to highlight particular issues and congressional divisions, especially those between Republicans and Southern Democrats, on the one hand, and northern Democratic liberals on the other.

"Keeping Score to Win the War," for example, professed concern with the war effort in its very title but only included votes relating to the "home front" of that war, presumably since many Southern Democrats had records supportive of the president on international matters.[132] On the domestic side, however, the "southern Poll Tax Democrats" had been "joined by an almost solid Republican vote in support of the Smith-Connally Bill," an article introducing the score-card explained, forming an "unholy alliance" that had also worked "against all efforts of President Roosevelt to maintain a stable home front."[133] This alliance was dominating Congress, the CIO argued, and a "counter-offensive" was ur-gently needed.[134] Similarly, the 1944 scorecard reproduced in the *CIO News* contained just one international issue out of seven evaluated (describing the vote on US participation in the United Nations Relief and Rehabilitation plan as "a fair test of isolationism against cooperation in the war and in the peace"), while highlighting other votes such as poll tax repeal and Roosevelt's veto of the Smith-Connally Act, on which the conservative coalition would be evident.[135]

By highlighting enemies in both parties, the CIO and P.A.C. could bolster their claim to "nonpartisanship" despite their overt support for the Democratic standard-bearer. As a July 1944 *CIO News* editorial declared, the CIO was not "becoming a tail to the Democratic Party's kite," since it opposed "the polltax anti-New Dealers"—that is, Southern Democrats—"with vigor."[136] Indeed, Hillman denied that P.A.C. had any desire to "capture" a party, as some in the press had charged, claiming instead that it hoped "to influence the thinking, the program, and the choice of candidates of *both parties*."[137] He even affirmed that P.A.C. would support both Democratic *and* Republican congressional candidates where their records were deemed favorable.[138] Yet ultimately P.A.C. gave its support lopsidedly to liberal Democrats, emphasizing the pos-itive record of northern Democrats in its scorecards and thereby encouraging endorsements and the provision of tangible campaign support to them. Among the congressional candidates endorsed by subnational affiliates for the general election, Republican senatorial hopeful Wayne Morse of Oregon was a lonely, if prominent, exception. As Hillman admitted in a press conference just before the election, P.A.C. had backed "only a few" GOP candidates, "since the Republicans don't have such a good record that we could endorse very many of them."[139]

By such an account, P.A.C.'s lopsided support for Democrats was merely in-cidental, a byproduct of the way lawmakers' views lined up, since there were simply more liberals on the Democratic side. Though the outcome might appear partisan, this line of reasoning suggested, the intent was not, since support had been determined based on a lawmaker's record, not his or her party label. Yet as previously noted, the scorecards portraying those records were far from neutral instruments, with votes carefully selected to emphasize the positive qualities of northern Democrats and to offer broadly negative characterizations of the Republican Party as a whole. And behind closed doors, P.A.C. was more explicit about its partisan intentions.

Cowan, Brophy, and Walsh, in their memo establishing the basic framework for P.A.C., explicitly recommended "that work be carried on largely within the Democratic Party." "Labor cannot continue with its old-time non-partisan attitude of rewarding individual friends and punishing individual enemies," they wrote, "for the fundamental policies of the major parties are too dissimilar."[140] Rewarding individual liberal Republicans, they seemed to say, might no longer be helpful to labor's larger aims. Their claim of stark differences in the "fundamental policies of the major parties," moreover, might suggest a clear and decisive extant party division that was prompting the CIO to pick a side. Yet the CIO's parallel concern with the "unholy alliance" of Southern Democrats and conservative Republicans belies such a characterization of the party system at that time. Rather, the authors' subsequent comments are more suggestive of a nascent division emerging around a polarizing president, which the CIO could help to publicize and promote. "We should not pretend that there is the slightest possibility of our achieving genuine influence in the Republican Party. Our influence in the Democratic Party, on the other hand, is already large and can be increased greatly if the proper methods are followed."[141] The Republican Party was a lost cause, in essence, while the Democratic Party offered a tantalizing prospect: a party in which sympathy to labor and liberalism more broadly was already growing; a party with a leader in the White House projecting a powerful liberal vision; a party that might, with P.A.C.'s assistance, be remade to better align with that vision, to become *more* liberal.

The "proper methods" would require active involvement in Democratic primary contests, Cowan and colleagues emphasized. The 1942 general election experience had suggested that "labor's choice was all too frequently confined to equally unsatisfactory candidates in the two major parties."[142] "These considerations, taken together," they concluded, "mean that labor should be thinking at this time of an independent political league" which would direct its attention mainly to the primaries of the Democratic Party.[143] Thus primary campaigns *against* Southern Democrats were in accord with this overarching partisan purpose, as by supporting liberal Democrats and opposing conservative ones in both primary and general election campaigns, P.A.C. hoped to reshape the Democratic Party in a more cohesively liberal direction. It set out, therefore, not to create a majority of liberal lawmakers in Congress per se, but to ensure a liberal majority within the Democratic Party.[144] Such a transformation, Cowan and colleagues believed, would ensure labor's influence within party circles and promote their policy aims.

Of course, "[a] certain flexibility of policy as regards methods of achieving political influence" would also be "desirable," they acknowledged; in states where the Republican Party was dominant, for example, or where there was a chance to aid "individual progressive Republicans" or defeat "reactionaries," circumstances might counsel pragmatism. There might even be "occasional independent and third party candidates who should have support."[145] But support would *not* flow automatically to such candidates on the basis of their issue positions alone. Rather, other "long-range considerations" would come into play.[146] In the bigger picture, those considerations would be partisan ones, as reasoning offered in the UDA/*New Republic*'s 1942 scorecard helps to illustrate. If Republicans ever regained congressional majorities, then individual liberal Republicans could help to bring about conservative outcomes with which they substantively disagreed, since they would vote to uphold GOP procedural control. "Even the best Republican candidates will carry this stigma upon them," the *New Republic* explained.[147] The lesson was clear: electing a *good* Republican could pave the way for a *bad* party.

In sum, even if there were fewer liberal Republicans to whom P.A.C. could offer support in the first place, the overall thrust of this approach was to ensure there were fewer still, with P.A.C. energy and activism poured into liberalizing the Democratic side. P.A.C.'s approach, first outlined in the Brophy memo, thus represented a firmer commitment to the dynamic partisanship with which the LNPL had experimented but ultimately abandoned in 1940. It suggested a stronger embrace of the existing two-party system and a new understanding of how it might be changed from within rather than transformed from without through the entry of a third party. As CIO leaders repeatedly affirmed, P.A.C. was not a stalking horse for a coming third-party effort. "It is definitely *not* the policy of the CIO to organize a third party," Philip Murray had announced in 1943, but rather "to abstain from and discourage any move in that direction." A third party "would only serve to divide labor and progressive forces," Murray warned, "resulting in the election of political enemies."[148] P.A.C. and NCPAC director Sidney Hillman would echo these claims in his appearance before the Anderson Committee in 1944, even as he served as chairman of a third party in New York State, the American Labor Party (ALP).[149] In fact, Hillman himself had once hoped for an independent labor party at the national level, but his views appear to have changed.[150]

As he explained it, the ALP was less of a third party than it initially appeared. Formed with CIO support in 1936 as effectively the New York branch of the LNPL, it took advantage of the fusion voting permitted in the state (which allowed candidates to appear on the ballot multiple times for different parties) and thus often backed major party candidates rather than putting forward its own. When the ALP did nominate its own candidate for governor in 1942,

Hillman had actually supported the Democratic nominee, he told the Anderson Committee.[151] He believed that the ALP and, for that matter, P.A.C., "ought to support the best man from either one of the parties," or so he publicly professed.[152] It just so happened that as far as P.A.C. was concerned, the "best man" was usually a Democrat.[153]

Indeed, whatever its rhetoric, journalists and commentators in 1944 largely treated P.A.C.'s electoral foray as partisan in orientation. For all it might try to frame its support for Roosevelt in individualistic terms, P.A.C.'s endorsement "made clear that it would function, for the present, mainly within the Democratic Party," a contemporary observer noted in the *Washington Post*.[154] CIO leaders and P.A.C. officials, moreover, played important roles at the Democratic convention at which Roosevelt was renominated and pushed hard to retain Vice President Henry Wallace—a prominent labor ally—as his running mate.[155] When it became clear that Wallace was unpalatable to a majority of convention delegates, Roosevelt tapped Missouri senator Harry Truman instead. Still, as Arthur Krock of the *New York Times* reported, he told his aides to "clear it with Sidney," referring to Sidney Hillman.[156] Whether or not Roosevelt uttered this possibly apocryphal line, it captured a sense that the CIO and P.A.C. were increasingly important players in Democratic Party politics, while registering little interest on the Republican side. Indeed, though Hillman made much of P.A.C.'s efforts to present its program before the platform-writing committees at both party conventions, it appeared to intentionally delay the GOP request so as to provoke a refusal.[157] The resulting "snub" generated media attention, but as the *Washington Post* noted, CIO officials were hardly perturbed by the Republican rebuff. "After all," one explained, "it was like asking them to hear the Democratic Party."[158] And indeed, in its organizational efforts and impact, some believed P.A.C. had outdone that party in 1944.

The Impact of P.A.C.

"The participation of labor in the political life of the Nation, while not a new development, was never more pronounced than it was in the election of 1944," the Senate's campaign expenditure committee announced in its final report.[159] As the *CIO News* observed after the election, "[t]his was American labor's first big organized effort in the political field," and it had "demonstrated its effectiveness beyond all expectations."[160] The journalist Samuel Grafton appeared to concur, noting that "[t]he organization of labor on a large scale has profoundly altered the American electioneering process, perhaps forever."[161]

The full extent of P.A.C.'s influence in 1944 and beyond is difficult to assess, given the role of local organizations and limited information on the scope of national assistance. The national P.A.C. certainly spent heavily in the election, even after switching to voluntary funds. Considered together, P.A.C. and the NCPAC spent just over $1.3 million during 1944, at least as far as was reported to the Clerk of the House of Representatives.[162] P.A.C. accounted for the majority of that amount, spending just under $1 million over the course of the year, split relatively evenly between about $478,000 in trade union funds used prior to the summer and nearly $471,000 in voluntary funds after that point. Considering that the Democratic National Committee (DNC) itself spent just over $2 million, this was a sizable contribution to the overall Democratic effort—both presidential and congressional—even without taking into account subnational PAC spending.[163]

In terms of results, the congressional picture was somewhat mixed. In a few notable contests, at least, P.A.C. enjoyed a taste of revenge. Its opposition to HUAC chairman Martin Dies in his Texas Democratic primary was widely credited with prompting his withdrawal and ultimate retirement from the House.[164] Another HUAC member, Representative Joe Starnes of Alabama, was defeated in his Democratic primary by a candidate the CIO had intentionally recruited.[165] Several other legislators pointed the finger at P.A.C. to explain their electoral defeats in 1944.[166] But the national headquarters did not publish complete listings of local and state endorsements, perhaps to avoid its claims of influence being put to the test.[167] Rather, a post-election overview appeared in the *CIO News* that was geared toward showcasing victories, suggesting that local CIO groups had backed at least 112 successful congressional candidates (of whom 107 were Democrats) and noting just 18 losses (including one Republican).[168] Overall, the resulting Congress was a slight improvement on 1942 from the CIO's perspective, in terms of the strength of pro-labor Democratic forces and the defeat of some prewar "isolationists," but the conservative coalition remained strong.[169]

At the presidential level, however, the results were clearer. The national P.A.C.'s favored presidential candidate won handsomely, if not quite as resoundingly as in his three previous victories. And labor's efforts on Roosevelt's behalf as he sought an unprecedented fourth term, especially P.A.C.'s contribution, were given significant credit in the post-election analysis, particularly in comparison to the contribution of the formal Democratic Party apparatus.[170] P.A.C. was described as better organized and more effective, for example. One journalist considered "friendly" to P.A.C.'s efforts observed that its national headquarters "was more businesslike, produced more smart literature, and generally had more brains and practicability at the helm than did Democratic National headquarters."[171] But even less-than-friendly observers found themselves paying homage to P.A.C. For example, Raymond Moley, once a key member of Roosevelt's "Brains Trust" who had since turned against the New Deal, described P.A.C.'s methods as "too thorough, too intense, and too surprising for the improvised, routine methods of the traditional Republican party."[172] Roosevelt, for his part, seemed to recognize where gratitude was due, sending a personal letter of thanks to Sidney Hillman.[173]

Among its "surprising" methods, P.A.C.'s emphasis on voter mobilization was deemed especially novel by contemporary observers. As E. E. Schattschneider noted in an unpublished essay, "P.A.C. and Party Organization," "The older types of party organization were based on assumptions concerning a great public indifference to politics. . . . What was remarkable about P.A.C. and largely about the whole Roosevelt drive was the confident assumption that many millions of Americans who had never voted before really cared about the result and really wanted to see Mr. Roosevelt get reelected."[174] The small-d democratic goal of maximum participation thus coincided, in this election, with P.A.C.'s goal of returning the capital-d Democratic president to the White House and hoping his congressional Democratic allies would benefit from his coattails. "P.A.C. had the new idea of this campaign," concurred Radford Mobley in the Detroit Free Press: "P.A.C. says that not for a long time again will any political machine try to win an election on the basis of not disturbing the voters. From now on it feels that elections will be won by maximum voting."[175]

With maximum voting, however, would come the increased costs of campaigning within an ever-expanding electorate. And it would increasingly bring P.A.C. into territory traditionally occupied by the political parties alone, such as organizing volunteers in local wards and mounting get-out-the-vote operations.[176] These party-like activities brought P.A.C. into contact, and sometimes conflict, with the regular party apparatus. Though DNC chairman Robert Hannegan denied any "ill feelings," Schattschneider concluded that the relationship was "complex and not without friction," since P.A.C. had duplicated some of the regular party's activities and challenged its traditional claim to sole local authority.[177] Journalist Thomas L. Stokes concluded after the election that labor was "an ally—not always politely accepted" by the regulars. It had "earned the right to partnership in the Democratic party," he remarked, but would likely "have to struggle for recognition."[178]

This talk of "partnership" or "alliance," however uneasy, points to the partisan orientation P.A.C. demonstrated in 1944, but also to a sense of greater depth or endurance than a fleeting campaign fling. P.A.C. was designed from the outset to be a permanent organization that would not, as many campaign committees did, disappear after the election. Instead, it would "carry on our educational work," as Hillman told the Anderson Committee, shifting to issue-based publicity campaigns and indirect lobbying as sustaining activities while also maintaining a focus on off-year state and local elections as well as future federal contests.[179] Indeed, when the CIO convention voted in November 1944 to continue P.A.C., it did so with instructions "to intensify its program of political education, and to prepare the ground work for extensive participation in the local, State, and congressional elections of 1946."[180] The NCPAC too, which had initially been envisaged as a temporary campaign committee, would also see its life extended.[181]

But the elation of 1944 would turn to disappointment in 1946. The war was now over, and the president on whom the CIO had staked so much was dead. Like many liberals, CIO and P.A.C. leaders were wary of his successor, Harry Truman, whose border South roots and background in Missouri machine politics led them to question his New Deal credentials. But in this midterm contest there would be no Democratic president atop the ticket in any case, no coattails on which to ride, however uncertain their direction. The CIO and P.A.C. would have to promote their vision of a liberal Democratic Party without its presidential proponent, and in a rapidly changing political context at home and abroad. On the one hand, the storm clouds of the Cold War were fueling greater concern with Communism in the United States and blurring the distinction between liberal and radical Left in the public mind. On the other, a massive increase in strikes following the end of the war sparked a public backlash against labor unions and entities associated with them. The resulting conservative wave saw Republicans retake unified control of Congress for the first time in sixteen years, while Southern Democrats enjoyed greater electoral security than their liberal counterparts, reinforcing the conservative coalition.[182]

P.A.C. had certainly tried to prevent the liberal bloodshed. The national arm spent nearly $400,000 in 1946 (partly on its ongoing overhead as a permanent organization).[183] Again it refrained from making direct contributions to candidates, but it continued to utilize treasury funds up until early September, its officials arguing, as they had in 1944, that union money could be utilized during the primaries for any other purpose they chose.[184] Accordingly, it tried to unseat southern conservatives in at least ten Democratic House primaries, as well as one "anti-labor" Democrat and two Republicans elsewhere.[185] As Kroll informed the 1946 House campaign expenditure committee, chaired by Representative J. Percy Priest (D-TN), local affiliates had "called upon" the national P.A.C. for "assistance of manpower and advice" in several southern states, including Alabama, Georgia, North Carolina, Texas, and Virginia, where only the Democratic primary mattered.[186] (It was more even-handed on the Senate side, at least, reporting involvement in two GOP and three Democratic primary contests in August 1946, for example.)[187] Yet despite some encouraging primary results, the general elections did not go P.A.C.'s way. As Truman noted, in some cases association with P.A.C. itself counted against candidates, with endorsements viewed as a "kiss of death" when "unaccompanied by effective mobilization of the vote on election day."[188]

As the *New Republic* summed up the discouraging results from a liberal perspective, "We Were Licked!" Where P.A.C. had received praise in 1944, the editorial deemed its efforts "poor" this time around. Still, the editorial rated the Democratic organization "much worse."[189] The problem, in all respects, was a lack of preparation, which must be resolved through ongoing ground-level efforts, not just a permanent national organization. "Political action is year-round-every-year work," the editorial chided. "The slogan that 'Elections Are Won Between Campaigns' is obviously one that belongs in every PAC primer."[190] It belonged elsewhere too, for the *New Republic* observed that other "independent political action organizations" had been active in 1946, even describing a "political action movement"—suggesting a growing coalition of actors modeling themselves after P.A.C. and working toward similar aims, including NCPAC and PACs created by several individual unions.[191] Indeed, the Priest Committee sent questionnaires to a variety of groups and tried to compile information on them, noting similar patterns of structure and technique.[192] For all its deficiencies in 1946, P.A.C. offered an attractive organizational blueprint that permitted electoral participation without forming a third party, and even existing third parties took note. Thus in 1944 the Communist Party of the United States (CPUSA) temporarily dissolved and reconstituted itself as the Communist Political Association, an independent "political committee" supporting Franklin Roosevelt for president, in line with the P.A.C. example.[193] The CPUSA's experiment would prove to be short-lived. But P.A.C. would soon be joined by a more enduring ally, one that had previously opposed overt "political action" and much that the CIO stood for. For when the newly elected 80th Congress demonstrated the legislative costs of electoral failure, the American Federation of Labor would join the fray.

Taft-Hartley and the AFL

The AFL had kept its distance from P.A.C. since its first outing in 1944, concerned that its endorsement of Roosevelt and the partisan thrust of its activities violated the AFL's now "traditional" nonpartisan policy.[194] But the new 86th Congress took steps that strained and ultimately broke the AFL's commitment to that policy. Many returning and newly elected lawmakers had faced explicit or implicit opposition from P.A.C. or its subnational affiliates in their campaigns, and emboldened by their newfound majority status, Republicans and their Southern Democratic allies were in no mood to forgive and forget. The Labor Management Relations Act of 1947—more commonly known by the names of its Republican sponsors, Senator Robert Taft of Ohio and Representative Fred Hartley of New Jersey—was their legislative revenge.

Passed over the veto of President Truman, the Taft-Hartley Act looked to weaken unions in a number of respects, both organizationally and politically.[195] In organizational terms, it struck at the heart of the labor movement: union security agreements (contracts with management that built in certain union prerogatives). The act outlawed the most "secure" of such agreements—the "closed shop"—in which union membership was a condition of employment. And though Taft-Hartley permitted the "union shop," in which new employees were required to join the union within a set time frame, it did so only where state law allowed, thus making state "right-to-work" laws banning the union shop a possibility. It also made changes to the "check-off," the practice of automatically deducting union dues from a payroll, which was viewed as another important pillar of union security. Now workers would have to sign cards explicitly authorizing the union to deduct their dues. In addition, Taft-Hartley placed limitations on expanded forms of union protest by outlawing secondary boycotts, *common situs* picketing, and jurisdictional strikes.

But the Taft-Hartley Act also contained provisions affecting union political activity. The Smith-Connally Act's prohibition on union political contributions in federal elections had been a temporary war measure, set to expire six months after the cessation of hostilities.[196] Taft-Hartley now made that provision permanent, while also extending the ban to primary as well as general elections.[197] More important, it extended the prohibition to union *expenditures* too, in an effort to undermine the legal rationale upon which P.A.C. and some individual unions had continued to spend treasury money in the electoral arena, particularly in primaries or prior to party presidential nominating conventions.[198]

Hartley's House version of the bill had actually wanted to go further and outlaw any union-connected political activity whatsoever, including PAC activity funded by voluntary donations, since such organizations still received and used some treasury money from unions.[199] But Taft's more restrained Senate version prevailed in conference on this issue, simply adding the word "expenditures" to the existing contribution ban.[200] Taft's measure was intended to curtail the use of treasury funds while conceding that voluntary funds were likely protected on free speech grounds. Taft even offered a legal endorsement of PACs, in terms of the voluntary account concept, on the Senate floor: "If the labor people should desire to set up a political organization and obtain direct contributions for it, there would be nothing unlawful in that," he noted.[201]

Nonetheless, the CIO's leaders and lawyers cried foul, characterizing the measure as a broad attack on free speech. It was one thing to limit a union's ability to make campaign contributions to candidates or parties, they said, but quite another to limit how much it could *spend* on their behalf or, by extension, *say* about them. For in a large territorial nation, to communicate one's views involved some expenditure of money—whether for advertising, travel and logistics, or the costs of producing leaflets and posters.[202] The CIO, for example, published its own newspaper, the *CIO News*, which featured editorials on partic- ular candidates and campaign issues during election season, much as other com- mercial newspapers did. To proscribe such expenditures, they argued, would violate the First Amendment, much as Attorney General Biddle had indicated in 1944.[203] And they took heart from a Massachusetts Supreme Court decision in *Bowe v. Secretary of Commonwealth* (1946), which had struck down a sim- ilar state prohibition on independent expenditures, proposed by referendum, as unconstitutional.[204]

The CIO soon had opportunity to voice its concerns in court, when the gov- ernment brought suit over a *CIO News* editorial urging support for a congres- sional candidate. When that case reached the Supreme Court, however, the justices avoided the thorny constitutional issues and instead offered a statutory construction, focused on considerations of audience. In *United States v. Congress of Industrial Organizations* (1948), the Court ruled that editorials appearing in union publications were *internal* communications aimed at members, so even if they advocated for particular candidates, Congress had not intended to proscribe such expenditures.[205] The Court chose not to rule on whether similar commu- nications aimed at an *external* audience would be covered by the ban, though a subsequent case indicated its view. In *United States v. United Auto Workers* (1957), the Court discerned a congressional intent to proscribe *commercial* broadcasts—such as the television advertisements the UAW had sponsored in Michigan in this case (ads that advocated particular candidates, and for which the union had utilized treasury funds).[206] But in this case, the Court did not de- finitively rule on the merits, leaving the constitutional status of the expenditure ban unresolved. Thus intended audience would remain the most important cri- terion in campaign finance cases through the 1970s.

Despite the lack of constitutional ruling, unions took steps after the *CIO News* case to avoid potential litigation by monitoring their external communi- cations more closely. With the prominent exception of the UAW in Michigan, unions and labor PACs generally sought to avoid explicit candidate advocacy in their public communications, if paid for with treasury funds.[207] But that did not mean they avoided *all* kinds of advocacy or proffered no opinions. Here "political education" could save the day. Interest groups had long made "edu- cational" claims as a way to enhance their status and justify their activities, tap- ping into the cultural power of the concept. Some, like the Anti-Saloon League, had even used such claims to try and bypass the disclosure requirements of earlier corrupt practices legislation.[208] But amid significant changes to the reg- ulatory environment for interest groups in the late 1940s, political education would take on a specific meaning that helped avoid the proscriptions imposed by new laws.

In addition to Taft-Hartley, there was the Federal Regulation of Lobbying Act to consider, after all, passed in 1946 following a massive upswing in lobbying as Congress debated significant postwar legislation. This explosion of importuning and influence-seeking on a range of bills, from veterans' housing to national health insurance, price controls, and public power, finally persuaded lawmakers to pass a comprehensive measure intended to constrain "lobbies," something that had first been mooted three decades before.[209] The Federal Regulation of Lobbying Act required individuals and organizations that undertook lobbying activities to register with congressional officials and disclose some of their financial activities. But its narrow focus on a traditional conception of lobbying meant that loopholes were evident from the outset. Most prominently, it failed to effectively regulate *indirect* lobbying via issue-based publicity campaigns and grassroots appeals to a lawmaker's constituents (a 1954 Supreme Court ruling would affirm that the statute only applied to direct lobbying).[210] To the extent political education involved advocacy of particular issues or policies, it was indirect, and therefore groups engaging in it could avoid the registration and disclosure requirements of the law.

Political education was more geared to shaping the electoral environment, however, than pushing specific bills—highlighting certain policy issues so as to aid lawmakers who took favorable stances on them, from the group's perspective, without *explicitly* urging passage or defeat of particular measures or the election or defeat of particular candidates. "Where two candidates are identified with quite sharply differentiated policies, propaganda that on its face is wholly concerned with the issues may contribute significantly to the success of the aspirant whose position on the issues is similar to the propagandist's," David Truman acknowledged in 1951, citing P.A.C. propaganda as an example.[211] Not only did this type of communication offer implicit support to certain candidates, but it also provided a means of evading the Taft-Hartley Act's prohibition on union electoral spending. By avoiding explicit advocacy of candidates, unions and their PACs could argue that these were "educational" broadcasts or publications rather than electioneering communications and could thus be paid for with treasury funds.[212]

Though such propaganda had the disadvantage of being less clear and direct, Truman noted other advantages to the groups that produced it. From a legal perspective, he emphasized tax law rather than campaign finance regulations per se, since many nonprofit groups enjoyed tax benefits premised on their supposedly "non-political" status.[213] But it also had normative and strategic value, Truman said, "for only by maintaining a 'nonpartisan, nonpolitical' façade can the group avoid threats to its internal cohesion and minimize the effects of the *low prestige* of openly one-sided appeals among undecided voters."[214] Thus in Truman's view, the appearance of outright "politicking" was still sufficiently controversial that interest groups took pains to deny it—even as the "façade" might be wearing thin. In the late 1940s, then, "political education" still had a more wholesome ring to it than "political action." And this stature perhaps helps to explain the choice of name for a new political vehicle created in 1948, when the Taft-Hartley Act inspired the American Federation of Labor to finally and fully "enter politics."

The passage of Taft-Hartley had drawn a line in the sand for the AFL. Its restrictions on union security agreements posed a direct threat to the labor movement that even the AFL could not ignore, and its prohibition on practices like *common situs* picketing outraged the building trades unions, which were particularly powerful within the AFL. Though it had previously criticized the CIO's political activities and the formation of P.A.C., these direct threats would now induce the AFL to abandon its traditional political policy for good.[215]

Frustration with that policy had been growing for some time. The CIO's more assertive political stance had seen it thrive organizationally in the late 1930s and early 1940s. By 1937, its affiliated membership had grown to be larger than that of the AFL.[216] But the AFL, still marked by its ill-fated past involvement in electoral affairs and being predisposed to appreciate incremental gains, such as those enjoyed during Roosevelt's time in office, had been reluctant to change. Taft-Hartley altered that calculation, with the AFL choosing to form its own counterpart to P.A.C. The AFL's response to what might be considered the CIO P.A.C.'s failure in 1946, then—P.A.C.'s inability to prevent the election of hostile congressmen, resulting in Taft-Hartley's passage—was more political action. Yet reflecting some continued unease with electoral involvement and a concern for "optics," as modern political professionals might label it, the AFL called its new PAC Labor's League for Political Education (LLPE), not *political action*. Nomenclature aside, the LLPE prepared to wade actively and assertively into the 1948 elections, with Taft-Hartley serving as the "acid test" for its congressional support.[217] The year 1948 would thus see the maturing of a liberal "political action movement" that P.A.C. had initiated five years before, and would reveal in far starker terms its partisan aims.

P.A.C. and Partisanship

In 1954 an internal CIO memo characterized the "history of labor political action" as alternating "spasmodically" between two different strategies, neither of which had proven particularly successful for the labor movement. "Either they plunged with fervor into the building of a separate labor or 'third' party," the memo noted, "or else they religiously refrained from participation in the political processes and sought to exert their influence only in specific instances and on specific issues."[218] The approach had been third-party politics or no "politics" at all, avoiding the rough and tumble of the electoral arena and seeking to "plead the justice of their cause" by lobbying legislators directly.[219] But neither approach had delivered. As much as third parties had spectacularly failed, pleading offered little more hope of success, as a last-minute CIO effort to avert the Smith-Connally Act graphically illustrated.[220] P.A.C. and its vision of permanent political action represented a third way, not a third party.

With P.A.C. and the NCPAC, the CIO had created a new type of political organization and placed interest group electoral activity on a nationalized and permanent basis, thus dramatically expanding the scale of such activity and altering its strategic orientation. In their public rhetoric, P.A.C. officials sought to downplay the novelty of its organizational model and the methods it pioneered. "Labor has always been in politics," one early champion of P.A.C. proclaimed, a claim that seemingly ignored the early history of the movement and reframed labor political action as a story of continuity rather than change.[221] P.A.C. directors repeatedly claimed their organization was "nonpartisan" as another means of denying change, while also seeking the normative and reputational benefits of that label. Yet P.A.C. *was* new in its approach and orientation. True, it had built upon the LNPL's experiments, but it had come closer to a sustained vision of dynamic partisanship in which Democratic Party change took center stage, and it had accordingly moved away from the punitive dynamic that had still to some extent animated the LNPL's efforts. Its legal theories and accounting methods, as well as the growth of CIO unions themselves, permitted a consistent stream of resources it could use to influence every stage of the electoral process: to cultivate and encourage candidates to run, to shape public opinion in their favor, to wage primary and general election campaigns on their behalf, and to deliver voters to the polls. For P.A.C., political action was not about threatening to punish lawmakers as a means of improving their future votes but about installing supportive lawmakers in the first place: representatives and senators who would be *precommitted* to the CIO's liberal aims and who, in theory at least, would never need to be persuaded on any legislative measure.[222]

For a combination of reasons—personalistic, in terms of loyalty to a charismatic Democratic president; contextual, in perceiving a larger liberal base to work with on the Democratic side; procedural, in that a party majority conveys structural benefits in the legislative process; and efficient, in aiming to maximize the impact of limited resources—the CIO, through P.A.C., chose to pursue such aims within the Democratic Party. Where the key to influence in the old punitive model was the *votes* an interest group controlled, or at least the *threat* that they could deploy an electoral bloc, P.A.C. sought to make its resources into a new currency of influence: the money and manpower that it could bring to campaigns and help a candidate to win. To be sure, votes would still be important, but in the threat model a group had to be willing to deliver its votes elsewhere. P.A.C. was not willing to do that, as the Brophy report had made clear, since CIO did not view the GOP as a credible alternative. It therefore needed a different approach to building influence within a party it would not abandon at the polls.

Indeed, the strength of that commitment was becoming clearer as the 1940s progressed. In 1946 the National Association of Manufacturers (NAM) sent two staffers undercover to attend an NCPAC "campaign school," to better understand the new methods of "political action" that P.A.C. and its allies had developed. The NCPAC instructors declared their work "nonpartisan," one reported, but "it seemed obvious . . . that they realize their program can only be affected through political agitation within the Democratic party."[223] Despite "repeated warnings or hints that a Republican victory this fall appeared likely" the other attendee noted, "they didn't seem interested in the possible strategy of jumping the fence and working inside the Republican party to get the 'right' candidates, whom they would then have a chance of electing."[224] If you want to build a majority in your favor, these NAM observers seemed to say, why not try to persuade *everyone*?

In 1944 the assistant chairman of P.A.C. (and also the NCPAC) had claimed it would do just that. "We are not in favor of a third party," C. B. Baldwin said. "We want liberals and progressives to do all they can to liberalize the two parties."[225] But by 1946, P.A.C. director Kroll hinted that while it "hope[d] to influence the decisions of both political parties," it would also "be ready to follow whatever course of action the future may find proper."[226] Behind the scenes in 1948, P.A.C.'s new assistant director, Tilford Dudley, declared explicitly just what that course might be. In an internal memo following the Democratic convention, he stressed P.A.C.'s "hope of liberalizing the Democratic Party and making it the instrument of the so-called common people of the country."[227]

There were risks involved in such a project, of course, not least that the CIO would become a "captured" group, as modern interest group scholars would characterize it, in which case the favored party would feel confident of the CIO's support without conceding much in policy terms.[228] But to the extent that concern had yet been anticipated, the emphasis on precommitted candidates could theoretically offset the risk. With its dynamic partisan strategy, P.A.C. sought to reshape the Democratic Party's composition through primary and general election activity, with the aim of finding and electing candidates who would be precommitted to the CIO's legislative goals. A party so composed would have internalized those goals and would pursue them automatically, effectively building in CIO influence from the outset. In the language of representation, such lawmakers would act like *delegates* for the CIO while believing themselves to be *trustees*. Thus liberalization itself would replace bipartisan electoral threat as the method of ensuring the CIO's ongoing influence, in theory at least.

This strategy of dynamic partisanship, developed in the 1940s by P.A.C. and subsequently adopted by some of its labor and liberal allies, was in essence a realignment project. It sought to reward Democratic friends and defeat Democratic enemies, or in some cases, to shift them into the Republican column and thereby reshape the Democratic Party in a more liberal direction, thereby realigning the axis of party conflict from within. Though never fully articulated as such, at heart this was a different vision of realignment than that which had been commonly understood little more than a decade before, which required the entry of a new party around which the system would reset.

That the CIO had fully abandoned any lingering desire for an "independent" party and instead committed itself to realigning the existing parties through "independent" political action was evident from its stance in the presidential race in 1948. It was not simply that the CIO Executive Committee, acting on the advice of P.A.C., once again endorsed a Democratic candidate for president, in this case Harry Truman. It was that in doing so they refused to support the independent presidential candidacy of a longtime "friend" to labor, former vice president Henry Wallace. That their reasons for doing so were both pragmatic and distinctly partisan, as explored in the next chapter, suggests the full realization of a new strategy.

A Labor-Liberal Constellation

When CIO president Phillip Murray had announced the formation of P.A.C. at the CIO convention in 1943, he had emphasized both the "magnitude of the work before us" and a goal toward which they should strive: "nominating and electing a candidate such as Vice-President Henry A. Wallace for the Presidency in 1944, and electing a Congress disposed to support him."[1] A progressive Republican whom Roosevelt had tapped as his secretary of agriculture in 1933, Wallace was an ardent New Dealer who had switched his party registration by 1938 and was made the Democratic nominee for vice president in 1940. When it became clear that Franklin Roosevelt would top the ticket again in 1944, however, Wallace's place was far from assured, having feuded with cabinet members and rankled the Democratic Party establishment. Yet P.A.C.'s national leaders fought hard at the convention to retain him. Even as they acquiesced in the eventual nomination of Harry Truman as vice president, P.A.C. officials did not abandon Wallace.

Instead, they proved instrumental in engineering his confirmation as commerce secretary, a position Wallace would hold until 1946, when his increasingly vocal criticism of US policy toward the Soviet Union led Truman, who by that point had become president, to demand his resignation.[2] Freed from the political strictures of a cabinet position, Wallace would transform his critique of the emerging Cold War into a full-fledged assault and a clarion call for a third party in 1948. "Progressives can no longer work within the traditional parties," Wallace declared, since both parties were still "harnessed to the car of monopoly" and attentive to big business interests.[3] "The decisive mistake of the New Deal," Wallace argued, "was its failure to recognize that it had to break through the limitations of the old parties to forge a new party of the people if its program was to be developed and carried forward."[4] By that rationale, the CIO's decision to work primarily within the Democratic Party, to seek to liberalize it via P.A.C., was equally a mistake. Indeed, as Brophy, Cowan, and Walsh had acknowledged in 1942, if "the control of reactionary interests over the Democratic Party is too strong to be broken" then a third party might be the only reasonable alternative.[5] But the CIO and P.A.C.'s leaders chose not to follow Wallace

The Rise of Political Action Committees. Emily J. Charnock, Oxford University Press (2020). © Oxford University Press.
DOI: 10.1093/oso/9780190075514.001.0001

into what they might once have regarded as the political promised land, as he sought to revive the Progressive Party. Rather, their continued support for the Democratic presidential nominee, and Democratic candidates more generally in 1948, demonstrates the strength of their partisan commitment, if still envisaged in dynamic terms. And that model of dynamic partisanship, premised on sustained electoral activity, was increasingly adopted by other organized actors on the center left of the political spectrum, with P.A.C. becoming a central node in a nascent party network.

P.A.C. might once have left open the narrow possibility of third-party action, but 1948 showed that the calculus had now permanently changed. International developments played a significant role in this assessment, particularly the crumbling relationship between the United States and the Soviet Union in the wake of World War II. As Moscow consolidated control in Eastern Europe, President Truman had adopted an increasingly hardline stance that divided liberal opinion, as Wallace's burgeoning critique had revealed. But as growing public hostility to the USSR translated into a full-fledged "Red Scare," liberal organizations were fearful of being tagged with a "Communist" label if they criticized Truman's policy. Wallace's presidential campaign itself would be dogged by charges that he harbored Communist sympathies, or, at the very least, that his supporters did. The re-formed Communist Party of the USA (CPUSA), after all, had declared its support for Wallace as soon as he announced his candidacy, instructing members and sympathizers, including some CIO-affiliated union leaders, to do the same.[6]

The resulting reputational concerns drove the CIO's leadership to take a more definitive stance against Wallace, despite their sympathy to some of his policy goals and initial reluctance to embrace Truman. Behind closed doors, a group of high-level CIO officials formulated new stances on foreign policy and political action that offered stronger support to Truman's approach, on the one hand, and on the other defined the organization's commitment to nonpartisanship "so as to exclude third party politics," as Zieger summarizes.[7] Despite opposition from pro-Soviet union leaders, the CIO Executive Committee formally adopted these new resolutions, which effectively forbade any member unions from endorsing or aiding Wallace's campaign. Ultimately the CIO's leaders would expel the Communist-leaning unions that supported him in the 1948 presidential contest.[8] (They also dissolved uncooperative state and local PACs that refused to abandon their commitment to Wallace.)[9] Pragmatism, it seemed, was winning out over pure principle in the determination of the CIO's political support.[10]

"We do not agree with the argument that a third-party Presidential campaign would mean a larger vote and a greater possibility of electing progressive Senators and Congressmen," the new political resolution declared.[11] Wallace's candidacy would simply sow "confusion and division," Phillip Murray claimed in a radio address a few months later.[12] Instead, CIO leaders were "convinced that the CIO's best hope for advancing its agenda lay within the Democratic Party, although not necessarily with support for Truman's 1948 bid for reelection," Zieger explains.[13] They had even approved a plan to draft Dwight D. Eisenhower to run as the Democratic standard-bearer—back when no one was entirely sure which way his partisan proclivities lay.[14] And many liberals from outside the labor movement had also been feeling torn between their anti-Communism and their concerns about Truman as a guardian of Franklin Roosevelt's legacy.[15] The Americans for Democratic Action (ADA), for example, was founded in early 1947 by liberal activists worried about both. Personal and partisan loyalties had been so intermingled in the figure of FDR that his successor was bound to face challenges. But these hesitant actors would ultimately fall into line, as Truman made overtures to the Left by creating the President's Committee on Civil Rights and vetoing the Taft-Hartley Act, though he was soon overridden.[16]

Events at the Democratic convention in July would also serve to reinforce the CIO's party orientation. And here the newly formed ADA played a role. It successfully pushed for a platform plank on civil rights, prompting segregationist senator Strom Thurmond of South Carolina to bolt the convention, with many Southern Democrat delegates leaving with him. They soon formed the States' Rights or "Dixiecrat" party and nominated Thurmond for president. Another third-party threat risked further dividing the Democratic vote, opening the door to a Republican president and a strengthened GOP grip on Congress. With Taft-Hartley solidifying the antilabor reputation of the Republican Party for many union members, the need to shore up Truman's support—and his coattails— took on additional importance for the CIO. At the same time, the Dixiecrat bolt raised the tantalizing prospect that Southern Democrats might abandon the party of Jefferson and Jackson for good, leaving behind a much purer liberal vehicle to be built upon.

Thus in August 1948, following Truman's nomination, the CIO executive board reaffirmed its stance against "the so-called Progressive Party" and voted to endorse President Truman.[17] Nonetheless, they still framed the CIO and P.A.C.'s broader political posture in 1948 as "independent and non-partisan," promising to give "support to the progressive forces in both major parties . . . basing its judgment of candidates solely on their records and their stand on the important issues of the campaign."[18] Their use of "independent" showed the organizational meaning that a term once identified with third-party politics had come to have. Their claim to nonpartisanship, meanwhile, was now little more than a coded reference to the CIO's implicit Democratic orientation, according to Zieger, and to its efforts to promote a liberal agenda within that party, which it considered "the only plausible arena" for doing so.[19]

Not all of its labor and liberal allies joined with P.A.C. outright. The ADA did publicly endorse Truman, but the AFL, still new to the arena of direct political action and more constrained by its traditional philosophy (not to mention its earlier history of failed presidential endorsements), chose not to endorse at all.[20] Neither the AFL Executive Committee nor Labor's League for Political Education (LLPE) would officially back Truman, though a number of AFL leaders formed a separate Committee of Labor Executives to offer their personal support.[21] Ironically, a liberal electoral group that the CIO had helped to foster actually became the organizational basis for Wallace's campaign. The Progressive Citizens of America (PCA) had been formed, in part, out of the old National Citizens Political Action Committee, which had remained active after the 1944 campaign. In the wake of what liberals viewed as disastrous 1946 midterms, however, the NCPAC determined to pool resources with other liberal organizations in an effort to unify, concentrate, and improve their electoral efforts for 1948, banding together as the PCA.[22] (The new name itself suggested the toll conservative criticism had taken in 1946, since the organizers had hoped to retain "political action" somewhere in the title, but members from the West and Midwest protested, citing "prejudice" in their communities against the term.)[23]

Reflecting its parentage, the NCPAC's chairman, Frank Kingdon, was named as cochairman of the new organization at the PCA's founding convention in New York, while CIO president Phillip Murray was chosen as a vice chairman.[24] Henry Wallace had even addressed the meeting, urging PCA activists at that point to focus on making the Democratic Party "out and out progressive."[25] But, as the *Chicago Daily Tribune* reported, the convention did not rule out "the possibility of a new political party whose fidelity to our goals can be relied on."[26] The PCA would ultimately pursue that latter path, morphing into the pseudo-party structure that nominated Wallace. Yet the PCA, tied to Wallace's campaign, eventually sank with it. The Progressive Party candidate pulled in less than 2.5 percent of the popular vote in November and won nothing in the electoral college.[27] Dixiecrat Strom Thurmond did little better, polling similarly in the popular vote, though his geographically concentrated support secured four states in the Deep South and thus thirty-nine electoral votes.

In Congress, moreover, the Democrats recaptured control of both chambers, with a large influx of northern Democrats, including many P.A.C.-backed candidates. Placing the vote on Taft-Hartley at the forefront of its congressional campaign, P.A.C. affiliates had endorsed 239 House candidates and 21 Senate candidates in the general election and claimed success rates of 71 percent and 81 percent, respectively. By the P.A.C. Research Department's own calculations, then, its successful candidates comprised 35 percent of the newly elected 81st Congress. And that P.A.C.-supported bloc showed a strong partisan leaning, with 94 percent of the successful candidates being Democrats.[28] (A greater emphasis on Democratic primary contests was also apparent, with local affiliates backing at least 105 candidates in Democratic contests, compared to 14 in Republican primaries.)[29] Yet the celebrations were somewhat diminished by the return of Southern Democrats who had supported the Dixiecrat ticket, who would gain influential committee positions due to their seniority. (Demonstrating the weakness of party disciplinary mechanisms, few punitive measures were taken against these former Dixiecrats.)[30]

Nonetheless, the overall results of the 1948 election would serve to vindicate the CIO and P.A.C.'s position and to close off any lingering third-party dreams among labor leaders. United Automobile Workers (UAW) president Walter Reuther, for example, had expected Republican nominee Thomas Dewey to win, whereupon he was ready to launch a drive for a new labor party. Instead, Truman's surprise victory scrapped those plans and put Reuther on a path that would see him become a staunch advocate of the Democratic Party and its broader electoral success.[31] Like many of his colleagues, however, Reuther would not so much abandon the goal of a labor party as look for new ways to fashion it from existing material—to make the Democratic Party, in essence, into a substitute. Events in 1948 thus showed the maturing of that vision of dynamic partisan commitment and the new vision of party realignment that went alongside it.

Unlike the CIO, Wallace had been unconcerned that his candidacy might deliver the White House to a conservative Republican, believing that a reactionary administration "would sharpen the issues between conservatives and liberals and hasten the political realignment which he desires," as two contemporary commentators explained.[32] For Wallace, a true party realignment could only be achieved from without and would emanate from the top down. But for the CIO, P.A.C., and the growing constellation of labor and liberal electoral actors, it could be brought about from within, steadily, progressively, through partisan political action in Congress. Indeed, their public denials of partisanship were wearing increasingly thin, though they continued to offer some token support to liberal Republicans. In 1948 P.A.C. affiliates had backed a handful of Republican candidates, generally those who had voted to uphold Truman's veto of Taft-Hartley.[33] But they were inconsistent even there, withholding support from at least two GOP House members who had voted to uphold the veto and thus belying a purely issue-based approach.[34]

By the following year even P.A.C.'s most prominent Republican "friend"— Senator Wayne Morse of Oregon—had begun to question its support for him and to suspect partisan intentions. Morse was one of three Republican senators who had voted against Taft-Hartley in 1947 and was now facing a re-election contest in 1950. But as Foster relates, Morse felt that labor support was distinctly lacking, unleashing "a bitter barrage of criticism" in a letter to P.A.C. director Jack

Kroll late in 1949. "I think you people in the CIO are going to have to make up your minds in respect to my candidacy for reelection as to whether or not you want any liberals in the Republican Party," he wrote. Indeed, Morse was beginning to sense that "at least some of you in the CIO want liberals only in the Democratic Party," a situation that Morse felt would worsen rather than help the cause of labor.[35] Morse even attributed outcomes such as Taft-Hartley to P.A.C.'s failure to actively support key liberal Republicans, noting that it could have done far more to aid Robert La Follette Jr., for example, the influential Wisconsin senator who was defeated in 1946.[36]

In Foster's telling, the underlying question was one of partisanship versus ideology. "Did the CIO and the PAC really want a liberal Congress, or did they support Democratic candidates regardless of ideology?"[37] This formulation is slightly misleading, however, for P.A.C. did not support Democratic candidates *regardless* of their ideology, but it did elevate support for liberal Democrats over liberal Republicans, showing far less regard for ideology in the latter case. Indeed, P.A.C. had come to see a liberalized Democratic Party as the key to a liberal Congress. Liberal Republicans were at best irrelevant and at worst dangerous to that plan; as the 80th Congress had shown, they would still uphold procedural control for a Republican majority, allowing numerous conservative measures to pass despite their substantive opposition. Thus P.A.C. might encourage occasional support for them as a means of bolstering its "nonpartisan" claims in public or for local pragmatic reasons, but in the bigger picture, its national officials hoped such lawmakers would either switch party affiliation or be replaced by liberal Democrats. Morse himself seemed to get the message, becoming an independent around 1952, before joining the Democratic Party in 1955. Likewise, since defeating them had proved so difficult, P.A.C. increasingly hoped the Dixiecrats would make the opposite switch, ridding the Democratic Party of its most conservative element. This process would not, however, move as quickly or as smoothly as P.A.C. and its allies hoped.

The Perils of Partisanship

"[T]he problem of moving the Republicans into the Republican Party is still with us," P.A.C.'s assistant director Tilford Dudley would bemoan following the 1952 elections, articulating his conviction that conservative Democrats were really Republicans in disguise.[38] Numerous conservative Democrats had again been re-elected that year, and the GOP itself had enjoyed a clean sweep, gaining majority control of Congress and winning the White House for the first time in twenty years, with Dwight D. Eisenhower as the nominee. The CIO had once again backed the Democratic presidential candidate, Adlai Stevenson, and even the AFL had endorsed Stevenson in 1952, moving beyond the separate committee it had set up to offer its support to Truman in 1948.[39] Despite these setbacks, Dudley was encouraged by reports that the newly elected Eisenhower administration would distribute patronage to the Dixiecrats, thus drawing conservative Southern Democrats closer to the Republican Party and perhaps even enticing them to switch sides. "This is an important step in building the Republican Party in the South," Dudley wrote. "CIO has always favored building a two party system in the South. Ike thus helps in the realignment of parties which we seek, which might give us a Congress of better consistency when the Democrats win."[40]

But partisan politics was not without its frustrations, even when that "consistency" was starting to materialize. A perceived lack of full support from liberal party leaders and the internal influence Southern Democratic legislators continued to enjoy emerged as key concerns in late 1955 when Walter Reuther, by this point president of the CIO, asked Jack Kroll to provide a frank assessment of P.A.C's relationship with the Democratic Party. The resulting memo urged a *recommitment* to the partisan policy rather than stepping back or returning to earlier models of interest group influence, primarily that of bipartisan electoral threat.[41] Indeed, the memo provides the strongest evidence of P.A.C's very unwillingness to threaten the Democratic Party with electoral defection, which had underpinned the old "friends and enemies" model.

Asking Dudley to prepare an initial draft, Kroll highlighted some of the problems.[42] "You know the money we spent and the efforts put forth and the results we get in successful elections," Kroll wrote. "The cooperation we get from the Party is not commensurate with these things." Dudley's draft should mention "some of the outstanding rebuffs we have received on the Hill," consider who should present these "grievances" and to whom, and evaluate "what is it that we should ask to be done?"[43] Accordingly, Dudley's draft systematically examined the various components that made up "the party" as conceived at that time—including the convention, the national committee, and the congressional delegation—and sought to untangle where the major problems lay. The CIO's problem was not, he assessed, with the convention delegates or the "leading Democrats" in that body.[44] Nor was it with the Democratic National Committee (DNC), at least in terms of outlook. "Its publications are right down our line," Dudley wrote. "Its emphasis is the same as ours. Its officers make our kind of speeches; listen to our advice; are anxious to get along with us," and would "generally do what we ask them to do, as long as it does not get them in trouble elsewhere." But the DNC still lacked significant power in the decentralized party system, even though it had become a more permanent and active entity. "Our real problem," Dudley thus concluded, "is with the Congress." "Here we are not dealing with the Democratic Party as a whole," in which "the liberals and the friends of labor" were dominant, he asserted, "but only with those who get elected. That is a significant difference."[45]

The key question therefore, was how to make the congressional delegation more reflective of the party "as a whole." "How can we tighten up the Democratic Party?" Dudley asked. "How can we make it into an organization? How can we refine its ingredients so as to make then purer liberals? How can we improve its discipline or sense of responsibility so that wandering congressmen can be tied to the party line?"[46] These blunt questions revealed how far P.A.C.'s outlook really was from the tired claim that its partisanship was merely incidental: the notion that its lopsided support for Democratic candidates merely stemmed from a greater profusion of liberals on that side. Indeed, Dudley admitted that the election of liberal Republicans rather than Democrats actually hurt P.A.C.'s objectives, since it made the composition of the Democratic congressional delegation even less reflective of the broader party, as Dudley assessed it.[47]

Given that the problem was largely a congressional one, Dudley's solutions were also focused on that body. He presented an array of suggestions "for making the congressmen more responsible to the Party as a whole," such as biannual national conventions to adopt a party platform; enhanced use of the party caucus in Congress; abolition of seniority rules (which advantaged long-serving Southern Democrats); and a "Party Council" consisting "of important Senators, Congressmen, Governors, and leaders of the National Committee," which could provide unity and guidance on issues and policy.[48] The use of the term "responsible" here is significant, since the suggestions Dudley offered were essentially identical with those recommended five years earlier by the Committee on Political Parties of the American Political Science Association (APSA).[49] The APSA Committee, chaired by E. E. Schattschneider, had expressed concern over the lack of party discipline in the United States, which they argued impeded government accountability to citizens and precluded the kinds of coherent public policy programs they deemed necessary in the modern age. The Committee's report thus considered ways to enhance party discipline so as to make parties more "responsible" to their membership and to the voters at large.

Some members of the APSA Committee had, in fact, sought feedback on their initial drafts from individuals working in the political sphere—and Dudley was one of those solicited.[50] In addition to serving as P.A.C.'s assistant director, he was also the alternate Democratic National Committeeman for the District of Columbia, in which capacity he wrote to other DNC members and state chairmen to promote the APSA report.[51] But Dudley also sent them free copies of the report, with the tab picked up by P.A.C.[52] He even corresponded directly with Schattschneider about the report and the idea of responsible parties (Dudley was an alumnus of Wesleyan University, where Schattschneider taught for most of his career, although it does not appear that Dudley was a former student of his).[53] The APSA report, this evidence suggests, served as both a source of justification and a tool to promote the strategy of dynamic partisanship to which P.A.C. was already committed.

Indeed, the major problem with P.A.C.'s extant approach, Dudley claimed, was that it was *not partisan enough*. "So far. Labor has been inclined to stay out of the Party's internal affairs and to avoid working from within, or through official, organizational bridges," Dudley summarized. "Our inclination has been instead to bargain with the Party from the outside, as with an employer."[54] The AFL, he claimed, was even more committed to this "bargaining from a distance" approach than the CIO (a point that suggests the continued influence of its "nonpolitical" heritage and later conversion to partisan political action).[55] "The Basic Question for Labor," then, was whether to seek more formal integration into the Democratic apparatus, more like the Trades Union Congress in the British Labour Party. Remaining somewhat distant "has the advantage of saving us money and embarrassing responsibilities. But it also means that the Party thinks it has fulfilled its obligation when it presents us with candidates and platforms that come within our general concept of acceptability, or at least are significantly better than the Republicans." "If we don't participate in the day to day problems of the party, why should they bother to consult with us on such matters?" Dudley asked.[56] Without such day-to-day involvement, moreover, P.A.C.'s visibility was diminished, making "it hard for the elected office-holder or the party leader to measure our contributions and the strength of our pressures." "It is clear to us that we spend huge sums in the campaigns and turn out millions of voters," Dudley explained, "[b]ut how does he know that to be true?"[57] The task was rendered more difficult, he continued, because so much of their support was "immeasurable."[58]

In at least some cases, however, P.A.C.'s support would be tangible, since by 1952 the national committee gave financial contributions directly to candidates, a practice national P.A.C. officials had denied in congressional testimony in 1944 and 1946 but appear to have begun in 1948.[59] Though there were no comparable congressional investigations of campaign expenditures in 1948 or 1950, some relevant information for 1952 was compiled by Professor Alexander Heard as part of a subsequent investigation—discussed later in this chapter—that drew on campaign finance disclosure reports filed in accordance with the Corrupt Practices Act. Records reproduced by Heard show that P.A.C. made direct contributions to at least sixteen candidates (all Democrats) in twelve states in 1952, for a total of $31,650.[60] Meanwhile, the AFL's LLPE gave at least $14,500 to three Senate candidates (again, all Democrats), two of whom P.A.C. had also contributed to.[61] The full amounts were probably much higher. (Internal CIO documents show that for the 1954 midterms, for example, the national P.A.C. contributed $83,500 to nineteen Democratic senatorial candidates, including Democrats challenging liberal Republicans such as Clifford P. Case in New Jersey and Leverett Saltonstall in Massachusetts.)[62] In total, P.A.C. spent over $500,000 in the 1952 campaign, split between direct contributions to candidates or committees and independent spending of its own, plus over $400,000 on additional "educational" expenses, all heavily oriented to aiding liberal Democrats.[63]

Withholding this financial largesse might make the point clearer, Dudley contemplated at one point in the memo—suggesting that a form of electoral threat, even if not the threat of defection at the polls, might still be relevant. "Maybe the present policy of 'bargaining from a distance' might work better if we really tried it," he mused, raising the possibility that threatening to sit out the 1954 elections entirely might have induced the congressional Democratic leadership to strip the Southern Democratic chairmen of their power. (The emphasis was therefore still on abstention, not on taking labor support elsewhere.) "But Labor did not do that; nor did the CIO. We spoke too late and too softly," Dudley concluded. But there was still time in 1956, Dudley added. "If we really did this, and meant it, it would be a thrilling revolution in American politics," he summed up, before acknowledging, "[b]ut we won't do it."[64]

Ultimately, Dudley recognized that the CIO was unwilling to threaten the Democratic Party in any real sense, since it effectively had nowhere else to go; there was little prospect of better policies from the Republican Party, and its leaders had ruled out third-party politics. Dudley was searching for options, then, for a "captured" interest group. In the final version of the memo, Kroll even speculated about abandoning politics altogether, retreating from the electoral field entirely and returning to earlier methods of influence through collective action and lobbying alone. Yet as Foster argues, Kroll probably did not consider this a "viable alternative."[65] Indeed, these methods had failed to deliver for labor in the past, inducing labor groups to "go into politics" in the first place. There was little reason to think they would be any more effective now. Thus, as the rest of Dudley's memo makes clear, further liberalization of the Democratic Party was seen as the only solution, and to achieve it, the CIO and P.A.C. must become more deeply enmeshed in the structures and procedures of the regular party apparatus.[66]

Formal integration need not go as far as the British Labour Party model, he noted, acknowledging that P.A.C. and most unions might prefer to maintain some organizational distance.[67] (Indeed, Dudley claimed that P.A.C. had never made "direct, open financial contributions to the Party," though archival information shows that it had, in fact, given over $10,000 to the DNC between 1951 and 1954, as well as donating to affiliated presidential campaign committees.)[68] But the unions did not need an official position in order to infiltrate the party apparatus more fully, Dudley explained. A benefit of the decentralized American party structure, for all its lack of party discipline, was its permeability. It was possible to gain representation in party bodies informally if labor union members were elected to serve on them, a path the CIO could do more to encourage. "We sometimes tend to support such activity by recommending 'participation in the party of your choice,'" Dudley observed "but our recommendations have been so mild, unwritten, secretive and half-hearted that they have been ineffective."[69] A more assertive effort could increase this source of internal strength, while also having the advantage of not appearing so official or visible, reducing liability in terms of labor's association with party actions.[70]

In several ways, P.A.C. would work behind the scenes to bolster Democratic "responsibility." In the wake of the 1948 Dixiecrat bolt, for example, it lent support to a push from some party officials for a "loyalty oath" at the next convention, which would commit delegates to listing the convention's nominees under the regular party label in their state.[71] In the mid-1950s, moreover, it sought to increase circulation of the Democratic Digest, a new national committee publication that portrayed a distinctly liberal vision of the party. "Being an organ of the National Committee," Dudley later noted, "it represents the Committee and the Convention—which are on *our side.* By pushing its circulation widely, we could push what is in effect *our concept of the Democratic Party*."[72] Indeed, P.A.C. was increasingly utilizing other national committee publications for its own work, particularly those of the research division, which the party had now heavily invested in. The DNC had begun to compile its own voting records, for example, in this respect taking a leaf from P.A.C.'s playbook. P.A.C. accordingly adopted these records as its own, with research director Mary Goddard instructing her staff not to duplicate what the DNC was already doing but merely to adapt and expand the information to address labor-specific concerns.[73]

But if the CIO expressed concern about its relationship with the Democratic Party late in 1954, its once-frosty relationship with the AFL, at least, was improving. In 1955 the two union federations would merge, ending two decades of hostility and conflict within the labor movement. The timing of Dudley's memo, in fact, suggests it was written in preparation for this merger, since the united AFL-CIO would combine its separate political action groups into one.[74] If anything, the combined group presented the possibility of enhanced party influence, offering a way to pool resources, talent, and experience into an electoral powerhouse that could be a dominant player in the burgeoning Democratic coalition. But it would also create an enlarged target for conservative critics of labor and its growing role in the political process, whose attacks became increasingly strident in the 1950s.

Coping with the Merger

A number of factors converged in the early 1950s to encourage the AFL and CIO merger, including politics. The election of Eisenhower as president in 1952 had put both federations on the defensive, since his incoming administration was "considered unfriendly by most labor unions," according to Zeigler.[75] The CIO, for its part, had never dealt with a Republican president, and in endorsing Stevenson appeared to reject any preference it might once have had for Eisenhower. Riding Eisenhower's coattails, Republicans had also recaptured control of both chambers of Congress. Fearing further legislation hostile to labor organizations, stronger AFL and CIO cooperation seemed imperative, since disunity had been partly blamed for the passage of Taft-Hartley and subsequent failures to repeal it. At the same time, past barriers to cooperation were diminishing.

The CIO's more radical leanings had diminished with the expulsion of Communist-dominated unions in 1950 (those that had supported Wallace's 1948 candidacy) and an internal "purge" of the national organization, bringing it closer philosophically to the AFL.[76] The creation of the LLPE and the AFL's embrace of a more assertive political posture also reduced practical political barriers to coordination with the CIO, as Hower points out.[77] And the AFL's longtime hostility to industrial unionism was itself abating. By the early 1950s it had permitted some craft unions to reformulate along industrial lines and even begun to charter new industry-wide unions.[78] This move, in fact, threatened to undermine the CIO altogether, which had lost its earlier advantage and was by the mid-1950s roughly half the size of the AFL.[79] Finally, a more cooperative attitude was stimulated by a change in leadership, with the election of George Meany as AFL president following the death of William Green in 1952, and the elevation of Walter Reuther at the CIO following Philip Murray's death the same year. With new occupants in the top offices less scarred by the original split than their predecessors had been, new possibilities were opening up for the AFL and CIO.[80] Indeed, some CIO union leaders had backed Reuther's bid for the presidency on the condition that he push for a merger, fearing its dissolution otherwise.[81] The stage was thus set, and after lengthy negotiations—and seventeen years apart—the AFL and CIO reunited in 1955.

From the perspective of political action, the merger would have concrete and immediate implications. The newly formed AFL-CIO moved to establish a unified political action committee to replace the operations of P.A.C. and the LLPE, making the 1954 congressional contests their last as separate entities. In 1955 they were merged into the Committee on Political Education (COPE) and prepared for the 1956 presidential and congressional elections as one. Soon enough this new political entity would find itself in the congressional spotlight, though for reasons outside of its control. A scandal had erupted early in the year when Senator Francis Case (R-SD) claimed he had been offered a large campaign contribution from an oil company in exchange for supporting an energy bill then under consideration in Congress.[82] This was exactly the kind of quid pro quo that had long animated concern about the corrupting potential of campaign contributions.[83] The incident would inform the work of two Senate investigations, the first an examination of 1956 campaign expenditures conducted by Senator Albert Gore (D-TN), under the auspices of his Privileges and Elections Subcommittee (part of the larger Senate Rules and Administration Committee), and the second a special investigation chaired by Arkansas Democrat John McClellan. The latter would be the first formally charged with examining campaigning and lobbying together. The Case scandal, after all, involved a contribution being deployed as a tool of lobbying.[84]

For his investigation, Gore recruited academic specialists to serve as consultants, including political scientists Alexander Heard and Herbert Alexander.[85] Heard and Alexander would go on to form the Citizen's Research Foundation, a nonprofit organization dedicated to compiling, analyzing, and publicizing what limited campaign finance information was then available and urging stronger legislation to record and regulate it.[86] In highlighting concerns about the influence of large individual donors in American politics, moreover, the Gore Committee helped to forge a coalition of liberal reformers who would push forward such changes, as Zelizer describes, eventually yielding the major campaign finance reforms of the 1970s.[87] But the committee's hearings and research also shed light on the role of electorally oriented organizations in campaigns, not just individual donors, including COPE and its predecessors.

COPE spent nearly $700,000 in the 1956 campaign, with a further $180,000 coming out of the old P.A.C. and LLPE accounts, presumably to empty them.[88] Intriguingly, this figure was slightly less than P.A.C. and the LLPE's combined spending in 1954, despite the presidential contest, suggesting that pooled resources did not necessarily translate into doubled spending. Nonetheless, the variation may reflect their stronger concern in the midterms with winning back control from the Republicans (the Democrats would ultimately secure majorities in both chambers), or COPE personnel may simply have assessed Eisenhower's chances of re-election and chosen not to invest heavily in his Democratic opponent in 1956, Adlai Stevenson once again. Indeed, the Democrats would ultimately retain control of Congress in 1956 despite Eisenhower's re-election, the first time since 1848 that a presidential candidate had won without his party securing a majority in either chamber.[89] Of course the information gathered by the Gore Committee and other sources, as shown in Table 6.1, may not actually reflect the true amount spent; campaign finance scholars regularly complained

Table 6.1 **Disbursements by AFL/CIO PACs, 1952–1958**

		1952	1953	1954	1955*	1956	1957	1958
AFL LLPE		249,258	28,737	485,082	53,969	148,080	No data	—
CIO P.A.C.	Individual Contributions Account	505,722	29,747	415,042	18,038	23,220	No data	—
	Educational Account	433,259	321,455	339,992	108,940*	8134		—
COPE		—	—	—	—	670,985	No data	709,813
Total		**$1,188,239**	**$379,939**	**$1,240,116**	**$180,947**	**$850,419**	No data	**$709,813**

*January 1 to May 31, 1955.

Sources: Data for 1953 and 1955 from "Labor Union Political Expenditures," Staff of the Senate Republican Policy Committee, November 1955, NAM Records, accession no. 1411, series V, box 62a, Hagley Library. Data for 1952, 1954, 1956, and 1958 from Alexander Heard, *The Costs of Democracy* (Chapel Hill: University of North Carolina Press, 1960). See "Table 21: Continuing Labor Political Committees, National Level: Gross Receipts and Disbursements, 1952, 1954, 1956, and 1958," 180–181. After the creation of COPE, the CIO P.A.C. and LLPE still made some expenditures in 1956, reported by Heard, presumably emptying their accounts.

about the accuracy of reporting, after all. Nor does it include the amount expended by other labor political action groups, of which there were 17 operating nationally by this point, according to Zelizer, and a further 155 at the state and local levels.[90]

In other respects beyond COPE's finances, the Gore hearings shed light on its operations and orientation, showing how it reconciled some of the differing practices of its predecessors, for example. Originally, the directors of both P.A.C. and the LLPE were appointed as joint codirectors of COPE, and they worked out new practices for the combined organization. On endorsements, for example, COPE adopted the CIO's decentralized structure, in which local and congressional district PACs made endorsements for all offices but the presidency. As COPE codirector James L. McDevitt explained, recommendations for subnational offices were the responsibility of state and local organizations and voters, who "would and properly do resent any attempt to have an outside judgment imposed upon them."[91] His comments suggest continuing popular sensitivity to "outside" intervention in elections, with McDevitt carefully framing COPE's activities so as not to inflame such concerns. McDevitt made similar rhetorical maneuvers to defend other aspects of COPE's activities. COPE did not have "any purge list either public or secret," he told the committee, another nod to popular concerns.[92] And he proclaimed once more, as P.A.C. and LLPE officials had previously asserted, that COPE was "nonpartisan" in word and deed—still trying to tap into the rhetorical and normative power of that term, even as COPE's actions and internal dialogue suggested otherwise.[93] McDevitt even assured the committee that COPE supported candidates of both parties, though he did not provide a full list of endorsements with which the claim could be assessed.[94] From a financial standpoint, *Congressional Quarterly* revealed in November that "[v]irtually all national labor campaign funds so far reported in 1956 benefited Democrats."[95] Indeed, given the readiness with which former P.A.C. officials had admitted their Democratic commitments behind closed doors, it is perhaps unsurprising that COPE's publicly nonpartisan posture was deemed "nothing but a lot of hog wash" by Indiana's commissioner of labor, for one. "It is time people began to realize that the organized labor movement of America is fast becoming an arm of the Democrat Party," he said in 1956.[96]

COPE officials had at least anticipated such an attack. "It will be charged that COPE has either taken over the Democratic party or is about to take over the Democratic party, nationally and locally," an internal memo discussing preparations for the coming campaign noted, though it offered no specific denial or evidence to rebut this charge. Indeed, COPE officials expected to be "subjected to a more concentrated and bitter attack by some elements in the 1956 campaign that have heretofore been directed at either the PAC or LLPE," the memo noted.[97] To admit publicly what they might in private, therefore, was risky. And yet on a practical level, COPE sought to advance the liberalization of the Democratic party—the push for greater "responsibility"—much as its predecessors had.

In a larger sense, that push involved standardization and nationalization, ensuring a more uniform political product nationwide. And even before it had the APSA seal of approval, P.A.C. and its allies had developed tactics to promote that aim, challenging the traditional geographic decentralization and ideological diffusion of the American party system. The scorecards such groups produced based on voting records, for example, served as a standardized framework within which every lawmaker, from any district, could be evaluated. Indeed, COPE would expand on and elaborate this practice. The LLPE had already produced more assertive scorecards than P.A.C. by marking votes "R" or "W," thus boldly proclaiming its vision of "Right" or "Wrong."[98] COPE used the same notation and now added "box scores," calculating the number of times lawmakers had voted right or wrong on issues of concern to the AFL-CIO.[99]

This seemingly minor change made voting records much easier to interpret at a glance, making them more accessible to the average member, while summarizing complex legislative records across multiple congressional sessions or even careers.[100] COPE soon produced an extensive compilation of roll-call analysis, surveying votes between 1947 and 1956 on a range of issues, from labor bills in particular to "general welfare legislation" and other aspects of both domestic and foreign policy.[101] This broad substantive scope was meant to show that the AFL-CIO had concerns beyond economic self-interest. As an essay accompanying the analysis explained: "The AFL-CIO does not judge Congressmen on selfish narrow lines but with the broad public interest in mind."[102] And that conception of the public interest fit with a larger liberal worldview. Accordingly, box scores could be used to quickly identify liberal, pro-labor lawmakers who would presumably have more right stances than wrong. They could be used to quickly characterize the parties, too. As *Congressional Quarterly* summarized, COPE's records showed that 38 of 49 Senate Democrats voted "right" most of the time, while 43 of 47 Senate Republicans voted "wrong."[103] (In the House, 168 Democrats out of 207 voted "right," and 175 of 195 Republicans voted "wrong.")[104]

These kinds of innovations, in fact, helped to transform voting records into sharper instruments of partisan change, even as they appeared ostensibly "objective." Box scores provided a shorthand way of identifying the "right" kind of Democrat—the *liberal* kind—while portraying conservative southerners as "outliers" from a desired ideal. Meanwhile, if the GOP was to be the party of conservatism, liberal Republicans could be cast as outliers too, with the implication that their kind should be eliminated, not encouraged. These trends could be propelled, moreover, through the targeted provision of campaign resources toward liberal Democrats, as identified through voting records. Research and resources, then, would become intertwined in ways that served to bolster national authority in otherwise decentralized organizations and to promote partisan change. If labor had helped to point the way, however, it would be other groups infused with a liberal purpose that made the most significant tactical innovations.

Ideology and Electioneering

Labor unions were not the only organizations to begin experimenting with political action in the 1940s. In 1946 the Priest Committee had expressed concern that "[p]olitical activities on an extensive scale are being engaged in by many organizations, most of whom are motivated by the desire to elect to Congress Members whose views and manner of voting conform to the ideologies adopted by the respective organizations."[105] Beyond economic interest groups themselves, whose viewpoints were increasingly aligned with ideological perspectives, purely "ideological" groups had also emerged on both sides of the political spectrum, groups whose memberships were not formally anchored in economic interests. In addition to their political differences, these groups would seek to impress their views upon the political scene in distinctive ways. While conservative groups pursued their aims through ideological publicity campaigns, they stopped short of providing direct financial assistance to candidates, offering endorsements, or even producing legislative "scorecards" to aid voters in making their choices. In sum, they chose a highly ideological form of political education over the most overt forms of political action. Liberal groups, in contrast, were more willing to embrace overtly electoral activities, emulating the labor PACs whose aims they largely shared. Thus, much as the CIO had formed the NCPAC to try to tap into a broader liberal sensibility, so independent liberal groups would move into that space as the NCPAC dissolved. And while they would emulate their labor allies, liberal groups would also offer their own innovations in the realm of political action, exerting an important long-term impact on the political scene.

The Americans for Democratic Action, for example, had been founded in early January 1947 by, among others, Eleanor Roosevelt and Walter Reuther, as a new vehicle for anti-Communist liberals.[106] The ADA had actually emerged out of the former Union for Democratic Action (UDA), which banded together with several similar organizations to try to strengthen their influence amid the "political crisis" of the early Cold War.[107] Like P.A.C., the ADA would oppose the Wallace presidential campaign and make liberalization of the Democratic Party its central goal.[108] And it resembled P.A.C. to some extent in means as well as ends, adopting a similar set of tactics to pursue this aim.

Testifying before the Gore Committee in 1956, the ADA's Executive Committee chairman, Robert R. Nathan, described his group as "a permanent, liberal, independent, political organization," one that was "not affiliated with any political party" and "concerned primarily with issues, with research and education on issues, and with candidates only on the basis of their stands on the issues."[109] What he described, in essence, were the operations of a political action committee, though the ADA did also engage in some direct lobbying. Nonetheless, it contributed money directly to candidates, issued endorsements, undertook voter mobilization efforts, and engaged in general "political educa-tion" as a sustaining activity between elections and as a form of independent campaigning in election contests themselves.[110] The ADA paid for the latter from a separate "nonpolitical" account which, like that of labor PACs, was kept dis-tinct from voluntary member contributions. Indeed, this nonpolitical account was largely funded by labor unions and hence could only be used for educa-tional activities or internal advocacy communications in the wake of Supreme Court decisions like *CIO News*.[111] According to Nathan, this relationship with labor unions was based on shared policy commitments, since liberal programs promoted "the well-being of the union membership."[112]

Despite its protestations of nonpartisanship, the ADA's congressional support went overwhelmingly to Democrats—over 90 percent at each election since its formation, Nathan admitted.[113] And at the presidential level, it had only ever supported Democratic candidates.[114] In 1956 the organization had endorsed Democrat Adlai Stevenson in his second bid for the presidency, even though, as Nathan acknowledged, "*both* the Republican and Democratic candidates for President have embraced liberal proposals long advocated by ADA."[115] Eisenhower's commitments had been deemed less trustworthy, Nathan con-tinued, trying to rationalize why the ADA's endorsement had gone elsewhere.[116] Much like P.A.C., the ADA grounded its public claim of nonpartisanship more in its willingness to oppose conservative Democrats than in any documented support for liberal Republicans.[117] But as noted elsewhere, this fact did not sug-gest a lack of partisan commitment so much as a dynamic variant attuned to reshaping the composition of that party.

In fact, the ADA's very formation had been intertwined with Democratic Party politics, amid concerns over Truman's leadership and the vitality of New Deal liberalism. It had played a prominent role at the 1948 Democratic convention—pushing the civil rights platform plank that would ultimately prompt the Dixiecrat "bolt"—and its members and officials served in an array of party positions, as convention delegates, local party chairs, or DNC staffers.[118] The ADA was essentially the liberal Roosevelt wing of the Democratic Party and thus more like a faction than a pressure group.[119] And yet it was also a different kind of faction, taking intraparty conflict outside the halls of Congress or the national convention and giving it new organizational form. Where earlier factional entities like the American Democratic National Committee of 1944 had been temporary campaign vehicles (in that case sputtering out even before the election), the ADA would be a permanent mass-membership group pushing a liberal vision of the Democratic Party.[120]

In the mid-1950s, moreover, the ADA would introduce a seemingly minor tactical innovation that would have a major impact in shaping that party and the political world more generally: the ADA Index score or Liberal Quotient (LQ).[121] Continuing the practice of congressional scorecards that the UDA had helped to pioneer, the ADA had tracked roll calls on issues it deemed important and published legislative scorecards in its newsletter, the *ADA World*, since the group's inception in 1947. But in the mid-1950s it began to summarize each lawmaker's record as a percentage, explaining the resulting score as an indicator of his or her liberalism. As the longest-running measure of this kind, these scores have been widely utilized in political science as a proxy for ideological liberalism and employed for a range of quantitative research purposes.[122] But these scores were not so much neutral metrics as honed political instruments, serving to transform a purportedly *educational* tool into a tool of political *action*.

The move to percentages was sufficiently controversial that the ADA rolled out the new practice slowly, providing some scores in press releases but choosing not to feature them in the newsletter for several years. This hesitation points to a range of criticisms swirling around the practice of scorekeeping that had been articulated with greater force since the 1940s, when scorecards were first widely publicized. Critics argued that scorecards, and particularly the move toward box scores and ultimately percentages, misrepresented lawmakers. Groups selected only a handful of votes according to their own purposes, leading the Republican Congressional Committee to blast COPE's 1956 voting record as a "political blackball" containing just "2% of the Record!," "Plenty of Distortion," and "Old Stuff."[123] Reaching back to votes from past Congresses was a regular point of criticism, since lawmakers had subsequently been re-elected, and thus their actions had presumably been approved by their constituents.[124] Even fellow liberals had some qualms about the reductive quality of percentage scores, especially, which could not capture the nuances and subtleties of legislative decision-making. As late as 1958, the Massachusetts chapter of the ADA warned against summary scores in its own statewide "Legislative Supplement."[125] "We trust the form of presentation will not lure the hasty reader to count +'s and −'s and rate his legislators in percentage fashion," it warned.[126]

Amid such concerns, interest groups that produced scorecards were careful to frame them in informational or educational rather than instructive terms, as a guide for voters from which they could make up their own minds, as noted in the previous chapter. But summarizing the record as a single score seemed to reduce the necessary effort on the reader's part, which had helped to support that educational claim. A single score also came closer to resembling an endorsement, veering into political territory without explicitly doing so. Indeed, ADA officials continued to claim that voting records were "educational" efforts and thus might be paid for out of their nonpolitical account.[127] Yet implicitly, a high score indicated a lawmaker of whom the ADA approved, thus encouraging its members to support that lawmaker without the ADA having to make official pronouncements. Since endorsement decisions were decentralized in the ADA's organizational structure, moreover, scorecards allowed the national headquarters to convey its own opinion directly to the membership.[128] Hence the ADA was slow and careful about promoting its innovation, only publicizing its scores in full beginning in the early 1960s.

Nonetheless, that innovation would have important effects. As Senator Carl T. Curtis of Nebraska—the sole Republican member of the Gore Committee—claimed in 1956, the ADA's voting guides were designed "pretty much to show how an individual measures up to the Democratic position."[129] By this he meant the *liberal* Democratic position, the views espoused by the national committee and other allied groups like COPE. Much like COPE's box scores, a high LQ could indicate the right kind of *Democrat* from the ADA's perspective, in both general and primary election contests, serving in the latter context as a signal that the formal party apparatus could not provide. The ADA even issued press releases characterizing Democrats in both chambers as "far more liberal" than their Republican counterparts, noting that Senate Democrats took its preferred liberal positions 72 percent of the time in 1956, compared to 30.5 percent for Senate Republicans, while House Democrats voted the ADA way 70.6 percent of the time, compared to 40.5 percent for House Republicans.[130] Scores also helped to guide practical campaign support from the national ADA, with financial and other material aid directed toward "deserving" candidates as identified by their LQs.[131] Again, such support went lopsidedly to liberal Democrats, aiming to advance their representation within the congressional party. Indeed, the ADA's preference was made particularly clear in 1957 when voting analysis revealed that the average Democratic LQ had actually *dropped* to its lowest recorded point, just 57 percent, compared to a 73 percent average in 1947, while the Republican average had reached "a liberal high" of 43 percent, compared to just 17 percent ten years before.[132] Rather than seek to promote this seemingly encouraging GOP trend, the ADA's chairman, Robert Nathan, urged the redoubling of its efforts to promote Democratic liberals.[133]

While the ADA maintained its public posture of nonpartisanship, other pronouncements betrayed some of the thinking behind its privately partisan stance. "Our aim is non-partisan," the *ADA World* had proclaimed in 1947 when introducing the first congressional scorecard, describing its mission as "to elect liberal Congressmen and Senators regardless of party affiliation." But as it quickly informed readers, "the voting record makes it fairly clear in which party such Congressmen are most likely to be found." In 1947, after all, "liberal opinion" had "failed to express itself in a politically significant way through the Republican party."[134] Rather than inspire an effort to improve liberal standing within the GOP, it was the Democratic Party, the ADA said, that could and should be improved.[135] "[T]he Democratic Party presents the most likely medium for the progressives in this country," Arthur Schlesinger Jr. had told an early ADA meeting. "[T]he surest way to make the Democratic Party a liberal party is to go into the Democratic Party," Franklin Roosevelt Jr. had added.[136] The attractions of Franklin's father had undoubtedly brought many progressives to the Democratic side, but essentially the argument was presented in terms of *efficiency*: since liberals were already more numerous in the Democratic Party, the cause could be more easily advanced in that forum. And progressive strategists were beginning to recognize another way that focusing on a single party could be more efficient.

As Thomas Amlie, formerly of both P.A.C. and the UDA, acknowledged in the early 1950s, it was no longer possible "to work through the Republican Party," as "sincere liberals" such as he himself had once hoped.[137] The continued election of liberal Republicans, moreover, "serves only to confuse the issue," he said, and could even bolster an overall *reactionary* picture in Congress in certain situations.[138] Amlie was pointing to another reason liberal groups pursued a dynamic partisan rather than truly nonpartisan strategy (in which liberal Republicans would have received similar levels of support as their Democratic counterparts). The organization of Congress was constructed around parties, with the majority gaining built-in institutional and procedural advantages such as committee chairmanships and influence over the agenda. Focusing on liberalization of the Democratic party could thus be more efficient, especially if majority status could be achieved or retained, while supporting a minority of liberals in the Republican party could be self-defeating, since they would uphold GOP procedural control that would empower their conservative colleagues, who could then advance conservative aims even without the liberals' substantive support.

Still, if the Democrats were to be the party of liberalism, the southern wing continued to prove a thorn in the side.[139] Roll-call analysis thus served a twofold purpose: to show that the GOP was a lost cause for liberals and to identify those conservatives who must be driven from the Democratic Party—whether through electoral defeat or party defection. As Amlie later wrote, it would help impress upon the public "that a Republican is someone who votes like a Republican."[140] Indeed, summary scores based on roll-call votes were developed with both members and the wider public in mind, with the device generating significant publicity by the early 1960s, when other organizations came to adopt it. The ADA's move to percentage scores, then, created a readily understandable device that served as an ideological shorthand, conveying signals in Democratic primaries and general elections and enhancing the influence of the national organization. Indeed, this type of measure helped to nationalize the contours of political debate, serving as a standardized ideological yardstick that could be applied across the country. In these respects and more, the ADA's adoption of scores would have a profound political impact.[141]

It would not be the only liberal group, moreover, to make important tactical innovations, this time in terms of campaign finance itself. The National Committee for an Effective Congress (NCEC) had emerged around the same time as the ADA and could also count Eleanor Roosevelt as a founding member. Unlike the ADA, however, which engaged in a variety of lobbying and publicity activities alongside direct political action, the NCEC focused almost exclusively on congressional races in pursuit of a Congress that would fulfill its vision of "effectiveness," and it generally avoided lobbying. That effectiveness was cast in overtly liberal terms, as was made clear when its chairman, Sidney Scheuer, appeared before the McClellan Committee hearings on lobbying and electoral activities in 1957.[142] As emerged in the testimony, the NCEC's main activity was raising and distributing money nationally to support particular candidates, particularly for US Senate seats, though Scheuer was less than transparent as to how it identified which candidates to support. While the ADA was experimenting with its liberal quotient, Scheuer expressed concern that relying on a "statistical record" could produce "a very unfortunate and unfair evaluation" of candidates, though he acknowledged that voting records were relevant to NCEC assessments.[143] In fact, at this point one particular Senate vote appeared to dominate such considerations: the censure in December 1954 of Joe McCarthy, the Wisconsin senator who had done so much to fan the flames of anti-Communism in the early 1950s. The NCEC had helped to bring the vote about, working directly with lawmakers in the only instance of "lobbying" that Scheuer would admit.[144] This had led the NCEC to offer its electoral support to at least one Republican, Senator Ralph Flanders of Vermont, who had sponsored the censure resolution.[145] But as Republican senator Barry Goldwater of Arizona inferred, those lawmakers who, like himself, had voted against the resolution—conservative Republicans and Southern Democrats in the main— would "receive the blessing of your bullets, come election time."[146]

Goldwater's assessment viewed NCEC activity through the lens of the old "friends and enemies" strategy, but this was to some extent a misunderstanding of its approach.[147] The McCarthy censure had been something of an exceptional case. The NCEC did not really set out to punish lawmakers at all nor threaten to punish them as a means of ensuring better legislative outcomes, in accordance with a traditional pressure group strategy. Rather, it tried to ensure a larger number of supportive lawmakers in Congress from the outset, through the provision of direct financial assistance to candidates sympathetic to its general aims. That was one of the reasons Scheuer denied that the NCEC engaged in lobbying: it did not use the promise of electoral support as a means of inducing favorable votes by lawmakers.[148] Indeed, it did not try to persuade them to take any particular positions. Rather, the NCEC tried to build in congressional effectiveness from the start by aiding candidates who would reliably support a liberal agenda once in office.

This approach required participation in some primary contests, mostly in the South where general election results were more or less assured.[149] In so doing, the NCEC largely reinforced labor and ADA efforts to liberalize the Democratic Party. On a national level, however, the NCEC went further than these counterparts in pooling voluntary contributions centrally and redistributing them across the country. The NCEC thus helped to pioneer new methods of national fundraising and targeted redistribution to key congressional districts, using a combination of ideological consistency, financial need, and electoral prospects to guide its decisions.[150] Yet it was this seemingly straightforward and pragmatic development that elicited the strongest critique from Goldwater, who denounced the nationalization of political action on normative and even constitutional grounds.

By distributing its financial support to certain candidates irrespective of the views of those living in the district and the choices they might have expressed in a party primary, the NCEC, in Goldwater's view, was violating cherished norms of local self-governance.[151] "[T]here is a great question in my mind of the propriety of groups operating outside of States for the election of people that they have no concern in," Goldwater said, other than seeking to forge a "liberal group" in Congress.[152] This critique showed a continued hostility to "outside" involvement in elections, particularly evident among conservatives, which had been previously directed against presidential intervention in local contests, such as Roosevelt's purge campaign of 1938, as well as against various electoral groups.[153] In 1914 the Senate's Committee on Privileges and Elections had even reported out a bill limiting how much money could be "sent from one State to another State" in federal elections, though it did not proceed further.[154] Goldwater now offered a constitutional rationale that might justify legislation, in terms of House elections at least.[155] Since Article I required that representatives be chosen "by the People of the several States" and specified residency requirements for candidates, indicating the Founders' emphasis on local ties, there were "legitimate questions" about the role of "outside organizations" that lacked such connections, he said.[156] For Goldwater, the very mechanisms by which national PACs like the NCEC operated—by aggregating contributions and then redistributing them to where they might be most helpful—was subverting the geographic integrity of the electoral process.

Though it was hardly a robust constitutional case, Scheuer acknowledged the objection as a "troublesome one."[157] But he identified a general trend toward the nationalization of politics, wherein economic emergency and war had enlarged the scope of legislators' interests beyond their local constituencies, making geographic boundaries less meaningful.[158] If local contests involved national issues, then a national organization could presumably take part. The NCEC's twofold commitment to national fundraising and targeted redistribution, in fact, rested on a reconfiguration of political connections in terms of ideology rather than geography. It sought to pinpoint "individual Americans all over the country" who shared its values, in the words of NCEC executive secretary George E. Agree, and to get "their support for individual candidates" in whom the NCEC was ideologically invested, foreshadowing the hyper-targeted campaign methods of today.[159] In this the NCEC suggested a nationalized conception of representation, too, in which citizens might look beyond their own representatives to achieve policy aims that could have nationwide effects.

Scheuer also justified the NCEC's actions by analogy, noting that the party committees aggregated money nationally and then reallocated it to candidates across the country.[160] But Goldwater, then-chairman of the National Republican Senatorial Committee, bristled at Scheuer's suggestion. "You cannot compare a national party, I hope we cannot, with the Committee for an Effective Congress or any other group that operates in that manner," Goldwater objected.[161] The national party committees were traditionally charged with the task of general fundraising and financing, he noted, and did so with transparency and according to fixed rules.[162] What Goldwater appears to have been referring to is the custom of party committees distributing funds to candidates on the basis of need, not ideological sympathies, support for the president, or any other litmus test. Groups like the NCEC, in contrast, targeted their financial support so as to promote liberalization of the Democratic Party. Nonetheless, though he rejected Scheuer's analogy, the discussion seemed to clarify for Goldwater the essence of his objection: that the NCEC and similar groups were beginning to operate more like "splinter parties," which Goldwater described as a dangerous development.[163]

Goldwater's critique of national intervention and splinter groups seemed to apply whatever their ideological orientation—a suggestion that would sit poorly with his later actions following the 1964 election, as discussed in chapter 8. But in its time and place, his perspective fit within a larger set of criticisms of political action emanating from conservative sources. Those critiques were undoubtedly shaped by the liberal leanings of its main practitioners: labor and liberal groups. Since conservative-leaning groups largely avoided explicit involvement in the electoral sphere, such "principled" criticisms could be leveled without the practical complications of opposing one's own. Yet it was in part those ideological objections that inhibited conservative groups from greater electoral involvement, as explored in the next two chapters, which consider both conservative ideological groups and business groups with an economically conservative orientation, so prominent in other political contexts such as lobbying. For their objections to political action were embedded in a larger conservative critique of labor unionism gathering steam in the late 1940s and early 1950s, one that stressed the collectivism and compulsion inherent in such organizations, inspired by a new strain of economic thought that effectively linked economic, political, and social freedoms.

Cash versus Coercion

For labor unions, political action was still framed in the terms *New Republic* journalist George Soule had identified in 1935, as a means of fulfilling "the right of the industrial citizen to have a share, through democratic procedure, in the decisions that govern his life."[164] Beginning in the 1940s, union leaders had emphasized that the very concept of PACs fulfilled this mission. With each member giving small and equal amounts, the act of contributing to campaigns was recast in civic terms, as a form of democratic participation. But as the costs of campaigns increasingly became the costs of mediated communications—as newspapers, radio, and ultimately television advertising came to the fore—the amounts needed to run a national campaign skyrocketed, for candidates, parties, and outside groups.[165] By the 1950s the parties themselves had launched publicity drives portraying campaign contributions as a civic duty and encouraging citizens to donate to "the party of your choice."[166] Yet an important element emphasized in all such schemes was their voluntary nature. Citizens should give money so as to uphold a healthy two-party democracy. Union members should donate to P.A.C. out of a sense of solidarity. But it should be their *choice* to do so. And it was regarding this issue that conservatives launched an increasingly successful attack on labor PACs at midcentury, questioning how "voluntary" the contributions made by union members really were and how wide the scope for member dissent could be when union treasury funds were involved.

In 1944, for example, two Republican members of the Green Committee— the Senate's investigation of campaign expenditures that year—expressed concern about the rights of union members who did not support the candidates P.A.C. was aiding.[167] At that time, their worry only applied to "union funds"— that is, money derived from member dues that might be used for publicity activities in support of a candidate. Where union members *chose* to give money, these senators argued, they must accept the risk of its being used to support candidates they might not personally prefer.[168] By the 1950s conservative critics were increasingly pushing this idea that union members' rights were being violated by the use of dues money for political purposes they might not agree with. As Senator Curtis put it during the Gore Committee hearings: "In other words, you got money paid in by people that had to pay it to hold their jobs, and they may not believe that any of the things you stand for are good for America."[169] Together with Senator Goldwater, Curtis launched an attack in the mid-1950s on the "violation of political freedoms" they perceived in union organizations.[170]

But such critics now added a further argument to their attack, challenging the notion that PAC contributions could ever be truly voluntary. Most members felt obliged to contribute, they argued, or had little say in the matter. The "checkoff" was a point of particular contention: an important feature of union security often negotiated into contracts, whereby employers would agree to automatically deduct union dues from a worker's paycheck, ensuring a reliable stream of income to the union.[171] Often, union leaders simply added on a political contribution, leaving the worker with no effective choice in the matter. Ultimately, the problem was *coercion*, whether "voluntary" contributions given under duress or union dues themselves, which conservatives regarded as coerced payments in all but "right-to-work" states, where job security was not predicated on union membership.

The benefit of this "coercion" argument was that it was difficult to level against business groups or other nonlabor interests. As Curtis pointed out, if businessmen disagreed with the National Association of Manufacturers' agenda, they could simply refuse to pay their dues, but without a majority uprising among the membership, union members had to accept the use of their dues for whatever purpose their leaders chose, at risk of losing their jobs.[172] This was a form of compulsion that, opponents argued ever more vociferously, went against the "American Way." Individual workers were made into "political prisoners," Curtis claimed.[173] "How it can be defended under our American system is just beyond me."[174] For their part, union leaders and liberal activists defended their actions in terms of internal union democracy, pointing out that if their political stances were sufficiently unrepresentative of the membership, the current leaders could be voted out at the next union election.[175] Yet in the late 1950s the internal workings of unions were coming under congressional scrutiny too, as two Senate investigations exposed the seedier side of union life.

The most famous was the Senate's Select Committee on Improper Activities in Labor or Management Field, informally known as the "Rackets Committee," formed in 1957 and chaired by Senator John L. McClellan, a prominent opponent of organized labor. The committee's televised hearings would generate huge publicity, with staff counsel Robert F. Kennedy famously dressing down Teamsters president Jimmy Hoffa and introducing the viewing public to a world of apparent union corruption and links to organized crime. John F. Kennedy and Barry Goldwater were also members of this committee, which severely damaged the reputation of organized labor at large.[176] But concerns about how unions were being run had first emerged the previous year in McClellan's investigation into lobbying and campaigning, which had raised serious questions about the health of union democracy in relation to political action.[177]

The impact of this first McClellan committee, coming on the heels of the 1956 Gore investigation, was to turn union leaders into strident opponents of campaign finance reform. Where they had once pushed for legal changes that might lessen restrictions on their activities—repeal of the expenditure ban in Taft-Hartley, for example—they now sought to protect the PACs and legal workarounds they had formulated. "[U]nion leaders perceived campaign finance reform as a tool for conservatives to emasculate their political power," Zelizer explains, fearing that new laws would regulate PACs and reduce their electoral influence.[178] Unions escaped such changes in the 1950s and 1960s, at least, but other legislation considered damaging to unions would become law in 1959, largely as a response to the second McClellan committee's findings. The Labor Management Reporting and Disclosure Act or Landrum-Griffin Act was intended to shore up democratic procedures within unions, requiring secret ballots in elections (subject to federal review) and more transparent financial accounting. But the act also owed something to the first McClellan committee in its move to protect the rights of individual union members, partly through secret ballots but also through a "bill of rights" that explicitly guaranteed members' freedom of speech. These guarantees would subsequently be used to garner refunds for union members of the portion of their dues used for politically oriented purposes.

Assessing Liberal-Labor Political Action

"We in America are undergoing a profound political revolution," P.A.C. director Jack Kroll told the ADA's convention in 1952, foretelling an array of important political developments that would characterize the twentieth century and situating P.A.C. at their heart:[179]

> It is a re-shifting of alignments, a re-orientation by our political parties, a groping by large groups of people for a clearly-charted course of action. How long it will take to reach its climax I do not know. Nor do I profess to know what form that climax will take. I do say that it is underway and that its effects will be felt in the elections this year. As far as I am concerned, I welcome the development. I think CIO-PAC, in

giving labor political expression, had something to do with it. I think
we will play a role in future developments . . . a role that will depend to
a large degree upon how well we carry on our work of political organization. And I think in doing that we are making a contribution to the
political life of America. We are making a contribution to the practical
functioning of our democracy.[180]

The political realm was dramatically transformed by labor political action.
Other labor groups emulated the P.A.C. model, such as the LLPE in 1947 and
ultimately the AFL-CIO Committee on Political Education, active from 1956
onward, along with various PACs established by international unions and
subnational affiliates. The formation of key liberal groups such as the ADA in
1947 and the NCEC in 1948 also suggests the importance of the P.A.C. model.
Yet political action, it seemed, had not secured the policy aims for which it was
intended. Despite massive expenditures of money and manpower throughout
the 1940s and 1950s, restrictive labor legislation like the Taft-Hartley Act, along
with the failure to repeal it, plus the Landrum-Griffin Act of 1959 are usually
cited as evidence of labor's lack of political success.[181]

The Landrum-Griffin Act of 1959 passed despite a major Democratic success
at the polls in 1958 and an influx of liberal members, seemingly confirming the
concern Jack Kroll had expressed in 1954, that labor might not gain all it desired
from its relationship with the Democratic Party. As a result of the 1958 election
there were optimistic assessments that "a clear majority in both chambers would
be 'pro-labor.' "[182] But electoral action in this case appeared insufficient. The conservative coalition could still close ranks both to frustrate or foster legislation,
as they did with Landrum-Griffin. And many apparent liberals had gone along,
demonstrating the fallibility of installing apparent allies from the get-go. Their
initial willingness to pursue the issue of union racketeering was perhaps attrib-
utable to the prominence of the Teamsters in the investigation, which had a reputation as a Republican-leaning union.[183] But the popular and legislative fallout
affected *all* unions, and such liberals may have felt constrained by public opinion
to support the bill. Even John Kennedy ultimately voted for it, though his role as
a moderating force in the conference committee helped him to secure AFL-CIO
support for his successful presidential candidacy in 1960. Yet the experience had
suggested that even with a Democrat back in the White House, favorable legislation was by no means guaranteed.[184] In such circumstances, labor organizations
continued to pursue other strategies of influence.

Thus partisan electioneering did not entirely supplant direct legislative
lobbying, for example, or traditional collective action. In fact, it was through
the latter route that labor made some of its most important gains during this
period—the UAW's famous 1950 contract with General Motors, the "Treaty of

Detroit," being a prominent example.[185] And yet labor organizations persisted in their electoral efforts, rather than retreat from the field, even as the theory of dynamic partisanship, on which their electoral strategy rested, failed to produce the results they had envisaged. Their story of increasing electoral investment without apparent policy reward, whether the repeal of Taft-Hartley or the defeat of Landrum-Griffin, points to an important dynamic of political action: its insatiable quality, a tendency to believe that the answer to a failed electoral effort is always to do *more* next time. But there were other important dynamics in play, relating to both competition and context, producing changes in the wider political realm that in some ways trapped labor into that strategy. And ironically, it was labor's own innovations that helped to bring that about.

By the mid-1950s the diffusion of political action had begun to spread to labor's competitors as much as its liberal admirers. The Americans for Constitutional Action, for example, was formed in 1958 as a self-proclaimed conservative counterweight to the ADA, and it was soon joined by other similar ideological groups. By the late 1950s, moreover, labor political action had also sparked a dramatic reaction within the business community, which would come to exemplify Clemens's warning that a group's enemies might turn successful organizational innovations against their originators, and do so more effectively.

When Business Is Not "Businesslike"

"The forces outside Labor have no counterpart to Labor's League and the P.A.C.," a US Chamber of Commerce brochure warned in 1949.[1] "Business men and their friends" were thus "compelled to decide whether they should remain quiescent in the face of these events or devise their own program of affirmative action."[2] To speak of "business men," of course, was to use a "dangerous" label, as Truman observed, since it presumed a unity of profession and purpose that may not always exist.[3] But the two national organizations most prominently associated with business interests appeared to recognize a common cause in the response they now devised. The US Chamber and the National Association of Manufacturers (NAM) were certainly not content to "remain quiescent," if they ever had been. But the "program of affirmative action" they developed was not a program of political *action*—at least not at first. The Chamber and the NAM, in fact, had spent much of the 1940s and early 1950s attacking the very idea of political action as practiced by labor and liberal groups. They had instead, joined by a growing number of conservative "friends," met political action with political education alone.

Through much of the immediate postwar period, they devoted their energies to waging the "free enterprise campaign," a publicity program infused with conservative ideology, which would educate Americans in the economic, social, and political benefits of capitalism. It linked business-friendly politics to a broader vision of individualism and freedom, a vision with purportedly universalist appeal.[4] Yet even without campaign contributions, endorsements, and voter mobilization activities, this ostensibly "educational" campaign was not unconcerned with electoral affairs. Rather, it involved an extension of the sophisticated publicity techniques developed by lobbyists and pressure groups since the 1920s, with the goal of influencing the broader political context in ways that might aid particular candidates or pieces of legislation, but without expressly advocating for them, thereby avoiding "the harsh glare of electoral politics," as Phillips-Fein puts it.[5] The free enterprise campaign was thus a long-term effort to ensure the status of business within American society and political culture, to cultivate a

The Rise of Political Action Committees. Emily J. Charnock, Oxford University Press (2020). © Oxford University Press.
DOI: 10.1093/oso/9780190075514.001.0001

context in which legislators sympathetic to business could be elected, and to sustain that positive environment given the rocky experiences of the 1930s. Combined with traditional lobbying, this publicity-based approach would be dominant among business interests for the next two decades.

That business groups and their allies launched such a publicity campaign does not, however, explain why they avoided direct political action in the period when labor and liberal electoral groups were first mobilizing. Traditional interest group theory might point to resources or organizational structure as considerations here; business groups lacked mass memberships but typically enjoyed significant financial resources. Without a large pool of potential volunteers or voters among their members, therefore, they might be naturally oriented toward publicity activities rather than ground-level electoral activities. Their officers, moreover, typically possessed their own substantial monetary resources and might thus make large campaign contributions as individuals. Since business groups were usually incorporated and thus prohibited from making contributions or expenditures "in connection with" federal elections, this offered an alternative means of engaging financially in campaigns without the need to create PACs (one that labor unions, in theory, did not enjoy). Yet corporations and business groups *did* ultimately create PACs, despite the consistency of these features, rendering them insufficient as explanations.

This trend became more noticeable in the mid- to late 1960s, and especially in the 1970s, from which point scholars have documented an enormous growth in corporate political action.[6] But the foundations were laid in the 1950s. As that decade drew to a close, business groups changed course and began to embrace political action, amid criticism that "business" was not taking a truly "businesslike" approach to meeting the perceived threat of labor and liberal political action. To some extent, legal uncertainty conditioned their initial reluctance, which court decisions had gradually clarified. But far more important was a combination of status, experience, ideology, culture, and electoral competition in shaping the "business viewpoint" toward political action over time, counseling against it in the 1940s and early 1950s, as discussed in this chapter, and moving toward it beyond that point, as discussed in the next.

The Reputation of Business

By the mid-1930s the "business civilization" of the 1920s lay in ruin. Businessmen and bankers were the objects of popular scorn, and the nation's premier business organizations—the NAM and the US Chamber of Commerce—found their position as "insiders" in the halls of political power attenuated. While the Chamber and the NAM had initially leant their support to the National Industrial Recovery Act (NIRA), they had become increasingly hostile toward it, and to New Deal measures more generally, as Franklin Roosevelt's first presidential term wore on. This kind of hostility emanating from the business community, Weed argues, informed the oppositional stance adopted by the Republican Party in the run-up to the 1936 election, one that went against the traditional expectation that political parties would moderate in response to defeat.[7] Yet Weed sees Wendell Willkie's candidacy in 1940 as evidence of a more moderate GOP stance, which he in turn attributes to a softening of business opposition—a change, he suggests, that had much to do with the coming of Keynesianism.

First published in early 1936, John Maynard Keynes's *General Theory of Employment, Interest, and Money* offered a new theoretical framework through which to understand government's role in the economy and a new language with which to discuss and justify it—assets that Roosevelt was quick to take advantage of. But Keynes's argument for increased government spending during economic downturns "was not incompatible with the interests of private corporations," Weed suggests.[8] Thus it also served to take the edge off business hostility to the New Deal, he argues, promoting an "intellectual transformation" within the business community that aided a Republican return to the center.[9] In this account, growing business receptivity to Keynesianism "would eventually lead to both the acceptance of government macroeconomic management and the emergence of the modern welfare state after the conclusion of the Second World War"—promoting what Arthur Schlesinger Jr. would dub the "vital center" and setting the stage for President Dwight D. Eisenhower's moderate "modern Republicanism."[10]

Yet beneath the apparent consensus in postwar politics lay much more antagonistic ideological currents, within the business community as much as beyond. Certainly some elements were becoming more reliably supportive of New Deal measures and of an enhanced role for the federal government at large. Ferguson, for example, has argued that business leaders identified with particular industrial sectors, such as banking, the tobacco industry, and even oil interests—sectors that were less sensitive to changes in labor law and welcomed greater international engagement—became important financial backers of the Democratic Party during the 1930s.[11] But at the same time, other parts of the business community were becoming intractably opposed to Roosevelt's liberal initiatives, not least among the labor-intensive, domestic-focused industries that form Ferguson's comparison group. So too were the major "spokesmen for business"—the US Chamber and, especially, the NAM. As Cleveland calculated, the NAM opposed thirty-one of the thirty-eight major laws passed between 1933 and 1941, more than 80 percent of the initiatives associated with the various "New Deals."[12] Thus Zeigler concludes that "[w]ith the coming of the New

Deal there was a manifestation of the shift of business goals from a position of dominance to one of a militant opposition."[13]

Indeed, historical scholarship, such as that of Fones-Wolf and Phillips-Fein, has challenged Schlesinger's vision of postwar consensus in the political realm altogether, pointing to pockets of resistance to the New Deal among "business conservatives"—opposition that bubbled under the surface during the 1950s, exploded into the open with Barry Goldwater's 1964 presidential campaign, and eventually fueled the conservative resurgence of the 1970s and beyond.[14] The NAM, and to some extent the US Chamber, might thus be viewed as incubators of this oppositional stream—a stance they soon found had organizational benefits. The booming economy and largely sympathetic political environment of the 1920s, in fact, had made for complacency among their existing and prospective members.[15] The Chamber's membership, steadily rising since its founding in 1912, had plateaued in the early 1920s, while the NAM's began to plummet.[16] As Zeigler concludes, "the 'normalcy' of the 1920's was, in fact, nearly disastrous for the NAM."[17] In this light, hostility to the New Deal would reinvigorate their organizations, arresting their membership decline and providing a new sense of purpose.[18] In fact, when opponents of the New Deal achieved a stunning legislative reversal with the Taft-Hartley Act in 1947, the NAM's membership actually declined once again.[19] The perpetuation of political conflict, it seemed—stressing constant vigilance against the possibility of external threats—was becoming essential to organizational maintenance.[20]

Opposing the New Deal, in fact, would animate an array of new ideological groups forged purely for that purpose, beyond those like the Chamber and the NAM that had formal ties to economic interests. For if the labor movement found itself part of a growing network of organizations sympathetic to liberal causes and the Democratic president, it did not want for opponents. Yet these emerging conservative groups seemed to take lessons from the failures of the Liberty League—from the reputational dangers of appearing to shill for the economically advantaged and the electoral dangers of outright involvement in a campaign, even when framed as "nonpartisan opposition" to a presidential candidate. Thus where liberal groups plunged deeper into political action and developed new techniques that further embedded them in the electoral scene, conservative groups largely kept within the hazy boundaries of "political education": claiming to educate voters about specific issues or broader political themes without explicitly *advocating* for specific bills or individual candidates, while still intending to shape the broader legislative and especially electoral context. In this manner, publicity would be extended from a grassroots lobbying technique to a form of indirect electoral activity.

The substance of the message promoted, however, would change in important ways over time. Conservative groups would initially seek to broaden the appeal of "Liberty League Liberty," which journalist George Soule had identified largely with property rights and constitutional traditionalism, by framing it in avowedly patriotic terms, seeking to tap into popular sentiment as Europe, and eventually the United States, hurtled toward war. But in the aftermath of that conflict, business groups in particular would draw upon new philosophical impulses, shaped by wartime encounters with totalitarian regimes, to place their economic goals within a broader philosophical framework embracing individual and political liberties too, offering a positive message with wider popular appeal, premised upon an all-encompassing concept of "freedom."

The "Patriotic Action Committees"

If the anti–New Deal groups of the 1930s had emphasized their commitment to "the Constitution," the international crises and conflict of the early 1940s would see their successors frame that commitment in terms of patriotism. The Committee for Constitutional Government (CCG) was one such group, a new entity forged from the embers of Frank Gannett's National Committee to Uphold Constitutional Government (NCUCG), which had folded in April 1941. A similar group also came to prominence at this time, the Constitutional Educational League (CEL), which described itself as one of the first "patriotic" and antisubversive groups.[21] Indeed, the patriotism these groups proclaimed was often expressed through opposition to whatever they deemed *unpatriotic*, manifesting variously as strident anti-Communism, fervent isolationism, or outright anti-Semitism.[22] And they pursued these fixations in the public sphere, though both stopped short of direct involvement in elections and in that sense sought to deny their work was "political."

Thus when Gannett appeared before the House campaign expenditures investigation in September 1944, chaired by Representative Clinton Anderson (D-NM), he proceeded to describe the CCG as a purely educational and nonpartisan organization formed "to support and protect our Constitution."[23] In the service of that aim it had distributed "more than 80,000,000 pieces of literature" across the country, seeking to educate the public "on constitutional principles and the fundamentals of our system of free, competitive enterprise."[24] Such activity, Gannett argued, was not partisan and thus not "political" as far as the Corrupt Practices Act was concerned. (The Internal Revenue Service had seemed to disagree, at least when it came to the CCG's predecessor, revoking the NCUCG's tax-exempt status and contributing to its demise.)[25] There was a significant difference between "partisan politics" and "politics in general," Gannett insisted, defining the latter as "working for the good of government" and placing the CCG's activities firmly in that camp.[26] On this basis, he denied that the

CCG was a "political committee" of any sort, quite different from the Congress of Industrial Organization's (CIO's) P.A.C. It did not endorse candidates, offer them financial aid, or wage independent campaigns on their behalf, but simply promoted its perspective on "the good of government," drawing on its substantial funds (in the region of "several hundred thousand dollars this year") raised from individuals who willingly contributed.[27] In contrast, Gannett emphasized, P.A.C. still utilized dues money irrespective of CIO members' political opinions. "It is sort of a coercive movement to raise a vast sum to be used frankly for the election of President Roosevelt," Gannett remarked. "That I should say, is politics."[28]

A CEL pamphlet described the organization in similar terms, as being "just what its name implies—an educational organization with a patriotic objective: the preservation of constitutional government. The league is not a political movement. It takes no part in partisan politics. It considers the fight for Americanism above politics."[29] The CEL thus described itself as a "patriotic action committee" that would give the American people "the facts" and thereby ensure the nation's safety.[30] It made no candidate endorsements, exhibited no party preference, and had a membership "composed of both Democrats and Republicans in every walk of life," CEL's executive vice chairman Joseph Kamp told the Anderson Committee, to which he had also been called to testify.[31] Kamp was himself a registered Democrat, he noted.[32] The CEL's activities had been "strictly *nonpartisan*," he emphasized, "and by nonpartisan I mean *for America*."[33] Patriotism and nonpartisanship were one and the same.

For Kamp, nonpartisanship was still compatible with outright opposition to the Communist Party, however, and the "kindred subversive groups which it dominates."[34] The CPUSA was simply *not* a political party in his view, since it forfeited that legal status by advocating un-American objectives.[35] Since this argument conveniently encompassed any group linked to the CPUSA—whether in actual fact or merely by reputation—opposing them was equally nonpartisan and patriotic. Thus did Kamp excoriate the trifecta of "Sidney Hillman, the C.I.O., and the Communist Party."[36] These forces may have managed to "take over" his Democratic party, he said, but the CEL was determined to prevent their "taking over the country" altogether.[37]

Given this attitude, the CEL and indeed the CCG were widely viewed as groups supportive of the Republican Party and its candidates.[38] But Kamp denied that he saw the GOP as a vehicle for beating back the Communist assault. The CEL had "exposed the attempt on the part of subversive elements to bore from within *both* political parties," Kamp said.[39] Nor had they stopped boring on the Republican side, he believed, when asked explicitly by the committee's counsel. "[I]t would not be to their advantage" to do so, Kamp explained. "If they can take over the Republican Party they are going to do that."[40] Why would the "radical elements" cease their activities within one party?, his answer seemed to ask. Why reduce their chances of success by focusing only on one? In this respect, the CEL's "nonpartisanship" was actually arrayed against the pernicious *bipartisanship* of these Communist infiltrators, as Kamp saw it.

Nor did the CEL's hostility to such infiltration reach the level of "political" activity, Kamp argued. While its overt opposition to the CIO might be construed as encouraging opposition to P.A.C.-backed candidates, Kamp claimed the CEL merely provided information to citizens on which they might base their decisions.[41] Since the CEL did not actively endorse anyone, he appeared to argue, it was not explicitly seeking to direct a citizen's vote and thus remained within the realm of "education."[42] The difference was one of command and compulsion over cultivation and suggestion. Kamp even articulated what became an important standard for classifying campaign advertising in the modern era: the presence of "magic words" urging support for or opposition to a specific candidate.[43] As he asserted, "if I came out and said, 'Now, vote for Roosevelt,' or 'Vote for Dewey,' then I would be engaging in political activity; I would not be asking them to use their own judgment; I would be asking them to follow my advice."[44] In this view, CEL pamphlets with such unsubtle titles as "Vote C.I.O. and Get a Soviet America" were not giving any electoral advice at all.[45]

"[E]ducation and political activities are two different things," Kamp stated bluntly to the Anderson Committee, leading an exasperated John Sparkman (D-AL), then a congressman, to remark: "That is what we have been told by every organization that has come before us"—including the CIO.[46] Indeed, as noted in previous chapters, "educational" claims were often invoked for cultural and strategic reasons, as well as legal ones. In this case, Kamp used the claim to explicitly deny that his organization was a "political committee" under the meaning of the Corrupt Practices Act and even to contest the Anderson Committee's legal authority to investigate it.[47] The CCG's executive director, Edward A. Rumely, adopted a similar stance but to little practical effect. When Kamp and Rumely refused to comply with subpoenas for their organizations' financial information, both were held in contempt of Congress.[48]

But the kind of political education undertaken by groups like the CEL and the CCG was less concerned with a narrow range of specific issues, as some of the earliest examples of this technique had been, and more infused with a broader ideological worldview, reflecting the fact that issue positions themselves were coming to cohere in more systematic ways. "[T]he New Deal is not a political party, it is a philosophy of government," Kamp had asserted in his testimony.[49] And waging war on a philosophy might be framed as an *intellectual* endeavor above an *electoral* one. Yet to do so effectively required an intellectual apparatus more systematic and compelling than "Americanism" alone. Conservative thinkers shaped by the horrors of war would soon provide one, offering a

framework that connected economics and politics in ways that brought anti–
New Deal groups and business organizations like the NAM and the Chamber
closer together. This perspective, identified with the Austrian school of economics, linked hostility to domestic economic regulation—particularly in terms
of labor—to opposition to Communism abroad, through an emphasis on coercion and collectivism. Much as Keynesianism had offered a new language of
justification for proponents of government intervention, its opponents now had
their own powerful message with wide prospective appeal: the inextricable link
between free markets, free individuals, and free societies.

The "Free Enterprise" Campaign

Beginning in the late 1930s and accelerating after World War II, the business community launched an "intellectual reconquest" of America, Fones-Wolf argues: a
sustained effort to reshape American political culture away from the liberalism
of the New Deal, respond to the threat posed by an increasingly active labor
movement, and promote economic expansion.[50] Where the Landon-Liberty
League efforts of 1936 had "revealed the political bankruptcy of business conservatism," Phillips-Fein suggests, in which "the support of wealthy businessmen
became its downfall," the new publicity efforts of the 1940s aimed to restore the
account.[51] But they would not do so by hiding an association with businessmen
so much as by reducing the stigma of that association; they would make business
into something *everyone* could identify with.

In part, their efforts benefited from a kind of economic patriotism stemming
from the American war effort. If the prestige, status, and influence of business
had been imperiled in the 1930s by the Great Depression, it was restored in the
1940s, due in large measure to America's entry into World War II.[52] The "miracle
of production" that enabled US factories to rapidly turn out the planes, ships,
munitions, and materiel necessary for the American war effort (and even beforehand, for the Lend-Lease program) had served to demonstrate the massive
capabilities of America's industrial core and helped to undo some of the negative reputational effects of the Depression. It had also put business leaders firmly
back in the lobbying game, as they vied for the enormous government contracts
that paid for that "miracle." The NAM and the Chamber were back in business,
so to speak, their voices resurgent in the inner councils of government, their traditional approach—direct lobbying—restored. But the 1930s had revealed how
fragile this position could be. Insider status also depended on outside support,
they had learned. "Business" would have to remain popular too.

Business leaders would thus look for a better message than the "Liberty
League Liberty" that Soule had condemned a decade earlier in the *New Republic*

as little more than a self-interested defense of property rights. The Liberty League and its sympathizers had actually tried to frame its arguments in more universal terms, but disingenuously and unsuccessfully, in Soule's view. They had stressed individual rights, for example—a worker's right to contract for the hours and wages he saw fit or to choose to bargain through a company union rather than an independent one—but only in ways that benefited business interests.[53] They had also attacked centralized government for infringing upon individual freedom as well as violating the Constitution, but this fell flat next to Roosevelt's arguments that citizens needed government help to make use of their freedoms.[54] In the mid-1940s and beyond, however, a new vision of liberty was being formed and articulated by business leaders. They would offer more effective arguments about the societal value of business, linking the realms of employment and politics. They would emphasize *freedom* over constitutionalism, *profit* over property, and the benefits that free markets could bring to all. The message that everyone's freedom, in all contexts, was linked to the freedom of business to act and prosper was one the Liberty League had not quite managed to convey.[55]

The Austrian school of economics provided much of the intellectual foundation for this new approach. Friedrich von Hayek's *The Road to Serfdom* was first published in the United States in September 1944 and summarized in *Reader's Digest* the following April, bringing his gospel of free markets over controlled economies to a wide audience. Two years later, Henry Hazlitt's primer *Economics in One Lesson* appeared and quickly became a bestseller. The "one lesson" was stated at the outset: "The art of economics consists in looking not merely at the immediate but at the longer effects of any act or policy; it consists in tracing the consequences of that policy not merely for one group *but for all groups*."[56] This was business universalism in a new guise. Only the actions or policies that aided business and its long-term productive capacity, in essence, had the ability to improve the lives of everyone through economic growth. Thus, where Liberty Leaguers had been castigated as "apostles of greed," the new businessmen would be "apostles of ideas," as Chamber of Commerce executive vice president Arch N. Booth envisaged in 1951.[57] And this new approach, as both Phillips-Fein and Fones-Wolf suggest, would be much more successful.

At the forefront of the free enterprise campaign were the Chamber of Commerce and the NAM, retooling their internal structures and devoting substantial resources to their publicity efforts as the 1940s progressed.[58] As early as 1934, the NAM had created a publicity committee designed to promote a pro-business message, the National Industrial Information Committee (NIIC). As NAM president Robert M. Gaylord informed the Anderson Committee in 1944, the NIIC had been established to address the "vital need" for a better understanding among the public, and within the business community itself, "of the economic relationship of business to society at large."[59] In this sense it was a defensive move, "a byproduct of the great depression of the thirties" which "had raised doubts among a large section of our people as to the desirability of maintaining free enterprise as the keystone of a modern economic system."[60] By the early 1940s, the NIIC was spending over $1 million a year promoting the cause.[61]

Other groups would also take up the free enterprise mission, including some of the earlier "constitution-saving" groups, who would appropriate the principles and promote their most virulent anti-Communist formulation. The basic point of the free enterprise message, after all, was "to promote the capitalistic system as opposed to communism or socialism," as Gaylord conceded.[62] Thus the CCG and the CEL, for example, continued their activities throughout the 1940s—beyond Roosevelt's tenure in the presidency and into the postwar world—by partly integrating this message. New organizations also sprang up to proselytize for free enterprise, including "think tanks" like the Foundation for Economic Education and the American Enterprise Association (forerunner of the American Enterprise Institute).[63] A nascent conservative constellation was thus emerging around these ideas.

With the exception of the American Enterprise Association, representatives from all of these organizations would be called to testify before one or more of the various congressional investigations into campaign expenditures or lobbying conducted in the 1940s and 1950s, suggesting their efforts to disseminate economic principles were making waves politically.[64] Gaylord's testimony in 1944 marked the first time the NAM had appeared before such a committee in thirty years, and it would be back again two years later.[65] Yet Gaylord would claim, as indeed was claimed by all of these groups in various ways, that their activity was in some sense *nonpolitical.* At the very least, none could be properly classified as PACs. When denying that the NIIC was a "political organization," for example, Gaylord noted that it "makes no contributions to candidates for public office or to any political organizations."[66] Rather, it was engaged in educational work for the NAM, he claimed, a status that would be likewise claimed by others, much as the CCG and the CEL had done.

Gaylord acknowledged a political dimension to this work, at least at the systemic level, since it was designed to "promote the capitalistic system as opposed to communism or socialism," but qualified that this was "asked in no *partisan* political sense."[67] Indeed, he characterized the NAM itself and the activities of the NIIC as entirely nonpartisan, noting that the NAM had members from both political parties and that both parties had included platform planks pledging support for the free enterprise system.[68] If the NAM was to engage as an organization in partisan politics, he told the committee, his "life would not be worth living."[69] Indeed, Gaylord criticized those organizations that did aid partisan causes, suggesting they had "not found out yet they cannot dictate to their members."[70] "You cannot tell the American people, you cannot tell the American Congressmen or other public servants, how they ought to vote," he said, drawing electioneering and direct lobbying together. "You can give them the facts and they are going to do want they think is right. But when you attempt to tell them how to do it, you only defeat your own purposes."[71] The free enterprise perspective, after all, celebrated those who "dare to think as individuals and do not think as a group dominated by the opinion of one small set of brains."[72] Actively directing voters toward a particular kind of candidate, even one who believed in such principles, would be self-contradictory.

That the NAM avoided the electoral arena directly was an important part of its "nonpolitical" claim. Organizations such as his went "[i]nto the field of politics insomuch as you try to influence public opinion," Gaylord conceded. "But we cannot go into the field to contribute to or endorse candidates or political parties."[73] The NAM would be taking no active part in the 1944 election campaign, he affirmed, or any other, for that matter.[74] It did occasionally provide information on congressional roll-call votes to its members, he admitted, though he was careful to distance this practice from any indication of candidate preference. Only if a vote concerned a matter vital to industry that had not been widely publicized in the press would it be circulated in the NAM's newsletter, Gaylord said.[75] Such records would include an explanation of the measure and the NAM's perspective but no characterization of a lawmaker's position as "right" or "wrong," he explained—that was "a matter of the conscience of the individual Congressman so far as we are concerned."[76] The NAM did not publish multivote scorecards or urge support for or opposition to particular lawmakers based on their records, he indicated.[77] Indeed, when Congressman Anderson asked whether the NAM provided a legislator's voting record "to help him or to hurt him" in an electoral sense, Gaylord affected surprise. "It never occurred to me in that light," he told the committee.[78]

Gaylord framed the NAM's sharing of such research in terms of *lobbying*, providing its member companies and trade associations with information on which their executives might act directly. "What we are trying to do," Gaylord explained, "is to provide a general reminder that, if you believe in the legislation that was adopted, or defeated, and your Congressman voted differently, you ought to talk with him and show him why you believe as you do."[79] The NAM was encouraging members be their *own* lobbyists, in effect. Of course the executives who effectively filled its membership roster were in a better position than most to talk directly with a legislator. But when Anderson quipped that the obvious alternative was to "retire him to private life by a large and enthusiastic majority," Gaylord offered a curt response. "Manufacturers do not retire anybody to private life," he said. "We have less influence in elections than anybody."[80]

They certainly did not command a "large and enthusiastic majority" of voters, since their members were primarily institutional, with a small number of individual members in the case of the Chamber. But they did control sizable monetary resources, which had become as much of a crucial resource in elections as manpower. Yet as Gaylord told the committee, the NAM had no plans at all "for the raising of any funds, either through the association or through voluntary contributions, for the purpose of educating the people as to how they should vote on issues, or candidates, at the coming election," nor had it "sent individuals into any congressional district in the recent primaries, or in past general elections, to organize or speak in behalf of candidates, or to recommend them to . . . individual members."[81] As an incorporated association, of course, the NAM could not undertake such activities directly, but Gaylord had instantly dismissed, he said, any talk of setting up its own PAC.[82] He shared with the committee his written response to one such suggestion in June 1944, after Attorney General Biddle had approved the basic structure of the CIO P.A.C., in which he professed shock at the very idea and rejected its legality. "The Federal Corrupt Practices Act prevents organizations such as ours from making political contributions," Gaylord had written. "The fact that an Attorney General has approved the actions of the Congress of Industrial Organizations Political Action Committee *has not changed that law.*" Moreover, even without legal considerations, to use NAM funds in political campaigns would be "highly improper," he added, since it meant redirecting money that contributors had given for other purposes and might go against their partisan political preferences, he implied.[83]

In any case, Gaylord was convinced that the law plainly meant to prohibit corporations (including incorporated associations) and labor unions from electoral activity, and he disagreed with any and all "subterfuges" to get around that basic meaning, or so he said.[84] "Even if you take the law off the books," he proclaimed, "we would not do it." On the matter of campaign contributions, he was especially clear: "I do not think business has any right doing that."[85] Yet he did believe in the *individual's* right to participate in political activity, including individual businessmen who, as citizens, "must take an interest in politics."[86] Under further questioning from the committee, Gaylord denied that this position was in itself a subterfuge of sorts, in that wealthy individuals associated with particular corporations might make large contributions legally. "If it is done within the law *as individuals,*" then it was perfectly proper, he said.[87] But he was quick to point out that the NAM did not actively try to encourage such individual donations.[88]

In contrast, Gaylord was prepared to admit that the NAM actively lobbied. That was simply "a modified right of petition," in his view.[89] It might even engage in indirect lobbying via publicity and broader "educational" activities, but it did not *electioneer,* was the claim. The Chamber of Commerce, meanwhile, was re-luctant even to admit to lobbying, let alone electioneering. After passage of the Federal Regulation of Lobbying Act in 1946, it refused to register as a group seeking to influence legislation on the grounds that its activities were purely educational—showing once more the legal as well as normative uses of that term. The NAM's and the Chamber's aversion to outright electioneering thus accorded with that of broadly conservative groups emerging in the 1940s, such as the CCG and the CEL. In the campaign expenditure hearings of the 1940s, in fact, only one conservative group even came close to approximating the form that P.A.C. had pioneered: American Action Inc. But it also disappeared almost as soon as its representative had appeared before the House electoral investiga-tion in 1946, chaired by J. Percy Priest of Tennessee.

American Action's executive director, Edward A. Hayes, described it as "an American, non-partisan, non-sectarian organization dedicated to uphold and defend America against communism, fascism, anti-Semitism, and all alien or anti-American groups that are attempting to destroy our form of government and our American way of life."[90] It intended to make direct contributions to candidates, Hayes noted, and was meant to be "a permanent organization."[91] American Action, therefore, seemed to fulfill the major requirements of PAC status. Indeed, according to Cook it was "specifically a political action orga-nization," conceived as the electoral arm of the National Economic Council (NEC)—though the relationship would be much less openly acknowledged than the CIO's connection to its PAC.[92]

The NEC itself was an "educational" advocacy group that had been incorpo-rated in New York in 1939, expanding to a national basis in 1943.[93] Its orientation was much more explicitly economic than the "constitution-saving" or "patriotic" groups of the 1944 election cycle.[94] The formation of American Action, Cook suggested, reflected the NEC's recognition of "the limitations of influencing in-dividual Congressmen," even where the group may have established personal contacts with them.[95] Even a friendly legislator could be constrained by the climate of opinion in his constituency, a concern that the NEC's own efforts of "education and opinion formation" could help assuage to some extent. But there were more basic problems with the "standard lobbying techniques" that employed individual contact, relationship building, and persuasion.[96] Personal relationships were all well and good, but they did not serve to convert legislators not already sympathetic to the group's concerns, Cook observed.[97] And it was difficult to build such "friendly personal relationships" with the less sympathetic members in the first place.

The NEC thus had two options for dealing with hostile or borderline legislators, Cook summarized: "It can bring pressure to bear through their constituencies or it can attempt to prevent his re-election."[98] In essence, it could utilize the tools of indirect lobbying or turn to political action, she suggested, seemingly ignoring the possibility of political education to alter the wider electoral environment. American Action, she suggested, was the NEC's attempt to engage in political action, but through an ostensibly separate group that would obscure its involvement.[99] While she pointed to some legal considerations to explain why it created a new group, she also brought in a normative dimension: that the NEC feared a backlash against perceived electoral intervention.[100] "[S]omething like fear of 'guilt by association' may have been operating, at least for a while," Cook noted.[101]

But it is unclear how far into the electoral realm American Action actually proceeded. Hayes appeared before the Priest Committee only a few weeks after the group's founding and thus had no concrete activity to report. There is little extant information, moreover, concerning the scope of its activity that fall. Writing in the mid-1950s and primarily concerned with a subsequent congressional investigation into lobbying groups, Cook characterized the NEC's ideological orientation as conservative and pointed to working relationships with members of the Republican Party's "right-wing."[102] But she offered nothing to assess how partisan any support provided by American Action in 1946 might have been. What is clear, however, is that it did little *beyond* 1946. For all its claims to permanence, American Action was nowhere to be seen in the next election cycle. In 1948, in fact, the NEC's president, Merwin K. Hart, bemoaned the absence of a conservative electoral group. Writing to a friend, he suggested that "the present trend in public affairs" might be "arrested and turned back" by an organization along the lines of "the old Anti-Saloon League."[103] In this, however, he seemed influenced more by the old ideas of rewarding and punishing so as to influence congressmen in *both* parties in a favorable direction.

Congressman Ralph Gwinn (R-NY), at least, had absorbed some of the new ideas; as he wrote Hart the following year: "Politically speaking, literally there is nothing for all patriotic groups to do, so important as organizing themselves into an army of volunteers at the election district level."[104] "Your forces must become election district leaders," Gwinn emphasized. "Where that is not practical, they must be lieutenants in the district. *They must influence the selection of the candidates in the first place*, and after electing them, support them by a *permanent organization*, one that is articulate."[105] The NEC's ground troops must, in sum, reclaim local party machinery for the Right. But in attempting to do so, they should not look only to one side: "Gradually the infiltration of good men and women for the right will take over the regular party machinery and thus replace the Socialist infiltration that has already succeeded 80% of the Democratic Party and 20% into the Republican Party."[106] The point was to recapture *both* parties, even if one was further in the hole than the other.

Indeed, it was the very absence of concern for both parties in labor political action that seemed to strike business-affiliated observers as odd. In 1946, for example, the NAM had engaged in covert activity to ascertain how the labor-liberal PACs were functioning, sending two young staffers to attend the National Citizens Political Action Committee School, an early training program for PAC operatives. As one of the undercover staffers noted in a confidential report, "While the NCPAC leaders declared they did not represent labor and that this school was non-partisan, it seemed obvious that they consider the labor groups as the most fertile ground for their doctrine *and that they realize their program can only be affected through political agitation within the Democratic party.*"[107] Other attendees noted "repeated warnings or hints that a Republican victory this fall appeared likely," yet, they observed, "they didn't seem interested in the possible strategy of jumping the fence and working inside the Republican party to get the 'right' candidates, whom they would then have a chance of electing."[108] They even speculated that the NCPAC might try such a bipartisan strategy in 1948, "if Republicans capture the House this year."[109] Republicans did capture the House in 1946, but as discussed in the previous chapter, the labor-liberal PAC approach did not change.

Gwinn, in contrast, was calling for a change in the general approach of "patriotic" groups and their allies in the business community, to move away from political education and embrace political action, if in a bipartisan form. But his recommendations still faced resistance from business organizations, especially, despite greater legal clarity and access to relevant resources, suggesting that other factors accounted for their unwillingness to create a PAC.

Why No "Business" PAC?

In his appearance before the Anderson Committee in 1944, NAM president Robert Gaylord had expressed serious legal reservations when it came to corporate political action, despite the attorney general's approval of the P.A.C. concept for labor unions and the implication that corporations might create a similar device. Indeed, by 1947 Senator Robert Taft—coauthor of the Taft-Hartley Act and "Mr. Republican" himself—had accepted the basic idea of a PAC. As noted in the last chapter, he found "nothing unlawful" in labor unions choosing "to set up a political organization and obtain direct contributions for it."[110] But Taft had not confined his reasoning to labor organizations. "[I]t seems to me the conditions are exactly parallel, both as to corporations and labor organizations," Taft said, speaking from the Senate floor on June 5, 1947.[111] And those parallel conditions extended to business associations too, Taft specified:

If the labor people should desire to set up a political organization and obtain direct contributions for it, there would be nothing unlawful in that. If the National Association of Manufacturers, we will say, wanted to obtain individual contributions for a series of advertisements, and if it, itself, were not a corporation, then, just as in the case of PAC, it could take an active part in a political campaign.[112]

By the mid-1950s the NAM's own counsel had been asked to clarify the laws on corporate political activity, as amended by Taft-Hartley, and reached the conclusion obvious to most outside observers, that since the attorney general's approval of the P.A.C. scheme had stood essentially unscathed in the ensuing years, and the statute as written applied to both labor unions and corporations equally, then the constraints and opportunities were the same for both. "Under the statute what is sauce for the goose is sauce for the gander," the NAM's Law Department concluded in a 1956 memo.[113]

The Law Department's analysis came as a new legal challenge was wending its way through the judicial system: *United States v. United Auto Workers.* That case, as discussed in chapter 5, involved UAW sponsorship of television broadcasts in Michigan, which explicitly urged support for senatorial candidates during the 1954 midterms. The UAW had used treasury funds to pay for the broadcasts, seemingly violating Taft-Hartley's ban on union political expenditures and leading the Department of Justice to bring suit. But at the time of the NAM's analysis, the District Court had dismissed the indictment, a decision that, had it stood, might have effectively authorized any political activity short of direct contributions to candidates using treasury funds. Indeed, the NAM's memo noted that the decision "makes it far easier for the newly merged AFL-CIO to carry out its announced objective of engaging in more intensive political activity."[114] As it was, the Supreme Court took up the case and outlined stronger constraints in its 1957 opinion: discerning a congressional intent to proscribe commercial broadcasts (though not internal communications, as it had decided in the *CIO News* case). The Court made no formal ruling on this issue, however, instead remanding the case back to lower courts for trial.

Still, however broad the permissible political activity, the conclusion the NAM's lawyers drew still held true: "It would seem to follow that corporations may well be entitled to engage in the identical types of activities apparently permitted to labor organizations."[115] Much as Taft had indicated, they noted that the law did not explicitly preclude corporations or incorporated business associations from creating PACs, in line with what labor unions had done. And unincorporated business associations were free from restriction under the Corrupt Practices Acts altogether, they observed (though other statutory frameworks, such as the tax code, might inhibit their political behavior to some extent).[116] By 1956, then, NAM leaders were clearly aware that there were no legal impediments to their creating a PAC.

What is more, very few legal challenges to labor political action had even emerged, and there were still fewer convictions. And for improper corporate political activity the numbers were even lower.[117] Between 1950 and 1956, for example the Department of Justice received fifty-four complaints concerning possible violations of the law restricting union and corporate financial involvement in elections. Thirty-nine of the complaints involved labor organizations, eleven involved national banks or corporations, and only four involved private corporations.[118] Of those four, an indictment was only sought in one case, and the grand jury refused to grant it. Of the entire fifty-four cases reviewed, the only one brought to trial involved a labor union and resulted in acquittal.[119] The UAW complaint, originally filed in December 1954, was not included in the data, as a final decision was still pending at that time, though the eventual outcome would be identical.[120]

Still, since both of those cases involved labor unions, some corporate counsel remained cautious, hesitating to draw generalizable conclusions from them.[121] The problem was that while the law might apply equally, labor unions, business associations, and corporations were not entirely equivalent in their organizational structures. Thus in 1958 the NAM Legal Department produced a handy memo on corporate political activity entitled "What Corporations Can and Can't Do." Having emphasized the rights of businessmen as *individuals* to participate in elections, the memo sought to clarify the corporate angle.[122] The *CIO News* case had excluded internal communications from a labor union to its members from the restrictions of the Corrupt Practices Act, however political those internal communications might be. But who counted as a "member" of a corporation? And what constituted *internal* communications? For incorporated business associations like the NAM or the Chamber, the answers were more straightforward, since they had clear members. For corporations it was reasonable to assume that stockholders could be considered "members" in some sense, such that communications with them would be properly internal. But an even more crucial question in terms of the potential reach of corporate electoral influence was whether *employees* might count. "Still untested is whether a corporation may safely urge employees to support a political party or candidate," the NAM memo reported, before outlining a possible rationale on the basis of informing "its stockholders, employees and others of danger or advantage to their interest in the adoption of measures, or the election to office of men espousing such measures."[123]

The "untested" nature of this justification may have served to discourage corporations from making political appeals to employees. After all, the Corrupt Practices Act imposed criminal liability on corporate directors convicted of violations, who could face a fine or even imprisonment.[124] There were also state laws and restrictions to consider.[125] But as both NAM memos suggest, a corporate

PAC seeking voluntary contributions from officers or even stockholders would have passed legal muster. By 1958 even party groups such as the Young Republicans were promoting the idea that corporations could engage in direct political action. "THERE IS NO PENALTY, NOT EVEN LOSS OF TAX EXEMPTION!" a report produced by the GOP affiliate emphasized, suggesting that businesses "can engage in any form of political activity as long as the expenditures do not come from dues money or general funds."[126] Yet neither the NAM nor its member corporations took such a step at this time. So what else might explain their inaction?

To the extent Phillips-Fein offers an explanation for business conservatives avoiding "the harsh glare of electoral politics," she points to the financial resources they typically possessed. Corporations could provide substantial funds to support their representative business associations, and "[m]oney could, after all, support ideas, print legislative analyses, and hire scholars, far more easily than it could create a mass following in support of conservative economic policies."[127] Fones-Wolf also points to financial resources that gave business an advantage in the realm of publicity—one that labor could not hope to match, she claims—which enabled business groups to essentially *purchase* dominance for their political vision.[128] Such comments reflect long-standing ideas about the nature of business resources and their possible uses.[129] They also suggest a natural fit between the configuration of resources available to business associations and corporations and the modes of activity they pursued.

Indeed, it was widely argued by mid-century scholars of interest groups such as Schattschneider, Key, and Truman, among others, that the kinds of financial resources enjoyed by the NAM and its fellow business organizations leant themselves to certain activities, like publicity, that only required money to pay for them. In contrast, these corporations and groups lacked the manpower and organizational capacity to mount electoral efforts. The NAM's limited membership made it ill-suited to electoral activity, Truman argued: "Its fifteen or twenty thousand members are too few and too widely distributed over the country to do this work effectively."[130] In essence, they lacked a sufficiently large membership to make a difference in terms of votes and similarly had little to offer in terms of grassroots mobilization. Of course there were some concerns about informal efforts by corporate executives to influence the votes of their employees, but business groups themselves had no mass membership to mobilize.[131] The emphasis on votes they might directly command thus reveals how these scholars continued to see electioneering through the lens of "pressure politics," idealizing the strategy of the Anti-Saloon League at its peak, when it threatened to deploy a voting bloc and swing an election to either side. Since business groups could not replicate this model, the best they could do, as one mid-century scholar put it, was "offer their services as proselytizers of a larger public."[132]

But even if we think in terms of the emerging alternative model of influence secured through campaign contributions, the configuration of business financial resources would remain relevant. Much as financial resources might orient business groups toward publicity activities, those available to their individual members might also have implications for broader group strategy. One of the reasons labor unions had created PACs, after all, was to pool the limited funds possessed by each member. But as scholars such as Zelizer point out, wealthy corporate executives could make large campaign contributions as individuals— comprising the cadre of "fat cats" who still provided a large proportion of party and candidate campaign funds at mid-century.[133] The Hatch Act amendments had imposed a $5,000 cap on individual contributions to political committees or candidates, but this amount could be given to multiple recipients, while the practice of "bundling" contributions from family members offered a way of circumventing the cap to some extent. As such, it might appear that corporations themselves had no need for a PAC to aggregate funds, since they could rely on the individual contributions of executives to get around the law.[134] (Indeed, in a more legally dubious practice, some corporations were accused of paying their top employees special "bonuses" with the understanding they would be contributed to particular candidates.)[135] By extension, business groups could rely on the contributions of their officers and prominent members.

These arguments, then, suggest that the preference of corporations and business associations for political education over political action was conditioned by resources; they were better suited to publicity activities, on the one hand, and had no need for a PAC, on the other.[136] And yet though such arguments may appear reasonable on the surface, it is not clear that resources *did* shape the activities of corporations and business associations so neatly or definitively. Indeed, it is not clear that the business financial advantage itself was quite so commanding. Hacker and Aberbach, for example, claimed that if national and local business donations were combined, "it is safe to assume that these form a greater total than that provided by labor unions."[137] But the data available to assess such claims were very limited, and such characterizations were therefore driven as much by expectations as evidence. Just because individual businessmen could *afford* to make large campaign contributions did not necessarily mean that they *did* so.

Alexander Heard, for example, one of the few political scientists who collected campaign finance data in the postwar decades, assessed "business" money in politics by examining the contributions of high-level executives in the top one hundred largest US corporations. Looking at election cycles in the 1950s, Heard found that such individuals had donated just over $1 million in 1952 and almost $2 million in 1956.[138] Yet Heard found that disbursements from fifteen national labor PACs (those that were in continuous operation from 1952 to 1958) came to almost $2 million in both 1952 and 1954, dropping slightly to $1.7 million in

1956 and to $1.6 million in 1958.[139] While "business" might draw on a narrower population than labor unions to deliver these amounts, the differences in absolute terms were quite limited.

Moreover, the extent to which a distinct "business interest" could have been discerned from such contributions at the time is unclear, given the laborious work Heard had to undertake to identify individuals associated with corporations and to systematically collate their contributions. Would national party committees really have an overarching sense of such activity? Would individual politicians? They might be aware of contributors identified with prominent local corporations, for example, but not this overarching picture of "business" financial activity. This is important because the impact of labor PACs came from more than just their bundling of small donations to permit substantial campaign contributions. Rather, they made those contributions more readily identifiable with a sponsoring union or federation; parties and politicians who received such largesse knew exactly where the money was coming from. Considered as a sector, "business" thus lacked the same kind of identifiable impact.

Even the impact of business associations like the NAM or the Chamber was limited in terms of individual contributions. Despite their personal wealth and likely interest in political matters, individuals with leadership roles in these organizations did not contribute in particularly high numbers. As shown in table 7.1, Heard found that just 36 percent of officers and directors of the Chamber

Table 7.1. **Chamber of Commerce & NAM Officials, Contributors in 1952 & 1956**

	# Names Checked	Rep.	Dem.	Other	Actual Contributors
			1952		
Chamber	14	5	1	0	5* (36%)
NAM	171	29	3	0	32 (19%)
			1956		
Chamber	18	4	0	0	4 (22%)
NAM	130**	17	0	0	17 (13%)

Notes: *One individual gave to both parties, hence the total number of contributors is reduced by one.

** For 1956, Heard only provides information on NAM directors, excluding officers and vice presidents which are included in the 1952 data.

Source: Adapted from Table 7, "Known Campaign Contributors of $500 and Over Belonging to Selected Organized Groups, 1952 and 1956," in Alexander Heard, *The Costs of Democracy* (Chapel Hill: University of North Carolina Press, 1960), 100–102.

of Commerce made campaign contributions of $500 or more in 1952, and only 22 percent did so in 1956. For the NAM, Heard found that 19 percent of its officials—including regional and honorary vice presidents—had made campaign contributions of over $500 in 1952. In 1956, when he looked solely at NAM directors, only 13 percent had made such contributions.[140] When so many association officials *were not* making campaign contributions—at the federal level at least—why should we assume that so many corporate executives *were*?

The group-level financial advantage of business associations, moreover, might not have been quite so great as supposed. Bauer and colleagues, for example, found that many trade associations lacked the resources for effective lobbying typically ascribed to them.[141] Even "[t]he famed purse of the National Association of Manufacturers has a bottom somewhere," Calkins acknowledged, "and its popular vote has definite bounds. No group has unlimited resources. None is utterly invincible."[142] At the same time, through treasury funds, labor unions and PACs had significant financial resources available to them for publicity and political education, alongside campaign contributions from voluntary funds. Thus where the NAM's NIIC spent approximately $1 million on free enterprise publicity in 1943 and $1.4 million in 1944, the merged AFL-CIO spent about $1 million in the late 1950s on pro-union publicity designed to undo the negative fallout from the McClellan "rackets" committee.[143] Adjusting for inflation, the AFL-CIO's outlay is still somewhat lower but nonetheless a significant expenditure on publicity aside from its other political activities.[144]

Perhaps most important, even if business organizations like the NAM *did* enjoy a financial advantage in reality, they did not necessarily *perceive* that advantage. In 1959, for example, NAM officials expressed anxiety about the "virtually unlimited" funds available to unions to spend "in every channel of communication":[145]

> The labor unions, thanks to the check-off, have hundreds of millions of dollars in their war chest with which to fight the battle of ideas. . . . By comparison, in terms of dollars, the NAM literally has "chicken feed." The NAM cannot hope to match its competition in funds. It is futile even to think in these terms. The only practical way the NAM can compete is to counterbalance opposition money with ideas.[146]

In the effort to counterbalance money with ideas, moreover, business associations did not necessarily believe they were gaining ground, even as Fones-Wolf suggests they were increasingly dominating the public debate. Far from feeling the NAM had won the publicity war, a survey of its membership in 1959 showed that members dramatically underestimated the "NAM's good standing with the public," leadings its authors to conclude that "[l]abor leaders and left-wing columnists have fooled members into thinking NAM has a bad name with the public."[147]

In essence, it is not clear that financial advantages, whether organizational or individual, real or imagined, led business associations to favor political education and avoid outright political action in the 1940s and 1950s. Certainly the static nature of these features cannot account for the change in practice by the early 1960s, when the NAM moved to establish a PAC, as discussed in the next chapter. Nor did the legal framework of campaign finance in which corporations and business associations were operating change in this time frame, which might account for a shift in behavior. Indeed, the significant growth in corporate PACs from the mid-1970s onward has been attributed largely to the campaign finance reforms of the 1970s, and especially to the Federal Election Commission's *Sun Oil* decision in 1975, which clarified exactly who within a corporate structure might be permitted to contribute. Yet some corporations, including incorporated business associations like the NAM, had already taken this step *prior* to such legal clarification, while several companies such as Gulf Oil, Union Carbide, Ford, and General Electric were experimenting with discrete "PAC-like operations" by the mid-1950s, as Zelizer describes.[148] If resources and law did not determine business group political activity, therefore, what inhibited their engagement in direct electioneering in the immediate postwar period? And what would begin to encourage it in the mid-1950s? The answer to the first question, I argue, involves past experience, political culture, and ideology, as discussed in the following section, while context and competition propelled change, as explored in the next chapter.

Constraining Business Political Action

"[N]othing is more stupid, than for an organization of big businessmen to get out and carry a flag in a political parade," the RNC's then-chairman had concluded of the Liberty League's failed campaign in 1936.[149] The painful lessons of that experience would not be lost on business groups as they contemplated their political strategies in the 1940s, and partly counseled against an overt electoral effort modeled after the CIO's P.A.C. But there was more to their initial rejection of PACs than a fear of backlash. When NAM president Robert Gaylord questioned the legality of the P.A.C. form in his 1944 congressional testimony, he reflected and channeled a number of themes that would recur in conservative rhetoric over time, even as that legality itself became more widely accepted. Conservative hostility to PACs involved more than a just a distaste for the unions who pioneered them, reflecting broader normative and ideological concerns that led some to oppose organized political action itself, regardless of who might be pursuing it.

Gaylord, after all, had employed ideological criteria to warn against directing voters toward particular candidates. Were business interests to do so, he had argued, they would go against the very principles for which they were arguing: individual freedom of thought and action over stultifying collectivism and a coercive state. Thus the individualism inherent in the American conservative persuasion—as influenced by the Austrian school—impeded the adoption of any strategy premised on directing voters toward a particular end. Gaylord had also hinted toward concerns about minority rights in the use of corporate funds for political purposes, suggesting that it would be "grossly unfair" to contributors, some of whom were "Democrats, some Republicans, and some New Dealers"—an intriguing intermediate category.[150] As later articulated by Senators Goldwater and McClellan in relation to union members, as discussed in the previous chapter, the underlying concern was the use of money to support political causes with which the contributor might not agree. In the union case the problem was of particular concern to conservatives, since members might be required to contribute through dues payments or even coerced into giving to PACs. As Raymond Moley quipped, union members were giving contributions to PACs "voluntarily," but only "after specific and pointed requests."[151]

As the NAM's chairman, Cola G. Parker, summarized his organization's position in 1956, "the NAM upholds the right of union leaders, as individuals, to state their views on candidates, parties and issues, and to try to persuade their own members that their official position is right. But, we do not believe union leaders should be permitted to use union funds and union organizations for partisan political purposes."[152] During the McClellan labor management hearings in 1957, the NAM even launched a public relations campaign on "labor abuses" that claimed, among other apparent misdeeds, growing resentment among rank-and-file members that their unions promoted candidates and causes against their preferences.[153] To the extent that political education efforts verged into this territory, it was a largely accurate critique, in that compulsory union dues *were* being used to promote the union's particular message. Thus the overall lack of voluntariness in union political activity was simply another reflection of the lack of individual choice inherent to unionism, as NAM leaders and other conservative critics saw it, cutting against the vision of freedom and individualism they were seeking to promote.

In the "fusion" that was 1950s conservatism, however, that atomistic vision of individualism lived alongside a holistic vision of society in which business was at one with the people at large. It was this universalistic view, along with the long-term experience of business interests in the political arena, that shaped a very different perspective on political action than that held by labor leaders—and one that involved a differing attitude toward partisanship. The CIO P.A.C. and the LLPE, as argued in previous chapters, embraced direct political action as a means of reshaping the Democratic Party. Despite their protestations of "nonpartisanship," their political activities were deeply intertwined with a partisan cause. In contrast, throughout the 1940s and early 1950s business groups like the NAM and the Chamber of Commerce rejected an explicitly partisan approach. Rather than being nonpartisan per se, they were effectively *bipartisan* in their dealings with lawmakers and party organizations, working with both sides and expecting support from both sides, despite the Republican leanings of many business leaders themselves.

Many journalistic observers, of course, discerned a partisan impulse behind the free enterprise campaign, as well as an electoral objective. *Fortune* magazine reporter William Whyte Jr., for example, writing in 1952, suggested that "the businessman engaged in the campaign is not sure *what* he is trying to communicate," but he was clear about the *why*.[154] "[T]o oversimplify, he is doing it because he is sincerely worried over what has been happening at the polls," Whyte wrote. "What he is after, to put it bluntly, is a Republican victory."[155] Though the groups behind the free enterprise campaign denied such partisan favoritism, Whyte dismissed their protests: "The claim of nonpartisanship simply makes business look silly."[156] Yet his own analysis suggested this claim was less a conscious misrepresentation than a self-delusion; the typical businessman had long "cherished the illusion that he can be politically persuasive and nonpartisan in the same breath," Whyte remarked.[157] In effect, businessmen might truly see themselves and their aims in nonpartisan terms, as something *both* parties should pursue.

This self-conception reflects the strain of universalistic thinking that had marked business attitudes since the early twentieth century, in which business did not conceive of its aims as self-interested or class-based but as promoting the interests of all.[158] This perspective had been reinforced by the free enterprise campaign, connecting an unrestricted economy to a free society and emphasizing the greater economic benefits of free markets for everyone. As General Motors CEO Charles E. Wilson famously put it in 1953, during Senate hearings following his nomination as President Eisenhower's defense secretary: "[F]or years I thought what was good for our country was good for General Motors, and vice versa. The difference did not exist. Our company is too big. It goes with the welfare of the country."[159] Since business identified its interests with those of society at large, its representative groups expected to enjoy an elevated position of influence within *both* parties.

As noted earlier, NAM personnel had expressed surprise in 1946 that the NCPAC did not seek to influence *both* parties through political action. And both parties made appeals to the business community at large. In 1958, for example, DNC chairman Paul Butler spoke at a NAM event and emphasized his party's pro-business credentials. Among Democrats, there were "more businessmen in Congress than any other occupational group except lawyers," Butler noted.[160]

(Indeed, a large number of legislators in *both* parties hailed from a business background, in contrast to the scarcity of politicians with labor connections.)[161] And in a nod to his audience's prime concern, he framed his party—through the actions of Democratic presidents and Democratic majority congresses—as the true savior of the free enterprise system, given its near collapse during the Depression. Once prosperity had been restored, he said, "certain businessmen got the strange idea that the Republican Party was responsible for it all and that the G.O.P. was the great friend of the businessman."[162] To some extent, then, businessmen were encouraged to see *both* parties as receptive to their aims and concerns.

And even if they might disagree with Butler's equation of New Deal economic management and the free enterprise system, even the most conservative businessman in the 1940s and 1950s knew there were some Democrats—mostly southern conservatives—who would uphold their economic vision in Congress. Indeed, the conservative coalition of Southern Democrats and northern Republicans was a central factor shaping business attitudes to politics in general and the political behavior of business groups in particular. If labor unions went "into politics" to liberalize the Democratic Party and realign the party system, business groups "kept out of politics" for much of the 1940s and 1950s because they were happy for it to remain as it was. Since much of their concern involved *stopping* the federal government from taking action, the conservative coalition served them well. Only when they perceived the weakening of that coalition— which they attributed to labor and liberal political action—did they contemplate an electoral response, though not, at first, a partisan one. Since business groups conceived their aims as something both parties should pursue, they were more reluctant to cast their lot with one side and essentially write the other party off. If the Democratic Party had fallen under the sway of labor and liberal interests, then it must be *saved* from those interests, they felt. When their efforts to reinforce the conservative coalition appeared unsuccessful, however, they began to embrace a more partisan response, looking to make the Republican Party a conservative counterweight. Thus partisan dynamics and interest group competition, more so than legal or financial considerations, help to explain the changing contours of business political behavior, eventually drawing business fully into the electoral realm, as explored in the next chapter.

A Tale of Two PACs

"The labor unions themselves have blazed the trail for the rest of us," the executive vice president of the National Association of Manufacturers (NAM), Charles Sligh Jr., told his colleagues in 1958, pointing to labor's political activities. "We must do as they have done."[1] Yet it would be five more years before the NAM took steps to fully emulate labor's example by establishing its own political action committee (PAC). It took two decades, therefore, for this important mode of political organization, first created by a major labor federation in 1943, to be adopted by a leading business group.

Though business groups had been reluctant to embrace direct political action in the postwar years and had focused their efforts on political education instead, calls for them to adopt a more assertive approach became more frequent and more strident as the years passed. Throughout the 1950s they would move, cautiously, hesitantly, in that direction. By the mid-1950s the US Chamber of Commerce and to some extent the NAM had ventured into new territory, seeking to build a grassroots political network by urging businessmen to get involved in election campaigns for either party, though they stopped short of direct financial involvement in elections. By 1963, however, the NAM chose to abandon its hostility to the very concept of political action and formed its own PAC—the Business-Industry Political Action Committee (BIPAC), setting the stage for an electoral contest between interest groups. If the 1936 election had seen business and labor take their economic rivalry into the electoral realm through nascent political "leagues," the 1964 election would see the organizational culmination of that conflict, now expressed through PACs.

What brought this shift about had as much to do with perception as reality in American politics. More than anything, it was spurred by a belief that labor and liberal groups were successfully altering the composition of the Democratic Party, that they were accordingly weakening the conservative coalition and thereby imperiling the causes and concerns that business groups held dear. These perceived changes in the wider political context, combined with their

The Rise of Political Action Committees. Emily J. Charnock, Oxford University Press (2020). © Oxford University Press.
DOI: 10.1093/oso/9780190075514.001.0001

competitive hostility to labor and liberal groups, led major business groups and their organized conservative allies to re-evaluate their approach. New conservative ideological groups such as the Americans for Constitutional Action (ACA) would lead the way and help nudge the NAM toward direct political action—at first to try to shore up the conservative coalition, but eventually to make the Republican Party into a counterweight.

As Sligh warned another audience of businessmen in 1959, "in recent years, the money and manpower of the vast American trade union movement have been thrown into the balance on the side of wrong-headed so-called liberalism."[2] It was the "negligence" of the business community that had "allowed" these spendthrift and, importantly, *Democratic* politicians to be elected, he continued, and he urged businessmen to "organize ourselves for a sales job" at the grassroots level.[3] BIPAC would become part of that sales force, adopting the model and methods first pioneered by the CIO P.A.C. but using them for opposite ends, ultimately seeking to reshape the Republican Party in a conservative direction. As part of a broader conservative political mobilization and embrace of direct political action, BIPAC's emergence and orientation would have important long-term implications for the party system.

Business Puts Down Roots

In 1950 Senator Karl Mundt—a conservative Republican from South Dakota—wrote dejectedly to Edward Rumely of the Committee for Constitutional Government (CCG). "We still have not been able to develop the closely knit and effective type of organization on our side of this fight for freedom that the CIO PAC and Americans for Democratic Action have been able to develop for their side of the controversy," Mundt complained, clarifying that "their side" was "the side favoring big government."[4] Conservatives must therefore "stay with this task until we are positive that we have just as many doorbell ringers and vote getters in our organization as they have in theirs."[5] Since the 1940s, Rumely's organization had been active in the political arena through a campaign of political education intended to promote conservative values and portray liberalism as essentially un-American, thereby discouraging citizens from voting for liberal candidates. But words alone were no longer enough in Mundt's assessment. Speaking to the manpower rather than monetary side of P.A.C. or Americans for Democratic Action (ADA) activities, Mundt's attitude suggested "a significant lack of confidence in existing party organizations" to perform tasks that had once been their exclusive responsibility, as Cook observed.[6] But such concerns would soon lead business organizations, if slowly and tentatively, to try to redress the balance.

The first signs appeared during the 1950 midterms at the state level, in which LaPalombara observed a newfound "inclination on the part of certain business groups to become involved in the campaigns." The Chamber of Commerce in Colorado, he noted, "actually participated in the campaign in a manner not characteristic of traditional Chamber activity," and in Ohio businessmen and professionals formed "The Ohio Voters," a citizens' group that "entered politics on an unprecedented scale and used techniques that differed radically from what one is accustomed to expect in American campaigns."[7] There, they sought to bolster the re-election campaign of Republican senator Robert Taft, who, as coauthor of the Taft-Hartley Act, was one of labor's key targets for electoral retribution. To offset this expected onslaught, a group of trade association executives quietly formed a committee, hoping to aid Taft's re-election through coordinated *individual* activity. They identified "local influentials" in every county and community and asked them "to arrange meetings, to register Taft supporters and get them to the polls, and to have voters visited by members of their professions," as Zeigler described.[8] Those "influentials," moreover, "actually included Republicans, Democrats, and Independent voters who put their interests as businessmen above any party affiliation," as LaPalombara reported.[9] This was a nascent attempt by "businessmen" to register and mobilize pro-business voters at the grassroots level, irrespective of their party affiliation. And it appeared to be a successful one, since Taft was re-elected by a substantial margin and went on to become Senate majority leader in the following Congress, before his untimely death in 1953.

At the national level, the NAM was also beginning to look beyond political education alone to voter registration campaigns, as a grassroots activity that could be justified in civic rather than political terms but might still augment its other efforts. Thus in late 1951 NAM staffers proposed a voter registration drive that they described as a "purely public service campaign," but noted that it "would fit into our plans on more specific issue campaigns exceedingly well," essentially by identifying and priming potentially sympathetic citizens.[10] By 1956 they looked beyond even this combination of voter registration and educational publicity on legislative issues, developing a new initiative aimed at mid-level business employees which appeared to take inspiration from the 1950 Ohio effort.

In the run-up to the presidential election, a broader plan for business electoral mobilization was sketched out and brought to the attention of the NAM, possibly developed by those involved with the "Ohio Voters" or at least modeled after that group. Termed "The Ohio Plan" or "The 1956 Plan" in its national form, it was "based upon the knowledge that there are a lot of right-thinking business and professional people who don't vote."[11] Some 30 percent of salaried industrial employees were not even registered to vote, an outline of the plan stated, while 40 percent of registered voters considered themselves independents who could only be won over "by approaching them intelligently."[12] This meant untapped voters, potentially in sympathy with business aims, who just needed to be energized. "There are enough of these people to provide the balance of power in any election," the outline continued, "AND THEY CAN BE REACHED AND INFLUENCED BY THE LEADERS OF INDUSTRY AND BUSINESS." Such leaders, the plan's authors argued, should try to mobilize a voting bloc.

The plan proceeded in three stages, color-coded so as to produce a patriotic "red, white, and blue campaign," which emphasized local business leaders recruiting others and educating them in practical politics, nonpartisan registration and get-out-the-vote campaigns conducted on their business premises, and a final "partisan" stage in which they would supply information to local party committees on potential activists from among their employees. Like the "Ohio Voters," then, the emphasis was on decentralized individual action through local leaders, minimizing the visible role of any sponsoring organization. Thus unlike the Liberty League campaign of 1936, which had been hampered by a visible business identity and identification with a party side, the Ohio Plan of 1956 assured business leaders some distance from the final "partisan" stage; they would essentially prime workers for campaign activity and channel them into party organizations, but without being visibly associated with partisan activity. The memo did not even specify *which* party should receive the benefit, at least by name, except to urge support for the candidate and party who "stand for Americanism as opposed to Socialism."[13]

Suggesting the influence of these ideas, the NAM soon approved a new "public affairs" program—a new term coming into vogue that described a distinctly *political* brand of public relations—which also followed a three-stage plan, emphasizing in-plant training and education in the first two and encouraging managerial employees to get more actively involved in political affairs.[14] The Chamber of Commerce was spreading a similar message, sending speakers out to local companies throughout 1956 who emphasized the civic duties of businessmen and even creating a "Committee on Political Participation" to consider ways of increasing turnout within this constituency and spurring ongoing political involvement.[15] Yet neither group embraced the third partisan stage of the Ohio Plan, which would funnel activists into local party organizations. At most, the NAM's program outlined the possibility of creating voluntary citizens' committees for "short-range, immediate action" in election years, but the emphasis was firmly placed on the earlier stages.[16]

Although such plans were being developed, there appears to have been limited progress in implementing them in the mid-1950s, with existing efforts marked by a lack of coordination and focus. As journalist Elizabeth Churchill Browns observed in August 1958, writing in the conservative magazine *Human Events*, "Businessmen in this arena approach the fight in a haphazard manner which they would never dream of using in business."[17] But becoming more *professional* in their approach to politics did not mean, in Browns's assessment, becoming more open or direct about their activities. "It would pay America's capitalists to hire experts to teach them how to fight carefully, intelligently, unobtrusively," she wrote. They needed to learn how to "utilize the flank attack."[18]

The NAM, it seems, took such advice to heart, becoming "quietly active" in thirteen regions across the country in the run-up to the 1958 congressional elections, as subsequently described by journalist Victor Riesel, by launching voter mobilization drives centered in local manufacturing plants.[19] In each region, researchers selected districts where conservative candidates had potential to win, then worked with local manufacturers to conduct seminars encouraging political involvement in their plants, much as the Ohio Plan had called for.[20] But these seminars were almost *too* quiet, with the NAM revealing no details of the program until after the election. Where COPE had publicly and directly backed more than three hundred candidates, the NAM had undertaken what even its own executive vice president deemed "an amateurish effort."[21]

And such amateurism had not paid off. The 1958 midterms appeared to many business leaders to augur a negative political shift, since they swept into office a swathe of younger liberal Democrats. The problem, from the perspective of such leaders, was not so much the party affiliation of these new members in and of itself but that their election weakened the bipartisan conservative coalition that had reliably protected business interests in Congress. Party control in Congress had changed hands several times since passage of the Taft-Hartley Act in 1947, but throughout those transitions the informal coalition of Southern Democrats and northern Republicans had remained relatively strong, with Republicans upholding the procedural rights of Southern Democrats—which they utilized to stifle civil rights legislation—in return for reciprocal support on economic and labor measures, often to the advantage of business.[22] Following Truman's re-election in 1948, for example, in which the Democrats had recaptured control of Congress, the coalition had prevented the repeal or weakening of Taft-Hartley. And it had become stronger still after the 1950 midterms, in which Republicans had made modest gains at the expense of more liberal Democrats.[23]

Indeed, so important had the coalition become that Senator Karl Mundt suggested in 1951 that it be made a formal alliance, even potentially the basis of a new political party. In a series of interviews that summer, Mundt outlined a plan urging selection of a Southern Democrat as running mate on the 1952 Republican presidential ticket. If this combination were successful, he proposed that a new party be formed, which would thereby induce liberals to form their own.[24] "Then you'd have two real political parties," Mundt said in one interview. "Each would stand for something definite." "We don't have any basic difference between our two political parties as they now operate," he complained. If his plan were implemented, "[t]he voter would get a choice."[25] Mundt's suggestion thus mirrored the drive for "responsible parties" that had been taken up with enthusiasm by labor and liberal activists, urging a realignment of the party system into liberal and conservative sides, though in this case via the instrument of a new party.

But Mundt's proposal also points to a disconnect between perception and reality. According to Rosenfeld, Mundt believed that "the fragmentation of conservative forces in America had enabled the creeping socialistic bent of the New Deal-Fair Deal agenda to drive policy unchecked."[26] Yet CQ analysis suggests that at the time Mundt was formulating his plan, the influence of the conservative coalition had never been higher.[27] It was still stopping liberal legislation, though perhaps the very effort involved led conservatives to fear for the future. In any case, Mundt's plan did not go anywhere; he gained support from a handful of conservative Republicans, but Southern Democrats were notably quiet on the subject.[28] Meanwhile, liberal Republicans such as Senator Wayne Morse of Oregon and Representative Clifford Case of New Jersey were viscerally opposed (thus proving obstacles to party realignment in a different guise). Case condemned the plan as "a sorry mess of pottage for which the party of Abraham Lincoln is asked to sell its birthright."[29] But he also rejected the whole notion of party realignment, suggesting that broad, catch-all parties produced stable government and peaceful transitions of power, while ideological parties would exacerbate economic and social divisions.[30]

Mundt's traditional vision of realignment by third party did not entirely disappear from conservative thought thereafter.[31] But whether for idealistic reasons such as those Case presented, pragmatic reasons such as the feasibility of prizing Southern Democrats away from their party (as Frank Gannett had earlier questioned), or ideological reasons connected to a universalist outlook on business, many business group leaders and conservatives continued to look to the informal congressional coalition to defend their interests. Yet as the decade wore on, its standing began to look more tenuous. Though Republicans had briefly won back congressional control in 1952 on Eisenhower's coattails, they lost it again in 1954 and saw their numbers slide further in 1956, despite Eisenhower's landslide re-election. A severe economic downturn then helped Democrats increase their majorities in 1958, with Republicans losing forty-eight seats in the House and thirteen in the Senate—the largest single-year party shift in Senate history.[32] Since liberal Democrats gained many of these seats, Rohde points to the emergence of a clear "ideological gap" between junior and senior members at least in the House of Representatives.[33] In the Senate, moreover, Southern Democrats now found themselves outnumbered by colleagues from the North and West, eroding their position of strength within the Democratic delegation, though it would be many years before their grip on power would be truly broken.[34]

Nonetheless, the conservative coalition was weakened and began to look less like a permanent guarantor of business interests. "For the next two years, the conservative coalition in Congress, the Northern Republicans and the Southern Democrats, will continue to fight a holding operation, slowing down America's march to the left," the NAM's Charles Sligh Jr. acknowledged, attributing liberal gains to trade union money and the groundwork of COPE. But more than a just "holding operation" was needed. "Let us give thanks to these men from North and South, because they are ones who are going to give us—the businessmen of America—one last big chance to do what we should have done 20 years ago," Sligh said. "These men are going to give us some time to get organized so that we may assume our full obligations as citizens of our country before the great test of the 1960 Presidential and Congressional elections."[35]

Sligh did not clarify what assuming these "full obligations" meant, nor what they should have done twenty years before, back when Labor's Non-Partisan League was beginning to expand its horizons beyond presidential contests, laying some of the foundations for the CIO P.A.C. But his words hinted of more overt political action. As early as 1954 there had been explicit calls for some kind of business PAC to counteract those of labor and liberal groups. Journalist and former Brains Truster Raymond Moley had made just such a suggestion in his syndicated column, arguing that business needed to promote the interests of capital, just as union PACs did for workers.[36] "[W]hat is wrong about a nationwide stockholders' PAC?" he asked.[37] And in April 1958 James Brubacker denounced the absence of such a vehicle in *Human Events*. "What business lacks" he asserted, "is leaders . . . men with intelligence and courage, and above all, the *will* to climb the mountain named 'The Business PAC.'"[38]

But business group leaders, at least, continued to lack that will. Their immediate response to the setbacks of 1958 was not the creation of a PAC but an expansion of the corporate political education programs they had experimented with on a small scale in 1956. Where the "free enterprise" publicity campaign sought to promote a pro-business message to the general public, hoping to create a favorable political climate for conservative candidates at election time, this new initiative would seek to transform businessmen themselves into political activists and campaign operatives. The "businessmen in politics" movement, as it became known, encouraged mid-level managers and corporate executives "to get into politics," as Hacker and Aberbach reported, so as "to act as a countervailing force against trade union power and the general trend towards socialistic legislation." And it "began in earnest" when the 1958 election returns came in.[39] The NAM and the Chamber would be at the forefront of this effort, but their "countervailing force" would still not amount to a direct organizational counterpart to COPE.

The "Businessmen in Politics" Movement

The prime targets of this new movement were the "salaried industrial employees" who, as observed in the 1956 Ohio Plan memo, often failed to vote. This description reflected a largely new category of workers that had expanded dramatically after World War II, essentially middle management and white-collar corporate employees. These workers "were impervious to unionization," Hacker and Aberbach explained, and often self-identified as "businessmen" themselves, "albeit of the managerial rather than the entrepreneurial variety."[40] And they had been neglected as a potential political force.

That business groups now looked to realize this potential reflected more than just unease with the strength of the conservative coalition. Corporations and business associations had long relied on direct lobbying efforts, alongside publicity-based indirect lobbying and political education, to help advance or impede legislation relevant to their affairs. But as the 1950s wore on there was a growing sense of disconnect between big business leaders and lawmakers. Hacker pointed to distinct social, educational, and attitudinal differences between these two "elites" and noted a concern among corporate leaders that even legislators considered sympathetic to business concerns had no real understanding of the specific issues or challenges they faced, particularly in large business enterprises such as those the NAM represented. Even though many lawmakers identified as businessmen, few came from the world of large corporations, and they tended to be more provincial in their origins, Hacker observed.[41] This feeling of being misunderstood shaped business leaders' perceptions, resulting "in the repeated assertion that Congress is dominated by labor unions," as Zeigler noted, "in spite of the fact that the trend since passage of the Taft-Hartley Act has been to place further restrictions on unions."[42] "The 'businessmen in politics' movement," was thus "a further symptom of this dissatisfaction."[43]

It began at the local level in 1957, in upstate New York, when the Syracuse Manufacturers Association launched its "Task Force on Practical Politics" to come up with ways to improve the business climate in the state. Rather than an educational publicity campaign, the group developed a training program that would teach middle management executives the nuts and bolts of political organizing, help them to better understand the workings of the local party organizations, and encourage them to get involved in political campaigns.[44] "Practical politics" was not so much about mobilizing businessmen to vote as about getting them to become actively involved in their local party organizations—even to take them over. It thus resembled the third "partisan" stage of the Ohio Plan, which encouraged such involvement on both sides.

Local General Electric (GE) executives had played an important part in developing the Syracuse variant, and GE in general was becoming much more politically engaged in the 1950s. Its vice president, Lemuel Ricketts Boulware, believed in a "ceaseless education campaign in the ideology of the free market," as Phillips-Fein describes, and the company would be the incubator for Ronald Reagan's conservative awakening when they hired him as a celebrity spokesman and host for GE-sponsored television programming.[45] As GE marketing consultant Willard Merrihue later explained, such courses could counter an aversion to politics evident among executives. "During the 19th century and the first two decades of the 20th, business exercised an overwhelming influence in politics and government," he acknowledged to a journalist. "But power always begets power, and business leadership inevitably overstepped the bounds of public morality in special-interest actions," he continued, in an unusual admission of self-interest. This had led to a decline in business influence but had also "unwittingly immobilized" corporate executives, "who sensed it was impolitic to identify prominently with politics."[46] Intent on reversing this trend, the NAM and the Chamber would draw on the Syracuse blueprint to promote "businessmen in politics" programs nationwide, exhorting white-collar employees to "get into politics" at the local level and beyond.[47]

The Chamber's program emphasized executive seminars, producing an "Action Course in Practical Politics" that corporations could use for staff training. Hacker and Aberbach reported that over one hundred corporations were using it by the end of 1959 in more than five hundred communities across forty-seven states. In total, about 100,000 people would participate in these programs at their peak in the late 1950s and early 1960s.[48] The NAM also developed "practical politics" courses such as "Citizen at Work," which it rolled out for the 1960 elections.[49] As Sligh explained in 1958, the NAM's role would be limited to providing the tools for political activity through its practical politics instruction courses and helping to shape the environment in which such activity would take place through publicity efforts; the groundwork must be done by individuals and organizations at the state and local levels.[50] "We are only too well aware that any kind of success will depend on what is done much nearer the grassroots than any national organization such as ours can reach," he added.[51]

Though the emphasis remained on individual action, these new programs suggest a shift in the strategic thinking of business leaders, moving away from the voting bloc mentality of the Ohio Plan, in which pro-business voters might swing an election either way (and the mere *threat* of doing so might keep a lawmaker in line). Instead, through practical politics and involvement in party affairs, businessmen would be "in a position to help determine that the right men occupy the seats in council, in the legislature and in the Congress" Sligh said, which was "a much better way to insure a good economic climate than trying to convince the wrong men to do right once they are elected by others."[52] This came closer to the emphasis union leaders and liberal activists placed on the cultivation and promotion of sympathetic electoral candidates—those who, in theory, would never need to be lobbied. But even if business group leaders had begun to view political strategy in a similar way to that of their rivals, their ideological commitments constrained them from taking a comparable dynamic partisan approach, focused on a single party.

Instead, their practical politics courses encouraged individuals to participate in the "party of your choice," whether Democratic or Republican (they were, at least, clear in their hostility to third parties, which had "proved mostly ineffective," as one NAM leaflet proclaimed).[53] Through such engagement, the Chamber and the NAM hoped to build a cadre of activists within both parties who were committed to their viewpoint. If anything, they placed a greater emphasis on participation in *Democratic* Party politics at this point, hoping to counteract the liberalizing efforts of COPE and the ADA from within rather than looking to push the Republican Party rightward. As Hacker and Aberbach observed of one course, it "was bipartisan at all times even if the syllabus was less than sympathetic to labor unions," though "the organizers of the program . . . felt that it was the Democratic Party that especially needed a conservative leaven and that the infiltration of businessmen could achieve this end." "The theory, in short, was one of infiltration," they concluded, through which "both major parties would be brought to nominate candidates sympathetic to business."[54] Whether this approach worked in practice, however, was another matter. Hacker and Aberbach concluded that the courses had limited impact at the individual level, at best activating those who already had some prior interest in politics.[55]

Nonetheless, the approach shows that the bipartisan ideal, stemming from a universalistic self-conception among business leaders, was still very much in evidence in these businessmen in politics programs. In 1959 Raymond Moley even articulated a variation on this theme, based on a pamphlet he had privately published three years earlier entitled *The Political Responsibility of Businessmen*. Though Moley had suggested a "capital PAC" in 1954 to take on labor PACs visibly and directly, he now offered a more nuanced view. Moley claimed that "decades of political attacks upon business" had led business leaders to feel not simply that their "talents were unsuited to political management," but that their involvement could result in "actual injury to the candidates and causes" they cared about. Conversely, a belief had arisen that "it hurts business competitively to take sides in political affairs."[56] Business leaders now needed to reject these shibboleths, Moley argued, and embrace their "political responsibility." Doing so required organizing on the ground, since "[m]anpower, rather than money is the major factor in winning elections," and he commended the practical politics programs for advancing this aim, channeling volunteers into party organizations and thereby helping to strengthen them.[57] But businessmen should *not* set up their own pseudo-party vehicles like COPE, nor should they challenge COPE directly, Moley now advised.[58]

As far as Moley was concerned, the Democratic Party was becoming the "prisoner' of COPE and thereby being transformed into "a special-interest or class organization."[59] Whereas political parties were traditionally "instruments of a classless society" in Moley's idealistic vision, the COPE-backed Democratic Party now threatened to unleash a barrage of class legislation against which the weakened Republican Party could provide little resistance.[60] Yet Moley did not propose that business offer support and succor to the beleaguered GOP in an effort to offset the COPE-Democratic threat, since to do so would propagate the very societal divisions to which he objected. "A counter movement to the unions centered in business as business, would merely invite class conflicts inimical to an orderly society," he explained. Rather, "[w]hat is needed is to activate *all Americans*, especially those with marked capacity for organization and leadership, to behave as good American citizens."[61] Urging businessmen to embrace their political responsibility did not mean "that there should be a businessmen's party or government," then, but rather that they could help to prevent the formation of a *labor* party, in effect.[62] In a sense, Moley denied that business was itself a "special interest," or at least believed it should not *act* like one.[63] As such, it should not be partisan and should not create a PAC.

The extent of business political action thus encompassed some of the grassroots activities in which PACs like COPE engaged: registering and turning out voters and providing volunteers for campaign activities (though in the latter case, to be channeled through existing party organizations). The businessmen in politics programs thereby addressed the manpower side of the coin, as Moley had advised, but not the monetary side, in terms of direct financial contributions to candidates. Business groups might provide some indirect financial assistance through educational publicity campaigns, but even in their publicity efforts, they continued to hold back from utilizing a key technique that labor and liberal electoral groups had adopted: the analysis and publication of congressional roll-call votes. Business group leaders might be more interested in electing the "right" men for office from the start, but they remained unwilling to tell their members or supporters just *who* those men might be.

As noted in the last chapter, the NAM's then-president Robert M. Gaylord told a congressional committee in 1944 that his organization rarely publicized individual roll-call votes to members and never urged support for or opposition to particular lawmakers on that basis.[64] Meanwhile, labor and liberal groups had increasingly fashioned roll-call analysis—a signature "educational" activity defended as scientific and "objective" analysis—into a tool of political action. Since the early 1940s they had created widely publicized scorecards that reviewed lawmakers' records on carefully selected issues and encouraged members and the wider public to use them in making their electoral choices. By the mid-1950s COPE and the ADA were experimenting with box scores to summarize those records, and even percentage scores in the ADA's case, which was gradually promoting its Liberal Quotient (LQ) as an overall measure of a lawmaker's liberalism. By that same point in time, NAM researchers had begun to compile roll-call data for internal purposes, at least, using this information to assess lobbying prospects and shape their legislative strategies.[65] But they did not share that information externally. A 1954 report detailing voting records was marked "confidential" and "not for publication or wide-spread dissemination" by the NAM's director of public affairs, Carl L. Biemiller, who urged colleagues to take care in handling it. The analysis was not even to be made available to the NAM's own members. Thus its hesitance in the political realm was apparent once again.

But if corporations and business groups were reluctant to venture into scorecard territory themselves, perhaps concerned about producing anything that named lawmakers explicitly, new conservative organizations in the late 1950s proved far more willing.[66] Thus in 1959 a former Chamber of Commerce staffer and author of its "Action Course" helped to compile the first conservative scorecard—"The Free Citizens Voting Record"—for a new group, Civic Affairs Associates, Incorporated.[67] Though conservative voices had once denounced scorecards as "blacklists," more positive perspectives on the practice now emerged, perhaps recognizing the need for sharper weapons with which to take on COPE. Even Raymond Moley, recently so careful in recommending how business should respond, was happy to endorse what Civic Affairs Associates had done, calling the new record a "perfectly legitimate and proper means by which to carry on the work of political organization."[68] But the Free Citizens Voting Record would be a short-lived effort, soon eclipsed by the work of a more prestigious and prominent conservative group: Americans for Constitutional Action, which produced a scorecard in 1960. Explicitly modeled after Americans for Democratic Action and emulating its liberal namesake, the ACA would push conservative political action further than its predecessors, closer to the activities of a PAC and closer toward the Republican Party.

The Rise of the Right

Much popular and scholarly attention has been paid to the conservative movement that exploded onto the national political scene in 1964, when Barry

Goldwater won the Republican presidential nomination—a victory engineered by a network of right-wing activists—and launched an unabashedly conservative campaign. Though Goldwater ultimately lost in a landslide to Democratic incumbent Lyndon Johnson, his campaign is often portrayed as planting the seeds of later victory as activists steadily built upon the almost 40 percent of the popular vote he received, culminating in the election of Ronald Reagan as president in 1980. As various historians have shown, however, the foundations of that movement had been laid in the years and even decades preceding Goldwater's run, as a new vision of American conservatism arose in the wake of the New Deal that blended constitutionalism and traditional religious or social values with free market economics and radical antistatism: a "fusion" of traditionalist and libertarian strands of thought, promoted by new conservative intellectuals like William F. Buckley, that was sealed with the staunch anti-Communism of the early Cold War.[69]

The 1950s saw a proliferation of new conservative institutions inspired by these ideas, including Buckley's founding of the *National Review* in 1955, as well as grassroots organizations formed by new activists, many of whom had become politically engaged through their wartime experiences, religious awakenings, or suburban lifestyles. Where an earlier wave of postwar conservative mobilization had centered on think tanks formed to promote free enterprise, including the Foundation for Economic Education and the American Enterprise Association, these newer organizations, particularly from the early 1960s, would be much more politically active, in large part responding to what they viewed as the threat from liberal and labor PACs.[70] Yet the PAC-inspired form and tactical repertoire adopted by these conservative organizations has been little noted in other scholarship. Nor has the complexity of their relationship with the Republican Party been fully appreciated, particularly in comparison to that of their liberal counterparts with the Democrats. Far from an inevitable partnership, it was at first a more hesitant, though ultimately just as passionate, embrace.

The appearance of the group For America before the Senate's Privileges and Elections Subcommittee in 1956, for example, during its probe of campaign activities, was suggestive of the changing outlook among conservatives. Formed as an "educational organization considerably right of center" in 1954, it "went political" after the IRS denied it tax-exempt status, according to the testimony of its national director, retired US Army brigadier general Bonner Fellers, and subsequently backed the States' Rights Party in the 1956 presidential campaign, thereby pursuing a variant of Mundt's plan to reconstitute the conservative coalition as a third party.[71] The party barely registered in the results, however, and For America dwindled into obscurity. But two years later Fellers became involved with a new organization that would have much greater significance both strategically and substantively: the ACA, for which he served as a trustee.

The ACA was officially formed in Pittsburgh in August 1958 and was headed up by retired US Navy admiral Ben Moreell, a past chairman of the Jones and Laughlin Steel Corporation. Former president Herbert Hoover was also a trustee, along with Edgar Eisenhower and an assortment of businessmen and other former military leaders such as Fellers.[72] As its name suggested, the new organization was explicitly designed "to be a conservative version of Americans for Democratic Action," the *Christian Science Monitor* informed its readers.[73] But if the ADA sought to liberalize the Democratic Party, the ACA did not immediately look to transform the Republican Party in the opposite direction. Rather, as its first press release explained (inserted by Senator Mundt into the *Congressional Record*), the new group would try to "force back together the conservative coalition which for over 20 years successfully stopped the greatest excesses toward statism in this country."[74] That coalition had been "torn apart" in the summer of 1957 by disagreements over public power and civil rights, an ACA internal document noted, and needed to be reinforced.[75] The ACA would do so by cultivating and aiding the election of "constitutional conservative" candidates regardless of party, thus emulating the ADA's methods if not its mission.[76]

Olson classified the ACA as an "electoral group," which is a "special variation of the interest group."[77] It was a special variation that, as Diamond summarized, "was an early effort to channel conservative movement support toward selected candidates."[78] And to select those candidates, the ACA now adopted a prominent tool of both the ADA and COPE: the congressional scorecard. The ACA would "fight fire with fire, or, more exactly, roll call with roll call," the *Milwaukee Journal* explained, in its efforts to counter their influence.[79] As noted in chapter 6, the ADA by the mid-1950s had come to summarize its scorecards in percentage terms, producing the LQ. Despite some initial hesitation about promoting those scores, ADA leaders gradually overcame their concerns and began distributing them to newspapers. By 1964 LQ scores for every lawmaker were published annually in the *ADA World,* serving as accessible signals of a lawmaker's liberalism, with high scores essentially functioning as endorsements. The ACA thus set out to provide a comparable measure that would assess a lawmaker's conservatism and showed no reservations about packaging the results as a percentage. Analyzing lawmaker stances "on questions vital to the survival of our free society" and drawing on votes from across several Congresses, the first "ACA Index" appeared in 1960.[80]

Despite their earlier criticism, conservatives now welcomed this initiative. Senator Goldwater, for example, who had once denounced "so-called voting records" and warned against evaluating Congress "by our feelings," publicly endorsed the ACA project as "the finest work of its kind ever put between covers," commending how "it tells the truth about each Member of Congress without bias of any kind."[81] Where liberal scores were once castigated as biased and self-interested, applying a conservative standard of assessment was now deemed acceptable, even "objective" in some sense. But this volte-face suggests less a conscious double standard when it came to political practices as a growing perception of threat among conservatives, who saw labor and liberal political action groups urging a "race toward statism" and the implementation of "piecemeal socialism."[82] The need to arrest these perceived developments now appeared sufficiently pressing that it overcame other objections, and conservatives became more willing to adopt some of their opponents' techniques.

Of course, to some extent conservatives could have simply used ADA scores in reverse fashion: if a high LQ meant a liberal legislator, then a low LQ indicated a conservative one.[83] But the selection of votes on which the ADA based its ratings was reflective of the liberal concerns of that organization, not necessarily the issues more important to conservatives. In addition, having the high score on the liberal side seemed to cede an important psychological and rhetorical advantage. As the Reverend I. E. Howard explained in *Christian Economics*, the ACA Index was "a help to the conservative senator or representative" because it "gives him a positive platform," being framed as a set of measures he had voted *for*, not against.[84] Substantively, too, it allowed the ACA to define the legislative contours of its conservative agenda rather than accept the ground on which liberal groups chose to fight, and to refine its approach as strategically necessary.

Indeed, following initial publication of the Index in 1960, the ACA received complaints from rural representatives—including midwestern Republicans and Southern Democrats—who objected to the negative evaluation of agricultural bills in calculating the scores.[85] Mississippi congressman William Colmer noted "much criticism" of the 1960 Index among Southern Democrats, for example, and expressed concern over his 66 percent score in updated ACA ratings released in 1961.[86] "Since I regard myself as a conservative and am frequently referred to as such and since according to my own scoring, I should be nearer 100%, I find it difficult to understand your methods," he wrote to an ACA staffer. In response, the ACA actually took steps to downplay agricultural issues in subsequent years so as to aid lawmakers from farm areas in the South and West. "At one time there was sharp criticism because of too much emphasis on agriculture," Executive Director Charles McManus explained to the ACA's trustees in early 1963. "There were three or four votes given on agricultural bills. We have corrected that."[87] Though their antistatist views meant they wanted to expose those merely "posing as conservatives," this suggests the continued importance to ACA leaders of sustaining the conservative coalition.[88]

To reinforce that coalition, the ACA also engaged in campaign activity intended to aid conservative candidates, utilizing scores to identify those deserving of support.[89] The ACA was a more hierarchical (and less extensive) organization than the ADA and made formal endorsements at the national level, though it was careful to avoid doing so when this official imprimatur might work against rather than for a candidate.[90] In such cases, the score alone would serve as a signal to interested voters, and its staffers would provide campaign assistance behind the scenes without publicly declaring their involvement.[91] That assistance, in general, was "in kind"; the ACA provided "manpower and other material aid to candidates rather than money contributions," including hiring temporary personnel to work on campaigns, writing speeches and press releases for candidates, and purchasing direct mail lists on their behalf.[92] In 1964 the ACA spent over $100,000 on such activities.[93] It did not, however, make direct financial contributions—citing practical rather than legal concerns "that cash contributions to candidates whose campaign organizations are managed by political amateurs are frequently wasted."[94] In that sense, the ACA operated more like the CIO P.A.C. in its early phase. Nevertheless, since it made expenditures to aid specific candidates, the ACA still registered as a political committee and filed reports with the Clerk of the House of Representatives.[95] According to Herbert Alexander, who consulted those reports, the ACA spent nearly $190,000 in 1960 and more than $200,000 in 1964, becoming one of the most significant nonparty spenders in congressional elections.[96]

Liberals responded to the ACA with an attack on its message but not its methods. Much as conservatives had once denounced them as communistic, liberals portrayed the ACA as a part of an extremist "radical Right" with links to controversial groups like the John Birch Society (JBS).[97] (ACA leaders claimed they represented the "responsible" Right and denied any official connection to the JBS, though the unofficial links were somewhat murky.)[98] Named for an American missionary killed by Chinese Communists in 1945, the John Birch Society had been founded in 1958—the same year as the ACA—to fight Communist infiltration in the United States and any hint of "collectivism" on the domestic front.[99] It was a far more secretive organization than the ACA, however, and far more conspiratorial in its outlook, reflecting the views of its founder, candy manufacturer Robert Welch (a former vice president of the NAM), who alleged that Communist infiltration had reached President Eisenhower himself.[100] In return, Eisenhower's successor, John F. Kennedy, was sufficiently concerned about the radical Right that he authorized a secret probe of right-wing organizations and their funding (an idea that had, in fact, come from UAW president and former CIO president Walter Reuther).[101]

The ACA was monitored as part of this effort, though it is unclear if it was targeted in the Kennedy administration's boldest move to counteract growing conservative activism, the Ideological Organizations Project within the Internal Revenue Service (IRS), which launched "politically motivated financial audits," as Andrew explains, intended to strip right-wing organizations of tax exemptions and thus undermine their financial viability.[102] This secret and illegal program was eventually revealed by a congressional investigation chaired by Senator Frank Church in the mid-1970s—the Select Committee to Study Governmental Operations with Respect to Intelligence Activities—which was established in the wake of the Watergate scandal.[103] Nonetheless, the White House kept tabs on the ACA's activities, including its campaign spending and assistance, and tracked its electoral successes.

An internal White House memo calculated that 74 percent of the candidates the ACA backed in the 1962 midterms had been elected, for example, warning that the "right wing-seems to have been more successful, politically, than is generally realized."[104] This chimed with the ACA's own internal analysis, which showed that it had endorsed 180 candidates in the general election, of whom 131 had won—suggesting a high success rate, though some were in relatively safe seats.[105] In party terms, the ACA had endorsed 170 Republicans and just 10 Democrats, revealing a far more partisan orientation to its activities than the ACA professed (though not quite as lopsided as COPE's had been in the reverse direction).[106] As *Congressional Quarterly* observed in its own assessment, "ACA endorsed conservative Northern Republicans," but it also "selected the most conservative candidate in Southern districts without too much regard to party label."[107] Indeed, the Democrats the ACA supported were almost all southerners, showing that its efforts to bolster the conservative coalition were still relevant. It even provided campaign support to a further four Alabama Democrats whom it did not publicly endorse, all of whom won election in November.[108]

Two years later, the ACA made slightly fewer endorsements, though it backed slightly more Democrats (17 out of 173 candidates), at least in public. According to internal documents, the ACA supported 27 more candidates behind the scenes, all Republicans.[109] With controversy swirling around Barry Goldwater's presidential candidacy, many candidates felt uncomfortable receiving the imprimatur of the radical Right. "[C]onservative legislators have been subjected to great pressures to reject the endorsement and aid of ACA," Moreell noted at the time.[110] Congressman John Lindsay of New York, whom the ACA regarded as a "flaming liberal," had described such endorsements as a "kiss of death" in 1964.[111] Certainly the ACA saw a much lower overall success rate among those who did accept its endorsement that year, dropping to 55 percent according to *Congressional Quarterly*.[112] Although CQ calculations suggested that ACA and COPE efforts had effectively canceled each other out in 1962, COPE appears to have done much better in 1964, particularly in marginal districts, and liberals made gains in Congress.[113] Yet ACA officials took comfort in their own assessment that, among Republicans, the most conservative incumbents—those with ACA scores of 65 percent or higher—had fared better.[114]

Among Democrats, the ACA had once again offered its support primarily to southerners (with the exception of Congressman Walter Baring of Nevada), but it backed some southern Republicans too, apparently torn between its desire to reinforce the conservative coalition as an institutional bulwark against liberalism and a recognition that Southern Democrats were not always the "truest" conservatives, even as they appeared to be far to the right of their northern counterparts. Indeed, in two southern congressional districts, the ACA even endorsed *both* the Republican and Democratic candidates—an equivocation that might suggest that equally conservative candidates were running.[115] But it might also point to ACA confusion over its purposes and partisanship. Since Eisenhower's first election in 1952, in which he won four southern states, the GOP had sought to strengthen its position in the once "solid South" and promote a viable two-party system. In 1957 the Republican National Committee (RNC) had launched "Operation Dixie" to aid nascent Republican organizations on the ground, and GOP congressional candidates were beginning to make headway in some urban areas.[116] In providing resources to such candidates the ACA could help to further that process, though it would likely mean the erosion of the cross-party conservative coalition over time. In backing candidates from both parties, then, the ACA could hedge its bets. But behind closed doors, if slowly and hesitantly, it was coming to embrace a much more partisan vision.

Just prior to the 1964 election, Moreell provided analysis to the ACA's trustees that showed stark party differences in terms of average ACA scores. While the Republicans had a 77.8 percent average, he noted, the Democrats languished at just 21.3 percent. "The Republican Party, as a whole, is the Party of constitutional conservatism and individual freedom," Moreell concluded from this comparison.[117] The Democratic Party, in contrast, stood for "democratic socialism, government intervention in the people's affairs and regimentation of the citizens."[118] There were exceptions, he acknowledged, but "the preponderance of each of the Parties is as I have stated." That there remained some outliers compared to these averages—liberal Republicans and conservative Democrats—Moreell continued, "confirms the view of many students of political science that the time is here for a re-alignment of the two Parties into conservative constitutionalists and liberal centralists."[119] Moreell reaffirmed this point after the election, noting that there were far more Republicans with ACA scores of 65 percent and above than Democrats, despite some "conspicuous exceptions."[120] That lopsided distribution, he said, explained why the ACA tended to back Republicans, a claim that its apparently partisan leaning was incidental.[121] Yet Moreell went further, noting that such analysis "serves to encourage the hope that eventually there will be a realignment of the Parties on the basis of conservatism versus modern liberalism."[122]

Rather than a rearguard action against Democratic liberalization, Moreell's assessment suggests that the ACA was coming to embrace realignment as its own. It was not simply the *view* of political scientists but now the *hope* of the

ACA. Indeed, the ACA had distributed copies of its party comparison chart to voters so as to emphasize the point about ideological differences and implicitly encourage change.[123] As much as the ACA urged voters to evaluate a lawmaker's individual record and score, emphasizing such party differences cast Southern Democrats in an unflattering light, less as heroic defenders holding back the liberal tide in their party than as outliers who should either join their ideological brethren on the opposing side or be replaced by conservative Republicans. As the editors of the *Richmond News Leader* had concluded after examining the first set of ACA Index scores, there was a much larger ideological difference between the parties than they had realized, and it raised questions about the South's commitment to the Democratic Party.[124] "[I]f the Republic ever comes to its political senses," they reflected, "we will choose up sides all over again."[125]

The ACA, it seemed, was now choosing sides too. Goldwater's presidential candidacy may have helped to convince its leaders, in the way it energized a conservative base nationwide and made the GOP appear a receptive partisan vehicle. The prominent switch of South Carolina senator Strom Thurmond from Democrat to Republican may have been a factor too, highlighting as it did the potential for personal partisan conversions to bring greater conservative cohesion to the GOP. Thurmond's switch was itself an important signal of the weakening ties between Southern Democrats and their national party, as the Kennedy and then Lyndon Johnson presidencies pushed liberal social measures, especially civil rights legislation. Thurmond had changed affiliation shortly after the Civil Rights Act of 1964 was signed into law, and there was no question that its passage under unified Democratic government tore at the deeply emotional party loyalty of white lawmakers and voters in the South—forged in the embers of the Civil War and suffused with racial antipathy—leading them to reconsider their enmity toward the GOP.[126] In the presidential contest, Goldwater carried five states in the Deep South (and just one other, his native Arizona). Over time, this fissure opened the South to steady Republican gains, both through party conversion among lawmakers and the electoral replacement of Democrats with Republicans.[127] The extent to which racial animus played a role in the ACA's own partisan shift is unclear; certainly its leaders were willing to work with segregationist lawmakers whose opposition to centralized government aligned with their own, but ACA internal documents provide little insight into their racial views. Ostensibly they opposed the Civil Rights Act on constitutional grounds, as an illegitimate exercise of federal power. At the very least it affirmed, perhaps definitively, their belief that a commitment to New Deal "statism" had progressed too far in the Democratic Party to be undone.[128]

Thus Moreell's statements suggest that the ACA was now committed to the same realignment that the ADA had long sought to bring about and that Mundt had proposed a decade before.[129] Its earlier support for the conservative coalition would recede from view, replaced by a desire to transform the GOP into a conservative counterweight to a liberal Democratic Party. Though it continued to avoid explicit involvement in presidential contests (it did not endorse in either 1960 or 1964, though it lent support to Goldwater by publicizing his high ACA score), the ACA became more active in Republican primary contests—in which it had previously engaged only occasionally—and began providing financial resources to candidates more directly.[130] And the ACA Index would provide a key tool for directing these activities, for the ACA itself and a growing constellation of conservative organizations. According to Richard Viguerie, a pioneering conservative fundraiser active from the late 1960s onward, the ACA's ratings gave conservatives "a precise way of knowing which Republicans to support or oppose . . . and they used these ratings to help change the face of the GOP."[131]

One Step Closer

One organization that had utilized ACA Index scores from the start was the NAM, pointing to the ideological sympathy between leading business organizations and conservative groups. In 1960, with a conservative rating now available, the NAM's public affairs division decided to distribute information on congressional voting and scores to its member firms.[132] But in keeping with the NAM's emphasis on individual choice in politics, its public affairs staff provided several different ratings from both "leading 'conservative' and 'liberal' organizations," including the ACA, the ADA, and COPE.[133] And they offered no explicit guidance about which came closest to the NAM's own viewpoint.[134]

Nor was it apparent that calls for greater political involvement among businessmen were producing greater individual financial participation by this point, even among the NAM and the Chamber's own officers. The proportion contributing to candidates or parties remained relatively low, much as it had been in the 1950s. Data gathered by Herbert Alexander showed that out of sixty or more officers and directors of the Chamber, just five made campaign contributions in 1960, while seven did so in 1964. In comparison, 21 and 22 NAM officials made contributions in those respective years, but this remained a small proportion of the 172 potential contributors in 1960 or 158 in 1964. Nonetheless, what contributions were made had a distinctly Republican orientation. All of the Chamber-associated contributions in both years went to Republicans, while the majority of NAM-association donations did also.[135] Of the nearly $61,000 that NAM officers contributed to major party committees and candidates in 1964, for example, 95 percent went to Republican causes (though half came from a single donor and his wife, Liberty League veteran J. Howard Pew).[136]

By the early 1960s some corporations had also moved beyond public affairs and begun to experiment with informal political action funds financed by contributions from their executives, suggesting a desire to imprint campaign contributions with a clearer corporate identity.[137] But if business associations were not yet following that lead, a professional group was about to take a significant step further. In 1961 the American Medical Association (AMA) did something no traditional interest group except labor federations had yet done: it created a formal PAC. The formation of AMPAC was thus a watershed moment in the rise of political action, demonstrating its diffusion across both the interest group environment and the ideological spectrum. The AMA's political motivations, after all, fit with a more conservative worldview. It opposed federal government involvement in healthcare, and it had discerned renewed danger in a 1958 legislative proposal to provide federal health insurance for the elderly, as well as the election of Kennedy in 1960, who had supported it.[138] AMPAC was formed in response to this distinct legislative threat, suggesting the AMA no longer trusted that lobbying alone would protect its interests. But its formation pointed to something else: the diminution of cultural boundaries on political action more generally. Just ten years earlier, political scientist David Truman had singled out the medical profession as being culturally constrained from political activism. "Doctors aren't expected to act that way," he had observed.[139] Now they were urged to do so, with the AMA's leaders perhaps emboldened by the growing commitment to political action among conservative ideological groups. In turn, AMPAC served to further that trajectory among traditional interest groups.

Unlike the AMA, business groups did not face an existential legislative threat in the early 1960s. The Taft-Hartley Act had survived repeated onslaughts. Right-to-work laws had passed in several states. The Landrum-Griffin Act of 1959 had placed further restrictions on unions, despite the influx of liberal legislators in 1958. And while a northern Democrat might have won the White House in 1960, John Kennedy was neither an ardent ally of labor nor an unabashed tax-and-spend liberal. He had served on the McClellan rackets committee, and his brother Robert, now attorney general, had been its crusading legal counsel. As a young senator in 1953, moreover, he had revealed in an interview that he was "not a liberal at all.... I never joined the Americans for Democratic Action or the American Veterans Committee. I'm not comfortable with those people."[140] He appointed prominent businessmen to his cabinet, such as Ford Motor Company president Robert McNamara. And as president, he pushed through substantial tax *cuts* for both individuals and corporations amid an economic recovery from the recession of 1958.

And yet perceptions of the wider political climate among business group leaders were marked by fear and uncertainty, a point that scholars might easily dismiss as a "paranoid style" or outlook without acknowledging its impact.[141] As the NAM's Charles Sligh noted after passage of the Landrum-Griffin Act: "The new law presents an advance, but that . . . advance is threatened by labor political activity."[142] Much as their publicity deified free enterprise and portrayed any infringement of that ideal as a step toward socialism, business leaders saw the pernicious influence of labor's political activism at every turn. They did not need a clear existential threat in the present to fear one in the future. Indeed, they saw their major legislative victories as vulnerable and viewed minor losses as the harbingers of creeping statism. Above all, they feared the impact of COPE and its allies on the political scene. The NAM's entire public affairs strategy in 1962, for example, was to be "based upon the challenge to industry presented by the AFL-CIO through its political arm, COPE."[143] But COPE, especially, was increasingly viewed as a force that publicity campaigns and political education alone could not confine. These perceptions more than any objective reality, along with an underlying competitive dynamic in the interest group environment, helped to fuel more urgent calls for business involvement in political action to protect its interests and lessened the constraining influence of older cultural or ideological objections. And so it was that a small item appeared on the agenda for the NAM's January 1963 executive committee meeting: to be discussed was a proposed "direct political action organization under the sponsorship of NAM."[144]

Shortly thereafter, in April 1963, the NAM's board of directors approved $100,000 in seed money for a new political action organization that would take the business message directly into the electoral battlefield. "At Last—A Political Organization for Businessmen," the *NAM News* soon announced.[145] The Business-Industry Political Action Committee (BIPAC as it would come to be known) had arrived, and with it began a new wave of business political action. BIPAC "was established to serve as a political education and action arm of American business and industry," a press release announced (later inserted into the *Congressional Record* by Republican Senate minority leader Everett Dirksen).[146] It sought "to promote a system of government in which the individual liberties of all citizens would be of paramount concern," to which end it would "encourage and assist individual citizens in organizing themselves for more effective political action."[147] More bluntly, it would "raise money to assist House and Senate candidates sympathetic to the business point of view and to conduct a program of political information at the local, state and national levels," a NAM spokesman explained.[148]

In so doing, BIPAC was both modeled after and intended to counter COPE. It was "planned as the management counterpart of COPE," one journalist observed, and meant "to give business the same organized national focus that COPE gave labor," as a BIPAC official later recalled.[149] Indeed, antilabor rhetoric was now utilized in new ways to justify the NAM's venture. Conservative critics had long derided closed or union shops as "labor monopolies," for example, which operated without competitors and denied their members a free choice to join.[150] In a pointed inversion, they now extended that assessment to the political sphere. As one of BIPAC's founding directors noted in 1964, "The leaders of big labor unions . . . have achieved also what amounts to a political monopoly in most of the nation's congressional constituencies."[151] As in the economic sphere the answer was competition, and business associations could provide it. As Hall noted, the formation of AMPAC and BIPAC meant that "the battle between groups representing labor, business, and professions has been made public, and the public should stand to profit from the open competition."[152]

Structurally, BIPAC was formally separate from its parent organization though informally connected, much like COPE. "[A]fter BIPAC is set up and functioning, it will have no official relationship to the NAM," the spokesman elaborated when announcing its formation.[153] Yet BIPAC was initially funded by the NAM, staffed with former NAM personnel (including Robert L. Humphrey, the NAM's director of public affairs, who became its first executive director), and its board was populated with NAM directors.[154] NAM officials even expressed internal concern about participation from other groups in BIPAC's management or planning "because this would risk turning it into a debating society instead of an action group," though they appear to have encouraged some Chamber of Commerce and AMPAC involvement.[155] Like COPE, BIPAC was also a permanent body, because "[o]ne-shot political action programs would not produce lasting results," a leaflet explained.[156] NAM lawyers had even sought copies of COPE's constitution and bylaws to consider in formulating their own.[157]

There were some differences, however. For a start, BIPAC asked for larger contributions than labor PACs did, offering different types of "membership" costing from $10 to $5,000.[158] Unlike COPE, moreover, BIPAC did not encourage subnational affiliates, intending to work with existing groups on the ground that shared its aims.[159] In this respect it more closely resembled the ACA, which placed a greater emphasis on the national level, though it did forge ties with nearly three hundred trade and business groups across the country.[160] NAM lawyers also sought out advice from AMPAC personnel as they planned their new organization, and Humphrey attended AMPAC events early in 1963, suggesting that it too provided a model for BIPAC and even a further spur to political action.[161] And of course, any similarity to COPE ended at the organizational level. "BIPAC's economic and political principles differ in that they reflect the views of the business community generally," a press release explained.[162]

With the formation of BIPAC, the NAM pursued a dual approach to the political realm: continuing its political mobilization courses, which now targeted the wives of executives as well as businessmen themselves, while also encouraging direct political action through a PAC.[163] The NAM's 1964 course, for example, entitled "The Bill Boyntons Go into Politics," featured a suburban couple becoming involved in a local political campaign. The goal of such technical instruction was "to produce effective manpower within critical congressional districts," an internal memo explained. If successful in 1964, it continued, then the NAM would "get a lion's share of the credit since it has been responsible for creating BIPAC (money) and Bill Boynton (manpower)."[164] In theory, that success would be measured in terms of victories for conservative congressional candidates—those who articulated "a sound philosophy of government"—in "critical" or close races.[165] Much like their labor and liberal counterparts, BIPAC officials publicly declared that their activities were strictly nonpartisan. "BIPAC is nonpartisan," the initial press release declared. "It is not affiliated with any political party."[166] But much like these other groups, the reality looked far more partisan than the rhetoric.

According to BIPAC's public pronouncements, candidates would be selected on the basis of their "platform, voting record and electability," without regard to party affiliation.[167] But the "voting record" that BIPAC utilized was the ACA Index, meaning that more Republicans were likely to receive support, and at that the most conservative ones.[168] As Robert Humphrey admitted in a newspaper interview, BIPAC also intended to oppose incumbents rated highly by COPE, who were almost exclusively Democrats.[169] In allocating electoral support on such a basis, BIPAC implicitly promoted a rightward shift in the GOP more than in the Democratic Party. More generally, reporters widely observed that Republican candidates and local party organizations were the likely beneficiaries of all enhanced corporate political activity.[170]

Nonetheless, BIPAC officials sought to bolster their nonpartisan claims in another way, by emphasizing the bipartisan composition of the board and of the panel that would determine which candidates to support.[171] Indeed, a former Democratic congressman from Alabama, Laurie C. Battle, was made acting director prior to the permanent appointment of Humphrey, who had himself served as the RNC's campaign director before moving to the NAM.[172] Yet this simply made clear that the nature of BIPAC bipartisanship resembled the conservative coalition of northern Republicans and Southern Democrats—a coalition that was weakening as both lawmakers and individual citizens reassessed their party loyalties. At the very least, BIPAC did not intend to participate in the presidential race and thus could not be tainted with a claim of presidential partisanship through endorsement or other modes of support.[173] This was perhaps of benefit organizationally, since Goldwater's candidacy was divisive even within the business community, never a unified bloc in the first place. Where the NAM and BIPAC stood firmly to the right, Goldwater's push for extremism over moderation induced many normally Republican business executives to abandon their party's presidential ticket.[174]

Ultimately, BIPAC supported seventy-eight House candidates and twelve Senate candidates in the 1964 general elections, almost all of whom were Republicans.[175] It supported just nine House Democrats, all southerners.[176] It did, however, provide financial aid in six Democratic primary elections, mostly in the South (compared to just one Republican primary in Michigan), suggesting that pragmatism remained a relevant factor in one-party states where conservative Democrats faced more liberal challengers.[177] Still, BIPAC supported Republican general election candidates across the South, in Alabama, Florida, Georgia, North Carolina, and Virginia, many of whom were elected.[178] Indeed, the unusual dynamics of the 1964 presidential race may have scrambled BIPAC's pragmatic calculations elsewhere; in Mississippi, for example, it backed a Democratic incumbent who lost to a Republican when Goldwater swept the state, in what was deemed "Mississippi's biggest Congressional upset in a century."[179] Outside the South, a backlash against Goldwater contributed to a poor performance for BIPAC candidates; just twenty-eight of its seventy-eight House candidates won election, a success rate of 36 percent (though BIPAC's executive director stressed that many of the races were marginal to begin with).[180] BIPAC's Senate performance was worse. Of the twelve candidates it had backed (all Republicans), just one won election: Paul Fannin in Arizona, running for the seat Barry Goldwater had vacated to run for the presidency.

As much as these figures point to BIPAC's operational partisanship, such patterns were only apparent *after* the general election, and then only for those who cared to look, since BIPAC's board prohibited the release of any financial information beforehand.[181] Indeed, BIPAC did not make public endorsements as the ACA did or publicize its contributions widely to signal its preferences, a level of secrecy that suggests some lingering concern about visible business involvement in politics. Other earlier concerns, both legal and ideological, appear to have shaped BIPAC's approach also. It was more financially cautious than other PACs, for example. Thus Alexander reported that it used voluntary funds to pay for all operating costs close to elections, which most other PACs no longer did.[182] It also consistently emphasized individual choice in its publications, suggesting awareness of the tension between collective political action and the individualist ethos conservatives espoused. In its constitution, BIPAC's mission was framed in terms of assisting "individual citizens in *organizing themselves* for more effective political action."[183] In promotional materials, BIPAC was described as "a voluntary movement of citizens acting on their own deep-seated beliefs as individuals."[184]

Yet placing this emphasis on individual choice and action made it difficult to explain why businessmen should act through BIPAC. "Certainly you can give directly to any candidate," one brochure clarified, acknowledging that there was a "dire need" for more individual involvement in politics.[185] But contributing to

BIPAC could make that involvement more "tangible and fruitful," the brochure suggested. BIPAC had "specialized information" and undertook vast "organizational planning" so as "to carry on in a purposeful, business-like manner this vital phase of effective, political action on a national basis."[186] It offered "a practical and realistic approach to politics for every individual who wants to preserve the individual rights and privileges embodied in the Constitution."[187] Individual action could be made more effective, in sum, by channeling support toward particular candidates and associating that support more clearly with business. For all the parsing, BIPAC gave the NAM an important collective tool: a singular identity in politics.

With BIPAC, a business group had met labor political action in kind on the electoral battlefield, if on a smaller scale. The business group spent a little over $200,000 in the 1964 elections, while COPE spent nearly $1 million.[188] But the NAM's venture was not greeted warmly across the entire business community. George Romney, the former president of General Motors turned Republican governor of Michigan, expressed concern with programs encouraging businessmen to place special interest identity above citizenship at large, something that business had long claimed to oppose.[189] And a former state politician and utility executive in Connecticut offered a more portentous, if contradictory warning. Though he generally supported public affairs programs, he worried about initiatives explicitly designed to combat COPE. "If this becomes an extension of the battle between management and labor it will fall flat as a pancake," he warned, suggesting the inefficacy of such an approach. But at the same time, he worried about the implications of success. "A real tragedy will befall us if we become a two-party system consisting of a business party and a labor party."[190]

The results of the 1964 election were meant to discount such a possibility: a business party versus a labor party, a conservative party versus a liberal one. Goldwater's "extremism" had been defeated, many journalists and politicians assumed. Moderates had regained control of the RNC.[191] Any incentives for Southern Democrats to defect were supposedly lessened by the resounding victories of a Democratic president and majority status in Congress.[192] Yet some contemporary observers noted continued energy on the right.[193] Conservative activists had largely brought about Goldwater's nomination, and his loss had not dampened their enthusiasm.[194] As Wildavsky had noted prior to the election, many of these activists were "purists" who cared less about victory than promoting their principles.[195] Goldwater's campaign helped convince them to pursue that aim within the Republican Party. Numerous new conservative organizations sprang up in the wake of the campaign, set upon shifting the GOP steadily rightward, leading the RNC's new chairman, Ray Bliss, to denounce them as "splinter groups" that were "destructive of party unity."[196] The congressional ratings and targeted financial backing that groups like the ACA and BIPAC could provide became tools through which conservative standards could be applied to the GOP from the outside. In practice, these PACs had become part of a broader constellation of conservative groups that, openly or otherwise, looked to shape the GOP into a counterweight to a liberalized Democratic Party.

BIPAC's activities in 1965 are telling. That year it gave $1,000 to the National Republican Congressional Committee, a clear violation of its nonpartisan pretensions.[197] And despite 1965 being an off year, it also made a significant campaign donation, backing Republican candidate Albert Watson in a special congressional election in South Carolina.[198] Watson was, in fact, a former Democratic incumbent who had endorsed Goldwater in 1964 and won re-election. Stripped of his seniority by the Democratic caucus (in itself suggestive of a more resolute party compared to 1948), he had resigned and promptly switched parties, running for his old seat again as a Republican.[199] BIPAC's support for Watson was symbolic of a broader shift among business group leaders and conservative activists who had long placed their faith in the conservative coalition but now increasingly looked to the Republican Party to protect their interests—a party they would help to remake.

Conclusion

The House That P.A.C. Built

In the wake of the 1964 presidential election, erstwhile Republican nominee Barry Goldwater offered a suggestion for the future of American politics. While vacationing in Jamaica after his electoral drubbing, Goldwater held an impromptu press conference during a round of golf and called for "a real realignment" of the American party system into "two new teams": Liberals and Conservatives.[1] He did not suggest new parties so much as new labels for the old parties, once fully re-sorted by ideology.[2] There had been a trend in this direction since 1928, Goldwater said, he merely wanted to formalize the shift.[3] To promote that vision, Goldwater would himself turn to political action—looking to the example of labor and liberal groups that he had once denounced and forming his own PAC, the Free Society Association (FSA).[4]

The story of American politics since Goldwater's loss has come to be told as the steady growth and eventual triumph of the conservative movement in the GOP, exemplified by the election of Ronald Reagan as president in 1980 and leading to the polarized party system we see today. We know much about the ideas and individuals that animated the movement, the groups that publicized them, and the ways voting behavior steadily changed, as the South shifted ever more Republican in the wake of the 1964 Civil Rights Act.[5] We know that each party's congressional delegations became increasingly uniform in their ideological viewpoints and increasingly distant from each other, with liberal Republicans and conservative Democrats almost extinct species by the 1990s.[6] Yet we often overlook an important organizational dimension of that story: the very *mechanisms* that brought about change and the reactive, competitive dynamics that fueled them.[7] Electoral activity undertaken by oppositional interest groups—"political action" as it came to be known—animated by a strategy of dynamic partisanship and ultimately implemented through political action committees (PACs), is a crucial and neglected factor for understanding this major transformation in American party politics.

The Rise of Political Action Committees. Emily J. Charnock, Oxford University Press (2020). © Oxford University Press.
DOI: 10.1093/oso/9780190075514.001.0001

From controversial origins in the early twentieth century, interest group electioneering became more entrenched and extensive over time, coming to be formalized in PACs and similar entities by the 1940s, partly in response to legal changes, but also to the increasingly technical and specialized nature of electoral activity and the increasing importance accorded it. Legal and cultural controversy continued to shape its development, conditioning the careful public presentation and pretensions to nonpartisanship. Yet there were differences in the way interest group leaders and activists on the left and right of the political spectrum approached political action and PACs. Dissatisfied with the results of lobbying and inspired by a Democratic president, labor union officials and liberals more generally were quicker to embrace a dynamic partisan vision of political action focused on the Democratic Party, where PACs could help to push the party leftward and effect an ideological realignment without recourse to a third party. In contrast, business group leaders and many conservatives, chastened by their failed electoral experiment in 1936, restored to a position of political privilege after the war, and invested in the gospel of individualism, initially placed their faith in the bipartisan conservative coalition and resisted the call of realignment for some time. Their eventual forays "into politics" in the late 1950s and early 1960s reflected their eroding confidence in that coalition and their growing belief that the liberalization of the Democratic Party could no longer be stopped. Instead, it must be met with a more conservative Republican Party, which a range of business and conservative PACs would seek to realize over time.

The new chair of the Republican National Committee (RNC) would now accuse Goldwater himself of fostering "splinter parties"—a charge the senator had once leveled against liberal groups in the 1950s.[8] At that time, Goldwater had emphasized party loyalty over ideological purity, but he later altered his position with the encouragement and assistance of conservative groups. Perhaps he too had come to see the GOP as the only vehicle for conservative success and to appreciate that, unlike the formal party machinery, interest groups possessed the tools to promote partisan change. As V. O. Key had explained to his students in 1957, American parties had "no system of quality control so as to be able to deliver a standard product under their trade-mark." "The customer has to beware," he warned.[9] But interest groups and PACs could offer a kind of "quality control," developing ways of identifying the "right" kind of party candidates and helping them get elected.

* * *

After Goldwater's loss, a wave of editorials denounced his vision of the party system and offered chilling pronouncements of what it might mean. They warned of "polarization" rather than principled partisanship. "Nobody knows for sure," said the *Charlotte Observer*'s editorial board, "but conceivably it could divide the nation into two warring ideological camps where compromise on matters of political principles would be regarded as akin to treason."[10] It might even "drive the nation's political temperature toward the boiling point and thus endanger the whole system of party government."[11] Yet little over a decade earlier, political scientists had proposed a similar plan, to wide intellectual acclaim. (Goldwater had even addressed the American Political Science Association's annual meeting in Chicago just two months before the election, when he warned of partisan "me-tooism"—much as the famous APSA report had done.)[12] Inspired by a vision of Democratic liberalization, E. E. Schattschneider and his colleagues did not fully reckon with the prospect of a more conservative GOP. Nor did they appreciate how far opposing ideological "purism" might go.[13] Schattschneider's responsible parties were meant to be ideologically distinctive but still open to differing ideas and interests, with party leaders reconciling various demands with a broader conception of the public good. But as Wildavsky described, the "ideal party" for the new activists of the 1960s was "a distinct and separate community of co-believers who differ with the opposition party all down the line."[14]

Schattschneider's earlier scholarship had also portrayed interest groups, or "pressure groups" as he labeled them, as a pernicious force in American politics that would be tamed by more "responsible" parties. He did not anticipate that they might play a role in bringing about more ideologically distinct and cohesive parties. Nor did he anticipate *how* they would do it. Schattschneider, Key, and others had suggested interest groups would largely *avoid* the electoral realm, in part to avoid any taint of "partisanship." Only if parties somehow became more distinct, taking opposing positions on an interest group's key concerns, would a group be forced to pick a side, Key had suggested, at which point it "might as well" join the electoral fray. Otherwise the reputational toll and prospect of internal divisions were considered prohibitive. As this book has shown, the reverse was often true: interest groups *chose* to engage in electoral activities, despite the risks, in order to *promote* uniformity within a single party on their issues of concern, which they thought would better secure their aims in the long run.

Interest group electioneering did not effect an immediate shift in the party system, nor is it entirely responsible for the dramatic changes we have seen. In some ways, the story told here is focused more on intentions than on results. But it offers a tangible way of connecting different processes and phenomena identified by political scientists as relevant to party realignment and polarization: the gradual "secular realignment" of voting behavior that Key described elsewhere in his scholarship, which informs Black and Black's account of change among southern voters; the ideological "sorting" of voters nationally into the "correct" party that Fiorina and colleagues have described since the 1970s, along

with a similar process through individual party conversions and electoral replacement that Theriault discerns among lawmakers; and the suggestion, first
developed by Aldrich, that ideological activists used primary elections to promote more extreme candidates, thus presenting general election voters with
more polarized choices.[15] Interest group political action is the thread that binds
them together: in the identification and cultivation of candidates through ideological rating systems, the use of these scores as well as formal endorsements to
signal to activists and primary voters which candidate to support, and the provision of financial resources and indirect campaign assistance to those candidates,
complemented by broader publicity campaigns designed to "educate" voters in
the liberal or conservative worldview.[16]

This model, pioneered by labor and liberal groups in the 1940s and early
1950s and emulated by conservative and business groups in the late 1950s
and early 1960s, has since been adopted by a range of issue-oriented advocacy groups that proliferated in the 1970s—a time when the number of PACs
itself exploded after passage of the Federal Election Campaign Act and subsequent amendments.[17] Consider the National Rifle Association (NRA) and the
National Abortion Rights Action League (NARAL), which both created PACs
in the 1970s.[18] Both rate lawmakers according to their issues of concern, make
public endorsements, and provide material aid to selected candidates. Both
claim to be nominally "nonpartisan" in doing so.[19] Yet both lopsidedly support
Republicans and Democrats respectively and have acquired a partisan reputation.[20] Indeed, reflecting a scholarly shift that now sees interest groups as central to understanding contemporary parties, they are viewed as part of a broader
organizational "network" surrounding each party. The activities of both groups
suggest that far from exhibiting partisan leanings because the distribution of
issue positions happens to fall that way, they have actively tried to promote
an asymmetry. The NRA sees its interests as best served by a Republican majority in Congress, one official told Skinner, and thus it favors Republicans over
Democrats even when their "grades" are the same.[21] Likewise, when NARAL had
an opportunity to support a pro-choice Republican in the 2012 Massachusetts
Senate election, it demurred, even though the Democratic challenger had no
congressional record to assess.[22] Much as the Union for Democratic Action
warned in 1942, groups like NARAL fear that a *good* Republican can pave the
way for a *bad* party, showing how institutional considerations inform a strategy
of dynamic partisanship.[23]

Some advocates of reproductive rights, however, have questioned NARAL's
Democratic allegiance, claiming that "[w]omen in the Democratic Party have
been taken for granted and have lost their bargaining power as a result."[24] This
articulates the traditional fear of "capture," in which groups lose influence by
allying with a party because, knowing the captured group's voters have "nowhere

else to go," the party makes only minimal policy concessions. The strategy labor leaders initially forged was meant to override that concern, maintaining influence through the provision of campaign resources rather than the threat of electoral defection, while enhancing the prospects for policy gains by installing sympathetic Democratic allies to begin with. They expected to achieve more through a liberalized Democratic Party, provided it held majority status, than through nonpartisan lobbying or other methods of influence. Yet it is not clear the strategy has worked as they hoped. The electoral successes COPE enjoyed in 1958, for example, did not translate into legislative gains for labor, as the passage of Landrum-Griffin showed. The 86th Congress had "fulfilled few of labor's optimistic expectations," as *Congressional Quarterly* noted in 1960.[25] COPE's response to this discouraging outcome, however, was *more* partisan political action, not less. Meanwhile, business group leaders perceived policy gains such as Landrum-Griffin as mere rearguard actions, sure to eventually crumble in the face of labor's electoral "juggernaut." Panicked by their own cataclysmic predictions, they sought to build their own electoral army. To some extent, then, the problem associated with partisan political action has not so much been *capture* as *counteraction*, with each side becoming trapped in an escalating and increasingly costly electoral conflict without securing the policy gains it expected.

Some might argue that the balance has now been firmly tipped in favor of business political action, since the Supreme Court's 2010 *Citizens United* decision and a subsequent Circuit Court ruling made possible the formation of expenditure-only "super PACs."[26] Though *Citizens United* overturned restrictions on both corporate and labor union electoral spending (using treasury rather than voluntary funds), the substantial decline of labor union membership in the later twentieth century meant it unlocked far greater corporate resources. For labor, there is a bitter irony here, since it did so much to pioneer and legitimize the kind of activities that can now be used against it. Indeed, at a time when union political power appeared in the ascendancy in the 1940s, the CIO's lawyers rejected the notion that the Court could constitutionally restrict union electoral spending, offering a rationale not unlike that proffered in *Citizens United,* though they chose not to test it at the time.[27]

Irrespective of legal issues, the debate over super PACs suggests an important shift in popular attitudes toward interest group political action since its origins in the early twentieth century. Current controversy generally centers on the *amounts* spent and the mechanisms of financing, rather than on the fundamental idea that groups organized around economic or ideological interests can play an active role in elections. The attempts to defend and justify political action in the face of early public hostility, to downplay its novelty—and often its partisan dimension—have served to render it more culturally acceptable over time. Indeed, the very campaign finance framework that *Citizens United* revisited—the

Federal Election Campaign Act of 1971 and its 1974 amendments—both reflected and furthered this broader process of legitimization, formally codifying the structure of PACs and their acceptable realm of activity.

* * *

"Political action determines the course of national history," a 1958 instructional manual encouraging businessmen to engage in politics had declared.[28] Over the course of the twentieth century, interest group electioneering developed from a broadly nonpartisan practice premised on the threat of electoral punishment over reward, to be delivered via a bloc of voters, to an instrument of dynamic partisanship advanced by the selective provision of both money and manpower in election campaigns, with the aim of drawing an entire party closer to a group's views and goals. Each approach implicated lobbying in different ways; electioneering was designed to complement and bolster lobbying efforts in the former case, while it would be rendered unnecessary if the latter approach were perfectly implemented.

Many of the groups that invented these practices remain active today—including the AFL-CIO's Committee on Political Education, the Americans for Democratic Action (ADA), the National Committee for an Effective Congress (NCEC), the American Medical Association Political Action Committee (AMPAC), and the Business-Industry Political Action Committee (BIPAC). Goldwater's Free Society Association, however, was a short-lived entity, while the Americans for Constitutional Action (ACA) had disappeared by the early 1980s.[29] Nonetheless, numerous conservative electoral groups emerged in the late 1960s and 1970s, including some associated with the American Conservative Union (ACU), which adopted many of the ACA's practices and effectively superseded it, remaining prominent on the right today.[30] All continue to engage in electoral activities on behalf of favored parties, their conflicts reflecting an underlying ideological divide initially forged in response to the New Deal. This conflict of organized interests—of business against labor, conservative versus liberal, Republican versus Democrat—previewed in the 1936 election and first fully realized, through PACs, in 1964, continues to shape American politics today.

Not all of the interest groups considered here, however, created fully fledged PACs or embraced overt political action in the same period. The US Chamber of Commerce, for example, despite its involvement with "businessmen in politics" programs in the 1950s and 1960s, continued to primarily emphasize lobbying until the late 1990s, at which point it became "a dominant player in election financing," according to Herrnson.[31] By 2014 the Chamber's political director acknowledged that its "No. 1 priority" was to ensure a Republican majority in Congress.[32] It followed the same trajectory as the NAM, therefore, just at a later date. In contrast, major agricultural organizations like the American Farm Bureau Federation have not formed PACs, though it does compile a congressional scorecard.[33] The Farm Bureau's stance may reflect its early policy gains during the New Deal, reducing the need for its leaders to seek alternative political approaches beyond legislative and bureaucratic lobbying.[34] Perhaps more crucially, the lack of a clear external opponent in the interest group world helped to protect its policy gains and further reduced electoral incentives.[35] The Farm Bureau also enjoyed institutional advantages, with its ties to the US Department of Agriculture and strong relationships with lawmakers on congressional agriculture committees.[36] Meanwhile, the cultural status of farmers in the American ideal served to make agricultural policy less divisive than labor or business policy, which in turn reduced the scope for partisan division.[37] All of this combined to make political action, particularly in its partisan form, less necessary for the Farm Bureau. Similarly, the American Association of Retired Persons (AARP), which lacks an organized interest group opponent and represents a constituency with cultural stature—many of its members receive significant distributive benefits from the federal government—has become a major lobbying group, but it does not engage in political action.[38]

Political action need not, in theory, be conducted on a partisan basis. But its emergence in the mid-twentieth century was foundationally associated with a strategy of dynamic partisanship. The CIO P.A.C. and its imitators aimed to create more ideological, nationally uniform parties, thus "realigning" the party system around a new dimension of conflict: the scope of federal government power. As P.A.C. director Jack Kroll told the ADA convention in 1952, America was "undergoing a profound political revolution," "a re-shifting of alignments" and "re-orientation by our political parties," which P.A.C. had both desired and helped propel.[39] Its goal reflected a new vision of party realignment, which had long been understood in terms of third parties. Only an "independent party" could disrupt the status quo and break apart the existing alignment, leftist radicals in the early twentieth century believed.[40] The example of Franklin Roosevelt's 1938 "purge" had pointed to a different way—of slowly changing a party from within. Yet even he had subsequently contemplated a more traditional effort to effect systemic change from without. As speechwriter Samuel Rosenman recalled, Roosevelt had opened a dialogue in 1944 with his former Republican opponent, Wendell Willkie, proposing a third party composed of Democratic and Republican liberals, though Willkie died before any plans could come to fruition.[41] Likewise, some conservatives, such as Republican senator Karl Mundt, had contemplated an inverse plan in the early 1950s.[42] The repeated failures of such efforts, however, led activists on both sides of the political spectrum to largely abandon independent parties as an instrument of change and embrace "independent" political action—that is, electoral activity conducted independently of a major party, though intended to both alter and advance its cause.[43]

* * *

If "realignment" means a shift in the central dimension of party conflict, then we might be seeing the makings of another one now. The presidency of Donald Trump has scrambled ideological categories to some extent, challenging the now "establishment" Republican orthodoxy on small government and free markets—some of the very attitudes that business and conservative groups worked so hard to instill in GOP lawmakers.[44] Yet Trump's attempt to rebrand the Republican Party illustrates some of the central themes of this book. For a start, he chose not to mount an independent presidential campaign in 2016 or to build a third party, looking instead to capture the Republican presidential nomination and then reshape the existing GOP from the top down. To some extent, he has since mounted a "purge" campaign as Franklin Roosevelt once did, weighing in on Republican primary contests and urging defeat of his critics.[45] But, like Goldwater, he has also looked to PACs to achieve his vision. In an unprecedented move for a serving vice president, Mike Pence created a PAC to support pro-Trump Republican candidates in the 2018 midterms, where formal party committees cannot selectively intervene.[46] Pence's effort, most likely undertaken at the president's behest, shows the continuing importance of a tactical template first contemplated more than eighty years ago.

Even if Trump successfully shifts the meaning of Republicanism, however, the parties are likely to remain bitterly divided or "polarized" for the foreseeable future. Partisan rancor has become deeply ingrained in Congress and beyond, such that a new dimension of conflict may simply reinforce old divisions rather than replace them. Yet the electoral model Trump is channeling in the pursuit of partisan change—the model pioneered by interest groups in the mid-twentieth century—might equally be used to *reduce* polarization as much as exacerbate it. Much as ideologically motivated activists used congressional ratings and selective campaign support to promote a more extreme vision of each party, moderates might use the same techniques to cultivate more centrist candidates and support them in *both* parties.[47] This is not to suggest a return to the conservative coalition of old but to recognize the contemporary pathologies of polarized partisanship—legislative gridlock, growing societal distrust, and the discrediting of political opponents—and to propose a practical, if undoubtedly challenging, solution.[48] As the liberal Republican Clifford Case observed in 1951:

The worst political disaster that could happen to us would be a sharply defined division of our parties along economic and class lines. Such a division would solve no problems. It would bring us in sight of the day when the losers in an election would begin throwing up barricades in the streets. The reason why the American people, winners and losers alike, accept the results of an election is that they all know the successful party represents no threat to the vital interests of any of them.[49]

The current party division does not perfectly match these economic or class lines, but many Americans now see their "vital interests" as threatened when either side takes office. Compromise is often viewed as tantamount to treason, and short-term electoral incentives preclude long-term resolution of crucial policy problems. If interest group competition and the emulation of new electoral techniques helped to get us here, new centrist groups might also emerge that— through sustained political action over time—could reverse engineer the process of partisan polarization itself. It would be neither quick nor easy; energizing the middle ground never is. But with the health of American democracy in the balance, it is essential to try.

ACKNOWLEDGMENTS

One accumulates numerous debts in the writing of any book, and there are many individuals and institutions I am glad of the opportunity to acknowledge. First, I was fortunate in pursuing my graduate education at the University of Virginia, where my dissertation adviser and committee members—Professors Sidney Milkis, Brian Balogh, James Ceaser, and Paul Freedman—provided valuable insight and guidance while also allowing me the intellectual space to fully explore my interests. I was also fortunate to receive several grants and fellowships as a graduate student and since then that have aided in the research and completion of this book. I am grateful to the Jefferson Scholars Foundation, which provided me a graduate fellowship at the University of Virginia; to the Miller Center at the University of Virginia, which awarded me a dissertation fellowship while I was writing up; and to Selwyn College, University of Cambridge, where the Keasbey Research Fellowship in American Studies enabled me to transform the dissertation into the final book form. I am also grateful to the Hagley Museum and Library, which provided a research grant at an early stage, and to the Friends of the University of Wisconsin-Madison Libraries for a grant later on in the process, enabling me to undertake archival work at the Wisconsin Historical Society that did much to hone my thinking. I am especially glad that the ideas I developed there appealed to David McBride at Oxford University Press and am grateful to him and to the anonymous reviewers whose feedback helped me to refine the manuscript, as well as to Emily Mackenzie for her help in the production process.

Of course a book is a reflection not just of the research and ideas you have formulated, but the life you have lived while you're writing it. I have been fortunate to find wonderful communities in the various institutions I've been part of and places I've called home. To my friends and colleagues at the University of Virginia, especially Hilde Restad, Kate Sanger, Kyle Lascurettes, Nadim

Khoury, Brandon Yoder, and the late Joshua Scott, I am grateful for your enthusiasm and encouragement through graduate school and beyond. Likewise, I am very grateful to my family and friends in the UK, who have supported me in so many ways throughout this process. I have been lucky to have inspiring mentors in Dr. Barbara A. Perry of the University of Virginia's Miller Center and Dr. Kathryn Dunn Tenpas of the Brookings Institution, for whose advice and generosity I am extremely thankful. I also want to thank the radio producers and staff at BackStory, where I came to better appreciate the power of narrative while working as a researcher, and the members of the American history seminar at the University of Cambridge, who helped me to rethink a political science project in more explicitly historical terms. I am especially grateful to one particular member of that seminar—my husband, Charlie—who offered encouragement and reassurance as I undertook the sometimes painful process of post-dissertation editing. Our wonderful daughter Eliza was born during the final stages of editing, and I want to thank her for napping sufficiently in her early months to get the book over the line! Finally, the biggest of all acknowledgments goes to my mother, who has kept a space on her shelf for a very long time awaiting this volume—thank you for everything. This book is for you.

NOTES

Introduction

1. *Report and Hearings of the Subcommittee on the Judiciary, U.S. Senate, 65th Cong.*, vol. I, *Brewing and Liquor Interests and German and Bolshevik Propaganda* (Washington, DC: Government Printing Office, 1919), 4.
2. A. Mitchell Palmer, for example, at that time the custodian of alien property, had denounced the Brewers' Association as a "vicious interest" that had been "pro-German in its sympathies and its conduct" and therefore "unpatriotic" (*Brewing and Liquor Interests*, 1). On the perceived pro-German sympathies and unpopularity of the Brewers, see David E. Kyvig, *Repealing National Prohibition* (Chicago: University of Chicago Press, 1979), 36. On their depiction as a source of twin dangers—"Kaiserism abroad and booze at home"—see Peter H. Odegard, *Pressure Politics: The Story of the Anti-Saloon League* (New York: Columbia University Press, 1928), 71.
3. *National Security League: Hearings Before a Special Committee of the House of Representatives*, 65th Cong., 3rd sess. (December 19, 1918) (Washington, DC: Government Printing Office, 1918). See also John Carver Edwards, "The Price of Political Innocence: The Role of the National Security League in the 1918 Congressional Election," *Military Affairs* 42, no. 4 (December 1978): 190–196.
4. See US Senate, "Presidential Campaign Expenditures," Report of the Special Committee Investigating Presidential Campaign Expenditures, February 28, 1929, S. Rep. No. 70-2024 (Washington, DC: Government Printing Office, 1929).
5. This threat was made by William A. Brady, president of the National Association of the Motion Picture Industry, before a Chicago legislative commission in 1919. See *Report of the Chicago Motion Picture Commission* (Chicago City Council: September 1920), 176.
6. A Senate judiciary subcommittee held a hearing to consider the movie industry's "alleged political activities" in 1922 but ultimately chose not to proceed with a fully fledged investigation. See *Proposed Investigation of the Motion-Picture Industry: Hearings before the Senate Committee on the Judiciary, Subcommittee on Senate Resolution 142*, 67th Cong., 2nd sess. (Washington, DC: Government Printing Office, 1922).
7. See, for example, Larry J. Sabato, *PAC Power: Inside the World of Political Action Committees* (New York: W.W. Norton, 1984); Paul S. Herrnson, Ronald G. Shaiko, and Clyde Wilcox, eds., *The Interest Group Connection: Electioneering, Lobbing, and Policymaking in Washington*, 2nd. ed. (Washington, DC: CQ Press, 2005); Richard M. Skinner, *More Than Money: Interest Group Action in Congressional Elections* (Lanham, MD: Rowman & Littlefield, 2007); Clyde Wilcox and Rentaro Iida, "Interest Groups in American Elections," in *The Oxford Handbook of American Parties and Interest Groups*, ed. L. Sandy Maisel, Jeffrey M. Berry, and George C. Edwards III (New York: Oxford University Press, 2010); and Mark J. Rozell, Clyde Wilcox, and Michael M. Franz, *Interest Groups in American Campaigns: The New Face of Electioneering*,

3rd ed. (New York: Oxford University Press, 2011). Public websites such as the Center for Responsive Politics' OpenSecrets.org and the National Institute on Money in Politics (https://www.followthemoney.org/) also track and analyze data made available by the Federal Election Commission.

8. Elisabeth S. Clemens, *The People's Lobby: Organizational Innovation and the Rise of Interest Group Politics in the United States, 1890–1925* (Chicago: University of Chicago Press, 1997).

9. On the ideal of the reluctant candidate in American civic life, see Gil Troy, *See How They Ran: The Changing Role of the Presidential Candidate*, rev. ed. (Cambridge, MA: Harvard University Press, 1996).

10. For an overview of these kinds of criticism—made against both interest groups and political parties as different species of "faction"—see Richard Hofstadter, *The Idea of a Party System: The Rise of Legitimate Opposition in the United States, 1780–1840* (Berkeley: University of California Press, 1969), chapter 1. On an "ideal of social harmony" as an important strain in nineteenth-century American political culture, see also Richard L. McCormick, "Political Parties in American History," in *The Party Period and Public Policy: American Politics from the Age of Jackson to the Progressive Era* (New York: Oxford University Press, 1986), 159, 173.

11. Rozell, Wilcox, and Franz, *Interest Groups in American Campaigns*, 24.

12. See, for example, V. O. Key, *Politics, Parties, and Pressure Groups* (New York: Crowell, 1942), 212.

13. This phrase, cited as the fundamental mantra of the "political action movement," appeared in the *New Republic* in 1946. "We Were Licked!," *New Republic*, November 18, 1946, 656.

14. Rozell, Wilcox, and Franz, *Interest Groups in American Campaigns*, 24.

15. See especially McCormick, "Political Parties in American History," 170. See also note 10.

16. E. E. Schattschneider, *Party Government* (New Brunswick, NJ: Transaction, 1942; repr. 2004), 27.

17. Key, *Politics, Parties and Pressure Groups* (1942), 212.

18. Ibid.

19. E. E. Schattschneider, "Pressure Groups versus Political Parties," *Annals of the American Academy of Political and Social Science* 259 (1948): 17–23.

20. Ibid., 18.

21. Schattschneider, *Party Government*, 192.

22. American Political Science Association (APSA), Committee on Political Parties, "Toward a More Responsible Two-Party System," *American Political Science Review* 44, no. 3, pt. 2 (1950): 1–96. For more on the APSA committee's activities and aims and the idea of "responsible" parties more generally, see Sam Rosenfeld, *The Polarizers: Postwar Architects of Our Polarized Era* (Chicago: University of Chicago Press, 2017), esp. chapter 1; and Mark Wickham-Jones, *Whatever Happened to Party Government?* (Ann Arbor: University of Michigan Press, 2018).

23. Daniel Tichenor and Richard Harris describe how this interpretation became "common wisdom" in the discipline, though E. E. Schattschneider made a more limited claim: that interest groups might *take advantage* of national party weakness to promote their aims but did not directly *cause* that weakness. See Daniel J. Tichenor and Richard A. Harris, "The Development of Interest Group Politics In America: Beyond the Conceits of Modern Times," *Annual Review of Political Science* 8, no. 1 (2005): 265; and Schattschneider, "Pressure Groups versus Political Parties," esp. 18, 23.

24. See, for example, Nicol C. Rae, "Be Careful What You Wish For: The Rise of Responsible Parties in American National Politics," *Annual Review of Political Science* 10 (2007): 169–191; and Rosenfeld, *The Polarizers*, esp. conclusion.

25. For an overview of both Key's and Schattschneider's early scholarship, see Tichenor and Harris, "The Development of Interest Group Politics in America"; and Michael T. Heaney, "Linking Political Parties and Interest Groups," in *The Oxford Handbook of American Political Parties and Interest Groups*, ed. L. Sandy Maisel and Jeffrey M. Berry (New York: Oxford University Press, 2010), 568–587.

26. See E. E. Schattschneider, *The Semi-Sovereign People: A Realist's View of Democracy in America* (Stamford, CT: Wadsworth Publishing, 1960; repr. 1988), 55–56; and V.O. Key, *Politics, Parties, and Pressure Groups*, 5th ed. (New York: Crowell, 1964), 156–157.

27. Schattschneider, *The Semi-Sovereign People*, 93. The same phrase appears in a book chapter by Schattschneider published in 1956, while the APSA committee offered similar reasoning in 1950, in anticipation of a hoped-for strengthening of the party system. "Any tendency in the direction of a strengthened party system encourages the interest groups to align themselves with one or the other of the major parties," its report explained. See E. E. Schattschneider, "United States: The Functional Approach to Party Government," in *Modern Political Parties: Approaches to Comparative Politics*, ed. Sigmund Neumann (Chicago: University of Chicago Press, 1956), 214; and APSA, Committee on Political Parties, "Toward a More Responsible Two-Party System," 19–20.

28. Key, *Politics, Parties, and Pressure Groups* (1964), 160. Emphasis added.

29. Lecture 7, "Political Tactics and Aims of Organized Labor," updated February 18, 1957, Personal Papers of V. O. Key, accession no. 2000-078, box 9, "Writings: 'Politics, Parties, and Pressure Groups,'" folder "Chap. III, 'Workers,' mss. notes and revisions," John F. Kennedy Presidential Library, Boston, MA.

30. Schattschneider, *The Semi-Sovereign People*, 87–93. See also Schattschneider, "United States," 206–209.

31. See, for example, Mildred A. Schwartz, *The Party Network: The Robust Organization of Illinois Republicans* (Madison: University of Wisconsin Press, 1990); Matt Grossmann and Casey B. K. Dominguez, "Party Coalitions and Interest Group Networks," *American Politics Research* 37, no. 5 (2009): 767–800; Gregory Koger, Seth Masket, and Hans Noel, "Cooperative Party Factions in American Politics," *American Politics Research* 38, no. 1 (2010): 33–53; Richard M. Skinner, "Do 527's Add Up to a Party? Thinking About the 'Shadows' of Politics," *Forum* 3, no. 3 (2005): Article 5; and Richard M. Skinner, *More Than Money: Interest Group Action in Congressional Elections* (Lanham, MD: Rowman & Littlefield, 2007).

32. Kathleen Bawn, Martin Cohen, David Karol, Seth Masket, Hans Noel, and John Zaller, "A Theory of Political Parties: Groups, Policy Demands and Nominations in American Politics," *Perspectives on Politics* 10, no. 3 (September 2012): 571–597.

33. For Bawn et al., "Lobbying works reliably only for policy demands that officials already favor," hence a better approach "is to get a genuine friend nominated and elected to office," which leads a group into partisan electoral activity ("A Theory of Political Parties," 575). Partisan electioneering is thus a superior strategy to nonpartisan lobbying. As Cohen, Karol, Noel, and Zaller explain in a related work: "Groups of policy demanders focus on nominations because it is easier to achieve their goals by electing politicians who share their views than by winning over truly independent politicians after they have taken office. They form parties because they need to cooperate with one another in order to get their candidates elected." Marty Cohen, David Karol, Hans Noel, and John Zaller, *The Party Decides: Presidential Nominations Before and After Reform* (Chicago: University of Chicago Press, 2008), 362.

34. Bawn et al., "A Theory of Political Parties," 580. Describing how the Democratic Party came to promote civil rights for African Americans in the second half of the twentieth century and the Republican Party came to adopt a strongly pro-life position, they argue "that policy demanders rather than office-holders initiated these important changes."

35. Since Bawn et al. view lobbying as an inferior strategy to the nomination and election of already sympathetic lawmakers, they offer an electoral logic that leads interest groups to effectively *create* two competing party coalitions. The idea of nonpartisan electoral activity is absent from their theory. See Bawn et al., "A Theory of Political Parties," 573–575.

36. A wave of recent scholarship has sought to illuminate different aspects of party–interest group relationships—once described by Tichenor and Harris as "one of the most glaring lacunae of the discipline"—and the argument developed here complements this literature through a comparison of labor, business, and ideological organizations and an emphasis on electoral *tactics* in effecting change. Schlozman, for example, also points to the role of labor unions in forging a more liberal Democratic Party and a more polarized system, characterizing them as an "anchoring group" that played a crucial role in twentieth-century party development. Schlozman's approach differs from mine, however, in his focus on social movements rather than interest groups per se and his emphasis on the power of parties themselves to resist or accept partnership with potential anchoring groups. My account stresses the electoral mechanisms by which interest groups alter the composition of the party and gradually expel

opponents of their cause, thus creating the conditions for partnership themselves. Other recent works suggesting the role interest groups can play in promoting party transformation include those by Baylor and Schickler, who place an emphasis on the area of civil rights in particular, as well as those by Krimmel, Elinson, and DiSalvo, who also examine aspects of the labor–Democratic Party relationship or the business-Republican Party connection, among other party-group relationships, but do not directly compare the two in the timeframe explored here. See Daniel J. Tichenor and Richard A. Harris, "Organized Interests and American Political Development," *Political Science Quarterly* 117, no. 4 (Winter 2002): 266; Daniel Schlozman, *When Movements Anchor Parties: Electoral Alignments in American History* (Princeton, NJ: Princeton University Press, 2015); Christopher Baylor, *First to the Party: The Group Origins of Political Transformation* (Philadelphia: University of Pennsylvania Press, 2018); Eric Schickler, *Racial Realignment: The Transformation of American Liberalism, 1932–1965* (Princeton, NJ: Princeton University Press, 2016); Katherine Krimmel, "The Efficiencies and Pathologies of Special Interest Partisanship," *Studies in American Political Development* 31, no. 2 (October 2017): 149–169; Katherine Krimmel, "Special Interest Partisanship: The Transformation of American Political Parties" (PhD diss., Columbia University, 2013); Gregory A. Elinson, "Shifting Coalitions: Business Power, Partisan Politics, and the Rise of the Regulatory State" (PhD diss., University of California, Berkeley, 2015); and Daniel DiSalvo, *Engines of Change: Party Factions in American Politics, 1868–2010* (New York: Oxford University Press, 2012).

37. *Proposed Investigation of the Motion-Picture Industry*, 4.

Chapter 1

1. Quoted in Robert A. Caro, *The Years of Lyndon Johnson: The Path to Power* (New York: Vintage Books, 1981), 46.
2. The 1872 *Crédit Mobilier* scandal, for example, revealed that numerous congressmen had profiteered from the construction of the transcontinental railroad. Three years later the "Whiskey Ring" scandal exposed members of President Ulysses S. Grant's administration who had colluded with whiskey distillers and distributors to divert liquor tax revenue for their own personal benefit. See Melvin I. Urofsky, "Campaign Finance Reform Before 1971," *Albany Government Law Review* 1, no. 1 (2008): 8.
3. Urofsky, "Campaign Finance Reform Before 1971," 9. See also Richard L. McCormick, "The Discovery That Business Corrupts Politics," *American Historical Review* 86, no. 3 (1981): 247–274.
4. Michael E. McGerr, *The Decline of Popular Politics: The American North, 1865–1928* (New York: Oxford University Press, 1986), esp. 30, 40–41. On the enthusiastic and enduring partisan loyalties of the age, which were "[b]ased on cultural and communal identities as well as memories of the civil war," see also Richard L. McCormick, "Political Parties in American History," in *The Party Period and Public Policy: American Politics from the Age of Jackson to the Progressive Era* (New York: Oxford University Press, 1986), 171.
5. The Pendleton Act of 1883 introduced merit-based appointment to the US civil service. See Urofsky, "Campaign Finance Reform Before 1971," 8–9; and Paula Baker, "Campaigns and Potato Chips; or Some Causes and Consequences of Political Spending," *Journal of Policy History* 14. no. 1 (2002): 18. On the reformers who took aim at parties, see McCormick, "Political Parties in American History," esp. 170.
6. Urofsky, "Campaign Finance Reform Before 1971," 11–12. As Urofsky explains, Hanna imposed a system of assessments on banks and major corporations, based on a percentage of their capital or a flat rate. The GOP collected $250,000 from Standard Oil alone, a donation that almost equaled Bryan's entire campaign war chest.
7. On this investigation and New York's legislative response, see Robert E. Mutch, *Buying the Vote: A History of Campaign Finance Reform* (New York: Oxford University Press, 2014), 33–47.
8. Urofsky, "Campaign Finance Reform Before 1971," 14–15; Theodore Roosevelt, "Fifth Annual Message to Congress," December 5, 1905, in *The American Presidency Project*, ed. Gerhard Peters and John T. Woolley, https://www.presidency.ucsb.edu/documents/

fifth-annual-message-4. Roosevelt had first sounded the disclosure theme in his 1904 annual address, repeating it again in 1905 and adding the call for a corporate ban.

9. Mutch, *Buying the Vote*, 46–47.

10. Tillman Act of 1907, 34 Stat. 864 (January 26, 1907). The act forbade corporations to make "a money contribution in connection with any [federal] election." It also banned national banks and congressionally chartered corporations from making political contributions in *any* elections, federal and below (otherwise state law prevailed). The act included both corporate and individual fines and even potential imprisonment for the officers or directors of corporations that violated the law. See Anthony Corrado, "Money and Politics: A History of Federal Campaign Finance Law," in *Campaign Finance Reform: A Sourcebook*, ed. Anthony Corrado, Thomas E. Mann, Daniel R. Ortiz, Trevor Potter, and Frank J. Sorauf (Washington, DC: Brookings Institution Press, 1997), 27–28.

11. In this case, it was the actions of Roosevelt's successor, William Howard Taft, that helped propel the move. The populist crusader William Jennings Bryan had been nominated as the Democratic presidential candidate for the third time in 1908 and was seemingly intent on making the financing of the campaign an issue in itself. Accordingly, both Taft and Bryan chose to voluntarily disclose contributions to and expenditures of their national party committees, setting a precedent that eased the way for congressional legislation. See Mutch, *Buying the Vote*, 60–62, 74–76.

12. Publicity Act of 1910, 36 Stat. 822 (June 25, 1910). As Corrado explains, the Publicity Act applied only to House elections, requiring "political committees" active in such contests to file financial reports with the Clerk of the House of Representatives (disclosing their contributions and expenditures) and imposing fines and/or imprisonment on violators ("Money and Politics," 37–38).

13. 1911 Amendments to the Publicity Act, 37 Stat. 26 (August 19, 1911); Corrado, "Money and Politics," 39–41. Though senators would not be uniformly elected by popular vote until ratification of the Seventeenth Amendment in 1913, some states had already passed laws requiring popular input on the state legislature's choice, thus accounting for the extension to Senate contests. For candidates themselves, maximum expenditures were set at $5,000 for House candidates and $10,000 for Senate candidates, with this sum designed to embrace both the nomination and general election campaigns.

14. As Corrado explains, the Publicity Act of 1910 defined a "political committee" to include "the national committees of all political parties and the national congressional campaign committees of all political parties and all committees, associations, or organizations which shall in two or more States influence the result or attempt to influence the result of an election at which Representatives in Congress are to be elected" ("Money and Politics," 37). In this particular bill, the definition applied only to House elections, but it would be expanded to other contexts by subsequent legislation. See also Urofsky, "Campaign Finance Reform Before 1971," 18; and Julian E. Zelizer, "Seeds of Cynicism: The Struggle over Campaign Finance, 1956–1974," *Journal of Policy History* 14, no. 1 (2002): 76.

15. On labor, farm, and women's groups in this period, see Elisabeth S. Clemens, *The People's Lobby: Organizational Innovation and the Rise of Interest Group Politics in the United States, 1890–1925* (Chicago: University of Chicago Press, 1997). On trade associations, the US Department of Commerce produced an annual directory that listed seven hundred national trade associations in 1919 and more than two thousand by 1929, as noted in Ellis W. Hawley, "Herbert Hoover, the Commerce Secretariat, and the Vision of an 'Associative State,' 1921–1928," *Journal of American History* 61, no. 1 (1974): 139. For an example of an early "issue" group, see Peter H. Odegard, *Pressure Politics: The Story of the Anti-Saloon League* (New York: Columbia University Press, 1928). For an overview of the associative impulse in the United States and various waves of organizational development, see Arthur M. Schlesinger, "Biography of a Nation of Joiners," *American Historical Review* 50, no. 1 (1944): 1–25.

16. Labor Management Relations Act of 1947, 61 Stat. 136 (June 23, 1947).

17. Federal Election Commission press release, "PAC Count—1974 to Present," updated July 1, 2012, http://www.fec.gov/press/summaries/2011/2011paccount.shtml; and Federal Election Commission press release, "Statistical Summary of 24-Month Campaign Activity of

the 2017–2018 Cycle," March 15, 2019, https://www.fec.gov/updates/statistical-summary-24-month-campaign-activity-2017-2018-cycle/.

18. David B. Truman, *The Governmental Process: Political Interests and Public Opinion* (Berkeley, CA: Institute of Governmental Studies, 1951/1993), 33, 37. Defining interest groups in terms of "shared attitudes" rather than a specific type of underlying interest encompasses traditional economic interests alongside groups organized around specific policy areas or larger ideological commitments—sometimes labeled "issue," "advocacy," or "ideological" groups—under the same label.

19. On the importance of "noncollective" benefits such as insurance for membership groups like unions, see Mancur Olson, *The Logic of Collective Action: Public Goods and the Theory of Groups* (Cambridge, MA: Harvard University Press, 1971), 72–73.

20. Consider Herrnson, for example, who states that "[t]he modern political action committee (PAC) . . . emerged during the 1970s," while Heaney and Strolovitch and Tichenor also emphasize the 1970s for PAC development. See Paul S. Herrnson, "Interest Groups and Campaigns: The Electoral Connection," in *The Interest Group Connection: Electioneering, Lobbing, and Policymaking in Washington*, 2nd ed., ed. Paul S. Herrnson, Ronald G. Shaiko, and Clyde Wilcox (Washington, DC: CQ Press, 2005), 26; Michael T. Heaney, "Linking Political Parties and Interest Groups," in *The Oxford Handbook of Political Parties and Interest Groups*, ed. L. Sandy Maisel, Jeffrey M. Berry, and George C. Edwards III (New York: Oxford University Press, 2010), 573; and Dara Z. Strolovitch and Daniel J. Tichenor, "Interest Groups and American Political Development," in *The Oxford Handbook of American Political Development*, ed. Richard Valelly, Suzanne Mettler, and Robert Lieberman (New York: Oxford University Press, 2016), 555.

21. The 1970 count comes from "List of National Political Action Committees," in *The Political Marketplace*, ed. David L. Rosenbloom (New York: Quadrangle Books, 1972), 376–383. The 1964 information is reconstructed from Herbert E. Alexander, *Financing the 1964 Election* (Princeton, NJ: Citizens Research Foundation, 1966). In tables 13 and 14, Alexander lists thirty "Labor National Committees" and twenty-six "Miscellaneous National Committees" (64–65). Most of the labor committees appear to have been fully fledged PACs that contributed directly to candidates in elections, while some of the miscellaneous committees were politically active without fulfilling this direct contribution criterion. As such, I have made a conservative estimate of "at least thirty" being PACs, primarily based on the labor examples, though the actual number was likely higher. There are a handful of other sources listing PACs prior to 1974. See, for example, "List of National Political Action Committees," 376–383; and Judith G. Smith, ed., *Political Brokers: Money, Organizations, Power, & People* (New York: Liveright, 1972).

22. For brief sketches of PAC development mentioning some or all of these examples, see Corrado, "Money and Politics," 30; Richard M. Skinner, *More Than Money: Interest Group Action in Congressional Elections* (Lanham, MD: Rowman & Littlefield, 2007), 6; and Mark J. Rozell, Clyde Wilcox, and Michael M. Franz, *Interest Groups in American Campaigns: The New Face of Electioneering*, 3rd ed. (New York: Oxford University Press, 2011), 60–61.

23. Hawley discusses 1919 and 1929 data on trade associations drawn from a directory produced by the Commerce Department. In 1923 this directory identified slightly more than eleven thousand trade associations at all levels, of which fifteen hundred were "interstate, national, and international," and it listed over nineteen thousand overall by 1931, as noted by Bonnett. In 1949 the Commerce Department cast its eye over "national associations" in general, estimating there to be more than four thousand national, trade, professional, civic, and other associations. See Ellis W. Hawley, "Herbert Hoover, the Commerce Secretariat, and the Vision of an 'Associative State,' 1921–1928," *Journal of American History* 61, no. 1 (1974): 139; US Department of Commerce, Bureau of Foreign and Domestic Commerce, *Commercial and Industrial Organizations of the United States*, rev. ed. (Washington, DC: Government Printing Office, 1923), III; Clarence Bonnett, "The Evolution of Business Groupings," *Annals of the American Academy of Political and Social Science* 179 (1935): 5; and US Department of Commerce, *National Associations of the United States* (Washington, DC: Government Printing Office, 1949), cited in Truman, *The Governmental Process*, 58.

24. The *Encyclopedia of Associations* has been published continuously by Gale Research since 1956. The first and second editions appeared as the *Encyclopedia of American Associations*. Other widely utilized directories include *Congressional Quarterly's Washington Information Directory*, published since 1975, and *Washington Representatives* (a directory of associations with Washington offices) since 1977. *Washington Representatives* is also known as the *Directory of Washington Representatives of American Associations & Industry*.

25. Notably, Walker drew a sample from the 1980 *Washington Information Directory* and traced back their formation dates. See Jack L. Walker, "The Origins and Maintenance of Interest Groups in America," *American Political Science Review* 77, no. 2 (June 1983): 390–406.

26. Tichenor and Harris used the Congressional Information Service's *U.S. Congressional Committee Hearings Index*, which provides information on hearings from 1833 onward, including the topic of the hearing and the organizations that testified. Using this method, they found far more early twentieth-century interest groups than Walker did. See Daniel J. Tichenor and Richard A. Harris, "Organized Interests and American Political Development," *Political Science Quarterly* 117, no. 4 (Winter 2002): 594–595, 599.

27. See, for example, Pendleton Herring, *Group Representation Before Congress* (Washington, DC: Brookings Institution, 1929), 19.

28. Belle Zeller, "The Federal Regulation of Lobbying Act," *American Political Science Review* 42, no. 2 (April 1948): 242. According to Zeller, concern arose among legislators about extensive lobbying on measures such as "veterans' housing, price control, public power projects, and strikes," along with national healthcare proposals.

29. Congress periodically published compilations of registrants, for example, and *Congressional Quarterly* soon began to report on registrations. See, for example, "Lobby Index 1946–1949: An Index of Organizations and Individuals Registering and/or Filing Quarterly Financial Reports under the Federal Lobbying Act," Report of the House Select Committee on Lobbying Activities, US House of Representatives, 81st Cong., 2nd sess., December 15, 1950, H.R. Rep. No. 3197 (Washington, DC: Government Printing Office, 1950); "Lobby Index 1950: An Index of Organizations and Individuals Registering and/or Filing Quarterly Financial Reports under the Federal Lobbying Act," Report of the House Select Committee on Lobbying Activities, US House of Representatives, 81st Cong., 2nd sess., December 29, 1950, H.R. Rep. No. 3234 (Washington, DC: Government Printing Office, 1950; and "Lobby Financial Reports," in *CQ Almanac—1948* (Washington, DC: Congressional Quarterly, 1949), 440–448.

30. In relation to primaries, the *Newberry* decision was reversed by *United States v. Classic* (1941). See *Newberry v. United States*, 256 U.S. 232 (1921) and *United States v. Classic*, 313 U.S. 299 (1941).

31. Federal Corrupt Practices Act of 1925, 43 Stat. 1070. The 1925 legislation also sought to close loopholes exposed by the Teapot Dome scandal of the early 1920s, in which oil executives had evaded disclosure requirements by making large political contributions in nonelection years, to which earlier legislation did not apply. See Corrado, "Money and Politics," 29.

32. As discussed later in this chapter, the 1940 Amendments to the 1939 Act to Prevent Pernicious Political Activities (Hatch Act) imposed a cap on political committee spending, while the War Labor Disputes Act of 1943 (Smith-Connally Act), temporarily banned labor union contributions in connection with federal elections, which the Labor Management Relations Act of 1947 (Taft-Hartley Act) later made permanent and further extended to "expenditures."

33. In 1920 House Clerk William Tyler Page took it upon himself to "inform" likely political committees of their status under the law, asking the Library of Congress to compile a list of organizations that appeared to be engaging in electoral activities. But even here, he was careful to explain his role as "purely ministerial," insisting that such organizations must still determine for themselves whether they were required to file. See Testimony of William Tyler Page, February 21, 1924, "Additional Publicity of Campaign Contributions made to Political Parties, and Limiting Amount of Campaign Expenditures by Amending Corrupt Practices Act," *Hearings before the House Committee on Election of President, Vice President, and Representatives in Congress*, US House of Representatives, 68th Cong., 1st sess., February 21, 28, and March 13, 1924 (Washington, DC: Government Printing Office, 1924), 2. Otherwise compliance was limited and self-selective. Nonetheless, some of these reports (filed between

1912 and 1970) are preserved at the National Archives' Center for Legislative Archives in Washington, DC, though as an unprocessed collection.

34. *Brewing and Liquor Interests and German and Bolshevik Propaganda*, vol. I of *Report and Hearings of the Subcommittee on the Judiciary*, US Senate, 65th Cong. (Washington, DC: Government Printing Office, 1919).

35. To some extent, the 1950 Buchanan Committee also blurred this distinction, since it considered both direct and *indirect* lobbying, where the latter involved appeals to the public in relation to specific pieces of legislation, which might then have broader electoral implications whether intended or not.

36. The senator in question was Francis Case (R-SD), who called attention to the $2,500 donation during debates over amending the Natural Gas Act. Though in favor of the contents of the bill, President Eisenhower ultimately vetoed it due to the ensuing controversy surrounding its passage. On the Case scandal, see Zelizer, "Seeds of Cynicism," 78.

37. In 1960 and 1964 the House created committees that held hearings, but only pertaining to subnational issues. From then on House investigating committees were formed biennially, corresponding with their electoral calendar, but either did not hold hearings or only did so on subnational issues.

38. On debates over pre-FECA legislative proposals beginning in the mid- to late 1960s, including the Long Act of 1968 (which established a basic framework for public funding of presidential campaigns, though it was never implemented), see Zelizer, "Seeds of Cynicism."

39. A Senate investigation was planned for 1916, for example, but partisan maneuvering led to fears that both national party committees would be embarrassed by revelations it might make, leading to the investigation being dropped. In 1932 both chambers created investigating committees to consider expenditures relating to the election, though neither held national-level hearings or issued relevant reports. The House committee appears to have been simply kept "in reserve" in case of allegations of specific violations, while the Senate committee became embroiled in a controversial Senate election in Louisiana and failed to report on the presidential expenditures it was also authorized to examine. In 1936 the Senate's campaign expenditures committee compiled an array of relevant national data, based on questionnaires sent to party committees and other electoral groups, and produced an extensive report but did not hold hearings. On 1916, see "Will Investigate Money in Campaign," *New York Times*, November 15, 1916, 1; "Dual Election Probe," *Washington Post*, November 15, 1916, 2; and "Kenyon to Urge Inquiry on All Campaign Funds," *Chicago Daily Tribune*, December 12, 1916, 10. On 1932, see H.R. Rep. No. 1508 (June 6, 1932) and H.R. Rep. No. 1679 (June 21, 1932); and "Senatorial Campaign Expenditures, 1932 (Louisiana)," Report of the Special Committee on Investigation of Presidential and Senatorial Campaign Expenditures, US Senate, 73rd Cong., 2nd sess., January 16, 1934, S. Rep. No. 191, 2. On 1936, see "Investigation of Campaign Expenditures in 1936," Report of the Special Committee to Investigate Campaign Expenditures of Presidential, Vice Presidential, and Senatorial Candidates in 1936, US Senate, 75th Cong., 1st sess., March 4, 1937, S. Rep. No. 151 (Washington, DC: Government Printing Office, 1937).

40. These data were initially compiled from the Lexis-Nexis congressional hearings database, now "Proquest Congressional." For consistency, I identified organizational witnesses on the basis of descriptions in the Lexis-Nexis metadata, which were originally drawn from headings in the published congressional hearings. These divide sections of testimony by introducing the name of a new witness and typically including any relevant organizational affiliation. There may, of course, be some witnesses whose organizational ties were not so identified, but I hope to have captured as many as possible through this systematic method.

41. The tables identify only *national* organizations, though some subnational groups did appear in the witness data, despite the exclusion of committees that solely looked to the subnational level. The exclusion of subnational groups here reflects my primary analytic interest in the contours of interest group activity on the *national* political scene.

42. To briefly explain the classification method here, in both types of hearings, groups were categorized on the basis of organizational connections to official party committees, whether formal—in the case of party auxiliaries—or merely financial, in the case of some "candidate-centered" groups. Some groups classified as "candidate-centered" may have had informal

connections to demographic, economic, or professional communities, such as the National Committee for Agriculture in 1940, which was partly financed by individual contributors. The fact that it was also partly funded by the Democratic National Committee (DNC), however, suggests it was not a fully independent effort emerging *out of* the agricultural community but was rather nurtured *by* the DNC so as to promote its presidential candidate within farming constituencies. Organizations listed in the "Economic Interests" category, therefore, had to be fully financially independent of the party (even if they promoted a major party's presidential candidate) and had to have a formal organizational or financial link to a preexisting organized economic interest group or to constitute such an interest group in themselves *outside* of the campaign context. Similarly, "Issue/Ideological Interests" had to be financially independent of the parties and had to have a formal organizational or financial link to a preexisting organized advocacy group—whether issue based or more broadly ideological—or to constitute such a group in themselves. At times there is some slippage between the economic and issue/ideological categories, where groups appear to be promoting particular policies or political outlooks that also have potential economic benefits for the members or supporters of the group. In some cases where there is a clear economic benefit or strong links to industry, as with most pro-tariff organizations identified in the early lobbying hearings, I have classified these as "economic interests." (An exception here is the National Tariff Commission Association noted in 1913, which appears to have been more of an advocacy group seeking a technocratic solution to the tariff question, through formation of a new tariff commission, rather than a group motivated by self-interested economic concerns.) Similar slippage emerges in the wake of the New Deal, when a range of anti–New Deal groups emerged, often financed by an interlinked network of prominent business executives. In these cases, although the political outlook they promoted promised economic benefits for these individuals and their businesses, I have classified such groups as "ideological" because they went beyond the purely economic in their aims and arguments. (An exception here is the American Liberty League, an early example of such anti–New Deal groups, which was widely viewed in the public sphere as a business-backed entity, as discussed further in this and later chapters.) Finally, in some cases, evidence about specific organizations is murky, in which case I have used my best judgment in classifying them, or in two cases excluded those organizations because their activities could not be confirmed (the Maryland Committee in 1940 and 1944 and the Democratic State Councils of Americans of Italian Origin in 1940).

43. This occurred in 1936 and 1948, for example, though the latter report was less extensive than that of 1936. See "Investigation of Campaign Expenditures in 1936"; and Report of the Special Committee on Campaign Expenditures, US House of Representatives, 80th Cong., 2nd sess., H.R. Rep. No. 80, 2469 (Washington, DC: Government Printing Office, 1948).

44. See, for example, James K. Pollock, *Party Campaign Funds* (New York: Alfred A. Knopf, 1926), 56, which includes some information on the 1916 campaign.

45. Overacker drew on disclosure reports filed with the House Clerk, and on the reports of congressional investigating committees. See Louise Overacker, "Campaign Funds in a Depression Year," *American Political Science Review* 27, no. 5 (1933): 769–783; "Campaign Funds in the Presidential Election of 1936," *American Political Science Review* 31, no. 3 (1937): 473–498; "Campaign Finance in the Presidential Election of 1940," *American Political Science Review* 35, no. 4 (1941): 701–727; and "Presidential Campaign Funds, 1944," *American Political Science Review* 39, no. 5 (1945): 899–925. The *APSR* also included a similar article on the 1928 election: James K. Pollock, "Campaign Funds in 1928," *American Political Science Review* 23, no. 1 (February 1929): 59–69. Overacker's book-length treatment, *Money in Elections* (New York: Macmillan, 1932) also covers the 1928 election. See also her *Presidential Campaign Funds* (Boston: Boston University Press, 1946); and "Labor's Political Contributions," *Political Science Quarterly* 54, no. 1 (1939): 56–68.

46. Overacker, "Campaign Funds in a Depression Year," 478; "Campaign Finance in the Presidential Election of 1940," 709; and "Presidential Campaign Funds, 1944," 902. She also mentions one national example in the 1932 article (the "National Progressive League") and one subnational example (the "Chicago Citizens Committee"). See "Campaign Funds in a Depression Year," 770, 772.

47. The Center for Responsive Politics, for example, describes "outside groups" as organizations that exist separately from a candidate's official campaign committee but are nonetheless "devoted to getting him or her elected." See Center for Responsive Politics, "Behind the Candidates: Campaign Committees and Outside Groups," https://www.opensecrets.org/pres16/outside-groups.

48. Overacker determines importance on the basis of financial impact, assessed retrospectively, whereas the committees typically called witnesses during the campaign period, at which point financial impact was not necessarily clear. As such, they were assessing a group's importance, notability, or wider significance in somewhat different terms. Nonetheless, while the overlap is imperfect, many of the groups Overacker lists do appear in the witness data.

49. For a brief discussion of the Citizens Research Foundation, see Zelizer, "Seeds of Cynicism," esp. 80. For more on Gore's investigation, see Julian E. Zelizer, *On Capitol Hill: The Struggle to Reform Congress and Its Consequences, 1948–2000* (New York: Cambridge University Press, 2004), 52. Heard later published some of his Gore committee research as a monograph. See Alexander Heard, *The Costs of Democracy* (Chapel Hill: University of North Carolina Press, 1960).

50. The CRF was originally associated with Vanderbilt University, before moving to Princeton and finally to the University of Southern California. Following its closure (sometime in the late 1980s or early 1990s), the majority of its records were acquired by the Institute of Governmental Studies at the University of California, Berkeley (others ended up in the possession of the Campaign Finance Institute in Washington, DC). The Institute of Governmental Studies holds the "Overacker-Heard Campaign Finance Data Archive," which consists of thousands of index cards detailing specific contributions from individuals and organizations to candidates, parties, and other political groups, with dates ranging from 1904 to the late 1960s. Overacker used these cards to produce her 1932 book *Money in Elections* and various *APSR* articles, and Heard adopted the same approach for his 1960 monograph, *The Costs of Democracy*.

51. Herbert E. Alexander, *Financing the 1960 Election* (Princeton, NJ: Citizens' Research Foundation, 1962), 42–43; and Herbert E. Alexander, *Financing the 1964 Election* (Princeton, NJ: Citizens' Research Foundation, 1966), 64–65. In 1960 Alexander identified seventeen labor committees and three more that he did not name, plus a further fifteen "miscellaneous" committees and four unnamed others, for a total of thirty-nine. In 1964 he identified thirty labor committees and twenty-six miscellaneous committees, for a total of fifty-six.

52. See Overacker, "Presidential Campaign Funds, 1944," 902n10 for this financial benchmark to determine "important" independent committees in the presidential campaign. If the $100,000 expenditure requirement were applied to Overacker's 1936 list, then the Progressive National Committee, the Progressive Republican Committee for Franklin D. Roosevelt, the Democratic Senatorial Campaign Committee, the Young Democratic Club of America, and the Women's National Republican Club would all be excluded. If it were applied in 1940, then all the Democrat-leaning groups except the National Committee of Independent Voters and the National Committee for Agriculture would be excluded, as would all the party auxiliaries. On the Republican side, the Willkie Clubs, Democrats for Willkie, the National Committee to Uphold Constitutional Government, the Citizens Information Committee, and another group called the Maryland Committee would survive from Overacker's original list. This latter entity, however, is excluded from table 1.6 because little information was available to verify its activities, and it appears from fragmentary information to have been a Maryland-based group and likely a subnational entity, despite its extensive spending.

53. Some 1,049 different organizational witnesses appeared across the committees I have classified as "major" investigations of campaign finance or lobbying (648 before the campaign committees and 401 before the lobbying committees), representing 102 different organizations. These figures refer to *witnesses* rather than appearances and thus exclude instances in which individuals testified more than once (usually doing so before the same committee, but sometimes across different committees in different Congresses).

54. In a statement submitted to the 1957 congressional committee investigating campaigns and lobbying, political scientist Stanley Kelley Jr. dated the emergence of permanent national committees, undertaking ongoing public relations and publicity activities, to "about 1930."

"Campaign Contributions, Political Activities, and Lobbying," *Hearings before the Special Committee to Investigate Political Activities, Lobbying, and Campaign Contributions*, US Senate, 84th Cong., 2nd sess. (Washington, DC: Government Printing Office, 1957), Appendix, 1255 (hereafter cited as McClellan Committee Hearings).

55. The America First Party was formed in 1943 by Gerald L. K. Smith, the right-wing political organizer who had taken over Huey Long's "Share Our Wealth" societies following Long's assassination in 1935, and helped to form the Union Party for the 1936 election. Where Long had opposed Roosevelt from a leftist-populist position, Smith's opposition took a far-right form infused with white supremacy and anti-Semitism. The America First *Party* he formed in 1943 was distinct from the America First *Committee* that had existed from 1940 to 1941 to oppose US intervention in World War II, but the similar name reflected its isolationist posture. Initially, Smith aimed at preventing Roosevelt's renomination at the Democratic convention but then ran as a presidential candidate himself, receiving just 1,781 votes in the 1944 election. Meanwhile, the American Democratic National Committee (ADNC) was an anti-Roosevelt Democratic splinter group formed in February 1944. As Kennedy describes, it also had isolationist ties and connections to the "Christian Front," a remnant of Father Coughlin's political movement. It was largely driven by southerners who aimed to prevent Roosevelt's presidential renomination, first by placing independent electors on the Democratic ballot in southern states, and when that proved unsuccessful, by backing Virginia senator Harry F. Byrd for president at the Democratic convention. When Roosevelt was renominated the ADNC devolved into a pseudo-third-party effort, spending $132,736 on electoral activities, as its treasurer told the Anderson Committee, though it was ultimately unable to get a candidate onto the ballot. See Stetson Kennedy, *Southern Exposure: Making the South Safe for Democracy* (Tuscaloosa: University of Alabama Press, 2010), 143–147, 150–151; Testimony of Gleason L. Archer, Treasurer of the American Democratic National Committee, October 6, 1944; "Campaign Expenditures," *Hearings before the Committee to Investigate Campaign Expenditures*, part 8, US House of Representatives, 78th Cong., 2nd sess. (Washington, D.C.: Government Printing Office, 1944), 557 (hereafter cited as Anderson Committee Hearings); and Testimony of Gerald L. K. Smith, October 3, 1944, Anderson Committee Hearings, part 6, 326.

56. On the background to this shift, see Robert Minor, *The Heritage of the Communist Political Association* (New York: Workers Library Publishers, 1944), University of Pittsburgh Digital Collections, "American Left Ephemera Collection," http://digital.library.pitt.edu/islandora/object/pitt%3A31735061537571.

57. A military physician who had served as military governor of Cuba and army chief of staff, Wood had been urged to run by former president Theodore Roosevelt. Wood managed to win the New Hampshire primary, while Hoover removed himself from consideration when he realized his own prospects had dimmed. At the convention in June, however, Wood lost the nomination to Warren G. Harding.

58. The Hoover Club of 1920 was ostensibly a draft movement formed by a fellow Stanford alumnus rather than the candidate himself. In 1928, however, the "Hoover for President Association" was a network of volunteer campaign groups, independent of the regular Republican party structure, that Ritchie suggests Hoover had quietly encouraged. See Donald A. Ritchie, *Electing FDR: The New Deal Campaign of 1932* (Lawrence: University Press of Kansas, 2007), 42.

59. Pollock points to the "Woodrow Wilson Independent League" and the "National Hughes Alliance," for example, as financially independent groups which promoted the 1916 Democratic and Republican nominees respectively. See Pollock, *Party Campaign Funds*, 56.

60. The Publicity Act Amendments of 1911 imposed limitations on the amounts congressional candidates might spend on their own campaigns but also stated that a candidate must not "*cause to be* given, contributed, expended, used, or promised" money in excess of those limitations either—that is, by individuals other than himself. Envisaging an electoral world in which candidates would typically self-finance their campaigns, this language was intended to bring under the spending caps whatever financial aid "friends" of the candidate might occasionally provide, whether by giving money to him directly or purchasing goods or services on his behalf. The scale of assistance from such "friends," however, was made plain by the

1921 *Newberry* case, in which 1918 Republican primary candidate Truman H. Newberry successfully appealed a conviction for excess spending under the Publicity Act to the Supreme Court. The majority ruled in Newberry's favor on the grounds that Congress lacked the authority to regulate primary elections, but a dissenting opinion pointed out that much of the money in Newberry's campaign had been spent by others. These justices believed that for a candidate to bear responsibility for such excess financing, he must "actually participate" in the spending of it—not simply know about it or acquiesce in its spending. In its legislative response to *Newberry*, the Federal Corrupt Practices of 1925, Congress took note of this dissenting opinion by specifying that campaign expenditure caps only applied to the candidate's own spending, and required him to disclose the expenditures of others only if "made with his knowledge or consent"—a slightly less stringent standard. As such, Overacker explained that the limitations "serve no useful purpose," for they effectively did nothing to prevent large sums being spent on a candidate's behalf, providing he denied knowledge of this activity. See Louise Overacker, *Money in Elections* (New York: Macmillan, 1932), 242–243, 271–273. See also Urofsky, "Campaign Finance Reform Before 1971," 18.

61. Overacker reported that in 1936 the Roosevelt Agricultural Committee spent $272,609, of which $244,087 was received from the Democratic National Committee (about 90 percent of its funds). Overacker reported that in 1940 the National Committee for Agriculture spent $131,489, of which $54,000 came from the DNC (approximately 41 percent of its funds). Overacker, "Campaign Funds in the Presidential Election of 1936," 478; and "Campaign Finance in the Presidential Election of 1940," 709.

62. Overacker notes that the National Progressive League for Roosevelt received up to $57,000 from the DNC, while in her 1937 article she indicates that the Progressive National Committee of 1936 received nothing (it spent $54,5460). Overacker, "Campaign Funds in a Depression Year," 770; and "Campaign Funds in the Presidential Election of 1936," 478.

63. The Associated Willkie Clubs was formed "during 1940" according to the Gillette Committee report, but was active prior to the Republican convention in June 1940, while the Hatch Act Amendments of 1940 were signed into law on July 19, 1940. In addition to the Hatch Act Amendments, the 1925 Federal Corrupt Practices Act had also encouraged the formation of electoral committees to some extent, as a way to evade the disclosure requirements it had imposed on donations of $100 or more going to a single committee. On the Willkie Clubs, see "Investigation of Presidential, Vice Presidential and Senatorial Campaign Expenditures, 1940," Report of the Special Committee to Investigate Presidential, Vice Presidential, and Senatorial Campaign Expenditures, 1940, US Senate, 77th Cong., 1st sess., February 15, 1941, S. Rep. No. 47 (Washington, DC: Government Printing Office, 1941), 7. On the proliferation of political committees, see Corrado, "Money and Politics," 30; and "Note, Registration of Groups Tending to Influence Public Opinion," *Columbia Law Review* 48 (1948): 598. The National Committee of Independent Voters received some of its money from trade unions— $54,100 of $25,455 or more than 20 percent, according to Overacker—but it was primarily an effort to appeal to independent progressives in the vein of the National Progressive League of 1932 or the Progressive National Committee of 1936, rather than an explicit labor project like Labor's Non-Partisan League in 1936. As such, I have classified it as a candidate-centered committee rather than a labor union vehicle. Overacker, "Campaign Finance in the Presidential Election of 1940," 709. For more on the NCIV, see Mason Williams, *City of Ambition: FDR, LaGuardia, and the Making of Modern New York* (New York: W. W. Norton, 2013), viii.

64. "Investigation of Campaign Expenditures in 1936," Report of the Special Committee to investigate Campaign Expenditures of Presidential, Vice Presidential, and Senatorial Candidates in 1936, US Senate, 75th Cong., 1st sess., March 4, 1937, S. Rep. No. 151 (Washington, DC: Government Printing Office, 1937), 25.

65. On December 21, with the United States now at war, the club's main organizer, Oren Root Jr., announced it would suspend activities during the conflict. "Willkie Boosters Suspend for War," *Washington Post*, December 22, 1941, 6.

66. For more on Citizens for Eisenhower and its relationship with the formal Republican Party apparatus, see Daniel J. Galvin, *Presidential Party Building: Dwight D. Eisenhower to George W. Bush* (Princeton, NJ: Princeton University Press, 2010), esp. 50–57.

67. Testimony of Charles B. Shuman, President; Roger W. Fleming, Secretary-Treasurer; Hugh F. Hall, Legislative Assistant; and Matt Triggs, Assistant Legislative Director, American Farm Bureau Federation, October 8, 1956, McClellan Committee Hearings, 640–664.

68. Similarly, in the lobbying investigations, the "Farmers Independence Council of America" was revealed in 1935 testimony to have lesser ties to the agricultural community than to the "Liberty League," a business-backed organization that played a prominent role in the 1936 election campaign, as discussed later in the chapter. See James C. Carey, "The Farmers' Independence Council of America, 1935–1938," *Agricultural History* 35, no. 2 (April 1961): 70–77.

69. Kile suggests that the Independent Agricultural League was a Farm Bureau offshoot, but the Senate's 1928 campaign expenditure committee did not call Farm Bureau personnel to testify about it, and it appears to have largely operated in midwestern states. The league is referenced in the committee's report, however (as the "Smith Independent Organizations Committee, George W. Peak, chairman"), revealing it was entirely financed by the DNC. This example is discussed more in the next chapter. See Orville Merton Kile, *The Farm Bureau through Three Decades* (Baltimore, MD: Waverly Press, 1948), 147; and "Presidential Campaign Expenditures," Report of the Special Committee Investigating Presidential Campaign Expenditures, US Senate, 70th Cong., 2nd sess., S. Rep. No. 2024 (1929), 26.

70. Senator John L. McClellan (D-AR) indicated in 1956 that a Farmers' Union representative would be testifying before his dual investigating committee, but this does not appear to have happened. See Testimony of Charles B. Shuman, President of the American Farm Bureau Federation, October 8, 1956, McClellan Committee Hearings, 650.

71. Trade associations account for 15 percent of the total witnesses in lobbying hearings, while labor accounted for just 1 percent (a similar level to farm groups). More generally, witnesses with a corporate connection made up 21 percent of the total in these lobbying hearings and 12 percent in the electoral hearings, but it is difficult to identify when their appearance relates to a distinct business interest or is simply a descriptor of their occupation. Organizational affiliations are only offered, however, when the witness testifies on behalf of that group.

72. A witness from a sector-specific trade association, the Association of Foreign Language Newspapers, also appeared in 1912, but this stemmed from a particular question the committee had in regard to payment for advertising in the newspapers he represented. The appearance of representatives from the National Retail Liquor Dealers Association in 1920 was more indicative of the temperance politics of the era, as discussed later in the chapter.

73. Labor unions accounted for 11 percent of the total witnesses in electoral hearings, while trade associations accounted for 5 percent.

74. The Plumb Plan League had been formed initially as a pressure group to oppose the Transportation Act of 1920, which would return the railroads to private ownership after federal control during World War I. It became active in the 1920 election when that effort failed. The name referred to an alternative legislative plan formulated by the Brotherhoods' legal counsel, Glenn E. Plumb. See Erik Olssen, "The Making of a Political Machine: The Railroad Unions Enter Politics," *Labor History* 19, no. 3 (1978): 373–396.

75. Testimony of L. E. Sheppard, President of the Order of Railway Conductors, October 30, 1924, *Hearings before the United States Special Committee on Campaign Expenditures, held in Chicago, IL*, vol. 2 (unpublished), 161–164. Olssen notes that the nearly six hundred branches of the league would form the organizational basis for the "Conference for Progressive Political Action," a pseudo third party that backed La Follette's independent presidential candidacy in 1924. See Olssen, "The Making of a Political Machine," 375–76.

76. The Brotherhood of Railroad Trainmen was also the main sponsor of the "Public Affairs Institute," examined as part of the 1950 lobbying investigation. See "Lobby Investigation," in *CQ Almanac—1950*, 6th ed. (Washington, DC: Congressional Quarterly, 1951), 752–766, https://library.cqpress.com/cqalmanac/document.php?id=cqal50-1376390.

77. Overacker, "Campaign Funds in the Presidential Election of 1936," 478.

78. Mark J. Rozell, Clyde Wilcox, and Michael M. Franz, *Interest Groups in American Campaigns: The New Face of Electioneering*, 3rd ed. (New York: Oxford University Press, 2011), 4.

79. "Campaign Expenditures Committee," Report of the Special Committee on Campaign Expenditures, US House of Representatives, 80th Cong., 2nd sess., December 30, 1948, H.R. Rep. No. 2469 (Washington, DC: Government Printing Office, December 30, 1948), 12.

80. Ibid, 13. It listed the CIO Political Action Committee, Labor's League for Political Education (AFL), Labor's Non-Partisan League (sponsored by the United Mine Workers), the Trainmen's Political Education League (sponsored by the Brotherhood of Railway Trainmen), and Railway Labor's Political League (for unaffiliated railroad workers).

81. Alexander, *Financing the 1960 Election*, 42; and *Financing the 1964 Election*, 64. Representatives of the CIO appeared before the Buchanan Committee to discuss lobbying issues in 1950, for example, but only representatives of P.A.C. ever appeared at campaign hearings in 1944, 1946, and 1952. Similarly, the AFL would come to be represented by Labor's League for Political Education before campaign expenditure investigations after 1947, and the merged AFL-CIO would be represented by the Committee on Political Education (COPE) after 1955.

82. Testimony of Miles D. Kennedy, October 8, 1956, McClellan Committee Hearings, 699.

83. The Willkie War Veterans' national chairman was Harry Colmery, a delegate to the Republican convention in 1936 and national commander of the American Legion in the mid-1930s. See Meredith Hindley, "How the GI Bill Became Law in Spite of Some Veterans' Groups," *Humanities* 35, no. 4 (July/August 2014), https://www.neh.gov/humanities/2014/julyaugust/feature/how-the-gi-bill-became-law-in-spite-some-veterans-groups. On its emphasis on Willkie's veteran status, see Theodore W. Cousens, *Politics and Political Organizations in America* (New York: Macmillan, 1942), 414–415.

84. Poen observes that the NPC was officially separate from the American Medical Association, but most of its officials were AMA members, and the AMA officially endorsed the NPC in 1942. See Monte M. Poen, *Harry S. Truman Versus the Medical Lobby: The Genesis of Medicare* (Columbia: University of Missouri Press, 1979), 46–48.

85. Overacker, "Campaign Finance in the Presidential Election of 1940," 709.

86. On the AMA's campaign utilizing the services of political consulting firm Whitaker and Baxter, see Adam Sheingate, *Building a Business of Politics: The Rise of Political Consulting and the Transformation of American Democracy* (New York: Oxford University Press, 2016), 122–126.

87. "General Interim Report of the House Select Committee on Lobbying Activities," US House of Representatives, 81st Cong., 2nd sess., October 20, 1950, H.R. Rep. No. 3138 (Washington, DC: Government Printing Office, 1950), esp. 8, 10, 49, 51, 65.

88. The principals of the public relations company that the AMA had hired for its anti-federal healthcare campaign, Clem Whitaker and Leone Baxter, also appeared before this committee. See Testimony of Dr. David Allman, President-Elect of the AMA; C. Joseph Stetler, Director of the Law Department; Dr. Cyrus Maxwell, Legislative Representative; and James W. Foristel, Counsel, Washington Office, October 8, 1956; and Testimony of Clem Whitaker and Leone Baxter of the Public Relations Firm of Whitaker & Baxter, San Francisco, Calif., January 22, 1957, McClellan Committee Hearings, 664–693, 1187–1216.

89. Testimony of Allman and Foristel, October 8, 1956, 681, 684–685.

90. Skinner, *More Than Money*, 77.

91. See, for example, Rozell, Wilcox, and Franz, *Interest Groups in American Campaigns*, 61.

92. As explained in note 42, most pro-tariff groups are primarily classified as *economic* pressure groups, given their strong association with industries receiving material benefits from protection. The "National Tariff Commission Association" of 1913, however, is classified as an issue/ideological group, since it appears to have been more of an advocacy group seeking a technocratic solution to the tariff question through formation of a new tariff commission. Groups concerned with tariff policy, in general, present a difficult case where issue and economic categories overlap to some extent, as with later anti–New Deal ideological groups.

93. See "League to Enforce Peace (U.S.)—Additional Records," MS Am 785, Houghton Library, Harvard University, https://hollisarchives.lib.harvard.edu/repositories/24/resources/1261.

94. The National Civic League was another temperance organization that had been organized within New York in 1910, and nationally in 1922, as their president explained before the committee. Though the Ku Klux Klan was a secret society primarily associated with virulent racism, it also had a public organizational face in the 1920s and a legislative program

that included a strong commitment to Prohibition, driven in part by its fervent anti-Catholicism. See Testimony of Rev. Olaf R. Miller, June 2, 1928, "Presidential Campaign Expenditures," *Hearings before the Special Committee Investigating Presidential Campaign Expenditures*, part 3, US Senate, 70th Cong., 1st sess. (Washington, DC: Government Printing Office, 1928), 857.

95. On "purposive" incentives see James Q. Wilson, *Political Organizations* (Princeton, NJ: Princeton University Press, 2004), 312.

96. As explained in note 42, the Liberty League is classified as a business organization given its widely publicized association with the business community, such that it became a kind of business pressure group in itself even as it articulated an ideological message opposed to the New Deal.

97. Alexander lists $147,605.20 in "gross disbursements" by the ADA in 1960 and $136,757.20 in "direct expenditures," since they transferred at least some money to other entities. He lists $179,063 for gross disbursements in 1964 and $177,913 in direct expenditures. Alexander, *Financing the 1960 Election*, 43; and *Financing the 1964 Election*, 65.

98. Alexander lists ACA gross disbursements of $187,923.48 in 1960 and direct expenditures of $187,182.46. He lists $203,905.00 in both categories in 1964. Alexander, *Financing the 1960 Election*, 43; and *Financing the 1964 Election*, 65.

99. The ACA was also outspent in both 1960 and 1964 by the "Christian Nationalist Crusade," an anti-Semitic white nationalist group whose founder, Gerald K. Smith, had also formed the "America First" party and served as its 1944 presidential candidate; it also had earlier links to Huey Long's populist organization in the 1930s—the "Share Our Wealth" clubs—as discussed in the next chapter. See also note 55.

100. BIPAC's gross disbursements were $203,283 in 1964, though its direct expenditures were just $19,952, having transferred out much of its money to other organizations or candidates. See Alexander, *Financing the 1964 Election*, 65.

101. I have found only two chapters in edited volumes that deal explicitly with BIPAC: Jonathan Cottin, "Business-Industry Political Action Committee," in *Political Brokers: Money, Organizations, Power, & People*, ed. Judith G. Smith (New York: Liveright, 1972), 121–143; and Candice J. Nelson, "The Business-Industry PAC: Trying to Lead in an Uncertain Election Climate," in *Risky Business? PAC Decisionmaking and Congressional Elections*, ed. Robert Biersack, Paul S. Herrnson, and Clyde Wilcox (Armonk, NY: M. E. Sharpe, 1994), 29–38. Smith's *Political Brokers* was a compilation of profiles of important PACs, party committees, and other interest group entities, first featured in *National Journal* in the run-up to the 1972 presidential election. The other groups included are the ADA, the ACA, AMPAC, COPE, the National Committee for an Effective Congress (NCEC), the National Republican Congressional Committee, the Ripon Society, the Democratic National Committee, and Common Cause.

102. As Cousens observed, "Certain auxiliary organizations of national political parties some-times resemble pressure groups," and while many were established only for one campaign, they "need not be temporary and some of them *may even become* actual pressure groups" he said, citing Labor's Non-Partisan League as such an example. See Cousens, *Politics and Political Organizations in America*, 46–47 (emphasis added).

103. This is not to suggest that third parties entirely disappeared (a handful do appear in Alexander's 1960 and 1964 data, though they are excluded from the analysis due to the small sums of money they spent), but perhaps that third-party efforts became somewhat less common than they might have been were it not possible for discontented Americans to seek electoral change via PACs. See also note 43 in the conclusion to this book.

104. John J. Raskob, for example, became a director of the US Chamber of Commerce in 1927, while Burk describes the strong organizational and financial ties between the DuPont company—whose top executives were key players in the Liberty League—and the National Association of Manufacturers. See note on File 369 in "John J. Raskob Papers—Finding Aid," Manuscripts and Archives Department, Hagley Museum and Library, http://findingaids. hagley.org/xtf/view?docId=ead/0473.xml; and Robert F. Burk, *The Corporate State and the Broker State: The Du Ponts and American National Politics, 1925–1940* (Cambridge, MA: Harvard University Press, 1990), 7, 145, 205.

Chapter 2

1. On formation of the Grange (or the "Patrons of Husbandry") in 1867 and the Knights of Labor in the late 1860s, see Elizabeth Sanders, *Roots of Reform: Farmers, Workers, and the American State, 1877–1917* (Chicago: University of Chicago Press, 1999), 33–41, 105–108.

2. See Richard Franklin Bensel, *Sectionalism and American Political Development, 1880–1980* (Madison: University of Wisconsin Press, 1987).

3. On Grange membership decline after about 1880, see D. Sven Nordin, *Rich Harvest: A History of the Grange 1867–1900* (Jackson: University Press of Mississippi, 1974); on the Knights of Labor (from more than 700,000 members in 1886 to 100,000 by 1890), see Sanders, *Roots of Reform*, 50.

4. Elisabeth S. Clemens, *The People's Lobby: Organizational Innovation and the Rise of Interest Group Politics in the United States, 1890–1925* (Chicago: University of Chicago Press, 1997).

5. Ibid., 177.

6. Quoted in Samuel P. Huntington, "The Election Tactics of the Nonpartisan League," *Mississippi Valley Historical Review* 36, no. 4 (1950): 619.

7. The GOP's commitment to a high protective tariff, for example, was generally favored by northern businessmen, whose industrial and manufacturing concerns it largely benefited, while southern businessmen were less enamored, bonded to the Democratic Party by the scar tissue of the Civil War, and imbued with the free trade principles of an agricultural exporting region. Even after 1896, when the populist fervor of Democratic candidate William Jennings Bryan prompted many businessmen to switch allegiances, business support for the Republican Party was never monolithic; it continued to be filtered through individualism, sectionalism, and pragmatism. On the sectional dynamics of support for the tariff, see Richard Franklin Bensel, *The Political Economy of American Industrialization 1877–1900* (New York: Cambridge University Press, 2000).

8. Melvin I. Urofsky, "Campaign Finance Reform Before 1971," *Albany Government Law Review* 1, no. 1 (2008): 9.

9. Clemens, *The People's Lobby*, esp. chapter 6.

10. Ibid., 34.

11. Ibid., 293.

12. Ibid., 172.

13. Ibid., 29, 314, 325. "[T]he pursuit of special interests" had been viewed as "culturally corrupt" under the nineteenth-century party system, Clemens notes (29), but in the early twentieth century, the parties too became culturally suspect.

14. Ibid., 173, 177. As Clemens describes the key features of this mode of organization in terms of the Farmers' Union (founded in 1902), it involved "the rejection of partisanship; the establishment of ties to the legislature, other pressure groups, and state agencies; and the articulation of specific demands to be met by new laws, public spending, or the strengthening of state agencies" (173).

15. The United States Brewers' Association was formed in 1862, for example, while the National Association of Manufacturers (NAM)—the first major industrial "peak" association— appeared in 1895. On the emergence of national trade associations in the mid-nineteenth century, see Harmon Zeigler, *Interest Groups in American Society* (Englewood Cliffs, NJ: Prentice-Hall, 1964), 96. See also Cathie Jo Martin and Duane Swank, *The Political Construction of Business Interests: Coordination, Growth, and Equality* (New York: Cambridge University Press, 2012).

16. Adam Sheingate, *Building a Business of Politics: The Rise of Political Consultants and the Transformation of American Democracy* (New York: Oxford University Press, 2016), esp. 36–37.

17. Testimony of Senator Robert La Follette, June 3, 1913, "Maintenance of a Lobby to Influence Legislation," *Hearings before a Subcommittee of the Committee on the Judiciary*, part 1, US Senate, 63rd Cong., 1st sess. (Washington, DC: Government Printing Office, 1913), 197 (hereafter cited as Overman Committee Hearings).

18. Ibid.

19. On the development of such publicity methods, see Christopher M. Loomis, "The Politics of Uncertainty: Lobbyists and Propaganda in Early Twentieth-Century America," *Journal of Policy History* 21, no. 2 (2009): 187–213.

20. "Where Are Those Lobbyists?," *Washington Post*, March 22, 1912, 6, quoted in Loomis, "The Politics of Uncertainty," 193.

21. Most scholars describing the activities of interest groups in this period emphasize the nonelectoral aspects of their activity. McCormick, for example, describes a restructuring of political participation at the turn of the twentieth century in which party-line voting and overall turnout declined at the same time that "interest-group organizations of all sorts successfully forged permanent, non-electoral means of influencing the government and its agencies." (251). Clemens also emphasizes the legislative and bureaucratic lobbying in which "modern" interest groups engaged, although she does not entirely ignore electoral activity, discussing "extra-partisan direct democracy" as another possible replacement for partisan politics (beyond nonpartisan lobbying), which utilized new institutional tools such as the initiative, the referendum, recall elections, and primaries (27, 172). Her main emphasis remains on lobbying techniques, however. See Richard L. McCormick, "The Discovery That Business Corrupts Politics," *American Historical Review* 86, no. 3 (1981): 251; and Clemens, *The People's Lobby*, esp. 27, 172–173.

22. In a time before polling could gauge local opinion, whether lawmakers heeded their call was a matter of organizational credibility, the lawmakers' sense of electoral vulnerability or aversion to risk, and their own personal "read" of their districts. On interest groups as a source of district intelligence prior to polling, see Brian Balogh, "'Mirrors of Desires,' Interest Groups, Elections, and the Targeted Style in Twentieth-Century America," in *The Democratic Experiment: New Directions in American Political History*, ed. Meg Jacobs, William J. Novak, and Julian E. Zelizer (Princeton, NJ: Princeton University Press, 2003), 222–249.

23. E. E. Schattschneider, *Party Government* (New Brunswick, NJ: Transaction, 1942/2004), 27; V. O. Key, *Politics, Parties and Pressure Groups*, 1st ed. (New York: Crowell, 1942), 212. See also David B. Truman, *The Governmental Process: Political Interests and Public Opinion* (Berkeley, CA: Institute of Governmental Studies, 1951/1993), 295.

24. As Key explained, "The theory underlying such a campaign is that the threat of retaliation at the polls makes an official more sympathetic toward the viewpoint of the organization concerned" (*Politics, Parties and Pressure Groups*, 1st ed., 212).

25. Schattschneider even formulated a "law of imperfect mobilization," which stated that groups could never deliver the votes they claimed to control, while Key noted how rare it was empirically, citing the Anti-Saloon League as an important exception. See Schattschneider, *Party Government*, 87; and Key, *Politics, Parties and Pressure Groups*, 1st ed., 211.

26. Mark J. Rozell, Clyde Wilcox, and Michael M. Franz, *Interest Groups in American Campaigns: The New Face of Electioneering*, 3rd ed. (New York: Oxford University Press, 2011), 24.

27. On the 1912 election and Roosevelt's role in particular, see Sidney M. Milkis, *Theodore Roosevelt, the Progressive Party, and the Transformation of American Democracy* (Lawrence: University Press of Kansas, 2009).

28. "Campaign Contributions," *Testimony before a Subcommittee of the Committee on Privileges and Elections*, vol. I, US Senate, 62nd Cong., 3rd sess. (Washington, DC: Government Printing Office, 1913), 3 (hereafter cited as Clapp Committee Hearings). As Mutch observes, the attempt to use the investigation to aid Taft's prospects did not go as planned, since Senator Clapp was actually a Roosevelt ally and conducted the hearings so as to minimize damage to Roosevelt's campaign. Robert E. Mutch, *Buying the Vote: A History of Campaign Finance Reform* (New York: Oxford University Press, 2014), 77–78.

29. Zeigler, *Interest Groups in American Society*, 110–112. Truman described the NAM's shift in focus toward labor concerns as so significant that it essentially "marked the beginning of a new organization" (*The Governmental Process*, 81).

30. At the time of Schwedtman's testimony he was vice president of the NAM's Missouri branch and had served as Van Cleave's secretary during his presidency from 1906 to 1909. Van Cleave was also head of Buck's Stove and Range Co. of St. Louis, in which capacity he pursued a major legal case against the American Federation of Labor and its president, Samuel Gompers. See

Testimony of Ferdinand C. Schwedtman, October 11, 1912, Clapp Committee Hearings, vol. I, 858–864; and "Van Cleave Is Dead; Was Foe of Gompers," *New York Times*, May 16, 1910, 9.

31. Testimony of Ferdinand C. Schwedtman, Clapp Committee Hearings, vol. I, 859–861.

32. Ibid., 861, 864. "Prior to 1896 Mr. Van Cleave was a very ardent Democrat, and so was I," Schwedtman told the committee (864).

33. Ibid., 861.

34. Ibid.

35. Ibid., 862.

36. Wilson's remarks are noted in "Maintenance of a Lobby to Influence Legislation," Overman Committee Hearings, 3. The tariff bill Wilson had recommended—debated and ultimately passed in a special session that the president called in April 1913—imposed a major reduction across tariff rates, plus an income tax to make up the resulting difference in federal revenues, taking advantage of the newly ratified Sixteenth Amendment. Both chambers of Congress would ultimately launch investigations into the frenzied lobbying on this measure: a Senate committee chaired by Lee S. Overman (D-NC) and a House committee chaired by Finis J. Garrett (D-TN).

37. Noted in Edgar Lane, "Some Lessons from Past Congressional Investigations of Lobbying," *Public Opinion Quarterly* 14, no. 1 (1950): 16–17.

38. See "The Tribune Turns Searchlight On the 'Invisible Government,'" *Chicago Tribune*, June 29, 1913, 1, for an overview of Mulhall's allegations. The NAM acted through a spinoff group, the National Council of Industrial Defense (NCID), in much of this activity, according to the *Tribune*. The NCID was created in 1908, supposedly at Mulhall's suggestion, and was ostensibly a separate alliance of more than two hundred local manufacturers' groups and citizens' organizations, forged around commitment to the "open shop." In reality, it was a "paper organization" serving as a supplementary lobbying arm for the NAM itself, with the two sharing key personnel (its main officers were senior NAM officials) and maintaining the same office in Washington. According to Zeigler, the NCID would later be renamed the National Industrial Council and "became the lobbying arm of the NAM." See Zeigler, *Interest Groups in American Society*, 112.

39. The *Tribune* identified three distinct streams of activity in which Mulhall engaged: "lobby, political, and strike breaking work." See "The Tribune Turns Searchlight On," 2.

40. Ibid., 1–3. "System of campaigning" is on p. 2.

41. Ibid., 4. Mulhall also charged that he supplied Democratic voters with alcohol intended to prevent their voting in a Maine congressional election, as noted during testimony before the House investigating committee. See "Charges Against Members of the House and Lobby Activities of the National Association of Manufacturers of the United States and Others," *Hearings before the Select Committee Appointed under Resolution 198*, vol. 4, US House of Representatives, 63rd Cong., 1st sess. (Washington, DC: Government Printing Office, 1913), 2739, 2414 (hereafter Garrett Committee Hearings).

42. "The Tribune Turns Searchlight On," 4.

43. Mulhall had never held an official position with the NAM, working instead for one of its associates who ultimately fired him. He subsequently maintained an informal position by appealing directly to Van Cleave, until 1908, when he "saw that my services were gradually narrowing down" ("The Tribune Turns Searchlight On," 2–3). As the Garrett Committee concluded in its report, Mulhall "entertained an animus toward many of those against whom he made allegations," but they still bore some responsibility for the actions in which he engaged, the committee felt. See "Charges Against Members of the House and Lobby Activities," Report of the Select Committee Appointed under House Resolution 198, US House of Representatives, 63rd Cong., 2nd sess., December 9, 1913, H.R. Rep. No. 113 (Washington, D.C.: Government Printing Office, 1913), 18 (hereafter Garrett Committee Report).

44. Testimony of Ferdinand C. Schwedtman, August 29, 1913, Overman Committee Hearings, part 54, 4383 (emphasis added). To some on the committee, this smacked of a plan to evade the Tillman Act, though most of the contests to which Mulhall referred had taken place prior to its passage or were nonfederal races outside of its bounds (see p. 4433).

45. Testimony of Charles Littlefield, September 19, 1913, Garrett Committee Hearings, vol. 4, 2740.

46. Ibid., 2741.

47. As former NAM president John Kirby Jr. testified before the Overman Committee, he and his fellow officers had "endeavored both to elect and defeat candidates for office" *as individuals*—something they considered "a duty which we owe to our country"—but he denied any electoral involvement in his official capacity. Testimony of John Kirby Jr., September 2, 1913, Overman Committee Hearings, part 56, 4502.

48. Testimony of Ferdinand C. Schwedtman, August 30, 1913, Overman Committee Hearings, part 55, 4437.

49. Testimony of Samuel Gompers, September 10–11, 1913, Garrett Committee Hearings, vol. 4, 2412.

50. Ibid., 2505. At first Gompers suggested that the federation spent between $400 and $500 in Maine for traveling and accommodation expenses and to circulate literature (2414). Later, on consulting AFL accounts, he revised this figure to about $1,500 (2505). AFL "electioneering" involved paying for local organizers; speakers to attend mass meetings; and limited circulation of literature, including overviews of an incumbent's voting record in terms of his or her "friendliness" toward labor (2462, 2547).

51. Ibid., 2428, 2443, 2469. According to Gompers's testimony, the AFL received $8,225.94 in 1906—mostly from local unions and a handful of individuals (including Gompers himself) in response to an appeal for "voluntary financial assistance"—and spent $8,147.19. In 1908 the AFL received $8,531.97 and spent $8,469.98, including some expenditures on the presidential campaign. In 1910 it received $3,609.48 and spent $3,590.28 ("[V]oluntary financial assistance" is on 2421). In terms of locations, Gompers acknowledged AFL participation in Littlefield's Maine district in both 1906 and 1908 (though it "was not very conspicuous" in 1906), as well as other districts in Indiana, Illinois, Michigan, New York, New Jersey, Connecticut, Massachusetts, California, Colorado, Pennsylvania, and Maryland, among others, in 1908. Gompers did not identify specific districts beyond this but alluded to involvement in various other contests from 1906 to 1912 (2415, 2443, 2461–2462).

52. Ibid., 2423, 2473. The AFL was *not* incorporated, Gompers confirmed, but was a voluntary association (2423). Gompers also admitted that the AFL did use some general funds for campaign publications in 1908 but not in other years (2473).

53. Ibid., 2462, 2472, 2418.

54. Ibid., 2418.

55. On the typical characterization of the AFL as "nonpolitical" in this early period, see Julie Greene, *Pure and Simple Politics: The American Federation of Labor and Political Activism, 1881–1917* (New York: Cambridge University Press, 1998), 2.

56. Zeigler, *Interest Groups in American Society*, 139.

57. Greene, *Pure and Simple Politics*, 66–69.

58. See Stephen J. Scheinberg, "Theodore Roosevelt and the A.F. of L.'s Entry into Politics, 1906–1908," *Labor History* 3, no. 2 (1962): 132n4; and Greene, *Pure and Simple Politics*, 66–67.

59. Greene, *Pure and Simple Politics*, 111; "systematic effort" is from Testimony of Samuel Gompers, Garrett Committee Hearings, 2462. See also Zeigler, *Interest Groups in American Society*, 142.

60. Gompers mentioned various lawsuits against labor unions, a court decision requiring unions to pay damages for strike actions on antitrust grounds, and the injunction procured by the Buck's Stove and Range company against an AFL boycott, which had resulted in a lengthy legal battle and Gompers being charged with contempt of court, though this was ultimately overturned by the Supreme Court. Testimony of Samuel Gompers, Garrett Committee Hearings, 2462. On this wider context, see also Zeigler, *Interest Groups in American Society*, 142; and Scheinberg, "Theodore Roosevelt and the A.F. of L.'s Entry into Politics, 1906–1908," 132.

61. On the AFL's "friends and enemies" strategy, see Clemens, *The People's Lobby*, 124–125.

62. Quoted in Scheinberg, "Theodore Roosevelt and the A.F. of L.'s Entry into Politics, 1906–1908," 136 (emphasis added). Cannon was speaking in Littlefield's district.

63. Testimony of Samuel Gompers, Garrett Committee Hearings, 2417–2418.

64. Scheinberg, "Theodore Roosevelt and the A.F. of L.'s Entry into Politics, 1906–1908," 134–135.

65. Testimony of Samuel Gompers, Garrett Committee Hearings, 2462.

66. Ibid., 2462, 2472.

67. As Gompers noted elsewhere, labor was becoming at most "partisan to a principle," not "partisan to a political party." Quoted in Greene, *Pure and Simple Politics*, 178.

68. Ibid., 161, 165.

69. Testimony of Samuel Gompers, Garrett Committee Hearings, 2418.

70. Zeigler, *Interest Groups in American Society*, 142.

71. Testimony of Samuel Gompers, Garrett Committee Hearings, 2530–2531.

72. Greene, *Pure and Simple Politics*, 175.

73. Testimony of Samuel Gompers, Garrett Committee Hearings, 2472, 2479.

74. Ibid., 2472.

75. On Roosevelt's letters, see Scheinberg, "Theodore Roosevelt and the A.F. of L.'s Entry into Politics, 1906–1908," 148; on rank-and-file discontent with such voting instructions, see Greene, *Pure and Simple Politics*, 175–176, 192; on the broader damage to the AFL's campaign, see Greene, 176.

76. Testimony of Samuel Gompers, Garrett Committee Hearings, 2472.

77. Ibid. "We had accomplished much that we desired, and that was publicity for our grievances and to arouse public attention to the relief which we sought," Gompers explained.

78. Ibid., 2472–2473. Gompers singled out the NAM's "hostile effort to anything we attempted to do" in previous campaigns (2472).

79. Ibid., 2472–2473. The AFL's political activity "ceased in 1910 systematically and comprehensively," Gompers said (2473), though he acknowledged at least one congressional campaign in 1912 in which, he asserted, the AFL "bore no expenses," but simply highlighted the incumbent's voting record in the *American Federationist* and *Weekly News Letter* (2505).

80. Ibid., 2428, 2443, 2469. See detailed figures in note 51.

81. Testimony of Frank Morrison, Secretary of the American Federation of Labor, September 11, 1913, Garrett Committee Hearings, vol. 4, 2538.

82. Greene, *Pure and Simple Politics*, 160.

83. Testimony of Frank Morrison, Garrett Committee Hearings, 2536. On information about a candidate's "friendliness" to labor, provided by the national office, see Testimony of Samuel Gompers, Garrett Committee Hearings, 2476, 2505. Morrison noted that he had encouraged state and local federations to cultivate union members to *stand* as candidates, in which cases the AFL tried to provide additional, if still limited, assistance. Testimony of Frank Morrison, Garrett Committee Hearings, 2536–2537, 2551.

84. Indeed, to the extent the national AFL was active in the districts, it was only on the invitation of local working people, both Gompers and Morrison affirmed. Garrett Committee Hearings, 2478 (Gompers), 2538 (Morrison).

85. Testimony of Arthur E. Holder, March 20, 1914, Overman Committee Hearings, 4888.

86. Albion Taylor, *Labor Policies of the National Association of Manufacturers* (Urbana: University of Illinois Press, 1928), 22–23, quoted in Grace R. Conant, "An Analysis of the Campaign of 1928" (master's thesis, Loyola University, Chicago, 1946), 88.

87. Ibid.

88. Controversy over intensive lobbying on a proposed federal estate tax in the 69th Congress (1925–1927) had prompted a new wave of proposals to regulate lobbying in the late 1920s, and Caraway had himself called for another inquiry into lobbying in 1927. His resolution, reintroduced in 1929, was given further impetus during Senate debate on the Smoot-Hawley Tariff bill that year, when it emerged that Senator Hiram Bingham (R-CT) had employed a tariff "expert" who was simultaneously employed by the Manufacturers' Association of Connecticut. See Edgar Lane, "Some Lessons from Past Congressional Investigations of Lobbying," *Public Opinion Quarterly* 14, no. 1 (Spring 1950): 21–22.

89. On the Chamber's formation, see Zeigler, *Interest Groups in American Society*, 113–114; and Donald R. Hall, *Cooperative Lobbying: The Power of Pressure* (Tucson: University of Arizona Press, 1969), 215.

90. Testimony of Julius H. Barnes, December 17, 1929, "Lobby Investigation," *Hearings before a Subcommittee of the Committee on the Judiciary*, vol. II, US Senate, 71st Cong., 2nd sess. (Washington, DC: Government Printing Office, 1931), 1614 (hereafter cited as Caraway Committee Hearings).

91. As Morrison had admitted in his 1913 testimony, while "the policy of the federation is non-partisan," there were "some people who believe it is better to have a labor party, the same as they have in England." Testimony of Frank Morrison, Garrett Committee Hearings, 2548. Strouthous has pointed to several third-party efforts at the subnational level in this period, suggesting the desire for an independent labor party was never entirely expunged. Andrew Strouthous, *U.S. Labor and Political Action, 1918–24: A Comparison of Independent Political Action in New York, Chicago and Seattle* (London: Macmillan, 2000).

92. *Presidential Elections Since 1789*, 2nd ed. (Washington, DC: Congressional Quarterly Press, 1979), 86.

93. An older leftist party, the Socialist Labor Party (SLP), also contested the 1912 presidential election, for example, polling only 0.19 percent of the vote (one of its representatives had appeared before the Clapp Committee that year to discuss its finances). The SLP's origins went back to the 1870s, though it was constituted more formally after 1890 under the leadership of Daniel DeLeon, along Marxist lines. Debs helped establish two rival parties to the SLP, first the Social Democratic Party in 1898 and then the Socialist Party in 1901. Debs's Socialist Party lacked the revolutionary impulse and commitment to overthrow capitalism that marked the SLP and tried to offer a more "Americanized" version of socialism. The Socialist Party would itself split in 1916 over the pacifist stance taken by Debs toward World War I, with the dissatisfied members breaking out to form the Social Democratic League of America. There was also persistent division among Communist adherents over whether to form their own party or seek to capture the extant Socialist organization, resulting in the formation of two new and distinct parties in 1919: the Communist Labor Party and the Communist Worker's Party. By 1920, having alienated supporters on both the right and the left of the Socialist spectrum, the Socialist Party itself would focus on forming a Labor Party in the European mold. On Debs's vision of socialism, see Milkis, *Theodore Roosevelt, the Progressive Party, and the Transformation of American Democracy*. On splits between Socialist parties, see Conant, "An Analysis of the Campaign of 1928," 62–63.

94. "1916 Presidential General Election Results," in *US Election Atlas*, http://uselectionatlas.org/RESULTS/national.php?year=1916.

95. "1920 Presidential General Election Results," in *US Election Atlas*, http://uselectionatlas.org/RESULTS/national.php?year=1920.

96. Testimony of Parley P. Christensen, September 1, 1920, "Presidential Campaign Expenses," *Hearing before a Subcommittee of the Committee on Privileges and Elections*, part 10, US Senate, 66th Cong., 2nd sess. (Washington, DC Government Printing Office, 1920), 1438–1439.

97. On the Farmer-Labor Party, see Richard M. Valelly, *Radicalism in the States: The Minnesota Farmer-Labor Party and the American Political Economy* (Chicago: University of Chicago Press, 1989).

98. For an account of the Railroad Brotherhood's campaign, see Erik Olssen, "The Making of a Political Machine: The Railroad Unions Enter Politics," *Labor History* 19, no. 3 (1978): 373–396.

99. Ibid., 375–376. On the limited nature of the 1924 Progressive "party," see Robert Elliott Kessler, "The League for Independent Political Action, 1929—1933" (master's thesis, University of Wisconsin, Madison, 1967), 17.

100. L. E. Sheppard of the Order of Railway Conductors appeared before the Senate's committee, chaired by William Borah (R-ID), as did Frank P. Walsh, Joseph W. Miller and John M. Nelson, representing La Follette's campaign.

101. James H. Shideler, "The Disintegration of the Progressive Party Movement of 1924," *Historian* 13, no. 2 (1951): 192. Gompers died soon after the election.

102. Coolidge received 54 percent of the popular vote in 1924 and 71.9 percent of the electoral college. His Democratic opponent, John Davis, won 28.82 percent of the popular vote, while La Follette won 16.62 percent. "1924 Presidential General Election Results," in *US Election Atlas*, https://uselectionatlas.org/RESULTS/national.php?year=1924.

103. On the renewal of the AFL's traditional hostility to third parties after 1924, see Kessler, "The League for Independent Political Action, 1929–1933," 63; and Richard J. Brown, "John Dewey and the League for Independent Political Action," *Social Studies* 59, no. 4 (1968): 160.

104. Kessler observed that in the late 1920s, "[o]ld third party warriors in the labor movement" had "abandoned independent political action." As Kessler described, the president of the Chicago Federation of Labor, John Fitzpatrick, explained "that he had learned his lesson in the early nineteen-twenties, and like 'a burned child who dreads the fire,' he was not ready to re-embark on the quest for political realignment" ("The League for Independent Political Action, 1929—1933," 63).

105. Clemens, *The People's Lobby*, 173.

106. For more on the NPL, see Robert L. Morlan, *Political Prairie Fire: The Nonpartisan League, 1915–1922* (Minneapolis: University of Minnesota Press, 1955); and Michael Lansing, *Insurgent Democracy: The Nonpartisan League in North American Politics* (Chicago: University of Chicago Press, 2015).

107. In the case of the NPL, at least, its absence from congressional hearings may relate to the lack of investigation in 1916, which was during its electoral heyday, though it still does not appear in Pollock's brief analysis of campaign finance in the 1916 election. See James K. Pollock Jr., *Party Campaign Funds* (New York: Knopf, 1926), 56.

108. Loomis, "The Politics of Uncertainty," 200.

109. Clarence J. Hein, "The Adoption of Minnesota's Direct Primary Law," *Minnesota History* 35, no. 2 (December 1957): 341–342; and Charles E. Merriam and Louise Overacker, *Primary Elections* (Chicago: University of Chicago Press, 1928), 61.

110. Merriam and Overacker, *Primary Elections*, 142.

111. Loomis, "The Politics of Uncertainty," 200. See also David B. Truman, "Party Reform, Party Atrophy, and Constitutional Change: Some Reflections," *Political Science Quarterly* 99, no. 4 (Winter 1984–1985): 647–648; and Peter F. Galderisi and Benjamin Ginsberg, "Primary Elections and the Evanescence of Third Party Activity in the United States," in *Do Elections Matter?*, ed. Benjamin Ginsberg and Alan Stone (Armonk, NY: M. E. Sharpe, 1986), 116.

112. Huntington, "The Election Tactics of the Nonpartisan League," 623.

113. Ibid., 618–619.

114. Ibid., 613–614. See also Hugh A. Bone, "Political Parties and Pressure Group Politics," *Annals of the American Academy of Political and Social Sciences* 319 (1958): 81. Bone described its "tactics of infiltration rather than third-party politics." State nonpartisan leagues were active in Minnesota, Wisconsin, Idaho, Colorado, and Montana, for example.

115. Huntington, "The Election Tactics of the Nonpartisan League," 615–619, 632.

116. In 1920, for example, sixteen Democratic primaries were held and selected 44.6 percent of the convention delegates, while twenty Republican primaries were held, selecting 57.8 percent of the delegates. The impact of primaries on convention outcomes was lessened, however, by the prevalence of "beauty contest" primaries, in which the result was not binding on delegates, or "favorite son" candidacies, in which state party leaders urged support for a popular local officeholder in the primary, thus giving them control of a bloc of delegates at the convention. On delegate counts, see *Congressional Quarterly's Guide to U.S. Elections*, 5th ed. (Washington, DC: CQ Press, 2005), 318.

117. On wartime agricultural prosperity, see Zeigler, *Interest Groups in American Society*, 173, and Conant, "An Analysis of the Campaign of 1928," 30–31; on the "red scare," see Kessler, "The League for Independent Political Action, 1929—1933," 19, 21.

118. On the postwar collapse of agricultural prosperity, see John D. Hicks, "The Third Party Tradition in American Politics," *Mississippi Valley Historical Review* 20, no. 1 (1933): 23–24; Zeigler, *Interest Groups in American Society*, 173, and Conant, "An Analysis of the Campaign of 1928," 30–33; on membership decline and internal disagreements, see Kessler, "The League for Independent Political Action, 1929—1933," 20–21, and Zeigler, *Interest Groups in American Society*, 172, 179; and on animosity toward the NPL's methods, see Huntington, "The Election Tactics of the Nonpartisan League," 626–627.

119. For the Farm Bureau's founding, see Testimony of Chester Gray, February 26, 1930, Caraway Committee Hearings, vol. II, 3018; on its membership, see Testimony of Gray Silver, January

21, 1921, "Farm Organizations," *Hearing before the Committee on Banking and Currency*, US House of Representatives, 66th Cong., 3rd sess. (Washington, DC: Government Printing Office, 1921), 37.

120. The extension program was established by the Smith-Lever Act of 1914 (38 Stat. 372).

121. See Zeigler, *Interest Groups in American Society*, 175–176.

122. Testimony of Gray Silver, 46. The House Banking Committee's 1921 investigation of farm organizations was narrowly framed and focused on a specific sector; thus it does not appear in the larger dataset of witnesses. For more on this investigation see Zeigler, *Interest Groups in American Society*, 176–177; and John Mark Hansen, *Gaining Access: Congress and the Farm Lobby, 1919–1981* (Chicago: University of Chicago Press, 1991), 29.

123. Testimony of Gray Silver, 46, 56–57, 75.

124. Testimony of Chester Gray, February 25, 1930, Caraway Committee Hearings, 2965.

125. Zeigler, *Interest Groups in American Society*, 176. See also Clemens, *The People's Lobby*, 146, on a bureaucratic orientation evident across agricultural groups.

126. Silver explained that the Farm Bureau submitted referenda to their county organizations to gauge opinion on particular issues and then communicated the results to Congress. Testimony of Gray Silver, 46.

127. Zeigler, *Interest Groups in American Society*, 177–179.

128. After 1926, Zeigler says, "the influence of the bloc slumped badly" due to internal disagreements, poor legislative management, and hostility from the Republican administration (*Interest Groups in American Society*, 178–179).

129. Zeigler, *Interest Groups in American Society*, 180. Farmers were to be charged an "equalization fee" (a kind of tax) should the government agency charged with marketing the surpluses have to sell them at a loss.

130. Kenneth Finegold and Theda Skocpol, *State and Party in America's New Deal* (Madison: University of Wisconsin Press, 1995), 78.

131. As Truman noted, Hoover was "more objectionable" to the Farm Bureau than even Coolidge had been ("Party Reform, Party Atrophy, and Constitutional Change," 302).

132. As Orville Merton Kile, a longtime Farm Bureau operative, posed the problem in his 1948 book on the Farm Bureau, how could its leaders aid Smith's campaign in the Midwest "while at the same time avoiding the appearance of 'dragging their organizations into politics?'" See Orville Merton Kile, *The Farm Bureau Through Three Decades* (Baltimore: Waverly Press, 1948), 148. This quote is also reproduced in Truman, "Party Reform, Party Atrophy, and Constitutional Change," 302–303.

133. Kile suggests that the effective demise of the Grange after supporting Bryan in 1896 was a cautionary example for the Farm Bureau (*The Farm Bureau Through Three Decades*, 147).

134. Ibid., 148–149. Also quoted in Truman, "Party Reform, Party Atrophy, and Constitutional Change," 303.

135. Kile, *The Farm Bureau Through Three Decades*, 149.

136. In his in-depth examination of the Farm Bureau in this period, for example, Hansen does not discuss Peek's role in the 1928 election at all (*Gaining Access*).

137. On these financial interactions, see the report of the Senate's 1928 campaign expenditures committee: "Presidential Campaign Expenditures," Report of the Special Committee Investigating Presidential Campaign Expenditures, US Senate, 70th Cong., S. Rep. No. 2024 (Washington, DC: Government Printing Office, 1929), 26–27. "Agricultural Leagues" are listed in "Table XI—Committees and Organizations Receiving and Expending Money in Behalf of the Democratic Party" (26). A further breakdown is provided in "Table XII—Smith Independent Organizations Committee, George W. Peak, chairman" (26–27), showing that this effort was entirely financed by the DNC ($400,000 in total).

138. On Smith's somewhat indeterminate position in relation to McNary-Haugen, see Gilbert C. Fite, "The Agricultural Issue in the Presidential Campaign of 1928," *Mississippi Valley Historical Review* 37, no. 4 (March 1951): 662, 666–667. On Hoover's farm policy exhibiting his "preference for associationalist cooperation over economic competition," see Finegold and Skocpol, *State and Party in America's New Deal*, 79.

139. Fite, "The Agricultural Issue in the Presidential Campaign of 1928," 664. McVeigh, Myers, and Sikkink explore a similar phenomenon in 1924 through the lens of the Ku Klux Klan in

Indiana, where the Klan's racial and religious obsessions, including Prohibition, trumped its opposition to high tariffs and support for progressive economic measures. Accordingly, it urged its supporters among Indiana farmers to back conservative Republican incumbent Calvin Coolidge in the presidential election rather than Robert La Follette, since Coolidge had proffered no opinion on the Klan while La Follette had condemned it outright. Rory McVeigh, Daniel J. Myers, and David Sikkink, "Corn, Klansmen, and Coolidge: Structure and Framing in Social Movements," *Social Forces* 83, no. 2 (2004): 653–690.

140. Truman, "Party Reform, Party Atrophy, and Constitutional Change," 303.

141. According to Kile, the Farm Bureau's "paid-up membership fell to a low of 163,246 in 1933," a substantial drop from the 1.5 million membership that Gray Silver had asserted in his 1921 congressional testimony, and lower even than the 317,000 members that Hansen indicates the Farm Bureau had in 1919. See Kile, *The Farm Bureau Through Three Decades*, 172; Testimony of Gray Silver, 37; and Hansen, *Gaining Access*, 29.

142. Kile discusses this limited 1932 effort, dubbed a "Battle of the Ballots," in which Farm Bureau leaders generally urged members to vote for candidates who had shown support for farm relief. Records of congressmen and pledges of challengers were sought and circulated to members through the Farm Bureau's monthly magazine, *The Bureau Farmer*. Kile, *The Farm Bureau Through Three Decades*, 184, 188.

143. Zeigler, *Interest Groups in American Society*, 185.

144. Finegold and Skocpol suggest that Roosevelt's campaign strategy focused on appealing to southern and western farm voters "on economic rather than ethnocultural grounds," but they make no mention of electoral partnerships with the Farm Bureau or other farm groups (*State and Party in America's New Deal*, 81–83).

145. On the success of the AAA in this respect, despite farmers disliking its emphasis on production control, see Finegold and Skocpol, *State and Party in America's New Deal*, esp. 13–20. Finegold and Skocpol credit preexisting state capacity at the USDA and land-grant colleges as an important factor in the AAA's long-term success. In turn, Sanders points to the role of farm groups in helping to create that very capacity, by promoting policies that powerfully shaped the Progressive Era administrative state. See Sanders, *Roots of Reform*, 392.

146. Hansen, *Gaining Access*, 12.

147. Ibid., 5. Thus the House Agriculture Committee became more favorable to Farm Bureau policies in the mid-1920s, Hansen says, because "[e]lectoral outcomes had indicated that alliances with the farm groups were becoming more advantageous" between 1924 and 1926 (49).

148. Ibid., 58, 89. Although Hansen acknowledges the possibility that interest groups might offer "electoral assistance," including "donations of money, personnel and exposure" (15), he finds little evidence of actual electioneering. In discussing the 1926 congressional elections, for example, Hansen writes: "The farm organizations' maneuvers in these elections appear remarkably subtle. If the farm groups deployed money or manpower, the practice was not extensive enough or unusual enough for anyone to comment on it" (58). Similarly, in discussing 1936, Hansen asks: "What did the farm organizations actually do in these elections?" "In terms of pressures, as traditionally conceived, they did precious little. The farm groups may have contributed money; they may have contributed manpower; but if they did, they did so silently" (89). In Hansen's telling, then, the farm organizations were brokers of electoral *information* rather than providers of electoral *services*—they acted "as barometers of farm opinion" for incumbents and challengers and "signaled their assessments of candidates' performance" to voters, though the *mechanisms* through which they did so are not always identified (89).

149. Ibid., 227.

150. Ibid.

151. Ibid., 230.

152. Ibid., esp. 101, 104–105.

153. Ibid., 83, 87, 90–92, 97.

154. Ibid., 20, 119–124, 152–156. Republicans supported a more flexible approach to price supports during this partisan phase, with fewer restrictions on production, while Democrats preferred high, fixed payments to farmers and strict production controls.

155. Ibid., 7, 112.
156. Ibid., 5, 13–14, 223. Since parties and interest groups are both potential sources of information in Hansen's model, lawmakers choose whichever offers "greater advantages or lower costs" (13). Where lawmakers favor interest groups, they do so "*at the expense of political parties, national leaders, and perhaps the greater good,*" Hansen says, channeling Schattschneider (14). But if interest groups offer the same information as parties, Hansen suggests, there is no reason to favor them, and lawmakers will look to their party (223). In such circumstances, "[p]arty politics subsumes interest group politics," he says (223).
157. Testimony of Charles B. Shuman, President; Roger W. Fleming, Secretary-Treasurer; Hugh F. Hall, Legislative Assistant; and Matt Triggs, Assistant Legislative Director, American Farm Bureau Federation, October 8, 1956, McClellan Committee, 640–664.
158. Hansen does point to the rise of a consumer lobby in the 1960s, which provided some opposition to agricultural groups, but this tended to be dispersed rather than monolithic opposition, especially as individual commodity organizations replaced overarching agricultural groups as the key representatives within the sector (*Gaining Access*, 177–187).
159. In the early 1930s, for example, all the major agricultural groups came together in support of the AAA. Even the disagreement over price supports in the 1960s was on the *nature* of those supports, not whether they should be offered at all.
160. Institutionally, the manner in which the Farm Bureau was interwoven into the administration of the AAA was important too, offering a privileged position from which to guide policy (see Hansen, *Gaining Access*, 86).
161. From a membership perspective, the Farm Bureau's numbers actually *increased* steadily after World War II (from less than half a million in the mid-1930s, to nearly 3.5 million in 1980), as Hansen observed in a 1985 article, despite a wider decrease in the overall farm population, as noted in his book (*Gaining Access*). Increased membership, in theory, would have provided greater resources for a traditional "bloc voting" approach, had its leaders chosen to pursue one or offered potential manpower in campaigns. This suggests that available resources in themselves do not determine the nature of political activity, as discussed more in chapter 7 in relation to business groups. See John Mark Hansen, "The Political Economy of Group Membership," *American Political Science Review* 79, no. 1 (March 1985): 84. On the declining farm population from the mid-twentieth century more generally, see Hansen, *Gaining Access*, 182–183.
162. Following passage of prohibition laws in several states, Congress had in 1913 banned the transportation of liquor into "dry" states, over President Taft's veto (the Webb-Kenyon Act). In December 1917 both chambers of Congress approved a prohibition constitutional amendment with large bipartisan majorities and sent it to the states for ratification. A wartime prohibition law was put into effect even before ratification was achieved, early in 1919. Finally, in late 1919, Congress passed the Volstead Act, the Eighteenth Amendment's enabling legislation, which brought Prohibition into effect on January 17, 1920. See David E. Kyvig, *Repealing National Prohibition* (Chicago: University of Chicago Press, 1979), 5–12.
163. K. Austin Kerr, *Organized for Prohibition: A New History of the Anti-Saloon League* (New Haven, CT: Yale University Press, 1985), 37, 43, 53.
164. Peter H. Odegard, *Pressure Politics: The Story of the Anti-Saloon League* (New York: Columbia University Press, 1928).
165. Ibid., 43–44.
166. W. M. Burke, "The Anti-Saloon League as a Political Force," *Annals of the American Academy of Political and Social Science* 32 (1908): 28–29, 33. Burke was a California Anti-Saloon League official and explained that these liquor representatives "had early learned that party affiliation must be secondary to trade protection" and had organized so as to hold "the balance of power between the parties" in elections. In turn, the Anti-Saloon League had "learned well the lesson," he said, and adopted similar methods.
167. K. Austin Kerr, "Organizing for Reform: The Anti-Saloon League and Innovation in Politics," *American Quarterly* 32, no. 1 (Spring, 1980): 51.
168. Odegard, *Pressure Politics*, 5; and Burke, "The Anti-Saloon League as a Political Force," 34. As Burke noted, "The league never undertakes to have any opinion upon any question except those concerning the saloon."

169. Burke, "The Anti-Saloon League as a Political Force," 33.

170. Odegard, *Pressure Politics*, 75, 76. Odegard calculated that some 245 million pieces of liter-ature were produced by the League's "American Issue Company" between 1909 and 1923, amounting to an unprecedented "campaign of education and agitation" by such a group.

171. Ibid., 105.

172. Ibid., 73.

173. As Kerr explains, the importance of elections as a backstop to pressure had soon become ap-parent to Anti-Saloon League founder Howard Russell. When the Ohio "local option" law initially failed to pass, Russell told supporters they would need to dig in for the long haul, and that legislative victories would come only by "carefully marshalling popular support and teaching recalcitrant politicians that votes for dry legislation were beneficial on elec-tion day" ("Organizing for Reform," 51). On ASL electoral techniques, see Kyvig, *Repealing National Prohibition*, 7, 12; and Burke, "The Anti-Saloon League as a Political Force," 27, 33, 35. As Burke explained, the League sought written pledges from candidates who had not previously held office but preferred to base its recommendation on an existing legislative record (35).

174. Burke, "The Anti-Saloon League as a Political Force," 33, 35. See also Ernest Hurst Cherrington, *History of the Anti-Saloon League* (Westerville, OH: American Issue Publishing Company, 1913), 91–92. Cherrington was the editor of the League's newspaper, the *American Issue*.

175. See Burke, "The Anti-Saloon League as a Political Force," 33, for an overview of its tactical hierarchy.

176. J. C. Jackson, "The Work of the Anti-Saloon League," *Annals of the American Academy of Political and Social Science* 32 (1908): 24. Jackson's estimate was a "conservative" one, he said, but took into account "the elections of state officers, legislators and local officers having to do with temperance matters."

177. Kyvig, *Repealing National Prohibition*, 10; and Kerr, *Organized for Prohibition*, 52.

178. *Brewing and Liquor Interests and German and Bolshevik Propaganda*," vol. I of *Report and Hearings of the Subcommittee on the Judiciary*, US Senate, 65th Cong. (Washington, DC: Government Printing Office, 1919). At one point the Brewers sought to channel tem-perance sentiment toward their economic rivals by promoting beer as a less intoxicating beverage than hard liquor and urging prohibition only of the latter. See Kyvig, *Repealing National Prohibition*, 37.

179. The Brewers had, in fact, faced the first conviction for illegal campaign contributions in a 1916 District Court decision, upholding the constitutionality of the Tillman Act's corpo-rate ban. See *United States v. United States Brewers Association*, 239 Fed. 163 (1916). See also Louise Overacker, *Money in Elections* (New York: Macmillan, 1932), 240.

180. Harry M. Chalfant, "The Anti-Saloon League—Why and What?," *Annals of the American Academy of Political and Social Science* 109 (1923): 282.

181. Odegard, *Pressure Politics*, 163; and Kerr, *Organized for Prohibition*, 253.

182. Kerr, *Organized for Prohibition*, 251; and Kyvig, *Repealing National Prohibition*, 12.

183. Kyvig, *Repealing National Prohibition*, xiii.

184. "Best known wet politician" is from Kerr, *Organized for Prohibition*, 253. On Catholicism, see Conant, "An Analysis of the Campaign of 1928," 125, 128.

185. Kerr, *Organized for Prohibition*, 254.

186. "Anti-Saloon League Politics," *Chicago Daily Tribune*, October 17, 1926, 10.

187. Ibid. The *Tribune* article highlighted an example in Ohio.

188. Ibid.

189. On the ASL's unincorporated status, see Testimony of Wayne Wheeler, July 1, 1926, "Senatorial Campaign Expenditures," *Hearings before a Special Committee Investigating Expenditures in Senatorial, Primary and General Elections*, part 1, US Senate, 69th Cong., 1st sess. (Washington, DC: Government Printing Office, 1926), 1325 (hereafter cited as Reed Committee Hearings). The League's publishing arm, the "American Issue Company," was incorporated.

190. As the Clerk, William Tyler Page, explained in congressional testimony, he had contacted various groups that appeared to be involved in politics to inform them of the law's

requirements and encourage filing. The Anti-Saloon League had accordingly filed a report but protested that its activities were "educational, scientific, and charitable rather than political as intended by the law." Statement of William Tyler Page, February 21, 1924, *Hearings on Additional Publicity of Campaign Contributions, House Committee on Election of President, Vice President, and Representatives in Congress,* 68th Cong., 1st sess. (Washington, DC: Government Printing Office, 1924), 22. For the Anti-Saloon League's protest, see *Congressional Record—House,* April 4, 1922, 5015. See also Overacker, *Money in Elections,* 258. Holman and Claybrook point to the Anti-Saloon League's protest as an early attempt to distinguish between "educational and campaign advertising," a distinction that was reframed and given a specific legal meaning after the 1976 *Buckley* decision as "issue" versus "electoral" advertising, where the latter had to contain words of "express advocacy" for a candidate. See Craig Holman and Joan Claybrook, "Outside Groups in the New Campaign Finance Environment: The Meaning of BCRA and the *McConnell* Decision," *Yale Law and Policy Review* 22 (2004): 239–240.

191. Urofsky, "Campaign Finance Reform Before 1971," 19. In *Newberry v. United States* (1921), a case stemming from a 1918 Senate primary election in Michigan, the Supreme Court struck down the application of the 1911 Publicity Act Amendments to primaries. The *Newberry* case also raised questions about its application to Senate elections more generally, since the existing campaign finance laws had been passed prior to ratification of the Seventeenth Amendment, mandating direct election of senators. In response, Congress passed a reformulated comprehensive law, the Federal Corrupt Practices Act of 1925 (43. Stat. 1070), which strengthened disclosure requirements (requiring all contributions over $100 be reported) but also raised campaign spending limits.

192. Testimony of Wayne Wheeler, June 17, June 23, June 26, and July 1–3, 1926, Reed Committee Hearings, part 1, 722–832, 1077–1090, 1161–1163, 1310–1457.

193. Testimony of Wayne Wheeler, June 17, 1926, Reed Committee Hearings, part 1, 826. If both candidates stood right, Wheeler explained, then "we keep hands off," and the same if both stood wrong, since "you can not get much moral enthusiasm up in a campaign between such candidates."

194. Ibid., 827. For Reed's response, see 1336.

195. Testimony of Wayne Wheeler, July 1, 1926, Reed Committee Hearings, part 1, 1334. As Wheeler later explained, the ASL's main activities involved "building public sentiment for total abstinence, for temperance, and sobriety, and law enforcement" and then "for a short time we are in the campaign" (1339).

196. Ibid., 1386. The ASL filed reports on that political activity, Wheeler said, noting that they had raised more than $8,000 so far for the 1926 primary campaigns (and had appealed to supporters for at least $50,000 for the general too), while their opponents had asked for $300,000.

197. Ibid., 1339–1340. For more on this modern debate, see Holman and Claybrook, "Outside Groups in the New Campaign Finance Environment," 239–240.

198. The $2 filing is noted in later testimony of Francis Scott McBride, who became the Anti-Saloon League's National Superintendent in 1924. Testimony of Francis Scott McBride, May 21, 1930, Caraway Committee Hearings, vol. IV, 4462. Senator Caraway pushed the point about ongoing political activity, suggesting that money raised in 1929 might be used in the 1932 campaign (4465).

199. Kyvig, *Repealing National Prohibition,* xv. Other anti-Prohibition pressure groups that appeared at this time included the "Crusaders"—an organization for young men—and the Women's Organization for National Prohibition Reform.

200. For more on the AAPA, see Kyvig, *Repealing National Prohibition;* and John C. Gebhart, "Movement Against Prohibition," *Annals of the American Academy of Political and Social Science* 163 (September 1932): 176.

201. Kyvig, *Repealing National Prohibition,* 46. As Kyvig explains, the AAPA sought pledges from its members to only vote for candidates who backed repeal of the Eighteenth Amendment, and it even planned to *publicize* the size of the pledged voter blocs so as to deter dry candidates and encourage wets—thus stressing the threat of punishment over overt electoral action.

202. Ibid., 39, 43, 48. See also Kerr, *Organized for Prohibition*, 236. The AAPA was incorporated in Washington, DC, in December 1920 (Kyvig, *Repealing National Prohibition*, 45).

203. Kyvig, *Repealing National Prohibition*, 48. The AAPA approved 249 candidates in 1922 and 169 in 1924, but "a number" of the candidates "repudiated its endorsement," Kyvig says (48).

204. Ibid., 46–48.

205. Ibid., 49. Not all of these prominent members were Protestant; Raskob, for example, was Catholic. Stayton discusses the elite strategy in his testimony before the Reed Committee. See Testimony of William H. Stayton, July 6, 1926, Reed Committee Hearings, part 1, 1482.

206. Ibid., xiii–xiv, 11. Drys claimed at the time, as have several historians since, that these wealthy individuals were solely motivated by personal economic interest, particularly the avoidance of income tax. But the attitudes of wealthy businessmen toward Prohibition were not monolithic. As Kyvig notes, some had supported it in the 1910s as an industrial effi- ciency and safety measure (10). For others, like John D. Rockefeller Sr. and his son, it spoke to their deeply held religious beliefs and claimed their support until the mid-1920s, when, as Kerr notes, concerns about lawlessness and social instability weakened their commitment (*Organized for Prohibition*, 248).

207. Kyvig, *Repealing National Prohibition*, 2; and Kerr, *Organized for Prohibition*, 277.

208. Kyvig, *Repealing National Prohibition*, 2–3. The meetings took place in December 1927 and January 1928 and were attended by William H. Stayton, Pierre du Pont, and former senator James Wadsworth, among others.

209. Testimony of William H. Stayton, Reed Committee Hearings, 1486.

210. Testimony of Gorton C. Hinkley, National Secretary and Treasurer of the Association Against the Prohibition Amendment, May 28, 1928; and Testimony of Edward B. Dunford, Attorney for the Anti-Saloon League of America, June 4, 1928, "Presidential Campaign Expenditures," *Hearings before the Special Committee Investigating Presidential Campaign Expenditures*, part 3, US Senate, 70th Cong., 1st sess., May 28, 29, 31 and June, 1, 2,4,5, and 6, 1928 (Washington, DC: Government Printing Office, 1928), 685–689 and 933–955 (hereafter cited as Steiwer Committee Hearings). The Senate's 1928 campaign investigation held hearings on the preconvention campaigns and embraced the full picture of the general election in their reports. The House of Representatives also formed a committee to examine aspects of the 1928 election, chaired by Rep. Frederick R. Lehlbach (R-NJ), which called witnesses from Prohibitionist and anti-Prohibition groups, but that investigation was con- fined to issues in particular states.

211. Testimony of Edward B. Dunford, Steiwer Committee Hearings, 933.

212. Ibid.

213. Kerr, *Organized for Prohibition*, 256–257. As Kerr explains, the ASL pushed for "law enforce- ment" rather than an outright *endorsement* of Prohibition due to fears the latter might fail at both conventions and would then "logically lead to calls for support of a third party, some- thing the league was never prepared to accept" (256).

214. Ibid., 257. The Democratic platform promised "an honest effort to enforce the eighteenth amendment" and its associated laws.

215. Ibid. Raskob was himself previously registered as a Republican; thus his selection gave af- front to party regulars as well as dry sentiment. Smith had initially promised to enforce the Prohibition law if elected president, but he switched gears after the convention, advocating modification of the Volstead Act and even a change to the Eighteenth Amendment that would effectively allow states to "opt-out" of Prohibition. See Conant, "An Analysis of the Campaign of 1928," 90, 114.

216. In February 1928 Hoover had personally declared his support for "vigorous and sincere en- forcement" of the law and described it as "a great social and economic experiment, noble in motive and far-reaching in purpose." The Republican Party platform itself pledged "the observance and vigorous enforcement" of Prohibition. Hoover even described himself as a "dry candidate" later in the campaign, though as a sop to the Eighteenth Amendment's critics (and in line with his favored administrative methods), he promised an independent commission to study the law and its problems. See "Hoover for Prohibition; Would Rigidly Enforce the 'Great Experiment,'" *New York Times*, February 24, 1928, 1; "Republican Party

Platform of 1928," June 12, 1928, in *The American Presidency Project*, ed. Gerhard Peters and John T. Woolley, http://www.presidency.ucsb.edu/ws/?pid=29637; and Kerr, *Organized for Prohibition*, 257.

217. V. O. Key, *Politics, Parties, and Pressure Groups*, 5th ed. (New York: Thomas Y. Crowell, 1964), 160.

218. There is some disparity in the ASL expenditure figures reported by different congressional committees. According to the report produced by the Senate's 1928 campaign expenditure committee, the ASL raised $172,468 and spent $165,326 in 1928, while the AAPA raised $478,038 and spent $453,700. In hearings before the Senate's 1929 lobbying investigation, however, the Anti-Saloon League's 1928 financial statement to the House Clerk was inserted, in which it reported raising $86,404.82 and spending $83,863.11. According to a different League financial report, also reproduced in the hearings, it spent $334,437.93 overall in 1928. (A "[s]pecial campaign" fund disbursed by E. B. Dunford is included as a line item in this report.) Similarly, McBride testified before the Caraway Committee that the League had spent over $80,000 on political activities, out of more than $330,000 of its total expenditure that year, but in a talk to ASL supporters on its role in the election, inserted in the *Congressional Record*, he suggests that the 1928 campaign fund was $100,000. The higher amount reported by the Senate campaign expenditure committee may reflect additional primary expenses, which the ASL may not have included in its report to the House Clerk, or it may include some spending by state or local affiliates. For the higher figures reported by the Senate's campaign expenditure committee, see "Table X—Committees and Organizations Receiving and Expending Money in Behalf of the Republican Party," and "Table XI—Committees and Organizations Receiving and Expending Money in Behalf of the Democratic Party," in "Presidential Campaign Expenditures," Report of the Special Committee Investigating Presidential Campaign Expenditures, US Senate, 70th Cong., 2nd sess., February 28, 1929, S. Rep. No. 2024, 26. See also Overacker, *Money in Elections*, 165. For the lower figures reported to the Clerk, see Report of Legal Department, Anti-Saloon League of America, March 5, 1929, reproduced in Caraway Committee Hearings, 4633; for overall expenditure, see "The Anti-Saloon League of America, Statement of Cash Receipts and Disbursements for Year 1928," reproduced in Caraway Committee Hearings, 4629. See also Testimony of Francis Scott McBride, May 21, 1930, Caraway Committee Hearings, 4463; and "Address by F. Scott M'Bride on 'The Anti-Saloon League and Elections,'" delivered on January 15, 1930, inserted in the *Congressional Record—Senate*, February 13, 1930, 3552.

219. See Kyvig, *Repealing National Prohibition*, 98, 102; and Kerr, *Organized for Prohibition*, 257–258.

220. Testimony of Edward B. Dunford, Steiwer Committee Hearings, 934, 942–946; and Conant, "An Analysis of the Campaign of 1928," 128.

221. Bishop James Cannon Jr., "Shall We Elect a Cocktail President?," *Nation*, July 4, 1928, reprinted in *Reform Bulletin* 19, no. 27 (July 1928), box 1, folder 16, "American Protestant Alliance, 1928," William H. Anderson and the Anti-Saloon League Papers 1903–1928, University of Chicago Library, Special Collections, http://www.lib.uchicago.edu/e/scrc/findingaids/view.php?eadid=ICU.SPCL. A former missionary from Maryland's Eastern Shore, Bishop Cannon had been superintendent of the Virginia Anti-Saloon League and served as the national League's lobbyist prior to Wheeler. He remained an ASL executive committee member and chairman of the Virginia Anti-Saloon League's executive and legislative committees, combining those roles with his chairmanship of the Methodist Board of Temperance and Social Service of the Methodist Episcopal Church South. See Conant, "An Analysis of the Campaign of 1928," 119; and Testimony of Bishop James Cannon Jr., June 3, 1930, Caraway Committee Hearings, vol. IV, 4760, 4786, 4788, 4791.

222. The Anti-Smith Democrats were formed in response to a July 18 "All-South Conference," held in Ashville, North Carolina, which had been organized by Cannon along with Southern Baptist reverend A. J. Barton. As Conant and Peel and Donnelly note, there had been widespread protest following Smith's nomination throughout the southern states. See Conant, "An Analysis of the Campaign of 1928," 115, 120; Roy V. Peel and Thomas C. Donnelly, *The*

1928 Campaign: An Analysis (New York: Richard R. Smith, 1931), 77; and Kerr, *Organized for Prohibition*, 258.

223. Conant, "An Analysis of the Campaign of 1928," 105–106. Conant itemizes $110,000 in contributions from Raskob to the party in 1928, given in three installments: two donations of $50,000 given on September 12 and October 3, and $10,000 on November 5.

224. Stayton to William H. Metson, September 5, 1928, reproduced in Testimony of William H. Stayton, May 2, 1930, Caraway Committee Hearings, vol. IV, 4239.

225. Hoover's victories included Florida, North Carolina, Tennessee, Texas, and Virginia, along with several border states. Smith received 40.8 percent of the popular vote (15,004,336 votes) but only 87 electoral votes; Hoover received 58.2 percent of the popular vote (21,432,823) and 444 electoral votes. "Table 1-7 Popular and Electoral Votes for President, 1789–2008," in *Vital Statistics on American Politics 2009–2010*, ed. Harold W. Stanley and Richard G. Niemi (Washington, DC: CQ Press, 2009), 17–21.

226. Totals reported in Kerr, *Organized for Prohibition*, 258. See also Donald A. Ritchie, *Electing FDR: The New Deal Campaign of 1932* (Lawrence: University Press of Kansas, 2007), 36.

227. S. Res. No. 20, reproduced in Caraway Committee Hearings, part 1 (1929), 1. The AAPA's president, Henry H. Curran, its board chairman, William H. Stayton, and director John J. Raskob all appeared, while the ASL's general superintendent, F. Scott McBride, and attorney Edward B. Dunford testified.

228. Senator Caraway questioned the AAPA's William H. Stayton, for example, on whether it had "authority" under its constitution to engage in electioneering (4135), and he asked AAPA president Henry H. Curran about its "publicity methods" (3830). Testimony of William H. Stayton, May 1, 1930, Caraway Committee Hearings, vol. IV, 4135; and Testimony of Henry H. Curran, April 16, 1930, Caraway Committee Hearings, vol. IV, 3830.

229. Testimony of Francis Scott McBride, May 9, 1930, Caraway Committee Hearings, vol. IV, 4342; and Testimony of Wayne Wheeler, July 1, 1926, Reed Committee Hearings, part 1, 1334.

230. Testimony of Francis Scott McBride, May 8 and 21, 1930, Caraway Committee Hearings, 4286, 4436. See also 4342, 4437.

231. "Address by F. Scott M'Bride on 'The Anti-Saloon League and Elections.'"

232. Testimony of Francis Scott McBride, May 8, 1930, Caraway Committee Hearings, 4288.

233. Ibid.

234. Mark J. Rozell, Clyde Wilcox, and Michael M. Franz, *Interest Groups in American Campaigns: The New Face of Electioneering*, 3rd ed. (New York: Oxford University Press, 2011), 24.

235. Testimony of Henry H. Curran, April 16, 1930, Caraway Committee Hearings, 3830.

236. "We are a nonpartisan organization, and we let party folks fight it out themselves," McBride was still telling the Caraway Committee in 1930, though Senator Caraway suggested they had a more Republican orientation. Testimony of Francis Scott McBride, May 21, 1930, Caraway Committee Hearings, 4462, 4406, 4286.

237. Kerr, *Organized for Prohibition*, 266. See also Ritchie, *Electing FDR*, 36.

238. The circumstances of Cannon's downfall are complex and involved stock speculation, charges of improper use of campaign funds, and a personal scandal including his second marriage (to his former secretary, with whom it was alleged he had conducted an affair prior to the death of his first wife). Virginia senator Carter Glass played a key role in bringing these issues to light, having taken offense at Cannon's threat in 1928 to electorally oppose Southern Democrats who supported Smith. Cannon was asked about some of these allegations during his 1930 Caraway Committee appearance but was further questioned by the Senate's 1930 campaign expenditure committee, chaired by North Dakota Republican Gerald P. Nye, which was specifically authorized to investigate Cannon's alleged violations of the Corrupt Practices Act. His failures to reveal large personal donations were then fully exposed, and though Cannon escaped prosecution in subsequent legal wrangling, his public stature rapidly diminished. See Michael S. Patterson, "The Fall of a Bishop: James Cannon, Jr., versus Carter Glass, 1909–1934," *Journal of Southern History* 39, no. 4 (November 1973): 493–518.

239. Kerr, *Organized for Prohibition*, esp. 213, 236, 242, 248.

240. Kyvig, *Repealing National Prohibition*, 130.

241. Ibid, 133. See also Kerr, *Organized for Prohibition*, 270.

242. Kerr, *Organized for Prohibition*, 269.

243. Ibid. The commission was headed up by former attorney general George Wickersham.

244. Ibid., 265.

245. The plank urged a constitutional amendment to this effect be submitted to popular conventions in each of the states, rather than going to the state legislatures for ratification—a procedural distinction that had generated intense debate since ratification of the Eighteenth Amendment in 1919, which had been approved by the legislatures. See Republican Party Platforms, "Republican Party Platform of 1932," June 14, 1932, in *The American Presidency Project*, ed. Gerhard Peters and John T. Woolley, http://www.presidency.ucsb.edu/ws/?pid=29638.

246. Kerr, *Organized for Prohibition*, 270.

247. Kyvig, *Repealing National Prohibition*, xvii.

248. Kerr, *Organized for Prohibition*, 266.

249. Roosevelt forces blocked Raskob's attempt to install Jouett Shouse as the convention chairman, which they foresaw as a maneuver intended to aid another Al Smith candidacy, yet the party platform appeared to reflect Raskob's stronger pro-repeal views. See Kyvig, *Repealing National Prohibition*, xvii; and Democratic Party Platforms, "Democratic Party Platform of 1932," June 27, 1932, in *The American Presidency Project*, ed. Gerhard Peters and John T. Woolley, http://www.presidency.ucsb.edu/ws/?pid=29595.

250. According to Kyvig, the only wet organization that publicly endorsed the Democratic nominee in 1932 was the Women's Organization for National Prohibition Reform (WONPR). The AAPA's campaign activities were focused on congressional contests, he says, where they leaned toward Democrats but supported Republicans who were for "unqualified repeal," but their broader efforts presumably contributed to the presidential campaign. See Kyvig, *Repealing National Prohibition*, 166.

251. See Kerr, *Organized for Prohibition*, 259, 270.

252. E. E. Schattschneider, *Party Government* (New Brunswick, NJ: Transaction Publishers, 1942/2004), 87; and Key, *Politics, Parties and Pressure Groups* (1942), 211–212. By 1964, however, Key referred to an "old stereotype of pressure group organization," characterized by the Anti-Saloon League, that no longer appeared accurate. See Key, *Politics, Parties and Pressure Groups* (1964), 156.

253. Kerr, for example, suggests that internal struggles in the 1920s, brought on by their new defensive posture, resulted in a loss of institutional capacity to mount the kinds of district-level campaigns through which they had previously found success. In his telling, using partisan connections and working with the GOP was to some extent an expedient alternative given this loss in capacity. At the same time, he suggests, northern Democratic politicians in the cities increasingly saw a wet stance as a way to attract immigrant voters. Kerr, *Organized for Prohibition*, 243, 259. Kyvig, however, does point to the "alliance forged between repeal organizations and the Democrat party" as an important factor in the larger shift in attitudes toward Prohibition, though he presents its partisan coloration in somewhat vaguer terms: "Maneuvering and leadership decisions which fixed a wet label on the Democrats and a dry one on the Republicans took place coincidentally but fatefully as party fortunes rose and fell because of the depression" (*Repealing National Prohibition*, xvii).

254. Neither Key nor Schattschneider references the AAPA—their inattention presumably a result of relying on Odegard for an account of the Anti-Saloon League, since Odegard only mentions the AAPA a handful of times and published his book early in 1928, prior to the AAPA's push in the presidential election.

255. Kyvig, *Repealing National Prohibition*, xvii. Kyvig points to "the alliance . . . forged between repeal organizations and the Democrat party" and its importance for shifting attitudes on Prohibition, ultimately achieving the Twenty-First Amendment.

256. Testimony of Francis Scott McBride, May 22, 1930, Caraway Committee Hearings, 4483.

Chapter 3

1. Max Lerner, "Roosevelt and His Fellow-Travelers," *Nation*, October 24, 1936, 471.

2. Ibid.

3. E. E. Schattschneider, *The Semi-Sovereign People: A Realist's View of Democracy in America* (Belmont: Wadsworth Publishing, 1960/1988), 87

4. J. I. Seidman, "Political Trends and New Party Movements," *Editorial Research Reports* I (1934), http://library.cqpress.com/cqresearcher/cqresrre1934051800.

5. Robert Elliott Kessler, "The League for Independent Political Action, 1929–1933" (master's thesis, University of Wisconsin, Madison, 1967), 100–106.

6. Thomas T. Spencer, "Democratic Auxiliary and Non-Party Groups in the Election of 1936" (PhD diss., University of Notre Dame, 1976), 16; and Donald R. McCoy, "The Progressive National Committee of 1936," *Western Political Quarterly* 9, no. 2 (1956): 459. The Minnesota Farmer-Labor Party's candidate for governor, Floyd B. Olson, was elected in 1930, and the Progressive Party of Wisconsin claimed gubernatorial success in 1934, returning Philip La Follette to the governor's mansion under its banner.

7. See Alan Brinkley, *Voices of Protest: Huey Long, Father Coughlin, and the Great Depression* (New York: Alfred A. Knopf, 1982), for detailed assessments of Townsend, and especially Long and Coughlin.

8. David R. Mayhew, *Electoral Realignments: A Critique of an American Genre* (New Haven, CT: Yale University Press, 2002). As Schlozman observes, "Mayhew attacks principally the claims about critical elections" as a means of understanding partisan change, rather than discrediting the idea of realignment—essentially, changes in the underlying basis of party competition—altogether. See Daniel Schlozman, *When Movements Anchor Parties: Electoral Alignments in American History* (Princeton, NJ: Princeton University Press, 2015), 20n, 21.

9. Quoted in McCoy, "The Progressive National Committee of 1936," 457.

10. Ibid.

11. Norris quoted in Loretto C. Mersh, "The Presidential Campaign of 1932" (master's thesis, Loyola University Chicago, 1937), 90. Formed in September 1932, its full title was the National Progressive League to Support Franklin D. Roosevelt for President. The NPL was one of only two nonparty committees that Overacker mentions in her overview of the 1932 election, and the only such organization active nationally. See McCoy, "The Progressive National Committee of 1936," 456; and Louise Overacker, "American Government and Politics: Campaign Funds in a Depression Year," *American Political Science Review* 27, no. 5 (1933): 770, 772–773, 775.

12. McCoy, "The Progressive National Committee of 1936," 456.

13. The Communist Party of the USA's adoption of the "popular front" strategy of 1935, in response to a Comintern directive to work with forces opposing fascism, would mark an important shift toward cooperation with the Socialist Party, but not until 1944 would it officially condone support for a major party candidate—Franklin Roosevelt—and then only temporarily, under wartime conditions.

14. Kessler, "The League for Independent Political Action, 1929–1933," 4. On the LIPA's organizational structure and membership, see esp. 41, 45, 55–57, 66, and 73.

15. Ibid, 8. See, for example, Dewey's 1931 articles in the *New Republic*, "The Need for a New Party," which framed the LIPA as a starting point for building one. Noted in Richard J. Brown, "John Dewey and the League for Independent Political Action," *Social Studies* 59, no. 4 (1968): 157.

16. Quoted in Kessler, "The League for Independent Political Action, 1929–1933," 53.

17. "Campaign of political education" is quoted in Brown, "John Dewey and the League for Independent Political Action," 158.

18. Kessler, "The League for Independent Political Action, 1929–1933," 60.

19. Ibid. In a 1913 speech, Norris had even advocated something he labeled a "non-partisan party," and he expressed little faith in a new party throughout his career. Quoted in Shirley Ann Lindeen and James Walter Lindeen, "Bryan, Norris, and the Doctrine of Party Responsibility," *Midcontinent American Studies Journal* 11, no. 1 (1970): 47.

20. In March 1931 Norris had joined with Senators Edward Costigan (D-CO), Bronson Cutting (R-NM), Robert La Follette Jr. (R-WI), and Burton Wheeler (D-MT) to call a conference of the country's progressive leaders in anticipation of the 1932 presidential election. Third-party

aspirations were explicitly ruled out, and the LIPA was excluded from the conference alto-gether. See McCoy, "The Progressive National Committee of 1936," 455.

21. "[W]e are firmly opposed to giving aid and comfort to any men within the old parties no matter how promising they seem," the LIPA's assistant secretary Norman Studer wrote in 1930. "A 'good' man in a party that is controlled by interests that control the Republican and Democratic parties is impotent no matter how much he may aspire to," he added. Quoted in Kessler, "The League for Independent Political Action, 1929–1933," 94.

22. Mersh, "The Presidential Campaign of 1932," 90.

23. McCoy, "The Progressive National Committee of 1936," 456.

24. According to McCoy, the National Progressive League's Western Committee Headquarters received nearly $9,000 from the Democratic National Campaign Committee and a further $1,000 from the DNCC's vice chairman, amounting to almost 90 percent of its income ("The Progressive National Committee of 1936," 456n7).

25. In total, non-major-party candidates received just under 3 percent of the popular vote in 1932, while Roosevelt secured more than 57 percent. This was a slight improvement over third-party performance in 1928, when the combined support for minor party candidates slipped to its lowest in sixty years, at just 1 percent of the popular vote, but it was far from the heights of 1924 or 1912. The LIPA had ultimately given its support to Socialist candidate Norman Thomas in 1932, who polled about 885,000 votes (information compiled from http://uselectionatlas.org/).

26. McCoy, "The Progressive National Committee of 1936," 457, 463–464.

27. Ibid., 458. Norris did ultimately become an honorary chairman of the resulting Progressive National Committee.

28. Ibid., 458–460. The PNC's founding conference was held in Chicago on September 11, 1936.

29. Ibid., 459, 462, 465.

30. Ibid., 460.

31. Quoted in McCoy, "The Progressive National Committee of 1936," 465.

32. Ibid. The speakers' manual described "the American idea," to which the PNC was committed, as "the Progressive and the Liberal idea," as against "the selfish, grasping irresponsible dicta-torship of the few."

33. McCoy notes that the conferees in Chicago had pledged $10,000 to help get the campaign started ("The Progressive National Committee of 1936," 460).

34. "Investigation of Campaign Expenditures in 1936," Report of the Special Committee to Investigate Campaign Expenditures of Presidential, Vice Presidential, and Senatorial Candidates in 1936," US Senate, 75th Cong., 1st sess., March 4, 1937, S. Rep. No. 151 (Washington, DC: Government Printing Office, 1937), 25 (emphasis added) (hereafter cited as Lonergan Committee Report).

35. Louise Overacker, "Campaign Funds in the Presidential Election of 1936," American Political Science Review 31, no. 3 (1937): 477 (emphasis added).

36. The Good Neighbor League, for example, received nearly $35,000 from the DNC in the form of direct transfers or loans, as Overacker shows, plus a further $47,000 in debt assump-tion after the campaign, as McCoy notes, for a total of $82,000 in party funds, but it raised almost $169,000 more from individual donors. See Overacker, "Campaign Funds in the Presidential Election of 1936," 478; and Donald R. McCoy, "The Good Neighbor League and the Presidential Campaign of 1936," Western Political Quarterly 13, no. 4 (1960): 1019.

37. Thomas T. Spencer, "Auxiliary and Non-Party Politics: The 1936 Democratic Presidential Campaign in Ohio," Ohio History 90 (1981): 114. According to Spencer, auxiliaries were es-pecially active in key midwestern states such as Ohio, Illinois, Indiana, and Michigan (127).

38. McCoy, "The Good Neighbor League and the Presidential Campaign of 1936," 1011–1021. As McCoy observes, there was a demographic aspect to the Good Neighbor League's appeal, since "those groups open chiefly to idealistic solicitations" were envisaged as "liberal-minded businessmen, educators, Negroes, religious leaders, social workers, and women" (1011).

39. Spencer, "Auxiliary and Non-Party Politics," 122.

40. In 1938, for example, the National Federation of Republican Women was formed to provide a national umbrella for the array of GOP women's clubs that had emerged since ratification of the Nineteenth Amendment, and the Women's National Republican Club appears to have

been incorporated within it. The NFRW, which still exists today, has greater autonomy than some auxiliaries but maintains a formal and explicit connection to the party. See Josephine L. Good, *The History of Women in Republican National Conventions and Women in the Republican National Committee* (Washington, DC: Republican National Committee, 1963).

41. Clyde P. Weed, *The Nemesis of Reform: The Republican Party During the New Deal* (New York: Columbia University Press, 1994), 85. The sectional view incorporated economic interests to the extent that it identified them with a particular geographic area and thus viewed competition between interests in *regional* terms.

42. Brian Balogh, "'Mirrors of Desires': Interest Groups, Elections, and the Targeted Style in Twentieth-Century America," in *The Democratic Experiment: New Directions in American Political History*, ed. Meg Jacobs, William J. Novak, and Julian E. Zelizer (Princeton, NJ: Princeton University Press, 2003), 222–249; and Adam Sheingate, *Building a Business of Politics: The Rise of Political Consulting and the Transformation of American Democracy* (New York: Oxford University Press, 2016).

43. As Weed concludes, "by 1937 the New Deal was not deploring 'special interests'—it was attempting to utilize them in an effort to develop an effective political coalition" (*The Nemesis of Reform*, 189).

44. Overacker, "Campaign Funds in the Presidential Election of 1936," 489. See Table VI, "Contributions of Organized Labor to the Democratic National Committee and Other Groups in the 1936 Campaign." Overacker notes that the LNPL raised over $195,000 but spent a little under $170,000 (478, 489).

45. James Truslow Adams, "A Business Man's Civilization," *Harper's Monthly* (July 1929), quoted in Grace R. Conant, "An Analysis of the Campaign of 1928" (master's thesis, Loyola University Chicago, 1946), 2.

46. James W. Prothro, *The Dollar Decade* (Baton Rouge: Louisiana State University Press, 1954), viii, quoted in Harmon Zeigler, *Interest Groups in American Society* (Englewood Cliffs, NJ: Prentice-Hall, 1964), 113.

47. As journalist Frederick Allen observed in 1935, looking back over the previous decade: "One of the choicest ironies of this period was that many, if not most, of the new measures which interfered with business freedom were passed under the heavy pressure of groups of business men who professed to hate interference." See Frederick Lewis Allen, *The Lords of Creation* (New York: Harper & Bros., 1935), 223–224. A similar insight underpins the "corporate liberal" school of historical scholarship. See the discussion in Louis Galambos, "The Emerging Organizational Synthesis of Modern American History," *Business History Review* 44 (1970): 280.

48. Ellis W. Hawley, "Herbert Hoover, the Commerce Secretariat, and the Vision of an 'Associative State,' 1921–1928," *Journal of American History* 61, no. 1 (1974): 116–140. See also Zeigler, *Interest Groups in American Society*, 100–101.

49. Weed, *The Nemesis of Reform*, 23, 27.

50. Ibid., 27.

51. Ibid., 129–131.

52. Zeigler, *Interest Groups in American Society*, 100, 106–108.

53. Weed, *The Nemesis of Reform*, 57–58, 61–63, 156–157, 160. See also Albert U. Romasco, *The Politics of Recovery: Roosevelt's New Deal* (New York: Oxford University Press, 1983), 208. Romasco points to a "Joint Business Conference for Economic Recovery," held in December 1934 and cosponsored by the Chamber and the NAM, which passed official resolutions amounting to "a severe critique of New Deal recovery policies" (208). Weed adds that the Chamber's annual convention in 1935 delivered a similar verdict, opposing continuation of the NRA, the Social Security Act, and the Utility Holding Company Act and seeking the "withdrawal of government agencies from activities properly the function of trade associations" (65). Citing Alfred Cleveland's research, Zeigler notes that the NAM opposed thirty-one of the thirty-eight major laws passed between 1933 and 1941 (*Interest Groups in American Society*, 116). See Alfred S. Cleveland, "NAM: Spokesman for Industry?," *Harvard Business Review* 26, no. 3 (1948): 357. How extensive and how intensive this opposition was within the wider business community is still a matter of debate. See, for example, the debate between Thomas Ferguson and Michael J. Webber on support or opposition among different

industrial sectors. Thomas Ferguson, "From Normalcy to New Deal: Industrial Structure, Party Competition, and American Public Policy in the Great Depression," *International Organization* 38, no. 1 (1984): 41–94; Michael J. Webber, "Business, the Democratic Party, and the New Deal: An Empirical Critique of Thomas Ferguson's 'Investment Theory of Politics,'" *Sociological Perspectives* 34, no. 4 (1991): 473–492; Michael J. Webber and G. William Domhoff, "Myth and Reality in Business Support for Democrats and Republicans in the 1936 Presidential Election," *American Political Science Review* 90, no. 4 (1996): 824–833; and Michael J. Webber, *New Deal Fat Cats: Business, Labor, and Campaign Finance in the 1936 Presidential Election* (New York: Fordham University Press, 2000).

54. Weed, *The Nemesis of Reform*, 62, 65.

55. Ibid., 65.

56. See "Violations of Free Speech and Rights of Labor: Employer Associations and Citizens' Committees—National Association of Manufacturers," *Hearings Before a Subcommittee of the Committee on Education and Labor*, part 17, US Senate, 75th Cong., 3rd sess. (Washington, DC: Government Printing Office, 1938), 7375.

57. Overacker, "Campaign Funds in the Presidential Election of 1936," 475–476.

58. Frederick Rudolph, "The American Liberty League, 1934–1940," *American Historical Review* 56, no. 1 (1950): 21.

59. Ibid.

60. Hamilton Basso, "The Liberty League Writes," *New Republic*, July 22, 1936, 320–321. This part of the "dialogue" is also reproduced in Rudolph, "The American Liberty League," 32.

61. The Liberty League was incorporated in the District of Columbia on August 15, 1934. The timing suggests that the Securities and Exchange Act of March 1934 was a particularly important impetus. See George Wolfskill, *The Revolt of the Conservatives: A History of the American Liberty League, 1934–1940* (Boston: Houghton Mifflin, 1962), 26.

62. As noted in chapter 1, note 104, Raskob had become a director of the US Chamber of Commerce in 1927, while the du Ponts had strong ties to the National Association of Manufacturers.

63. John J. Raskob to R.R.M. Carpenter, quoted in Rudolph, "The American Liberty League," 19.

64. Ibid.

65. Quoted in Weed, *The Nemesis of Reform*, 58.

66. Basso, "The Liberty League Writes," 32.

67. The Twenty-First Amendment, repealing Prohibition, was ratified December 5, 1933.

68. Intraparty rivalries may have also animated Raskob and Shouse's break with FDR, since Roosevelt maneuvered to replace Shouse as presiding officer at the 1932 convention, installing an ally of his own instead. Roosevelt did not entirely clean house at the DNC, however, keeping on Charley Michelson as director of the DNC's Publicity Division. Despite being hired by Shouse, Michelson would turn his firepower upon Smith, Raskob, and Shouse when they bolted the party. See Mersh, "The Presidential Campaign of 1932," 4, 49–51, 70–71.

69. See "Smith-Roosevelt Break Traces to Start of Presidential Rivalry," *New York Times*, January 27, 1936, 3. See also Mersh, "The Presidential Campaign of 1932," 27, 80, 101. In terms of Smith's more constrained progressive sensibilities, Lippmann described Smith in 1925 as "the most powerful conservative in urban America." Walter Lippmann, *Men of Destiny* (New York: Macmillan, 1927), 6, quoted in Mersh, 27.

70. Wolfskill, *The Revolt of the Conservatives*, 37, 54. The quotation was taken from a resolution passed at the last meeting of the AAPA directors, on December 6, 1933, and appears also in George Soule, "Liberty League Liberty—II: Liberty in Politics (Continued)," *New Republic*, September 2, 1936, 98. See also J. S. Cullinan to Jouett Shouse, December 27, 1935, Records of the American Liberty League 1929–1948, accession LMSS, box 1301, folder 66, Hagley Museum and Library, Wilmington, Delaware (hereafter cited as Liberty League Papers).

71. When Raskob placed the DNC on a permanent basis in the late 1920s, Shouse had become chairman of the Democratic Executive Committee. See Sean J. Savage, "Franklin D. Roosevelt and the Democratic National Committee," *Social Science Journal* 28, no. 4 (1991): 451–465.

72. Wolfskill, for example, points out that the Liberty League did not want to be seen as trying to influence the 1934 election, at least (*The Revolt of the Conservatives*, 26).

73. Alfred E. Smith, "The Facts in the Case," speech delivered to the American Liberty League Dinner, January 25, 1936, Washington, DC.

74. Wolfskill, *The Revolt of the Conservatives*, 65.

75. Rudolph, "The American Liberty League," 21n5, 25. On the Liberty League's publicity efforts generally, see Wolfskill, *The Revolt of the Conservatives*, 65–67.

76. On the innovations of popular associations, see Elisabeth S. Clemens, *The People's Lobby: Organizational Innovation and the Rise of Interest Group Politics in the United States, 1890–1925* (Chicago: University of Chicago Press, 1997). On the new techniques of the 1920s and the creation of "artificial" opinion, see Christopher M. Loomis, "The Politics of Uncertainty: Lobbyists and Propaganda in Early Twentieth-Century America," *Journal of Policy History* 21, no. 2 (2009): 203.

77. Membership statistics are included in "Memorandum for Mr. Knudsen from W. H. Stanton," March 6, 1936, Liberty League Papers, box 1301, folder 56.

78. Rudolph, for example, suggests that during the 1930s "an organization with 'sound' American principles might have been expected to attain a membership of more than 150,000 at its peak." The League's own expectations were also much greater, with Shouse telling reporters in 1934 that he expected to attract several *million* members ("The American Liberty League," 25–26).

79. Wolfskill, *The Revolt of the Conservatives*, 61. The first state division was formed in Delaware (unsurprisingly given the du Pont connection).

80. Ibid., 67–68. See also Rudolph, "The American Liberty League," 25n19.

81. Rudolph, "The American Liberty League," 26.

82. Ibid., 25–26.

83. Wolfskill, *The Revolt of the Conservatives*, 121. "The League is opposed to any attempt to divide this country into classes and blocs," Shouse affirmed.

84. Letter from William H. Stanton to William S. Knudsen, Esq., 1501 Balmoral Drive, Detroit, Michigan, March 9, 1936, Liberty League Papers, box 1301, folder 56.

85. "Shows Du Pont Aid to Liberty League," *New York Times*, January 11, 1935, 9. The exact figures were $104,830.92 in receipts and $95,062.21 in expenditures. The *Washington Post* also noted that these donations had come from eighty-three individuals. See "Liberty League Paid $104,830 by Supporters," *Washington Post*, January 11, 1935, 2.

86. "Reporting of Contributions to and Expenditures by Political Organizations," *Unpublished Hearing before a Subcommittee of the House Committee on Judiciary*, US House of Representatives, 74th Cong., 2nd sess., February 21, 1936, 7–8.

87. "Speech of Jouett Shouse, President American Liberty League, Before the Bond Club of New York, November 20, 1934," 8, press release, November 20, Liberty League Papers, box 1301, folder 26.

88. "Shows Du Pont Aid to Liberty League," 9.

89. "Speech of Jouett Shouse." "Partisan" is spelled "partizan" in the original document, but is altered here for consistency.

90. As an Associated Press journalist summarized Shouse's explanation of the financial report, he "said any organization which sought to influence legislative action was political. Quickly he added the league was in no way partisan." "Liberty League Paid $104,830 by Supporters," 2.

91. Among the League's directors were Republicans James Wadsworth Jr. and Nathan Miller, as well as Democrats Al Smith and John W. Davis. See Spencer, "Democratic Auxiliary and Non-Party Groups in the Election of 1936," 17; Donald A. Ritchie, *Electing FDR: The New Deal Campaign of 1932* (Lawrence: University Press of Kansas, 2007), 187; and Daniel J. Tichenor, "The Presidency and Interest Groups: Allies, Adversaries, and Policy Leadership," in *The Presidency and the Political System*, 8th ed., ed. Michael Nelson (Washington, DC: CQ Press, 2006), 324.

92. Quoted in Rudolph, "The American Liberty League," 29.

93. Roosevelt had been happy to oblige, noting that few could oppose such noble sentiments as the League expressed. See Wolfskill, *The Revolt of the Conservatives*, 27.

94. "Liberty League Paid $104,830 by Supporters," 2.

95. Wolfskill, *The Revolt of the Conservatives*, 210.

96. George Soule, "Liberty League Liberty—I: Liberty in Politics," *New Republic*, August 26, 1936, 64–65.

97. Ibid., 63. Elsewhere Soule describes several of these groups as "precursors" to the Liberty League. The Sentinels, for example, was a "charitable corporation" originally formed in 1922 to oppose federal government encroachment following ratification of the Prohibition and women's suffrage amendments. It waged a largely successful war against the Sheppard-Towner Maternity Act and the Children's Bureau, expanding its activities in the early 1930s to New Deal legislation. The Crusaders was formed in 1929 to promote repeal of Prohibition. See Soule, "Liberty League Liberty—II," 95–98; and Julia Bowes, " 'Every Citizen a Sentinel! Every Home a Sentry Box!' The Sentinels of the Republic and the Gendered Origins of Free-Market Conservatism," *Modern American History* 2, No. 3 (2019): 272.

98. Rudolph, "The American Liberty League," 32.

99. Soule, "Liberty League Liberty—II," 98.

100. Ibid., 96. See also Soule, "Liberty League Liberty—I," 65. In June 1936 Black inserted into the *Congressional Record* a financial overview that showed links between the Liberty League and many of the groups opposed to the holding company bill called before his committee. See *Congressional Record—Senate,* June 20, 1936, 10,492.

101. Soule, "Liberty League Liberty—II," 95.

102. Rudolph, "The American Liberty League," 32.

103. Ibid. See also Soule, "Liberty League Liberty—II," 98; and "Shows Du Pont Aid to Liberty League," which discusses a $9,000 donation from the Liberty League to the Crusaders.

104. Soule, "Liberty League Liberty—I," 63.

105. George Soule, "Liberty League Liberty—III: Liberty in Industry," *New Republic*, September 9, 1936, 121–122.

106. Ibid., 122. Section 7(a) required all codes of fair competition approved under NIRA to guarantee employees "the right to organize and bargain collectively through representatives of their own choosing," stipulated that they be free from coercion in selecting said representatives, and forbade requiring employees to join a company union.

107. Ibid., 125.

108. Soule, "Liberty League Liberty—I," 64.

109. See *Schechter Poultry Corp. v. United States*, 295 U.S. 495 (1935).

110. See Wolfskill, *The Revolt of the Conservatives*, 72; Rudolph, "The American Liberty League," 31; and Soule, "Liberty League Liberty—II," 98, and "Liberty League Liberty—III," 122, on support provided by the League's Lawyers' Committee, which had also deemed the NRA and the AAA unconstitutional.

111. Clement E. Vose, "Litigation as a Form of Pressure Group Activity," *Annals of the American Academy of Political and Social Science* 319, no. 1 (1958): 20, 24–25. Vose also notes the National Consumers' League as pursuing similar tactics.

112. Reed quoted in Wolfskill, *The Revolt of the Conservatives*, 72.

113. Rudolph, "The American Liberty League," 31; and Soule, "Liberty League Liberty—III," 122.

114. Evidence that the NAM's approach was less aggressive comes from the testimony of the NAM's counsel, John C. Gall, before a Senate subcommittee in 1938. He claimed that the NAM legal staff had not considered the Wagner Act to be "unconstitutional in its entirety," and that while they had advised members that it did not appear "applicable to local employment relations," they had always felt that its general principles would be upheld. Testimony of John C. Gall, March 2, 1938, "Violations of Free Speech and Rights of Labor: Employer Associations and Citizens' Committees—National Association of Manufacturers," 7394.

115. James A. Emery quoted in Weed, *The Nemesis of Reform*, 66. Phillips-Fein also points to legal opposition to the Wagner Act by the NAM. See Kim Phillips-Fein, *Invisible Hands: The Making of the Conservative Movement from the New Deal to Reagan* (New York: W. W. Norton & Company, 2009), 14–15.

116. J. S. Cullinan to Jouett Shouse, December 27, 1935, Liberty League Papers, box 1301, folder 66. Despite his reservations, Cullinan still sent a contribution.

117. Quoted in Wolfskill, *The Revolt of the Conservatives*, 198.

118. "Reporting of Contributions to and Expenditures by Political Organizations," 5–6. The letter was received February 20, 1936, and urged all House members to oppose the

Bankhead-Jones bill, which proposed federal financing to assist tenant farmers in pur-chasing land but which the People's Lobby believed would actually hurt small farmers and consumers.

119. Ibid., 6.

120. Ibid., 5 (emphasis added). The question came from Representative Francis Walter (D-PA), referring to fellow representative Patrick J. Boland (D-PA).

121. Ibid., 8.

122. Ibid., 2.

123. Smith "carefully refrained from accepting Liberty League sponsorship" (Rudolph, "The American Liberty League," 31.

124. Ibid.

125. Wolfskill, *The Revolt of the Conservatives*, 198.

126. Ibid., 205.

127. Both quoted in Wolfskill, *The Revolt of the Conservatives*: Coughlin on p. 30, and Harrison on p. 210.

128. E. E. Schattschneider, *Party Government* (New Brunswick, NJ: Transaction Publishers, 1942/2004), 88.

129. Quoted in Rudolph, "The American Liberty League," 29.

130. The League's earlier statement is described in "'Nonpartisan' Fight on Roosevelt Is Opened by the Liberty League," *New York Times*, July 1, 1936, 1, 17.

131. Wolfskill, *The Revolt of the Conservatives*, 206.

132. Rudolph implies that the League did not endorse Landon upon the request of the Republican Party ("The American Liberty League," 31). Yet Wolfskill reports Shouse claiming "that strong pressure was brought to have the League endorse the Republican ticket even be-fore the convention met or a candidate was nominated, pressure brought, among others, by Henry Fletcher, chairman of the Republican National Committee, and this despite Fletcher's statements that there would be no combination with the League" (*The Revolt of the Conservatives*, 205).

133. Quoted in Wolfskill, *The Revolt of the Conservatives*, 198 (emphasis added).

134. Ibid., 198 (emphasis in original). "Everyone, it seemed, dismissed the nonpartisan claims of the Liberty League," Wolfskill remarked (35).

135. Rudolph, "The American Liberty League," 30, 33. See also 29.

136. Ibid., 29.

137. Ibid., 30.

138. Lerner, "Roosevelt and His Fellow-Travelers," 471.

139. "Washington Notes: Can Big Business Buy This Election Too?," *New Republic*, September 9, 1936, 129.

140. Lerner, "Roosevelt and His Fellow-Travelers," 471.

141. The CIO was originally formed in November 1935 at the AFL convention (and would have ten affiliated unions by September 1936, the point at which the AFL suspended them). On the formation of the CIO, see Zeigler, *Interest Groups in American Society*, 149.

142. Ibid., 149.

143. V. O. Key, *Politics, Parties, and Pressure Groups* 1st ed. (New York: Crowell, 1942), 86.

144. *Labor's Non-Partisan League: Its Origin and Growth* (Washington, DC: Labor's Non-Partisan League, 1938), 4, The Len and Caroline Abrams DeCaux Collection, accession no. 332, series IV, box 15, "LNPL and PAC Related Reference Materials," folder 5, "Plan for 1940 Congressional Campaign," Walter P. Reuther Library, Wayne State University, Detroit, Michigan (hereafter cited as *LNPL: Its Origin and Growth*).

145. Raymond Moley quoted in Kenneth Finegold and Theda Skocpol, *State and Party in America's New Deal* (Madison: University of Wisconsin Press, 1995), 72. This agrarian strategy in 1932 replicated the approach that had won Roosevelt the governorship of New York.

146. Finegold and Skocpol, *State and Party in America's New Deal*, 72.

147. Philip Taft, "Labor's Changing Political Line," *Journal of Political Economy* 45, no. 5 (1937): 634.

148. Ibid. On interregional competition, see 638–639; on employer coercion and the injunction, see 640.

149. Ibid., 643.

150. Ibid.

151. Ibid.

152. Ibid., 642. Key also described the League as "a new departure in the political role of labor" operating on a much more active basis and a wider scale then previous labor efforts (*Politics, Parties, and Pressure Groups*, 1st ed., 86).

153. Joseph E. Hower, "'Our Conception of Non-Partisanship Means a Partisan Non-Partisanship': The Search for Political Identity in the American Federation of Labor, 1947–1955," *Labor History* 51, no. 3 (2010): 458. The AFL pursued a policy of "endorsing the candidacy of President Roosevelt by indirection" Taft observed ("Labor's Changing Political Line," 641).

154. Hugh A. Bone, "Political Parties in New York City," *American Political Science Review* 40, no. 2 (1946): 277.

155. See Anthony Corrado, "Money and Politics: A History of Federal Campaign Finance Law," in *Campaign Finance Reform: A Sourcebook*, ed. Anthony Corrado, Thomas E. Mann, Daniel R. Ortiz, Trevor Potter, and Frank J. Sorauf (Washington, DC: Brookings Institution Press, 1997), 29.

156. Lonergan Committee Report, 127–128. Unions gave $195,393.13 to LNPL's national organization and a further $32,000 to the state divisions, plus $40,300 to the Progressive National Committee and $180,558.03 to the American Labor Party.

157. Ibid., 127. Unions gave $62,517.50 to the Nominators' Division. For more on this Democratic fundraising group see Webber, *New Deal Fat Cats*, 125.

158. Lonergan Committee Report, 128. Contributions of $50,000 were recorded on October 8 and October 21 in Table 1(a), "Direct Cash Contributions to Democratic National Committee."

159. Ibid., 127.

160. Ibid., 27.

161. Melvin I. Urofsky, "Campaign Finance Reform Before 1971," *Albany Government Law Review* 1 (2008): 23–24. Urofsky recounts the tale of John L. Lewis hand-delivering a $250,000 check to Roosevelt, which he refused to accept for fear of appearing too close to the unions, while the DNC quietly accepted the check and many more from the same source.

162. The report states: "The United Mine Workers alone, it will be remembered, contributed $500,000 to the Democratic Party in the 1936 campaign." Nathan E. Cowan, John Brophy, and J. Raymond Walsh, "Memorandum to President Philip Murray," December 30, 1942, 20, Wayne County AFL-CIO Papers, box 25, CIO Political Programs folder, Walter P. Reuther Library, Wayne State University, Detroit, Michigan.

163. Taft, "Labor's Changing Political Line," 641.

164. Lonergan Committee Report, 26 (noted in "Receipts and Expenditures by Miscellaneous Committees of National Scope").

165. McCoy notes that Lewis, Hillman, and Philip Murray attended the PNC's founding conference, and that unions were a significant funding source. The Lonergan Committee report shows that of the approximately $60,000 that the PNC raised, over $40,000 had come from unions, of which $35,000 was contributed by Lewis's UMW alone. See McCoy, "The Progressive National Committee of 1936," 459–460, 468; and Lonergan Committee Report, 26, 131.

166. McCoy, "The Progressive National Committee of 1936," 464.

167. McCoy, "The Good Neighbor League and the Presidential Campaign of 1936," 1017.

168. Quoted in Wolfskill, *The Revolt of the Conservatives*, 189, 210.

169. Jouett Shouse to Pierre S. du Pont, June 4, 1936, Liberty League Papers, box 1301, folder 66, "771–3 American Liberty League—Jouett Shouse 1936."

170. As Wolfskill summarized, "[T]he plan promised about as much success as the chain-letter idea after which it was modeled" (*The Revolt of the Conservatives*, 216). Nonetheless, a League supporter was still urging it in late October. See Charles S. Johnson, October 22, 1936, Liberty League Papers, box 1301, folder 66.

171. On this point see also Wolfskill, *The Revolt of the Conservatives*, 216.

172. Pierre S. Du Pont to Jouett Shouse, June 6, 1936, Liberty League Papers, box 1301, folder 66, "771–3 American Liberty League—Jouett Shouse 1936."

173. In June, for example, Shouse gave a radio speech in which he said, "Democrats . . . left without a party in present circumstances, must decide the course they will pursue. They owe no duty of loyalty to the New Deal . . . making under the name of the Democratic party, the machinery of which it has momentarily seized." The New Deal would be defeated in November, Shouse said, because "some two million Democrats will take a walk to vote Republican" (quoted in Wolfskill, *The Revolt of the Conservatives*, 200).

174. Ibid., 200.

175. "Spent $518,123 in 1936," 4. Ritchie notes that the Liberty League "wielded a bigger staff than the Republican National Committee, and it outspent it on anti-New Deal publicity" (*Electing FDR*, 187).

176. Tillman Act of 1907, 34 Stat. 864 (emphasis added). Wolfskill notes that the Liberty League was incorporated in the District of Columbia on August 15, 1934 (*The Revolt of the Conservatives*, 26). See also Robert F. Burk, *The Corporate State and the Broker State: The Du Ponts and American National Politics, 1925–1940* (Cambridge, MA: Harvard University Press, 1990), 141.

177. Du Pont contributions calculated from data provided in Wolfskill, *The Revolt of the Conservatives*, 207; RNC spending in Lonergan Committee Report, 27. From Wolfskill's information, the du Ponts contributed $530,370 to the RNC and the Pews $485,977, though he suggests there were more contributions than reported and notes that a large number of Liberty Leaguers were members of the Republican national finance committee, too (206–207).

178. Quoted in Wolfskill, *The Revolt of the Conservatives*, 207.

179. Ibid., 214.

180. Ibid., 254.

181. Ibid., 61–62, 254.

182. Paul W. Ward, "Washington Weekly: Farley Captures Labor," *Nation*, October 31, 1936, 512.

183. Ibid.

184. William Leuchtenburg, *Franklin D. Roosevelt and the New Deal, 1932–1940* (New York: Harper & Row, 1963), 189.

185. J. Thomas Butler to Jouett Shouse, October 12, 1936, Liberty League Papers, box 1301, folder 66, "771–3 American Liberty League—Jouett Shouse 1936."

186. Wolfskill, *The Revolt of the Conservatives*, 214, Rudolph, "The American Liberty League," 31; and Tichenor, "The Presidency and Interest Groups," 325.

187. For example, Wolfskill concludes that the League failed because of "what it seemed to represent" (*The Revolt of the Conservatives*, 260).

188. Quoted in Wolfskill, *The Revolt of the Conservatives*, 211. Representative John J. O'Connor even claimed that Landon's (nomination) acceptance speech was written by the NAM and edited by Shouse (214).

189. See, for example, Rudolph, "The American Liberty League," 26–27; and Wolfskill, *The Revolt of the Conservatives*, 121.

190. Rudolph, "The American Liberty League," 27.

191. Ibid.

192. Ibid., 30.

193. Quoted in Soule, "Liberty League Liberty—II," 95.

194. Soule, "Liberty League Liberty—II," 95 (emphasis added).

195. Pierre S. Du Pont to Jouett Shouse, September 21, 1936, Liberty League Papers, box 1301, folder 66.

196. George L. Buist to Jouett Shouse, October 17, 1936, Liberty League Papers, box 1301, folder 66. Buist was an attorney in Charleston, South Carolina.

197. Ibid.

198. *LNPL: Its Origin and Growth*, 4 (emphasis added).

199. Quoted in ibid., 5.

200. Ibid., 5.

Chapter 4

1. Paul W. Ward, "Washington Weekly: Farley Captures Labor," *Nation*, October 31, 1936, 512.
2. Ibid.
3. Ibid.
4. Ibid.
5. Ibid.
6. The Roosevelt administration had not sided with labor on all policy issues to that point either. As journalist Raymond Gram Swing noted in the *Nation*, for example, the National Recovery Administration had failed to consult with autoworkers when creating the industrial code for car manufacturing, under instructions from Roosevelt. The magazine also condemned the first six months of the National Labor Relations Board's activity as "a picture of impotence and futility" and described Roosevelt's message on the crucial provision of the National Industrial Recovery Act's section 7(a), guaranteeing collective bargaining rights, as "vague piety, and hopelessly ambiguous besides." See Raymond Gram Swing, "The White House Breaks with Labor," *Nation*, February 13, 1935, 181; and "Labor Notes: Two Boards, Two Reports," *Nation*, March 6, 1935, 280.
7. Ward, "Washington Weekly," 512 (emphasis added). In New York, Ward observed, the American Labor Party had not run any of its own congressional candidates, as it had originally promised, offering "a ticket bearing the names of only Roosevelt and Lehman."
8. Max Lerner, "Roosevelt and His Fellow-Travelers," *Nation*, October 24, 1936, 472.
9. The Union Party received 1.95 percent of the popular vote, the Socialist Party 0.41 percent, and the Communist Party 0.17 percent. "1936 Presidential General Election Results," in *US Election Atlas*, https://uselectionatlas.org/RESULTS/.
10. George Gallup founded the AIPO in 1935. Gallup Poll, December 16–21, 1936, iPOLL Databank, The Roper Center for Public Opinion Research, University of Connecticut, http://www.ropercenter.uconn.edu/data_access/ipoll/ipoll.html. The methodology utilized by polling companies at this time was less accurate than more modern methods, but the information reported here was available to actors at the time. For efforts to recalibrate early polls according to contemporary sampling standards, see Adam J. Berinsky, Eleanor Neff Powell, Eric Schickler, and Ian Brett Yohai, "Revisiting Public Opinion in the 1930s and 1940s," *PS: Political Science & Politics* 44, no. 3 (2011): 515–520.
11. On sources of tension between labor and the president, including his "seeming impartiality" in this struggle, see Donald R. McCoy, "The National Progressives of America, 1938," *Mississippi Valley Historical Review* 44, no. 1 (1957): 76–77
12. In the Ohio gubernatorial campaign, for example, John Bricker linked "the CIO to the New Deal administration," while Representative Martin Dies (D-TX) offered a resolution to investigate the sit-down strikes and their connection to the administration. See Clyde P. Weed, *The Nemesis of Reform: The Republican Party During the New Deal* (New York: Columbia University Press, 1994), 196, 198.
13. Quoted in Daniel J. Tichenor, "The Presidency, Social Movements, and Contentious Change: Lessons from the Woman's Suffrage and Labor Movements," *Presidential Studies Quarterly* 29, no. 1 (1999): 22.
14. John S. Forsythe, "Legislative History of the Fair Labor Standards Act," *Law and Contemporary Problems* 6 (Summer 1939): 464–490. A bill passed the Senate in July 1937, and a version with some amendments was reported out of the House in August, but the Rules Committee refused to issue a rule to allow floor consideration. The Democrats were unable to bring it to the floor by other means before the expiration of the session later that month. Roosevelt subsequently called for a special session, convened in November, in which wage and hour legislation was to be addressed, and a discharge petition was successful in bringing the bill to the floor. It was met with a drive to have the bill recommitted, however, and this measure passed on December 17, 1937.
15. These various factors are discussed in McCoy, "The National Progressives of America, 1938," 76–77. McCoy also points to labor disillusionment amid strong congressional opposition to New Deal measures and FDR's calls for increased military expenditures as a concern (77).

16. Harmon Zeigler, *Interest Groups in American Society* (Englewood Cliffs, NJ: Prentice-Hall, 1964), 149–150.

17. Ibid., 149.

18. Roper/*Fortune* Survey, May 1938, iPOLL Databank, The Roper Center for Public Opinion Research, University of Connecticut, http://www.ropercenter.uconn.edu/data_access/ipoll/ipoll.html.

19. Gallup Poll, December, 1936; Gallup Poll, July 1937; and Gallup Poll (American Institute of Public Opinion), January 1938, iPOLL Databank, The Roper Center for Public Opinion Research, University of Connecticut, http://www.ropercenter.uconn.edu/data_access/ipoll/ipoll.html.

20. *Labor's Non-Partisan League: Its Origin and Growth* (Washington, DC: Labor's Non-Partisan League, 1938), 7, The Len and Caroline Abrams DeCaux Collection, accession no. 332, series IV, box 15, "LNPL and PAC Related Reference Materials," folder 5, "Plan for 1940 Congressional Campaign," Walter P. Reuther Library, Wayne State University, Detroit, Michigan (hereafter cited as *LNPL: Its Origin and Growth*).

21. Ibid., 11–12.

22. Contemporary analysts noted successes for labor candidates in these states, some of whom were themselves CIO officials, and also noted Democratic primary victories in two Ohio mayoral races, which they attributed to League activity. See B. W. Patch and B. Putney, "Labor in Politics," *Editorial Research Reports* I (1940), http://library.cqpress.com/cqresearcher/cqresrre1940022300.

23. Philip Taft, "Labor's Changing Political Line," *Journal of Political Economy* 45, no. 5 (1937): 641(emphasis added).

24. Ibid. Taft explicitly makes this connection, saying the LNPL was "following the techniques originally used by the Farmers' Non-partisan League, which not only indorsed candidates but entered its own in the primaries."

25. Ibid., 644.

26. Ibid.

27. V. O. Key, *Politics, Parties, and Pressure Groups* 1st ed. (New York: Crowell, 1942), 86.

28. *LNPL: Its Origin and Growth*, 16.

29. Labor's Non-Partisan League, *The Voting Record of Senators and Congressmen on Major Labor, Farm, and Other Social Legislation* (Washington, DC: LNPL, 1938), New York Public Library. LNPL published this "scorecard" on March 6, 1938, but it subsequently circulated a list of "grades" rating lawmakers according to their favorability to labor. The latter was partially based on the earlier voting analysis but placed a stronger emphasis on the wages and hours recommittal vote. See Emily J. Charnock, "More Than a Score: Interest Group Ratings and Polarized Politics," *Studies in American Political Development* 32, no. 1 (April 2018): 4, esp. n20.

30. On the LNPL's greater emphasis on House contests, see Charnock, "More Than a Score," 8–9n62; on not entering every contest in which the LNPL had identified an interest, see *LNPL: Its Origin and Growth*, 22.

31. *LNPL: Its Origin and Growth*, 24.

32. Key, *Politics, Parties, and Pressure Groups* (1942), 87.

33. Discussing the voting record in a March article, the *CIO News* reported that the LNPL would also "broadcast generally a list of Congressmen and Senators it endorses for re-election," doing so "[s]ome time within the next few weeks" ("Labor Enters Politics: Non-Partisan League Gains Power in Many States," *CIO News*, March 26, 1938, 5. That later announcement appears to have been the list of "grades"—both "A" for those supported and "D" for those opposed—that was reported in, for example, George E. Reedy, "Lewis Launches Congress Purge, Issues Blacklist," *Philadelphia Inquirer*, July 16, 1938, 1, 4; "Lewis League Gives Indorsement to 42 Members of House," *Philadelphia Inquirer*, July 17, 1938, 1, 18; and "LNPL Lists Ratings of 80 Congressmen," *CIO News*, July 23, 1938, 5.

34. Of forty-two members on the "A" list, thirty-two were Democrats, five were Wisconsin Progressives, four were Democratic Farmer-Laborites in Minnesota, and one was a California Republican. See Reedy, "Lewis League Gives Indorsement to 42 Members of House," 18.

35. Of forty members on the "D" list, twenty-six were Democrats and fourteen were Republicans. See Reedy, "Lewis Launches Congress Purge, Issues Blacklist," 4.

36. While there had been some prior presidential engagement in congressional elections, Milkis and Nelson point out that Roosevelt's 1938 intervention was "conducted on an unprecedented scale and, unlike the previous efforts [of Taft and Wilson, for example], bypassed the regular party organization." Sidney M. Milkis and Michael Nelson, *The American President: Origins and Development, 1776–2007* (Washington, DC: CQ Press, 2008), 291.

37. "It is the view of the Presidential advisers," *Los Angeles Times* political columnist Frank R. Kent reported, "that the administration should place itself strongly behind the 100 per cent Roosevelt candidate in the primaries. The contention is that, the people being still with the President, they will rally to the support of the man known to be his friend." Frank R. Kent, "The Great Game of Politics," *Los Angeles Times*, May 27, 1938, 10.

38. James A. Farley, *Jim Farley's Story* (New York: Whittlesey House, 1948), 147, quoted in Susan Dunn, *Roosevelt's Purge: How FDR Fought to Change the Democratic Party* (Cambridge, MA: Belknap Press of Harvard University Press, 2010), 224–225.

39. Of the twenty-six House Democrats given "D" grades by the LNPL in 1938, eight were non-Southern. Key notes that the LNPL had supported the court-packing bill, yet neither votes on that measure nor the executive reorganization bill appeared in its 1938 scorecard, and they were not mentioned as factors influencing the "grades" it publicized, discussed in note 29. Nonetheless, of the administration's main electoral targets, as identified by Dunn, the LNPL also expressed opposition to Senator Walter George of South Carolina and Millard Tydings of Maryland, even though Tydings had actually voted for the wage-hour bill in the Senate. In this case, the LNPL's opposition seems to have been driven more by its support for Tydings's opponent—Representative David J. Lewis of Maryland—a former coal miner with strong ties to the labor movement. It also expressed some opposition to Senator Ellison D. Smith of South Carolina, an opponent of the wage-hour bill, though he did not appear to be included in the original announcement of LNPL targets. It is not clear how active the LNPL was in these Senate contests, and its announcements and activities were more heavily oriented to House candidates. Notably, it did not formally oppose Representative John O'Connor of New York, chairman of the Rules Committee and the only congressman targeted in Roosevelt's "purge," since he had voted *against* recommitting the wage-hour bill. On the LNPL's support for court-packing and its absence from the scorecard, see Key, *Politics, Parties, and Pressure Groups* (1942), 86; and Labor's Non-Partisan League, *The Voting Record of Senators and Congressmen on Major Labor, Farm, and Other Social Legislation*. On the various targets of Roosevelt's 1938 congressional campaign, see Dunn, *Roosevelt's Purge*. On LNPL opposition to George and Tydings, see Reedy, "Lewis Launches Congress Purge, Issues Blacklist," 4. For Smith as another target, see "Blacklisted Legislators Show Divided Reactions," *Philadelphia Inquirer*, July 17, 1938, 16. On the LNPL's electoral activities in 1938, see *LNPL: Its Origin and Growth*, 22.

40. "Political Note: Spring Gardening," *Time*, May 30, 1938. Lewis backed former miner and lieutenant governor Thomas Kennedy for the Democratic gubernatorial nomination against the wishes of Pennsylvania's regular Democratic organization and eventually joined forces with the state's junior senator, Joe Guffey, to support an alternative Democratic candidate for Pennsylvania's other Senate seat. Following a "savage" campaign, both the Guffey-Lewis backed candidates lost their primaries, while Republicans prevailed in the general election.

41. Frank R. Kent, "The Great Game of Politics," *Los Angeles Times*, May 24, 1938, 4.

42. Ibid. With Pennsylvania, Kent suggested, "[t]he idea that candidates with the Roosevelt blessing are invulnerable has been knocked out." See also Chapin Hall, "What Goes On?," *Los Angeles Times*, May 23, 1938, 2. Both Kent and Hall noted the involvement of the WPA in the Pennsylvania contest.

43. In the case of Gillette, Dunn (*Roosevelt's Purge*) notes that opposition was mounted indirectly by visits from Roosevelt's son James and other administration officials, rather than through a direct intervention by the president. Dunn also notes that Senator Claude Pepper (D-FL) received similar indirect support in his primary campaign. Otherwise the president also expressed support for Senators Alben Barkley (D-KY), Hattie Caraway (D-AR), Elmer Thomas (D-OK), Robert Bulkley (D-OH), and William G. McAdoo (D-CA), as well as Congressman Maury Maverick (D-TX), in their primary contests. Of those supported, all but McAdoo won their primaries and went on to win the general election.

44. As discussed in note 39, however, Tydings had supported wage-hour legislation in the Senate, suggesting the LNPL may have factored administration concerns into its expressed opposition here.

45. As Dunn details, the timing of WPA funding grants, the actions of individual WPA workers, and the role of its administrator—Harry Hopkins—were all subject to public and congressional scrutiny in relation to Roosevelt's effort. In Iowa, for example, where Roosevelt sought the defeat of incumbent senator Guy Gillette, Hopkins publicly declared his support for the challenger (Otha Wearin), provoking a firestorm of criticism that WPA funds were being used as "a political whip." In Georgia, where Roosevelt opposed incumbent senator Walter George, the WPA made a $53 million allocation to the state in the days before the primary—an action widely viewed as an effort to sway the results (*Roosevelt's Purge*, 115–116, 173). On May 25, 1938, Senator Burton K. Wheeler (D-MT) "declared on the Senate floor that the Roosevelt administration was responsible and could not deny responsibility for attempts made by W.P.A. Administrator Hopkins, P.W.A. Administrator Ickes, Postmaster-General Farley and other administration officials to dictate the choice of the voters in Democratic primaries." See "Senator Wheeler Assails Political Use of Aid Funds," *Los Angeles Times*, May 26, 1938, 1.

46. Robert Dale, "Labor's Prospects Bright in Fall Election Contests," *CIO News*, October 1, 1938, 8. A banner headline in the *CIO News* of September 24, 1938, was "Labor Forces Win in Primaries," *CIO News*, September 24, 1938, 5.

47. Dale, "Labor's Prospects Bright in Fall Election Contests," 8.

48. Information from Table 1-17, "Losses by President's Party in Midterm Elections, 1862–2006," in *Vital Statistics on American Politics 2009–2010*, ed. Harold W. Stanley and Richard G. Niemi (Washington, DC: CQ Press, 2009), 42, http://library.cqpress.com/vsap/vsap09_tab1-17; Schickler and Caughey, for example, find a "broadly based reaction against labor unions" from the late 1930s, using specially recalibrated polling data from the period. See Eric Schickler and Devin Caughey, "Public Opinion, Organized Labor, and the Limits of New Deal Liberalism, 1936–1945," *Studies in American Political Development* 25, no. 2 (2011): 162–189.

49. On the safety of southern seats, see Julian E. Zelizer, *On Capitol Hill: The Struggle to Reform Congress and Its Consequences, 1948–2000* (New York: Cambridge University Press, 2004).

50. Key, *Politics, Parties, and Pressure Groups*, 86.

51. LNPL statement reported in "League Surveys Election Results, Sees Need for Increased Activity," *CIO News*, December 5, 1938, 7.

52. Sean J. Savage, "Franklin D. Roosevelt and the Democratic National Committee," *Social Science Journal* 28, no. 4 (1991): 452–454.

53. Sidney M. Milkis, *The President and the Parties: The Transformation of the American Party System Since the New Deal* (New York: Oxford University Press, 1993), chapters 4–6. On the backlash to the "purge," see Dunn, *Roosevelt's Purge*.

54. See Milkis, *The President and the Parties*, 76–77; and Savage, "Franklin D. Roosevelt and the Democratic National Committee," 454. On the DNC's continued financial support for the GNL, see Donald R. McCoy, "The Good Neighbor League and the Presidential Campaign of 1936," *Western Political Quarterly* 13, no. 4 (1960): 1018.

55. "Campaign Expenditures: Allied Democrats, Friends of Democracy, Official Democratic County Assembly Committee of San Francisco, and United Labor Legislative Committee, Committee for Constitutional Government," *Hearings before the Committee to Investigate Campaign Expenditures*, part 10, US House of Representatives, 78th Cong., 2nd sess., October 12, 19, and 24, 1944 (Washington, DC: Government Printing Office, 1944), 1183 (hereafter cited as Anderson Committee Hearings). Like Senator Hatch, Congressman Clinton Anderson also hailed from New Mexico and would later succeed Hatch in the Senate.

56. Anthony Corrado, "Money and Politics: A History of Federal Campaign Finance Law," in *Campaign Finance Reform: A Sourcebook*, ed. Anthony Corrado, Thomas E. Mann, Daniel R. Ortiz, Trevor Potter, and Frank J. Sorauf (Washington, DC: Brookings Institution Press, 1997), 30.

57. See Dunn, *Roosevelt's Purge*, 116, for a discussion of the background to the Hatch Act.

58. Corrado, "Money and Politics," 30, 47. See 1940 Hatch Act Amendments, 54 Stat. 767 (July 19, 1940), section 6, amending section 20 of the Hatch Act.

59. Allison R. Hayward, "Revisiting the Fable of Reform," *Harvard Journal on Legislation* 45 (2008): 443. Hayward argues that this muddies a clear case for legislative *intent* in respect of this significant campaign finance reform.

60. Ibid., 443–444.

61. As Corrado observes: individual donors "could still donate large sums by giving to multiple committees or by making contributions through state and local party organizations, which were not subject to the $5,000 limit." ("Money and Politics," 30).

62. "Fletcher's Opinion on the Application of Hatch Act," *New York Times*, August 4, 1940, 2.

63. Ibid.

64. According to the Gillette Committee Report, eighty-nine independent committees supporting the Republican ticket in multiple states spent $2,832,167.41, compared to $2,242,742.47 spent by the RNC. The forty-one intrastate independent committees spent a further $754,900.81. "Investigation of Presidential, Vice Presidential, and Senatorial Campaign Expenditures, 1940," Report of the Special Committee to Investigate Presidential, Vice Presidential, and Senatorial Campaign Expenditures, 1940, US Senate, 77th Cong., 1st sess., February 15, 1941, S. Rep. No. 47 (Washington DC: Government Printing Office, 1941), 11 (hereafter cited as Gillette Committee Report).

65. Ibid., 10. According to the Gillette Committee Report, twenty independent committees supporting the Democratic ticket in multiple states spent $557,017.60, compared to $2,438,091.88 spent by the DNC. The twenty-one intrastate independent committees spent a further $311,558.49.

66. Ibid., 10–11. In addition to national party committees and both interstate and intrastate independent committees, Democratic state committees spent a further $2,785,659.82, for a total of $6,092,327.79 on the Democratic side, while Republican state committees spent $10,791,625.17, for a total of $16,621,435.86 on the Republican side.

67. Louise Overacker, "Campaign Finance in the Presidential Election of 1940," *American Political Science Review* 35, no. 4 (1941): 709. Overacker's list was drawn from the Gillette Committee Report and is essentially replicated in Key, *Politics, Parties, and Pressure Groups* (1942), 447n4. The Associated Willkie Clubs of America spent $1,355,604.

68. Overacker, "Campaign Finance in the Presidential Election of 1940," 709. According to Overacker's calculations using information in the Gillette Committee Report, Democrats for Willkie spent $416,808, and the National Committee to Uphold Constitutional Government spent $377,381. The National Committee of Independent Voters for Roosevelt and Wallace spent $250,455, $54,100 of which was contributed by trade unions, while the National Committee for Agriculture spent $131,489, of which $54,000 came from the DNC.

69. Quoted in Jennifer Burns, *Goddess of the Market: Ayn Rand and the American Right* (New York: Oxford University Press, 2009), 53.

70. Ibid.

71. Ibid. Burns suggests that "[t]he telegrams touted as spontaneous manifestations of his popularity turned out to be part of a carefully orchestrated corporate campaign."

72. Henry O. Evjen, "The Willkie Campaign: An Unfortunate Chapter in Republican Leadership," *Journal of Politics* 14, no. 2 (1952): 247. Evjen notes that Willkie also authorized another group, "Democrats for Willkie," while a number of unauthorized groups also emerged (247, 253).

73. Ibid., 252.

74. Ibid., 247–248.

75. Ibid., 241, 247, 249, 253.

76. On formation of the "Independent Clubs," see "REPUBLICANS: New Force?," *Time*, December 23, 1940. On its demise in December 1941, see "Willkie Boosters Suspend for War," *Washington Post*, December 22, 1941, 6.

77. "Investigation of Presidential, Vice Presidential, and Senatorial Campaign Expenditures, 1944," Report of the Special Committee to Investigate Presidential, Vice Presidential, and Senatorial Campaign Expenditures in 1944, US Senate, 79th Cong., 1st sess., March 15th, 1945, S. Rep. No. 101 (Washington, DC: Government Printing Office, 1945), 7 (hereafter cited as Green Committee Report).

78. Ibid.

79. Of the $131,489 spent by the National Committee for Agriculture, $54,000 had come from the DNC (approximately 41 percent of its funds), according to Overacker, "Campaign Finance in the Presidential Election of 1940," 709.

80. According to Overacker, the Roosevelt Agricultural Committee spent $272,609, of which $244,087 was received from the DNC (about 90 percent of its funds), while the Senate's 1928 campaign expenditure committee found that the Independent Agricultural League (referred to as the "Smith Independent Organizations Committee") had received all of its funds from the DNC (a $400,000 contribution). See Louise Overacker, "Campaign Funds in the Presidential Election of 1936," *American Political Science Review* 31, no. 3 (1937): 478; and "Presidential Campaign Expenditures," Report of the Special Committee Investigating Presidential Campaign Expenditures, US Senate, 70th Cong., February 28, 1929, S. Rep. No. 2024 (Washington, DC: Government Printing Office, 1929), 26. Testifying before the Gillette Committee, the National Committee for Agriculture's chairman, William Settle, indicated a relationship between the three groups: "In 1932, George Peake was chairman of that committee and made his effort in the campaign, and then in 1936 we operated again, and now in 1940," he explained. See *Hearings before the Special Committee Investigating Campaign Expenditures, 1940*, vol. 5, US Senate, 76th Cong., 3rd sess., November 4, 1940 (Washington, DC: Ward and Paul, 1940), 449 (hereafter cited as Gillette Committee Hearings).

81. As an internal memo produced during the Senate's 1944 campaign expenditure investigation put it: "However noble the purpose of this law has been, the result has led only to the horizontal growth of a number of independent committees." Special Committee on Campaign Expenditures, 1944, "Independent Committees," 1–2, 8E2/7/19/5, US Senate, 78th Cong., 1944 general file I-M, RG 46 box no. 2, Miscellaneous Camp. Exp. '44 (folder), National Archives and Records Administration, Legislative Archives Center, Washington, DC. See also "Note: Registration of Groups Tending to Influence Public Opinion," *Columbia Law Review* 48, no. 4 (1948): 598.

82. Gillette Committee Hearings, vol. 2, October 4, 1940, 113–114.

83. Richard Polenberg, "The National Committee to Uphold Constitutional Government, 1937–1941," *Journal of American History* 52, no. 3 (1965): 582. As Polenberg explains, the NCUCG viewed Roosevelt's attempts to reorganize the executive branch as a dictatorial power grab and his proposal to pack the Supreme Court as a subversion of the separation of powers (594).

84. Quoted in Polenberg, "The National Committee to Uphold Constitutional Government, 1937–1941," 583.

85. On these techniques, see Christopher M. Loomis, "The Politics of Uncertainty: Lobbyists and Propaganda in Early Twentieth-Century America," *Journal of Policy History* 21, no. 2 (2009): 189–200. On Rumely's background in lobbying, see Polenberg, "The National Committee to Uphold Constitutional Government, 1937–1941," 582.

86. Polenberg, "The National Committee to Uphold Constitutional Government, 1937–1941," 594–595. Rumely was called before the Senate's lobbying investigation in 1938, now chaired by Senator Sherman Minton (D-IN), who had taken over from Hugo Black upon his appointment to the Supreme Court. When asked to provide the committee with NCUCG financial documents, Rumely had refused on the grounds that its publicity activities had been purely educational. The argument earned Rumely a rebuke from Minton in open session, raking over his shady professional background and even his possible links to the Ku Klux Klan.

87. Ibid., 592–593.

88. Ibid., 594.

89. Ibid., 593.

90. Ibid.

91. Ibid.

92. Ibid., 594.

93. Ibid.

94. Testimony of Samuel B. Pettengill, Chairman of the National Committee to Uphold Constitutional Government, October 25, 1940, Gillette Committee Hearings, vol. 3, 226–227 (emphasis added).

95. Testimony of Frank E. Gannett of the Committee for Constitutional Government, September 7, 1944, "Campaign Expenditures: Committee for Constitutional Government," Anderson Committee Hearings, part 7, 406.

96. Ibid.

97. Ibid.

98. Polenberg, "The National Committee to Uphold Constitutional Government, 1937–1941," 596–597. The successor organization was the Committee for Constitutional Government, discussed further in chapter 8.

99. George L. Buist to Jouett Shouse, October 17, 1936, Records of the American Liberty League 1929–1948, accession LMSS, box 1301, folder 66, Hagley Museum and Library, Wilmington, Delaware (hereafter cited as Liberty League Papers).

100. George Wolfskill, *The Revolt of the Conservatives: A History of the American Liberty League, 1934–1940* (Boston: Houghton Mifflin, 1962), 189.

101. Ibid., 189–190.

102. Ibid., 190.

103. Ibid. The idea was to create "a coalition constitutional party," Wolfskill explains.

104. Ibid.

105. Ibid., 255.

106. Ibid., 247.

107. William H. Stanton to Pierre S. Du Pont, May 12, 1938, Liberty League Papers, box 1301, folder 4.

108. Wolfskill, *The Revolt of the Conservatives*, 247.

109. According to a review of the League's 1937 finances produced by its secretary, William Stanton, major contributions and loans were provided by Irénée du Pont ($12,500), Pierre du Pont ($15,500), and J. Howard Pew ($2,500), who together contributed more than 80 percent of the League's funding that year (William H. Stanton to Pierre S. DuPont, May 12, 1938, Liberty League Papers, box 1301, folder 4). The Liberty League's financial report—filed with the House Clerk in March 1938—showed total receipts of $15,332.35 for the first quarter of 1938, which included $5,000 from Lammot du Pont, then-president of the DuPont Company, and $2,500 from J. Howard Pew of Sun Oil. The balance on hand was $1588.95, suggesting continued outlays (unless debt was still being retired). "The American Liberty League of Delaware" also made a report. See "Farley Says Party Is Clear of Debt," *New York Times*, March 11, 1938.

110. Wolfskill, *The Revolt of the Conservatives*, 247.

111. "New Deal Foe Folds Up: American Liberty League Joins Other Extinct Political Bodies," *New York Times*, September 24, 1940, 20.

112. Overacker, "Campaign Finance in the Presidential Election of 1940," 715n44.

113. Tichenor, "The Presidency, Social Movements, and Contentious Change," 22. Tichenor explains that on the war, Lewis believed that it "would derail a progressive labor agenda. Lewis predicted that war production would swallow labor up in an efficient military-industrial state."

114. Key, *Politics, Parties, and Pressure Groups*, 1st ed., 86–87.

115. On Lewis's considering a third party in 1944 with the LNPL as its base, see Herbert Harris, *Labor's Civil War* (New York: Knopf, 1940), 105.

116. Roper/*Fortune* Survey, April 1940, iPOLL Databank, The Roper Center for Public Opinion Research, University of Connecticut, http://www.ropercenter.uconn.edu/data_access/ipoll/ipoll.html.

117. The UMW's split from the CIO was formalized in May 1941, when the UMW stripped Murray of membership and status as a vice president. Lewis continued to claim control of the LNPL, however, leading state LNPLs such as that in New Jersey to dissociate from the national organization. See Robert H. Zieger, *The CIO: 1935–1955* (Chapel Hill: University of North Carolina Press, 1995), 138; "Strike or Insurrection?," *Chicago Daily Tribune*, May 19, 1946, 20; and "Jersey Labor Unit to End Lewis Link," *New York Times*, May 24, 1942, 38.

118. Some 30 percent of respondents in an April 1941 Roper/*Fortune* poll, for example, agreed that "a national labor party ... would be a good thing for the country." Roper/*Fortune* Survey,

April 1941, iPOLL Databank, The Roper Center for Public Opinion Research, University of Connecticut, http://www.ropercenter.uconn.edu/data_access/ipoll/ipoll.html.

119. Key, *Politics, Parties, and Pressure Groups* (1942), 86.

120. Joseph G. LaPalombara, "Pressure, Propaganda, and Political Action in the Elections of 1950," *Journal of Politics* 14, no. 2 (May 1952): 317.

Chapter 5

1. Roosevelt referenced the no-strike pledge in a "Fireside Chat" addressing the miner's strike, led by Lewis. See Franklin D. Roosevelt, "Fireside Chat," May 2, 1943, in *The American Presidency Project*, ed. Gerhard Peters and John T. Woolley, https://www.presidency.ucsb.edu/documents/fireside-chat-0.

2. Section 9 of the Smith-Connally Act extended from corporations to unions the prohibition on making contributions "in connection with" federal elections, thus amending section 313 of the Federal Corrupt Practices Act. Roosevelt argued that this measure lacked "relevancy" to the main substance of the bill and urged more "careful consideration" of its duration and scope. Franklin D. Roosevelt, "Veto of the Smith-Connally Bill," June 25, 1943, in *The American Presidency Project*, ed. Gerhard Peters and John T. Woolley, http://www.presidency.ucsb.edu/ws/?pid=16420.

3. The provision banning labor contributions had been taken from a separate bill proposed by Congressman Gerald Landis (R-IN) and was inserted into the anti-strike measure during House floor debate, generating little substantive discussion. The amended bill passed amid significant parliamentary confusion. See Allison R. Hayward, "Revisiting the Fable of Reform," *Harvard Journal on Legislation* 45 (2008): 448, 450–451.

4. Accounts of the initial formation of the CIO P.A.C. are provided in Joseph Gaer, *The First Round: The Story of the CIO Political Action Committee* (New York: Duell, Sloan, and Pearce, 1944), 60; James Caldwell Foster, *The Union Politic: The CIO Political Action Committee* (Columbia: University of Missouri Press, 1975), 3; and Robert A. Garson, *The Democratic Party and the Politics of Sectionalism, 1941–1948* (Baton Rouge: Louisiana State University Press, 1974), 57.

5. Robert E. Mutch, *Buying the Vote: A History of Campaign Finance Reform* (New York: Oxford University Press, 2014), 107.

6. Melvin I. Urofsky, "Campaign Finance Reform Before 1971," *Albany Government Law Review* 1 (2008): 26.

7. As discussed in this chapter, P.A.C. did not *immediately* adopt a direct contributions approach, relying instead on legal arguments about its status (that it was not technically a "labor organization") and a specific interpretation of the 1944 electoral calendar (that the law did not apply until *after* presidential conventions) to justify continued use of treasury funds, providing it was for *expenditures* in campaigns rather than direct contributions. In its early years it also avoided making direct contributions in general election contests, even from voluntary funds.

8. Zieger, for example, states that "[s]ince its inception the CIO had been part of the Democratic coalition," and Chang observes that both the AFL and the CIO "shared a commitment to the Democratic party" by the early 1950s. See Robert H. Zieger, *The CIO: 1935–1955* (Chapel Hill: University of North Carolina Press, 1995), 267–268; and Tracy F. Chang, "The Labour Vote in US National Elections, 1948–2000," *Political Quarterly* 72, no. 3 (2001): 379–380.

9. Thirteen "standing committees" were noted in a 1945 organization chart submitted to the House Select Committee on Lobbying Activities of the 81st Congress, including the Political Action Committee and the Legislative Committee. See "CIO Organization, 1945," in "Housing Lobby," *Hearings before the Select Committee on Lobbying Activities*, part 2, US House of Representatives, 81st Cong., 2nd sess., April 19, 20, 21, 25, 26, 27, 28, May 3, 5, and 17, 1950 (Washington, DC: Government Printing Office, 1950), 152 (hereafter cited as Buchanan Committee Hearings).

10. See Testimony of Sidney Hillman, August 28, 1944, "Campaign Expenditures," *Hearings before the Committee to Investigate Campaign Expenditures*, part 1, US House of Representatives, 78th Cong., 2nd sess. (Washington, DC: Government Printing Office, 1944), 6 (hereafter cited as Anderson Committee Hearings); and "The CIO-PAC and How It Works," December

1954, esp. 2, CIO Political Action Committee (PAC) Collection Papers, 1943–1960s, accession no. 647, box 13, folder 18, "CIO/PAC History," Walter P. Reuther Library, Wayne State University, Detroit, Michigan (hereafter cited as CIO-PAC Papers). The latter document provides detailed information on P.A.C.'s initial formation, personnel, and organization.

11. Testimony of Jack Kroll, October 14, 1946, "Campaign Expenditures—CIO Political Action Committee," *Hearings before the Committee to Investigate Campaign Expenditures*, part 2, US House of Representatives, 79th Cong., 2nd sess. (Washington, DC: Government Printing Office, 1946), 95–96 (hereafter cited as Priest Committee Hearings).

12. Philip Taft, "Labor's Changing Political Line," *Journal of Political Economy* 45, no. 5 (October 1937): 634, 638.

13. Ibid., 637–639.

14. See, for example, Mark R. Wilson, *Destructive Creation: American Business and the Winning of World War II* (Philadelphia: University of Pennsylvania Press, 2016).

15. Garson, *The Democratic Party and the Politics of Sectionalism*, 56.

16. On concerns with wartime agencies, see Garson, *The Democratic Party and the Politics of Sectionalism*, 56; and Zieger, *The CIO*, 179. Relevant agencies included the National War Labor Board (1942–1946) in particular, but also the Office of Production Management (1941–1942)/War Production Board (1942–1945) and the Office of Price Administration (1941–1946), among others.

17. Testimony of Sidney Hillman, June 13, 1944, "Presidential, Vice Presidential, and Senatorial Campaign Expenditures, 1944," *Hearing before the Committee to Investigate Campaign Expenditures of Presidential, Vice Presidential, and Senatorial Candidates in 1944*, part 1, June 13, 1944, US Senate, 78th Cong., 2nd sess. (Washington, DC: Government Printing Office, 1944), 8 (hereafter cited as Green Committee Hearings).

18. Nathan E. Cowan, John Brophy, and J. Raymond Walsh, "Memorandum to President Philip Murray," December 30, 1942, 15, Wayne County AFL-CIO Papers, box 25, CIO Political Programs folder, Walter P. Reuther Library, Wayne State University, Detroit, Michigan (hereafter cited as Cowan-Brophy-Walsh Report).

19. Cowan-Brophy-Walsh Report, 15.

20. Ibid., 2.

21. Ibid., 7, 15.

22. Ibid., 1.

23. Ibid., 7.

24. Ibid., 7–8. "In most cases the state councils have established specialized agencies, usually political or legislative committees, to which political work is delegated," they noted.

25. Ibid., 5.

26. Ibid., 6.

27. Ibid.

28. Ibid., 9.

29. Quoted in Garson, *The Democratic Party and the Politics of Sectionalism*, 58. Hillman made a similar statement before the Anderson Committee in 1944. See Testimony of Sidney Hillman, Anderson Committee Hearings, part 1, 5.

30. The *New Republic* editorial, for example, proclaimed that "[p]olitical action is year-round-every-year work," and the parties should learn from this example. Thus the Democrats must "reverse their usual policy of cutting national headquarters down to a skeleton staff between elections and instead strengthen their forces" if they were to improve their fortunes in 1948. "We Were Licked!," *New Republic*, November 18, 1946, 656.

31. E. E. Schattschneider, *Party Government* (New Brunswick, NJ: Transaction Press, 1942/ 2004), 163.

32. Although an Anti-Saloon League "campaign committee" was set up in the 1928 campaign, it seems to have been purely an accounting matter.

33. Cowan-Brophy-Walsh Report, 15.

34. See Louis Galambos, "The Emerging Organizational Synthesis in Modern American History," *Business History Review* 44, no. 3 (1970): 280.

35. The Cowan-Brophy-Walsh Report did briefly consider whether the reporting requirements of the Federal Corrupt Practices Act of 1925 might have any bearing on the activities of state

CIO councils, thus necessitating a separation of state political committees, but concluded that any potential requirements were not sufficiently "serious" (11).

36. Cowan-Brophy-Walsh Report, 10.

37. Ibid.

38. Ibid. Permitting participation from non-CIO unions and liberal groups was "[t]he principal reason for the separation of the political agency from the state councils," the Cowan-Brophy-Walsh Report emphasized (10). It also noted elsewhere that "a national organization directed solely by the CIO" was "out of the question" (17).

39. This linkage was so strong that Cook describes the NCPAC as "the non-labor branch" of the CIO P.A.C., and as, "in effect, a subsidiary" of it. Gloria Resch Cook, "The Relationship Between Political Parties and Pressure Groups" (master's thesis, University of North Carolina, Chapel Hill, 1956), 219, 221.

40. "Investigation of Presidential, Vice Presidential, and Senatorial Campaign Expenditures, 1944," Report of the Special Committee to Investigate Presidential, Vice Presidential, and Senatorial Campaign Expenditures in 1944, US Senate, 79th Cong., 1st sess., March 15, 1945, S. Rep. No. 101 (Washington DC: Government Printing Office, 1945), 23 (hereafter cited as Green Committee Report). See also Cook, "The Relationship Between Political Parties and Pressure Groups," 212, 219, 221.

41. Testimony of Sidney Hillman, Anderson Committee Hearings, part 1, 12, 21. Like P.A.C., the NCPAC was "organized for the purpose of helping to elect Roosevelt and Truman and a progressive Congress" in 1944 and would provide financial support to congressional candidates, he said.

42. As the Green Committee reported, the NCPAC was organized "[a]s a possible means of broadening the source of individual contributions to the Political Action Committee fund" Green Committee Report, 23.

43. Cowan-Brophy-Walsh Report, 19.

44. See War Labor Disputes Act (Smith-Connally Act), 57 Stat. 163 (1943), section 9, amending section 313 of the Federal Corrupt Practices Act of 1925.

45. This point is often neglected, though both Zelizer and Hayward acknowledge that the CIO P.A.C. used treasury money almost exclusively at first. See Julian E. Zelizer, "Seeds of Cynicism: The Struggle over Campaign Finance, 1956–1974," *Journal of Policy History* 14, no. 1 (2002): 76; and Hayward, "Revisiting the Fable of Reform," 455n.

46. Testimony of Sidney Hillman, Anderson Committee Hearings, part 1, 16. According to Hillman's own financial report, these union contributions came to $671,214.11 in total.

47. Ibid., 8, 14. P.A.C. had "made a few modest contributions in connection with the primary campaigns of candidates after consultation with the local organizations of the CIO," Hillman acknowledged (8). A list was included in the published hearings that showed P.A.C. contributions to seventeen individual candidates in eight states, along with one political committee in New York—the "Committee for the Nomination of Win the War Candidates"—which supported state candidates endorsed by the American Labor Party and ALP congressman Vito Marcantonio. The total amount of these contributions was $32,058.44.

48. Foster, *The Union Politic*, 24. See also Green Committee Report, 21–23.

49. The national P.A.C. endorsed Roosevelt on May 17, 1944. See Testimony of Sidney Hillman, Anderson Committee Hearings, part 1, 8.

50. See Green Committee Report, 22; and Testimony of Sidney Hillman, Anderson Committee Hearings, part 1, 16.

51. Green Committee Report, 21.

52. Testimony of Sidney Hillman, Anderson Committee Hearings, part 1, 13, 17. Hillman explained that P.A.C. had both a "Trade-Unions Contributions Account" and an "Individual Contributions Account" for voluntary donations (13). From July 23, 1944 to August 15, 1944, the Individual Contributions Account had received $17,127.50 in donations, he told the committee (17). Modern "connected" PACs, that is, those established and administered by a labor organization or corporation, are also defined as "separate segregated funds," denoting the separation of their voluntary financing from the sponsoring organization's treasury accounts. See "Understanding Nonconnected PACs,"

Federal Election Commission, https://www.fec.gov/help-candidates-and-committees/registering-pac/understanding-nonconnected-pacs/].

53. Testimony of Sidney Hillman, Anderson Committee Hearings, part 1, 16. See also 22–23 and Green Committee Report, 22.

54. Testimony of Sidney Hillman, Anderson Committee Hearings, part 1, 17, 22. These loans came from individuals, Hillman asserted, rather than the unions themselves. Between July 23 and August 15, 1944, the Individual Contributions Account had received $39,750 in loans on top of the $17,172.50 in individual donations and had already disbursed $36,983.50, thus utilizing the loaned money. "Obviously, we did not have the funds," Hillman told the committee, "so we borrowed money from individuals" (22).

55. Ibid., 20.

56. Ibid.

57. Ibid., 22–23.

58. Ibid., 5.

59. Ibid., 30. "Our whole approach is on a nonpartisan basis," Hillman explained. "We do not care what party a candidate belongs to. We have got our program and we will support any Congressman who comes anywhere near supporting that program."

60. Foster, *The Union Politic*, 28–29; and Garson, *The Democratic Party and the Politics of Sectionalism*, 77.

61. The quotation is Biddle's summation of Smith's charge, made in his initial letter dated January 10, 1944. Alongside Smith, Congressman Martin Dies and Senator E. H. Moore also made complaints to Biddle about P.A.C., and copies of these various latters were obtained by the National Association of Manufacturers' legal counsel, Lambert Miller, in 1947. Attorney General Francis Biddle to Congressman Howard W. Smith, April 6, 1944, released by the Department of Justice on April 7, 1944, and sent to, among others, the NAM's legal counsel Lambert Miller. "OHP" to Lambert Miller, June 26, 1947, National Association of Manufacturers (NAM) Records, 1895–2001, accession no. 1411, series V, "Law Department Records," box 62a, Hagley Museum and Library, Wilmington, Delaware (hereafter cited as NAM Records).

62. Attorney General Biddle to Congressman Smith, April 6, 1944, NAM Records. The FBI investigation had revealed general expenditures for personnel, along with the costs of "a 'get out the vote' campaign . . . a campaign in favor of the soldiers vote bill, a full employment conference, and the preparation of a post-war program"—none of which were prohibited by the Smith-Connally Act. The investigation had also found a direct contribution to a gubernatorial candidate in New Jersey, a state election not covered by the law. The Senate's 1944 campaign expenditure committee offered a similar conclusion: "Except for the primary and local elections, the special committee was advised that in no instance did the Political Action Committee transfer any of its funds to a political candidate or committee, for use in connection with a Federal election." See Green Committee Report, 22.

63. Attorney General Biddle to Congressman Smith, April 6, 1944, NAM Records.

64. The Dies Committee began its investigation of P.A.C. in July 1943, according to the statement of its chief investigator, Robert Stripling, during hearings in September 1944. See "Investigation of Un-American Propaganda Activities in the U.S.," *Hearings before the Special Committee on Un-American Activities*, US House of Representatives, vol. 17, 78th Cong., 2nd sess., September 27–29, October 3–5, 1944 (Washington, DC: Government Printing Office, 1944), 10211–10212.

65. "Investigation of Un-American Propaganda Activities in the United States: Report on the CIO Political Action Committee," Report of the Special Committee on Un-American Activities, US House of Representatives, 78th Cong., 2nd sess., March 29, 1944, H.R. Rep. No. 1311 (Washington, DC: Government Printing Office, 1944) (hereafter cited as Dies Committee Report).

66. Attorney General Francis Biddle to Congressman Martin Dies, August 7, 1944, NAM Records, series V, box 62a. Dies had written to Biddle on August 4.

67. Ibid.

68. When polled about labor union political activities by the Roper organization in April 1940, 57 percent of respondents said labor should "keep out of politics altogether," for example,

rather than form a third party or work with the major parties. In August 1946, 52 percent of respondents selected that response. As Truman noted, even union members themselves were often uncomfortable with "political" rather than "collective" action, tending to view "collective bargaining and the strike as the proper sphere of union activity" and "election activity, especially partisanship, as outside this sphere." See Roper Survey, April 1940, and Roper Survey, August 1946, iPOLL Databank, The Roper Center for Public Opinion Research, University of Connecticut, http://www.ropercenter.uconn.edu/data_access/ipoll/ipoll.html; and David B. Truman, *The Governmental Process: Political Interests and Public Opinion* (Berkeley: Institute of Governmental Studies, University of California, Berkeley, 1951/1993), 295, 298–299.

69. Roper/*Fortune* Survey, April 1944, iPOLL Databank, The Roper Center for Public Opinion Research, University of Connecticut, http://www.ropercenter.uconn.edu/data_access/ipoll/ipoll.html.

70. Attorney General Francis Biddle to Senator E. H. Moore, September 23, 1944, NAM Records, series V, box 62a. Smith-Connally had utilized the definition of "labor organization" in the Wagner Act. As codified in section 610 of the US Code: "For the purposes of this section 'labor organization' means any organization of any kind, or any agency or employee representation committee or plan, in which employees participate and which exist for the purpose, in whole or in part, of dealing with employers concerning grievances, labor disputes, wages, rates of pay, hours of employment, or condition of work."

71. Testimony of Sidney Hillman, accompanied by John Abt, Counsel, August 28, 1944. Anderson Committee Hearings, part 1, 27.

72. Ibid.

73. Ibid.

74. As Hillman explained to the Anderson Committee, P.A.C. would not contribute directly to Roosevelt's campaign—that is, to the DNC, which was officially running it—nor to the RNC, as he added later. See Testimony of Sidney Hillman, Anderson Committee Hearings, part 1, 21, 37.

75. Attorney General Biddle to Senator Moore, NAM Records, September 23, 1944.

76. Ibid. Biddle quotes this from Moore's initial letter of August 30, 1944.

77. Ibid.

78. Ibid. Where Biddle denied the appropriateness of such a classification as applied even to the CIO P.A.C., the congressional committee tasked with investigating the 1946 elections (the Priest Committee) concluded that the CIO P.A.C *was*, in fact, a labor organization and thus was prohibited from making campaign contributions irrespective of the voluntary nature of its funds. See "Campaign Expenditures Committee," Report of the Special Committee on Campaign Expenditures, 1946, US House of Representatives, 79th Cong., 2nd sess., December 31, 1946, H.R. Rep. No. 2739 (Washington, DC: Government Printing Office, 1946), 43 (hereafter cited as Priest Committee Report).

79. Attorney General Biddle to Senator Moore, NAM Records, September 23, 1944.

80. Ibid. Moore questioned whether the CIO was itself "engaged in furthering, advancing, or advocating the nomination or election of any candidate" through its literature.

81. Ibid. Biddle's reference to section 9 of the Smith-Connally Act prohibiting *contributions* only applied to section 313 of the Corrupt Practices Act itself, and section 13 of the Hatch Act. CIO legal counsel wrote to P.A.C. regional directors in December 1943, with a similar message. The Smith-Connally Act only applied to federal general election contests, the letter asserted, and had "no application to primary elections, elections of delegates to political conventions, or elections of State or local officials" (21–22). Where it did apply, the act prohibited only "*contributions* of money or any other thing of value by a labor organization." Letter to CIO P.A.C. Regional Directors, December 9, 1943, reproduced in Green Committee Report, 22 (emphasis added).

82. Attorney General Biddle to Senator Moore, September 23, 1944.

83. Testimony of John J. Abt, Green Committee Hearings, part 1, June 13, 1944, 23; also quoted in Green Committee Report, 22. If using general funds to produce and distribute posters, pamphlets, or editorials promoting particular candidates was classified as making contributions subject to the FCPA, Abt also argued, then newspapers publishing editorials on particular candidates must be considered in violation too.

84. Letter to CIO P.A.C. Regional Directors, December 9, 1943, reproduced in Green Committee Report, 22.
85. Ibid.
86. Ibid. See also Melvin I. Urofsky, "Campaign Finance Reform Before 1971," *Albany Government Law Review* 1 (2008): 26.
87. See Louise Overacker, *Money in Elections* (New York: Macmillan, 1932), 242–243, 271–273.
88. Perhaps P.A.C. lawyers feared that such funds might be treated as union "contributions" after the primaries and conventions, since they were given to P.A.C. and used "in connection with" federal elections that now had candidates. Yet the logic underpinning the theory would seem to permit the CIO itself or other unions to make such expenditures. Indeed, that is exactly what Biddle was endorsing, in terms of the CIO paying for the production and distribution of its regular newspaper, for example, even if it contained editorials explicitly advocating for particular candidates. This very issue would, in fact, be considered in more detail by the Supreme Court in *United States v. CIO* (1948), the "CIO News" case, as discussed later in this chapter.
89. These figures are drawn from P.A.C.'s final financial report for 1944, as filed with the Clerk of the House of Representatives and reproduced in the Green Committee Report. It showed that P.A.C. had received $647,903.26 into its trade union account in 1944 and spent $478,498,82, while it had received $376,910.77 into the individual contributions account and spent $470,852.32. This deficit was presumably made up with loans, as Hillman had suggested in his testimony before the Anderson Committee. This final statement differs slightly from the testimony Hillman had given to the Anderson Committee, in which he noted that $671,214.11 had been received by the trade union account by July 23, 1944, of which P.A.C. had spent $371,086.56 ($67,320.48 of which was "expended or contributed in primary campaigns and State elections"). This disparity suggests that either Hillman did not have complete information when he testified before the Anderson Committee in August, or the trade union fund was not completely "frozen" thereafter, as he had assured that committee. See Green Committee Report, 23; Testimony of Sidney Hillman, Anderson Committee Hearings, part 1, 16, 22.
90. "People Not Money Power Behind PAC," *CIO News*, September 4, 1944, 4. The front-page headline for this same story was "Political Strength in People, Not in Funds—CIO PAC" (1).
91. Testimony of Sidney Hillman, Anderson Committee Hearings, part 1, 5.
92. Ibid., 6.
93. Ibid., 8.
94. Ibid., 6.
95. Quote from the CIO's 1943 convention, held November 4 in Philadelphia, reproduced in Attorney General Biddle to Congressman Smith, NAM Records, April 6, 1944.
96. Testimony of Sidney Hillman, Anderson Committee Hearings, part 1, 7.
97. Ibid. (emphasis added).
98. Ibid.
99. Ibid.
100. Ibid., 5. "We conceive of our task as that of political education in the deepest and most practical sense of that word," Hillman said, "education in the full and enlightened exercise of the responsibilities of citizenship."
101. Ibid., 8. See also Foster, *The Union Politic*, 25, on P.A.C.'s registration and turnout drive.
102. Testimony of Sidney Hillman, Anderson Committee Hearings, part 1, 8.
103. Cowan-Brophy-Walsh Report, 2; Garson, *The Democratic Party and the Politics of Sectionalism*, 56.
104. Foster, *The Union Politic*, 25, 42–44.
105. "Political Primer for All Americans" (ca. 1943), CIO-PAC Papers, box 15, folder 12, "PAMS—Politics & Voting, 1940s–1960s."
106. Testimony of Sidney Hillman, Anderson Committee Hearings, part 1, 8.
107. Testimony of Sidney Hillman, Green Committee Hearings, part 1, 12–13. See also Green Committee Report, 21. P.A.C.'s subsequent director, Jack Kroll, made a similar clarification before another congressional committee in 1946, while an internal P.A.C. document from 1951 offered further details: "It is important to realize that National PAC does not itself make any endorsements for Senators, Congressmen, etc. It merely compiles information as to the endorsements made by the state PACs. For obvious reasons it is very wary about

releasing even this data to the public. Thus, newspaper inquiries about endorsements are always shunted to the state PACs for answer." The national P.A.C. did, however, provide information and guidance in the making of these endorsements and could exert more active pressure if necessary. As the document further explained, the national P.A.C. did have "the authority to direct the work of the state PACs" but had "generally relied on advice and persuasion, rather than orders" when the state and national bodies disagreed. Testimony of Jack Kroll, October 14, 1946, Priest Committee Hearings, 93; and Confidential Agenda for CIO-PAC Executive Board Meeting, March 12 and 13, 1951, 4–5, CIO-PAC Papers, box 13, folder 24, "CIO-PAC Meetings, 1946, 1951."

108. Testimony of Sidney Hillman, Anderson Committee Hearings, part 1, 7.

109. Ibid., 8.

110. Ibid. Indeed, Hillman acknowledged the political power of voting records elsewhere in his testimony. Campaigning for Roosevelt and Truman would involve "the distribution of literature," he noted, which would "pay attention to the record of Mr. Dewey, or his lack of record" (21). Part of conducting "a political campaign," he added later, was trying to "bring out the record of the candidates and speak either for them or against them" (29).

111. See Testimony of Samuel Gompers and Frank Morrison, September 10–11, 1913, "Charges Against Members of the House and Lobby Activities of the National Association of Manufacturers of the United States and Others," Hearings before the Select Committee Appointed Under Resolution 198, vol. 4, US House of Representatives, 63rd Cong., 1st sess. (Washington, DC: Government Printing Office, 1913), 2478, 2505, 2547 (hereafter Garrett Committee Hearings).

112. Elisabeth S. Clemens, The People's Lobby: Organizational Innovation and the Rise of Interest Group Politics in the United States, 1890–1925 (Chicago: University of Chicago Press, 1997), 124. Clemens traces the first example at the state level to California in 1913. By 1916, she says, labor unions in several states had followed suit, adopting the "checking up system" as it became known (125, 174). At the national level, Rozell, Wilcox, and Franz attribute the first scorecard to the Farmers Union in 1919, but the National Security League appears to have used the device in the 1918 congressional elections, generating significant backlash. See Mark J. Rozell, Clyde Wilcox, and Michael M. Franz, Interest Groups in American Campaigns: The New Face of Electioneering, 3rd ed. (New York: Oxford University Press, 2011), 114; and John Carver Edwards, "The Price of Political Innocence: The Role of the National Security League in the 1918 Congressional Election," Military Affairs 42, no. 4 (December 1978): 191.

113. Clemens, The People's Lobby, 124–125 (emphasis in original).

114. Ibid.

115. Testimony of Samuel Gompers, September 10, 1913, Garrett Committee Hearings, vol. 4, 2420.

116. Amlie initially sought a federal appointment following his retirement from the House and was nominated to the Interstate Commerce Commission by President Roosevelt, but his nomination was blocked by a group of conservative former colleagues. Amlie ultimately requested it be withdrawn. See Robert E. Long, "Thomas Amlie: A Political Biography" (PhD thesis, University of Wisconsin—Madison, 1969); Foster, The Union Politic, 32; and Franklin D. Roosevelt, "Withdrawal of the Nomination of Thomas R. Amlie for the Interstate Commerce Commission," April 17, 1939, in The American Presidency Project, ed. Gerhard Peters and John T. Woolley, http://www.presidency.ucsb.edu/ws/?pid=15745.

117. Tom Amlie to Arnold Zander (President of S.C. & M. Employees), November 7, 1952, CIO-PAC Papers, box 11, folder 19, "Dudley Correspondence—Democratic National Committee, 1947–56, 1 of 4."

118. Ibid.

119. The UDA was formed at a meeting in New York on May 10, 1941. "Four Years of UDA," [n.d., ca. 1945], p. 1, Americans for Democratic Action Records 1932–1965 [MSS 3], series 1, Union for Democratic Action Administrative file, box 15, "Go-Ke," folder 1-15-7, "History of the UDA," Wisconsin Historical Society, Madison, Wisconsin (hereafter cited as ADA Records).

120. "A Congress to Win the War," *New Republic*, May 18, 1942 (Part II), 683, Thomas Amlie Papers [MSS 452], Public Papers, box 72, folder 2, "'A Congress to Win the War' (New Republic Supplement), Published version, May 1942," Wisconsin Historical Society, Madison, Wisconsin (hereafter cited as Amlie Papers).

121. On LNPL scorecards and grades, mentioned in the previous chapter, see Emily J. Charnock, "More Than a Score: Interest Group Ratings and Polarized Politics," *Studies in American Political Development* 32, no. 1 (April 2018): 4, 8.

122. *Editorial Research Reports*, for example, the forerunner of *Congressional Quarterly*, identified three "widely circulated compilations" of roll call votes in the 1942 campaign, one published in March by the national League of Women Voters, another by the *Christian Science Monitor* in May, and the UDA's compilation, published in the *New Republic*, also in May. The UDA compilation was "the one that has attracted most attention," the report observed. "Roll Calls in 1942 Campaign," *Editorial Research Reports* I (1942),http://library.cqpress.com/cqresearcher/cqresrre1942062000.

123. Amlie continued to be involved with the UDA, however; he was still a member of its board of directors in July 1944, for example. See Minutes of UDA Board of Directors Meeting, July 7, 1944, Amlie Papers, Public Papers, box 85, folder 10, "Union for Democratic Action (UDA)—Executive Board & Committee Meetings, 1942–1946."

124. "The Record of Congress and What It Means to You." Special legislative supplement, *CIO News*, June 19, 1944.

125. *Keeping Score to Win the War*, Publication No. 87 (Washington, DC: Congress of Industrial Organizations, 1943), "CIO Publications: Pamphlets," box 2, Political and Social Activism Pamphlet Collection, University of Illinois at Chicago Special Collections, Chicago, IL. This scorecard, based on twenty measures of concern to labor, was attributed by HUAC to P.A.C., but the inside cover of the pamphlet states that the roll-call analysis had initially appeared *in Ammunition*, the UAW's monthly magazine. The pamphlet, which included an introductory article alongside the voting analysis, was then circulated by the National CIO Special Committee on Congressional Action "in connection with the national campaign authorized by the CIO Executive Board." This scorecard is noted in the Dies Committee Report, 35.

126. "The Record of Congress and What It Means to You," H. According to Edwards, the National Security League *had* used right/wrong terminology in its 1918 "Loyalty Chart" for the House, which highlighted votes on eight "preparedness" measures relating to World War I, but its actions provoked fierce criticism among lawmakers and generated a congressional inquiry. For a comparable Senate chart, the League actually removed this terminology and simply recorded lawmakers' positions as "for" or "against." See Edwards, "The Price of Political Innocence," esp. 191–192, 194.

127. "If Rankins Rankle, It's Up to You to Change Them!," *CIO News*, October 2, 1944, 7.

128. The question was asked by Congressman Coe. Testimony of Jack Kroll, Priest Committee Hearings, part 2, 93.

129. Ibid., 99.

130. Ibid., 93.

131. The national P.A.C. distributed its voting records as a newsletter but also may have provided more extensive voting records to state and local PACs. As national P.A.C. research director Mary Goddard observed in the early 1950s: "Years of experimentation have brought general agreement that the most useful kind of voting record for political action are master records containing a maximum number of votes for each year together with a full but concise description of the meaning of the vote." Such "master records" were the most useful to subnational PACs, she noted, who then had some flexibility to emphasize the most important issues locally. Goddard, "Research for Political Action" [n.d. but ca. early 1950s], 5, CIO-PAC Papers, box 17, folder 22, "Political Research by Labor Unions." See also box 12, folder 4, "PAC Congressional Voting Record Newsletter, 1950–52."

132. In the UDA's 1942 scorecard, for example, Amlie purposely added domestic policy issues to what had initially been envisaged as a foreign policy scorecard, in order to improve the records of some liberals who had opposed US entry into World War II while making those of Southern Democrats—who were generally supportive of intervention—appear worse. See Charnock, "More Than a Score," 7.

133. *Keeping Score to Win the War*, 2.
134. Ibid.
135. "The Record of Congress and What It Means to You," E. The other issues detailed were the soldiers' vote, tax measures, poll tax repeal, the Smith-Connally Act, food subsidies, and price control.
136. "Partisan or Non-Partisan," *CIO News*, July 10, 1944, 4.
137. Testimony of Sidney Hillman, Anderson Committee Hearings, part 1, 5 (emphasis added).
138. Ibid. Speaking to journalists just before the election, Hillman told them that P.A.C. was not aiming to "capture or be captured by" the Democratic Party. See "Hillman Tells Press PAC 'Facts of Life,'" *CIO News*, November 6, 1944, 7.
139. "Hillman Tells Press PAC 'Facts of Life,'" 7.
140. Cowan-Brophy-Walsh Report, 21.
141. Ibid.
142. Ibid., 23.
143. Ibid., 22.
144. Ultimately, P.A.C. wanted both, but looked to achieve a liberal majority in Congress *via* a liberal Democratic majority.
145. Cowan-Brophy-Walsh Report, 22.
146. Ibid., 16.
147. "'A Congress to Win the War,'" 697.
148. Quoted in Gaer, *The First Round*, 61 (emphasis added).
149. Testimony of Sidney Hillman, Anderson Committee Hearings, part 1, 5. Both Murray and Hillman drew from the CIO's 1943 convention resolution on political action, which ruled out a third party in 1944.
150. Hillman had helped found the American Labor Party in New York State in the 1930s and had been involved with the Conference for Progressive Political Action in the 1920s. For a discussion of earlier subnational third-party efforts in New York, Chicago, and Seattle involving labor organizations, see Andrew Strouthous, *U.S. Labor and Political Action, 1918–24* (London: Macmillan, 2000).
151. Testimony of Sidney Hillman, Anderson Committee Hearings, part 1, 34.
152. Ibid., 36.
153. Zelizer, "Seeds of Cynicism," 76.
154. Mark Sullivan, "Communist, CIO Acts to Have Deep Effect on Political Parties," *Washington Post*, May 28, 1944.
155. Garson, *The Democratic Party and the Politics of Sectionalism*, 117. A number of CIO members served as delegates or alternates at the convention, too, with some holding positions of responsibility on important convention committees, Garson notes. See 116–122 for an extensive discussion of the CIO's 1944 convention efforts on behalf of Wallace. On CIO backing for Wallace, see, for example, "PAC-CIO Backs Wallace as FDR Running Mate," *CIO News*, June 19, 1944, 3.
156. Garson, *The Democratic Party and the Politics of Sectionalism*, 120, 123. The phrase was reported by Arthur Krock of the *New York Times*, though its veracity was questioned for some time.
157. Testimony of Sidney Hillman, Anderson Committee Hearings, part 1, 7.
158. Ben W. Gilbert, "GOP Snubs CIO Political Committee," *Washington Post*, June 26, 1944, 1.
159. Green Committee Report, 20.
160. "The CIO Plays Its Part," *CIO News*, November 13, 1944, 8.
161. Samuel Grafton, writing in the *Chicago Sun*, November 11, 1944, quoted in E. E. Schattschneider, "P.A.C. and Party Organization," ca. 1953, E.E. Schattschneider Papers, 1901–1907, call no. 1000-9, box 2, folder 37, "Political Action Committees and Party Organization, Notes and Drafts, circa 1953," Wesleyan University Special Collections and Archives, Middletown, Connecticut.
162. Green Committee Report, 23. According to this report, NCPAC "solicited contributions from the general public and filed a financial statement with the Clerk of the House of Representatives as the law required." It had received a total of $380,306.45 in contributions and made expenditures of $378,424.78. If added to the spending from both P.A.C. accounts

($949,351.14 when voluntary and trade union accounts were combined), the total expenditure from P.A.C. and NCPAC sources was $1,327,775.92 (23).

163. Ibid., 21. The $949,351.14 spent by the national P.A.C. did not include expenditures of state and local PACs, which the CIO claimed were separate intrastate bodies and thus not subject to the disclosure requirements of the Corrupt Practices Act (21). As detailed elsewhere in the Green Committee Report, the DNC spent $2,056,121.58 (79).

164. Garson, *The Democratic Party and the Politics of Sectionalism*, 76; and Foster, *The Union Politic*, 28. Foster points to Jack Kroll's belief that Dies actually *over*estimated CIO strength in his district.

165. Garson, *The Democratic Party and the Politics of Sectionalism*, 76. Starnes was defeated by Albert Rains, "a state legislator who had been cultivated by the CIO as the result of his open sympathy for organized labor," Garson notes.

166. Ibid. See also Foster, *The Union Politic*, 29.

167. Foster, for example, notes that P.A.C. "never published a complete list of its primary endorsements," while the national office staffers directed all inquiries about endorsements to state PACs rather than releasing comprehensive information themselves, according to a 1951 internal document. "For obvious reasons" the national P.A.C. was "very wary about releasing even this data to the public," it explained. See Foster, *The Union Politic*, 28; and Confidential Agenda for CIO-PAC Executive Board Meeting, March 12 and 13, 1951, 5, CIO-PAC Papers, box 13, folder 24, "CIO-PAC Meetings, 1946, 1951."

168. This is a state-by-state descriptive article, rather than a statistical summary. Drawing from the information it contains, at least 107 successful Democratic candidates for House and Senate elections had local CIO backing, as did a further 17 who lost (several more Democrats are mentioned in the overview, but CIO support is not explicitly confirmed). In contrast, CIO groups backed just five successful Republican candidates, including Senate incumbent George Aiken in Vermont and candidate Wayne Morse in Oregon, plus a congressional candidate in California and two in Ohio. One other Republican candidate with CIO support lost the general election (Elmer Gabbard in Kentucky). The overview also points to CIO interventions in two Republican primaries: successfully opposing William Lambertson in Kentucky and unsuccessfully opposing Gerald Nye in North Dakota, though Nye went on to lose the general election. "Exclusive! Labor Angle on FDR Sweep, State by State," *CIO News*, November 13, 1944, 6–7, 10.

169. The *CIO News* described "an improved Congress" with "[m]any CIO-backed candidates . . . returned" in its November 13 edition and pointed to "the change for the better of Congress' complexion" on November 20. *Editorial Research Reports* also stated that "[t]he leadership of the President . . . was strengthened by the congressional primaries and elections of 1944," but noted of the next congressional session that "the Truman program met resistance from the same coalition of conservatives that had obstructed much of the Roosevelt program." Democrats gained twenty seats in the House in 1944, while the composition of the Senate was unchanged by the election. Jordan suggests that Republicans fully expected to win majority control in 1944, and thus the marginal Democratic gains were more impressive than they might appear. See "Exclusive! Labor Angle on FDR Sweep, State by State," 6; "Political Action Big Success: Keep Your Eyes on Congress," *CIO News*, November 20, 1944, 4; "Record of the 78th Congress (Second Session)," *Editorial Research Reports* II (1944), http://library.cqpress.com/cqresearcher/cqresrre1944122000; "Record of the 79th Congress (First Session)," *Editorial Research Reports* II (1945), http://library.cqpress.com/cqresearcher/cqresrre1945122100; and David M. Jordan, *FDR, Dewey, and the Election of 1944* (Bloomington: Indiana University Press, 2011), 325.

170. "Labor, militant, alert, and organized as never before, deserves credit for President Roosevelt's reelection," Thomas L. Stokes concluded in the *Daily Oklahoman*, as reported by E. E. Schattschneider in an unpublished overview of the 1944 election and P.A.C.'s role. Schattschneider also pointed to the importance of foreign affairs and Roosevelt himself, in addition to labor's role. See Schattschneider, "P.A.C. and Party Organization," esp. 8. See also Truman, *The Governmental Process*, 313; and Tom Amlie to Arnold Zander, November 7, 1952, on credit given to labor and Roosevelt's own contribution.

171. Ernest Lindley, "FDR's Party Also Should Study Vote," *Washington Post*, November 19, 1944, B5. Schattschneider classifies Lindley as "friendly," and makes reference to this quote, in "P.A.C. and Party Organization," 4–5.

172. Raymond Moley, writing in the *New York Times*, November 17, 1944, quoted in Schattschneider, "P.A.C. and Party Organization," 2.

173. Noted in Garson, *The Democratic Party and the Politics of Sectionalism*, 129.

174. Schattschneider, "Samuel Grafton's Analysis," in "P.A.C. and Party Organization," 2.

175. Radford E. Mobley in the *Detroit Free Press*, November 12, 1944, quoted in Schattschneider, "P.A.C. and Party Organization," 7.

176. Journalist Marquis Childs, for example, observed in his post-election analysis that "[a] great deal of the work that a Democratic organization might have done was taken care of this time by the regional offices of the Political Action Committee." Marquis Childs in the *St. Louis Post-Dispatch*, November 13, 1944, quoted in Schattschneider, "P.A.C. and Party Organization," 3.

177. Schattschneider, "P.A.C. and Party Organization," 4. Schattschneider summarizes an interview with Hannegan, published in the *St. Louis Post-Dispatch* on November 17, 1944, in which "Hannegan said that his policy was to cooperate with the PAC and other groups such as . . . the American Labor Party, but he insisted that PAC did not dictate to Democratic national headquarters or interfere with campaign strategy. He insisted also that there were no ill feelings between PAC and the party organization, in spite of the efforts of opposition newspapers to start trouble."

178. Thomas L. Stokes, writing in the *Daily Oklahoman*, November 9, 1944, quoted in Schattschneider, "P.A.C. and Party Organization," 5.

179. Testimony of Sidney Hillman, Anderson Committee Hearings, part 1, 21.

180. Green Committee Report, 23.

181. As the Green Committee had reported, the NCPAC "was intended to function not later than November 7, 1944, in support of the candidacies of Franklin D. Roosevelt and Harry Truman, and 'progressive' candidates for the Senate and House of Representatives" (Green Committee Report, 23).

182. Republicans gained fifty-six House seats in 1946 and thirteen in the Senate. See Table 2-3, "Net Party Gains in House and Senate Seats, General and Special Elections, 1946–2006," in Norman J. Ornstein, Thomas E. Mann, and Michael J. Malbin, *Vital Statistics on Congress 2008* (Washington, DC: Brookings Institution Press), 54.

183. Priest Committee Report, 31.

184. Testimony of Jack Kroll, Priest Committee Hearings, part 2, 144, 147, 163. Without a presidential contest to structure its activities, P.A.C. had delayed switching to voluntary funds until September 3, Kroll explained in his testimony, at which point "most of the primaries were out of the way, and there were candidates in most of the States" (144). It still did not make direct contributions to candidates, he affirmed, and later denied that it solicited any contributions for candidates without handling the money itself (147, 163).

185. The *CIO News* reported that P.A.C.-backed candidates had defeated several Southern Democrats, listing various House contests in Florida, Georgia, Missouri, North Carolina, Oklahoma, and Virginia, plus an unsuccessful effort in Alabama. It also noted P.A.C. involvement in one Democratic primary outside of the South, in Wisconsin, where P.A.C. supported challenger Edmund Bobrowicz over "anti-labor" incumbent Thad Wasielewski, though Wasielewski had received local CIO support in 1944. In the two House Republican primaries mentioned, P.A.C. opposed incumbents Thomas Winter in Kansas and Robert Rodgers in Pennsylvania. See "16 Wins for PAC," *CIO News*, August 19, 1946, 8A. On CIO support for Wasielewski in 1944, see "Exclusive! Labor Angle on FDR Sweep, State by State," 10.

186. Testimony of Jack Kroll, Priest Committee Hearings, part 2, 150–151. Kroll also mentioned Missouri as a state where the national P.A.C. provided assistance in a primary (in Kansas City), and claimed it was active "in practically every one of the States in which there were primaries." Of the states Kroll mentioned specifically, only Texas was not listed in the overview of primary successes published in the *CIO News* on August 19, 1946. See "16 Wins for PAC," 8A.

187. "16 Wins for PAC," 8A. According to the *CIO News*, P.A.C. supported Republican Senate candidate Ralph Flanders, who won his primary in Vermont and went on to win the general election, and opposed incumbent Republican senator Henrik Shipstead of Minnesota (previously Farmer-Labor), who lost his primary. P.A.C. also opposed Democratic incumbents Charles Gossett in Idaho, George Radcliffe in Maryland, and Burton K. Wheeler in Montana, all of whom lost their primary contests.

188. Truman, *The Governmental Process*, 306.

189. "We Were Licked!," *New Republic*, November 18, 1946, 656.

190. Ibid.

191. Ibid.

192. See Priest Committee Report, 27–36.

193. As noted in chapter 1, the CPUSA was revived in 1945.

194. Garson, *The Democratic Party and the Politics of Sectionalism*, 58. In March 1944 the AFL announced that, unlike P.A.C., it would adhere to labor's traditional "nonpartisan" political policy of "rewarding our friends and punishing our enemies." See Louis Stark, "Labor Leaders Active in Pre-Campaign Moves: While AFL Continues 'Nonpartisan,' CIO Works for Roosevelt," *New York Times*, March 5, 1944, 6E.

195. See Harry S. Truman, "Veto of the Taft-Hartley Labor Bill," June 20, 1947, in *The American Presidency Project*, ed. Gerhard Peters and John T. Woolley, http://www.presidency.ucsb. edu/ws/?pid=12675.

196. See Anthony Corrado, "Money and Politics: A History of Federal Campaign Finance Law," in *Campaign Finance Reform: A Sourcebook*, ed. Anthony Corrado, Thomas E. Mann, Daniel R. Ortiz, Trevor Potter, and Frank J. Sorauf (Washington, DC: Brookings Institution Press, 1997), 30.

197. Urofsky, "Campaign Finance Reform Before 1971," 27. In *United States v. Classic* (1941), a case stemming from a Louisiana primary contest, the court had recently ruled that Congress *did* have the authority to regulate primary elections, in a departure from *Newberry v. United States* (1921).

198. Section 304 of the Taft-Hartley Act amended section 313 of the Federal Corrupt Practices Act of 1925 so as to prohibit any national bank, corporation, or labor organization from making "a contribution or expenditure in connection with" a federal election or primary, and included as an expenditure "a payment, distribution, loan, advance, deposit, or gift, of money, or anything of value, and includes a contract, promise, or agreement, to make an expenditure, whether or not legally enforceable." See Green Committee Report, 89.

199. This element had originated with the House campaign expenditures committee in 1946 (the Priest Committee), which had recommended classifying PACs as "labor organizations" themselves, since they received some funding from unions even if they also operated a "voluntary" account. See Priest Committee Report, 40, 42–43, 46; and "Labor-Management Relations Act, 1947," Report of the Committee on Education and Labor, US House of Representatives, 80th Cong., 1st sess., April 11, 1947, H.R. Rep. 245 (Washington, DC: Government Printing Office, 1947), 211.

200. Taft's version followed the recommendation of the Senate's 1946 campaign expenditure committee, chaired by Senator Allen J. Ellender (D-LA). As Ellender saw it, the move would neatly stem the use of treasury funds in and around election contests, preventing unions from expending such moneys themselves or doing so via their associated PACs, while still permitting the use of voluntary funds by PACs, which he felt could not be restricted on the grounds of free expression. See *Congressional Record—Senate*, 80th Cong., 1st sess., June 6, 1947, 6522; and Joseph E. Kallenbach, "The Taft-Hartley Act and Union Political Contributions and Expenditures," *Minnesota Law Review* 33, no. 1 (December 1948): 9n29. Also see the opinion in *Pipefitters v. United States*, 407 U.S. 385 (1972).

201. See *Congressional Record—Senate*, 80th Cong., 1st sess., June 5, 1947, 6439.

202. For this point, I am indebted to Paula Baker's (2012) unpublished paper, which details the ways campaign costs increasingly became the costs of *communication* in the early twentieth century: the costs of mass advertising and publicity. Paula Baker, "How Money Became Speech" (unpublished manuscript, July 1, 2012).

203. Summarizing the position of the CIO's executive board, CIO legal counsel Lee Pressman and John J. Abt described section 304 of the Taft-Hartley Act as unconstitutional and asserted the First Amendment rights of a labor organization to "disseminate information about and statements of its position on federal candidates" through its own publications or broadcasts. In an earlier memo making legal recommendations to the board, Pressman cited the opinion of Attorney General Biddle in response to the Smith-Connally Act, that he could "hardly conceive" any congressional intent to proscribe "expressions of opinion by labor unions or by newspapers." President Truman also referenced such concerns in his Taft-Hartley veto message, describing the expenditure restriction as "a dangerous intrusion on free speech" that could apply to media companies as much as unions. See CIO Legal Department (Lee Pressman and John J. Abt), "Memorandum on Political Activity under the Taft-Hartley Act," July 23, 1947, 1–2; and CIO Legal Department (Lee Pressman, Eugene Cotton, and Frank Donner), "Memorandum re: Taft-Hartley Bill, Presented to CIO Executive Board, June 27, 1947," 2, both in CIO-PAC Papers, box 13, folder 2, "Legal Department Correspondence, 1945–49." See also Attorney General Francis Biddle to Senator E. H. Moore, September 23, 1944, NAM Records, series V, box 62a; and Truman, "Veto of the Taft-Hartley Labor Bill," June 20, 1947.

204. *Thomas W. Bowe v. Secretary of the Commonwealth of Massachusetts*, 69 N.E.2d 115 (1946). This case is noted in Pressman and Abt's "Memorandum on Political Activity under the Taft-Hartley Act," July 23, 1947, 2.

205. *United States v. Congress of Industrial Organizations*, 335 U.S. 106 (1948). The editorial had been penned by CIO president Philip Murray, urging support for a Democratic congressional candidate in a Maryland special election. The government charged that the editorial had also been circulated at CIO expense outside of the membership and obtained an indictment against the union for the *expenditures* involved in publishing and circulating the newsletter using treasury funds. Initially, the US District Court for the District of Columbia dismissed the case, claiming the statute was unconstitutional on First Amendment grounds, but the Supreme Court avoided those issues on appeal, ruling internal communications exempt from the ban and finding evidence that the CIO had circulated the editorial more widely to be inconclusive. On the Court's opinion, see Urofsky, "Campaign Finance Reform Before 1971," 27.

206. *United States v. United Automobile, Aircraft and Agricultural Workers*, 352 U.S. 567 (1957). The UAW was indicted for using treasury funds to sponsor television broadcasts that allegedly urged support for certain congressional and senatorial candidates in Michigan during the 1954 elections. The District Court had dismissed the indictment, but the Supreme Court reversed the dismissal. The Court's majority opinion discerned a congressional intent to proscribe *commercial* broadcasts since they involved broad public dissemination, but it did not offer a definitive opinion, instead remanding the case back to the District Court for trial. The jury was instructed to consider whether the broadcast was *intended to* and *did influence* the general public, and found the UAW not guilty. See Urofsky, "Campaign Finance Reform Before 1971," 27. For an argument that the Court incorrectly depicted congressional intent on the issue of commercial broadcasts, see Hayward, "Revisiting the Fable of Reform," 421–470.

207. Offering legal guidance to a local union leader in 1954, for example, P.A.C. assistant director Tilford Dudley restated the CIO's official view that the Taft-Hartley prohibitions on union political expenditures were unconstitutional and that explicit candidate advocacy, paid for by union treasury funds, was theoretically acceptable. Nonetheless, he observed that "CIO unions usually have not gone this far in their activity" due in part to legal uncertainty, as well as a lack of funds to some extent. Tilford E. Dudley to Rollin Everett, July 29, 1954, 1, 3, CIO-PAC Papers, box 17, folder 11, "Union Political Activity/Campaign Expenditures— Legal Opinions, 1940s–50s."

208. On the Anti-Saloon League, see chapter 2, note 190. The 1944 Anderson Committee report also noted that many labor unions and corporations had "taken the position that they may engage in activities more or less verging on the political, during as well as between political campaigns, so long as they operate indirectly through organizations and programs which they regard as educational." See Anderson Committee Report, 9.

209. On the postwar context shaping passage of the Federal Regulation of Lobbying Act, see Belle Zeller, "The Federal Regulation of Lobbying Act," *American Political Science Review* 42, no. 2 (April 1948): 242. On various lobby registration proposals from 1913 onward, see Edgar Lane, "Some Lessons from Past Congressional Investigations of Lobbying," *Public Opinion Quarterly* 14, no. 1 (1950): 20–21. As Zeller notes, Congress had previously passed limited registration requirements in specific areas; for example, shipping interests that lobbied the US government were required to register with the United States Maritime Commission, while those who lobbied on behalf of foreign governments were regulated under the Foreign Agents Registration Act of 1938 (239–240).

210. See the ruling in *United States v Harriss,* 347 U.S. 612 (1954). See also Charles B. Nutting and W. Edward Sell, "Modern Lobbying and Its Control," *Rocky Mountain Law Review* 26, no. 4 (June 1954): 403; and Emanuel Celler, "Pressure Groups in Congress," *Annals of the American Academy of Political and Social Science* 319 (September 1958): 5–6. A Democratic congressman from New York, Celler was chairman of the House Judiciary Committee.

211. Truman, *The Governmental Process*, 311. He also characterized NAM propaganda in a similar light.

212. As P.A.C. assistant director Tilford Dudley explained in 1954, "[i]t is ... generally believed that educational work concerning economic and political issues can be carried on with the use of trade union funds" during campaign periods and that "[s]uch publications, programs, etc., may properly indicate the action or inaction, votes or other positions and attitudes of people in public life on the issues being discussed." The *records* of particular lawmakers could thus be highlighted as "simply a matter of reporting the facts of current public life." But, he added, "we do not recommend that educational publications or programs financed by union money include a recommendation as to how the reader should vote in a federal election," since to do so would be "legally uncertain." Dudley to Rollin Everett, July 29, 1954, 2.

213. Truman, *The Governmental Process*, 320. In this respect, the contemporary tax concerns appear more related to *lobbying* than to campaign activities, since restrictions on legislative advocacy by nonprofit or charitable organizations were first built into the tax code in the Revenue Act of 1934, while equivalent restrictions relating to *campaign* activity were not added until the Revenue Act of 1954 (the result of an amendment offered by then-Senate minority leader Lyndon Johnson). Nonetheless, interest groups that sought influence in both the legislative and electoral arenas, or those primarily attuned to the latter, may still have viewed political activities as an area of uncertainty in relation to their tax status and chosen a more cautious approach. Even in 1934, legislators had considered extending the prohibition to "participation in partisan politics," but the idea was dropped in conference— perhaps reflecting limited evidence of this problem at that time. See Judith E. Kindell and John Francis Reilly, "Election Year Issues," 2002 Exempt Organizations Continuing Professional Education (CPE) Text, 336, www.irs.gov/pub/irs-tege/eotopici02.pdf.

214. Truman, *The Governmental Process*, 320 (emphasis added).

215. Lecture no. 7, "Political Tactics and Aims of Organized Labor," updated February 18, 1957, in Personal Papers of V. O. Key, accession no. 2000-078, box 9, "Writings: "Politics, Parties, and Pressure Groups," folder "Chap. III, 'Workers,' Mss. Notes and Revisions," John F. Kennedy Presidential Library, Boston, MA (hereafter cited as V. O. Key Papers).

216. Harmon Zeigler, *Interest Groups in American Society* (Englewood Cliffs, NJ: Prentice-Hall, 1964), 149–150.

217. Minutes of the National Committee of Labor's League for Political Education, November 17, 1948, 1, in V. O. Key Papers, box 9, folder "Chapter III—4th ed. Materials Used. Folder 2 of 2." As explained at the AFL convention that year, "no matter how many favorable votes a Congressman had on other issues, an unfavorable vote on the Taft-Hartley Act disqualifies him from receiving L.L.P.E. support." See "AFL Proceedings, 1948," in box 9, folder "Chap. III, 'Workers,' Materials Used."

218. "The CIO-PAC and How It Works," 1.

219. Ibid., 1–2.

220. Foster, *The Union Politic*, 10–11.

221. Gaer, *The First Round*, 49. Gaer was P.A.C.'s publicity director. As LaPalombara observed, this claim was only valid "[i]f the terms 'politics' and 'labor' are used in a very broad sense."

See Joseph G. LaPalombara, "Pressure, Propaganda, and Political Action in the Elections of 1950," *Journal of Politics* 14, no. 2 (1952): 313.

222. See Cowan-Brophy-Walsh Report, esp. 23.

223. "Confidential—Report of NAM Representatives Who Attended National Citizens Political Action Committee School, Washington, D.C., June 26–29, 1946—General Impressions of Miss McKane," NAM Records, series 1, general files, box 307, "Folder—N.A.M.—Miscellaneous, National Citizens Action Political Action Committee School, 1946."

224. "Confidential—Report of NAM Representatives Who Attended National Citizens Political Action Committee School, Washington, D.C., June 26–29, 1946—General Impressions of Messrs. Swanson and Buergelin," NAM Records, series 1, box 307, "Folder—N.A.M.—Miscellaneous. National Citizens Action Political Action Committee School, 1946."

225. C. B. Baldwin, quoted in the *Springfield Republican,* November 12, 1944, in Schattschneider, "P.A.C. and Party Organization," 6.

226. Jack Kroll in the *New Republic,* October 21, 1946, quoted in Chamber of Commerce Employer-Employee Relations Department, *Labor in Politics* (Washington, DC: US Chamber of Commerce, 1950), 13, in V. O. Key Papers, box 9, "Writings: "Politics, Parties, and Pressure Groups," folder "Chap III—'Workers'—Political Tactics."

227. "A Day to Day Account of the Activities of CIO-PAC at the Democratic Convention" (1948), 7, CIO-PAC Papers, box 17, folder 12, "1948 Campaign & DNC." Dudley was an active party organizer who had served as the District of Columbia's delegate to the 1948 Democratic Convention. Approximately fifty-five CIO members served as delegates or alternates. See "CIO Members of State Delegations," CIO-PAC Papers, box 17, folder 12, "1948 Campaign & DNC."

228. On the risks of "capture," see Paul Frymer, *Uneasy Alliances: Race and Party Competition in America* (Princeton, NJ: Princeton University Press, 199); and Christopher Witko, "The Ecology of Party-Organized Interest Relationships," *Polity* 41, no. 2 (2009): 230.

Chapter 6

1. Quoted in Nathan E. Cowan, John Brophy, and J. Raymond Walsh, "Memorandum to President Philip Murray," December 30, 1942, 24, Wayne County AFL-CIO Papers, box 25, CIO Political Programs folder, Walter P. Reuther Library, Wayne State University, Detroit, Michigan (hereafter cited as Cowan-Brophy-Walsh Report).

2. On the circumstances of Wallace's dismissal, see Robert A. Garson, *The Democratic Party and the Politics of Sectionalism, 1941–1948* (Baton Rouge: Louisiana State University Press, 1974), 225–226.

3. Henry A. Wallace, "Why a Third Party in 1948?," *Annals of the American Academy of Political and Social Science* 259 (September 1948): 10.

4. Ibid., 15.

5. Cowan-Brophy-Walsh Report, 22.

6. See Robert H. Zieger, *The CIO: 1935–1955* (Chapel Hill: University of North Carolina Press, 1995), 268. Wallace announced his presidential candidacy on December 29, 1947.

7. Ibid.

8. Harmon Zeigler, *Interest Groups in American Society* (Englewood Cliffs, NJ: Prentice-Hall, 1964), 155.

9. In 1948 the national P.A.C. director had dissolved California's state PAC and local PACs in New York City and Newark, New Jersey, which had refused "to follow CIO policy instead of Wallace policy," and established replacement ones. See Confidential Agenda for CIO-PAC Executive Board Meeting, March 12 and 13, 1951, 4, CIO Political Action Committee (PAC) Collection Papers, 1943–1960s, accession no. 647, box 13, folder 24, "CIO-PAC MEETINGS, 1946, 1951," Walter P. Reuther Library, Wayne State University, Detroit, Michigan (hereafter cited as CIO-PAC Papers).

10. Schlozman makes a similar point, suggesting unions were paying the "price of alliance" with the Democrats. See Daniel Schlozman, *When Movements Anchor Parties: Electoral Alignments in American History* (Princeton, NJ: Princeton University Press, 2015), chapter 6.

11. Text of resolution quoted in Louis Stark, "CIO's Board Votes Against 3d Party for Aid Plan, 33-11," *New York Times*, January 23, 1948, 1.

12. Speech text included in Jack Kroll to Philip Murray, June 24, 1948, 9, in CIO-PAC Papers, box 13, folder 7, "Philip Murray Correspondence, 1945–51."

13. Zieger, *The CIO*, 269. See also Garson, who notes that the CIO went into 1948 having "allocated funds only to candidates for Congress," even though it had approved of Truman's veto of the Taft-Hartley Act (268). On liberal-labor concern with the Truman administration, see Sidney M. Milkis, *The President and the Parties: The Transformation of the American Party System since the New Deal* (New York: Oxford University Press, 1993), 156–159.

14. See Garson, *The Democratic Party and the Politics of Sectionalism*, 268–269; and "A Day to Day Account of the Activities of CIO-PAC at the Democratic Convention," 1948, 1, CIO-PAC Papers, box 17, folder 12, "1948 Campaign & DNC." As Garson notes, the Americans for Democratic Action (ADA) was also heavily involved with this effort to draft Eisenhower and to drop Truman from the ticket more generally (269).

15. Milkis, *The President and the Parties*, 156.

16. On Truman's efforts to win back liberal support, see Garson, *The Democratic Party and the Politics of Sectionalism*, 226–230. In particular, Garson points to a memo by Truman adviser Clark Clifford which recommended ignoring the South and focusing instead upon outreach to "the Negro and labor vote," which he thought would hold the balance of power in the election (230).

17. "Recommendations of the Executive Officers to the Meeting of the CIO Executive Board, Washington, D.C., August 30–31, 1948," 3, CIO-PAC Papers, box 17, folder 12, "1948 Campaign & DNC." The CIO Executive Board voted 35–12 to endorse Truman in August 1948. On the CIO endorsement, see David B. Truman, *The Governmental Process: Political Interests and Public Opinion* (Berkeley, CA: Institute of Governmental Studies, 1951/1993), 301.

18. "Recommendations of the Executive Officers," 3.

19. Zieger, *The CIO*, 267–268.

20. On the ADA endorsement, see Louther S. Horne, "Truman, Barkley Endorsed by ADA; Group Headed by Henderson Condemns Wallace and Dewey and Assails Congress," *New York Times*, August 30, 1948, 10; on the AFL nonendorsement, see Truman, *The Governmental Process*, 301.

21. Truman, *The Governmental Process*, 301.

22. This organization was formed from a merger of the NCPAC with the Independent Citizens Committee of the Arts, Sciences and Professions, along with eight smaller liberal groups, in December 1946. See William R. Conklin, "Wallace Charts Policies for 1948 in Liberal Merger," *New York Times*, December 30, 1946, 1, 9.

23. Conklin, "Wallace Charts Policies for 1948 in Liberal Merger," 9.

24. Ibid. See also "'Liberal' Bodies Merge and Hint at Third Party," *Chicago Daily Tribune*, December 30, 1946, 16.

25. Conklin, "Wallace Charts Policies for 1948 in Liberal Merger," 9.

26. "'Liberal' Bodies Merge and Hint at Third Party," 16.

27. Wallace won 2.38 percent of the popular vote in 1948, while Thurmond won 2.4 percent. Information from *Presidential Elections Since 1789*, 2nd ed. (Washington, DC: Congressional Quarterly, 1979), 89, 95.

28. According to internal P.A.C. documents, 169 of the 239 endorsed House candidates were elected, while 17 of the 21 endorsed Senate candidates won their races. Of the 535 newly elected members of the 81st Congress, 186 had thus received endorsements from P.A.C. Of these, 174 members were Democrats (158 of the 169 congressmen and 16 of the 17 senators). See CIO-PAC Research Department, "Congressional Elections Results, 1948," March 3, 1949, and "Members of Congress Supported by PAC," March 11, 1949, CIO-PAC Papers, box 17, folder 19, "Elections: PAC Research, 1948–54." Slightly different House results are reported elsewhere. Schlozman, for example, notes 215 endorsements and 144 successful House candidates, while a 1949 interview with Jack Kroll suggests 137 of the 215 endorsees won election, with both figures yielding a lower success rate of 64–67 percent. See

Schlozman, *When Movements Anchor Parties*, 140; and Hugh Morrow, "The CIO's Political Hotshot," *Saturday Evening Post*, March 5, 1949, 120.

29. "Summary of 1948 Primaries—August 27, 1948," CIO-PAC Papers, box 17, folder 12, "1948 Campaign & DNC." Of these 105 Democrats, 66 were successful in their primary contests, while 4 of the 14 Republicans won their nominations. This document also lists five other primary contests without indicating the party affiliation of the candidates. It is not clear if any of the four P.AC.-supported Republicans who were successful in their primaries also received P.A.C support in the general election, though at least one such candidate did: Margaret Chase Smith of Maine.

30. Truman did take support for Thurmond into account in awarding federal patronage, along with a lawmaker's support for his Fair Deal legislation, but Dixiecrats were not stripped of their congressional seniority or positions. See Sean J. Savage, "To Purge or Not to Purge: Hamlet Harry and the Dixiecrats, 1948–1952," *Presidential Studies Quarterly* 27, no. 4 (1997): 783.

31. Nelson Lichtenstein, *Walter Reuther: The Most Dangerous Man in Detroit* (Urbana: University of Illinois Press, 1995), 305–306.

32. R. Boeckel and L. Wheildon, "Third Party Movements," July 16, 1947, in *Editorial Research Reports* II (1947).

33. P.A.C. had supported six incumbent GOP representatives who had voted "no" on Taft-Hartley, including Jacob Javits of New York, and five other GOP challengers, including Gerald Ford of Michigan, presumably satisfied with their pro-labor commitments. See CIO-PAC Research Department, "Members of Congress Supported by PAC," March 11, 1949, CIO-PAC Papers, box 17, folder 19, "Elections; PAC Research, 1948–54."

34. P.A.C. did not offer support to at least two other Republican House members who had voted to uphold the veto, William Lemke of North Dakota and Thor Carl Tollefson of Washington. The issue in Lemke's case may have been his third-party associations as the Union Party presidential candidate in 1936. The Tollefson nonendorsement appears to have been linked to tensions between the CIO and AFL in Washington state and the partisan commitments of the local CIO, according to Tollefson's campaign manager, Norm Schut. "The CIO type people were Democratic, period," Schut reflected. See Norm Schut interview, Washington State Oral History Program Olympia, WA, 1989, www.apps.leg.wa.gov/oralhistory/view_resource.aspx?d=1009. Five other Republicans in the 80th Congress had voted "no," three of whom failed to win re-election to the 81st Congress: Homer R. Jones (WA), John C. Brophy (WI) (*not* the CIO official), and John C. Butler (NY). Three Republican senators also voted "no" on Taft-Hartley—Wayne L. Morse (OR), George W. Malone (NV), and William Langer (ND)—but none was up for re-election in 1948. Curiously, P.A.C. did offer support to one Republican senatorial candidate in 1948, Margaret Chase Smith of Maine, who had actually voted to *override* Truman's veto while serving in the House during the 80th Congress. This suggests another violation of a purely issue-based rationale but perhaps reflects the "flexibility of policy" required in a Republican-dominated state like Maine, which may have counseled local support for Smith, who was otherwise regarded as a labor supporter.

35. Quoted in James Caldwell Foster, *The Union Politic: The CIO Political Action Committee* (Columbia: University of Missouri Press, 1975), 197.

36. Ibid., 197–198.

37. Ibid., 198.

38. Memo from Tilford E. Dudley to Clayton Fritchey [Deputy DNC Chairman and Adlai Stevenson's press secretary], December 12, 1952, CIO-PAC Papers, box 11, folder 19, "Dudley Correspondence—Democratic National Committee, 1947–56, 1 of 4."

39. Noting opposition to the move, the *New York Times* reported that "delegations from five AFL locals silently protested this partisan action" at the convention. See A. H. Raskin, "Unanimous A.F.L. Backs Stevenson; But 5 Unions Silently Protest Group's Ending Tradition of Not Taking Sides," *New York Times*, September 24, 1952, 14. On the 1952 endorsement, see Kirk R. Petshek, "The Seventy-First Convention of the AFL," *Monthly Labor Review* 75 (November 1952): 499–501.

40. Tilford E. Dudley to William Millis, 12/19/1952, CIO-PAC Papers, box 11, folder 19, "Dudley Correspondence—Democratic National Committee, 1947–56, 1 of 4."

41. Dudley, "Relations with Democratic Party," copy included in Dudley's correspondence, sent to Roy Reuther, November 1, 1955, CIO-PAC Papers, box 11, folder 20, "Dudley Correspondence—Democratic National Committee, 1947–56, 2 of 4."

42. Foster, *The Union Politic*, 199–201. Kroll's version of this memo, located in Kroll's papers at the Library of Congress and discussed by Foster, appears largely based on Dudley's draft, if framed in stronger terms. Foster portrays Kroll as deeply troubled by the state of the relationship, emphasizing a bleak tone in his memo: "He blasted the Democrats for everything from refusing to give the CIO an official position on the national committee to allowing too many conservative congressmen the use of the party's name," Foster summarizes (199). According to Foster, Kroll outlined several alternatives to the existing political relationship between the CIO and the Democratic Party, all of which are evident in the Dudley draft, if less emphatically stated in some cases. Kroll's suggestions that the CIO might entirely "abandon politics," for example, is framed in Dudley's draft as withholding financial assistance. Kroll's suggestion of a return to a policy of "strict voluntarism," as Foster characterizes it, however, in which they would "endorse neither party" but "extend aid to only a few selected 'friends,'" does not appear evident in Dudley's draft. See Foster, 200-201.

43. Memo from Jack Kroll to Tilford E. Dudley, September 15, 1955, CIO-PAC Papers, box 12, folder 16, "Democratic National Committee, 1954–55, 1 of 2."

44. "The majority of the delegates are sufficiently friendly and the leading Democrats are sufficiently aware of the importance of the labor vote that they listen to our preferences," Dudley observed. While they did not always produce exactly what labor wanted, he believed they were generally responsive. Dudley, "Relations with Democratic Party," 2.

45. Ibid., 2–3.

46. Ibid., 3.

47. Ibid.

48. Ibid., 6–7.

49. APSA Committee on Political Parties, *Toward a More Responsible Two-Party System* (Washington, DC: American Political Science Association, 1950). See "Part II—Proposals for Party Responsibility."

50. Bertram M. Gross to Dudley, February 28, 1950, CIO-PAC Papers, box 11, folder 26, "Congressional Correspondence—1944–51." Gross—a member of the APSA Committee and, at that point, executive secretary of the Council of Economic Advisors—asked Dudley for his reaction to section II, especially, prior to publication of the report. Dudley's lengthy reply encouraged the authors to be more specific in their recommendations if they wanted to "produce results." See Dudley to Bertram Gross, March 6, 1950, 1, CIO-PAC Papers, box 11, folder 26, "Congressional Correspondence—1944–51."

51. Dudley to Democratic National Committee Members and State Chairmen, April 8, 1954, CIO-PAC Papers, box 12, folder 16, "Democratic National Committee, 1954–55, 1 of 2." Rosenfeld also notes the APSA report's influence on other Democratic leaders such as Paul Butler, who was elected as DNC chairman in December 1954. See Sam Rosenfeld, *The Polarizers: Postwar Architects of Our Polarized Era* (Chicago: University of Chicago Press, 2017), 20, 29.

52. Dudley to Ranald Hobbs, Rinhardt & Company Inc, March 17, 1954, and Dudley to Frederick Cushing, Rinehard & Co., Inc., April 26, 1954, CIO-PAC Papers, box 12, folder 16, "Democratic National Committee, 1954–55, 1 of 2."

53. E. E. Schattschneider to Dudley, April 15, 1954, CIO-PAC Papers, box 12, folder 16, "Democratic National Committee, 1954–55, 1 of 2." Dudley's biography, a copy of which is filed in his papers, says he graduated cum laude from Wesleyan in 1928. According to the finding aid for Schattschneider's papers at Wesleyan, he did not join the faculty until 1930. See CIO-PAC Papers, box 13, folder 26 and https://www.wesleyan.edu/libr/sca/FAs/sc1000-9.xml.

54. Dudley, "Relations with Democratic Party," 8.

55. Hower points to the AFL's nonpartisan heritage coming up against the new realities of the political scene as the dominant tension shaping the LLPE's development up to the merger with the CIO. Joseph E. Hower, "'Our Conception of Non-Partisanship Means a Partisan

Non-Partisanship': The Search for Political Identity in the American Federation of Labor, 1947–1955," *Labor History* 51, no. 3 (August 2010): 455–478.

56. Dudley, "Relations with Democratic Party," 8.

57. Ibid.

58. Ibid.

59. An interview with Jack Kroll refers to $300,000 of national P.A.C. funds in 1948 going "directly into the campaign funds of individual candidates in amounts up to $5000 per candidate." A confidential internal document also describes the CIO-P.A.C.'s procedure for making direct contributions to candidates in 1951, which involved making the check out to the candidate or his associates but then sending the check to the state PAC for local officials to deliver in person. See Morrow, "The CIO's Political Hotshot," 119; and Confidential Agenda for CIO-PAC Executive Board Meeting, March 12 and 13, 1951, 3, CIO-PAC Papers, box 13, folder 24, "CIO-PAC MEETINGS, 1946, 1951."

60. Heard's 1952 data file consists of individual index cards detailing contributor, recipient, amount, and state (in some cases a date is also recorded), reproduced by Heard and his research assistants from campaign finance reports filed with Congress. From these cards, P.A.C. appears to have directly contributed to Senate candidates in Connecticut, Massachusetts, Minnesota, Missouri, Montana, Nevada, Washington, West Virginia, Wisconsin, and Wyoming—all Democrats (as well as additional contributions to independent committees supporting Senate candidates in Connecticut, Montana, Nevada, and Wisconsin). P.A.C. also appears to have given to House candidates in Maryland, Ohio, and Wisconsin—again, all Democrats. The notation on these cards is sometimes unclear, however, presenting the possibility that some of these contributions came from state CIO P.A.C. affiliates rather than the national P.A.C. Nonetheless, at least $6,000 was definitively contributed by the national P.A.C., as indicated clearly on the index cards ($3,000 to Henry Jackson, a Democratic Senate candidate in Washington, and $2,000 to William Carlson, a Democratic-Farmer-Labor Senate candidate in Minnesota, as well as $1,000 to an independent committee supporting Democratic candidate Abraham Ribicoff for Senate in Connecticut). Information in Overacker-Heard Campaign Finance Data Archive, box 41, "1952 Democratic, Republican, Labor Party Committee Transfers"; box 42, "1952 Democratic and Labor Party Committee Transfers"; and box 45, "Transfers: Assorted 1952," Institute of Governmental Studies, University of California, Berkeley.

61. All of the LLPE contributions are marked "national," though one ($5,500 to the Committee for the Reelection of Senator Benton in Connecticut) is annotated by hand, "Could this be a state committee?" See box 41, "1952 Democratic, Republican, Labor Party Committee Transfers," Overacker-Heard Campaign Finance Data Archive.

62. In Massachusetts, P.A.C. gave $3,500 to Democrat Foster Furcolo's campaign against Saltonstall and $5,000 to Democrat Charles R. Howell in his campaign against Clifford P. Case in New Jersey. It also gave $1,000 to Edgar A. Brown in South Carolina, a Democratic challenging former Dixiecrat Strom Thurmond. "CIO-PAC Schedule of Contributions— Senatorial, January 1 through December 31, 1954," CIO-PAC Papers, box 13, folder 22, "PAC Contributions—Income and Expenses, 1948–54."

63. Alexander Heard, *The Costs of Democracy* (Chapel Hill: University of North Carolina Press, 1960). See "Table 21: Continuing Labor Political Committees, National Level: Gross Receipts and Disbursements, 1952, 1954, 1956, and 1958," 180–181.

64. Dudley, "Relations with Democratic Party," 8–9. The threat, as Dudley explained, would be to "refuse to support the Party and its candidates in 1956"—not to go elsewhere—"unless the Democrats in Congress agreed to drop the seniority system and to appoint committee chairmen and members on the basis of ability, loyalty to the program, etc." (9).

65. Foster, *The Union Politic*, 200–201. See also note 42.

66. As Dudley summarized his draft when sending it to Roy Reuther, "[t]he general theme is that to get results out of the Democratic Party we need to make it more disciplined or tightly knit and more responsible for carrying out its platform mandates." Tilford Dudley to Roy Reuther, November 1, 1955, CIO-PAC Papers, box 11, folder 20, "Dudley Correspondence— Democratic National Committee, 1947–56, 2 of 4."

67. Dudley, "Relations with Democratic Party," 1.

68. According to information in the Overacker-Heard Campaign Finance Data Archive, the national CIO P.A.C. contributed $8,400 to the DNC in 1952 and also made two other contributions to the DNC, in 1951 ($1,000) and 1954 ($1,000). The national group also contributed $12,500 to various pro-Stevenson committees that were closely aligned with the Democratic Party in 1952, including the Stevenson-Sparkman Forum Committee, the 1952 Campaign Headquarters Travel Committee, and the National Volunteers for Stevenson. See Overacker-Heard Campaign Finance Data Archive, boxes 35 and 42.

69. Dudley, "Relations with Democratic Party," 1.

70. Ibid., 2.

71. Ted Dudley, "The Loyalty Fight in Chicago," July 29, 1952 (sent "to unions in D.C."—pencil notation), CIO-PAC Papers, box 12, folder 18, "National Democratic Party, 1948–54."

72. Dudley, "Relations with Democratic Party," 7 (emphasis added).

73. Mary Goddard, "Research for Political Action" [n.d. but ca. early 1950s], 5, CIO-PAC Papers, box 17, folder 22, "Political Research by Labor Unions." See also box 12, folder 4, "PAC Congressional Voting Record Newsletter, 1950–52."

74. Foster suggests the opposite, claiming that a planned meeting of national, state, and local CIO leaders to determine which strategic alternative to pursue was derailed by merger negotiations, and that in the subsequent frenzy of activity Kroll's eventual recommendations essentially slipped away (*The Union Politic*, 201). This is a surprising conclusion given that the memo was produced in November 1955 and the merger convention occurred just a month later, on December 5, 1955. It is hard to imagine that the memo was not partly concerned with shaping the AFL-CIO's political strategy moving forward, especially since Kroll served as codirector of the newly formed Committee on Political Education (COPE) until his retirement in 1957.

75. Zeigler, *Interest Groups in American Society*, 155. Eisenhower's appointments to the National Labor Relations Board were considered evidence of the difficulties labor would face in this new political environment.

76. Ibid.

77. Hower, "'Our Conception of Non-Partisanship Means a Partisan Non-Partisanship,'" 455.

78. Zeigler, *Interest Groups in American Society*, 155.

79. Ibid., 149–150.

80. Ibid., 155.

81. Ibid.

82. The offer of $2,500 came from lobbyists of the Superior Oil Company. The legislation being debated was H.R. 6645, amending the Natural Gas Act so as to remove federal price regulation. Though President Eisenhower supported the measure, he ultimately vetoed it due to the scandal surrounding Case. See Dwight D. Eisenhower, "Veto of Bill to Amend the Natural Gas Act," February 17, 1956, in *The American Presidency Project*, ed. Gerhard Peters and John T. Woolley, http://www.presidency.ucsb.edu/ws/?pid=10736.

83. Julian E. Zelizer, "Seeds of Cynicism: The Struggle over Campaign Finance, 1956–1974," *Journal of Policy History* 14, no. 1 (2002): 78.

84. Zelizer suggests that the Case incident "increased congressional interest in the issue of campaign finance" and thus helped inspire the two investigations—with Gore conducting a more extensive examination of campaign expenditures in 1956 than most of the recurring investigations ("Seeds of Cynicism," 78). See also Robert E. Mutch, *Buying the Vote: A History of Campaign Finance Reform* (New York: Oxford University Press, 2014), 268–269n8.

85. Zelizer, "Seeds of Cynicism," 78.

86. Ibid., 78, 80.

87. Julian E. Zelizer, *On Capitol Hill: The Struggle to Reform Congress and Its Consequences, 1948–2000* (New York: Cambridge University Press, 2004). Zelizer points to Gore as an important player in this burgeoning movement for campaign finance reform—composed of liberal activists and allies—who saw greater regulation in this area as one way of reducing the electoral advantages enjoyed by conservative Democratic legislators from the South.

88. Heard, *The Costs of Democracy*, 180–181.

89. Milkis, *The President and the Parties*, 164.

90. Zelizer, "Seedsof Cynicism," 79.

91. Testimony of James L. McDevitt, Co-Director of the AFL-CIO Committee on Political Education, September 10, 1956, "1956 Presidential and Senatorial Campaign Contributions and Practices," *Hearings Before the Subcommittee on Privileges and Elections of the Senate Committee on Rules and Administration*, part 1, US Senate, 84th Cong., 2nd sess., September 10 and 11, 1956 (Washington, DC: Government Printing Office, 1956), 49 (hereafter cited as Gore Committee Hearings).

92. Ibid.

93. Ibid., 47.

94. Ibid., 57. Several local newspapers reported on November 1, 1956, that COPE was not distributing a complete list of its endorsees that year, and none was found in the *AFL-CIO News*. See, for example, "AFL-CIO Plans Big TV Political Rally," *Bismarck Tribune*, November 1, 1956, 21. In September, McDevitt offered a "rough guess" that up to twenty-five Republicans might win local endorsement, as reported in the *AFL-CIO News*, though he named only two House candidates endorsed so far (both in Pennsylvania), while his codirector, Jack Kroll, added that they had identified no liberal Republican candidates for the Senate. The *AFL-CIO News* did publish an overview of its electoral successes, however, noting that local affiliates had endorsed approximately 288 House candidates in 1956, of whom 159 won election, and 29 Senate candidates, of whom 15 were elected. McDevitt's guess is in "COPE Sets 'R' Weeks to Spur Registration," *AFL-CIO News*, September 1, 1956, 5. The electoral overview is in "Labor Efforts Aided Liberal Victories," *AFL-CIO News*, November 10, 1956, 1. These endorsements are described as coming from "local AFL-CIO political groups" or "major individual sections of local labor."

95. Less than 0.1 percent of labor funds had gone to Republican candidates, CQ calculated. See "Unions Take Credit for Democratic Congress," *CQ Weekly*, week ending November 16, 1956, 1374.

96. George F. Hinkle, Indiana Commissioner of Labor, "Union Bosses and Political Action Creates Second-Class Citizenship," Address before the Annual Meeting of the Council of State Chambers of Commerce, September 7, 1956, National Association of Manufacturers (NAM) Records, 1895–2001, accession no. 1411, series V, "Law Department Records," box 62a, Hagley Museum and Library, Wilmington, Delaware (hereafter cited as NAM Records).

97. "Political Program for 1956," 8, CIO-PAC Papers, box 11, folder 23, "PAC Program, 1952–53."

98. See, for example, Labor's League for Political Education, "The Record They Stand On" (1948), in CIO-PAC Papers, box 12, folder 6, "Congressional Voting Records, 1945–58."

99. COPE, "How Your Senators and Representatives Voted 1957–1958," CIO-PAC Papers, box 12, folder 6, "Congressional Voting Records, 1945–58." The 1957–1958 compilation itself presented information on thirteen House votes and sixteen Senate votes, but also a recapitulation of the 1947–1956 record. Here they provided a box score for each congressman, such as "5 right and 11 wrong."

100. Indeed, in 1956 the AFL-CIO sent COPE's voting records out to every member. See "COPE Sets 'R' Weeks to Spur Registration," *AFL-CIO News*, September 1, 1956, 5.

101. COPE's "How Your Senators and Representatives Voted 1947–1956" divided legislation into four categories: labor legislation, general welfare legislation, domestic policy, and foreign aid.

102. COPE, "How Your Senators and Representatives Voted 1947–1956," 1.

103. "AFL-CIO Lists 38 Democratic Senators as Voting 'Right,' 43 Republicans as Voting 'Wrong' on 20 Issues in 10 Years," *Congressional Quarterly Weekly*, week ending September 28, 1956, 1162.

104. "AFL-CIO Lists 168 Democratic Representatives as Voting 'Right,' 175 GOPS as Voting 'Wrong' on 19 Labor Issues," *Congressional Quarterly Weekly*, week ending September 28, 1956, 1160.

105. "Campaign Expenditures Committee," Report of the Special Committee on Campaign Expenditures, 1946, US House of Representatives, 79th Cong., 2nd sess., December 31, 1946, H.R. Rep. No. 2739 (Washington, DC: Government Printing Office, 1946), 42.

106. On the founding of the ADA, see Milkis, *The President and the Parties*, 156–57; and Hal Libros, *Hard Core Liberals: A Sociological Analysis of the Philadelphia Americans for Democratic Action* (Cambridge, MA: Schenkman, 1975), 12–18.

107. On the "political crisis," see National Board of Directors Meeting, Union for Democratic Action, Minutes, October 25, 1946; on the ADA's formation, see National Board of Directors Meeting, Union for Democratic Action, Minutes, January 5, 1947. Both in Americans for Democratic Action Records – Additions, 1943-1995 [M97-135], Union for Democratic Action, 1945-1947," box 1, folder 1/5, "UDA Minutes," Wisconsin Historical Society, Madison, Wisconsin (hereafter cited as ADA Records—Additions).

108. Where the Progressive Citizens of America had countenanced third-party possibilities at some future point, "[t]he ADA appeared to be headed toward working for New Deal aims within the Democratic Party." See "Third Party Chances Slim in '48," *Washington Post,* January 19, 1947, M12.

109. Testimony of Robert R. Nathan, Chairman of the Executive Committee of Americans for Democratic Action, October 10, 1956, Gore Committee Hearings, part 2, 282.

110. Ibid., 282, 283, 288–289. Nathan described a decentralized endorsement structure in which the national ADA endorsed only presidential and vice presidential candidates (282, 288–289). He pointed to the "political work of the local chapters" as being "concerned primarily in mobilizing independent voters on behalf of liberal candidates"—a task with which the national organization assisted through its publications and organizational support (283).

111. Ibid., 291. The ADA maintained both accounts, Nathan explained, "because we believe that ADA does engage in both political, direct political, activity, and a considerable amount of nonpolitical activity of an educational nature," such as preparing "material on issues" or testifying before Congress in relation to particular issues. In terms of labor financing, records compiled by Alexander Heard suggest that labor contributions to the ADA totaled $47,000.09 in 1952, while Nathan acknowledged that the UAW alone was contributing $1,000 per month to the ADA's fund in 1956. See Overacker-Heard Archive, box 43, "Republican Party Committee Transfers; Minor Parties and Misc. Groups: Transfers"; and Testimony of Robert R. Nathan, Gore Committee Hearings, part 2, 293.

112. Testimony of Robert R. Nathan, Gore Committee Hearings, part 2, 295.

113. Ibid., 289–290. Nathan offered this 90 percent characterization about each contest from 1948 to 1954, and though information on ADA endorsements in 1956 was not fully compiled at the time of the hearing, Nathan deemed it almost certain that "over 90% of our congressional support will go to Democrats."

114. Ibid., 288–289.

115. Ibid., 284 (emphasis added).

116. Ibid.

117. Nathan objected forcefully, for example, to one senator's characterization of the ADA voting guides as being designed "pretty much to show how an individual measures up to the Democratic position." "I think there is a big difference," Nathan responded, noting that Senator Eastland of Mississippi "would hardly warrant ADA support, although he is a Democrat, and I don't see how we could ever support him," thus demonstrating that "within the Democratic Party, there are very great differences; just the same, I think, within the Republican Party." See Testimony of Robert R. Nathan, Gore Committee Hearings, part 2, 290.

118. Berry discusses the platform fight, while Milkis notes that the DNC's "Research Division" was authorized by Truman and nominally run by the party but was actually under the supervision of White House counsel Clark Clifford and "dominated by liberal activists who were prominent in progressive organizations" such as the ADA, the American Veteran's Committee (AVC), and the NAACP. See Jeffrey M. Berry, *The New Liberalism: The Rising Power of Citizen Groups* (Washington, DC: Brookings, 1999), 10; and Milkis, *The President and the Parties,* 156.

119. Indeed, DiSalvo identifies the ADA as part of a "change faction"—the "Liberal-Labor alliance"—within the Democratic Party at midcentury, alongside the AFL-CIO and COPE, the UAW, the American Civil Liberties Union (ACLU), and the National Association for the Advancement of Colored People (NAACP). Daniel DiSalvo, *Engines of Change: Party Factions in American Politics, 1868-2010* (New York: Oxford University Press, 2012) 15.

120. See chapter 1, note 55, for more on the ADNC.

121. See Emily J. Charnock, "More Than a Score: Interest Group Ratings and Polarized Politics," *Studies in American Political Development* 32, no. 1 (April 2018): 2, 14–16.

122. ADA LQ scores, alongside comparable conservative measures such as those developed by the Americans for Constitutional Action (ACA) in the early 1960s (as discussed later in this chapter), have been particularly important in studies of congressional organization and have been used to show increasing ideological divergence between the parties in Congress. Both ADA and ACA scores are included in the University of Michigan's Inter-University Consortium for Political and Social Research (ICPSR) dataset of interest group scores from 1960 to 1982, which has been heavily utilized in this literature. For an overview of the use of scores in assessing theories of congressional organization, see E. Scott Adler, *Why Congressional Reforms Fail: Reelection and the House Committee System* (Chicago: University of Chicago Press, 2002), 48; on their use in measuring partisan ideological divergence, see Keith T. Poole and Howard Rosenthal, "Roll Call Voting and Interest Group Ratings," in *Congress: A Political-Economic History of Roll Call Voting*, ed. Keith T. Poole and Howard Rosenthal (New York: Oxford University Press, 1997), 165–183.

123. Republican Congressional Committee, "A Look At C.O.P.E.'s Political Blackball" (ca. 1956), NAM Records, series V, box 62a, folder "UAW (Political Activities and Misuses of Union Funds." A pamphlet matching the title and description is mentioned in "GOP Hits COPE Voting Record," *Congressional Quarterly Weekly*, week ending October 26, 1956, 1283.

124. The Union for Democratic Action's 1942 scorecard, for example, which had been published in the *New Republic*, was attacked for drawing upon votes from previous Congresses to make its case against "obstructionist" lawmakers. Similarly, when challenged by an ADA-backed candidate in 1948, Louisiana congressman F. Edward Hébert denounced the use of earlier votes in evaluating his record, pointing to the "ballots of confidence" his constituents had cast in re-electing him. As Thomas Amlie acknowledged in 1950, "there is a widespread attitude that it violates the cannons of good taste to explore too far into a politician's past record," and that "there is the implicit assumption that each election serves to wipe out past political sins and that the only thing that is properly relevant is what he may have done between elections." See "A Congress to Win the War," 684; Arthur Sears Henning, "New Deal–Red Alliance to Get Test at Polls," *Chicago Tribune*, May 18, 1942, in Thomas Amlie Papers [MSS 452], Public Papers, box 85, folder 11, "Union for Democratic Action (UDA)— General, 1942–1947 + n.d." Wisconsin Historical Society, Madison, Wisconsin (hereafter cited as Amlie Papers); F. Edward Hébert, Address No. 1, August 2, 1948, 3, Americans for Democratic Action Records 1932–1965 [MSS 3], series 7: Public Relations File box 91, folder 7-91-1, "Primaries, Campaigns, Elections, 1948," Wisconsin Historical Society, Madison, Wisconsin (hereafter cited as ADA Records); and Thomas R. Amlie, *Let's Look at the Record* (Madison, WI: Capital City Press, 1950), 19, in Amlie Papers, box 73, folder 3, " 'Let's Look at the Record'—Published Version, 1950."

125. "Legislative Supplement: Roll-Call Record of 1957–1958 General Court," *Bay State Citizen*, October 1958, ADA Records, series 6, Political File, 1944–1964, box 14, "1956 Elections to 1958 Elections," folder 6-14-3, "1958 Elections, ADA Political Questionnaires."

126. Ibid.

127. In his testimony before the Gore Committee, for example, Robert Nathan denied that the ADA's various voting guides were "political" documents within the meaning of the Corrupt Practices Act, even where they included information on particular roll-call votes and an indication of ADA preferences. Though he acknowledged that, at some level, all ADA publications had "the election of or the defeat of candidates" as an aim, and that such activities might be deemed "political" in the "generic" sense of the term, they were *educational* rather than *political* under the law. See Testimony of Robert R. Nathan, Gore Committee Hearings, part 2, 287–288.

128. The national ADA created a "political evaluation committee" in the late 1950s, in part to examine endorsement practices by local chapters, finding that "[t]he Congressional voting record prepared by the national organization was pretty generally used by the chapters, at least as one factor in endorsement determination." The picture was inconsistent, however, and the ADA stressed the need for greater national guidance. Report to the National Board from the National Executive Committee, May 1, 1959, 2, ADA Records, series 6,

Political File, 1944–1964, box 16, "1960 Elections," folder 6-16-1, "ADA Political Evaluation Committee, 1959."

129. Testimony of Robert R. Nathan, Gore Committee Hearings, part 2, 290. Nathan had denied this particular characterization, as discussed in note 117.

130. Eleven Democratic senators had a perfect record from the ADA's perspective, along with ninety-four House Democrats and seven Republicans. Two Republican senators had a completely negative record from the ADA's perspective, as did nineteen House Republicans and ten House Democrats. "ADA Rates Congressmen," *Congressional Quarterly Weekly*, week ending August 17, 1956, 1046.

131. From at least the early 1960s, the national ADA raised a general campaign fund to aid liberals, overseen by the "candidate support committee," with deserving candidates identified by scores. In August 1960, for example, a staffer compiled a list of fourteen incumbent legislators "deserving of ADA campaign support," almost all of whom had a "100% voting record." See, for example, John Kenneth Galbraith to Mrs. C. Girard Davidson, September 7, 1967, ADA Records—Additions, box 28, "Political Files, 1948–1992," folder 28–25, "Candidate Support Committee, Referendum '70"; and William L. Taylor to Violet M. Gunther, "List of Senators and Congressmen Deserving of ADA Campaign Support," August 16, 1960, ADA Records, series 6, Political File, 1944–1964, box 15, "1958 Elections to 1960 Conventions—Dem. and Rep," folder 6-15-8, "A.D.A. Activities, General Strategy & Corr., 1960, Jan—Nov."

132. Robert R. Nathan, "Memo," November 1957, 1, ADA Records, series 6: Political File, 1944–1964, box 14, "1956 Elections to 1958 Elections," folder 6-14-6, "1958 Elections, Congress."

133. Ibid.

134. "Report Card for 80th Congress," *ADA World*, August 26, 1947, 11.

135. Ibid.

136. Quoted in Steven M. Gillon, *Politics and Vision: The ADA and American Liberalism, 1947–1985* (New York: Oxford University Press, 1987), 19.

137. Amlie, *Let's Look at the Record*, 23.

138. Ibid. On liberal Republicans bolstering their conservative colleagues, see 21–23.

139. Ibid.

140. Tom Amlie to Arnold Zander, November 7, 1952. CIO-PAC Papers, Box 11, Folder 19, "Dudley Correspondence – Democratic National Committee, 1947-56. 1 of 4."

141. For more on the ways external metrics can transform the internal culture of organizations in nonpolitical settings, see Wendy Nelson Espeland and Michael Sauder, "The Dynamism of Indicators," in *Governance by Indicators: Global Power through Quantification and Rankings*, ed. Kevin Davis, Angelina Fisher, Benedict Kingsbury, and Sally Engle Merry (Oxford University Press, 2012), 86–109.

142. Testimony of Sidney H. Scheuer, Chairman of the National Committee for an Effective Congress, December 12, 1956, "Campaign Contributions, Political Activities, and Lobbying," *Hearings before the Special Committee to Investigate Political Activities, Lobbying, and Campaign Contributions*, US Senate, 84th Cong., 2nd sess. (Washington, DC: Government Printing Office, 1957), 1040, 1042 (hereafter cited as McClellan Committee Hearings). Scheuer was joined by NCEC executive secretary George E. Agree.

143. Ibid., 1040.

144. Ibid., 1043–1044. The censure idea did not originate with the NCEC, Scheuer noted, but acknowledged that Senator Ralph Flanders of Vermont had sought the organization's help in formulating it.

145. Ibid., 1040. The NCEC had endorsed Flanders several times, Scheuer noted, and though "we certainly did not agree with all of his votes" (Scheuer characterized Flanders as an "economic" conservative), "we did not change our views as to his qualities." Those qualities were presumably greatly strengthened by Flanders's opposition to McCarthy. On his sponsorship of the censure resolution, see Anthony Leviero, "Final Vote Condemns McCarthy, 67–22, for Abusing Senate and Committee," *New York Times*, December 3, 1954, 1.

146. Testimony of Sidney H. Scheuer, McClellan Committee Hearings, 1041.

147. Ibid., 1043–1044. Goldwater characterized the NCEC as attempting first "to effect the election of people who are friendly to your line of thought," and then afterward trying "to

influence the Congress in its decisions." Goldwater pointed to the McCarthy censure and made reference to "the China lobby situation" and the Nuremberg trials as instances of NCEC lobbying, supporting his contention that "you are trying to influence not only the selection of people to this congressional body, but you are then trying to influence their actions after they get here." Scheuer acknowledged that the NCEC sought to elect those "friendly" to its line of thought, but claimed it did *not* actively seek to influence legislators once elected, with the notable exception of the McCarthy censure.

148. Ibid., 1043–1044.
149. Ibid., 1042. As a general principle, Scheuer stated, NCEC was only active in primaries "in one-party States where the nomination is tantamount to election."
150. According to Alexander, the NCEC was among three committees that "accounted for about 80 per cent of gross disbursements of all miscellaneous committees" in 1960. (The others were Americans for Constitutional Action, a conservative group discussed in the next chapter, and the Christian Nationalist Crusade, a right-wing organization led by Gerald K. Smith, which may have grown out of his experiment with the America First party in 1944). While the NCEC claimed to be nonpartisan and to distribute funds to candidates of both parties, it did so primarily on the basis of ideological considerations. According to Poole, analyzing the efforts of the NCEC for the conservative Heritage Foundation in 1977, the group had had a "three-point test" for the distribution of funds: "Is he a self-starting, independent liberal? Does he need money? Can he get elected?" See Herbert E. Alexander, *Financing the 1960 Election* (Princeton, NJ: Citizens' Research Foundation, 1962), 44; and William T. Poole, *Institutional Analysis # 5: The National Committee for an Effective Congress* (Washington, DC: The Heritage Foundation. 1978), 2–3.
151. McClellan Committee Hearings, 1041–1042. "I see in your organization, and other similar organizations," Goldwater declared, "groups who are actually getting into State prerogatives, groups who operate completely outside of States."
152. Ibid., 1041.
153. "In any political entity, voters naturally and rightfully resent the unwarranted invasion of outsiders," Jim Farley had written of the purge. So strong was the reaction to Roosevelt's actions that Eisenhower had decried presidential "intervention" in congressional races on the campaign trail in 1952. See James A. Farley, *Jim Farley's Story* (New York: Whittlesey House, 1948), 147, quoted in Susan Dunn, *Roosevelt's Purge: How FDR Fought to Change the Democratic Party* (Cambridge, MA: Belknap Press of Harvard University Press, 2010), 224–225; and David B. Truman, "Party Reform, Party Atrophy, and Constitutional Change: Some Reflections," *Political Science Quarterly* 99, no. 4 (Winter 1984–1985): 639.
154. The committee had amended the bill so as to include this limitation, capped at $10,000. Though the report recommends "its immediate passage," further action on the bill is not apparent. "Publicity of Campaign Contributions," Report from the Committee on Privileges and Elections, US Senate, 63rd Cong., 2nd sess., August 25, 1914, S. Rep. No. 770, 1.
155. McClellan Committee Hearings, 1041–1043.
156. Ibid., 1042. The source of Goldwater's constitutional concerns was apparently the article I provisions relating to the election of congressmen and senators. Article I, section II, states that members of the House of Representatives are to be "chosen every second Year by the People of the several States" and specifies state residency requirements for those standing for the office. The Seventeenth Amendment, which altered the process for selecting senators laid out in article I, section III, suggests that the two senators for each state must be "elected by the people thereof." "[T]he intent of the Constitution relative to the Senate can be broadly interpreted," Goldwater admitted, but there were legitimate questions, he felt, as to "the properness, under the concept of our Constitution, of outside organizations getting into the selection of Members of the House of Representatives," at the very least (1042).
157. Ibid.
158. Ibid.
159. Ibid., 1031.
160. Ibid., 1043.
161. Ibid., 1042.
162. Ibid., 1043.

163. Ibid., 1042–1043.

164. George Soule, "Liberty League Liberty—III: Liberty In Industry," *New Republic*, September 9, 1936, 121.

165. See Paula Baker, "How Money Became Speech" (unpublished manuscript, July 1, 2012), and note 202 in chapter 5.

166. Bipartisan funding drives sponsored by the Advertising Council beginning in the 1950s, for example, aimed to make contributing to parties a habit for the average citizen. For more on these campaigns, which stressed contributing to the party "of your choice," see Robert Griffith, "The Selling of America: The Advertising Council and American Politics, 1942–1960," *Business History Review* 57, no. 3 (1983): 388–412.

167. This was a "Minority Comment" appended to the majority report, authored by Senators Joseph H. Ball (R-MN) and Homer S. Ferguson (R-MI). See Green Committee Report, 24.

168. "Minority Comment," Green Committee Report, 24. Ball and Ferguson therefore appeared to accept the legitimacy of a voluntary political fund.

169. Testimony of Robert R. Nathan, Gore Committee Hearings, part 2, 294–295. Curtis was referring to labor union contributions to ADA's nonpolitical fund.

170. The two called a press conference in December 1955, for example, at which they denounced such violations and highlighted stories of aggrieved workers. See Rose McKee, "Political Aid Protested by Union Men," *Washington Post and Times Herald*, December 16, 1955, 29.

171. On the checkoff, see Melvin I. Urofsky, "Campaign Finance Reform Before 1971," *Albany Government Law Review* 1, no. 1 (2008): 26. As Zelizer notes, "The right of unions to collect voluntary donations for campaign contributions remained contentious" ("Seeds of Cynicism," 76).

172. Testimony of Robert R. Nathan, Gore Committee Hearings, part 2, 294–295.

173. Ibid., 295.

174. Ibid., 294–295. Curtis described it as "involuntary money extracted from people to hold a job."

175. Ibid., 295. Nathan, for example, suggested that union leaders felt supporting the ADA was "consistent with the well-being of the union membership" and would be replaced by the rank and file if wrong in this belief.

176. The McClellan "Rackets Committee" held hearings from 1957 to 1959 and issued its final report in March 1960. The committee investigated, for example, allegations of bribery by the Teamsters in Kansas; violence in the UAW's boycott of Kohler Co. in Wisconsin; and perhaps most famously, the alleged connections between the Teamsters and organized crime. See Final Report of the Select Committee on Improper Activities in the Labor or Management Field, 86th Cong., 2nd sess., March 31, 1960, S. Rep. No. 1139 (Washington, DC: Government Printing Office, 1960).

177. Zelizer, "Seeds of Cynicism," 78.

178. Ibid., 78–80. Union leaders were comfortable with some reform measures, Zelizer suggests, especially the restriction of large individual donations, since they often highlighted the small contributions on which the PAC model rested, but they feared other measures designed to curb union political activity more generally.

179. Jack Kroll to ADA Convention [1952], 5. CIO-PAC Papers, Box 14, Folder 26, "1952 Elections."

180. Ibid., 5–7.

181. For a discussion of failed efforts to repeal Taft-Hartley, see Zeigler, *Interest Groups in American Society*, 153–154. On Landrum-Griffin, see R. Alton Lee, *Eisenhower and Landrum-Griffin: A Study in Labor-Management Politics* (Lexington: University Press of Kentucky, 1990).

182. This characterization was first offered in a 1958 *Congressional Quarterly* study based on an analysis of COPE contributions, noted in a 1960 article, suggesting that "238 House members and 58 Senators, a clear majority in both chambers, would be 'pro-labor.'" Rohde also notes "a large influx of northern liberal Democrats into the House as a result of the 1958 election." See "Labor Disappointed in 'Pro-Labor' 86th Congress," *Congressional Quarterly Weekly*, week ending August 19, 1960, 1464; and David W. Rohde, *Parties and Leaders in the Post-Reform House* (Chicago: University of Chicago Press), 7.

183. Teamsters president Dave Beck, for example, had opposed the AFL-CIO's endorsement of Stevenson in 1956, while serving as one of the federation's vice presidents, and was later ousted as a result of the investigation. See "What Political Role Will Labor Play in '56," *Congressional Quarterly Weekly,* week ending September 28, 1956, 1156.

184. As Ritchie describes, Kennedy had generally "steered a middle course" on labor issues. He had voted against Taft-Hartley while serving in the House, for example, but favored some labor reform legislation (34). What became the Labor Management Reporting and Disclosure Act of 1959 had actually originated with a relatively moderate Kennedy proposal in the Senate, though it had been significantly amended on the floor and replaced with the tougher Landrum-Griffin bill in the House. Kennedy worked in conference to remove some of the restrictions on unions and ultimately voted for the resulting legislation, his role as conciliator helping him to gain AFL-CIO support for his presidential ambitions while also enjoying the wider reputational benefits of voting for significant labor reform (45–46). The Teamsters, meanwhile, remained hostile to Kennedy during the campaign and throughout his administration, since Robert Kennedy, as attorney general, continued his investigation of that union. See Donald A. Ritchie, "Kennedy in Congress," in *A Companion to John F. Kennedy,* ed. Marc J. Selverstone (Chichester, UK: Wiley Blackwell, 2014), 33–50; and *CQ Fact Sheet on John F. Kennedy* (Washington, DC: Congressional Quarterly, 1960), https://www.jfklibrary.org/Research/Research-Aids/Ready-Reference/JFK-Fast-Facts/Voting-Record-and-Stands-on-Issues-Page-2.aspx

185. The "Treaty of Detroit" was a UAW contract with GM, signed in May 1950 and originally set to run five years; *Fortune* magazine gave it the label. See Nelson Lichtenstein, *Walter Reuther: The Most Dangerous Man in Detroit* (Urbana: University of Illinois Press, 1995), 280.

Chapter 7

1. Chamber of Commerce Employer-Employee Relations Department, *Labor in Politics* (Washington, DC: US Chamber of Commerce, 1950), 19, Personal Papers of V. O. Key, accession no. 2000-078, box 9, "Writings: 'Politics, Parties, and Pressure Groups,'" folder, "Chap III—'Workers'—Political Tactics," John F. Kennedy Presidential Library, Boston, MA (hereafter cited as V. O. Key Papers).

2. Ibid., 3.

3. David B. Truman, *The Governmental Process: Political Interests and Public Opinion* (Berkeley: Institute of Governmental Studies, University of California, Berkeley, 1951/1993), 63.

4. Chamber of Commerce, *Labor in Politics,* 1–2, 5.

5. Kim Phillips-Fein, *Invisible Hands: The Making of the Conservative Movement from the New Deal to Reagan* (New York: W. W. Norton & Company, 2009), 56. Indeed, Phillips-Fein does not emphasize direct political action in her account of "business conservatives" and their "ideological mobilization" in the mid-twentieth century, though she does point to some tangible activities beyond publicity, such as executive training to fight union drives and "businessmen-in-politics" programs, as discussed in this chapter (106–107). Similarly, Fones-Wolf stresses publicity campaigns as the key business response to labor union's political mobilization. See Elizabeth A. Fones-Wolf, *Selling Free Enterprise: The Business Assault on Labor and Liberalism, 1945–60* (Urbana: University of Illinois Press, 1994), esp. 50–51.

6. The creation of predecessor organizations in the 1960s, in fact, have been largely neglected due to the lack of systematic data collection prior to the creation of the Federal Election Commission in 1974. Exceptions include Zelizer, who acknowledges the formation of AMA and NAM PACs in 1961 and 1963 respectively and argues that their appearance helped to generate greater support for campaign finance reform among mainstream Democrats. Nonetheless, he does not explain why these groups decided to establish PACs at this time. Julian E. Zelizer, "Seeds of Cynicism: The Struggle over Campaign Finance, 1956–1974," *Journal of Policy History* 14, no. 1 (2002): 83.

7. Clyde P. Weed, *The Nemesis of Reform: The Republican Party During the New Deal* (New York: Columbia University Press, 1994), 65.

8. Ibid., 194.

9. Ibid., 193–194.
10. Ibid., 195. See Arthur M. Schlesinger Jr., *The Vital Center: The Politics of Freedom* (Cambridge, MA: Riverside Press, 1949); and David L. Stebenne, *Modern Republican: Arthur Larson and the Eisenhower Years* (Bloomington: Indiana University Press, 2006).
11. Thomas Ferguson, *Golden Rule: The Investment Theory of Party Competition and the Logic of Money-Driven Political Systems* (Chicago: University of Chicago Press, 1995), 120–124.
12. Harmon Zeigler, *Interest Groups in American Society* (Englewood Cliffs, NJ: Prentice-Hall, 1964), 116, referring to Alfred S. Cleveland, "NAM: Spokesman for Industry?," *Harvard Business Review* 26 (May 1948): 357; and John W. Jeffries, "A 'Third New Deal'? Liberal Policy and the American State, 1937–1945," *Journal of Policy History* 8, no. 4 (October 1996): 387–409.
13. Zeigler, *Interest Groups in American Society*, 116.
14. Fones-Wolf, *Selling Free Enterprise* (1994); and Phillips-Fein, *Invisible Hands* (2009).
15. With economic growth smoothing over intra-industrial conflicts and few political battles to fight, the need for membership in a peak association appeared far from pressing.
16. Zeigler, *Interest Groups in American Society*, 115. The NAM's membership, however, began to plummet at that point, falling from 5,700 members in 1922 to just under 1,500 a decade later. Zeigler puts the number at 1,469 members in 1933.
17. Ibid.
18. Ibid., 116.
19. Ibid.
20. Ibid.
21. The Constitutional Educational League was one of the first "patriotic" and antisubversive groups according to Kamp—formed in 1919 by disaffected veterans, who returned from fighting in Europe to find subversive Socialists in their midst. According to Kennedy, the CEL had links with the American Democratic National Committee of 1944, while the CCG had links to a related Gannett entity, the National Farm Committee. See Testimony of Joseph P. Kamp, September 20, 1944, "Campaign Expenditures," *Hearings before the Committee to Investigate Campaign Expenditures*, part 5, US House of Representatives, 78th Cong., 2nd sess. (Washington, DC: Government Printing Office, 1944), 248 (hereafter cited as Anderson Committee Hearings); and Stetson Kennedy, *Southern Exposure: Making the South Safe for Democracy* (Tuscaloosa: University of Alabama Press, 2010), 144.
22. See, for example, Testimony of Joseph P. Kamp, Anderson Committee Hearings, part 5, 272, in which he claimed that "[t]he central unit of the un-American gestapo is the Anti-Defamation League of B'nai B'rith."
23. Testimony of Frank E. Gannett, September 7, 1944, Anderson Committee Hearings, part 7, 377.
24. Ibid., 377–378.
25. The NCUCG had been refused tax-exempt status on the grounds that its purported educational efforts skirted too close to the "political" realm as far as the Internal Revenue Service was concerned. These tax issues were, in fact, the motivation behind the reformulation of the older National Committee to Uphold Constitutional Government as the CCG. While the NCUCG had been an unincorporated association, the Committee for Constitutional Government was an incorporated entity under DC law, and a parallel nonprofit foundation was established—the Constitution and Free Enterprise Foundation—for tax-deductible purposes. See Testimony of Frank E. Gannett, 425; and Gloria Resch Cook, "The Relationship Between Political Parties and Pressure Groups" (MA thesis, University of North Carolina, Chapel Hill, 1956), 24.
26. Testimony of Frank E. Gannett, Anderson Committee Hearings, part 7, 435.
27. Ibid., 436.
28. Ibid., 435.
29. From the 1937 CEL pamphlet, *Vote for John L. Lewis, and Communism*, reproduced in Anderson Committee Hearings, part 5, 251.
30. See Joseph P. Kamp, *How to Be an American, to Organize for America, to Fight Un-Americanism: The ABC's and the Do's and Don'ts for Constructive Patriotic Action* (New York: Patriotic Action Committee, Constitutional Educational League, 1946). "By

educating the American people, by letting them know what is going on, by giving them the facts," the CEL would attain its patriotic objectives, Kamp explained (255–256). The CEL was formed as an incorporated association under the laws of Connecticut (257).

31. Testimony of Joseph P. Kamp, Anderson Committee Hearings, part 5, 248.

32. Ibid., 249–250.

33. Ibid., 248 (emphasis added).

34. Ibid., 251. Kamp was reading here from the 1937 CEL pamphlet *Vote for John L. Lewis, and Communism*.

35. Ibid.

36. Ibid., 250. See also 261.

37. Ibid.

38. Yet beyond Gannett and his inner circle, the CCG *was* viewed in partisan terms. Key, for example, claimed it "operated in effect as an unacknowledged auxiliary of the Republican party" in the 1940s. V. O. Key, *Politics, Parties, and Pressure Groups*, 5th ed. (New York: Thomas Y. Crowell, 1964), 89.

39. Testimony of Joseph P. Kamp, Anderson Committee Hearings, part 5, 251 (emphasis added).

40. Ibid., 291.

41. Ibid., 257. "I would imagine that might be the implication," Kamp said.

42. Ibid., 275–276.

43. Footnote 52 of the Supreme Court's decision in *Buckley v. Valeo*, 424 U.S. 1 (1976)—which struck down parts of the Federal Election Campaign Act of 1971 and its 1974 amendments—identified a number of words and phrases such as "vote for" or "vote against," later dubbed "magic words," that had to be present for a communication to constitute "express advocacy" in a federal election context and thus make any expenditures to produce it subject to disclosure and reporting requirements. See Ciara Torres-Spelliscy, ed., *Writing Reform: A Guide to Drafting State & Local Campaign Finance Laws*, rev. ed. (New York: Brennan Center for Justice, 2010), 5, 14–15, https://www.brennancenter.org/sites/default/files/legacy/Writing%20 Reform%202010%20FINAL.pdf.

44. Testimony of Joseph P. Kamp, Anderson Committee Hearings, part 5, 276.

45. Ibid, 257. The CEL's earlier pamphlet, *Vote for John L. Lewis, and Communism*, had similar electoral overtones (251).

46. Ibid., 259.

47. Ibid., 248, 253, 258, 297, 308–309.

48. See Edward A. Rumely to Clinton P. Anderson, September 18, 1944, reproduced in Anderson Committee Hearings, part 7, 442–444. Rumely was willing to provide details of the CCG's expenditures, but not its contributors. Rumely refused on the grounds that the CCG was not, in his view, a political committee, and that his legal duty was to protect the identities of the group's contributors (a factor Kamp also raised).

49. Testimony of Joseph P. Kamp, Anderson Committee Hearings, part 5, 262.

50. Fones-Wolf, *Selling Free Enterprise*, 287.

51. Phillips-Fein, *Invisible Hands*, 19–20.

52. Ibid, 2. On the damage to the reputation of business, see also 9, 17. On its resurgence during the war, see 26–27.

53. George Soule, "Liberty League Liberty III—Liberty In Industry." *New Republic*, September 9, 1936, 121–122.

54. This theme was first articulated in Roosevelt's "Commonwealth Club" speech of 1932 and further developed in his 1936 convention address. See Sidney M. Milkis, *The President and the Parties: The Transformation of the American Party System since the New Deal* (New York: Oxford University Press, 1993), esp. 8–9, 39–43, 72–73.

55. On the "Free Enterprise" campaign generally, see Fones-Wolf, *Selling Free Enterprise*.

56. Henry Hazlitt, *Economics in One Lesson* (New York: Harper and Brothrs, 1946), 5 (emphasis added).

57. "You and the Public," Records of the Chamber of Commerce of the United States of America, 1912–1980, accession 1960, series IV, box 2, folder "Publicity Seminar," Hagley Museum and Library, Wilmington, Delaware (hereafter cited as Chamber of Commerce Records).

58. See Fones-Wolf, *Selling Free Enterprise*, esp. 7, 24–25; and Phillips-Fein, *Invisible Hands*, esp. 14, 66.

59. Testimony of Robert M. Gaylord, President of the National Association of Manufacturers, August 31, 1944, Anderson Committee Hearings, part 2, 99.

60. Ibid.

61. Ibid., 98–99.

62. Ibid., 117.

63. For more on the constellation of especially libertarian organizations founded at this time, see Jennifer Burns, *Goddess of the Market: Ayn Rand and the American Right* (New York: Oxford University Press, 2009), 204.

64. The NAM, CCG, and CEL were all called before the House campaign expenditures committee in 1944, and the NAM would appear again before its 1946 successor, alongside a new conservative group, American Action, Inc. The CCG and CEL also appeared before the House committee investigating lobbying in 1950, which also heard testimony from Foundation for Economic Education representatives, while the US Chamber of Commerce would be called before the Senate's campaign expenditure investigation in 1956 and its combined lobbying and electoral investigation in 1957.

65. NAM representatives had appeared before other kinds of congressional committee during this period, however, including Robert La Follette Jr.'s (I-WI) 1937 Senate investigation into the intimidation of labor organizers and activists. La Follette's investigation was conducted under the auspices of the Senate Committee on Education and Labor Subcommittee (Subcommittee on S. Res. 266), which held hearings from 1937 to 1939.

66. Testimony of Robert M. Gaylord, Anderson Committee Hearings, part 2, 101.

67. Ibid., 117, 122 (emphasis added). The NIIC's 1944 program, he said, was designed "to show the public that the enterprise and initiative of its individual citizens, not the super-planning of an all-powerful state, offer the key to the better world we all are seeking" (122).

68. Ibid., 102, 108.

69. Ibid. 108.

70. Ibid.

71. Ibid., 109.

72. Ibid., 102.

73. Ibid.

74. Ibid., 108.

75. Ibid., 105. See also 125.

76. Ibid.

77. Ibid., 106, 116.

78. Ibid., 125–126.

79. Ibid., 126.

80. Ibid.

81. Ibid., 108. The quotes were phrased as questions by Representative Clarence J. Brown (R-OH), and Gaylord replied to each in the negative. "In other words," Brown summed up, "you are telling our committee that you and your organization have in no way taken part in political activities—at least as far as parties, or candidates, or political issues are concerned—in the past and that you do not expect to do so in this campaign, or in future campaigns?," which Gaylord affirmed (108).

82. Ibid., 108–109. Gaylord acknowledged that at least some NAM members "would like to see some political activity," noting a letter from a member in June, "suggesting that since the Attorney General had given his blessing to the P.A.C, that we ought to take some of the money . . . from the N.I.I.C. program and appropriate it for political work" (108).

83. Ibid., 108 (emphasis added). Gaylord's reply was sent on June 26, 1944.

84. Ibid., 125. See 108, 110, and 124–125, for Gaylord's interpretation of the law.

85. Ibid., 109.

86. Ibid., 124.

87. Ibid., 111 (emphasis added).

88. Ibid., 116.

89. Ibid., 103.

90. "Campaign Expenditures: American Action, Inc.," *Hearings before the Committee to Investigate Campaign Expenditures*, part 5, US House of Representatives, 79th Cong., 2nd sess. (Washington, DC: Government Printing Office, 1946), 33.

91. Ibid. Formed as a nonprofit corporation in Delaware in 1946, American Action's contributors included Liberty League veterans like J. J. Raskob, but also newer conservative voices such as William Volker and William H. Regnery. On its corporate status, see Cook, "The Relationship Between Political Parties and Pressure Groups," 18, 28–29.

92. Cook, "The Relationship Between Political Parties and Pressure Groups," 34.

93. Ibid., 1. The NEC was primarily concerned with "influencing legislation," Cook noted, "and it therefore focuses most of its activities upon the legislative phase of the political process" (61). It was only "indirectly concerned with the election phase of the political process," she said (34).

94. Ibid., 18. Nonetheless, American Action did work quite actively with groups like the Committee for Constitutional Government in support of its economic aims. "[T]here is a wide area of agreement between the two organizations within which cooperative or supplementary functions are fulfilled on two levels of activity: action on specific issues and action in the broader, more generalized area of education and public opinion formation," Cook noted (19).

95. Ibid., 62.

96. Ibid., 63 for reference to "standard lobbying techniques."

97. Ibid.

98. Ibid., 64.

99. Ibid., 28.

100. Ibid., 36–37. The legal dimensions here are not entirely clear. Cook refers to the Federal Regulation of Lobbying Act of 1946 as a consideration, but as interpreted in *United States v. Harriss* 347 U.S. 612 (1954), it applied to direct lobbying only. From a tax perspective, though lobbying activities were restricted as of 1934, *campaign* activity by "charitable" organizations was not constrained until 1954, if the NEC was classified as such. American Action, meanwhile, was incorporated, so how it was meant to overcome prohibitions on direct political activity is unclear. See Emanuel Celler, "Pressure Groups in Congress," *Annals of the American Academy of Political and Social Science* 319 (September 1958): 8; and Judith E. Kindell and John Francis Reilly, "Election Year Issues," 2002 Exempt Organizations Continuing Professional Education (CPE) Text, 336, www.irs.gov/pub/irs-tege/eotopici02. pdf. See also chapter 5, note 213.

101. Cook, "The Relationship Between Political Parties and Pressure Groups," 37.

102. Ibid., 69–70. The NEC was "not an objective, educational enterprise," Cook concluded. It had "distinct political principles upon which its work and literature are based and its activities are geared to promote the philosophy embodying these principles" (69–70). It desired "a realignment of the political parties in such a way that their aims and objectives would coincide with those of the NEC," she said, qualifying that "the sort of party alignment it wants" was incorporation of its principles into a party platform, "probably the Republican" (70).

103. Merwin K. Hart to Retired Brigadier General Brice P. Disque, April 21, 1948, reproduced in "Lobbying, Direct and Indirect: National Economic Council, Inc.," *Hearings before the Select Committee on Lobbying Activities*, part 4, US House of Representatives, 81st Cong., 2nd sess., June 6, 20, 21, and 28, 1950 (Washington, DC: Government Printing Office, 1950), 330.

104. Ibid.

105. Ibid.

106. Ibid.

107. "Confidential—Report of NAM Representatives Who Attended National Citizens Political Action Committee School, Washington, DC, June 26–29, 1946—General Impressions of Miss McKane" (emphasis added), National Association of Manufacturers (NAM) Records, 1895–2001, accession no. 1411, series 1, box 307, "Folder—N.A.M.—Miscellaneous, National Citizens Action Political Action Committee School, 1946." Hagley Museum and Library, Wilmington, Delaware (hereafter cited as NAM Records).

108. "Confidential—Report of NAM Representatives Who Attended National Citizens Political Action Committee School, Washington, DC, June 26–29, 1946—General Impressions of

Messrs. Swanson and Buergelin," NAM Records, series 1, box 307, "Folder—N.A.M.—Miscellaneous, National Citizens Action Political Action Committee School, 1946."

109. Ibid.

110. *Congressional Record—Senate*, 80th Cong., 1st sess., June 5, 1947, 6439. Taft's opinion was even cited in the 1972 Supreme Court case *Pipefitters v. United States* and accorded strong weight as an indicator of legislative intent. See *Pipefitters Local Union No. 562 v. United States*, 407 U.S. 385 (1972).

111. Ibid.

112. Ibid. (emphasis added).

113. N.A.M. Law Department Memo, "Political Action and the Corrupt Practices Act, U.S. v. United Automobile Workers, CIO," February 24, 1956, NAM Records, accession no. 1411, series I, box B-5, folder "Political."

114. Ibid. The NAM memo was prepared in February 1956, after the District Court had initially dismissed the indictment against the UAW but before the Supreme Court had taken up the case. Indeed, it was unclear whether the Justice Department would appeal and, in even if it did so, whether the Supreme Court would reach a decision before the November 1956 elections. Accordingly, the NAM was basing its assessment on the idea that if the dismissal was upheld, then there were basically no effective limits on the kinds of political activities in which labor unions could engage.

115. Ibid.

116. During the debate over the Smith-Connally Act in 1943, the possibility of adding "management organization" to the statutory language was raised (presumably to embrace those unincorporated business associations that would not otherwise be restricted, or as a poison pill designed to defeat the legislation), but it did not make into the final bill. Senator Hatch subsequently introduced a separate bill that would have applied to such associations, but it went nowhere. See Joseph E. Kallenbach, "The Taft-Hartley Act and Union Political Contributions and Expenditures," *Minnesota Law Review* 33, no. 1 (December 1948): 5.

117. Overacker noted in 1932 that there had been very few prosecutions under the corrupt practices laws to that point, a rare example being *United States v. U.S. Brewers' Association* (1916), a District Court decision that upheld the constitutionality of the corporate contribution ban. See Louise Overacker, *Money in Elections* (New York: Macmillan, 1932), 240. In a 1964 overview of corporate political activity, US Chamber of Commerce general counsel William Barton also pointed to charges against various auto dealers in Michigan, in relation to the 1946 election, where pleas of nolo contendere were entered. See William B. Barton, "Corporations in Politics: How Far Can They Go Under the Law?," *American Bar Association Journal* 50 (March 1964): 228.

118. "Statistical Report of Complaints Received by the Department of Justice Concerning Alleged Violations of Section 610, Title 18, U.S.C. (Political Contributions by National Banks, Corporations, and Labor Organizations)" [1950–1956], NAM accession 1411, series V, box 62a, Hagley Library. Looking through the complaint descriptions, I calculated that of the fourteen complaints that were presented to a grand jury following DOJ investigation, nine involved unions. In all the other union cases they were either deemed not to warrant investigation or no evidence of a violation was found—except for one case in 1951, in which a possible labor violation was discerned but the statute of limitations had been exceeded.

119. Ibid. The International Hod Carriers Building and Construction Laborers Union was acquitted in 1951 after being accused of spending $20,000 in support of a congressional candidate.

120. Ibid.

121. Barton observed that court decisions provided "little help" in answering the questions of businessmen regarding political activity ("Corporations in Politics," 230).

122. "What Corporations Can and Can't Do," NAM Records, accession no. 1411, series I, box B-5, folder "Political," Hagley Library. "AS INDIVIDUALS, businessmen have the same political rights and privileges as all citizens," the memo noted. See also Barton, "Corporations in Politics," 228.

123. "What Corporations Can and Can't Do."

124. Barton warned that the Federal Corrupt Practices Act was *not* "a dead letter" despite the lack of convictions, and that the belief no one would be punished under the law was "without substantial foundation" and even "dangerous"—though he acknowledged that both "spokesmen for both business and labor" have expressed it" ("Corporations in Politics," 230–231).

125. Barton, "Corporations in Politics," 231.

126. "Elections—How Big Labor Wins—A Report on Labor's Political Mobilization—Ways to Combat It" [1958], 13, box 3H491, "1958 Senate Campaign General Files: COPE—"How Big Labor Wins"; COPE—contributors, 1958; COPE—Mahoney and Udall" folder, Stephen Shadegg/Barry Goldwater Collection, 1949–1965, The Dolph Briscoe Center for American History, The University of Texas at Austin. See also Fritz Randolph to Senator Barry Goldwater, September 12, 1958, in same folder, explaining the provenance of the report. Randolph was Goldwater's legislative assistant and also chairman of the DC Young Republicans.

127. Phillips-Fein, *Invisible Hands*, 56.

128. Labor "could never match the resources available to the leaders of American business," Fones-Wolf argues, yielding a postwar environment "increasingly dominated" by their "images and ideas" (*Selling Free Enterprise*, 287). On disparities between the NAM and labor publicity spending, see Fones-Wolf, *Selling Free Enterprise*, 43–44, 47–49.

129. As noted in previous chapters, the APSA Committee on Political Parties expressed this kind of opinion, as did Truman (*The Governmental Process*, 312), Zeigler (*Interest Groups in American Society*, 235), and many others.

130. Truman, *The Governmental Process*, 312. It was unlikely that the NAM could mount an electoral effort "even if it wished to," Truman said.

131. On efforts to influence employees, including special payments to be used for political purposes, see "Washington Notes: Can Big Business Buy This Election Too?," *New Republic*, September 9, 1936, 129; "Senator Wheeler Assails Political Use of Aid Funds," *Los Angeles Times*, May 26, 1938; and Anthony Corrado, "Money and Politics: A History of Federal Campaign Finance Law," in *Campaign Finance Reform: A Sourcebook*, ed. Anthony Corrado, Thomas E. Mann, Daniel R. Ortiz, Trevor Potter, and Frank J. Sorauf (Washington, DC: Brookings Institution Press, 1997), 29–30.

132. Zeigler, *Interest Groups in American Society*, 244.

133. Zelizer, "Seeds of Cynicism," 78–79.

134. For assertions that corporate officials made contributions as individuals, see Melvin I. Urofsky, "Campaign Finance Reform Before 1971," *Albany Government Law Review* 1 (2008): 29; Zelizer, "Seeds of Cynicism," 78–79; and Andrew Hacker and Joel D. Aberbach, "Businessmen in Politics," *Law and Contemporary Problems* 27, no. 2 (1962): 276. On the question of PAC formation, Urofsky specifically states that "company officials felt no need to do so" (29).

135. See Corrado, "Money and Politics," 29; Zelizer, "Seeds of Cynicism," 78–79; and Urofsky, "Campaign Finance Reform Before 1971," 28–29.

136. See, for example, Zeigler, *Interest Groups in American Society*, 234.

137. Hacker and Aberbach, "Businessmen in Politics," 276.

138. Net totals of known contributions came to $1,014,909 in 1952 and $1,936,847 in 1956. Of these totals, 92 percent went to Republicans in 1952 and 94 percent in 1956. Alexander Heard, *The Costs of Democracy* (Chapel Hill: University of North Carolina Press, 1960), 115.

139. Ibid., 180–181. National-level labor committee disbursements—including the AFL's Labor's League for Political Education, the CIO P.A.C., and the Committee on Political Education after their merger—amounted to $1,817,622 in 1952, $1,929,655 in 1954, $1,690,297 in 1956, and $1,576,525 in 1958.

140. Ibid., 101–102. In the table displaying this information, Heard identifies the percentage of NAM directors contributing in 1956 as 14 percent, but the raw numbers suggest the figure is 13 percent. For 1952, Heard found that 15 percent of the NAM's directors had contributed over $500 to federal campaigns, compared to 24 percent of the NAM's officers, 21 percent of its regional vice presidents, and the highest proportion—43 percent—of its honorary vice presidents. It is unclear why Heard excluded 1956 data on NAM officers and vice presidents, since he had compiled comparable information for the Senate's campaign

expenditure investigation that year, chaired by Senator Albert Gore (D-TN). That information may not have been finalised, however, as Heard describes the 1956 data used in *The Costs of Democracy* as "adjusted" from that shown in the Gore Committee's report. See "1956 General Election Campaigns," Report of the Subcommittee on Privileges and Elections, US Senate, 85th Cong., 1st sess. (Washington, DC: Government Printing Office, 1957), 86-89.

141. Raymond A. Bauer, Ithiel de Sola Pool, and Lewis Anthony Dexter, *American Business and Public Policy: The Politics of Foreign Trade* (New York: Atherton Press, 1963).

142. Fay Calkins, *The CIO and the Democratic Party* (Chicago: University of Chicago Press, 1952), 154.

143. On the NIIC's 1943 and 1944 spending, see Testimony of Robert M. Gaylord, Anderson Committee Hearings, part 2, 99. On the AFL-CIO's spending, see Zeigler, *Interest Groups in American Society*, 234.

144. The AFL's $1 million spending in 1959 dollars is about $600,000 in adjusted 1943 dollars, using the Consumer Price Index inflation calculator provided by the US Bureau of Labor Statistics at www.bls.gov/data/inflation_calculator.htm.

145. "Annual Report on NAM's Public Relations Policies and Programs" (presented at the February 11, 1959 meeting of the Political Relations Advisory Committee), NAM Records, series I, box 306, "Folder—Board of Directors—Public Relations Advisory Committee, General 1959."

146. "Memorandum—An Executive Control Research System for NAM," Opinion Research Corporation [1959?], NAM Records, series I, box 306, folder "Board of Directors—Public Relations Advisory Committee, 'Executive Control Research System,' 100-Q."

147. The survey was based on 598 personal interviews with "NAM correspondents," in the main, at 503 NAM member companies (cross-sectional sample), conducted in April 1959 by the Opinion Research Corporation of Princeton, New Jersey. While 58 percent of the public viewed NAM "favorably," only 20 percent of NAM members *thought* the public viewed NAM favorably. Conversely, while 11 percent of the public did have an unfavorable view of the organization, NAM members thought this figure was 45 percent. "Executive Control Research, NAM Members Look at NAM," Produced by the Opinion Research Corporation, Princeton, New Jersey, June 1959, NAM Records, series I, box 306, folder "Board of Directors—Public Relations Advisory Committee, 'Executive Control Research System,' 100-Q."

148. Zelizer, "Seeds of Cynicism," 79.

149. George Wolfskill, *The Revolt of the Conservatives: A History of the American Liberty League, 1934–1940* (Boston: Houghton Mifflin, 1962), 215.

150. Ibid., 108.

151. Raymond Moley, "A Capital PAC?," *Los Angeles Times*, December 14, 1954.

152. "The Political Future—An Address by Cola G. Parker, Chairman of the Board, National Association of Manufacturers, Director Kimberly-Clark Corporation, before the American Farm Bureau Federation, Miami, Florida, December 12, 1956," NAM Records, series I, box 5, folder "Political." (The original document reads "leader" instead of "leaders," an apparent typo corrected in the quote used here.)

153. Minutes of the Public Relations Advisory Committee, New York, NY, April 19, 1956, NAM Records, series I, box 306, folder "Board of Directors—Public Relations Advisory Committee, General 1956."

154. William H. Whyte Jr., *Is Anybody Listening? How and Why U.S. Business Fumbles When It Talks with Human Beings* (New York: Simon & Schuster, 1952), 11–12.

155. Ibid., 12.

156. Ibid., 11–12.

157. Ibid., 12. They were unwilling to acknowledge being "a partisan in the great debate," he added.

158. In his 1913 congressional appearance before the Overman Committee, for example, former NAM president John Kirby Jr. expressed his opposition to "vicious class legislation" while characterizing measures the NAM supported as "beneficial to the whole country and not to any particular class." Testimony of John Kirby Jr., September 2, 1913, "Maintenance of a Lobby to Influence Legislation," *Hearings before a Subcommittee of the Committee on the*

Judiciary, part 56, US Senate, 63rd Cong., 1st sess. (Washington, DC: Government Printing Office, 1913), 4501.

159. Testimony of Charles E. Wilson, January 15, 1953, *Hearings before the Committee on Armed Services*, US Senate, 83rd Cong., 1st sess. (Washington, DC: Government Printing Office, 1953), 25–26.

160. "The Lessons of the Election—An Address by Paul M. Butler, Chairman of the Democratic National Committee, before the 63rd Congress of American Industry, Sponsored by the National Association of Manufacturers, Hotel Waldorf-Astoria, New York, on Wednesday, December 3, 1958," press release, December 3, 1958, NAM Records, series I, box 5, folder "Political."

161. See Donald R. Matthews, *The Social Background of Political Decision-Makers* (Garden City, NJ: Doubleday, 1954), 30. Zeigler also refers to "the dominance of business and professional occupational origins of legislators" (*Interest Groups in American Society*, 134).

162. "The Lessons of the Election," December 3, 1958.

Chapter 8

1. Sligh was describing the NAM's new antilabor public relations campaign. See "Congress, Labor Unions, and the Public," July 31, 1958, National Association of Manufacturers (NAM) Records, 1895–2001, accession no. 1411, series I, box 530, file 58-2734, Hagley Museum and Library, Wilmington, Delaware (hereafter cited as NAM Records).

2. "In Politics, Default Means Defeat: An Address by Charles R. Sligh, Jr., Executive Vice-President of the National Association of Manufacturers" (1959?), 3, NAM Records, series I, box 5, folder "Political."

3. "Negligence" appears in Sligh, "In Politics, Default Means Defeat," 5; "organize ourselves for a sales job" appears in "Like It or Not, We're in Politics—Charles R. Sligh, Jr. Executive Vice-President of the National Association of Manufacturers" (speech), 5, received October 31, 1958, NAM Records, series I, box 5, folder "Political."

4. Senator Karl E. Mundt to Dr. Edward A. Rumely, January 13, 1950, reproduced in "Lobbying, Direct and Indirect: Committee for Constitutional Government," *Hearings before the Select Committee on Lobbying Activities*, part 5, US House of Representatives, 81st Cong., 2nd sess., June 27, 28, 29, and August 25, 1950 (Washington, DC: Government Printing Office, 1950), 437.

5. Ibid.

6. Ibid.

7. Joseph G. LaPalombara, "Pressure, Propaganda, and Political Action in the Elections of 1950," *Journal of Politics* 14, no. 2 (1952): 325.

8. Harmon Zeigler, *Interest Groups in American Society* (Englewood Cliffs, NJ: Prentice-Hall, 1964), 245–246.

9. LaPalombara, "Pressure, Propaganda, and Political Action in the Elections of 1950," 311.

10. Memo from John T. Thacher to Mssrs. Bunting, Miller, Robey, and Gilson, November 8, 1951, NAM Records, series I, box 5, folder "Get out the Vote."

11. "The Industrial Campaign for Competence and Honesty in Government" (n.d.), NAM Records, series I, box 5, folder "Get out the Vote." This text describes the "Ohio Plan," which was oriented to activity by businessmen in Ohio and refers to the 1952 election. By 1956 it was being circulated as a model for national activity, having been utilized by some National Industrial Council (a NAM affiliate) state councils in 1952. As another memo noted: "The 1956 Plan is the Ohio Plan under a more appropriate name for national use and incorporates the best ideas that were developed in other states that had used somewhat similar plans in previous years." See Bob DeVany to NIC State Associations, "'Ohio Plan' Material Available," May 31, 1956, and "A Brief Review of 'The 1956 Plan' and How the Second Phase Can Be Used Effectively by a State Sponsoring Organization" (dated May 23, 1956), NAM Records, series I, box B-5, folder "Political—Get Out to Vote Campaign—1."

12. "The Industrial Campaign for Competence and Honesty in Government."

13. Ibid.

14. Sligh, "Like It or Not, We're in Politics," 6. See also Raymond Moley, *The Political Responsibility of Businessmen: Its Neglect, the Consequences Thereof, and What Can Done About It*, rev. ed. (1959), 18–19, in V. O. Key Papers, box 10, "Writings: "Politics, Parties, and Pressure Groups," folder "Chap. IV—'Business' Materials Used, Folder 3 of 5," John F. Kennedy Presidential Library, Boston, MA. The pamphlet was originally written in 1956 and subsequently updated, Moley states in "A Note of Explanation."

15. Moley, *The Political Responsibility of* Businessmen, 19.

16. Sligh, "Like It or Not, We're in Politics," 6.

17. Elizabeth Churchill Browns, "The Secret of Political Success—How to Convert the Unconverted," *Human Events* 15, no. 34 (August 25, 1958): 1–4, NAM Records, series I, box 5, "Political—Misc. Booklets."

18. Ibid.

19. Victor Riesel, "NAM Seeks to Develop Art of Practical Politics," *Marion Star* [n.d., but published post-election in 1958], NAM Records, series I, box 5, folder "Political." As described by Riesel, NAM leaders disclosed *after* the election that they had been "quietly active" in thirteen regions during the campaign.

20. Ibid. Essentially, they held action courses in those regions and sought to aid small plant owners in merging their efforts "just as small unions joined in one COPE drive."

21. Ibid.

22. In 1946 the Republicans took both the House and the Senate. In 1948 the Democrats regained majorities in both chambers, and they retained control in 1950. In 1952 the Republicans took back the House and the Senate.

23. Reflecting on the Congress elected in 1950, Patch noted that "[t]he southern Democratic-Republican coalition has been more powerful in the 82nd Congress than at any time since it began to take shape about 15 years ago; in fact, it is now the effective majority in the national legislature." The Democrats had lost six Senate seats and twenty-nine House seats in the 1950 midterms. See B. W. Patch, "Southern Democrats and the 1952 Election," *Editorial Research Reports* II (1951), http://library.cqpress.com/cqresearcher/cqresrre1951090500; and Gerhard Peters, "Seats in Congress Gained/Lost by the President's Party in Mid-Term Elections," in *The American Presidency Project*, ed. John T. Woolley and Gerhard Peters, http://www.presidency.ucsb.edu/data/mid-term_elections.php.

24. Patch, "Southern Democrats and the 1952 Election."

25. "New Political Alliance—An Interview With Karl E. Mundt," *U.S. News & World Report*, August 3, 1951, 28. Quoted in Patch, "Southern Democrats and the 1952 Election."

26. Sam Rosenfeld, *The Polarizers: Postwar Architects of Our Partisan Era* (Chicago: University of Chicago Press, 2017), 69. For more on Mundt's proposal, see 69–74.

27. Patch, "Southern Democrats and the 1952 Election."

28. Ibid. Mundt gained support for his plan from other conservative Republican senators, including Joe McCarthy of Wisconsin, Robert Bennett of Utah, and Ralph Brewster of Maine, but Southern Democrats such as Harry Byrd of Virginia had not indicated their views.

29. Clifford P. Case, "Should the G.O.P. Merge with the Dixiecrats?," *Collier's*, July 28, 1951, 21, 54–57. Quoted in Patch, "Southern Democrats and the 1952 Election."

30. Ibid.

31. Even prior to Mundt, there had been at least some third-party stirrings among conservatives, including Frank Gannett's tentative plans in the late 1930s, as discussed in chapter 4. In addition, Patch briefly references a plan from the late 1940s involving Republican senator John W. Bricker of Ohio, though this is not mentioned by Rosenfeld in *The Polarizers*, and Patch offers no further details. Kennedy notes a "fusion" ticket proposed by the ADNC in 1944 that would have put forward Democratic senator Harry Byrd for president with Bricker as vice president, and this may be the reference. Following Mundt's suggestion, *Chicago Tribune* political commentator Chesly Manly called for "a new political party" in his 1954 book, *The Twenty-Year Revolution*, a view encouraged and echoed by the Tribune's publisher, Robert McCormick, as Hemmer describes. McCormick urged the formation of a new American Party to unite "Taftite Republicans and southern Democrats," and Hemmer points to other conservative media personalities, such as radio presenter Clarence Manion, who repeatedly sounded the theme of a new third party in the mid-1950s. By the late 1950s, however,

Hemmer hints that Manion's political vision had changed, embracing the Republican Party rather than a third party, as discussed in note 71. Nonetheless, former Dixiecrat standard-bearer Strom Thurmond voiced the possibility of a third party in 1960, "if both major parties nominated strong backers of civil rights legislation for the presidency." See Patch, "Southern Democrats and the 1952 Election"; Stetson Kennedy, *Southern Exposure: Making the South Safe for Democracy* (Tuscaloosa: University of Alabama Press, 2010), 150; and Nicole Hemmer, *Messengers of the Right: Conservative Media and the Transformation of American Politics* (Philadelphia: University of Pennsylvania Press, 2016), 132, 137. Thurmond comments reported in "Political Briefs—Third Party in 1960," *CQ Weekly*, week ending August 16, 1957, 995.

32. United States Senate Historical Office, "September 8, 1958 Mid-Term Revolution," http://www.senate.gov/artandhistory/history/minute/Mid_term_Revolution.htm.

33. David W. Rohde, *Parties and Leaders in the Post-Reform House* (Chicago: University of Chicago Press, 1991), 7–8.

34. On the chamber composition, see "September 8, 1958 Mid-Term Revolution." On the efforts to break the conservative coalition, see Julian E. Zelizer, *On Capitol Hill: The Struggle to Reform Congress and Its Consequences, 1948–2000* (New York: Cambridge University Press, 2004). The admission of Alaska and Hawaii as states in 1959 also brought three more non-Southern Democratic senators to Washington (plus one Republican).

35. Sligh, "Like It or Not, We're in Politics," 2.

36. Raymond Moley, "A Capital PAC?," *Los Angeles Times*, December 14, 1954.

37. Ibid.

38. James M. Brewbaker, "Men to Match my Mountains: A Blueprint for Business Political Action," *Human Events* 15, no. 14 (April 7, 1958): 1–4, NAM Records, series I, box 48, folder "Public Affairs Dept. Business-Industry Political Action Committee (BIPAC) 1963 100-Q."

39. Andrew Hacker and Joel D. Aberbach, "Businessmen in Politics," *Law and Contemporary Problems* 27 (Spring 1962): 266.

40. Ibid.

41. Andrew Hacker, "The Elected and the Anointed: Two American Elites," *American Political Science Review* 55, no. 3 (1961): 547–548.

42. Zeigler, *Interest Groups in American Society*, 134.

43. Ibid.

44. The Manufacturers Association of Syracuse began such courses in 1957 (Hacker and Aberbach, "Businessmen in Politics," 269).

45. On Boulware and the free-market campaign, see Kim Phillips-Fein, *Invisible Hands: The Making of the Conservative Movement from the New Deal to Reagan* (New York: W. W. Norton & Company, 2009), 100. On Reagan and GE, see 112, 147–148. General Electric and Gulf Oil had similar programs to the Syracuse one, Zeigler notes (*Interest Groups in American Society*, 121).

46. George Melloan, "Playing Politics: More Companies Train Employees for Political Chores, Officeholding," *Wall Street Journal*, February 17, 1964, 1.

47. Hacker and Aberbach, "Businessmen in Politics," 268.

48. Ibid. In 1962, the Chamber promoted the Action Course at their first public affairs conference in Washington, DC. Chamber of Commerce Records, series IV, box 2, folder "Public Affairs Conferences."

49. Sligh, "In Politics, Default Means Defeat," 5. See also "Politics and Progress—An Address by Charles R. Sligh, Jr., Executive Vice-President of the National Association of Manufacturers, before the Exchange Club, Grand Rapids, Mich., February 23, 1959," NAM Records, series I, box 5, folder "Political."

50. Ibid. The NAM was, for example, "working hard at obtaining public understanding of the kind of candidates who should be elected, regardless of party label."

51. Ibid.

52. Ibid.

53. Unidentified leaflet, NAM Records, series I, box 48, folder "Public Affairs—General 1958–59 100-Q."

54. Hacker and Aberbach, "Businessmen in Politics," 268, 271.

55. Ibid., 269, 272–275.
56. Moley, "A Capital PAC?," 16.
57. Ibid., 10, 22.
58. Ibid., 16, 22.
59. Ibid., 8.
60. Ibid., 8, 13. ("classless society" is on 13).
61. Ibid., 5–6 (emphasis added).
62. Ibid., 13.
63. Ibid., 37.
64. Testimony of Robert M. Gaylord, President of the National Association of Manufacturers, August 31, 1944, "Campaign Expenditures: National Association of Manufacturers," *Hearings before the Committee to Investigate Campaign Expenditures*, part 2, US House of Representatives, 78th Cong., 2nd sess., August 31, 1944 (Washington, DC: Government Printing Office, 1944), 105.
65. Stricker-Henning Report on the Composition of the 86th Congress—October 3, 1958, NAM Records, series I, box 5, folder "Political." This report used voting records of congressmen compiled during the Republican-controlled 83rd Congress.
66. A 1958 newspaper article suggests that Gulf Oil corporation may have compiled some type of congressional scorecard that year, though its scope and the extent of its distribution is unclear. See Lester Tanzer, "Business & Elections: More Companies Edge into Politics, Draft Bigger 1960 Ventures," *Wall Street Journal*, October 14, 1958.
67. "The Free Citizens Voting Record" scored votes according to "six principles of economic and political freedom": the free market, limited government, economy in government, economic growth with stability, equality under the law and the elimination of physical coercion, and national security. "The Free Citizens Voting Record," NAM Records, series I, box 5, folder "Political Misc. Booklets."
68. Raymond Moley, "A Look at the Record" (this article appears to have come from *Perspective* magazine). Back cover of "The Free Citizens Voting Record," NAM Records, series I, box 5, folder "Political Misc. Booklets."
69. See, for example, Phillips-Fein, *Invisible Hands*; Rick Perlstein, *Before the Storm: Barry Goldwater and the Unmaking of the American Consensus* (New York: Hill and Wang, 2001); Lisa McGirr, *Suburban Warriors: The Origins of the New American Right* (Princeton, NJ: Princeton University Press, 2001); John A. Andrew, *The Other Side of the Sixties: Young Americans for Freedom and the Rise of Conservative Politics* (New Brunswick, NJ: Rutgers University Press, 1997); and Gregory L. Schneider, *Cadres for Conservatism: Young Americans for Freedom and the Rise of the Contemporary Right* (New York: New York University Press, 1999). On the intellectual origins of "fusionism," see George H. Nash, *The Conservative Intellectual Movement in America Since 1945* (New York: Basic Books, 1976).
70. Mary C. Brennan. *Turning Right in the Sixties: The Conservative Capture of the GOP* (Chapel Hill: University of North Carolina Press, 1995), 61. The "American Enterprise Association" became the "American Enterprise Institute" or "AEI" in 1962. On these earlier organizations, see also Jennifer Burns, *Goddess of the Market: Ayn Rand and the American Right* (New York: Oxford University Press, 2009), 204.
71. *Chicago Tribune* publisher Robert McCormick, Sears Roebuck chairman Robert E. Wood, and conservative radio commentators Clarence Manion and Dan Smoot were influential in the founding of For America, which blended anti-Communist, isolationist, and states' rights impulses. Hemmer suggests that both McCormick and Manion were proponents of a new third party at the time that would bring together "Taftite Republicans and southern Democrats," but that Manion soon came to see the GOP as a better vehicle for channeling conservative hopes. See Testimony of Bonner Fellers, October 8, 1956, "1956 Presidential and Senatorial Campaign Contributions and Practices," *Hearings Before the Subcommittee on Privileges and Elections of the Senate Committee on Rules and Administration*, part 2, US Senate, 84th Cong., 2nd sess., October 8, 9, and 10, 1956 (Washington, DC: Government Printing Office, 1956), 296–297; and Hemmer, *Messengers of the Right*, 132–137.
72. Sara Diamond, *Roads to Dominion: Right-Wing Movements and Political Power in the United States* (New York: The Guilford Press, 1995), 61. Board members are listed in John J. Synon,

"The ACA-Index: How to Trap a Demagog," *Human Events* 17, no. 21 (May 26, 1960): 2. Americans for Constitutional Action Records, 1955–1971 [MSS 309], subject files, box 21, folder 21:2, "ACA Clippings, 1958–1967," Wisconsin Historical Society, Madison, Wisconsin (hereafter cited as ACA Records).

73. Robert S. Allen, "Inside Washington: New ACA Opposes ADA," *Christian Science Monitor,* October 27, 1957, Americans for Democratic Action Records 1932–1965 [MSS 3], series 7, Public Relations file, box 92, "Re—Ri," folder 7-92-3, "Right Wing Materials—Americans for Constitutional Action, 1957, Dec—1962, Oct," Wisconsin Historical Society, Madison, Wisconsin (hereafter cited as ADA Records).

74. The quotation comes from the ACA press release announcing its formation, as inserted into the *Congressional Record* by Senator Karl Mundt (R-SD), and noted in Diamond, *Roads to Dominion*, 61. See *Congressional Record,* August 4, 1958, 14,558, and "Group to Defend Free Enterprise," *New York Times,* August 5, 1958. See also *Group Research Report,* July 20, 1962, special report on ACA.

75. "The Case for an 'ACA'—Americans for Constitutional Action" [undated, ca. 1957/58], box 3H490, folder "1958 Senate Campaign General Files: Alexander Holmes, American Institute Language Center, Americans for Constitutional Action, Appointments, Arizona Cattle Growers' Association List," Stephen Shadegg/Barry Goldwater Collection, 1949–1965, The Dolph Briscoe Center for American History, The University of Texas at Austin.

76. As stated in an early leaflet, the ACA's major aim was "to assist in the re-election of members of Congress who, by their voting records, have shown their dedication to the principles of Constitutional Conservatism." In a 1965 chairman's statement, Moreell recalled his first address to the trustees in 1958, where he had stressed the need to aid both incumbents and new conservative challengers, who might otherwise "become discouraged and withdraw from the battle." See ACA, "Action, Campaign, Aims" leaflet [1960?], ACA Records, Publications, box 20, folder 10, "ACA Brochures, 1959–1968"; and "Minutes of the Meeting of the Trustees, Americans for Constitutional Action," January 16, 1965, 4, ACA Records, Board of Trustees Records, box 1, folder 2, "ACA Trustee Minutes, 1960–1965."

77. David M. Olson, "The Structure of Electoral Politics," *Journal of Politics* 29, no. 2 (1967): 359.

78. Diamond, *Roads to Dominion*, 61.

79. "ADA View Countered by Right Wing Group," *Milwaukee Journal,* May 22, 1960, 30.

80. Americans for Constitutional Action, *ACA-Index* (Washington, DC: Human Events, 1960). "Vital to the survival" appears in an explanatory broadsheet, "Reasons for the ACA Index" [1960], 1; "strengthen or weaken" in an "ACA Performance Fact Sheet" [1960], both in ACA Records, Publications, box 20, folder 20:4, "ACA Ratings of Congressmen, 1960."

81. Sen. Barry Goldwater to Admiral Ben Moreell, May 24, 1960, ACA Records, subject files, box 21, folder 21:12, "ACA Enclosures, Printed, 1959–1960." Goldwater's language is suggestive of a solicited and staff-guided endorsement, since ACA assistant director John J. Synon had earlier described the Index as "the most penetrating analysis of each member of Congress ever put between covers." See John J. Synon to DeWitt Wallace, May 13, 1960, ACA Records, subject files, box 22, folder 22:10, "ACA Voting Fact Sheet Mailing to Press, 1960." He repeated the language in his *Human Events* article, "The ACA-Index: How to Trap a Demagog," 4.

82. The need to reverse "the race toward statism" appears in the (Confidential) Report of the Executive Director [1959], 1, ACA Records, Executive Director's Records, box 3, folder 7, "Executive Director's Memoranda File, 1958-1962"; "Piecemeal socialism" appears in M. Stanton Evans, "ADA: The Enemy Within: How the Left Achieves Its Political Victories," *Human Events,* June 30, 1958, ADA Records, series 2, Administrative file, 1946-1965, box 73, "Pe - Po," folder 2-73-6, "Political Attacks on ADA Corr., 1958, Aug. - 1962, March."

83. The ACA did acknowledge using inverted ADA scores as a general *check* on its own estimate of a lawmaker's conservatism. See, for example, "Comments on the ACA CONSISTENCY INDEX CHARTS—by Ben Moreell," October 12, 1964, ACA Records, subject files, box 22, folder 22:8, "ACA Voting Index, Comments by Moreell, 1964." Later in the 1960s, the ACA also began to use ADA and COPE scores in a more comparative way, including them alongside their own ratings in various publications.

84. Rev. I. E. Howard, "A Standard for the People," *Christian Economics,* September 6, 1960. ACA Records, subject files, box 21, folder 21:2, "ACA Clippings, 1958–1967." To reinforce

this point, the first *ACA-Index* grouped together votes into policy areas, labeling these sub-indices the "FOR Sound Money and AGAINST Inflation Index," for example, or the "FOR Individual Liberty and AGAINST Coercion Index," among others. See "Reasons for the ACA Index" [1960].

85. See, for example, Rep. Wint Smith (R-KS) to Kenneth W. Ingwalson, June 2, 1960, ACA Records, Congressional Correspondence, 1959–1971, box 13, folder 13:5, "ACA Congressional Correspondence, 1960, Alphabetical."

86. William M. Colmer to Charles A. McManus, December 11, 1961, ACA Records, Congressional Correspondence, 1959–1971, box 13, folder 7, "Congressional Replies to New Ratings, 1961." (McManus had replaced Ingwalson as the ACA's executive director in 1961.)

87. Minutes of Meeting of Executive Committee of Americans for Constitutional Action, February 5, 1963, 21, ACA Records, Board of Trustees Records, box 1, folder 2, "ACA Trustee Minutes, 1960–1965."

88. On the way ACA ratings had been used to expose Southern Democrats "posing as conservatives" in Alabama, see "Minutes of the Meeting of the Trustees, Americans for Constitutional Action," January 29, 1966, 20, ACA Records, Board of Trustees Records, box 1, folder 3, "ACA Trustee Minutes, 1965–1966."

89. In 1960, ACA prioritized general election assistance for "incumbents rating relatively high in the ACA-INDEX" and "candidates who are attempting to replace some of those rating low in the ACA-INDEX," thus providing some level of support in ninety-four House and Senate contests. In subsequent years it formulated more complex guidelines, taking into account the competitiveness of districts and the strength of the opposing candidate, but scores still played a key role. See Kenneth W. Ingwalson to Admiral Ben Moreell, "Progress Report—September 15, 1960," 1; Charles A. McManus to Admiral Ben Moreell, "Annual Report, 1964," December 9, 1964, 7; and Thomas A. Lane to the ACA Board of Trustees, "Subject: Annual Report, 1966," March 1, 1967, 3, all in ACA Records, Publications, box 19, folder 19:8, "Annual and Semiannual Reports, 1958-1971 (incomplete)."

90. The ACA was originally formed as a purely national group and had only a handful of regional affiliates by the mid-1960s. On its original intent *not* to create local or state chapters, see "Executive Director's Report on Progress of ACA," July 1959, ACA Records, Publications, box 19, folder 19:8, "Annual and Semiannual Reports, 1958–1971 (incomplete)."

91. In 1966, for example, they provided campaign assistance to 225 candidates, but only publicly endorsed 135. Lane to the ACA Board of Trustees, "Subject: Annual Report, 1966," March 1, 1967, 4. See also "Group of Conservatives Assigns Secret Aides to 46 Candidates," *New York Times*, October 22, 1962.

92. Thomas A. Lane to the ACA Board of Trustees, "Annual Report, 1965," January 29, 1966, 2. For examples of the kinds of assistance provided, see "Minutes of the Meeting of the Trustees, Americans for Constitutional Action," January 16, 1965, 10; Charles A. McManus to Admiral Ben Moreell, "Annual Report, 1964," December 9, 1964, 7–8; "Minutes of the Meeting of the Trustees, Americans for Constitutional Action," May 26, 1965, 4; and Ben Moreell to Trustees of Americans for Constitutional Action, "Mid-year Report—January 1, 1966 through June 30, 1966," July 20, 1966. Minutes all in ACA Records, Board of Trustees Records, box 1, folder 2, "ACA Trustee Minutes, 1960–1965"; Reports all in ACA Records, Publications, box 19, folder 8, "Annual and Semiannual Reports, 1958–1971 (incomplete)."

93. In 1964, for example, the ACA hired seventy-five temporary employees for the duration of the campaign, beyond its five permanent staff members. They spent $109,000 of their $188,000 in 1964 receipts on direct campaign assistance. "Minutes of the Meeting of the Trustees, Americans for Constitutional Action," January 16, 1965, 10.

94. Lane to the ACA Board of Trustees, "Annual Report, 1965," January 29, 1966, 2. Concerns over their nonprofit tax status, however, may have been a further consideration.

95. The ACA was a "nonprofit trust" that self-identified as a political action group and filed reports with the Clerk of the House of Representatives, as required under the Federal Corrupt Practices Act of 1925. Olson, for example, classified the ACA as an "electoral group," which is a "special variation of the interest group" (359). See David M. Olson, "The Structure of Electoral Politics," *Journal of Politics* 29, no. 2 (May 1967): 352–367. On the

campaign finance reforms of the 1970s, see Robert E. Mutch, *Buying the Vote: A History of Campaign Finance Reform* (New York: Oxford University Press, 2014), esp. chapters 7–8.

96. Herbert E. Alexander, *Financing the 1960 Election* (Princeton, NJ: Citizens' Research Foundation, 1962), 44. Alexander identified three committees—the Christian Nationalist Crusade, the National Committee for an Effective Congress, and the ACA—as accounting for "about 80% of gross disbursements of all miscellaneous committees" in 1960. (The Christian Nationalist Crusade marked the return of Gerald K. Smith to the world of political action and may have grown out of his experiment with the America First party in 1944.) The ACA's disbursements came to $187,923 in 1960 and $203,905 in 1964. See Alexander, 43; and Herbert E. Alexander, *Financing the 1964 Election* (Princeton, NJ: Citizens' Research Foundation, 1966), 65.

97. Abcarian and Stanage as well as Koeppen classified the ACA as a "radical right" organization, though Scoble described its brand of "ultraconservatism" as slightly more "respectable" than that of the John Birch Society. On the House floor, Representative Ronald Cameron (D-CA) accused the ACA of being "a reactionary, right-wing extremist group" while trying to clothe itself and the JBS in "an aura of respectability." Gilbert Abcarian and Sherman M. Stanage, "Alienation and the Radical Right," *Journal of Politics* 27, no. 4 (1965): 776; Sheilah R. Koeppen, "The Republican Radical Right," *Annals of the American Academy of Political and Social Science* 382, no. 1 (1969): 74n1; Harry M. Scoble, "Political Money: A Study of Contributors to the National Committee for an Effective Congress," *Midwest Journal of Political Science* 7, no. 3 (1963): 243, 245; and "ACA Awards to Congressmen Stir Dispute in House," *Congressional Quarterly*, May 31, 1963, 847. ACA Records, Distinguished Service Awards (Series), box 14, folder 1, "Distinguished Service Award, 1963, 1965, 1967."

98. Despite denials of an official connection, some ACA trustees *were* connected to the JBS; General Bonner Fellers was "an endorser of the society," for example, and Charles Edison had connections to a Robert Welch–backed publication. The ACA denied that either was on the John Birch Society board, however, as an attack advertisement had claimed. See "This Is Not a Smear!" ad and ADA response [1963], 2, ACA Records, subject files, box 21, folder 21:13, "Extremism, Responses to Charges Of, 1960, 1963, 1964, 1967."

99. For more on the formation of the John Birch Society, see Rick Perlstein, *Before the Storm: Barry Goldwater and the Unmaking of the American Consensus* (New York: Hill and Wang, 2001), 116–119.

100. Phillips-Fein, *Invisible Hands*, 59.

101. See Andrew, *The Other Side of the Sixties*, 167, on investigations conducted by White House deputy special counsel Myer Feldman and assistant special counsel Lee White, and 153–154 on an initial memorandum authored by Reuther.

102. Ibid., 9; see also 160–163.

103. Ibid., 157.

104. Myer Feldman, "Memorandum for the President, Subject; Right-Wing Groups," August 15, 1963, 2, Papers of John F. Kennedy, President's Office files, box 106, file, Right Wing Movement Part I, John F. Kennedy Presidential Library, http://www.jfklibrary.org/Asset-Viewer/Archives/JFKPOF-106-013.aspx.

105. ACA News Release, October 22, 1962, ACA Records, subject files, box 21, folder 6, "Congressional Election Results, 1962, Synopsis of ACA Efforts." The news release has been hand-annotated with the election results, indicating that 131 candidates won and 48 lost, translating into a 73 percent success rate—just below the 74 percent calculated by the White House. The ACA annotations included some additional endorsed candidates not included in the original press release, which may account for the difference.

106. Ibid. The ACA's support for Democrats translates to 5.9 percent of its total 1962 endorsements, while COPE support for Republicans represents 1.7 percent of its total 1962 endorsements. The news release itself does not indicate the party affiliation of endorsed candidates, but this information has been reconstructed using the *Biographical Directory of the United States Congress* (bioguide.congress.gov) and checked against a *CQ Weekly* article that offers information on ACA endorsements. See "Mixed Election Results Scored by ACA and COPE Endorsees," *Congressional Quarterly*, week ending November 16, 1962, 2157.

107. "Endorsement Highlights," *Congressional Quarterly*, week ending November 16, 1962, 2157.

108. Charles A. McManus to Admiral Ben Moreell, "Annual Report, 1962," November 26, 1962, 6, ACA Records, Publications, box 19, folder 19:8, "Annual and Semiannual Reports, 1958-1971 (incomplete)." McManus provided a list of 184 candidates who had received various degrees of ACA assistance, naming four Alabama Democrats not included in its October 22 news release of public endorsements.

109. The ACA assisted two hundred Republicans and seventeen Democrats in the 1964 congressional elections, according to Moreell's post-election report to the board of trustees. For Senate seats, it backed seventeen Republicans and one Democrat. See "Minutes of the Meeting of the Trustees, Americans for Constitutional Action," January 16, 1965, 5.

110. "Minutes of the Meeting of the Trustees, Americans for Constitutional Action," January 16, 1965, 4.

111. Ibid., 5.

112. Some 95 of 173 ACA-endorsed candidates won in 1964 (55 percent), 81 Republicans and 14 Democrats. See "Liberals Gain Among Candidates Backed by COPE, ACA," *Congressional Quarterly Weekly*, week ending November 13, 1964, 2681.

113. In 1962, *Congressional Quarterly* noted that both COPE and the ACA had seen success rates of "slightly over 50% on the marginal House races in which they made endorsements," thus suggesting a similar overall impact (though COPE had "fared much better in the Senate races"). In 1964, however, COPE's success rate was 68 percent, with 259 of the 381 congressional candidates it endorsed winning election, and 61 percent in marginal House races (compared to 46 percent for the ACA in marginal races). See "How ACA, COPE Did," *Congressional Quarterly*, week ending November 16, 1962, iv; and "Liberals Gain Among Candidates Backed by COPE, ACA," *Congressional Quarterly Weekly*, week ending November 13, 1964, 2681.

114. "Minutes of the Meeting of the Trustees, Americans for Constitutional Action," January 16, 1965, 5.

115. Ibid. The two districts were the Alabama 6th and the Texas 22nd.

116. See Daniel Galvin, *Presidential Party Building: Dwight D. Eisenhower to George W. Bush* (Princeton, NJ: Princeton University Press, 2009), chapter 3.

117. "Comments on the ACA CONSISTENCY INDEX CHARTS—by Ben Moreell," October 12, 1964.

118. Ibid.

119. Ibid.

120. "Minutes of the Meeting of the Trustees, Americans for Constitutional Action," January 16, 1965, 5.

121. Ibid. "The far greater number of conservatives in the Republican Party explains the preponderance of ACA's support for Republicans," Moreell said (5). Similarly, as ACA trustee Edgar Foreman noted at a subsequent meeting, "When we are accused of being partisan in the sense that we favor Republicans, we can show these figures which demonstrate that the Republican Party is the more conservative of the two parties; that they are more dedicated to the spirit of the Constitution." "Minutes of the Meeting of the Trustees, Americans for Constitutional Action," May 26, 1965, 10.

122. "Minutes of the Meeting of the Trustees, Americans for Constitutional Action," January 16, 1965, 5.

123. Ibid.

124. "An Index to Conservatives," *Richmond News Leader*, May 31, 1960, 10, ACA Records, subject files, box 21, folder 21:2, "ACA Clippings, 1958–1967."

125. Ibid.

126. In fact, Moreell's October 1964 comments on the ACA scores were circulated to Thurmond, who had officially switched parties on September 16, 1964 (see annotation on "Memorandum from Admiral Ben Moreell," October 16, 1964, ACA Records, subject files, box 22, folder 22:8, "ACA Voting Index, Comments by Moreell, 1964."

127. See Sean M. Theriault, "Party Polarization in the US Congress: Member Replacement and Member Adaptation," *Party Politics* 12, no. 4 (2006): 483–503; and Earl Black and Merle Black, *The Rise of Southern Republicans* (Cambridge, MA: Belknap Press, 2002).

128. The term "statism" was used by, for example, ACA Executive Director Kenneth Ingwalson. See (Confidential) Report of the Executive Director [1959], 1.

129. As Moreell later confirmed, this analysis "serves to encourage the hope that eventually there will be a realignment of the Parties on the basis of conservatism versus modern liberalism." "Minutes of the Meeting of the Trustees, Americans for Constitutional Action," January 16, 1965, 5.

130. On noninvolvement in presidential contests, see Memo from Kenneth W. Ingwalson to Admiral Ben Moreell, "Subject: Report—Major Activities in 1960—ACA," ACA Records, Publications, box 19, folder 8, "Annual and Semiannual Reports, 1958–1971 (incomplete)"; and Charles A. McManus to Admiral Ben Moreell, "Annual Report, 1964," December 9, 1964. The ACA was "not normally active in field programs in Primary elections," McManus noted in early 1965, noting that it had endorsed sixteen primary candidates in 1964 (fourteen of whom won) and offered active campaign assistance to just one (Representative Walter Baring of Nevada, a conservative Democrat). In planning for 1966, however, the ACA hoped to offer "primary support for forty-three candidates," plus "conditional support" for a further seventeen (presumably conditional upon them winning their primaries, if challenged), "and active opposition to sixty-five." See "Minutes of the Meeting of the Trustees, Americans for Constitutional Action," January 16, 1965, 10; and "Minutes of the Meeting of the Trustees, Americans for Constitutional Action," May 26, 1965, 5. In 1966, ACA "inaugurated a program of special assistance to large contributors" which effectively recommended "worthy candidates" to whose campaigns they should donate, and the ACA in some cases handled and transmitted the checks. It expanded this initiative substantially in 1968—now labeled "Programmed Financial Support"—raising nearly $116,000 to be directly contributed to candidates (while spending a further $237,200 on in-kind campaign assistance), though, as the 1971 annual report noted, the whole operation was undertaken "in confidence." See Ben Moreell to friends of ACA, March 10, 1969, 3, and "ACA Annual Report, 1968," 8–9, ACA Records, Publications, box 19, folder 19:8, "Annual and Semiannual Reports, 1958–1971 (incomplete)"; Thomas A. Lane to the ACA Board of Trustees, "Subject: Annual Report, 1966," March 1, 1967, 8; and "ACA Annual Report, 1971," 3, ACA Records, Publications, box 19, folder 19:8, "Annual and Semiannual Reports, 1958–1971 (incomplete)."

131. Richard A. Viguerie and David Franke, *America's Right Turn: How Conservatives Used New and Alternative Media to Take Power* (Chicago and Los Angeles, Bonus Books, 2004), 68.

132. NAM Public Affairs Reporter, "Information on Congressional Races Now Available," August 17, 1960, NAM Records, series I, box 5, folder "Political 100 1960-62."

133. "Information on Congressional Races Now Available" and "Explanation of Voting Record: Information on Incumbent Congressmen," NAM Records, series I, box B-5, folder—Political 100 1960-62.

134. The NAM's public affairs division did include an overview of how lawmakers voted on "18 Selected Key Issues," but it is not clear why these issues were selected or where the NAM stood on them. At best, it is perhaps a score of *presidential* support, as the president's position is indicated. See "Explanation of Voting Record."

135. Alexander, *Financing the 1960 Election*, "Table 11—Contributions of Officials of 13 Selected Groups, 1960," 65; and Alexander, *Financing the 1964 Election*, "Table 21—Contributions of Officials of 13 Selected Groups, 1964," 91–92. In 1960, two NAM officials gave contributions to Democratic candidates or committees, while four did so in 1964.

136. Alexander, *Financing the 1964 Election*, 92. Information on Pew is drawn from the raw data Alexander compiled, filed in the Overacker-Heard archive at Berkeley. Those data also show a further $3,000 contribution to Americans for Constitutional Action. See "[1964?] Political Contributions [Contents uncertain]" (no box number), Overacker-Heard Campaign Finance Data Archive, Institute of Governmental Studies, University of California, Berkeley.

137. Julian E. Zelizer, "Seeds of Cynicism: The Struggle over Campaign Finance, 1956–1974," *Journal of Policy History* 14, no. 1 (2002), 78–79. Zelizer names Gulf Oil, Union Carbide, Ford Motor Company, and General Electric as among those corporations experimenting with "PAC-like operations" since the 1950s, but notes they did so "without public knowledge."

138. This was the Forand Bill, sponsored by Representative Aime Forand (D-RI), a proposal similar to Medicare.

139. David B. Truman, *The Governmental Process: Political Interests and Public Opinion* (Berkeley, CA: Institute of Governmental Studies, 1951/1993), 301.

140. Paul F. Healy, "The Senate's Gay Young Bachelor," *Saturday Evening Post*, June 13, 1953, 127.

141. Richard Hofstadter, "The Paranoid Style in American Politics," *Harpers*, November 1964, https://harpers.org/archive/1964/11/the-paranoid-style-in-american-politics/.

142. Sligh, "In Politics, Default Means Defeat," 2.

143. "NAM Public Affairs Program," Memo from Robert L. Humphrey to Mssrs. Bieber, Grier, Hammond, Rathbun, and Steinbrugge, November 28, 1962, NAM Records, series I, box 48, folder "Public Affairs Dept. 100-Q 1961-1962."

144. W. P. Gullander to the NAM Executive Committee, December 27, 1962, NAM Records, series I, box 48, folder "Public Affairs Dept. Business-Industry Political Action Committee (BIPAC) 1963 100-Q."

145. Edward I. Maher, "At Last—A Political Organization for Businessmen," *NAM News*, August 16, 1963, NAM Records, series I, box 48, folder "Public Affairs Dept. Business-Industry Political Action Committee (BIPAC) 1963 100-Q."

146. "Nature and Activities of Business-Industry Political Action Committee," introduced by Senator Everett Dirksen (R-IL), *Congressional Record—Senate*, February 27, 1964, 3858.

147. Ibid.

148. Quoted in Donald R. Hall, *Cooperative Lobbying—The Power of Pressure* (Tucson: University of Arizona Press, 1969/1970), 206. See also Resolution, undated, NAM Records, series I, box 48, folder "Public Affairs Dept. Business-Industry Political Action Committee (BIPAC) 1963 100-Q."

149. Melloan, "Playing Politics," 1; and Joseph J. Fannelli, "Corporate and Union Political Activity" (presented at the Conference on Congressional Campaigns and Federal Law, Political Campaign and Election Law Committee of the Federal Bar Association, Washington, DC, November 27–28, 1979, 122). Fannelli was BIPAC's president at that time, having been appointed in 1975. See also Hall, *Cooperative Lobbying*, 205.

150. Elizabeth A. Fones-Wolf, *Selling Free Enterprise: The Business Assault on Labor and Liberalism, 1945–60* (Urbana: University of Illinois Press, 1994), 259. See also the Opinion Research Corporation Public Opinion Index poll from March 1963, which asked respondents: "Would you say there are any labor union monopolies in this country or any unions that are pretty much like monopolies?" iPOLL Databank, The Roper Center for Public Opinion Research, University of Connecticut, http://www.ropercenter.uconn.edu/data_access/ipoll/ipoll.html.

151. Quoted in Hall, *Cooperative Lobbying*, 206.

152. Hall, *Cooperative Lobbying*, 208.

153. Quoted in Hall, *Cooperative Lobbying*, 206.

154. W. P. Gullander to the NAM Executive Committee, December 27, 1962. Robert L. Humphrey became director of public affairs for the NAM in 1962 and then executive director of BIPAC in 1963. Interview with Humphreys, NAM Records, series I, box 48, folder "Public Affairs Dept. Business-Industry Political Action Committee (BIPAC) 1963 100-Q."

155. Hall, *Cooperative Lobbying*, 206.

156. "Do You Have a Question About BIPAC?," NAM Records, accession no. 1411, series I, box 48, folder "Public Affairs Dept. Business-Industry Political Action Committee (BIPAC) 1963 100-Q."

157. AMPAC's executive director Joe Miller sent the NAM's legal counsel copies of a model constitution and bylaws for state and local COPEs, though he noted they had been unable obtain copies of the national committee's documents. See Joe D. Miller to Lambert H. Miller, November 2, 1962, NAM Records, series V, box 62a.

158. Melloan, "Playing Politics," 1.

159. "Do You Have a Question About BIPAC?"

160. Melloan, "Playing Politics," 1.

161. "Business Report for April 4–September 18, 1963," NAM Records, series 1, box 307, folder "Board of Directors. Sample Folder—Meeting Sept. 17 1963, Hot Springs, Va." Humphrey

attended the AMPAC Workshop, Chicago Illinois on April 18, 1963, and the AMPAC National Conference, Chicago, Illinois on April 18.

162. "Nature and Activities of Business-Industry Political Action Committee," *Congressional Record,* February 27, 1964, 3858.

163. The NAM also held "precinct action workshops" in targeted districts. See booklet, "Bill Boynton goes into Politics," received February 6, 1964; leaflet, "The Bill Boyntons go into Politics" (1964?); leaflet, "Announcing Precinct Action Workshop—A Work Conference for Leaders in Public Affairs and Political Action," received August 12, 1964; "Campaign Technique Manual," produced by NAM, received August 25, 1964; "Make Time for Politics" program, aimed at women, "Produced as a Public Service by the National Association of Manufacturers," NAM Records, series I, box 5, folder "Political Misc. Booklets."

164. Memo, July 1, 1964, NAM Records, series I, box 49, Political Education.

165. "Do You Have a Question About BIPAC?" The leaflet includes the statements, "Your BIPAC membership is aimed sharply to help specific candidates espousing a sound philosophy of government who have a genuine chance of victory," and "candidates will be supported only in districts and States where a close vote is anticipated."

166. "Nature and Activities of Business-Industry Political Action Committee."

167. Ibid.

168. Melloan, "Playing Politics," 1.

169. Ibid.

170. Ibid.

171. "Do You Have a Question About BIPAC?"

172. "Business-Industry Group to Aid House Candidates," *Washington Post,* August 5, 1963, A2. Humphrey had been the RNC's campaign director in 1956 and 1958 before going to work for the NAM.

173. Edward Cowan, "Industry Is Nonpartisan: Business Stepping Up Its Plans for Political Action Programs," *New York Times,* July 5, 1964, 1.

174. See, for example, Cowan, "Industry Is Nonpartisan," who reported that "a number of leading businessmen have said privately that they will vote for President Johnson." See also Earl Mazos, "Goldwater Sees Need to Realign 2 Major Parties," *New York Times,* November 15, 1964, 75, which noted that "normally Republican business leaders and suburban communities went Democratic" in 1964.

175. BIPAC supported Democratic candidates in Alabama, Mississippi, North Carolina, and Virginia. "BIPAC Supported Congressional Candidates: 1964 Election Results," *BIPAC Newsletter,* no. 5, December 1964, 2–3, NAM Papers, series I, box 48, folder "Public Affairs—BIPAC Newsletter 1964–67."

176. Ibid.

177. Ibid. BIPAC supported Democratic primary candidates in Missouri, Tennessee, Mississippi, Texas, and Nevada, along with a Republican primary candidate in Michigan.

178. Of eighteen candidates BIPAC contributed to in southern states, nine were Republicans and nine Democrats. Twelve of the candidates it backed won and six lost. Among both Southern Democrats and Southern Republicans, six candidates won, respectively, and three lost.

179. BIPAC backed eleven-term Democratic congressman William Winstead in the 4th District, who lost to the Republican candidate Prentiss Walker in a surprise defeat. Goldwater won 87.1 percent of the vote in Mississippi. See Joseph Crespino, *In Search of Another Country: Mississippi and the Conservative Counterrevolution* (Princeton, NJ: Princeton University Press, 2007), 104–105.

180. Robert L. Humphrey, "Executive Director's Report," *BIPAC Newsletter,* no. 5, December 1964, 1, NAM Papers, series I, box 48, folder "Public Affairs—BIPAC Newsletter 1964–67."

181. On this prohibition, see "BIPAC Support of Congressional Candidates," Received August 17, 1964, NAM Records, series I, box 48, folder "Public Affairs Dept. Business Industry Political Action Committee (BIPAC), 1964, 100-Q."

182. Herbert E. Alexander, *Financing the 1968 Election* (Lexington, MA: Heath Lexington, 1971), 201.

183. "Constitution and By-Laws" (emphasis added), NAM Records, series I, box 48, folder "Public Affairs Dept. Business-Industry Political Action Committee (BIPAC) 1963 100-Q."

184. "Do You Have a Question About BIPAC?"
185. Ibid. See also "The BIPAC Story," NAM Records, series I, box 48, folder "Public Affairs Dept. Business-Industry Political Action Committee (BIPAC) 1963 100–Q."
186. "Do You Have a Question About BIPAC?"
187. Ibid.
188. Alexander, *Financing the 1964 Election*, calculated COPE's gross disbursements as $988,810.00 and BIPAC's as $203,283 (64–65). BIPAC's spending is also noted in Humphrey, "Executive Director's Report," 1.
189. See Melloan, "Playing Politics," 1.
190. The quotation comes from Anthony E. Wallace, a former Speaker of the Connecticut House and assistant to the president at Connecticut Light & Power Co. Quoted in Melloan, "Playing Politics," 1.
191. A more moderate RNC chairman, Ray Bliss, was appointed in April 1965 to replace Goldwater's conservative pick, Dean Burch, despite Goldwater's initial opposition to the plan. See Philip A. Klinkner, *The Losing Parties: Out-Party National Committees 1956–1993* (New Haven, CT: Yale University Press, 1994), 73–77.
192. Aaron Wildavsky, "The Goldwater Phenomenon: Purists, Politicians, and the Two-Party System," *Review of Politics* 27, no. 3 (July 1965): 411–412.
193. See, for example, Donald Janson, "Rightists Buoyed by the Election; Open New Drives," *New York Times*, November 23, 1964, 1.
194. Goldwater's candidacy was largely engineered by leaders of new conservative organizations and owed much to the actions of F. Clifton White, a Cornell University political science professor who combined his academic life with that of a partisan and had organized the National Draft Goldwater Committee in 1961. See F. Clifton White, *Suite 3505: The Story of the Draft Goldwater Movement* (New Rochelle, NY: Arlington House, 1967); Charles Mohr, "Goldwater's Nine," *New York Times*, September 13, 1964; Alfred S. Regnery, *Upstream: The Ascendance of American Conservatism* (New York: Simon & Schuster, 2008), 96; and Phillips-Fein, *Invisible Hands*, 142.
195. Wildavsky had interviewed Goldwater delegates at the 1964 Republican convention and contrasted them to more pragmatic "politicians" ("The Goldwater Phenomenon," 393).
196. Cabell Phillips, "Bliss Denounces Goldwater Unit as Peril to Party," *New York Times*, June 19, 1965, 1. See also Klinkner, *The Losing Parties*, 78. Schoenwald describes the ACA as one of four "splinter groups" that "helped to carry the conservative agenda into the next decade" (the others were the American Conservative Union, Young Americans for Freedom, and the Free Society Association—a group created bty Goldwater and discussed in the conclusion). See Jonathan M. Schoenwald, *A Time for Choosing: The Rise of Modern American Conservatism* (New York: Oxford University Press, 2001), 12.
197. Contribution reported in "Selected 1965 Expenditures Reported by Committees," *CQ Weekly*, December 2, 1966, 2978.
198. Ibid.
199. See "Washington Report," *Life Magazine*, May 21, 1965, 448. Under the heading "Both Sides Embarrassed," this report notes that Watson's campaign was "frankly racist and right wing, not at all the image Republicans are trying to project these days." This suggests that BIPAC supported a continued push to the right within the GOP, despite calls for moderation in the wake of Goldwater's defeat. On Watson's public endorsement of Goldwater, see Crespino, *In Search of Another Country*, 104. On Watson's switch, see Kevin P. Phillips, *The Emerging Republican Majority*, updated ed. (Princeton, NJ: Princeton University Press, 2014), 224.

Conclusion

1. Earl Mazos, "Goldwater Sees Need to Realign 2 Major Parties," *New York Times*, November 15, 1964, 1.
2. Ibid., 75.
3. Ibid., 1.
4. Variously known as the Free Society Association or Free Society Committee, Goldwater's organization would in "no way be a third party movement," he explained, but would simply "attempt

to educate more and more American people into the values of the Republican party." That education, however, would proceed by offering financial support to conservative Republicans in their congressional contests. Quoted in Philip A. Klinkner. *The Losing Parties: Out-Party National Committees 1956–1993* (New Haven, CT: Yale University Press, 1994), 78.

5. As noted in chapter 8, note 69, an array of historical scholarship has documented the "rise of the Right." See, for example, Kim Phillips-Fein, *Invisible Hands: The Making of the Conservative Movement from the New Deal to Reagan* (New York: W. W. Norton & Company, 2009); Elizabeth A. Fones-Wolf, *Selling Free Enterprise: The Business Assault on Labor and Liberalism, 1945–60* (Urbana: University of Illinois Press, 1994); John A. Andrew, *The Other Side of the Sixties: Young Americans for Freedom and the Rise of Conservative Politics* (New Brunswick, NJ: Rutgers University Press, 1997); Jonathan M. Schoenwald, *A Time for Choosing: The Rise of Modern American Conservatism* (New York: Oxford University Press, 2001); Kevin Kruse, *White Flight: Atlanta and the Making of Modern Conservatism* (Princeton, NJ: Princeton University Press, 2005); and Elizabeth Tandy Shermer, *Sunbelt Capitalism: Phoenix and the Transformation of American Politics* (Philadelphia: University of Pennsylvania Press, 2013). For more on this transformation from the perspective of political science, see especially Eric Schickler, *Racial Realignment: The Transformation of American Liberalism, 1932–1965* (Princeton, NJ: Princeton University Press, 2016); and Earl Black and Merle Black, *The Rise of Southern Republicans* (Cambridge, MA: Belknap Press, 2002).

6. See, for example, Sean M. Theriault, *Party Polarization in Congress* (New York: Cambridge University Press, 2008); and Barbara Sinclair, *Party Wars: Polarization and the Politics of National Policy Making* (Norman: University of Oklahoma Press, 2014). For overviews of party polarization more generally, see Michael Barber and Nolan McCarty, "Causes and Consequences of Polarization," in *Political Negotiation: A Handbook*, ed. Jane Mansbridge and Cathie Jo Martin (Washington, DC: Brookings Institution Press, 2016), 37–90; and Geoffrey C. Layman, Thomas M. Carsey, and Juliana Menasce Horowitz, "Party Polarization in American Politics: Characteristics, Causes, and Consequences," *Annual Review of Political Science* 9 (2006): 83–110. Where elite polarization is widely accepted among political scientists, debates continue about the extent of mass polarization, especially the question of whether citizens' views have substantially diverged or simply become sorted by ideology into the "correct" party. See, for example, Morris P. Fiorina, Samuel J. Abrams, and Jeremy C. Pope, *Culture War: The Myth of a Polarized America* (New York: Pearson Longman, 2006); and Matthew S. Levendusky and Neil Malholtra, "(Mis)perceptions of Partisan Polarization in the American Public," *Public Opinion Quarterly* 80, no. 1 (2016): 378–391.

7. The role of "activists" is often stressed in accounts of polarization, but not necessarily their organizational context or tactics. See, for example, Geoffrey C. Layman, Thomas M. Carsey, John C. Green, and Richard Herrera, "Activists and Conflict Extension in American Party Politics," *American Political Science Review* 104, no. 2 (May 2010): 324–346. See also note 15.

8. Cabell Phillips, "Bliss Denounces Goldwater Unit as Peril to Party," *New York Times*, June 19, 1965, 1. For Goldwater's earlier criticism, see Testimony of Sidney H. Scheuer, Chairman of the National Committee for an Effective Congress, December 12, 1956, McClellan Committee Hearings.

9. Lecture no. 7, "Political Tactics and Aims of Organized Labor," updated February 18, 1957, V. O. Key Papers, box 9, "Writings: "Politics, Parties, and Pressure Groups," folder "Chap. III. 'Workers.' Mss. Notes and Revisions," John F. Kennedy Presidential Library, Boston, MA.

10. "Drastic Party Realignment Could Harm Entire System," *Charlotte Observer*, September 22, 1964, filed in Records of the Democratic National Committee, series I, box 38 [labeled "Negro Civil Rights Organizations Activities 1964], folder "Political Parties—Proposed Party Realignment As Result of 1964 Campaign, Called for by BMG, other Conservatives," Lyndon B. Johnson Presidential Library, Austin, TX (hereafter cited as DNC Records).

11. Ibid.

12. Goldwater had faced "a generally hostile audience of political scientists," according to the right-leaning *Chicago Tribune*. As the *New York Times* reported, he "deviated from his text" to warn of political "me-tooism," which Goldwater considered the bigger danger to the two-party system since it might bring about a "bastard" party, as he labeled it—describing a third party—"which can be born to a sad marriage." See "Senator Lashes Out at Abuse of Powers,"

Chicago Tribune, September 12, 1964; and "Goldwater Sees Presidency Peril," *New York Times,* September 12, 1964, 1, 10, both filed in DNC Records, series I, box 331 [labeled "Goldwater Files—Campaign Speeches and Domestic Issues"], folder "Goldwater, Sen. Barry—Speeches 1964 Chicago IL Sept 11 Issues—Expansion of Presidential Power Attacks Supreme Court, on School Prayer and Reapportionment, Two Party System, Extremism, Vote against Civil Rights Act to American Political Scientist Association."

13. See Nicol C. Rae, "Be Careful What You Wish For: The Rise of Responsible Parties in American National Politics," *Annual Review of Political Science* 10 (2007): 169–191.

14. Aaron Wildavsky, "The Goldwater Phenomenon: Purists, Politicians, and the Two-Party System," *Review of Politics* 27, no. 3 (July 1965): 398. In this case, Wildavsky was describing conservative activists involved in the Goldwater campaign, whom he described as "purists." See chapter 8, note 195.

15. V. O. Key, "Secular Realignment and the Party System," *Journal of Politics* 21, no. 2 (1959): 198–210; Black and Black, *The Rise of Southern Republicans,* 192, 205; Fiorina, Abrams and Pope, *Culture War,* esp. 61–63, 67–70, 178–179); Sean M. Theriault, "Party Polarization in the US Congress: Member Replacement and Member Adaptation," *Party Politics* 12, no. 4 (2006): 483–503; and John H. Aldrich, *Why Parties? The Origin and Transformation of Political Parties in America* (Chicago: University of Chicago Press, 1995), 180–193. As explicated in a 1983 article, Aldrich frames his analysis in terms of individual *activists* as a way to explain why the expectation that candidates would converge around moderate policy stances, drawn from Downsian spatial analysis, did not always hold. Poole and Rosenthal, however, briefly reference the *interest groups* that activists joined and the importance of the resources they provide to candidates as helping to explain why candidates took more divergent policy positions. Rae specifically cites interest group activity (and the role of large donors) in primaries as one of several factors pushing the polarization of parties today. See "A Downsian Spatial Model with Party Activism," *American Political Science Review* 77, no. 4 (1983): 974–990; Keith T. Poole and Howard Rosenthal, "The Polarization of American Politics," *Journal of Politics* 46, no. 4 (November 1984): 1075; and Rae, "Be Careful What You Wish For," 182.

16. Supporting this contention, La Raja and Schaffner have argued that the legal framework surrounding campaign finance has tended to advantage ideologically motivated donors and groups who support more extreme candidates. See Raymond La Raja and Brian F. Schaffner, *Campaign Finance and Political Polarization: When Purists Prevail* (Ann Arbor: University of Michigan Press, 2015).

17. As noted in chapter 1, the Federal Election Commission identified 608 national PACs in 1974 and 8,666 federal PACs in 2017. See Federal Election Commission press release, "PAC Count—1974 to Present," updated July 1, 2012, http://www.fec.gov/press/summaries/2011/2011paccount.shtml; and Federal Election Commission press release, "Statistical Summary of 24-Month Campaign Activity of the 2017-2018 Cycle," March 15, 2019, https://www.fec.gov/updates/statistical-summary-24-month-campaign-activity-2017-2018-cycle/.

18. The NRA's PAC, the Political Victory Fund, was created in 1976, while NARAL-PAC was formed in 1977. The NRA itself was founded in 1871, while NARAL traces its roots to the National Association for Repeal of Abortion Laws, formed in 1969. See Samuel C. Patterson and Keith R. Eakins, "Congress and Gun Control," in *The Changing Politics of Gun Control* ed. John M. Bruce and Clyde Wilcox (Lanham, MD: Rowman & Littlefield, 1998), 45–73, 61; and Suzanne Staggenborg, *The Pro-Choice Movement: Organization and Activism in the Abortion Conflict* (New York: Oxford University Press, 1994), 24, 84.

19. The NRA's website notes that the Political Victory Fund "ranks political candidates— irrespective of party affiliation," and a 2010 explanation of its endorsement policy, still available on the website, describes the PVF as "non-partisan in issuing its candidate grades and endorsements." In a 2008 memorandum, NARAL president Nancy Keenan described her group as "the nation's leading non-partisan pro-choice political organization," though notably, there are no current references to nonpartisanship on the NARAL website. For NRA statements, see https://www.nrapvf.org/grades/ and https://www.nrapvf.org/articles/20100510/nra-pvf-endorsement-policy. For NARAL, see Memorandum from Nancy Keenan, NARAL President, to Interested Parties, "Pro-Choice Victories in the 2008 Election,"

November 5, 2008, http://www.prochoiceamerica.org/assets/files/2008-election-victories.pdf.

20. Already by 1995, in fact, the NRA was described by *Nation* as "an appendage to the Republican Party," acknowledging that "liberal labor unions" bore a similar relationship to the Democrats. See Marc Cooper, "The N.R.A. Takes Cover in the G.O.P.," *Nation*, June 19, 1995, 877.

21. Richard M. Skinner, *More Than Money: Interest Group Action in Congressional Elections* (Lanham, MD: Rowman & Littlefield, 2007), 148–149. A Republican majority meant "a progun Speaker and progun committee chairmen," the official told Skinner.

22. NARAL chose not to back self-proclaimed "pro-choice" Republican Scott Brown in the Massachusetts Senate election, claiming that his record suggested he was "mixed choice" on the basis of three Senate votes NARAL had analyzed; it endorsed his Democratic challenger, Elizabeth Warren, whom it labeled "pro-choice" even though she had not voted on any of the measures. See "NARAL 2012 Voter Guide," http://www.prochoiceamerica.org/elections/2012/voter-guide/choice-position-explanations.html.

23. "A Congress to Win the War," *New Republic*, May 18, 1942 (part II), 687, Thomas Amlie Papers [MSS 452], Public Papers, box 72, folder 2, "'A Congress to Win the War' (New Republic Supplement), Published version, May 1942," Wisconsin Historical Society, Madison, Wisconsin.

24. See, for example, Amy Siskind, "Why Women's Orgs Must Become Non-Partisan," *Huffington Post*, posted November 8, 2009, updated May 26, 2011, https://www.huffingtonpost.com/amy-siskind/why-womens-orgs-must-beco_b_349970.html

25. "Labor Disappointed in 'Pro-Labor' 86th Congress," *Congressional Quarterly Weekly*, week ending August 19, 1960, 1464.

26. See *Citizens United v. Federal Election Commission*, 558 U.S. 310 (2010); and *Speechnow.org v. Federal Election Commission*, No. 08-5223 (D.C. Circuit 2010).

27. As P.A.C.'s assistant director Tilford Dudley stated in 1954, summarizing the CIO's legal viewpoint since passage of the Taft-Hartley Act in 1947: "The CIO took and still takes the position that the prohibition of our direct expenditures of trade union funds in a federal election is unconstitutional because it violates our rights of free speech and free assembly." Tilford E. Dudley to Rollin Everett, July 29, 1954, 2, CIO Political Action Committee (PAC) Collection Papers, 1943–1960s, accession no. 647, box 17, folder 11, "Union Political Activity/Campaign Expenditures—Legal Opinions, 1940s–50s," Walter P. Reuther Library, Wayne State University, Detroit, Michigan (hereafter cited as CIO-PAC Papers).

28. National Precinct Workers, Inc., "Now Is the Time" (1958), 16, box 3H492, folder "1958 Senate Campaign General Files: Glen Canyon Dam, Golston Loan, G.O.P. Facts, Governor's Office—Cost etc., Green, Al," Stephen Shadegg/Barry Goldwater Collection, 1949–1965, The Dolph Briscoe Center for American History, The University of Texas at Austin.

29. The ACA reconstituted itself as the Americans for Constitutional Action Research Institute in 1980, a tax-exempt 501(c)(3) "educational" organization, but it disappeared from view after 1984. See Americans for Constitutional Action Research Institute, *1981 ACARI INDEX: An Analysis of the Voting Record of Each Member in the Congress, 1st Session, 97th Congress* (Washington, DC: ACARI, 1981).

30. The ACU was formed in late 1964 under the guidance of conservative editor William F. Buckley Jr., and ACA leaders had some initial involvement (ACA president Ben Moreell was a member of its "Advisory Assembly," for example). Like the ACA, the ACU would look to the ADA for inspiration, though it initially focused on intellectual and educational activities rather than political action, since Buckley believed an overarching organization was needed to bring structure and leadership to the conservative constellation, as the ADA had for the liberal community. The ACU would eventually supersede the ACA, however, moving closer to the electoral realm by producing a congressional rating based on roll-call votes, for example, beginning in 1971. Even prior to this, beginning in 1967, it had produced the "DMV [Democratic Margin of Victory] Report," a scorecard intended to show how moderate and liberal Republicans contributed to Democratic legislative victories in Congress. Moreover, as Schoenwald notes, the ACU established the Conservative Victory Fund in 1969 to fundraise and distribute financial assistance to conservative congressional candidates. It also launched the Conservative Political Action Conference (CPAC) in 1973, which is still an

important conservative political forum. In 1971 Charles McManus (now ACA president) had complained that "rival" conservative groups were straining the ACA's finances, and by the end of the decade it was largely defunct. In 1985 *Congressional Quarterly Weekly Report* replaced ACA scores with ACU scores in its regular overview of congressional ratings. Today the ACU is a 501(c)4 nonprofit organization with an affiliated PAC and foundation. See "The American Conservative Union—A History," https://web.archive.org/web/20150716003551/http://conservative.org/acu-history/; "Minutes of the Meeting of the Trustees, Americans for Constitutional Action," January 16, 1965, 12, Americans for Constitutional Action Records, 1955–1971 [MSS 309], Board of Trustees Records, box 1, folder 2, "ACA Trustee Minutes, 1960–1965," Wisconsin Historical Society, Madison, Wisconsin (hereafter cited as ACA Records); "ACA Annual Report, 1971," 9, ACA Records, Publications, box 19, folder 19:8, "Annual and Semiannual Reports, 1958-1971 (incomplete)"; Andrew, *The Other Side of the Sixties*, 214; Schoenwald, *A Time for Choosing*, 241; and "The 99th Congress: 1985 Group Ratings," *Congressional Quarterly Weekly Report*, November 22, 1986, 2959–2966.

31. The Chamber did not create a PAC until about 1990, and it was relatively inactive until the late 1990s. As Herrnson notes "it was not a dominant player in election financing until the late 1990s," at which time it was "one of several large business associations that became more politically active, and more partisan." See Paul S. Herrnson, *Congressional Elections: Campaigning at Home and in Washington* (Washington, DC: Congressional Quarterly Press, 2011), 33. The earliest year for which the Center for Responsive Politics has Chamber-PAC financial data is 1990. See http://www.opensecrets.org/pacs/lookup2.php?strID=C00082040. The Chamber's electoral spending is partially made through its PAC and partially through direct spending as a 501(c)6 nonprofit group, which is compatible with its tax status as long as political activities remain under 50 percent of its expenditures.

32. Though its preference for Republicans was apparent, supporting Democrats was "a small but very real part" of the Chamber's political activity into the 2000s, Bland notes, though during the Obama presidency it had "dwindled to a fraction of its former self." Scott Bland, "Is the Chamber of Commerce No Longer Bipartisan?," *Atlantic*, March 31, 2014, https://www.theatlantic.com/politics/archive/2014/03/is-the-chamber-of-commerce-no-longer-bipartisan/434391/.

33. Many state Farm Bureaus do have their own PACs and super PACs, but the national organization itself has not formed one. The "Farm Bureau PAC" listed on OpenSecrets.org appears to be a Michigan state Farm Bureau super PAC. See https://www.opensecrets.org/pacs/lookup2.php?strID=C00532416&cycle=2018. For the Farm Bureau's congressional scorecard, see https://scorecard.fb.org/home.

34. Finegold and Skocpol, for example, observe that the Agricultural Adjustment Administration was one of the clearest success stories of the New Deal, helping to address the chronic economic instability farmers had long faced. Kenneth Finegold and Theda Skocpol, *State and Party in America's New Deal* (Madison: University of Wisconsin Press, 1995).

35. The Farm Bureau's main opponent in its early years was an "internal" one: the Farmers' Union, which represented tenant farmers and agricultural laborers. The consumer lobby that emerged in the late 1960s and early 1970s challenged some farm subsidies, but it did not clearly cohere in one organized grouping, and it did not face a dominant farm group, either. By that point the Farm Bureau's presence had diminished, with the agricultural sector represented by an array of commodity-based associations, as Hansen describes. See John Mark Hansen, *Gaining Access: Congress and the Farm Lobby, 1919–1981* (Chicago: University of Chicago Press, 1991), 182–183.

36. Farm groups are the classic example of the "iron triangle," in which interest groups, congressional committees, and executive departments have mutually reinforcing aims. See Adam D. Sheingate, *The Rise of the Agricultural Welfare State: Institutions and Interest Group Power in the United States, France, and Japan* (Princeton, NJ: Princeton University Press, 2003), 6.

37. This is not to say that partisan division was entirely eliminated. As Hansen describes, agricultural politics took on a more partisan cast in the late 1950s and early 1960s, reflecting disagreement over the nature and extent of agricultural subsidies. Though the Farm Bureau acquired a Republican-leaning reputation during this period and accordingly lost "access"

according to Hansen, it still did not venture into electoral politics. See Hansen, *Gaining Access*, 20, 119–124, 152–156. See also chapter 2, note 154.

38. As a web page explaining AARP's political advocacy states: "We are a nonpartisan organization. . . . [W]e never endorse candidates or political appointees. We don't have a political action committee, and we don't contribute to candidates or campaigns." Alongside its nonelectoral posture, AARP has a reputation for bipartisanship: "We have a long history of working with elected officials on both sides of the aisle," the article adds. John Hishta, "We Stand on Principle, Not Politics," AARP, February 10, 2017, https://www.aarp.org/politics-society/advocacy/info-2017/health-protecting-medicare.html.

39. Jack Kroll to ADA Convention [1952], 5–7, CIO-PAC Papers, box 14, folder 26, "1952 Elections."

40. On third-party aspirations in the 1930s, for example, see J. I. Seidman, "Political Trends and New Party Movements," *Editorial Research Reports* I (1934), http://library.cqpress.com/cqresearcher/document.php?id=cqresrre1934051800.

41. See Susan Dunn, *Roosevelt's Purge: How FDR Fought to Change the Democratic Party* (Cambridge, MA: Belknap Press of Harvard University Press, 2010), 106–109; and Sam Rosenfeld, *The Polarizers: Postwar Architects of Our Polarized Era* (Chicago: University of Chicago Press, 2017), 1.

42. See B. W. Patch, "Southern Democrats and the 1952 Election," *Editorial Research Reports* II (1951), http://library.cqpress.com/cqresearcher/cqresrre1951090500.

43. Hirano and Snyder, for example, have pointed to a significant drop in support for third parties from about 1930 and offer a "co-optation" hypothesis to explain it; namely, that "the Democratic Party co-opted the left-wing policy position beginning with the passage of the New Deal agenda," and since much of this third-party activity came from the Left, it accordingly declined. Their depiction of "co-optation" thus places initiative with the party and points to increased labor union campaign contributions as evidence that the Democratic Party was moving leftward. The argument made here offers a reverse perspective: that labor leaders made a *choice* to align with the Democratic Party and sought to transform it internally so as to approximate a labor party. PACs offered an instrument to do so and an alternative organizational vehicle into which to pour their energies. See Shigeo Hirano and James M. Snyder Jr., "The Decline of Third-Party Voting in the United States," *Journal of Politics* 69, no. 1 (February 2007): 1–2, 8–9.

44. As Evan McMullin, the independent Republican who challenged Trump in the 2016 election, asked the Twittersphere in May 2017: "In our Trumpian era, is there any longer a traditional right and left? Or are there only those who fight for liberty and those against it[?]" Quoted in E. J. Dionne, "The Anti-Trump Right Is Becoming a Breed of Its Own," *Washington Post*, May 31, 2017.

45. Just before South Carolina's Republican primaries in June 2018, for example, Trump published a tweet describing Representative Mark Sanford—who had been critical of his administration—as "nothing but trouble" and "very unhelpful" to his presidency. Sanford lost his primary, with the result widely attributed to the president's intervention. See, for example, Natasha Bach, "The Power of a Trump Tweet: Mark Sanford Defeated in Primary after President's Last-Minute Twitter Attack," *Fortune*, June 13, 2018, http://fortune.com/2018/06/13/trump-twitter-mark-sanford/]; and Alan Blinder, "In the Age of Trump, Mark Sanford's Political Career Fades," *New York Times*, June 12, 2018, https://www.nytimes.com/2018/06/12/us/politics/mark-sanford-trump.html]. Demonstrating the dramatic shift in attitudes to presidential campaigning since Roosevelt's purge, Trump's interventions—both positive and negative—have been widely accepted and even *encouraged* by party leaders. See Sean Sullivan and Michael Scherer, "GOP Eager for Trump Intervention in Contested Senate Primaries," *Washington Post*, May 9, 2018, https://www.washingtonpost.com/powerpost/mcconnell-west-virginia-primary-worked-out-very-well-attacks-on-me-didnt/2018/05/09/582e1394-5394-11e8-abd8-265bd07a9859_story.html?utm_term=.5cdd5ef22c06].

46. Pence's PAC, the Great America Committee, is one of a large number of "leadership PACs" formed by individual politicians that have emerged since the early 1980s. The Great America Committee spent $3,884,038 in the 2018 election cycle, including contributions of $739,700 to 104 Republican House candidates and 21 Senate candidates (plus a contribution of

$5,400 to Trump's re-election campaign). See Vaughn Hillyard, "Pence Creates PAC Ahead of 2018, 2020 Elections," *NBC News*, May 18, 2017, http://www.nbcnews.com/politics/ white-house/pence-creates-pac-ahead-2018-2020-elections-n761436; and "Great America Cmte—Contributions to Federal Candidates, 2018 Cycle," https://www.opensecrets.org/ pacs/pacgot.php?cycle=2018&cmte=C00640664.

47. This approach differs from two previous attempts to promote centrism or bipartisan cooperation, as articulated by Unity08 in the 2008 presidential election and Americans Elect in 2012—both of which utilized online platforms to offer expression to citizens disenchanted with the major parties and sought to promote a bipartisan presidential ticket. Both focused on presidential races and emphasized new technological innovations, rather than the gradual and mechanical process of reshaping each party from within, by cultivating and supporting moderate congressional candidates. More recently, the No Labels group comes closer to the model suggested here. A 501(c)4 organization founded in 2010, it has engaged in congressional primary and general elections in the past few cycles, making independent expenditures through a network of affiliated super PACs. See Kira C. Allmann, Daniel Maliniak, Ronald B. Rapoport, and Lonna Rae Atkeson, "The Internetilization of American Parties: The Implications of the Unity08 Effort," in *The State of the Parties: The Changing Rose of Contemporary American Parties*, 6th ed., ed. John C. Green and Daniel J. Coffee (Lanham, MD: Rowman & Littlefield, 2010), 149–162; Chris Cillizza and Aaron Blake, "Americans Elect and the Death of the Third Party Movement," *Washington Post*, May 18, 2012, https://www.washingtonpost.com/ blogs/the-fix/post/americans-elect-and-the-death-of-the-third-party-movement/2012/ 05/17/gIQAIzNKXU_blog.html; Lynn Sweet, "Bipartisan 'No Labels' Group's Super PAC Network Revealed: Mega Chicago Donors," *Chicago Sun-Times*, March 12, 2018, https:// chicago.suntimes.com/columnists/bipartisan-no-labels-2018-super-pac-network-chicagodonors/; and Ben Kamisa, "Bipartisan 'No Labels' Group Aims to Protect Moderates in Primary Fights," *The Hill*, March 25, 2018, http://thehill.com/homenews/campaign/ 380030-bipartisan-no-labels-aims-to-protect-moderates-facing-primary-fights.

48. On societal implications, see Cass R. Sunstein, "Partyism," *University of Chicago Legal Forum* 2015 (2016): article 2, http://chicagounbound.uchicago.edu/uclf/vol2015/iss1/2.

49. Clifford P. Case, "Should the G.O.P. Merge with the Dixiecrats?," *Collier's*, July 28, 1951, 21, 54–57, quoted in Patch, "Southern Democrats and the 1952 Election."

INDEX

Note: Tables are indicated by *t* following the page number

For the benefit of digital users, indexed terms that span two pages (e.g., 52–53) may, on occasion, appear on only one of those pages.